Train Ferries *of* EUROPE

STEVE BARRON

Published by:
Ferry Publications, PO Box 33, Ramsey, Isle of Man IM99 4LP Tel: +44 (0) 1624 898446 E-mail: ferrypubs@manx.net
Website: www.ferrypubs.co.uk

Ferry Publications

Contents

Produced and designed by Ferry Publications trading as Lily
Publications Ltd

First Edition: April 2021

Acknowledgements

In preparing this book, many people have let me use their photographs, delved in the archives or answered my questions. In particular, I would like to thank:

Laura Clow of the Institute of Engineers & Shipbuilders in Scotland and Kavan Stafford of the Mitchell Library, Glasgow, for unearthing old technical papers and patents. Douglas Yuill for his information and pictures of the Forth & Tay ferries.

Pieter Inpijn and Gena Anfimov for the use of their pictures.

Varvara Chaykovskaya of Baltiysky Zavod, Carola Kuhn of Schweizerische Bodensee-Schiffahrtsgesellschaft AG and Jean-Luc Rickenbacher of the Verkehrshaus, Luzern for providing information and pictures.

Laureano Garcia of Trasmedships, Gert Jakobsen of DFDS, Heidi Kämäräinen of Finnlines, Erik Lewenhaupt of Stena Line and Björn Boström of Ystad Hamn for answering queries.

Particular thanks to my wife Morna for improving my grammar and to John Bryant and Richard Kirkman for proof-reading, correcting various mistakes and also provided additional information. Special thanks to Miles Cowsill of Ferry Publications for encouraging me to prepare this book and for putting it all together.

Introduction

This book sets out to chart the history of train ferries in Europe. They first appeared in 1850, in the age of railway mania, when competing railway companies raced to connect Europe's cities. In the following 170 years, they became important links in the expanding railway network. They started small, crossing rivers and estuaries, and developed into large seagoing ships carrying long-distance sleeper cars between Europe's major cities.

Their design also has a wider importance as the ferries were the first ships to be integrated with another mode of transport. This required engineers from different disciplines to work together so that the ferry, the dock, the linkspan and the rolling stock all worked together. The ferries are also unusual in having the railway companies as reluctant owners. They would have much preferred the simplicity of a bridge or tunnel rather than a complicated and expensive marine operation.

Over a hundred train ferry routes around Europe are recorded, from Tinnsjø in the Norwegian mountains to the Caspian Sea. Most have now disappeared. The shorter crossings have been replaced by bridges or tunnels. Other routes have closed in the last few decades as freight has moved from rail to road and passengers have swapped long-distance trains for air travel. Today the train ferry is almost completely extinct in Northern and Western Europe and one of the oldest routes, across the Baltic from Sassnitz in Germany to Trelleborg in Sweden, came to an end in the spring of 2020.

The book is divided geographically. It starts with the first ferries in Scotland and the unsuccessful Victorian schemes for train ferries across the English Channel, before these were implemented in the First World War. It then moves to Scandinavia, where the ferries connecting Denmark's islands created a national rail network and expanded at the end of the 19th century with links first to Sweden and later Germany. Ferries operated both across the Baltic and around its coast, linking small islands and in the ports of Stettin, Danzig and St. Petersburg.

In the decades following the first ferries, others were operating on the Continent's main rivers, the Rhein, Elbe and Danube as well as Swiss, Austrian and Italian lakes. Further south, the last of the great passenger services still runs between Sicily and the Italian mainland after

The world's first purpose-built train ferry in 1850. The *Leviathan* crossed the Firth of Forth between Granton and Burntisland for forty years. *(Douglas Yuill Collection)*

more than 120 years. In contrast with their decline in Western Europe, new train ferry routes have opened in the past few decades on the Black Sea and Caspian linking the countries which emerged from the break-up of the Soviet Union.

The ferries themselves vary from small pontoon barges guided across the Rhein by wire ropes, to giant multi-deck freight ferries on the Black Sea and Baltic ferry-liners as big as the great ocean liners of the past. What they have in common as train ferries is that they make regular crossings between the same ports, day after day, sailings which can take a few minutes or several hours. Each train ferry is designed to match the ports it serves and often spends decades on a single route.

The history of each ferry route is told and, as far as possible, pictures and technical data are included for more than three hundred train ferries which have operated around Europe. Inevitably a few will have been missed.

The early years - 1850 to 1899

Looking back from the 21st century, it is difficult to visualise land transport before the railway age, when a horse and cart could move goods only a few miles per day. The rich could travel by horse or stagecoach and ordinary people seldom travelled as they had to walk. The development of the railways over the middle

Train ferries in operation

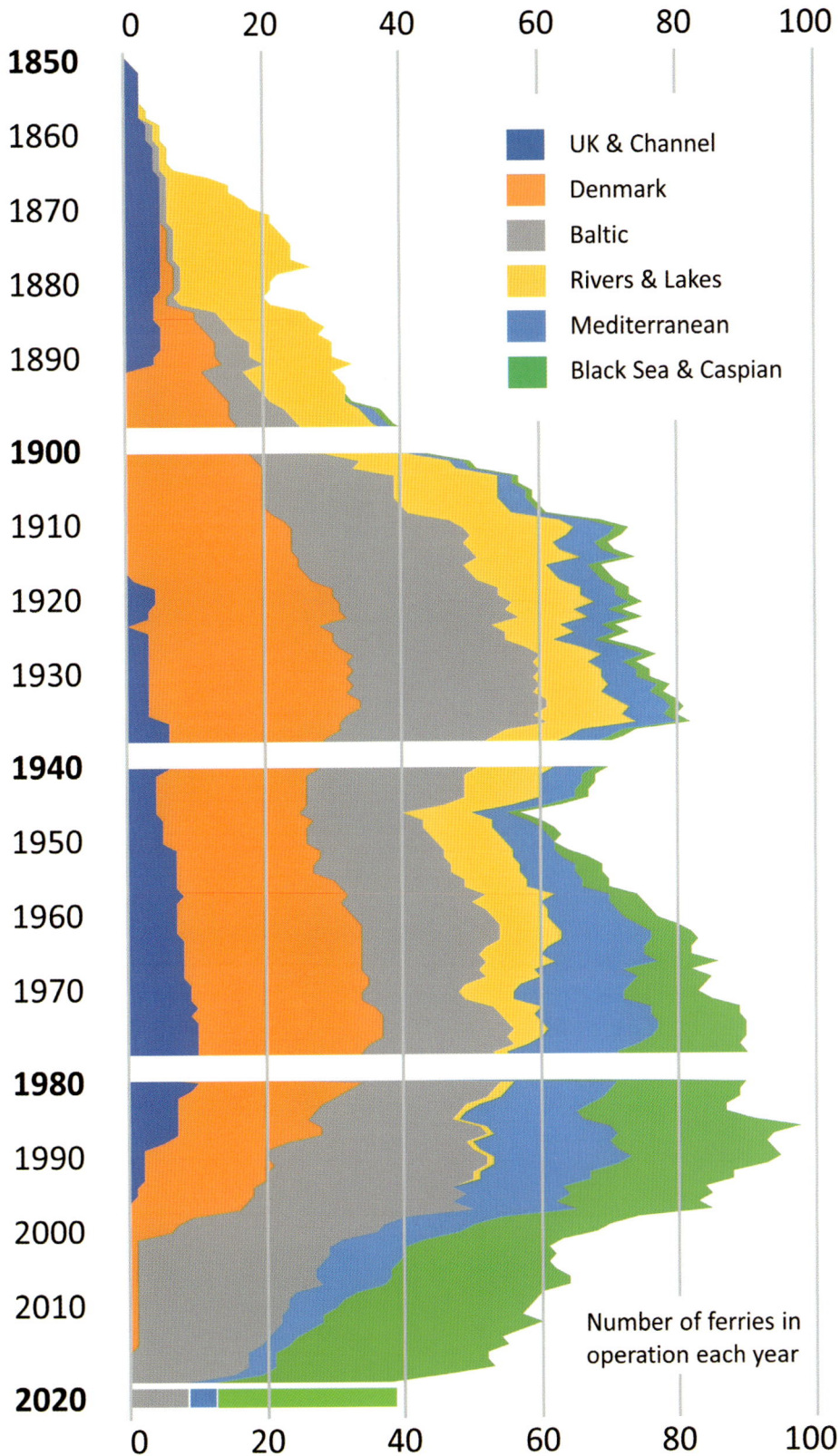

Legend:
- UK & Channel
- Denmark
- Baltic
- Rivers & Lakes
- Mediterranean
- Black Sea & Caspian

Number of ferries in operation each year

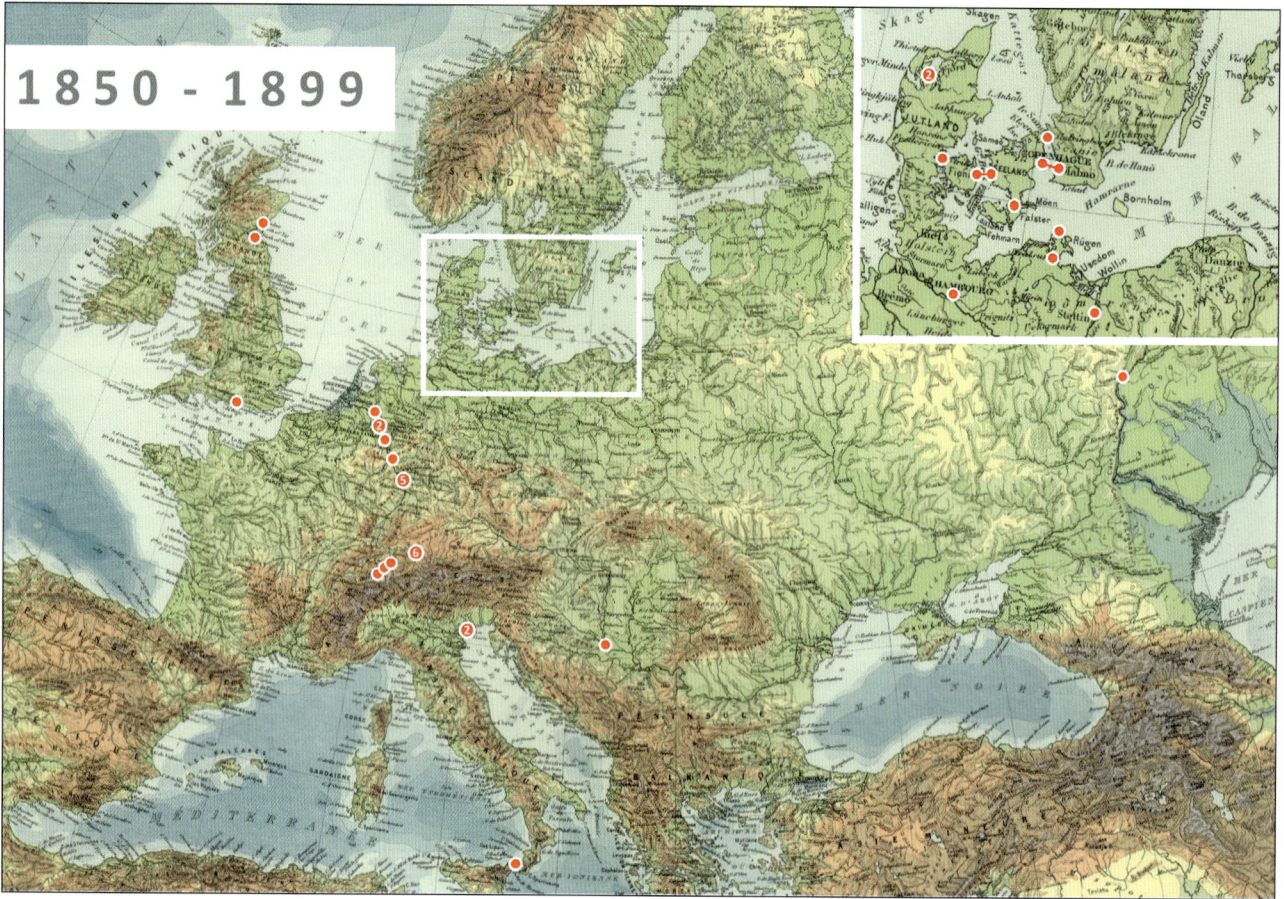

1850 - 1899

decades of the 19th century was a revolution. Hundreds of tons of goods could be moved quickly by train and with a cheap ticket, ordinary people could visit a distant city or holiday at the seaside.

However, once the railway reached a river, lake or sea, very little had changed. Ferries were generally small wooden boats, many still had sails or oars. Only on the busiest routes was there a mail steamer or packet boat. When it arrived in port, transferring cargo to the quayside could take several hours. Dock-labourers would carry goods on their backs and manhandle them from the hold to horse-drawn carts or railway wagons on the quay. Few loads would weigh more than 50kg and if there was a small hand-powered crane on the

dockside, it could only lift a few barrels. The transfer of goods between ship and quay had changed very little since Roman times.

The first ferries

The railway was invented to move coal. The growing industrial cities consumed hundreds of tons per day and for the first time a wagon could be loaded at the coalfield and arrive at a factory siding tens of miles away without the coal being handled along the way. At a time when many shipwrights followed plans inherited from their fathers, the railway engineers brought their practical engineering to the design of the first train ferries.

	Leviathan	Rorschach
Year built	1849	1966
Service	8km across the Firth of Forth	12km across the Bodensee
Dimensions (L x B x D)	51.1 x 10.5 x 1.98m	55.5 x 12.2 x 1.36m
Capacity	3 tracks / 20 wagons	2 tracks / 12 wagons
Loading	Bow and stern	Bow and stern
Arrangement	Central wheelhouse on gantry sheer on main deck deck	Central wheelhouse on gantry, sheer on main deck
Propulsion and steering	2x steam engines driving	2x diesel engines driving independent paddle wheels Voith-Schneider
propellers		
Power and speed	210 hp / 5 knots	1200 hp / 12 knots
Working life	40 years	10 years + 44 years as car ferry

The *Trajekteschiff I* was the first international train ferry in 1869, crossing the Bodensee between Germany and Switzerland. Her huge coal consumption made her very expensive to operate and she was laid-up in 1883. *(Stadtarchiv Friedrichshafen)*

The first Danish train ferry, the *Lillebælt,* was built in Newcastle in 1872. *(Museet for Søfarts)*

The earliest German ferries operated across the Rhein, here between Rheinhausen and Hochfeld in 1866. *(Berlin Architekturmuseum)*

Their objective was to transfer up to twenty wagons, each containing around five tons of coal, from shore to ship in a few minutes using only a handful of men. Two main problems needed to be solved. When coal was loaded from a chute, men with shovels would level it around the hold to keep the ship upright. Loading heavy wagons over the side would cause the ship to heel. This was at the least a problem for the mooring ropes, but if not carefully managed, the ship could capsize. The second problem was to allow for the difference in elevation between the quayside and the ship's deck which would change depending on the tide and the ship's draught. The wagons could be run down a ramp and winched back up to the quayside on a rope. But as they had no brakes this would be time-consuming and

potentially dangerous, depending on the gradient.

Crossing the Firths of Forth and Tay, on the east coast of Scotland, was the first time, civil and mechanical engineers and naval architects combined their skills to design a ferry, its dock and its loading arrangements as a system. Wagons were loaded over the ferry's bow and stern, it had engines and boilers on both sides to create a clear deck for the wagons. The tidal range was solved by the 'flying bridge', a horizontal platform which could move up and down a ramp, carrying several wagons at a time from the quayside to the ship's deck. A flexible ramp on the flying bridge connected to the ferry, linking the ship to the quayside. The first train ferry, the *Leviathan*, in 1850 was a

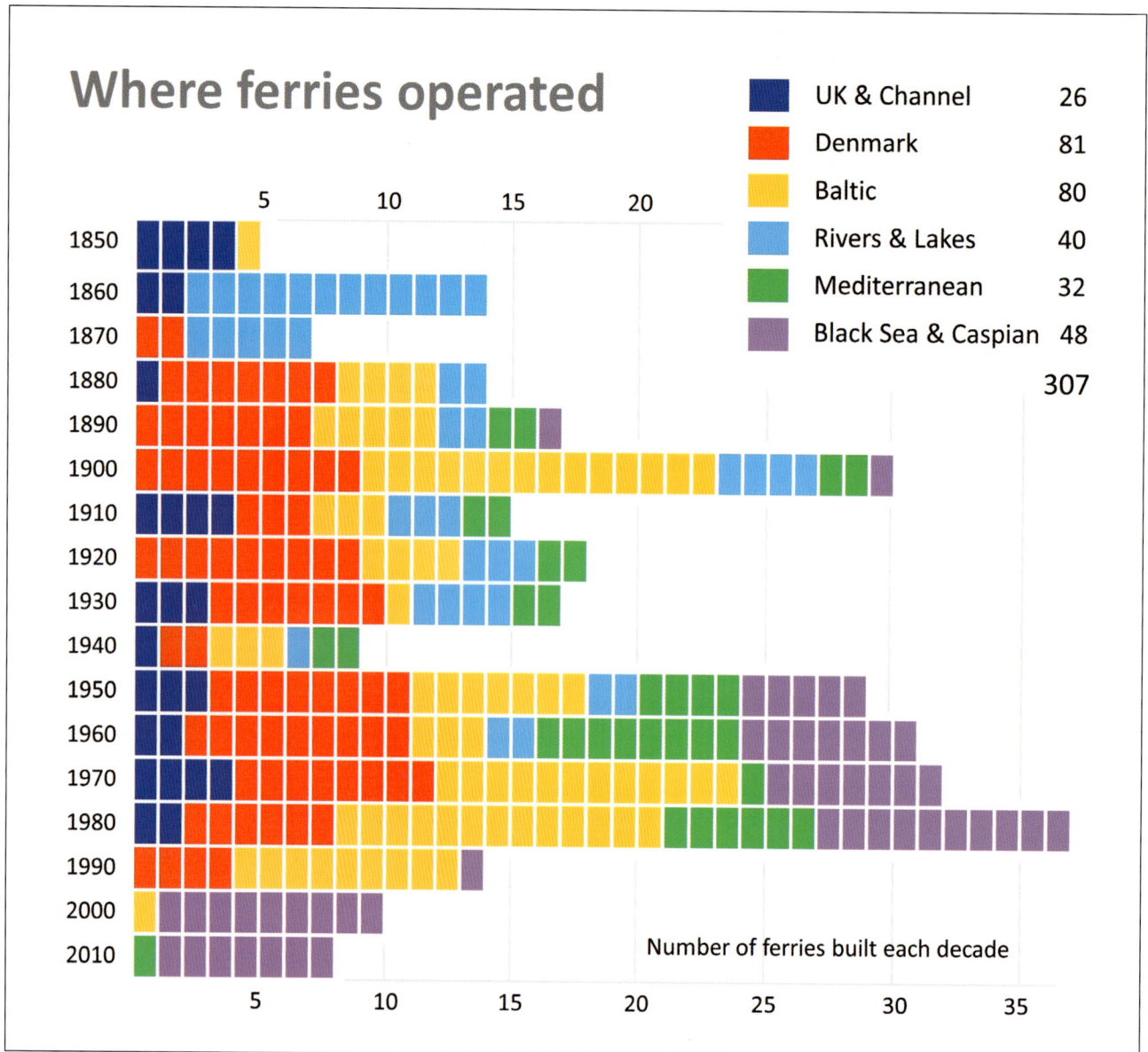

Where ferries operated

Legend		Count
■	UK & Channel	26
■	Denmark	81
■	Baltic	80
■	Rivers & Lakes	40
■	Mediterranean	32
■	Black Sea & Caspian	48
		307

Number of ferries built each decade

(Chart: stacked bar chart showing the number of ferries built each decade from 1850 to 2010, by region.)

Early routes

Train ferries were the creature of the railways, so their development followed the expansion of Europe's railway network through the mid-19th century. By 1870, German railway companies had built eleven ferry crossings on the Rhein and Elbe. They were the first reluctant ferry operators as their plans to build bridges were rejected by the Prussian military in case they were captured by an invading French army. Some of these ferries were tugs and barge, but others were steam-powered pontoons which pulled themselves across the river on a wire rope. After the Franco-Prussian war most were replaced by bridges and only four of the routes survived until the end of the century.

The original Forth and Tay ferries were described as 'waggon boats' and were not designed to carry passengers. Passenger steamers ran a parallel service between the stations on either side of the Firths. However, they did take passengers who had missed the steamer, though they had to stand on the deck between the coal wagons which must have been fairly miserable in the Scottish winter. The Rhein river ferries which followed a few years later were also designed for goods wagons. When they later carried passenger coaches, the passengers stayed in their coaches during the crossing.

The first international train ferry, the *Trajektschiff I*, ran across the Bodensee (Lake Constance), between Southern Germany and Switzerland in 1869. It was also the first specifically designed to carry passengers as well as goods and provided a promenade deck for them to take the air and enjoy the alpine scenery. Although the ferry did not last long, given its huge appetite for coal, the service across the lake continued for more than a

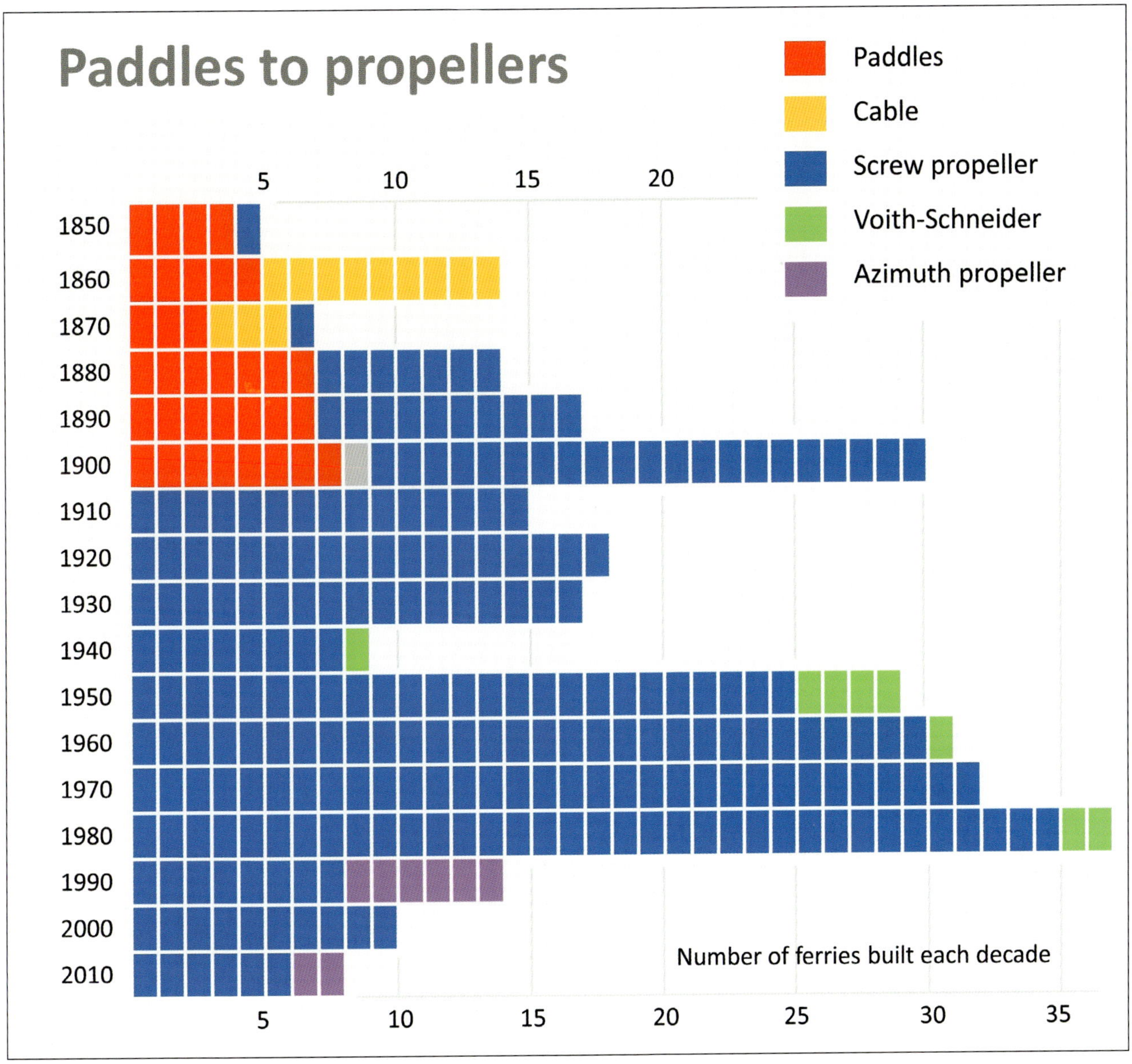

Paddles to propellers
Paddles
Cable
Screw propeller
Voith-Schneider
Azimuth propeller
5
10
15
20
25
30
35
1850
1860
1870
1880
1890
1900
1910
1920
1930
1940
1950
1960
1970
1980
1990
2000
2010
Number of ferries built each decade

century and spawned a number of smaller ferries on other Swiss lakes. Of the 57 train ferries built in the 19th century, 21 operated on rivers and lakes.

Denmark's first ferry was in 1872 and crossed the Lillebælt, between Jylland and the island of Fyn. With no tide in the Baltic, adjusting for small changes in sea level was comparatively simple. The *Lillebælt* also had accommodation for passengers with both 1st and 3rd class saloons below the train deck. With only tiny portholes and oil lamps, these saloons must have been fairly gloomy, but at least provided a warm and comfortable place to shelter during the crossing.

Danish Railways started four other ferry services in the following decade connecting the rail networks of all the larger islands. This included the Storebælt, which at 26 km, was the first ferry crossing taking more than an hour. In time, it became the busiest and probably the best-known train ferry service in Europe. The success of the Storebælt ferries led to international crossings between Denmark and Sweden in the last decade of the 19th century. By this time, the ferries had become larger and grander and the accommodation on the Danish flagship, the *Kjøbenhavn*, included Gentlemen's and Ladies' Saloons and a Dining Room, all with electric lighting, though still located below the train deck

The Germans followed the Danish lead with ferries in the port of Stettin and on the Baltic island of Rügen. While most of these routes were clustered in the north and west of Europe, two other train ferries started operation in the last few years of the 19th century. A large icebreaking ferry, the *Saratovskaya Pereprava*, was built in Newcastle to cross the Volga at Saratov and expand the Russian railway eastwards. In the south, a ferry connecting Sicily to the Italian mainland started in 1899 and remains in operation as the longest running train ferry service in Europe.

1900 - 1939

Paddles to propellers

One of the biggest technical risks taken by the designers of the *Leviathan* was to fit two steam engines, each independently driving one of the paddle wheels. Before this, paddles were always connected by a shaft, driven by the engine in the centre of the ship, which ensured the two paddles rotated together. Getting rid of the shaft between the paddles allowed the train deck to be lowered to improve stability. It also allowed the paddles to be used for steering, even rotating the ship in her own length by running one paddle forward, the other aft. The question was whether the two engines could be controlled well-enough for the ship to be steered in a straight line, particularly when the paddles were loaded unevenly as she rolled in a heavy sea. In the event, the design was a success and *Leviathan* could be steered safely even in bad weather. The design was copied by most of the ferries which followed, such as the *Trajektschiff I* and *Lillebælt*.

In addition to manoeuvrability, paddles allowed a shallower draught and a fuller hull shape which suited the early ferries and harbours. The biggest disadvantage in Denmark and the southern Baltic was that the paddles were damaged when breaking the winter ice. The other issue was that paddles are more efficient going forward than going astern. On a short crossing with a double-ended ferry, this was not important. On a longer crossing, such as the Storebælt or between København and Malmö, the ferries were

designed to operate double-ended but with experience found it quicker to turn and operate with the paddles in their more efficient direction.

The first ferry with a screw propeller was reportedly the *Pikas*, built in 1858 by AG Vulcan in Stettin, to transport wagons across the harbour from the rail sidings to their shipyard. The first screw ferry in public service was the *BB I*, built in 1873 by Escher Wyss for the Swiss lakes. Propellers quickly became the norm and the fourteen ferries built in the 1880s were equally split, seven had paddles and seven propellers. In the following decades, screw propellers were in the majority and the last paddle ferries built were the *Sicilia* and *Calabria* for the Strait of Messina in 1905.

Beyond the horizon 1900 to 1939

While the 19th century ferries stayed within sight of the shore, the 20th century opened with two new long-distance routes across the Baltic, connecting Germany to Denmark and Sweden. Warnemünde to Gedser in 1903 and Sassnitz to Trelleborg in 1909. These heralded the new age of long-distance through-trains and sleeper services connecting Berlin to København and Stockholm. These ferries also took passenger accommodation to the next level. The *Prins Christian*, built for Danske Statsbaner in 1903, was the first ferry to move the passenger saloons above the train deck, providing lounges and dining saloons for first-class passengers lit by large square windows and with access to a

promenade deck. Her profile with central funnels, an enclosed superstructure and forward wheelhouse created the model for most later ferries.

Small ferries were introduced to move goods wagons around harbours with Amsterdam, Danzig, and St. Petersburg following Stettin's lead. The ferry on Tinnsjø served a chemical plant in the Norwegian mountains. There was also a short-lived ferry service carrying an electric tram to the Stockholm suburbs.

The long-discussed train ferry across the English Channel was finally started by the British Army towards the end of the First World War to supply the Western Front. In the 1920s, these ferries started a commercial service taking goods wagons between Harwich and Zeebrugge. From 1936, the Southern Railway carried the London to Paris 'Night-Ferry' sleeper between Dover and Dunkerque.

In Denmark, several of the old services disappeared as bridges were built in the 1930s, though the Storebælt

Top: The *Kjøbenhavn* leaving her namesake city. By the end of the 19th century, train ferries had become larger, faster and far more comfortable for their passengers. *(Københavns Kommune)*

Above: The *Saratovskaya Pereprava*, leaving the Tyne for Russia in 1895, was the largest train ferry of her day and first to have four tracks on deck. Wagons were loaded using hydraulic lifts at the bow. *(Author's collection)*

Left: The *BB II* of 1886 (later renamed *D.G.V 2*) operated on the Swiss lakes and was one of the first propeller driven ferries. Amazingly, her hull is still in use as a gravel barge more than 130 years later. *(Author's collection)*

The Danish ferry, **Prins Christian**, was built for the Gedser to Warnemünde crossing in 1903. She became a model for later ferries with an enclosed superstructure and passenger saloons above the train deck. *(Author's collection)*

remained. New services were started to Denmark's Southern islands, mostly for farmers to send sugar beet for processing. In the last few months of peace, a new route opened between Kristiansand in Norway and Hirtshals in the north of Denmark, but like many services across Northern Europe this was soon a casualty of the Second World War.

Steam to diesel

Propellers had replaced paddles by the start of the 20th century, but virtually all ferries had steam engines until the 1920s. Nearly all were coal-burning, though a few, such as on the Volga and the British Army's cross-channel ferries, used oil.

The first train ferry in the world to have an internal combustion engine was the *Jasper von Moltzahn*, built in 1911 for the Wittower crossing on the German Baltic coast and fitted with a 45 hp petrol engine. She could carry three wagons and made the 10-minute crossing two or three times a day. The petrol engine proved much cheaper than burning coal all day to keep a boiler in steam. She was followed three years later by the *Spoorpont* operating across Amsterdam harbour and fitted with a 130 hp Kromhout 'hot-bulb' oil engine. This was an early form of the diesel engine that used an external vapouriser or 'hot-bulb' to ignite the fuel-air

It took only two decades to change from paddles to propellers. The Italian ferries **Sicilia** and **Calabria**, built in 1905, were the last paddle train ferries. *(Author's collection)*

mixture. The engines operated at low pressure, which made them large and heavy compared to later diesel engines, but had the advantages of being easy to repair and not too fussy about fuel quality.

These were both small ferries, but the Danish engineering company Burmeister & Wain pioneered large marine diesel engines and their first ocean-going motor ship, the *Selandia* was built in 1912. Her owners were

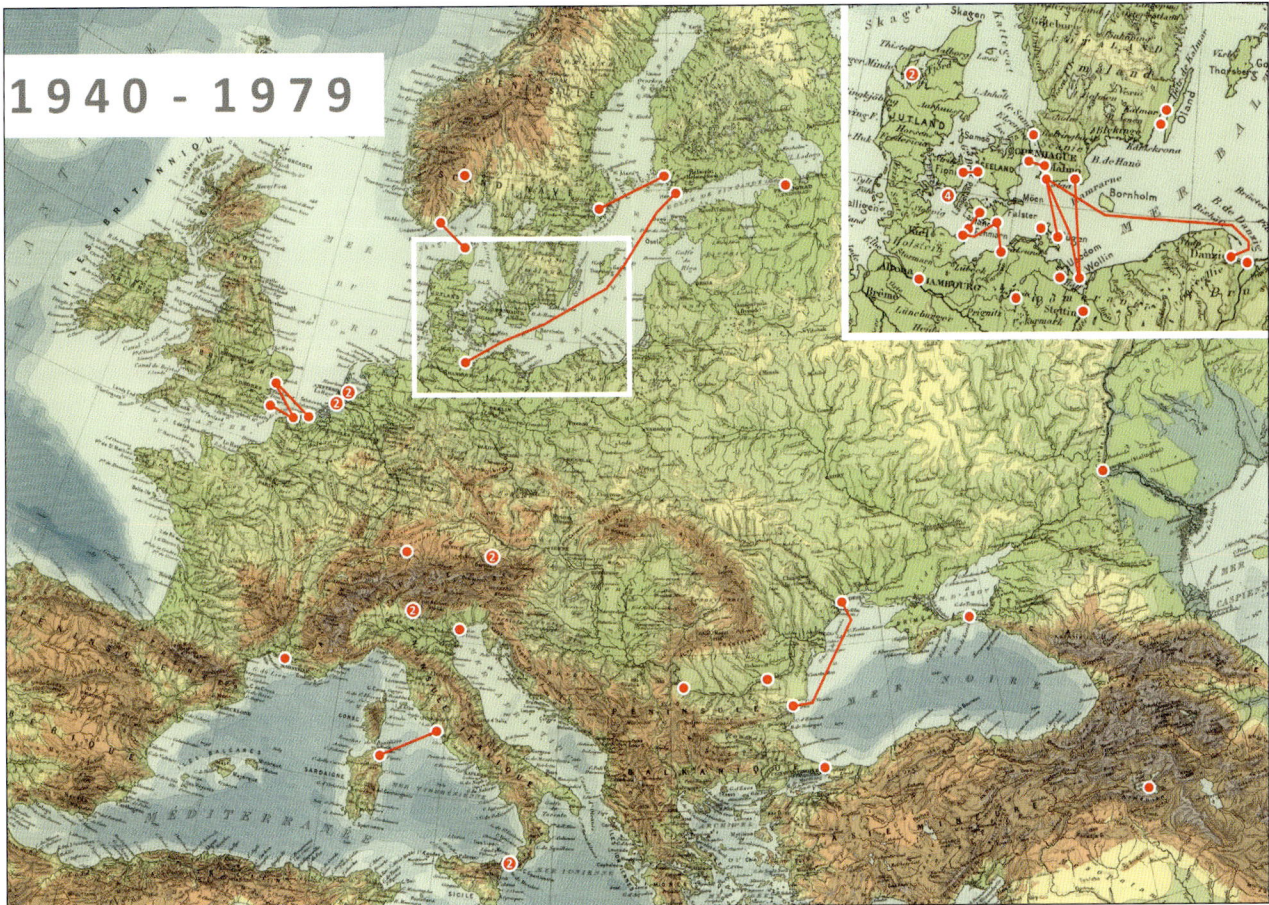

1940 - 1979

shareholders in the ferry company, A/S Mommark Færge, so it was not surprising that their first train ferry, the *Mommark*, was built with two Holeby diesels in 1922. Danske Statsbaner followed five years later with the much larger *Korsør* in 1927. The change from steam to diesel was almost complete within a decade. The most advanced ferries of their day were the *Scilla* and *Cariddi*, delivered to Italian Railways in 1932. They were the first to have diesel-electric propulsion and bridge control. Of the seventeen ferries built in the 1930s, thirteen were diesel powered. Three of the steam ships were Southern Railway's turbine-driven *Twickenham Ferry*, *Shepperton Ferry* and *Hampton Ferry*, which were the last large steam train ferries. The only steam ferry built after the war was a small shipyard ferry in Leningrad.

Ports and linkspans

Transferring rail wagons from the shore to the ferry is always more difficult than for road vehicles. Partly because the rails need to be accurately aligned, but also because rolling stock is only designed for small gradients. While the first ferries coped with the tide by loading wagons with a 'flying bridge', most train ferries operated in places with very little tidal range. The small differences in water level on the Baltic, Mediterranean and Black Sea could be accommodated by a hinged

linkspan. The same is true for the Caspian Sea and Alpine Lakes.

Rivers presented a different challenge as although there is no tide, the water level can vary between five or ten metres at different times of year. The ferry at Lauenburg on the Elbe used the flying-bridge design. The cable ferries on the Rhein had a long ramp with a gradient of 1:48 which could be used by locomotives. On the Volga, the *Saratovskaya Pereprava* was fitted with a hydraulic lift on the bow to raise wagons to the level of the shore track. Two terminals were built on each side of the river at different elevations and the ferry chose the one closest to the river level. In Hamburg, the whole deck of the ferries could be elevated to the quayside level. Other river crossings used long linkspans, such as at Giurgiu and Ruse on the Danube, where the linkspans were 200m long.

One of the highest tidal ranges is in the English Channel, with the level varying by 7m at Dover. This posed a problem for Southern Railway's ferries in the 1930s. At Dunkerque, the linkspan was located in a non-tidal dock entered through a sea-lock. At Dover, there was no space within the harbour to build a long linkspan, so the chosen solution was to build a ferry dock. This was matched closely to the ferries' dimensions and could be entered at any state of the tide. The dock gate then closed and the water level pumped-up to bring the ferry level to the quayside in less than 30

The **Deutschland** and **Drottning Victoria** started the first long distance service, from Sassnitz in Germany across the Baltic to Trelleborg in Sweden, in 1909. *(Järnvägsmuseet)*

minutes. As well as the delay, the dock also limited the size of the ferry. When the much larger *Nord Pas-de-Calais* was introduced between Dover and Dunkerque in 1988, the old ferry dock was replaced by a new quay and linkspan.

War and peace 1940 to 1979

Not only were many ferry services suspended during the Second World War, but many ships were lost. Ferries were sunk in the English Channel, Denmark, the Baltic and Sicily. The Volga ferry moved downriver to play an important part of the Battle for Stalingrad and the *Hydro* was famously sunk by the Norwegian Resistance in 1944 to destroy her cargo of heavy water. After D-Day, the British ferries transported locomotives and rolling stock to France assisted by a several US Navy LSTs temporarily converted to carry rail wagons. One new service started during the war, linking Bulgaria and Romania across the Danube.

At the end of the war most services restarted, though the Baltic ferries had to adjust to changes in national borders and the division of Europe into east and west separated by the 'Iron Curtain'. The services from Sweden to what had become East Germany remained and new services were started to Poland. In the Western Baltic, the 'Vogelfluglinie' connected West

The freight ferry **T.F.2** was one of three built for the British Army during the First World War. She later sailed between Harwich and Zeebrugge before being lost in 1940. *(Author's collection)*

Germany to Denmark, initially through Grossenbrode and later from Puttgarden to Rødbyhavn.

In the 1950s, the prisoners of Stalin's gulags built the Trans-Polar Railway with ferry crossings on Russia's two great Arctic rivers. The railway was never completed and the ferries went south, running across the Kerch Strait to Crimea in the Black Sea. A long-planned service also started in Turkey, crossing the Bosporus in

the Southern Danish islands, to the Swedish island of Öland and across Austrian lakes. However, a new service started in 1971 across Lake Van in the mountains of Eastern Turkey and is still in operation.

The most important development was the multi-deck ferries built for long-distance freight routes. Railship opened Europe's longest ferry route in 1975, 1,000km from Travemünde in Northern Germany to Hanko in Finland. This was followed in 1977 by similar large multi-deck ferries operating on the Black Sea between Varna in Bulgaria and Iliychevsk in Ukraine.

The multi-deck ferries

Determining the right size for a ferry is a balance of several factors. Ocean-going ships make voyages lasting days or weeks, much longer than the time to load or discharge in port. Thus, the best way to reduce cost is to make the ship bigger so that a single ship and crew can move more cargo. With a ferry designed for a short

Top left: The *Jasper von Moltzahn*, built in 1911, was fitted with a 45 hp petrol engine and was the first motor ferry in the world. She was renamed *Bergen* in 1949 and scrapped in 1997. *(Author's collection)*

Middle left: The *Spoorpont* carried rail wagons across Amsterdam harbour. She was built in 1914 with a 'hot-bulb' oil engine, a forerunner of the diesel engines which came into general use in the 1920s. *(Author's collection)*

Above: The first large diesel ferry was Danske Statsbaner's *Korsør*. She was built for the Storebælt in 1927 and followed by a sistership *Nyborg* in 1931. *(Author's collection)*

Left: The Dover train ferry dock was used to raise the ferry level with the quayside linkspan at any state of the tide. *(Ferry Publications Library)*

Istanbul and a tiny ferry carrying salt wagons in the south of France.

Two of the longest ferry crossings started in the early 1960s, both carrying passengers as well as rail wagons. Italian Railways introduced a ferry from Civitavecchia, north of Roma, 220 km to Golfo Aranci on the island of Sardegna. In the Soviet Union, a ferry service started across the Caspian Sea from Baku to Krasnovodsk.

Several small ferry routes came to an end in the 1960s as branch lines closed, including services between

crossing, it can take longer to load the ferry and manoeuvre out of the harbour than to make the crossing. The most efficient design will balance the size of the ferry with the number of trips it can make in a day, which can be further complicated where this needs to meet a railway timetable.

On crossings taking less than an hour, ferries have normally been double-ended and often with a single rail track on the centreline. This was not an efficient use of the deck space, but the area around the coaches could

The steam turbine *Twickenham Ferry* was delivered to the Southern Railway in 1934. She and her two sisterships were the last large steam ferries to be built in Europe. *(FotoFlite)*

The most advanced ferries of their day, the Italian sisterships, *Scilla* and *Cariddi*, were built in 1932 with diesel-electric propulsion and bridge control. *(Author's collection)*

No. of rail tracks

Legend:
- Single track (yellow)
- Twin tracks (orange)
- Three tracks (dark red)
- Four or more tracks (purple)
- Multi-deck (black)

Chart: Number of ferries built each decade, by decade from 1850 to 2010, categorised by number of rail tracks.

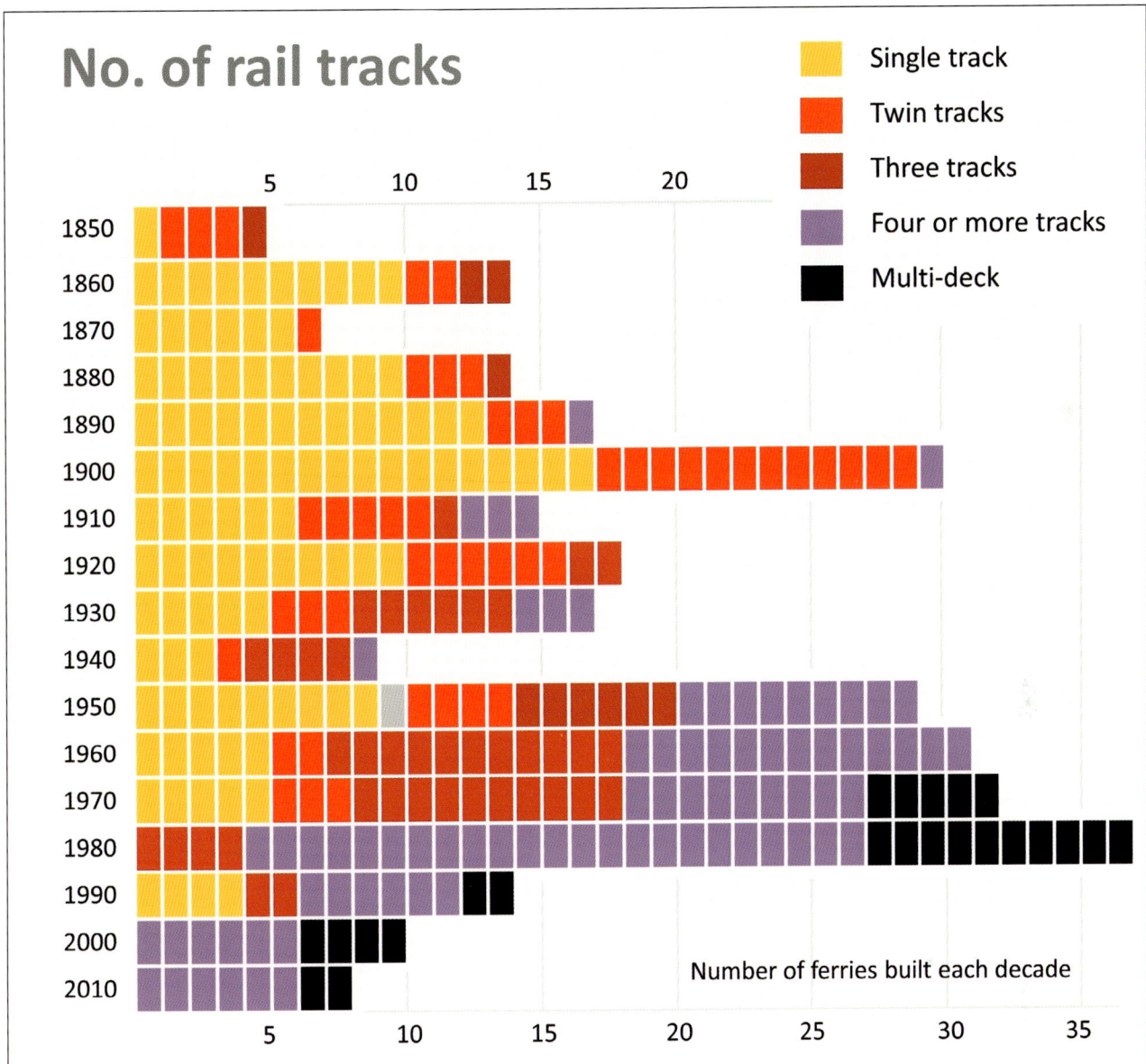

be filled with foot passengers or cars and the ferries could load quickly and had no need to turn in the harbour. Larger ferries carrying passengers had two tracks, but a third track made it difficult for passengers to get out of the coaches on the centre track.   Only freight ferries had multiple tracks on deck to pack the wagons as closely as possible. The *Leviathan* had three tracks and the first ferry with four tracks was the *Saratovskaya Pereprava*, on the Volga in 1895.

Large freight ferries on longer routes were pioneered on the U.S. Great Lakes towards the end of the 19th century, carrying wagons of coal, timber and grain up to 100 miles across Lake Michigan. The first European ferries to follow this model were the three ferries, *T.F.1, T.F.2* and *T.F.3*, built for the British Army during the First World War. They had four tracks on deck carrying 54 wagons on 334m of track. After the war, they were used between Harwich and Zeebrugge. Very few pure freight ferries were built in Europe, the Italian *Messina*

was built in 1924 and the *Suffolk Ferry, Norfolk Ferry* and *Essex Ferry* were built in the 1940s and 50s for the Harwich to Zeebrugge crossing. The only other similar ferry was the *Asa-Thor* built for Danske Statsbaner in 1965 for the Storebælt with space for 50 wagons on 413m of track. As ships got larger, and more importantly wider, they had sufficient stability to carry two decks of freight. The *Svealand* and *Götaland* were built in 1973 for Swedish Railways' service across the Baltic to Germany. They carried rail wagons on five tracks, still on a single deck, but also had an upper deck for trucks and trailers.

It was a small step to design a ship to carry rail wagons on several decks. The first ship with an elevator to move wagons between two decks was the *City of New Orleans*, built in 1959 for the Florida to Cuba service. This was taken to the next level by the *Railship I* delivered in 1975 to operate a 30-hour crossing from Travemünde on the German Baltic coast to Hanko in

Gross tonnage

▨	Less than 1000 gt		
▨	1000 to 5000 gt		
▨	5000 to 10,000 gt		
▨	10,000 to 20,000 gt		
▨	More than 20,000 gt		

Number of ferries built each decade

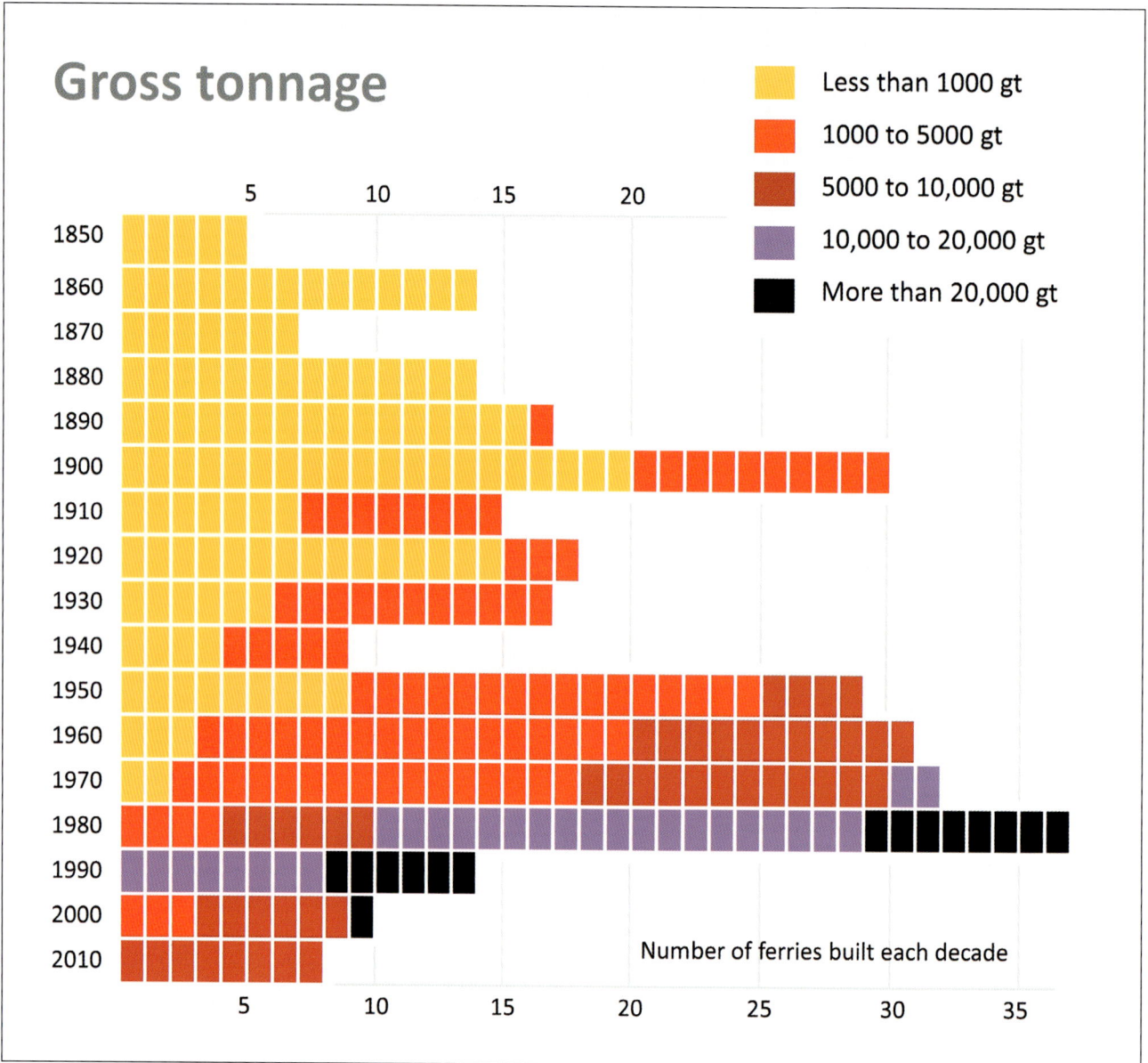

Finland. She had two main innovations for loading wagons, a two-deck lift moved wagons between the three decks and a switching rail fitted in the bow allowed wagons to transfer between the five tracks on the upper and lower decks. *Railship I* had 1,307m of rail rack, more than twice that of any previous ferry, and while it took a few hours to load and unload, this was not too important on a long crossing. She was followed by larger sisterships, *Railship II* and *III*.

The success of Railship was followed by four large ferries, two for Bulgaria and two for Soviet Ukraine, which ran between Varna and Iliychevsk on the Black Sea. Eventually twenty-three multi-deck ferries would be built.

The long decline 1980 to 2019

Thirty-seven train ferries were built in the 1980s, more than in any other decade, and the number of

The *Hydro* became famous when she was sunk by Norwegian Commandos in 1944 to destroy her cargo of heavy water. *(Anders Beer Wilse)*

Deutsche Bundesbahn's *Theodor Heuss* unloading at Grossenbrode Kai in the early 1960s. The division of Germany after the Second World War required new routes between West Germany and Denmark. *(Author's collection)*

ferries operating around Europe peaked at 98 in 1986. Since then, their numbers have declined steeply. There were only 68 by the year 2000 and by 2019 it had reduced to 38, the same as at the end of the 19th century.

The 1980s started with more multi-deck ferries. The *Garibaldi* was built for the Italian Railways' service to

Sardegna in 1982. She was followed by what was probably the greatest train ferry project, between Sassnitz and Klaipeda along the south Baltic coast. This linked East Germany directly to the Soviet Union to by-pass Poland's railways. The five ships were the largest train ferries in the world when the service started in 1986. The ferries were designed for a fast turnround in

The first new train ferry on the Dover to Dunkerque service after the war was SNCF's elegant *Saint-Germain*, built in Denmark in 1951. *(FotoFlite)*

Years in service

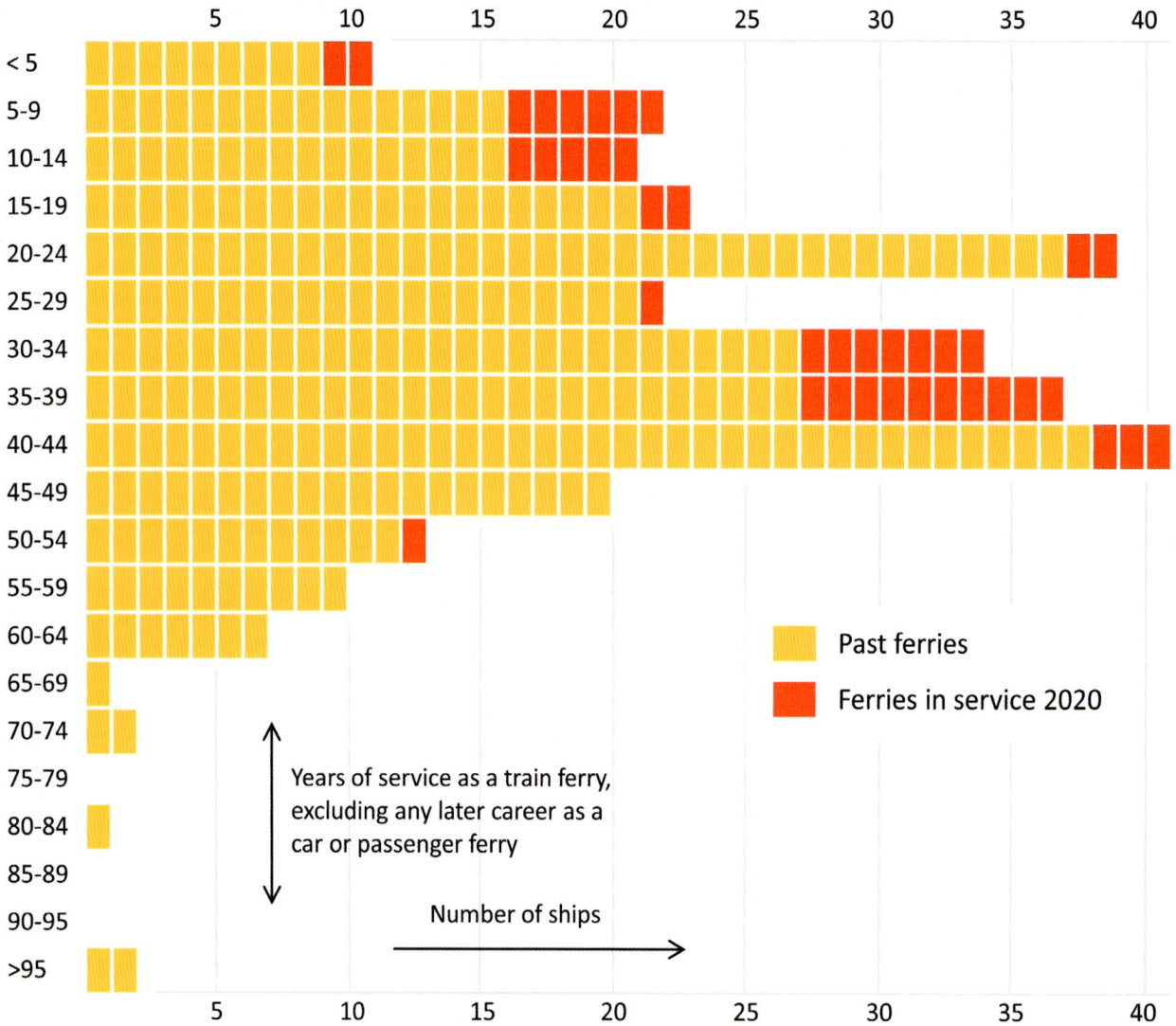

Years of service as a train ferry, excluding any later career as a car or passenger ferry

Number of ships

Past ferries

Ferries in service 2020

The **Sovietskiy Uzbekistan** was one of five sisterships built by the Soviet Union in the 1960s to cross the Caspian Sea. At the time, they were the largest train ferries in the world. (Author's collection)

Two little ferries, the **Beauduc** and the **Esquineau**, were built in 1958 to ship salt wagons across the Rhône. The linkspans were longer than the ferries. (Author's collection)

Freight ferries got larger in the 1970s with Swedish Railway's *Götaland* and *Svealand* which had an upper deck for trucks and trailers. *(Museet for søfarts)*

port and the East German designers decided not to fit a lift between decks, which they saw as a bottleneck. Instead, linkspans were fitted at two levels allowing wagons to be loaded directly to both the main and upper decks. A 640m-long earthworks ramp and bridge was built to provide a gentle gradient to the upper deck, although this filled only a small corner of the ferry terminal which covered five square kilometres.

A new ferry service was also started from Travemünde to Malmö to compete with the land route across Denmark and also routes from Eastern Sweden to Finland. At the same time, many of the longest established routes were replaced by tunnels and bridges. The Harwich to Zeebrugge service closed in 1987 and Dover to Dunkerque followed in 1995 after the opening of the Channel Tunnel. The Storebælt fixed link ended Denmark's internal train ferries in 1997 and in 2000 the ferries between Denmark and Sweden were replaced by the Øresund Bridge. The last train ferry service to Denmark, from Puttgarden to Rødbyhavn, closed to rail traffic in 2019 as the trains from København to Hamburg were rerouted over the Storebælt bridge.

Further south, the Bosporus rail tunnel opened in 2013, though a parallel ferry service continued to carry hazardous cargoes, and a new road-rail bridge from Russia to Crimea was opened across the Kerch Strait in 2019.

The *Railship I* was built in 1975 and was the first ferry to carry rail wagons on several decks. She had many imitators over the following decade. *(Jukka Huotari)*

In the 1990's and 2000's, a network of long-distance train ferry services started in the Black Sea following the break-up of the Soviet Union. These connected Ukraine, Romania and Bulgaria to Russia, Georgia and Turkey. The services carried a mix of trucks and rail wagons, but not all have survived and the Romanian ferries were laid-up in 2009. In the Baltic, Lithuania's independence from the Soviet Union left a Russian enclave at Kaliningrad and new long-distance services linked the port of Baltiyisk to Sassnitz and Ust-Luga, west of St. Petersburg.

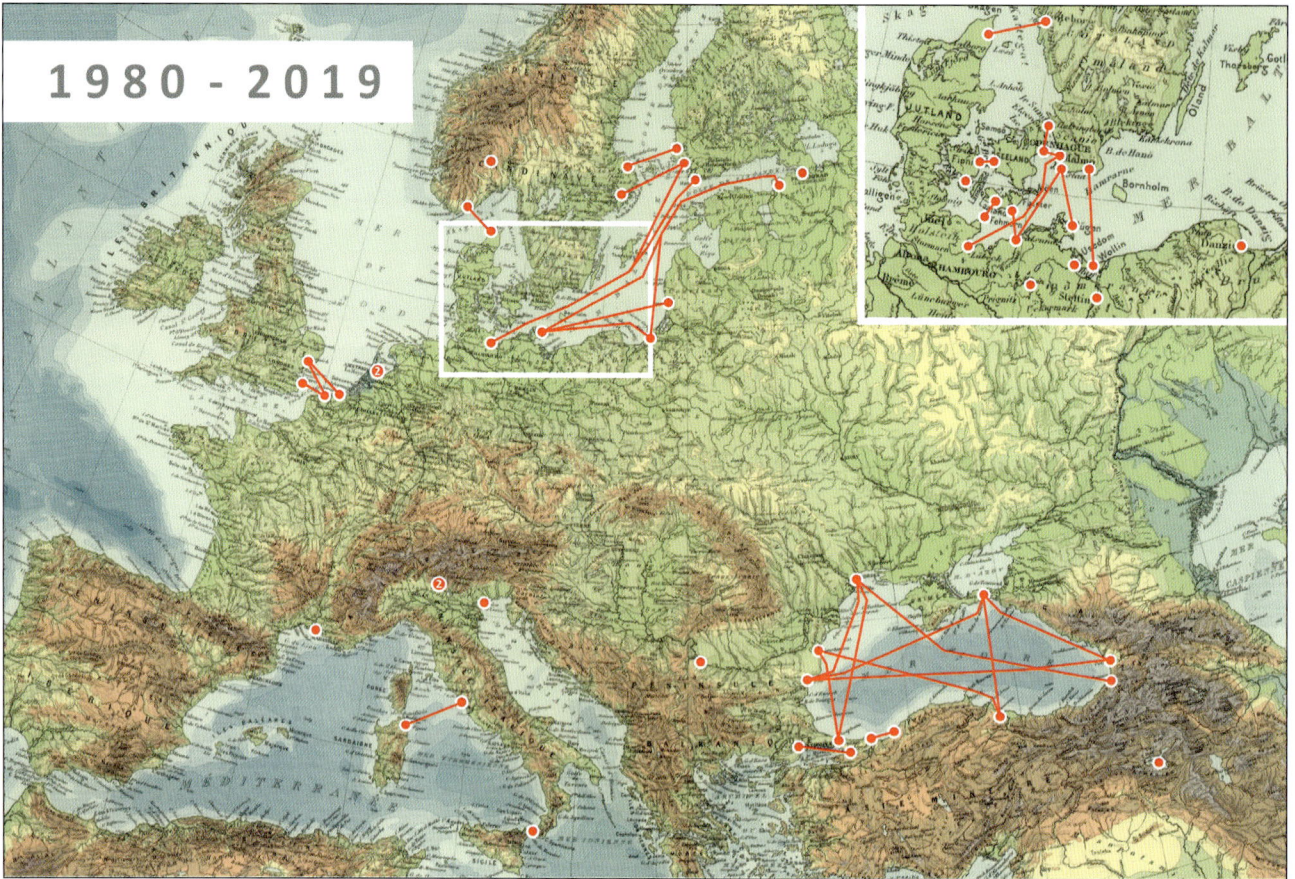

1980 - 2019

The *Essex Ferry*, built for British Rail's Harwich to Zeebrugge service in 1957, was a post-war example of a ferry built purely for freight. *(FotoFlite)*

The *Geroi Shipki* was one of four large multi-deck ferries built to run between Bulgaria and Soviet Ukraine. *(Gerolf Drebes)*

The Italian multi-deck ferry *Garibaldi* operated between the mainland and Sardegna from 1982 until 2009. *(Ian Boyle)*

The *Kong Frederik IX* was built in 1954 for Danske Statsbaner's services to Germany and the largest ferry at the time. *(Postcard – Author's collection)*

The Unity Line's service from Swinoujscie to Ystad came to end in 2019 and though the rail facilities at Swinoujscie port are being redeveloped there is a question mark on whether the service will restart.

The Azerbaijan Caspian Shipping fleet continued to grow and built six two-deck rail ferries for their routes across the Caspian. The original service from Baku, moved to a new terminal at Alat and the port of Krasnovodsk, now in Turkmenistan, was renamed Turkmenbashi. A new service was opened from Baku to Aktau in Kazakhstan in 1992.

Sadly, there were also disasters, with the sinking of the *Jan Heweliusz* in the Baltic and the *Mercuri-2* in the Caspian costing many lives.

Big, but not always beautiful

From the 1950s, the gross tonnage of ferries grew quickly. There were the multi-deck freight ferries and passenger ferries started carrying trucks and cars, as well as trains. More space was needed for car decks and passenger accommodation. The second factor is that gross tonnage is a measure of a ship's enclosed

British Rail's last passenger-train ferry, the **Vortigern,** operated both as a train ferry between Dover and Dunkerque and as a drive-through car ferry. *(Author's collection)*

volume. The train decks on pre-war ferries were generally open at the stern and thus their volume was not included in the gross tonnage. After the loss of the car ferry *Princess Victoria* in 1953, watertight bow and stern doors became normal practice. The train and car decks became an enclosed volume and thus gross tonnage rose very quickly.

The growth of the largest ferries since 1950 is shown in the table below. Although this is specifically lists train ferries, vehicle ferries saw a similar growth over the same period. The last and largest train ferry, the *Skåne*, is typical of the large cruise-ferries on the Baltic routes.

Longevity

If railway companies were reluctant to operate ferries, they were also reluctant to replace them. As ferries were often designed for a specific route, they had a limited resale value. As a result, they often stayed in

The Azerbaijan Caspian Shipping Co. operates the largest fleet of train ferries with thirteen ships. The **Mercuri-1**, previously the **Sovietskaya Gruziya**, is one of a class of eight ferries built in Croatia in the 1990s. *(Author's collection)*

service much longer than other types of ship. Their average working life was more than 32 years. The record being set by the *Stralsund* which worked on various routes on the German Baltic coast for 100 years, before being preserved as a museum ship. Italian railways' *Villa* also worked on the Strait of Messina for

The growth in train ferries since 1950				
	Year built	Gross tonnage	Service	Location
Kong Frederik IX	1954	4,084	Passenger / freight	Baltic
Sovietskiy Azerbaidzhan	1962	8,840	Passenger / freight	Caspian
Geroi Shipki	1978	10,096	Freight only	Black Sea
Railship II	1984	20,077	Freight only	Baltic
Mecklenburg-Vorpommern	1996	37,987	Passenger / freight	Baltic
Skåne	1998	42,705	Passenger / freight	Baltic

Top: The last and largest train ferry built for the English Channel was SNCF's *Nord Pas-de-Calais*. Too large for the Dover dock, she operated from a new linkspan until replaced by the Channel Tunnel in 1994. *(Pieter Inpijn)*

Above left: The *Sassnitz* operated across the Baltic between Sassnitz and Trelleborg until the service closed in 2020. *(Christian Kowalski)*

Left: The largest ever train ferry, the *Skåne*, sailing past the old ferry station at Warnemünde on her way out into the Baltic. She has two open vehicle decks above the main train deck. *(Author)*

One of the few large ferries still operating on the Baltic, the *Wolin*, previously the *Sky Wind* and the *Öresun*d, now operates as a passenger and vehicle ferry between Swinoujscie and Trelleborg. *(Pieter Inpijn)*

69 years. Many ferries also went on to have long second careers, generally as car ferries. The greatest survivor is the *BB II*, built in 1886 and still used as a gravel barge on the Swiss Lakes 134 years later.

2020 onwards

At the start of 2020 there were 38 train ferries operating in Europe. By the end of the year, only 36:

seven on the Baltic, four on the Strait of Messina, twelve in the Black Sea and Turkey and thirteen on the Caspian. The majority of these are more than 30 years old.

Only two passenger services remained in the Baltic, running from Germany to southern Sweden. Within a few months, the Sassnitz to Trelleborg service which had operated since 1909 was stopped, leaving only the route from Rostock to Trelleborg in operation. There is also the Russian freight service using two of the old Railship

The *Logudoro* was built for the Sardegna service in 1989 and a close sister to *Scilla* (IV) and *Villa* (II). She was laid-up when this service closed and transferred to the Messina Strait in 2012. *(Phil English)*

The Vogelfluglinie ferry *Deutschland* was converted to hybrid power in 2013-14. The train ferry service stopped in 2019 and she and her sisters are now purely car ferries. *(Frank Lose)*

Snow-capped alpine peaks form a backdrop for the double-ended ferry *Romanshorn* crossing the Bodensee between Switzerland and Germany. *(Schweizerische Bodensee-Schiffahrtsgesellschaft AG)*

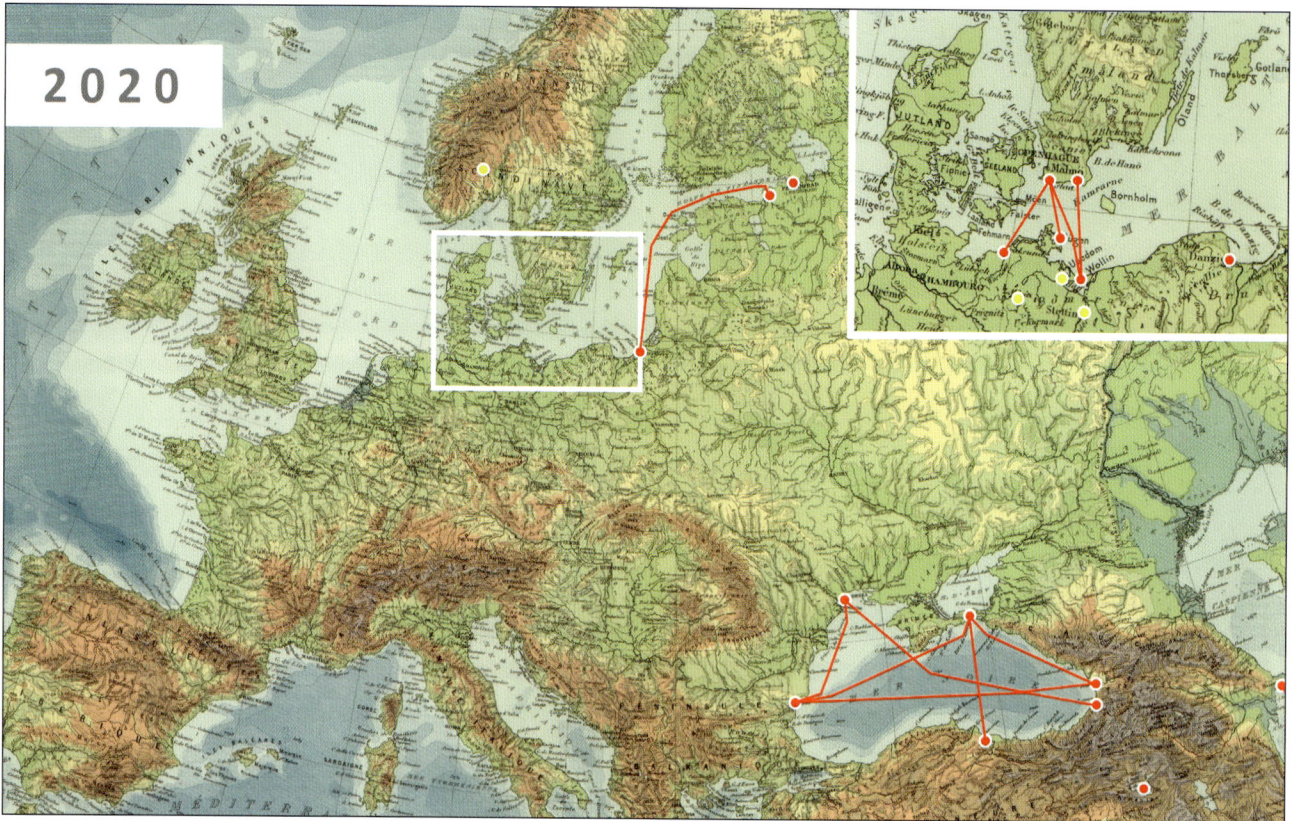

2020

Loading passenger coaches at Messina in Sicily, the last service in Europe to carry passenger trains. *(Authors collection)*

vessels between Baltiyisk in Kaliningrad and Ust-Luga, with two new ships being built to replace them.

Old shipyard ferries survive in Gdansk and St. Petersburg and four small ferries, including the *Stralsund*, have been preserved as museum ships, at Tinnoset, Fürstenberg/Havel, Wolgast and Szczecin, (marked as yellow dots on the map).

On the Mediterranean, there are still four ferries on the Messina Strait, the oldest route still in operation and the last to carry passenger coaches. Several projects to build a bridge between Sicily and the Italian mainland have come and gone but with no certainty on when it will be built, a new ship is under construction to replace the older ferries. Several freight services continue on the Black Sea, although only time will tell whether the older ferries will be replaced. The two ferries on the Kerch Strait also have an uncertain future with the opening of the bridge in 2019.

The largest fleet is the thirteen ships operated by the Azerbaijan Caspian Shipping Co., and while some of the ships built in the 1980s have been laid-up, others have recently been refurbished. New terminals have been built at the Caspian ports with capacity for overland traffic from China to increase. Exports are brought through Kazakhstan by rail and across the Caspian and Black Sea ferries to Europe.

Over the next few decades, transport will change to meet climate change objectives. Scandlines converted the diesel-electric propulsion on their Vogelfluglinie ferries to hybrid power in 2013-14, using a battery bank to reduce emissions. A reduction in the number of diesel trucks on Europe's roads may also lead to a revival of rail freight. Whether this will result in the busy ro-ro routes across the North Sea, Baltic and Mediterranean carrying rail wagons once again is a question for the future.

ONE

The first ferries

Forth & Clyde Canal Co.
Kirkintilloch – Grangemouth
1835 - unknown

Although this book is about railways, it starts in the canal age. Britain's industrial revolution accelerated through the second half of the 18th century. The cotton industry moved workers from their homes to new factories. James Watt developed the steam engine to become a practical source of power. Glasgow expanded quickly into an industrial city, powered by coal brought from the north Lanarkshire coalfields by the Monkland Canal. A major part of this new age of opportunity was the opening of the Forth & Clyde Canal in 1790. It ran for 56km across central Scotland linking the west and east coasts. It was deeper and wider than previous canals, designed to allow seagoing ships to travel from the Atlantic to the North Sea. Raw materials imported from the Americas could be processed in Glasgow's factories and exported to the North Sea ports without the long dangerous voyage around the north of Scotland.

The railway age

Where canals were not practical, colliery-owners built tramways. These were paved roads with gentle gradients that allowed a horse to pull a line of coal trucks. Initially, the tramways had grooves or simple plate rails to guide the trucks. Iron rails were introduced at the beginning of the 19th century and although there were several experiments with steam engines, it was George Stephenson who brought it all together. His railway from the Shildon colliery to the port of Stockton in the north-east of England opened in September 1825. For the first time, coal trucks were pulled by a steam locomotive running on wrought iron rails and the railway age was born.

At the same time, a group of colliery owners in central Scotland obtained approval to build the

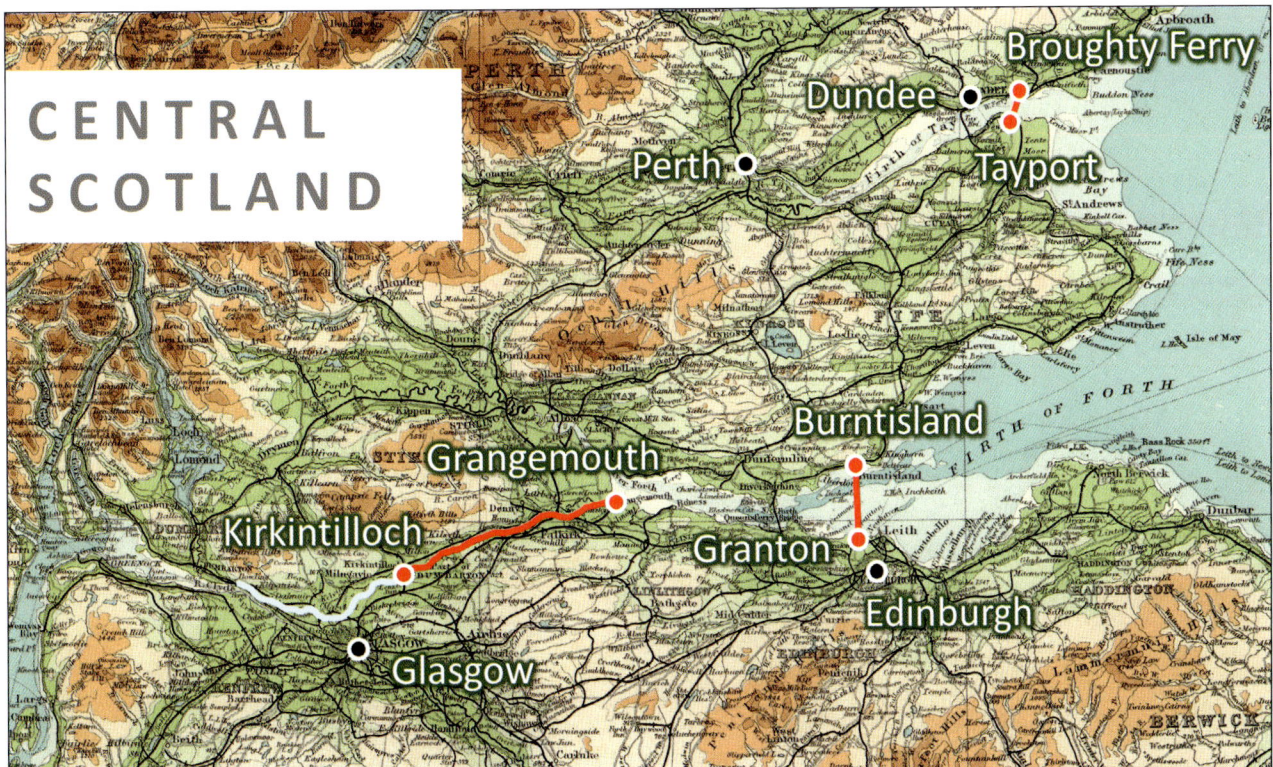

A train of wagons with 50 tons of coal being pulled by a Clydesdale horse named 'Dragon' on the newly opened Monkland & Kirkintilloch Railway, 1826. *(East Dunbartonshire archive)*

Monkland & Kirkintilloch Railway in 1824. The line was to run for around 10 miles, north from the coalfields around Coatbridge to the Forth & Clyde canal at Kirkintilloch. At Kirkintilloch, the coal would be loaded into barges and taken eastwards to the new port of Grangemouth on the Firth of Forth. They appointed a young engineer to oversee the work, Thomas Grainger had worked on several road projects though the Monkland & Kirkintilloch was his first railway. The shareholders were aware of developments in England and part of his brief was to build a railway that would be suitable for steam locomotives. He used iron rails, though unfortunately chose a gauge of 4' 6", (1,372mm) as opposed to Stephenson's 4' 8½", (1,435 mm) that became standard gauge. This may have been due to

poor communication or simply that at the time no-one envisaged a future where railways would be connected as a national network. Either way, Grainger's track was later changed to standard gauge at significant expense.

The Monkland & Kirkintilloch Railway started operation in 1826 using horse-drawn wagons belonging to the coal mines. The first steam locomotive was brought into service in 1831. The wagons were loaded at the mines and at Kirkintilloch the coal was unloaded into barges using chutes. Loading the barges was comparatively easy. Once the barges reached Grangemouth, shovelling the coal out of their holds and transferring it to waiting ships was hard manual work. A new railway taking coal from the Lanarkshire mines directly to customers in Glasgow was opened in 1831

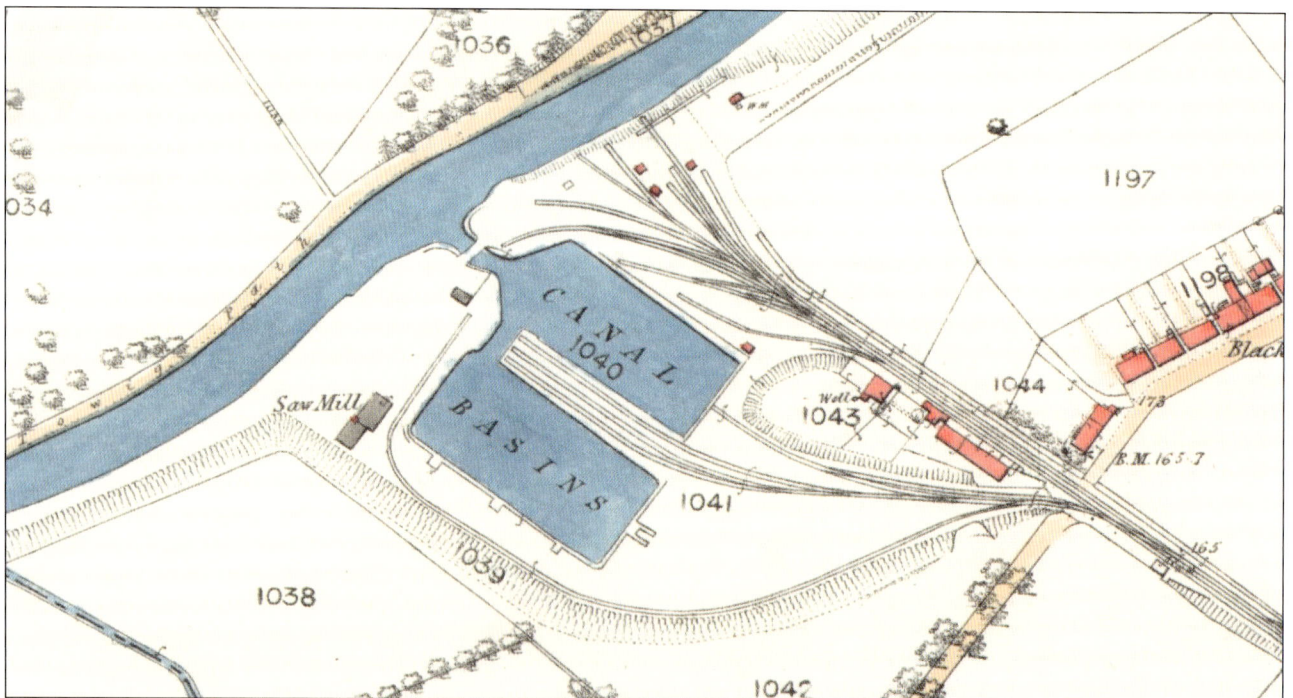

Map of the Monkland & Kirkintilloch Railway at the Forth & Clyde canal basin in Kirkintilloch. The line stopping at the quayside on the easterly basin may have been where the waggon boat was loaded

REID & HANNA,
SMITHS,
IRON BOAT BUILDERS,
GASHOLDER MAKERS,
AND GAS ENGINEERS,
8, SMITHHILL-STREET,
PAISLEY.

Advert for Reid & Hanna, builders of the waggon boat.

Thomas Grahame of Whitehill (1791-1866) inventor of the cart-boat and waggon-boat. The unacknowledged father of the ro-ro ferry. *(Glasgow Museums)*

and took much of the traffic from the Monkland Canal. The shareholders of the Forth & Clyde Canal were obviously worried that the new railways would soon threaten their coal trade to the east coast ports.

Thomas Grahame and the waggon-boat

The ro-ro ferry was the brainchild of Thomas Grahame of Whitehill, a retired army major in his early forties from a prosperous Glasgow merchant family. He was an energetic member of the Forth & Clyde Canal Committee and well aware of the threat from the new railways. Around 1830, he introduced fast horse-drawn catamarans for passengers on the canal. He also experimented with steam tugs, though these were less successful. His next scheme in 1833 was to persuade the canal company to introduce a 'cart-boat' to transport farm produce into Glasgow, which he described in a letter to a friend in Paris, dated March 1835. Farmers

close to the canal wanted to make regular deliveries of small quantities of dairy products, vegetables and grain to merchants in Glasgow. However, loading and unloading these goods from a canal boat led to damage and expense. Grahame's solution was to fit an old iron quarry barge with a flat open deck that could carry 16-18 carts. The horse-drawn cart-boat started early each morning, moving westwards along the canal. Farmers would take their carts to the canal-side and push them onboard. Once the boat reached Glasgow, the carts were unloaded and the canal company provided horses

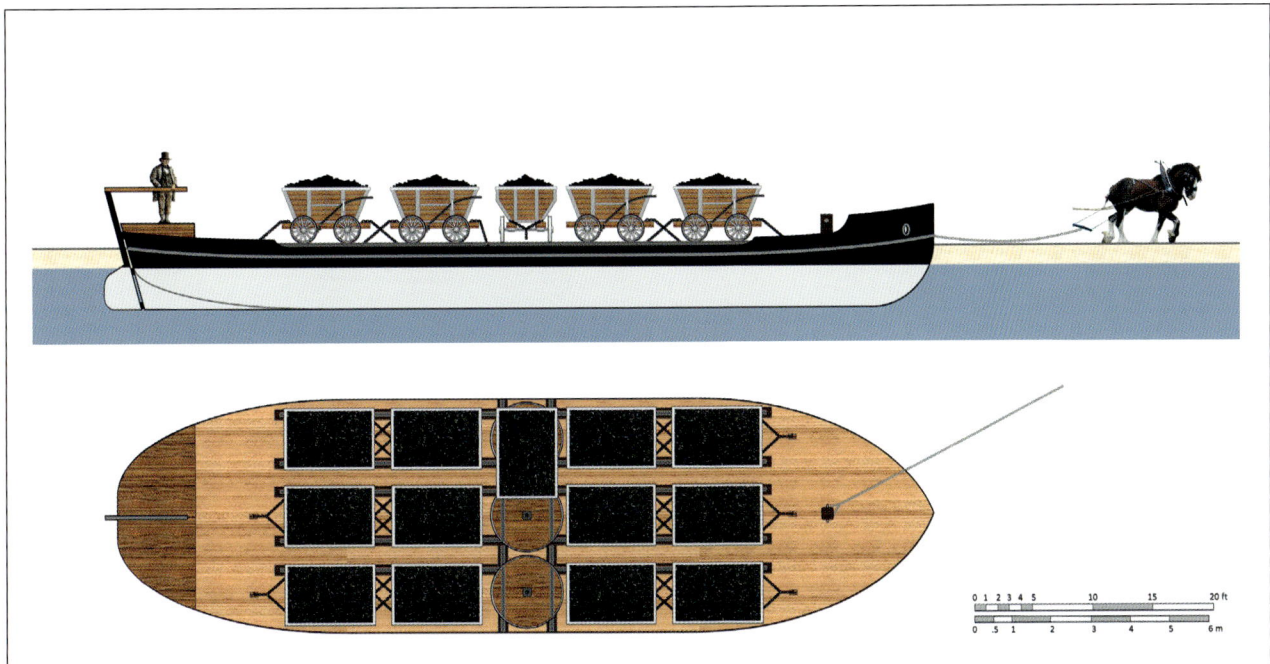

The waggon boat carried fourteen coal wagons with three girdles, or turntables, to load the wagons on to the fore and aft tracks. Maximum speed was walking pace with one horse-power. *(Author)*

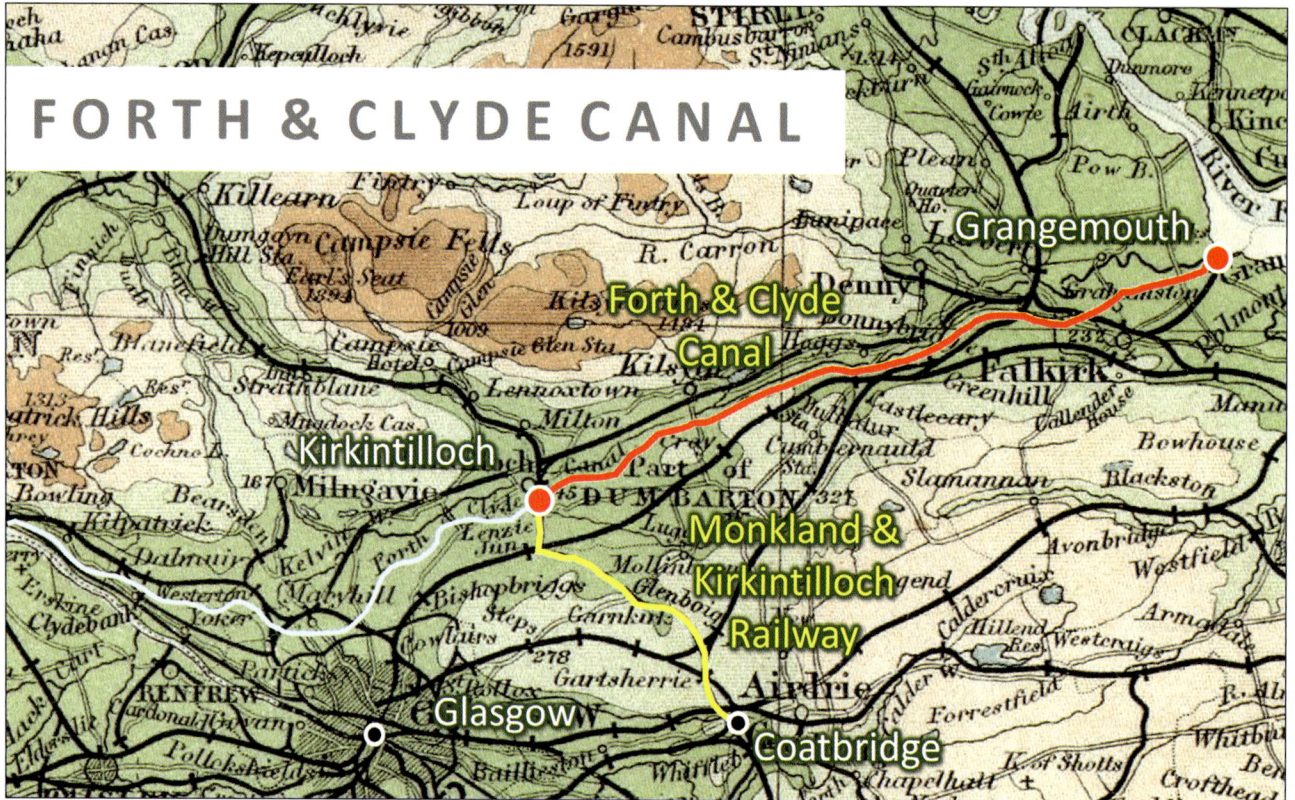

FORTH & CLYDE CANAL

to deliver them to merchants around the city. The empty carts, and some with manure travelling back to the countryside, were returned to the boat each afternoon and collected by the farmers as the boat travelled eastwards along the canal each evening.

The cart-boat was a great success and allowed Grahame to persuade the Forth & Clyde Canal Committee to use the same idea for transporting coal wagons from the railway at Kirkintilloch to the port at Grangemouth. As a loaded coal wagon weighed around four tons, twice the weight of a farm cart, this needed a specially designed boat. The 'waggon-boat' was ordered

from Reid & Hanna in Paisley, a company experienced in building iron boats for the canal, and its launching was reported in the Paisley Advertiser of Saturday, 3rd October 1835:

Iron Boat – *Monday last, an Iron Boat, of a peculiar construction, built by Messrs Reid and Hanna, and fitted up by the Messrs Walker, was sent off from the Quay here. She is built of iron, 3/16th in thickness, is 68 feet long, 19 feet broad, & 3½ feet depth of hold. The iron work of her weighs about 14 ton, the wood work about 10, and*

An old postcard showing a horse-drawn barge on the Forth & Clyde Canal, near the Falkirk locks, towards the end of the 19th century.

The Forth & Clyde Canal today, a bit more overgrown but still used for leisure boats and water sports.

she will carry about 60 tons. She is intended to ply between the Kirkintilloch railway and Grangemouth, with coals, not in bulk but in the railway waggons, of which she carries 14. Midway, between stem and stern, three girdles turning on pivots are placed abreast, and from these, three lines of parallel railways run both aft and foreward. The waggons are run on in midship, turned round on the girdles, and pushed two on each rail towards the stem, two on each rail towards the stern, and the last two put aboard remain in midships standing athwartships. By the use of this vessel a great deal of time and labour will be saved in lading coal vessels at Grangemouth, and much breakage of coal prevented.

The turntables are described as girdles, which in Scots are round iron plates used to cook bread or scones over a fire, (a griddle in current English). The great advantage of the waggon boat was to reduce the labour and cost of discharging the coal. At Grangemouth docks, the canal descends through a flight of locks to sea level. By taking the wagons off before the locks, they could be run to the dock at a higher elevation and the coal discharged directly to waiting ships from a coal staith.

There is no description of how the wagons were loaded on and off the boat. Some thought had obviously gone into the design, fitting the turntables midships allowed wagons to be loaded and stowed alternately forward and aft, port and starboard, to minimise changes in the boat's trim and heel. The advantage of a canal is that there is no tide to change the water level. However, the draught of the boat would increase by more than half a metre when the fourteen coal wagons were loaded, so there must have been some kind of adjustable ramp, even if only by packing or removing timbers under movable rails. There is no record of who was responsible for the engineering, whether Thomas Grahame got involved in the detail or whether Thomas Grainger, who was the railway's civil engineer was involved in the quayside arrangements. The only reference is in the Monkland & Kirkintilloch Railway accounts for December 1835: Waggon Boat, William Dodds for six new waggons and for cutting rails .. £81-3s.

The wagon boat was a commercial success and earned £540 in its first year of operation, though how long it lasted is not recorded. Over the next twenty years, many new railway lines were built and canal transport became increasingly uneconomic. By 1860 the Forth & Clyde Canal Co. built a branch line giving railway wagons direct access to their dock at Grangemouth. If the waggon boat was still in operation, that would certainly have been the end of its service.

The Firths of Forth and Tay

Edinburgh, Perth & Dundee Railway Co.	1850-1862
North British Railway Co.	1862-1890
Granton – Burntisland	1850-1890
Ferryport-on-Craig – Broughty Ferry	1851-53, 1859-80

Europe's first train ferry service, as we would recognise it today, was started on the Firth of Forth in 1850. The world's first train ferry was in the United States, when mail and luggage vans were shipped across the Susquehanna river in 1838.

The 1840s was a decade of railway mania. Dozens of railway companies were formed, each proposing new lines and trying to prevent their rivals from getting there first. Amongst these was the Edinburgh & Northern Railway Co., which planned to build a railway up the east coast of Scotland, from Edinburgh to the northern cities of Dundee and Aberdeen. Its competitor was the Caledonian Railway, which was building from Glasgow, north and east to Stirling, Perth and ultimately Dundee and Aberdeen. The E&NR's problem was that to push a line north from Edinburgh, it had to cross the two great estuaries of the Forth and Tay. The alternative was to take a long detour west via Stirling and Perth into the territory of the rival Caledonian Railway. The E&NR

Thomas Grainger, (1794-1852), engineer for the Monkland & Kirkintilloch Railway and designer of the Forth and Tay ferries with Robert Napier. *(ICE / Heriot-Watt University)*

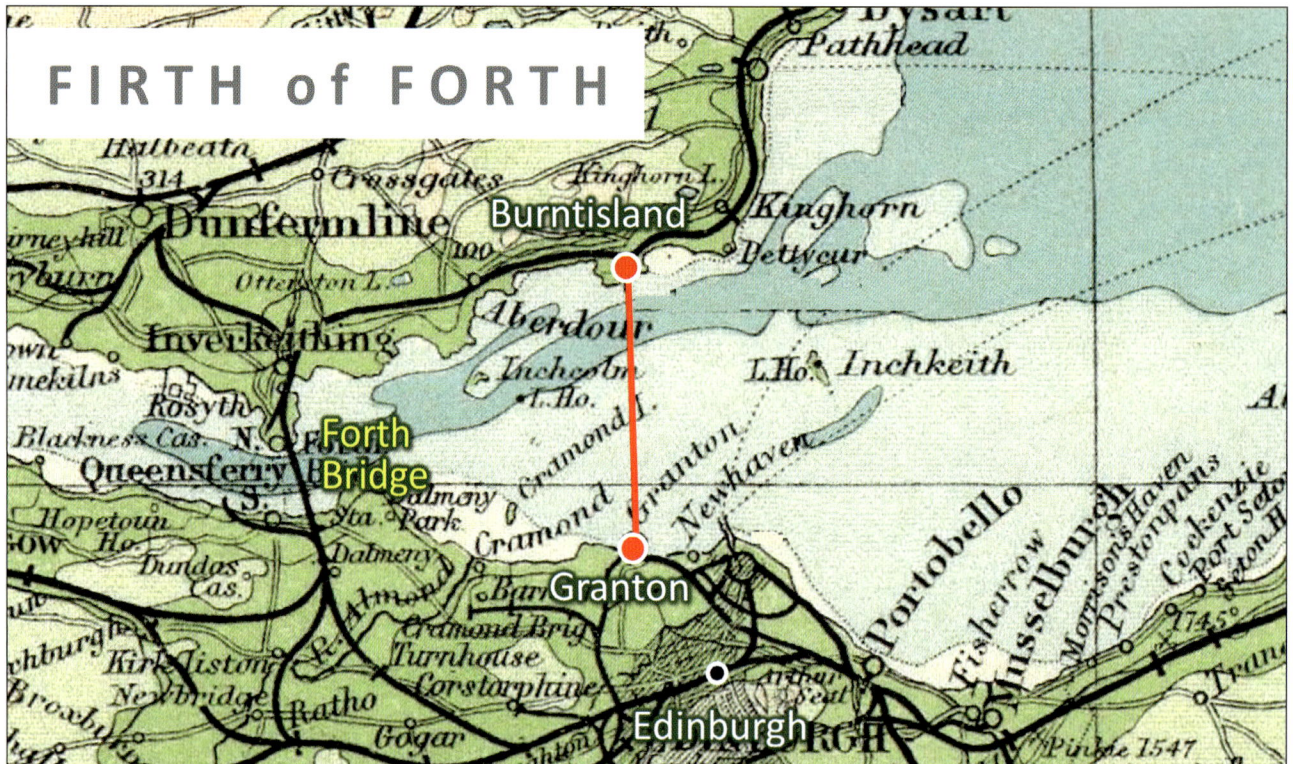

FIRTH of FORTH

settled on the direct route, building a line from Burntisland, on the south coast of Fife, north through the Fife coalfields. This would then cross the Tay by a bridge just east of Perth and connect with the Dundee & Perth Railway. At the southern end, this plan required a reliable ferry across the Firth of Forth connecting Edinburgh and Burntisland. Thomas Grainger was selected as the Chief Engineer for the project. He was by this time one of Scotland's leading civil engineers, building on his success with the Monkland & Kirkintilloch Railway twenty years earlier.

The original plan was to build a bridge across the Tay and various sites east of Perth were surveyed. However, Perth was still an active port and a high-level bridge that would maintain navigation was too expensive. Eventually the line was rerouted to enter Perth from the south which avoided the need for a new bridge. That still left the problem of a route to Dundee. The best route was to take the railway to Newport from where a ferry ran across the Tay direct to Dundee. However, in 1845 the Scottish Central Railway, which owned the line from Perth to Dundee, bought this ferry to frustrate the E&NR. The E&NR's solution was to extend the branch line they had planned to Cupar through to the north coast of Fife at Ferryport-on Craig. Here, a short ferry could cross the Tay to Broughty Ferry, around 5 km east of Dundee, and passengers could transfer to the Dundee & Arbroath Railway. Railway construction started in 1846 and locomotives were ordered from R.&W. Hawthorn Ltd in Newcastle. The line was opened in stages, from Burntisland to Cupar in 1847 and the lines through to Perth and Ferryport-on Craig in 1848. The E&NR bought

the rights to the Tay ferry for £12,600 in July 1847 and set about improving the harbours and providing new passenger steamers. The passenger service started with the paddle steamer *Express* in May 1848.

On the Forth, passenger steamers had been introduced in 1844 on the 5-mile crossing between Granton and Burntisland. The E&NR bought out the ferry company in 1847 for £90,000 and negotiated with the Duke of Buccleuch, who owned Granton harbour, to use the port as their southern terminus. To provide a through route from Granton to Edinburgh city centre, the E&NR also bought the Edinburgh, Leith & Granton Railway Co. in 1847.

As with the Forth & Clyde Canal, the economics of the railway relied on transporting freight, principally coal and farm produce, to the cities. Passengers were the jam, not the bread and butter. The railway provided the shortest route from the Fife coalfields south to Edinburgh and north to Dundee, which was a booming industrial city. However, for this to compete with the longer rail journeys via Stirling and Perth, it was vital to avoid having to handle the coal at the ferry crossings. As an initial experiment, rails were laid on the deck of passenger steamers and wagons lifted on and off by crane. Each steamer took up to 12 loaded wagons, weighing around 3½ tons each.

The floating railway

While this was commercially successful, handling loaded wagons by crane was slow and vulnerable to accidents. No doubt the passengers also objected to the

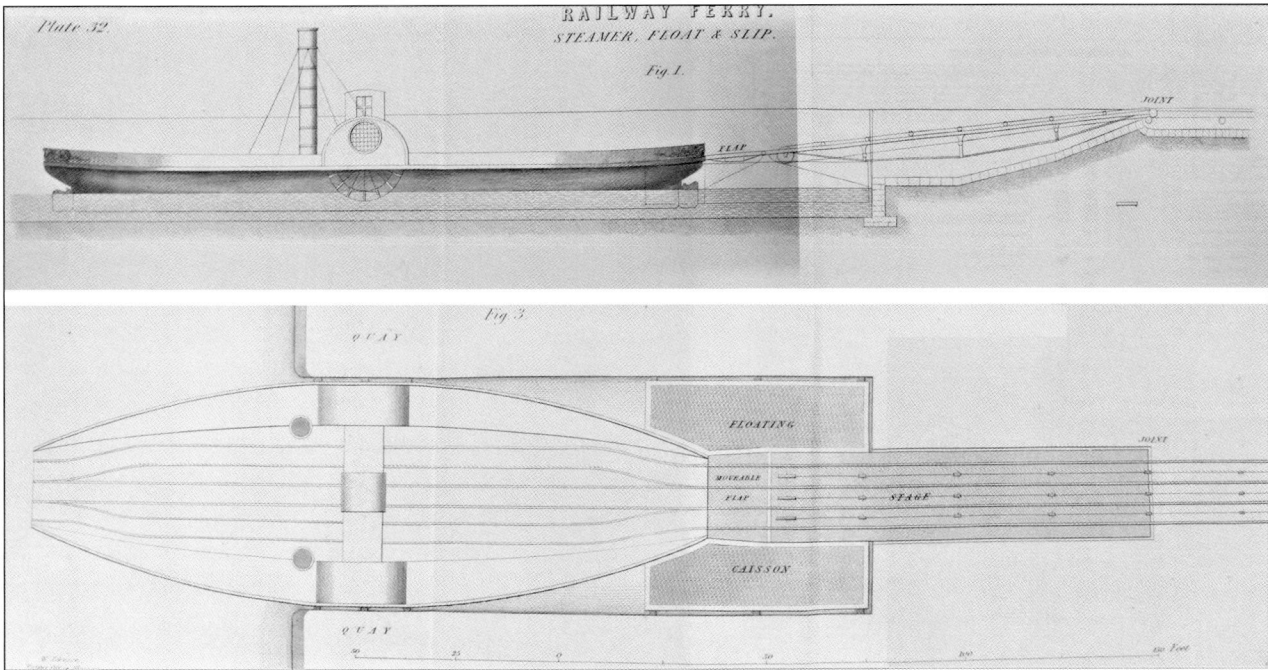

Grainger and Napier's original ferry and linkspan design for the Tay crossing. The linkspan rests on a floating caisson and a loop of chain driven by a stationary engines is used to pull the wagons up the slope. *(The Practical Mechanic's Journal – June 1849)*

coal dust. As a more permanent solution, Thomas Grainger's proposed to the E&NR Directors that they should construct a 'floating railway'. This required some ingenuity as unlike the previous experience on the canal, the Firths of Forth and Tay are fully exposed to the North Sea. Easterly gales create very rough seas as the waves are funnelled into the long tapering estuaries. The harbours also experience a tidal range of nearly 5 metres. Thomas Grainger's plan for the 'floating railway' had two parts. To build a steamer with rails fitted to a flat deck and to construct stages allowing wagons to be transferred on and off the steamer at any state of the tide.

To build this prototype ship, Thomas Grainger wisely chose Robert Napier and Sons, of Govan on the Clyde, one of the country's most experienced shipbuilders and marine engineers. Napier had built the engines for the first Cunard steamers which had crossed the Atlantic under power ten years earlier. The 'floating railway' steamer was ordered in 1848 and the initial plan was to put it into service on the Tay crossing, as reported by the Glasgow Herald of November 1848:

A Floating Railroad – . . . *as the Forth and Tay . . . . lie across the route of the great east coast line of railways which will shortly extend from London to Aberdeen, it became extremely desirable that some means should be devised by which these seas might be crossed without the troublesome necessity of passengers and goods changing carriages. We are happy to say that a plan has been devised for carrying the trains bodily across the Tay at Broughty Ferry, where it is about a mile*

and a half broad. Mr. Robert Napier is at present building in his yard at Govan, a Floating Railway, for the Edinburgh and Northern Railway Company. It is being built of iron, 180 feet in length, and 35 feet in breadth. It is to have three lines of rails on deck, so as to enable it to take on a railway train of 500 feet in length, and is to be propelled by engines of 250 horses' power. As the main line of railway on each side of the Tay is considerably above the level of the sea, stationary engines on either side of the Frith are to be employed to draw up or lower the trains. This rail-road steamboat is expected to be launched in a few weeks.

The ferry was launched on the 6th February 1849, though without any formal naming, it was still referred to as the 'floating railway'. Interestingly the vessel was launched broadside into the river. Until then, all steamers had followed a simple pattern. The engine was placed amidships driving a single shaft, with a paddle wheel on each side. The 'goods boat' was designed to be double-ended with a clear open deck, running the full length of the vessel. The steeple engines used at the time were too high to fit below the deck and thus two engines were provided, one either side. To operate in either direction, a rudder was fitted at each end with a device to lock the forward rudder.

More details of the engines were provided by The Dundee Courier of 28th February 1849:

The floating railway – . . . *Her power is about 200 horses, the diameter of her cylinders being 56 inches. These, as well as her two funnels are placed*

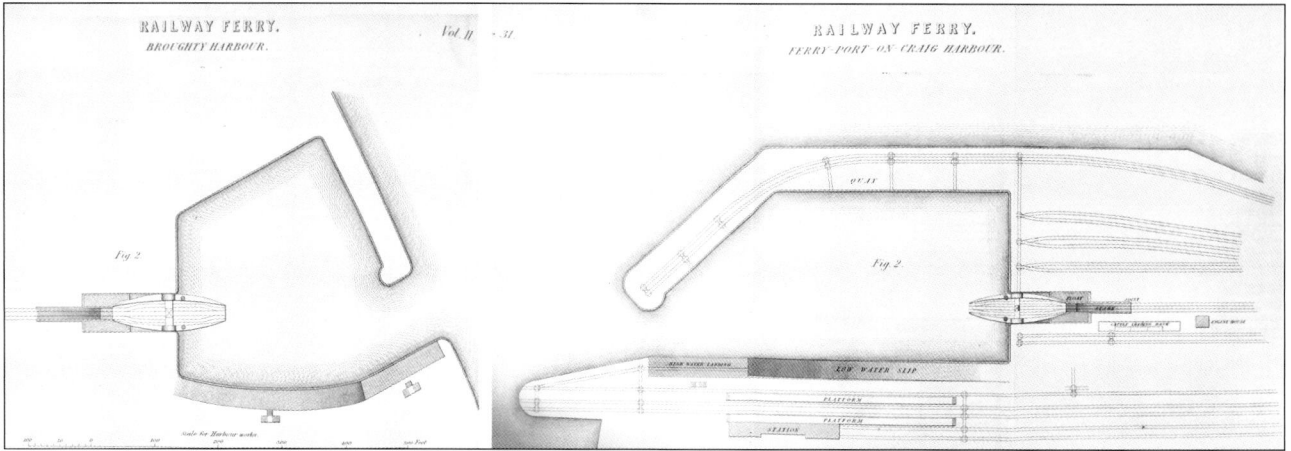

Plans of the harbours at Broughty Ferry and Ferryport on Craig, (later called Tayport) either side of the Tay. This shows the narrow dock aligning the ferry with the linkspan and floating caisson. This design was superseded by Bouch's 'flying-bridge' design. *(The Practical Mechanic's Journal – June 1849)*

on each side, close to the paddle boxes, so as to leave the middle space of her deck entirely clear.

. . . The engines will be totally unconnected with each other, and may be used singly or together, or the one may be going one way while the other is going another, or standing still, so as to turn the vessel quickly round in aid of the steersman.

While the ferry was a revolutionary design, the second part of the project was to devise a means of quickly loading and unloading the wagons at all states of the tide. Thomas Grainger's idea was to provide a floating caisson, designed to match the bow of the ferry. A hinged linkspan ramp, described as an 'inclined plane', connected the quayside to the floating caisson. At high tide, the rails on the caisson would be level with the quayside, with the angle of the linkspan becoming steeper as the tide went out. The linkspan was 100 feet (30m) long, with a gradient of 16% at low tide. To pull the wagons up the ramp, an endless loop of chain was driven by a windlass at the top of the linkspan. The chain

passed over a series of guides and a pulley wheel on the caisson. The whole arrangement was powered by a stationary engine on the quayside. To unload the ferry, the crew would push each wagon in turn from the deck to the caisson and then connect it to the travelling chain by a 'tail rope'. The wagon was then pulled up the ramp and disconnected when it reached the rails on the quayside. Friction brakes on the windlass were used to reverse the procedure and control wagons running down the linkspan on to the ferry. This was described in The Dundee Courier of 28th February 1849:

. . . On each side of this firth there have been formed by the railway company harbours for the particular reception of this vessel, there being, first, a basin into which she will run, and then a peculiarly formed pier, or rather groove, adapted for the admission of her prow. On being fixed into this groove, the bulwarks of the bow will be removed, and an inclined plane caused to descend, with its point towards the vessel and on a level with the rails, on her deck; and the carriages and trucks

The opening of the floating railway with the **Leviathan** loading wagons using the flying bridge in Granton harbour. *(Author's collection)*

being then affixed to a chain, they will be hauled by means of machinery at once up to the main line, where of course they may proceed on their journey, . . .

From a 21st century perspective the first train ferry looks unremarkable. However, that is because she became the prototype for hundreds of similar vessels built over the next two centuries. Grainger and Napier's design for the ferry and linkspan were a revolutionary departure from all previous ships and were the origin of many design features common to all small ferries to this day.

● A double-ended ship loaded over the bow or stern. All previous ships had berthed alongside a quay and loaded from the side.

● A clear cargo deck for the full length and breadth of the ship, uninterrupted by masts, funnels or superstructures. The engines and funnels were placed either side and the central steering position located on an elevated gantry.

● Integrated propulsion and steering. In this case, manoeuvrability was improved by having two engines, each driving an independent paddle wheel. Later ferries used steerable thrusters or Voith Schneider propellers.

● A linkspan to adjust for variations in elevation between the deck and quayside. This was hinged at the landward end, with the free end supported on a floating caisson. The caisson specifically designed to mate with the ferry's bow or stern. While later train ferries often had a gantry to support the linkspan, due to the weight of the rail wagons, a floating caisson is still commonly used for vehicle ferries.

On the 13th of January 1849, the E&NR appointed an ambitious young engineer, 26-year-old Thomas Bouch, as the railway's Manager and Chief Engineer. His role was push-through the railway and ferry construction and set-up the railway operations. Bouch inspected E&NR's operations over his first few days in the job and, at his first board meeting a week later, announced that he had sacked four members of staff for various misdemeanours. To reinforce his authority, he sacked a further seventeen staff when he visited the railway's Burntisland works two weeks later.

Grainger's linkspan design was published in more detail in The Practical Mechanic's Journal in June 1849. However, at some point over the summer of 1849, Bouch decided to cancel the caisson and linkspan arrangement and proposed a 'flying bridge' or travelling platform design instead. Part of the reason was the cost of the harbour works required for Grainger's design. It was also true that Grainger's design would be quite slow in operation as the wagons would be pulled up the linkspan one at a time. Looking from the 21st century, the procedure for connecting the wagons to a moving chain using a tail rope also looks quite dangerous, though that is unlikely to have worried Victorian engineers.

Thomas Bouch, (1822-1880), who took over as Chief Engineer of the Edinburgh, Perth & Dundee Railway in 1849 and was the designer of the flying bridge.

The flying bridge

Bouch's alternative design was for a 'flying bridge'. The design was based on a masonry slipway with a gradient of 1 in 6. Four heavy timbers were fitted along the length if the slipway, each supporting an iron rail. The moving platform, or flying bridge, was a solid wooden framework, 65 feet long by 21 feet wide, supported on 24 cast-iron wheels. The top surface of the platform had a slope of 1/100, just enough for wagons to roll under their own weight. Four wrought iron girders extended from the forward end of the platform, each 35 feet long, supported on hinges. The forward end of the girders was supported on a crossbeam linked by chains at either side, over a goalpost structure, to a gantry across the platform. On the gantry, two manual winches, allowed the girders to be lifted and lowered to connect to the ferry. At the top of the slipway, there was a windlass powered by a stationary steam engine, essentially a locomotive without wheels, which raised and lowered the flying bridge on the slipway. It also powered smaller winches to pull the wagons from the ship's deck on to the movable platform. The most ingenious part of the design was that the girder hinges contained a universal joint that allowed the girders to rotate slightly to adjust for

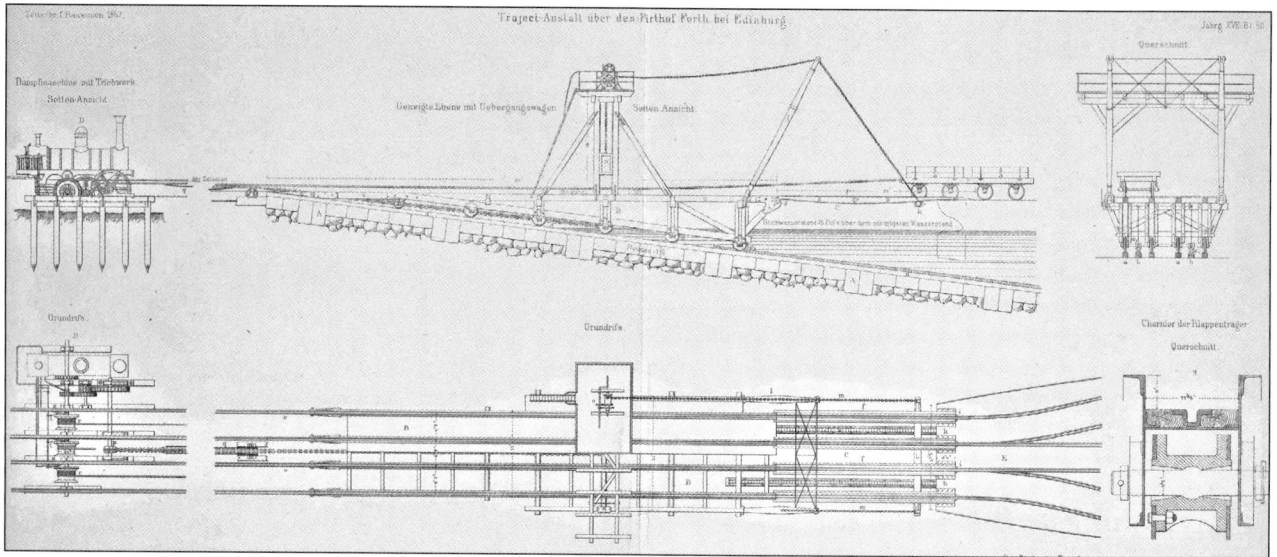

Drawing of the flying bridge, published in a German technical paper. (Berlin Architekturmuseum)

the heel of the ship.

Although this was a novel design, it is worth being aware of another engineering project completed in the second half of 1849. An inclined plane was built on the Monkland Canal at Blackhill in the east end of Glasgow. This is essentially an iron box, or caisson, on wheels which travels on rails up and down a ramp to carry a canal boat between two levels. Normally there are two caissons, side by side, connected by a wire or chain over a winch at the top of the ramp. As one caisson goes up, the other goes down, so the winching engine needs only to compensate for the friction in the system. Several had

been built on English canals in the 1780s and 90s. The inclined plane on the Monkland Canal bypassed a flight of eight locks and dropped the canal by 96 feet (29m). It had two caissons, each weighing around 90 tons and a steam winching engine. Many of the details of Bouch's floating bridge are similar to the Blackhill inclined plane, so it may have been the canal industry's last contribution to the railway age.

The flying bridge was described in a paper to the Institution of Civil Engineers in 1861 by William Hall, who had worked for Bouch on the design. As later events would show, Bouch was not an engineer who focused on

The slipway and flying bridge at Burntisland harbour. (Fife Cultural Trust - Kirkcaldy Libraries)

details, so much of the credit for building a working system probably rests with Hall. History has credited Thomas Bouch for designing the first train ferry, though in hindsight much of the work had been done by Thomas Grainger and Robert Napier before Bouch became involved. Unfortunately, Thomas Grainger was not around to clarify the record. He was injured in a train collision at Stockton-on-Tees in July 1852 and died a few days later.

The Leviathan

The ferry was completed in the summer of 1849 and made the voyage of over 500 miles around the north of Scotland, from the Clyde to the Forth, arriving at Granton in September. Given that the paddle wheels where not connected and each had a separate engine, matching the paddle speed to keep the ship in a straight line must have been a challenge. However, William Hall reported that this was not a problem even in heavy seas.

In 1849, the E&NR changed its name to the Edinburgh, Perth & Dundee Railway, (EP&DR). The ferry was ready, but the harbour works were not completed. Although the original intention was to start with the service on the Tay, it was decided to start the Forth crossing between Granton and Burntisland first. A second, smaller ferry was ordered from Robert Napier for the Tay crossing.

Early in 1850, the harbour works and the flying bridges at Granton and Burntisland were complete, though the final testing was not without incident. The flying bridge was secured to the slipway rails by a rack and pin arrangement when the weight was taken off the windlass. On Saturday, 26th January 1850, two men were working under the flying bridge at Burntisland and withdrew the pins without checking that the windlass was locked. As a result, the flying bridge broke loose and ran down the slipway into the sea. One of the men, John Forsyth, who worked for Hawthorn & Co, was trapped in the machinery

The *Leviathan* beached at low tide, showing the relatively fine hull shape despite the square deck. Despite the early drawings showing a wheelhouse, she had an open bridge.

The sign at Burntisland harbour commemorating the ferry service, though contemporary newspapers report the first voyage being on the 30th January 1850.

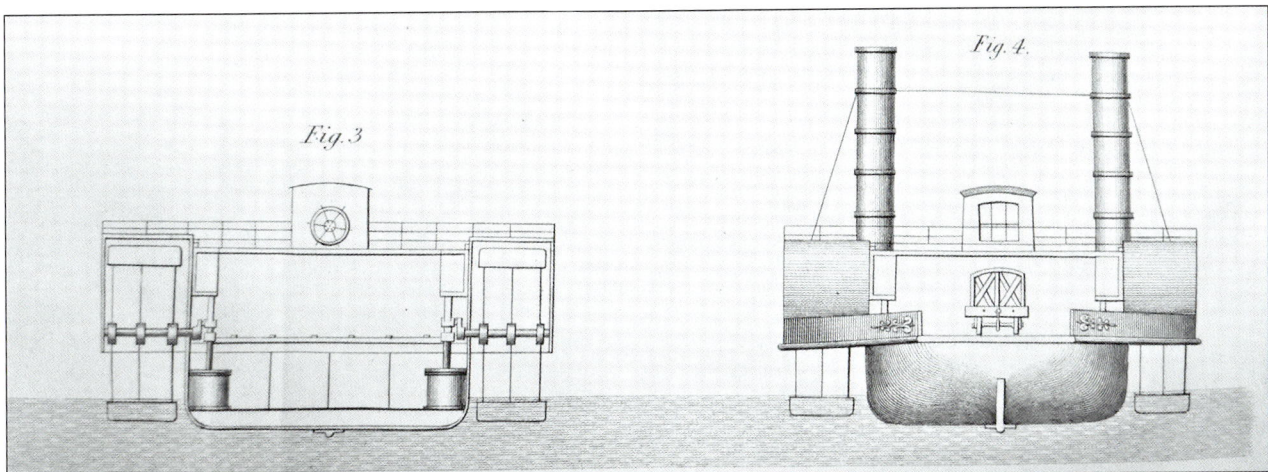

Sections through Grainger and Napier's ferry showing the three tracks on the rail deck with the wheelhouse above. The paddles on either side are driven by independent steam engines. The *Leviathan* was built to this design. (*The Practical Mechanic's Journal – June 1849*)

Forth and Tay ferries

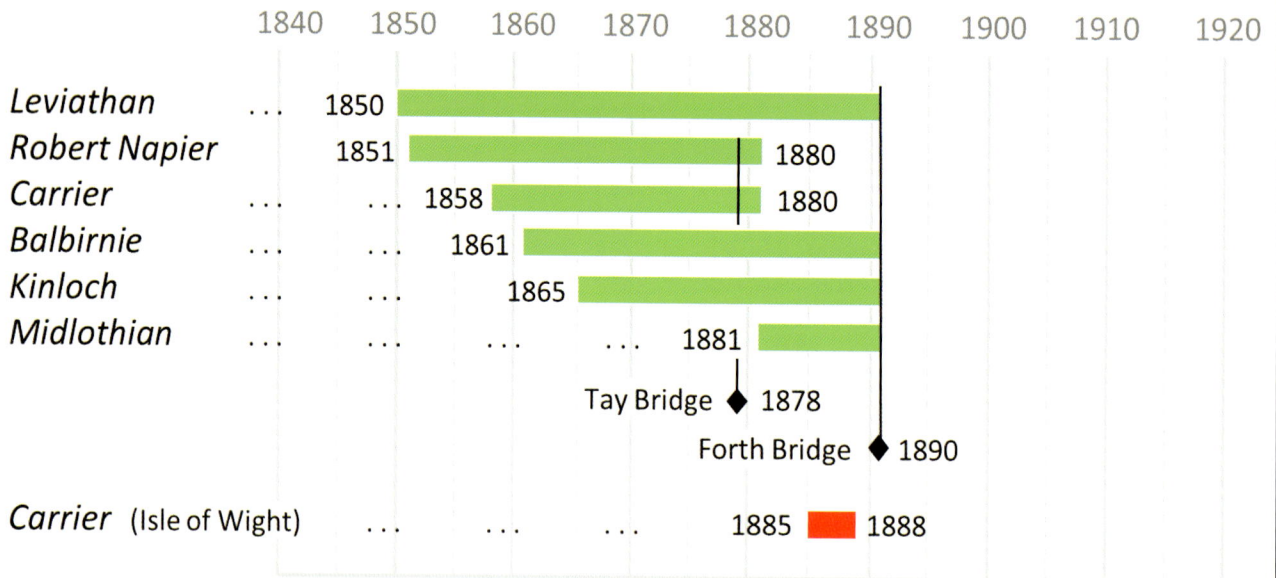

	1840	1850	1860	1870	1880	1890	1900	1910	1920

Leviathan ... 1850

Robert Napier 1851 — 1880

Carrier ... ... 1858 — 1880

Balbirnie 1861

Kinloch 1865

Midlothian 1881

Tay Bridge ◆ 1878

Forth Bridge ◆ 1890

Carrier (Isle of Wight) ... ... 1885 ▮ 1888

and killed. The second man escaped with minor injuries.

Despite this accident, the final trials were completed and the first crossings with wagons started on the following Wednesday, 30th January. Twelve wagons of coal and general merchandise were loaded at Burntisland in about seven minutes, the crossing took 25 minutes and the wagons were unloaded at Granton in three minutes, amidst the hearty cheers of a large crowd of spectators. This was the first time that the goods boat was referred to by name, as the *Leviathan*. After this successful trip, the EP&DR directors retired for a good lunch in the Granton Hotel, hosted by John Anderson the contractor for operating the ferry. *Leviathan* operated reliably and in March 1851 Bouch reported to the EP&DR board that the ferry had operated every single day since it began and had transported 29,000 wagons over the Forth in the first six months.

The second goods boat, named the *Robert Napier* in honour of its builder, arrived on the Forth in September 1850. She was similar to the *Leviathan*, though smaller. The *Robert Napier* was only 130 feet long (39.5m) with two lines of rails on deck, compared with the *Leviathan's* 168 feet (51.1m) and three lines of rails. One clever piece of design was that the four rails on the *Robert Napier's* deck were equally spaced, so that two lines of wagons could be loaded, port and starboard, or if there was little traffic, a single line of wagons could be loaded in the centre.

The *Robert Napier* started the Tay service between Ferryport-on Craig, (soon renamed Tayport), and Broughty Ferry in March 1851. Using the two ferries, the distance by rail from Edinburgh to Dundee was shortened

to 49 miles compared to 91 miles for the alternative route via Stirling and Perth. The goods boats only carried wagons and steamers ran in parallel taking passengers over the two crossings. However, if passengers had missed the steamer they were allowed to travel on the goods boat, provided they didn't mind standing out on the open deck exposed to the coal dust and weather.

The two goods boats operated reliably, but not without incident. The one main change from the original design was to fit permanent buffers at the stern of the vessels, so that they only loaded over the bow. William Hall reported that this change was 'to prevent wagons going overboard' during loading but did not reveal how often this had happened.

In 1853, the *Leviathan* could not cope with the traffic across the Forth, so the EP&DR decided to suspend the Tay service and transfer the *Robert Napier* to the Forth. An agreement was made to route goods wagons to Dundee via Perth over the Scottish Central Railway's tracks. This resulted in considerable loss of revenue, so the Company decided to order a third ferry to restart the Tay crossing. The *Carrier* was delivered in 1858 by Scott & Co. in Greenock and restarted the Tay crossing in 1859. She was similar in size to the *Robert Napier*, 125 feet long, with two tracks, able to carry 14 wagons.

As traffic increased on the Forth, a fourth goods boat, the *Balbirnie*, was delivered by S.& H. Morton & Co., in Leith in 1861. The *Balbirnie* was larger than the previous boats, 200 feet long, with three tracks and able to carry around 28 wagons. The following year, the Edinburgh, Perth & Dundee Railway was taken over by the North British Railway. The line across Fife was critical to the

The *Midlothian* at the flying bridge in Granton. The passenger ferry, *John Stirling*, which ran in parallel with the goods boats, is partly visible on the right. *(Fife Cultural Trust - Kirkcaldy Libraries)*

North British's vision of creating a north-south trunk route from Aberdeen via Edinburgh to Berwick and south to London. The Tay and Forth ferries had served their purpose, but the crossings took time and were uncomfortable in winter. To attract passengers away from their rival Caledonian Railway's longer route via Perth and Stirling, the ferries would need to be replaced by bridges.

Traffic continued to increase and by 1863 the *Balbirnie* was working the Forth crossing day and night. Two crews worked 12-hour shifts making six return crossings each shift. The North British ordered another goods boat, the *Kinloch*, similar to *Balbirnie*, but slightly longer at 216 feet and with capacity for 30 wagons. She was delivered in 1865 by A.& J. Inglis of Pointhouse in Glasgow and was distinctive in that her funnels were staggered, the starboard funnel aft of the paddle box and the port funnel forward. The service was not without incident and in 1865, the engineer on *Leviathan*, Robert Geddes, was working on the paddles when they were accidently set in motion. He was badly injured, but fortunately survived. In 1872, the crew of *Balbirnie* broke open some whisky casks but the engineer admitted the theft and kept his job, the rest of the crew were sacked.

The Tay bridge

Thomas Bouch had left the EP&DR in 1851 and gone into business as a consulting engineer. Over the next decade he built several railways in the North of England and developed a reputation for designing low cost railways and pioneering lightweight iron lattice girder bridges. He maintained his contacts with the North British Railway, so when they started seriously looking at building bridges over the Forth and Tay, Bouch was the obvious candidate. His first design for the Tay bridge was completed in 1864. As always, there were many interests to be placated and the process of agreeing the bridge's location and gaining political approval wore on until 1870. The Tay estuary is wide but shallow so the design was for a long snake of a bridge, 3,264m long with iron lattice girders supported on 73 piers. It was the longest bridge in the world and opened on the 1st June 1878 amidst great celebration. A year later, Queen Victoria crossed the bridge and its designer joined the elite of Victorian engineering by becoming Sir Thomas Bouch.

The new bridge increased traffic on the East Coast line making the Granton to Burntisland ferry even busier. Bouch had been working on his design for the Forth bridge and with the Tay bridge open, the foundation stone was laid in September 1878. The design for the Forth bridge was much more ambitious than for the Tay. The water depth in the Forth estuary required main spans of 1600 feet (488m) supported from 550 feet (168m) high towers. The loads in the chains supporting the bridge deck were too great for traditional wrought iron and

41

The goods boats laid-up in Burntisland in 1890 after the opening of the Forth Rail Bridge. The largest ferry, the *Midlothia*n in the foreground. *(Douglas Yuill Collection)*

high-tensile steel was proposed for the first time.

On 28th December 1879, a severe gale blew through the Firth of Tay. In the early darkness of a winter evening, people saw sparks from the wheels of the southbound train as the strong wind forced its wheels against the check rails as it crossed the bridge. The northbound train reached the bridge shortly after 7 pm, but by 7.30 it had not arrived in Dundee. In the darkness, it was impossible to see what had happed. Mr Roberts, the locomotive foreman at Dundee, set out across the bridge clinging to the rails against the force of the wind. He struggled on in the darkness, frequently on his hands and knees, until he came across a void with only the waves crashing on the bridge foundations 80 feet below. There was no sign of the train and its 75 passengers and crew.

The passenger and goods boat service from Ferryport-on-Craig to Broughty Ferry had continued after the opening of the Tay Bridge, but the traffic was considerably reduced. After the failure of the bridge, most freight was rerouted via Perth on the competing Caledonian Railway and the goods boat service ended on the 1st February 1880. The *Carrier* and *Robert Napier* were surplus to requirements. The *Carrier* was sold the following year, together with the 'flying bridges' and winching gear, to Samuel Lack Mason for a new service to the Isle of Wight. The *Robert Napier* was used as a workboat for the new Tay Bridge construction.

After the disaster, work on the Forth bridge stopped and the North British Railway resigned themselves to maintaining the Granton to Burntisland crossing for several more years. The North British had refurbished the old *Leviathan* in 1878, but without a date for a new bridge, they ordered their last and largest goods boat. The *Midlothian* was delivered by Ramage & Ferguson in

A recent aerial view of Granton harbour with Burntisland on the north shore of the Firth of Forth in the top left corner of the picture. The flying bridge slipway still exists, just above the white building with the blue top.

An aerial view of Broughty Ferry, on the North shore of the Tay, showing the flying bridge slipway in the harbour. The 15th century tower of Broughty Castle is at the bottom right of the picture.

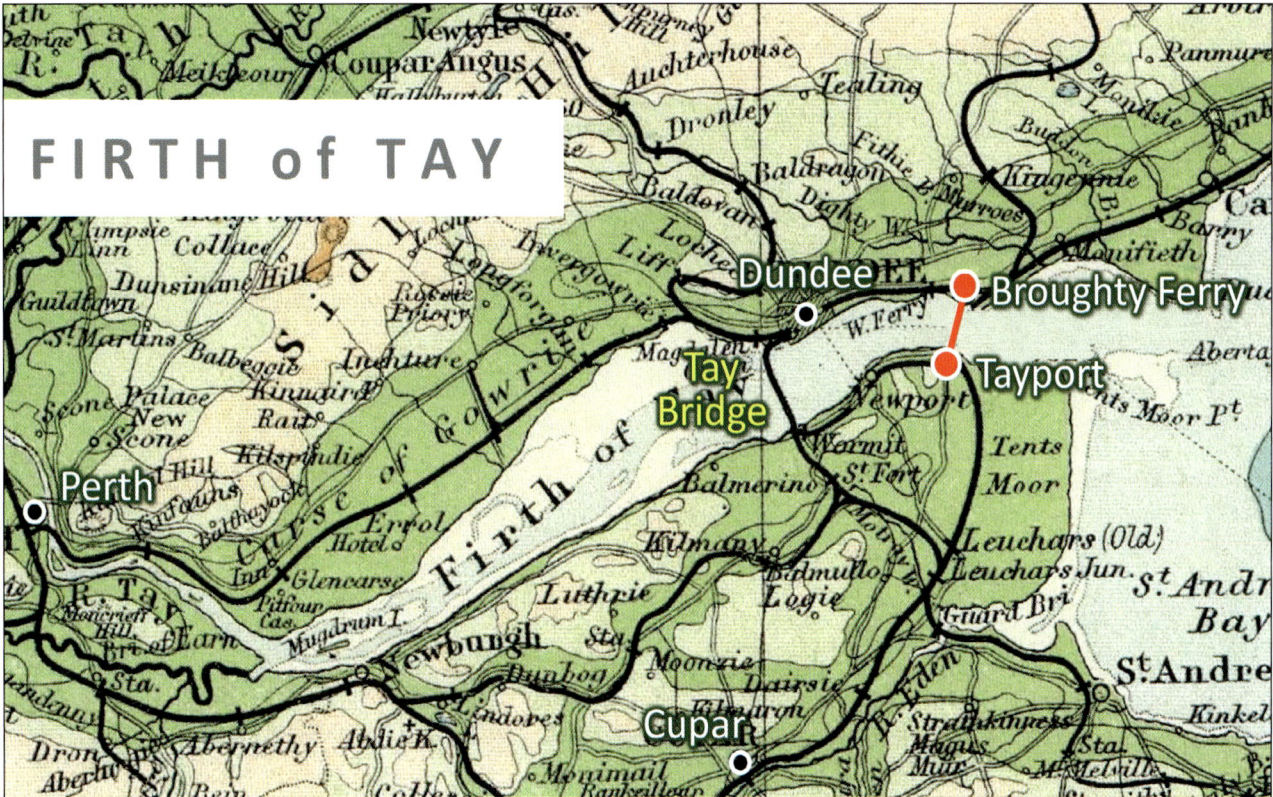

FIRTH of TAY

Leith in 1881. Although similar is design to the other goods boats, the *Midlothian* was 262 feet long (80m) and capable of carrying 40 wagons.

The inquiry into the Tay bridge failure inevitably put most of the blame on Sir Thomas Bouch. With hindsight, the disaster was most probably caused by carriages derailing in the high wind and striking the bridge structure. However, it was also true that much of the cast iron fabrication was of very poor quality. The inquiry found that the design had underestimated the wind force on the bridge and that fabrication and maintenance had not been adequately supervised. As superintending engineer, the responsibility rested squarely on Bouch's shoulders. He retired to his home and never recovered from the stress of the disaster and subsequent inquiry. He died a few months later in October 1880, a broken man. Sadly, Thomas Bouch is remembered for the Tay bridge disaster and his earlier contribution to developing the first train ferries is largely forgotten.

A new more robust design was developed for the Tay Bridge by William Barlow, replacing the lattice iron piers with solid iron columns and masonry. It reopened in June 1887 and the *Robert Napier*, now 37 years old was laid-up and sold for scrap the following year. A new design was also developed for the Forth Bridge, by Sir John Fowler and Benjamin Baker, using riveted steel tubes to create two cantilevered central spans, each 1,709 feet, (521m) in length. Construction started in 1882 and the Forth Bridge was opened to traffic in March 1890, the wonder of the age. Both the Tay and Forth Bridges remain in service today as part of the East Coast Main Line.

An aerial view of Ferryport on Craig, now called Tayport, on the south of the Firth of Tay with the remnants of the flying bridge slipway on the left.

The NBR was glad to see an end to the ferry service. Although it could transport over 500 wagons a day, the annual cost of £34,000 was a significant drain on revenue. They sold the four redundant goods boats, *Leviathan*, *Balbirnie*, *Kinloch* and *Midlothian*, to P&W McLellan of Glasgow for £11,700. The *Balbirnie* was scrapped in 1891. The *Leviathan*, which had been re-engined in 1886, and *Kinloch* were sold on to the Bank of Vera Cruz for further service in Mexico. However, this fell through and they were scrapped the following year. The newest and largest of the boats, *Midlothian*, was converted to a barge and sold for further service in Sweden and Russia, before being scrapped in 1907.

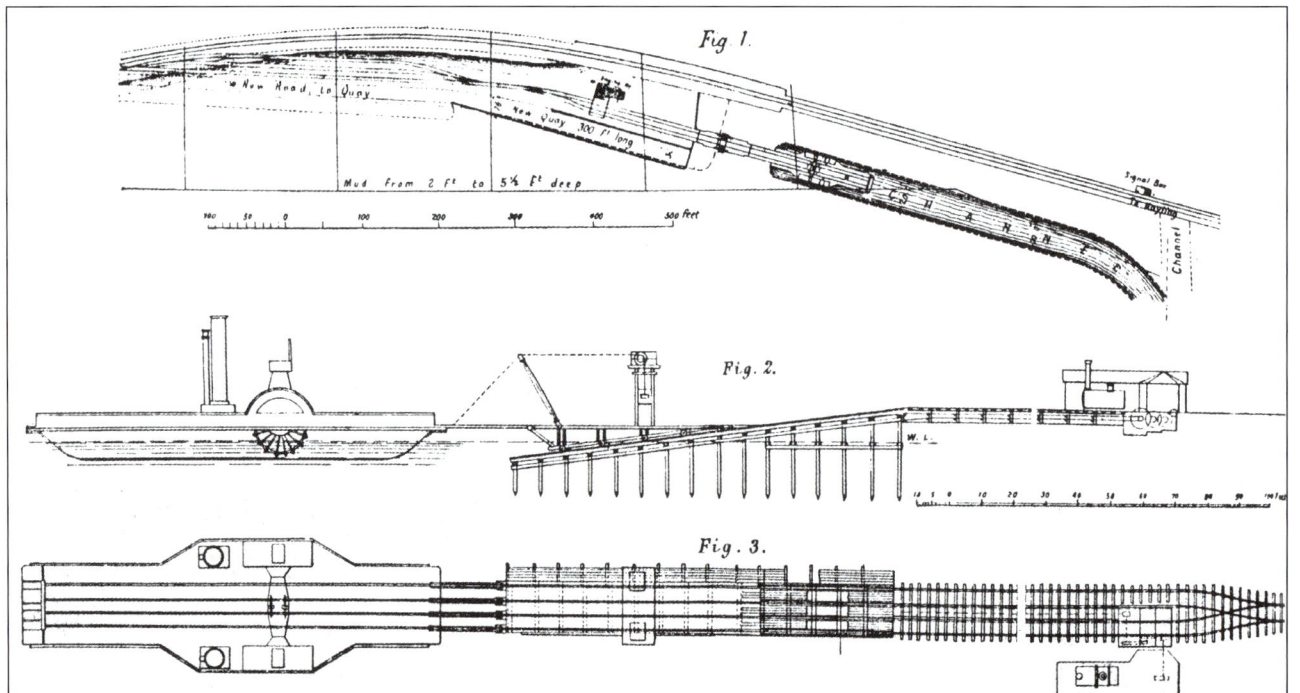

Drawings of the slipway, flying bridge and the Carrier at Langstone. The slipways appears to be built on timber piles, as opposed to the masonry structures used in Scotland.

Isle of Wight

Isle of Wight Marine Transit Co.
Langstone – Bembridge   1885-1888

During the 1860s and 70s, a network of railways was built on the Isle of Wight on England's South coast. The railways linked the ports of Ryde and Bembridge in the north-east of the island with towns such as Shanklin and Ventnor further south. As had been the case in Scotland thirty years earlier, goods from the mainland had to be handled twice, from rail to ship at the mainland port and back to rail on arrival in the Isle of Wight. This took time, added costs and damaged goods.

In 1881, Samuel Lack Mason proposed creating a train ferry to the Isle of Wight, similar to those operating in Scotland. He had first-hand experience of the Forth and Tay operations as General Manager of the North British Railway Co. from 1867 to 1874. After the Tay crossing closed, Mason bought the *Carrier* together with the flying bridges and winching gear for £3,400. He made agreements with the London, Brighton & South Coast Railway, (LB&SCR) and the Brading Harbour Improvement Railway & Works Co. to build ferry ports using the second-hand equipment at Langstone near Havant on the mainland and at Bembridge, near St. Helens on the Isle of Wight.

The Isle of Wight Marine Transit Co. was formed in 1884 and bought the agreements, the *Carrier* and the shore equipment from Samuel Mason for £28,425. The slipways and flying bridges from the Tay were rebuilt at their new locations and Captain Walker, one of the NBR ferry captains from the Forth, moved south to superintend the operations. The service began on 1st September 1885. Its main purpose was to transport agricultural produce from the Isle of Wight to mainland markets and return with bulk goods such as coal. In 1886, the Isle of Wight Observer recounted a record set by Sir Philip Rose, transporting his horses and carriages from London to his summer house at Shanklin. The horses and carriages were loaded on to LB&SCR railway trucks at Victoria station, leaving at 06.35 am. The train arrived at Langstone after 9 am and the trucks put aboard the *Carrier*, which sailed at 10.30 am. The ferry arrived at Bembridge around 12.35 pm and the trucks were unloaded, leaving Bembridge station at 1.12 pm and arriving at Shanklin at 1.38 pm. In reality, the service was not always so reliable and, as Sir Philip was the LB&SCR's solicitor, this was probably a publicity stunt.

The little *Carrier* struggled with the crossing. Langstone to Bembridge was around 11 miles, four miles in a channel dredged through the mud to the mouth of Langstone harbour, then seven miles of open sea crossing the Solent to the Isle of Wight. Even in good weather the *Carrier* could only make one return trip each day with 14 wagons. On a bad day, the service was cancelled and perishable goods had to be transferred to Portsmouth

An illustration of the *Carrier* leaving the slipway at Bembridge on the Isle of Wight. A heavy bulwark had been fitted over the bow to protect the wagons in heavy weather.

and taken over to Ryde on the passenger ferry. Not surprisingly, it did not make money. The LB&SCR was persuaded to take over the company's assets in 1886, but the service continued to operate at a considerable loss.

A Naval Review was held at Spithead in 1887 to commemorate the 50th anniversary of Queen Victoria's accession to the throne. The *Carrier* made a special trip taking LB&SCR staff and their families to view the ships, complete with three carriages and a meat wagon on deck. The trip was remembered for the wrong reasons when *Carrier* sailed ahead of the Royal Yacht, covering the dignitaries in thick black smoke. The losses mounted up and the service was eventually ended on 31st March 1888. The *Carrier* was laid-up in Newhaven and sold to Sweden in 1892, where she was broken up the following year. The terminal equipment at Bembridge was sold for scrap in 1900 for £75 cash.

As a postscript, there was a proposal to build a railway tunnel to the Isle of Wight in 1913, followed by a counter proposal for a train ferry. The ferry was strongly supported by Col. Hobart, Chairman of the Isle of Wight Chamber of Commerce, though the plan was overtaken by the war. The scheme was resurrected in 1919, but never turned into a workable project.

TWO

Channel ferry schemes

Channel ferry schemes

Early schemes

It is fair to say that England has had a conflicted attitude to mainland Europe over the past two millennia. The Romans, Saxons, Vikings and finally Normans all invaded and settled in England. Medieval English kings claimed sovereignty over much of France and held on to Calais until the 16th century. Attitudes to the ferry service across the English Channel suffered the same conflicts throughout the 19th century. On the one hand, merchants, travellers and later holidaymakers wanted a comfortable, reliable ferry service with mail delivered regularly between London and Paris. On the other, the military remained suspicious that anything that improved communication could be used by foreign powers to launch an invasion.

The first plan for a tunnel was proposed by a French mining engineer, Albert Mathieu-Favier in 1802, at a time when small sailing ships were completely at the mercy of the weather. The design was to provide a tunnel for horse-drawn coaches, lit by oil lamps. A second drainage tunnel would be bored below the main tunnel and an artificial island built on the Varne Shoals in the middle of the channel for changing horses. As this was at the time of the Napoleonic Wars, it is not surprising that nothing came of the scheme.

Suspicion that civil engineers would propose any scheme for a fee, unless there were competent people to judge their merits, was the subject of an editorial in 'The Scotsman' in 1841. Discussing alternative railway routes between Scotland and England, it stated:

'Without some such arrangement, capitalists would be in great danger of being allured into the support of impracticable or wasteful schemes, by designing individuals. The skill of civil engineers varies very much - the measure of their consciences even more - and we have seen enough to satisfy us, that for a good fee a Report might be got recommending as highly practicable and advantageous, a floating railway from Dover to Calais, or a tunnel under the Alps, to join France and Italy!'.

Aimé Thomé de Gamond, (1807-1876), was the Chief Engineer for the Department de Pas de Calais and spent much of his working life developing schemes for a cross-channel rail link.

Hopefully, the editor of the 'The Scotsman' lived long enough to see both projects become practicable and advantageous a generation later.

Aimé Thomé de Gamond

The first engineer to look at ways of connecting the English and French railways was Aimé Thomé de Gamond. He was born in 1807 and had studied to become a mining engineer in the Netherlands before being appointed as Chief Engineer for the Department of Pas-de-Calais. In 1834 he proposed his first idea for a tunnel between Dover and Calais using sheet-metal tubes. Over the next 30 years he devoted his time and wealth to developing five more schemes for tunnels, bridges and ferries:

In 1836, a huge granite bridge with 150m spans.

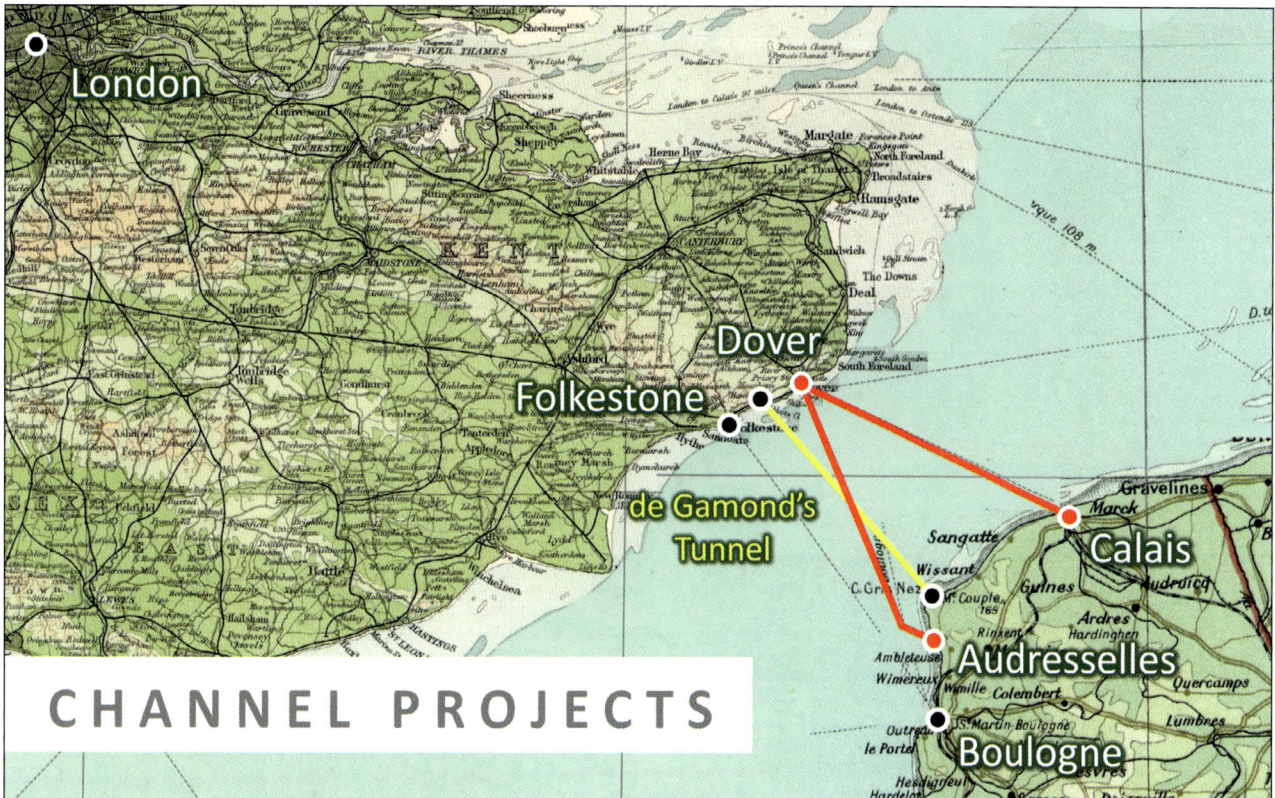

London

Dover

Folkestone

de Gamond's
Tunnel

Sangatte

Wissant

Calais

Gravelines

Audresselles

Boulogne

CHANNEL PROJECTS

In 1837, two 8 km long piers, built out from either side, with 'le bac flottant', a large double-ended steam ferry running between special docks at the end of each pier.

In 1840, a causeway across the Channel with openings for shipping channels close to each coast, crossed by pontoon bridges.

In 1856, a 34 km bored tunnel.

In 1866, a 36 km bored tunnel on a revised route, with a central island on the Varne Bank.

Thomé de Gamond was not just an armchair engineer. To collect soil samples, he personally dived 33m to the seabed from a small boat rowed by his daughter and on one occasion, he was attacked and bitten by conger eels. His tunnel proposal was presented to Napoleon III in 1856 and after various modifications finally accepted in 1867. A Franco-British Committee was formed to develop the proposals that included Sir John Hawkshaw, a prominent British civil engineer, who became a champion of later tunnel projects. The Committee's findings were presented to Queen Victoria and Prince Albert in 1868 and supported by important engineers of the day, including Brunel, Locke and George Stephenson. As always, politics intervened, and British interest waned with the outbreak of the Franco-Prussian War in 1870.

Thomé de Gamond's early idea of transporting trains on a floating platform is the most interesting in terms of this book, but there do not appear to be any drawings of his proposal. Interest in the tunnel project continued,

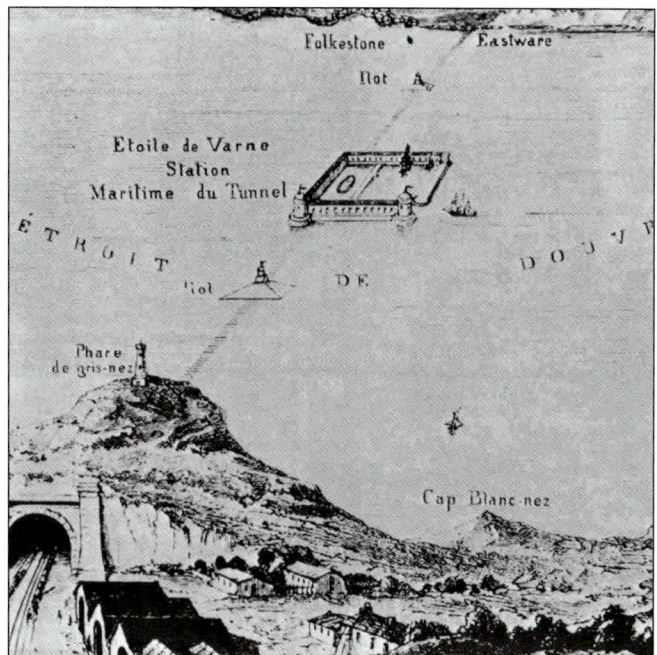

Thomé de Gamond's 1866 tunnel scheme proposed a port and station on an artificial island on the Varne Bank in the middle of the Channel.

though Thomé de Gamond was largely side-lined and died in poverty in 1876. His lasting contribution was to focus engineering minds on both sides of the channel on providing a railway link from London to Paris.

business, applying his inventive mind to manufacturing improved cotton spinning machinery. Over the next few years, he was granted many patents, for diverse and mysterious items such as the Self Stripping Carding Engine, the Derby Doubler or Lap Machine and the Loose Boss Top Roller. The business was successful, and he moved his factory from Ashton-under-Lyme to the Collyhurst Works in Manchester, selling his machinery throughout Britain and abroad.

Leigh first took an interest in marine engineering in 1849, patenting a system for steering ships by varying the power to twin screws, but to his disappointment, the Admiralty showed no interest. In 1861, he took a trip to the United States, crossing the Atlantic on the *Great Eastern*. He was impressed that even in a storm off Newfoundland the vessel did not appear to pitch, though it still had a heavy roll. He concluded that if a ship was long enough it would not pitch and that roll could be minimised if it were built on pontoons. This would be ideal for a Channel train ferry and he exhibited his ideas with models at the London International Exhibition of 1862.

In an article in Engineering in December 1866, Leigh proposed a fleet of four or six train ferries running between Dover and Calais, 800 feet (244m) long with a breadth of 160 feet (49m) but with a draught of only around 6 feet. The ships would be powered by two pairs of paddle wheels, one forward and one aft, with each of the four paddle wheels having its own pair of engines. Given the size of the ship he expected that,

'We should, at any rate, get a practically motionless ship, so far as rolling and pitching are concerned, and this in the roughest sea, supposing the vessel to have full way on her. That there would be absolutely no rolling we do not pretend, but it

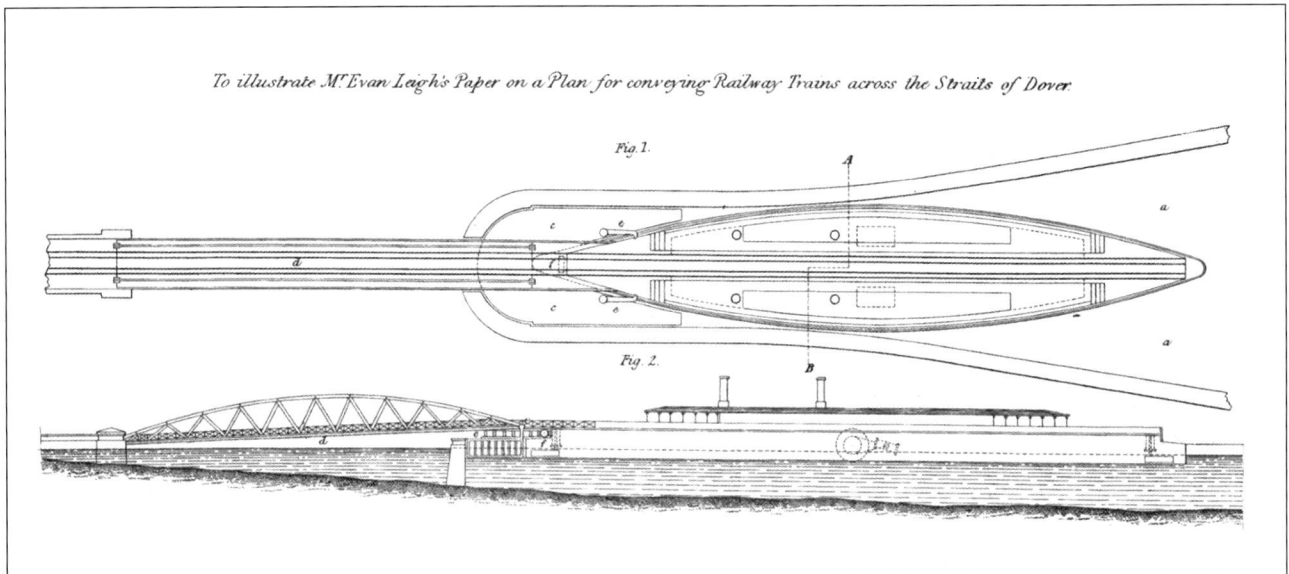

Evan Leigh, (1810-1876), was a Lancashire inventor who developed several designs for cross-Channel train ferries during the 1860s.

Evan Leigh

Evan Leigh was an unlikely train ferry pioneer. He was born in 1810 in Ashton-under-Lyme, Lancashire, the son of a wealthy cotton mill owner and left school aged 16 to spend two years in Europe studying engineering and science. When he returned to England, he took over as manager of his father's cotton spinning mill and remained there for about 25 years. Around 1850, he had got tired of cotton spinning and decided to start a new

To illustrate Mr Evan Leigh's Paper on a Plan for conveying Railway Trains across the Straits of Dover

Evan Leigh proposed ferries 800 feet long and 160 feet broad, (244m x 49m) but with a draught of only 6 feet. He also presented plans for a ferry port and linkspan in 1871. *(Institute of Naval Architects, 1871)*

Evan Leigh's ferry port had long 'V' shaped breakwaters and a linkspan bridge, stretching more than half a mile from the shoreline. Exactly where the ports would be built was not specified. The sketch also included a drydock for the ferries, which were much larger than any other ships of the time. *(Institute of Naval Architects, 1871)*

is not unreasonable to believe that this would be so little that not one passenger in fifty would be affected by it, any more than by the motion of the little craft upon which so many thousands ride daily and without internal disturbance, upon the Thames.'

The ships proposed were certainly enormous, longer and nearly twice the beam of the *Great Eastern*, and not surprisingly more than twice as long and around five times as broad as any existing Channel packet. One of the weaknesses of the proposal was that Leigh paid very little attention to the ports and transfer arrangements. Part of the reason for the very shallow draught was the limitation of the existing Calais harbour, which had very little water at low tide.

Evan Leigh's designs evolved over the following years and he presented a paper, 'On a Plan for Conveying Railway Trains across the Straits of Dover', to the Institution of Naval Architects in 1871. The ship had reduced in size, now 500 feet (152m) long and 88 feet (27m) breadth, though still with a shallow draught of 5 feet (1.5m). Instead of the previous design, with paddle wheels forward and aft, the ship had two pairs of paddle wheels either side. The paddle wheels were fitted inside the hull, extending through an opening in the bottom plating. The port and starboard paddle wheels were not connected and had separate engines so that they could be used for steering, similar to the *Leviathan* twenty years before. The other novel feature was that the paddle wheels were closed drums, with only small external blades acting on the water.

Leigh had also developed ideas for the docking arrangements, though these were fairly theoretical and didn't reflect the actual Channel ports. His design included 'V' shaped breakwaters with a floating caisson at the point of the 'V'. The caisson had a system of rollers and a pair of mechanical hooks to secure the ship

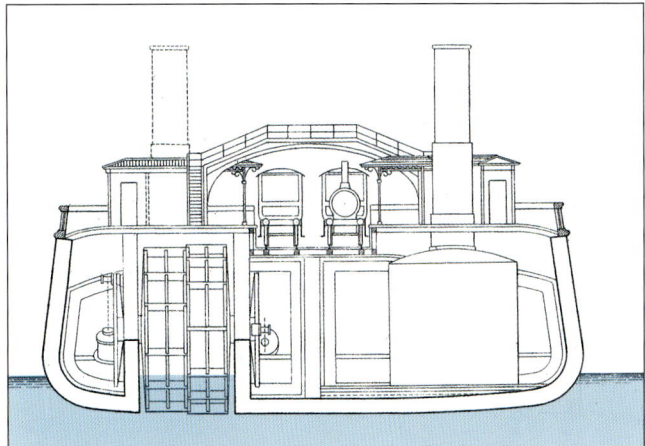

Evan Leigh's ferry had two rail tracks. Its great breadth was because the twin paddle wheels were fitted within the hull. Surprisingly for a ship designed not to roll, it did not have bilge keels. *(Institute of Naval Architects, 1871)*

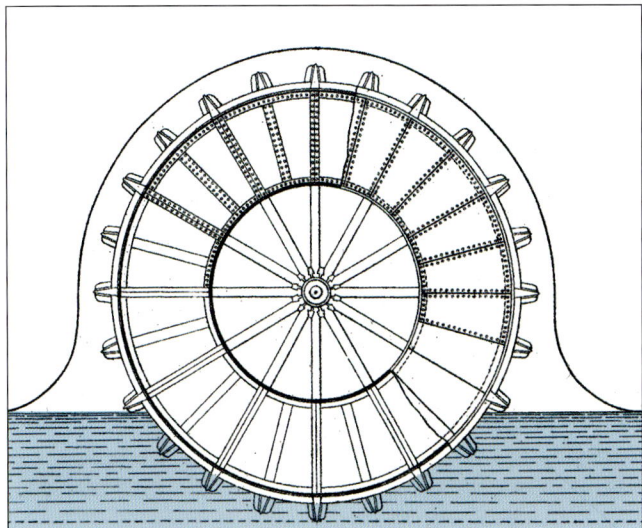

Evan Leigh's patented paddle wheel design consisted of a doughnut-shaped watertight iron drum with small blades on the outside circumference. *(Institute of Naval Architects, 1871)*

in place and also supported one end of a hinged linkspan, level with the ferry's deck. This was similar in concept to Thomas Grainger's original design for the Tay ferry, but Leigh's linkspan was around 315 feet (96m) long. As the spring tidal range at Dover is around 19 feet, (5.8m) this would have a workable gradient of ± 3%.

Leigh's paper got a bit of criticism, not least from John Scott Russell, who had worked with Brunel on the *Great Eastern* and the previous year had designed a train ferry for Lake Constance. There was scepticism on whether the paddles would be effective as they were largely enclosed within the hull. Also, that the long 'V' shaped breakwaters would act as a funnel and amplify the effect of the waves.

Leigh was undaunted by the criticism and the following year received a patent for 'Improvements in the Construction and Propelling of Ships for Railway Ferries and other Purposes'. His ideas had moved on and the ferry he proposed had four tracks rather than the previous two. The patent also incorporated several novel ideas:

● A complex method of flanging the edges of the hull plates, to provide integral stiffeners. In theory this would reduce the overall number of rivets required, though the patent does not explain how the plates could be made with sufficient accuracy to achieve a watertight construction.

● A double-hull construction with the paddle wheels contained within the outer hulls.

● Improved steering by connecting forward and aft rudders so that they operated together.

● Using the steering wheel to control a steam valve which would accelerate or decelerate the paddle wheels on either side of the ship.

None of these ideas were taken further, but Evan Leigh remained inventive to the end. In his later years he suffered from bronchitis and died at his home in 1876.

Fowler's project

If Evan Leigh was an engineering eccentric, John Fowler was a pillar of the Victorian engineering establishment. He was born in Sheffield in 1817, the son of a land surveyor, and at seventeen he was apprenticed as an engineer working on water supply and canal works. Like most ambitious young engineers of his generation, he soon moved to work on railway projects. After working as assistant on the London & Brighton Railway, he set himself up as a consulting civil engineer in 1844.

Over the next thirty years he supervised railway projects all over Britain and Ireland and later consulted on railways in Australia, India, Norway and Egypt. During the 1850s and 60s, he built the Pimlico Bridge, the first railway bridge across the Thames, and supervised the Metropolitan and Circle Lines of the

John Fowler, (1817-1898), was an experienced civil engineer who championed the Channel Ferry Project from 1865 through to 1872. Towards the end of his career, he was the supervising engineer on the Forth Railway Bridge. *(Wellcome Collection)*

London Underground.

Perhaps prompted by Leigh's train ferry model at the 1862 Exhibition, Fowler started taking an interest in developing a Channel ferry. Right from the start, he realised that the key to operating large ferries was to provide suitable harbours, protected from the worst of the weather and available at all states of the tide. In 1865, Fowler partnered with James Abernethy, an experienced harbour engineer, and with William Wilson they surveyed possible sites for harbours in both England and France. On the English side, they proposed creating an extension to Dover Harbour, building large new breakwaters to extend the enclosed area of the harbour to 95 acres, and provide a protected ferry terminal, or 'Water Station'. In France, they were disappointed by both existing ferry ports at Calais and Boulogne. Both harbours had narrow approaches obstructed by sandbanks and the harbours themselves were small and vulnerable to silting. Their recommendation was to build a new deep-water harbour and railway terminal close to the fishing village of Audresselles, around 12 km north of Boulogne.

Fowler's ferries

The ferries proposed were large double-ended paddle steamers, 450 feet (137m) long, 57 feet (17m) beam, 85 feet (26m) across the paddle boxes and with a draught of 12 feet (3.7m). Superficially they were similar to the

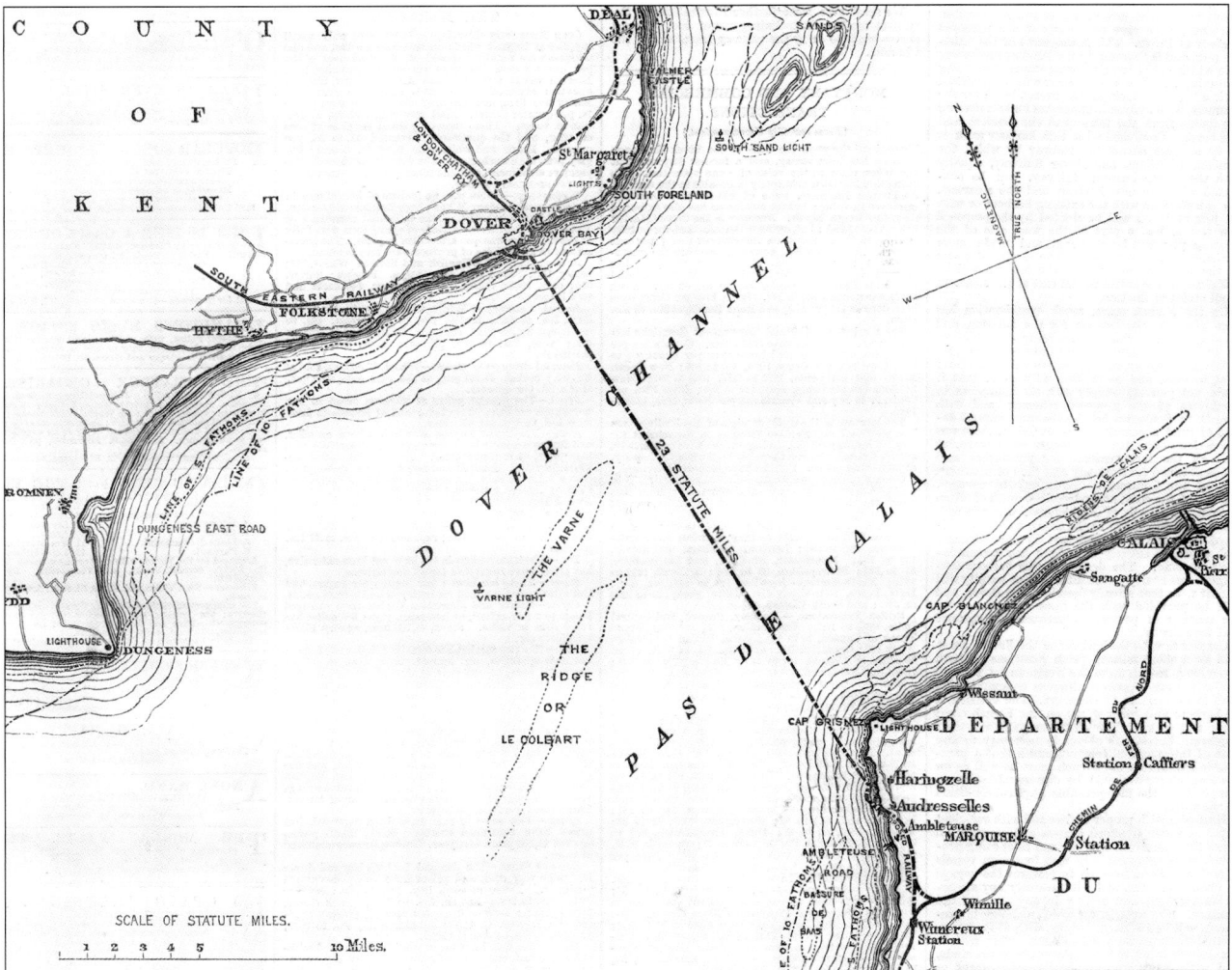

Fowler realised the importance of developing suitable harbours for large ferries. Rather than use Calais, her proposed building a new deep-water harbour at Audresselles, north of Boulogne. (*Illustrated London News*)

existing steam packets, only larger. The most obvious difference was that the train ferries had four funnels, two either side, unlike a passenger steamer where the engines are on the centreline. They also had hinged watertight bow and stern doors. The ferries were powered by four oscillating cylinder steam engines, two connected to each paddle wheel. The unobstructed train deck meant that the port and starboard paddle wheels were not connected, as with Leigh's design and the *Leviathan*. The total power was 10,000 hp, designed to drive the ship at 20 knots. There was a single track on the main deck to carry 16 passenger carriages. The concept was that the main deck of the ferry would be like a mainline railway station. Passengers could stay in their carriages during the crossing or alight to a platform where they could stroll and use refreshment and smoking rooms. There would also be a customs office. While the early drawings showed a single track of carriages, later descriptions stated that there would be two tracks. Goods wagons were carried on a lower deck, accessed by an internal ramp on the first designs, but later changed to a hydraulic lift.

Fowler was not afraid to involve experienced engineers and shipbuilders. The preliminary design for the ferries was developed with A.& J. Inglis & Co., of Pointhouse in Glasgow, who had just built the *Kinloch* for the Forth. His plan for the 'water stations', echoed the great railway terminals of London or Paris. The entire ferry dock was covered by a huge glass arched roof. Trains would be transferred from the quayside to the ferry by a hydraulic lift that coped with the tidal range. The lift consisted of a horizontal lattice girder platform, 200 feet (61m) long. The platform was moved up and down by hydraulic jacks at each end, driving chains and counterweights. The hydraulic jacks were designed by Sir William Armstrong & Co. in Newcastle, who stated that they would take about a minute to raise or lower the platform. John Fowler more cautiously stated that five minutes would be a reasonable delay. The total cost of the project, harbours and ferry boats, was estimated at £2.2 million and could be operational in three years.

In parallel with Fowler's ferry project, others were seeking support for a Channel Tunnel, based on Thomé

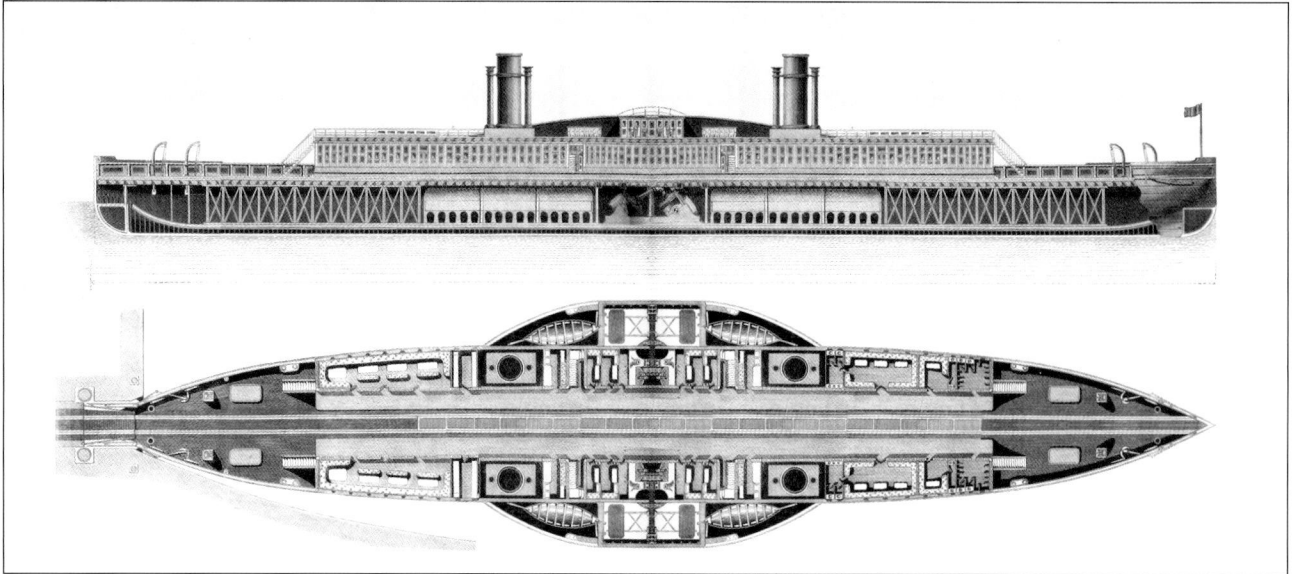

Fowler's first ferry design was developed by A&J Inglis & Co. in Glasgow. The ferry was 137m long, with a single rail track on the main deck and a station platform on either side. *(Engineering, Feb. 1869)*

de Gamond's proposals. Sir John Hawkshaw estimated the tunnel would cost £10 million and take 10 years to complete. When asked by Lord Richard Grosvenor, the Chairman of the Channel Tunnel Company, Fowler declined to give his support:

"I came to the conclusion, that at all events it was premature. Yes, and I declined to take the responsibility of adopting it. I thought it very much better that we should begin with something which at all events we could see our way to the end of. It may lead, in the course of fifty or a hundred years, to a tunnel being seriously proposed, but we are certainly not ready for a tunnel yet. The bridge is too ridiculous to discuss, as the bridge would

Fowler proposed a 'Water Station' in Dover's Western Docks with the ferry sailing into a covered berth to protect passengers from the weather. To the left of the Water Station, there was a drydock for maintaining the ferries. *(Engineering, Feb. 1869)*

The ferry was much larger than the existing Channel steam packets and was designed for a service speed of 20 knots, powered by four oscillating steam engines. *(Illustrated London News)*

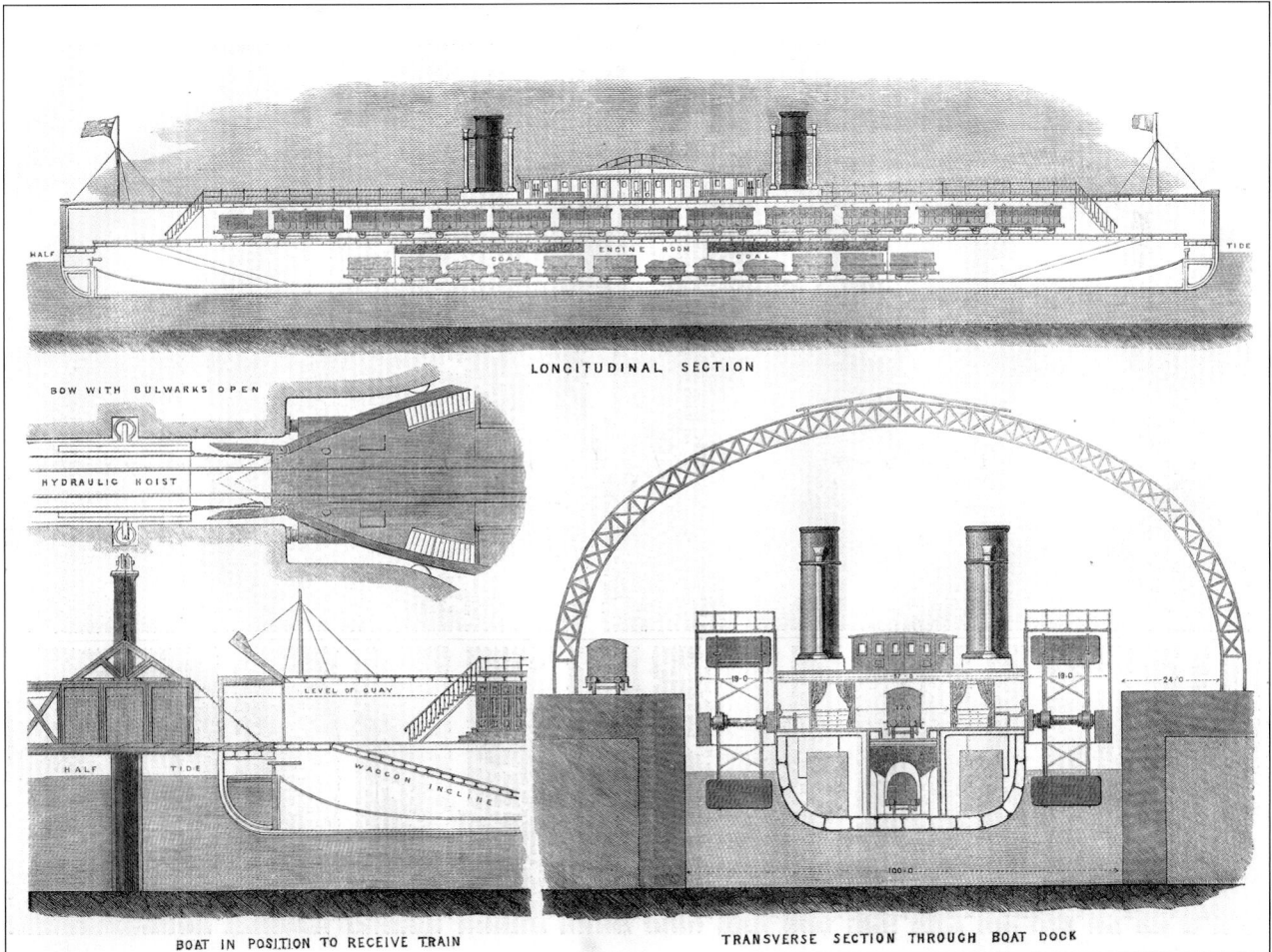

A revised ferry design added a lower train deck for goods wagons. The great arched roof over the ferry berth was similar to the main London stations. A hydraulic hoist platform was used to handle the train at any state of the tide. *(Illustrated London News)*

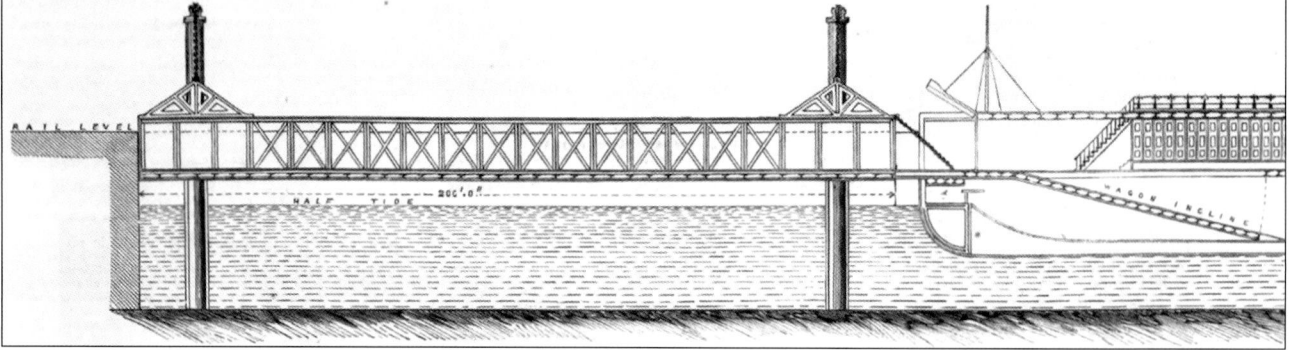

THE CHANNEL FERRY: HYDRAULIC LIFT AND LANDING STAGE.

MR. JOHN FOWLER, MR. J. ABERNETHY, AND MR. W. WILSON, ENGINEERS.

The hydraulic lift and landing stage was slightly less than half the length of the ferry, so that the coaches could be unloaded and raised to the level of the dockside in two operations. *(Engineering)*

consist of a number of piers, which would be rocks dangerous to navigation.

My proposal is parallel to a tunnel in this sense, that it is a continuous communication. The very essence of my proposal is that carriages, goods trucks, and mails should be carried across without

breaking bulk; that would be accomplished by a tunnel, but it will be accomplished much better, in my opinion, by proper boats."

To an experienced well-connected engineer like Fowler the technicalities of the ferry project were

Another view of the Dover 'Water Station', though this time without the drydock. *(Illustrated London News)*

LONGITUDINAL SECTION OF FERRY STEAMER

The final ferry design had evolved to have hydraulic lifts, forward and aft, for transferring the goods wagons between the main and lower decks. An idea that was revived by the *Railship I*, just over a century later. *(The Graphic)*

relatively straight-forward. The politics on both sides of the channel were much more complicated.

In Britain, a Bill had to be approved by Parliament to allow the modifications to Dover harbour. The 'International Communications Bill' was first introduced in 1865 but withdrawn under pressure from the Admiralty who opposed the harbour works. A second attempt in 1867 met a similar fate as the Admiralty felt that any improvements to Channel ports were an invitation to invasion. The ferry project was designed to connect to both railways serving Dover, the South Eastern Railway and the London, Chatham & Dover Railway. However, the South Eastern Railway opposed the project, partly because they had invested in Folkestone as a channel port, but also because their Chairman, Sir Edward Watkin, was a supporter of the tunnel. The project also struggled to get support in France as many were against the proposed new port at Audresselles, particularly the local authorities in both Calais and Boulogne who would lose the ferry traffic.

At its third attempt in 1870, the railways had withdrawn their opposition and the Bill was passed by the House of Commons. Final approval by the House of Lords was dependent on agreement with the French

Government for the necessary harbour works. Due to the Franco-Prussian War, this was overtaken by events and the Bill again withdrawn.

When peace returned, the project was again discussed with the French Government and railway companies. All parties were agreed and a fourth attempt to pass the Bill was made in 1872, again it was passed by the House of Commons. In the House of Lords, the Committee was evenly divided. The counsel for the promoters drew glowing pictures of the brilliantly-lit stations where invalids in search of warm climates were conveyed to the sunny south without risk of exposure to the weather, the abolition of sea-sickness, the vast increase of traffic and of strengthening the entente cordiale between England and France. All was in vain as the Chairman, Earl Belmore, used his casting vote to reject the Bill. Fowler was hugely disappointed. He never changed his opinion that the Channel ferry was a worthwhile project but decided he had spent enough time and money and was tired of politics. He moved on to other work, not least by partnering with Benjamin Baker to design and build the great new railway bridge across the Forth.

The problem was largely that not enough people

The final drawing of Fowler's plan for Dover harbour, this time with two covered berths. The proposal was submitted to Parliament for the fourth time in 1872 and rejected by the House of Lords. Fowler decided to move on to other projects. *(The Graphic)*

shared Fowler's view that a ferry and a tunnel were complementary. The ferry could be implemented in a few years and generate traffic and revenue that would justify the much longer and more expensive tunnel project. This is essentially what happened in the 20th century. However, from the 1870s through to the First World War, the proposers of the tunnel opposed ferry projects with the result that neither progressed.

Admiral Belcher's waterjets

Fowler's long campaign to push his train ferry project through parliament sparked the interest of many other engineers to explore other proposals. Though these were purely ideas for discussion, rather than serious projects, one of these was a ferry with waterjet propulsion.

The idea for a 'hydraulic reaction engine' was developed by John Ruthven and his son Morris sometime in the 1840s. John was a mechanical engineer and as a young man had spent some time in New York before returning to his native Edinburgh. He had worked with Alexander Craig in the 1830s, trying to develop a rotary steam engine. This never evolved into a practical machine and John, together with his son Morris, a

Vice-Admiral Sir Edward Belcher, (1799-1877), had retired from a long naval career when he proposed a train ferry with waterjet propulsion in 1870. *(Wellcome Collection)*

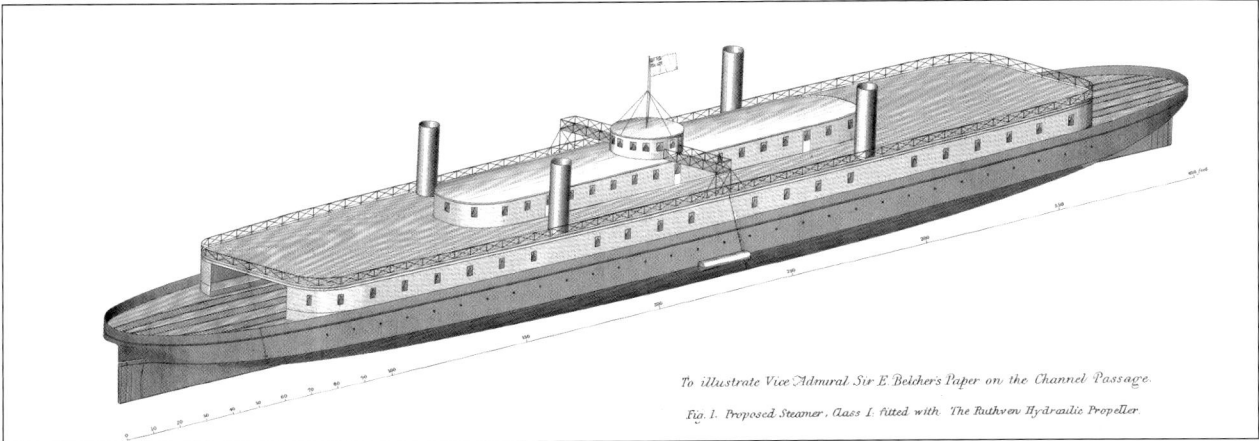

Admiral Belcher's train ferry was propelled by waterjets fitted amidships either side. It also had three lines of track on the main deck. *(Institution of Naval Architects)*

shipyard draughtsman, turned their minds to the hydraulic reaction engine. Their idea was to use a steam engine to drive a large centrifugal pump. Seawater was taken into the pump through the bottom of the ship and pumped out through nozzles fitted to the sides. These ejected the water aft, pushing the ship forward. At the time, virtually all steamships were powered by paddles. The first screw steamer, the *Archimedes*, had been built in 1840 and Brunel's *Great Britain*, was completed in 1845.

The Admiralty were hugely interested in alternative means of propulsion as paddles were very vulnerable to gunfire. In 1843 they conducted their famous experiment, building two similar sloops, *HMS Rattler*, fitted with a screw propeller, and *HMS Alecto* with paddles. In a tug-of-war, with a line between the sterns of the ships, the *Rattler* pulled the *Alecto* astern at 2 knots, proving the superiority of screw propulsion.

HMS Waterwich

In 1851, the Ruthvens built a working model of a ship propelled by their hydraulic engine. They continued with their experiments and eventually persuaded the Admiralty to conduct a full-size trial. In 1864, the Admiralty ordered three identical gunboats, *HMS Viper, Vixen* and *Waterwich*. The *Viper* and *Vixen* had conventional propellers, the *Waterwich* had a hydraulic engine built by J.& W. Dudgeon of Millwall, London. The pump impellor was 14 feet 6 inches (4.4m) in diameter, weighed 8 tons, and was driven by three steam engines, totalling 780 hp. Two nozzles were fitted on each side of the hull above the waterline, one pointing forward and one aft, with a valve which could almost instantly change the direction of the jet. While the ship was normally propelled by two jets pointing aft, the direction of a jet could change from aft to forward, simply by closing a valve, allowing the ship to turn in her own length. Comparative trials between the waterjet and screw propelled ships were carried out on the Solent in

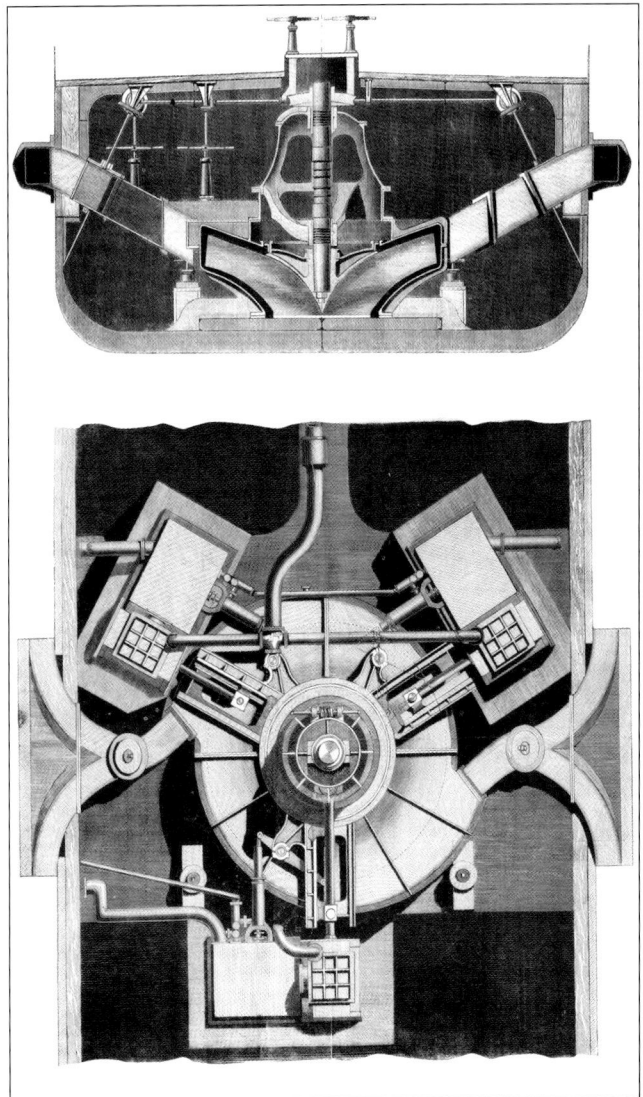

A section and plan of Ruthven's hydraulic engine fitted to *HMS Waterwich.* Water was pulled in through the bottom of the ship to a large centrifugal pump powered by three steam engines. The pump outlet was through two waterjets fitted to the sides above the waterline. A valve allowed the jet direction to be changed from forward to aft. *(The Engineer)*

1867. The waterjet performed impressively, the *Waterwich* achieved a similar speed to the screw ships and was much more manoeuvrable. The main disadvantage of the hydraulic engine was that it was larger and heavier than a conventional engine. Space was always at a premium in naval ships and the Admiralty did not pursue the invention.

In 1870, Vice-Admiral Sir Edward Belcher presented a paper to the Institution of Naval Architects proposing a waterjet powered train ferry. Belcher was aged 70, a retired Admiral who had carried-out the first British survey of Hong Kong harbour in 1841 and in 1852 led a rescue mission to find the lost Franklin expedition in the Canadian arctic. He was a supporter of Fowler's project and had a strong opinion that a seaworthy ship needed a draught of around 12 feet, as opposed to less than 6 feet on Leigh's design. However, Belcher proposed a number of improvements. In particular, he disliked the use of disconnected paddle wheels:

If the wind be abeam and the vessel roll in the trough of a heavy ground swell, even in calm, the rolling of one paddle out of the water would cause the engine to race, with great risk to the destruction of machinery. As to the over-immersed paddle, it loses considerable propelling power, at the same time as that of its opposite is utterly lost, thus diminishing half the propelling force and consequent loss of speed. ...
On this specific point, the hydraulic (engine) rejoices in her superiority over all other modes of propulsion; seeing that the orifice in the air performs equally, or better than that immersed.

Belcher proposed a ferry 400 feet (122m) long, 60 feet (18.3m) wide with a draught of 13 feet, (4m). It was double ended with three tracks on a single train deck. The centre track for goods or luggage wagons, the passenger carriages on the outside tracks being accessed from platforms, similar to Fowler's design. This was just an idea for discussion, but in many ways, it is a pity that it was not taken forward. Keeping the trains above the watertight deck, by removing the lower train deck, made loading and unloading much easier. The open deck-ends avoided the need for watertight bow and stern doors, which made the ship much safer. Simple shutter doors were proposed for the openings at each end of the superstructure simply to protect the carriages and platform from the weather.

The waterjet propulsion was probably every bit as efficient as paddles and the improved manoeuvrability would be a great benefit on a short ferry crossing. The size of the hydraulic engine would not really be an issue provided it fitted below the train deck. The only caveat would be that the pump seals may have eroded quite quickly if the ferry pulled sand through the hydraulic engine while manoeuvring in shallow harbours.

Henri Dupuy de Lôme, (1816-1885), was the most famous French naval architect of his generation and proposed a train ferry scheme using an artificial island off the coast at Calais. *(Alchetron)*

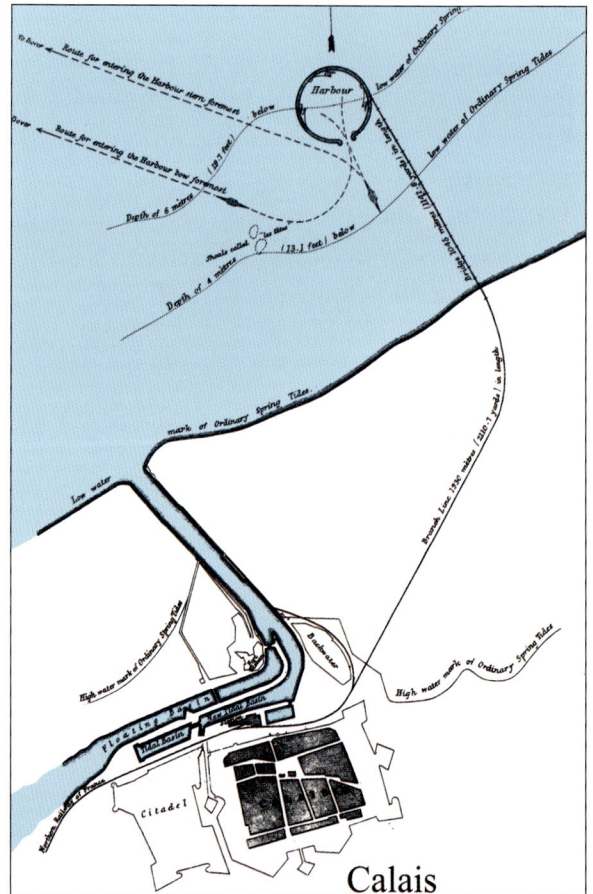

A plan of 400m diameter circular harbour, proposed by Dupuy de Lôme, to be built off the coast at Calais. *(Institution of Naval Architects,)*

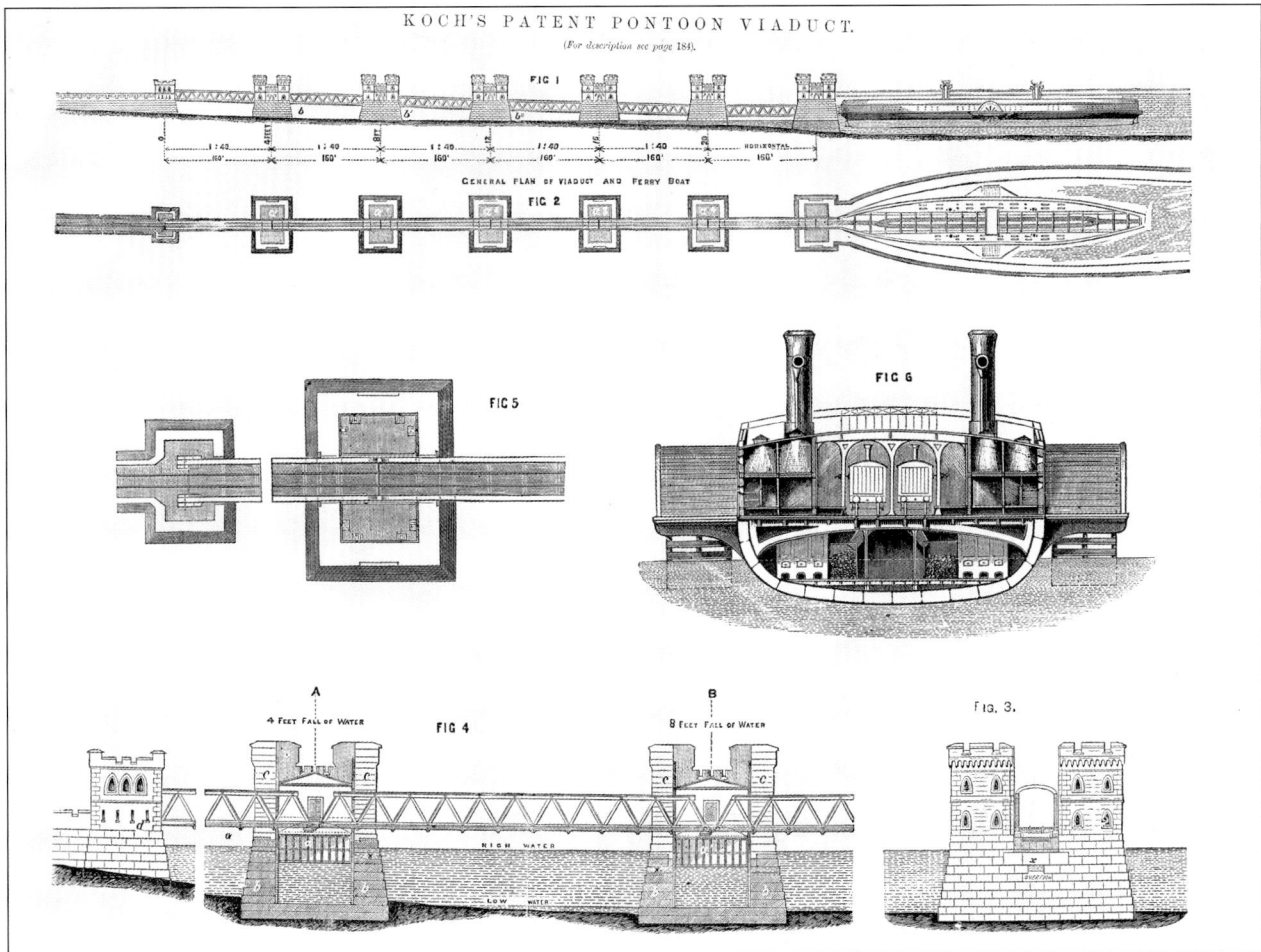

Koch's patent viaduct, complete with neo-gothic towers to restrain the pontoons. As it was more than twice the length of the ferry, it would need to be protected inside a very large harbour. *(The Engineer)*

Other schemes

Dupuy de Lôme

Through the eight years that Fowler's project was in the news, many other engineers came forward with ideas. Amongst the most serious of these was the French naval architect, Henri Dupuy de Lôme who developed a plan for a Calais-Dover train ferry. This was presented as a paper to the Société de Géographie in Paris, in 1874. Dupuy de Lôme was the most famous naval architect in France and had transformed the French Navy, introducing steam warships in the 1850s and 60s. In the 1870s he was largely retired, a Deputy in the National Assembly who spent much of his time making designs for navigable balloons and airships.

Dupuy de Lôme proposed a broadly similar scheme to Fowler's using three large paddle steamers, each 135m long, 11.2m breadth with a draught of 3.5m and displacement of 2,100 tons. The steamers were slightly simpler, in that they were not double-ended and loaded trains only through stern doors. He also explained why the channel packets of the day were famously

uncomfortable. He had calculated their natural roll period as 7-8 seconds, very similar to the dominant period of the waves in the Channel. His train ferry was designed to have a natural roll period of 12-13 seconds and would thus roll very little, other than in the most severe seas.

The main difference in his proposal was that the ferries would run between Dover and Calais, avoiding the need to build Fowler's new port and railway connections at Audresselles. Dupuy de Lôme accepted the problems with the existing Calais harbour, but proposed building a new offshore harbour around a kilometre off the Calais coast in a water depth of around 5m. His harbour was a circular breakwater around 400m in diameter with its entrance facing the shore to protect it from the weather and connected back to the mainland by a railway bridge. To avoid the complication of Armstrong's hydraulic platform, Dupuy de Lôme's proposal had three loading docks arranged around the inside circumference of the harbour. The elevation of each dock would vary from its neighbour by around 2.4m. Based on the state of the tide, the ferry would select the dock closest to the train deck elevation. A

30m hinged linkspan connected the dock to the ship and allowing for a difference of elevation of ±1.2m the maximum gradient would be 4%. A similar three-dock arrangement was planned for Dover, situated close to the Admiralty Pier.

The plan was that two ferries would be able to make four return trips per day, sixteen crossings in total. This would provide capacity for 800,000 passengers and 800,000 tons of freight each year. Dupuy de Lôme produced a convincing commercial proposal, requiring capital of nearly £1 million to implement the project, of which £560,000 was to build the new port at Calais.

Unfortunately, Dupuy de Lôme's proposals were made as an interested engineer. Without financial and political backing on both sides of the Channel his project was never going to progress.

Koch's pontoon viaduct

In 1872, a Mr Koch received a patent for a pontoon viaduct to allow trains to load and unload from a ferry at any state of the tide. His design involved a series of iron truss bridges, supported on floating caissons. Each bridge was 160 feet (49m) long and could adjust for 4 feet of tidal range with a 2.5% gradient. The number of bridges required would reflect the tidal range, thus for Dover six bridges were proposed to adjust for 24 feet, (7.3m). The whole viaduct would be 960 feet (293m) long, which would in turn have needed a substantial

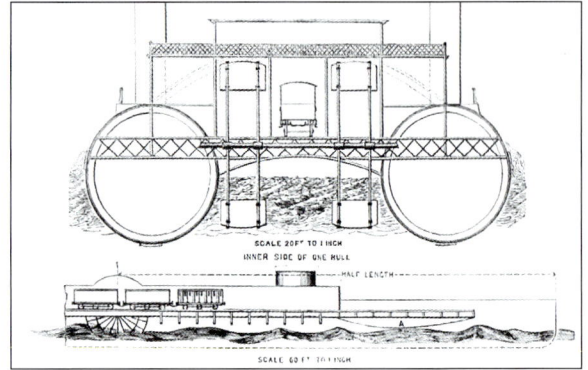

Alfred Goddard's idea for a catamaran train ferry in 1872. It had two cylindrical hulls, with the train and paddles supported on a platform between the hulls. *(The Engineer)*

breakwater to protect it. The design was never implemented, largely due to the space required and the cost of the harbour-works. However, the architectural detail with each caisson restrained within a little neo-gothic castle is quite charming.

Mr Goddard's catamaran

Alfred Goddard of Hastings' idea for a catamaran train ferry was published in 'The Engineer' in 1872. His plan was for a vessel with two cylindrical hulls, each 500 feet (152m) long and 25 feet (7.6m) diameter, connected by a series of transverse girders. Between the hulls a

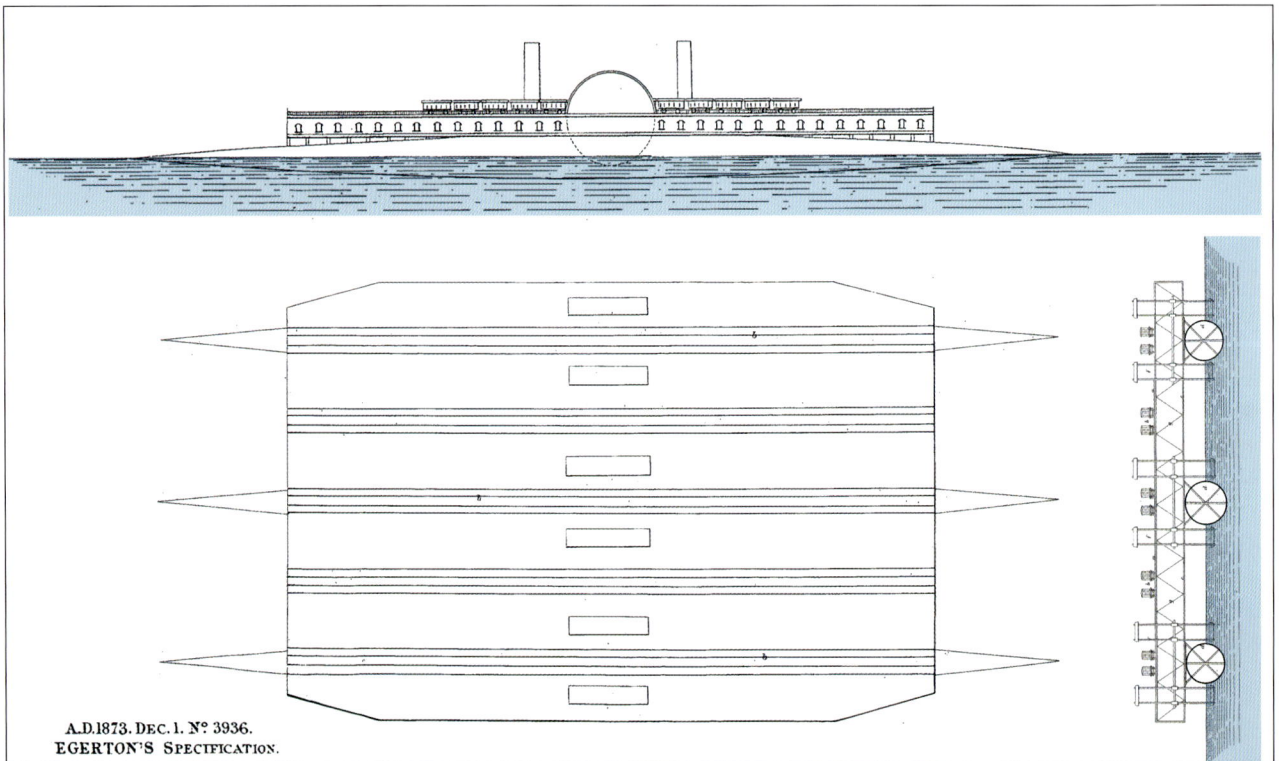

A.D.1873. DEC. 1. N° 3936.
EGERTON'S SPECIFICATION.

Hugh Egerton patented his giant trimaran train ferry in 1873. The deck was 134m long and 87m wide supported on three tapered cylinders. It was powered and steered by three pairs of paddle wheels, with ten rail tracks on the upper deck to carry 200 railway wagons. The patent was not clear on where the ferry would dock or how the wagons would be loaded. *(Patent 3936)*

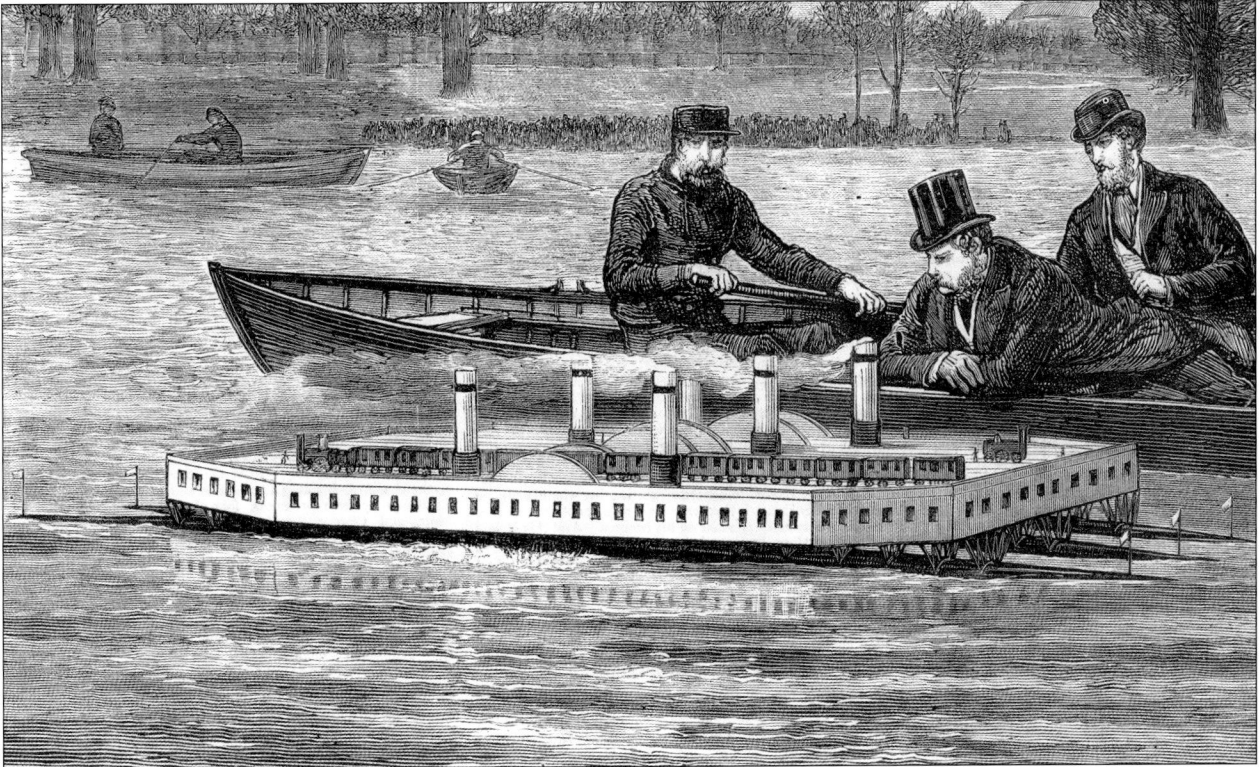

Hugh Egerton continued to develop and patent his trimaran designs. He is presumably the man in the top hat inspecting the model being tested on the Serpentine in 1876. *(The Graphic)*

platform deck, 400 feet (122m) long by 30 feet (9.1m) wide would support a central train track and provide space for passenger accommodation. The vessel was to be double ended, with engines, contained inside the cylindrical hulls driving internal paddle wheels. The main advantage claimed for the design was that the width across the two hulls would prevent the vessel rolling and allow the paddles to operate in calm water between the hulls.

Hugh Egerton's amazing trimaran

While Mr Goddard's idea may have been sketched in an afternoon, Hugh Egerton spent several years developing even more amazing proposals. Egerton was born 1834, the son of a Cheshire vicar. He left home looking for adventure, joining the army to fight in the Crimean War, then moving to South Australia to look for gold. In the 1860s he managed gold mines and set up as a stockbroker in Bendigo. It's not clear whether he made his fortune, but he returned to England in 1873. He may have had an uncomfortable voyage home, as his thoughts turned to developing huge multi-hull ships that would not pitch or roll at sea.

He registered a patent in 1873 for 'Improvements in the Construction of Ships, Ferry Boats and other Vessels'. It proposed:

To construct a floating vessel in such a manner

that while it will be capable of carrying or transporting very heavy and cumbrous loads, such as railway trains, carriages and animals on a deck, the vessel shall be of comparatively light draught and be incapable of pitching and rolling even in a rough of heavy sea.

To this end the buoyant or floating part of the structure is formed of three, four, or more long cylindrical or other suitably shaped pontoons made by preference of sheet iron, arranged parallel to each other, but at sufficient distance apart to receive between them paddle wheels for the propulsion of the vessel, and to allow of the easy escape of the tail water.

The superstructure is formed of strong horizontal girders, on which rests a platform or deck, on which may be erected cabins, engine houses and holds for the stowage of goods. . . .

A vessel constructed in this manner will be capable of receiving an entire railway train or other cumbrous load on the deck, and the vessel may be propelled at very great speed.

The vessel's hull was formed by three tapered cylinders, each 600 feet (183m) long and 26 feet (7.9m) in diameter. These tapered to a point, forward and aft, and were sealed to provide buoyancy. The cylinders were set 78 feet (24m) apart and connected by transverse lattice girders. These girders formed the

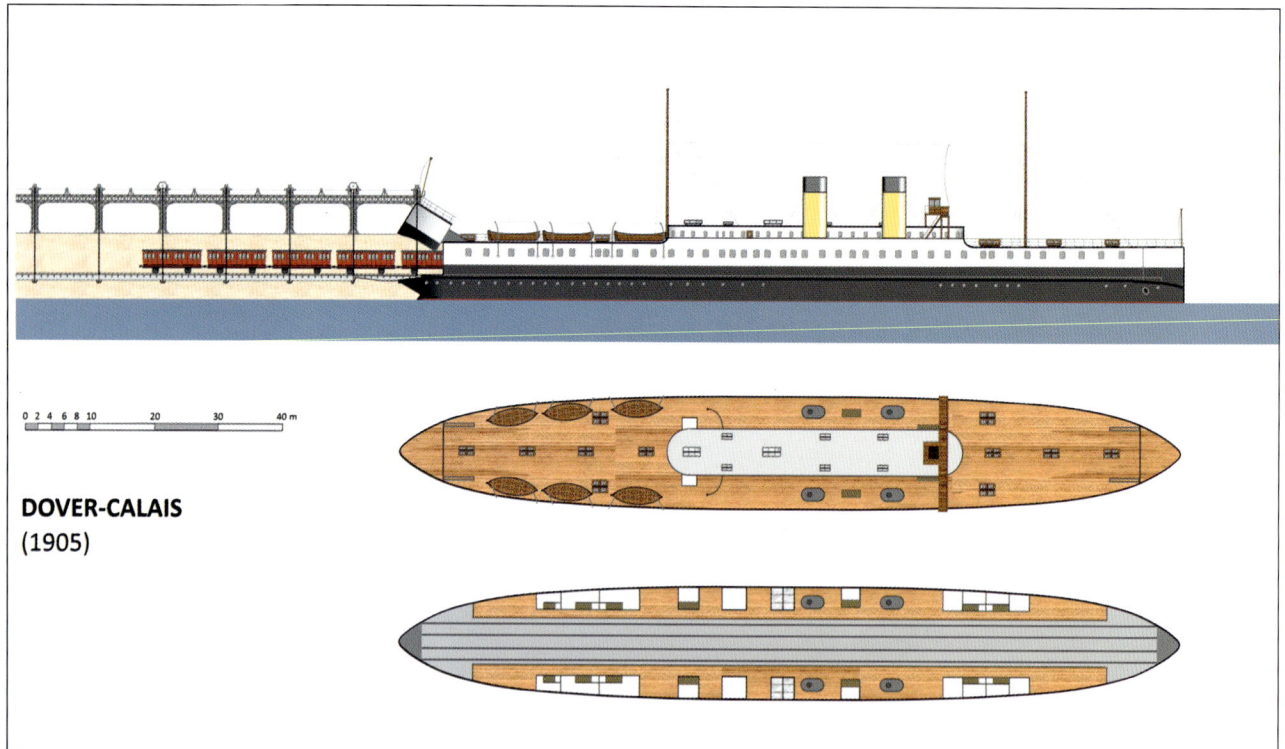

DOVER-CALAIS
(1905)

The steam-turbine ferry *Dover-Calais* was designed for the Intercontinental Railway Company in 1905. The plan was for two passenger ferries and two simpler ferries for goods wagons. As with previous ferry schemes, it was opposed by the supporters of a tunnel. *(Author)*

frame of a large deckhouse, 438 feet (134m) long, 286 feet (87m) wide and 20 feet (6.1m) in height. The deckhouse contained the engines and accommodation, with three pairs of paddle wheels, around 55 feet (17m) in diameter. On the roof of the deckhouse were ten parallel railway tracks, which would carry more than 200 railway wagons. The vessel was planned to have top speed of around 15 knots. There were no rudders, as it would be steered and be able to turn in its own length using the port and starboard engines.

Unfortunately, there were no details of what the harbours would look like or how the trains would be loaded and unloaded. Egerton continued with this design for many years, demonstrating a model on the Serpentine in Hyde Park in 1876. As with the other more adventurous schemes, it never went any further.

The 20th century

Through the last two decades of the 19th century various schemes for a Channel Tunnel were put forward, though all were rejected on defence grounds. It wasn't until the turn of the 20th century that there was a serious attempt to revive a train ferry project. The old rivalry between the two railways to Dover, which had worked against the previous ferry project, had been resolved. The South Eastern Railway and London, Chatham & Dover Railway had combined their operations in 1899. The Directors of the South Eastern &

Chatham Railway visited Denmark, Sweden and Germany in 1902 to survey train ferry operations. As a result, the Intercontinental Railway Company was formed the following year supported by the SE&CR in England and the Chemins de Fer du Nord in France. One of the leaders of the project was Sir Benjamin Baker, who had designed the Forth Bridge with John Fowler twenty years earlier. His old colleague having died in 1898.

The general principles of the plan were very similar to Fowler's scheme. The ferries would run between Dover and Calais. A new port was no longer needed in France as Calais harbour had been widened and deepened. As parliamentary approval was needed for the harbour improvements in Dover, the promoters lodged the Channel Ferry Railway and Quay (Dover) Bill in 1905.

The economic justification for the project was similar to the estimates prepared for Fowler's project thirty years earlier. The annual revenue was around £300,000 of which around 70% was in fares from 500,000 passengers, the balance from goods and mail wagons. The ferry provided an opportunity to transport fruit and cut flowers from France and Italy direct to London in a fleet of temperature controlled 'Aerothermic' goods wagons. British exporters, particularly of delicate goods such as china, saw the opportunity to avoid the damage caused by handling crates at the ports. One of the supporters of the project was the International Sleeping Car Company, better known by its French name Compagnie Internationale des Wagons-Lits, who were keen to run 'trains de luxe', on both day and night services, from London to Paris.

The Dover-Calais

The project proposed four train ferries, two principally for passenger carriages and two much simpler ships for goods wagons. The passenger ferries were designed by Sir W.G. Armstrong, Whitworth & Co., Newcastle and the goods ferries by the French shipbuilders Chantiers de St. Nazaire. The design of Armstrong's steamer had been evolved over many years by Sir William White, who later become Chief Constructor to the Admiralty. The steamer, provisionally named the *Dover-Calais*, was not too dissimilar from Fowler's ferry thirty years earlier. It was 400 feet (122m) long with a breadth of 56 feet (17m), with four funnels arranged two either side. Armstrong's had studied the design of the Lake Michigan train ferries in the United States and recently built the *Baikal* for Russia and the *Scotia* for Canada. This had led them to propose steam turbines driving twin screws, rather than the paddles in the previous design. Also, the bow and stern doors opened vertically, described as bascule doors, similar to the bow visors of modern ferries.

The *Dover-Calais* was designed by William White, (1845-1913), Chief Naval Architect for Armstrong Whitworth & Co. in Newcastle, based on their experience with the Lake Baikal ferry for Russia. He was later Chief Constructor to the Admiralty. *(Institution of Mechanical Engineers)*

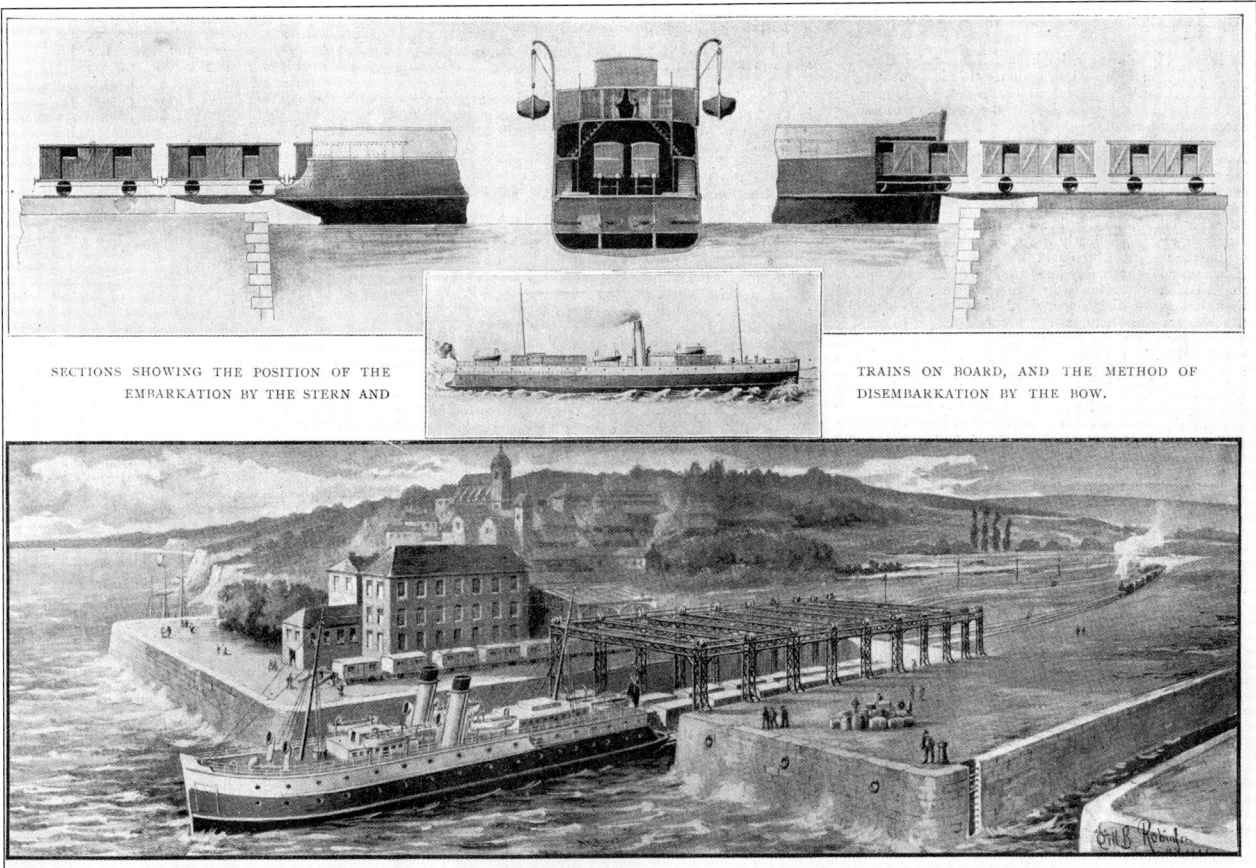

SECTIONS SHOWING THE POSITION OF THE EMBARKATION BY THE STERN AND

TRAINS ON BOARD, AND THE METHOD OF DISEMBARKATION BY THE BOW.

The goods ferries planned for the Intercontinental Railway Company's service also had two lines of track. The lower picture shows the gantry supporting the hydraulic platform which lifted the wagons from the ferry's deck to the quayside. *(Illustrated London News)*

The arrangement for loading the trains onboard was similar in concept to Fowler's design with a horizontal lift platform, supported in a gantry structure. The main difference being that the lift would be electrically powered to a design prepared by the Compagnie de Fives-Lille. Ernest de Rodakowski's book, 'The Channel Ferry', describes the process of loading trains as follows:

Upon arrival at the ferry station, the main line engine will be detached from the train. Then, either by means of a shunting engine at the back of the train, or possibly by haulage from electric capstans, half of the train will be moved on to the platform of the lift, which is 350 feet long, and is furnished with two parallel lines of rail. The train will then be divided, and its rear half in turn moved on to the second line of rail on the lift. This operation completed, the lift will be lowered to the level of the steamer lying berthed against the projecting arm of the quay, and the train transferred by means of electric capstans to the rails on the deck over a short steel bridge or flap, fitted to the end of the lift platform, and hinged in such a way as to allow for the movement of the ship in the water, caused by the slight alteration of its displacement as it receives or is relieved of the load of the train. Conversely, on the arrival of the ship bearing the train, the electric lift will await its advent at the proper height; the train will be transferred from the ship on to the lift by means of the electric windlasses; and the lift raised to the height of the land rails, where the main line locomotive will be coupled on, and the train removed from the lift in two instalments.

The internal arrangement of the *Dover-Calais* retained the concept of the Fowler ferry, with two lines of track close to the centreline and a station platform either side. Nine passenger carriages were carried on each track. Ernest de Rodakowski describes the passenger experience:

When the train has been shipped on board the steamer, the passengers will find themselves in what is to all intents and purposes an exceptionally well-arranged station; that is to say, they can alight on a wide platform, and walk under cover to a waiting-room, refreshment-room, smoking-room, or private cabin, all fitted up in a style with which the ordinary main line or even terminal station cannot compete.

It is not entirely clear why the 'station' concept was considered so important. It was a very inefficient use of the train deck, which could have had four rather than two tracks. There was also no reason why a whole deck above could not have been used for passenger facilities and accommodation. Even more surprisingly, the inefficient use of the train deck was also applied to the goods vessels, which also had two tracks, despite having space for three or even four.

The first version of the Channel Ferry Railway and Quay (Dover) Bill in 1905 proposed building the ferry dock in Dover's Commercial Harbour. The Admiralty objected to this and the Bill was withdrawn. A revised version of the Bill was resubmitted in 1906, proposing building the ferry dock to the west of the Admiralty Pier, and was passed by parliament.

In a re-run of the 1870s, progress with the ferry scheme was held pending resolution of a Bill proposing a Channel Tunnel, again supported by the SE&CR. The tunnel scheme was again rejected on the grounds of national security. However, the SE&CR remained reluctant to support the ferry plan and pressurised the Dover Harbour Board to oppose the developments that would provide more shunting space in the harbour. In 1909, a deputation of supporters of the ferry scheme urged Winston Churchill, the President of the Board of Trade, to intervene with the railway and harbour authorities. Churchill made statements in support of the ferry, but without support from the railways no action was taken.

Newhaven to Dieppe

As a last throw of the dice, the London, Brighton & South Coast Railway, in partnership with the Chemins de fer de l'État, formed the Channel Ferry Company in 1911. This company involved many of the individuals involved in the previous scheme and proposed to operate a train ferry between Newhaven and Dieppe. However, the project was overtaken by the outbreak of the First World War in 1914.

THREE

England to the Continent

The First World War

War Department (British Army)

Southampton – Dieppe	1917-1919
Richborough – Dunkerque / Calais	1918-1920
Southampton – Cherbourg	1918-1919

After all the projects and politics of the Victorian era, it was war that led to a train ferry service across the English Channel. The British Expeditionary Force went to France in 1914 with 250,000 men believing, "it would all be over by Christmas". Two years later there was an army of over two million volunteers and conscripts and as they became more experienced, their tactics and equipment became more sophisticated. When the German army was pushed back from the Hindenburg line in 1918, British troops advanced behind tanks, with a rolling artillery barrage and the enemy's positions plotted by aerial reconnaissance.

These military advances were made possible by an army logistics organisation that reliably delivered thousands of tons of supplies and ammunition to the front line. The transformation of railway and canal transport had its origins in August 1916 when the British commander, Sir Douglas Haig, invited a group of railway managers to France to advise on how to improve military transport. The leader of this group was Eric Geddes, already the Deputy General Manager of the North Eastern Railway, while still in his thirties. Haig was so impressed by Geddes, that he extended his stay in France and appointed him Director-General of Military Railways, with the rank of Major-General.

One of his first challenges was to provide more capacity at the Channel ports. The existing ports were fully stretched. Folkestone was the principal route for transporting troops to Boulogne and on to the army's huge transit camp at Étaples. Dover was under the control of the Admiralty and was the base for the fleet defending the Channel. A new port was needed to move large quantities of freight and Geddes was instrumental in developing the site at Richborough for both barge and ferry traffic. Richborough lies 15 miles north of Dover on the River Stour, close to Ramsgate. The Inland Waterways and Docks section of the Royal Engineers

Eric Geddes, (1875-1937), was appointed by General Haig as the first Director-General of Military Railways. He oversaw the development of Richborough port. *(Library of Congress)*

took over a flat marshy site of 2,200 acres, (890 hectares) to create the port. Within a few months, the course of the river was diverted, new basins dredged, a wharf was constructed with steel sheet piling and a navigable channel created out to sea through Pegwell Bay. A branch line was constructed from the South-Eastern & Chatham Railway and 60 miles of sidings were created within the Richborough base. Over time, wharves, workshops, foundries and power stations were added until there were 20,000 men working on the base. The sidings and railway yards had capacity to marshal over 3,000 wagons and a fleet of thirty-one tank locomotives were provided for shunting. The yards worked 24 hours a day, but with no lights as this could have attracted enemy aircraft. Despite this, by 1918 the port was handling nearly 1,500 wagons per day.

In December 1916 a cross-channel barge service was started towing barges from Richborough and taking them inland through the French and Belgian canal systems. By the end of the war in November 1918, there was a fleet of 50 tugs and 232 barges which had transported 1.25 million tons of freight.

Although the barge traffic was successful, it very quickly became clear that additional capacity was required. At the beginning of 1917, (now Sir) Eric Geddes was promoted to Inspector-General of Transportation and his position of Director-General of Military Railways was taken over by Sir Guy Granet. Like Geddes, Granet was a professional railway man. He had initially trained as a barrister, before moving to the Midland Railway and becoming its General Manager in 1906.

One of Granet's first actions was to present a proposal to the Army Council for the establishment of a train ferry service between England and France. This was not without opposition, the navy objected to anything maritime that was not under their control and the railways were concerned that British wagons would not be returned from France. The ferries would be vulnerable to attack and, as the shipyards were fully occupied replacing merchant ships sunk by German submarines, there were questions on how quickly the ferries could be built. The benefit of war is that decisions can be taken in weeks that would take years of wrangling in peacetime. On the 17th January 1917, an instruction was issued that three ferry steamers should be constructed, terminal ports be selected, and the necessary berths and other incidental facilities be provided with maximum despatch.

Sir Guy Granet, (1867-1943), succeeded Eric Geddes and pushed through the military train ferry project against resistance from the Admiralty. *(Library of Congress)*

The Army ferries

The train ferry designs developed by Sir W.G. Armstrong, Whitworth & Co. ten years earlier were dusted off and improved. A contract for two ferries was placed with Armstrong Whitworth in Newcastle. To

WORLD WAR 1

London

Richborough

Southampton

Calais

Dunkerque

BELGIUM

The Western Front 1917

Dieppe

Cherbourg

FRANCE

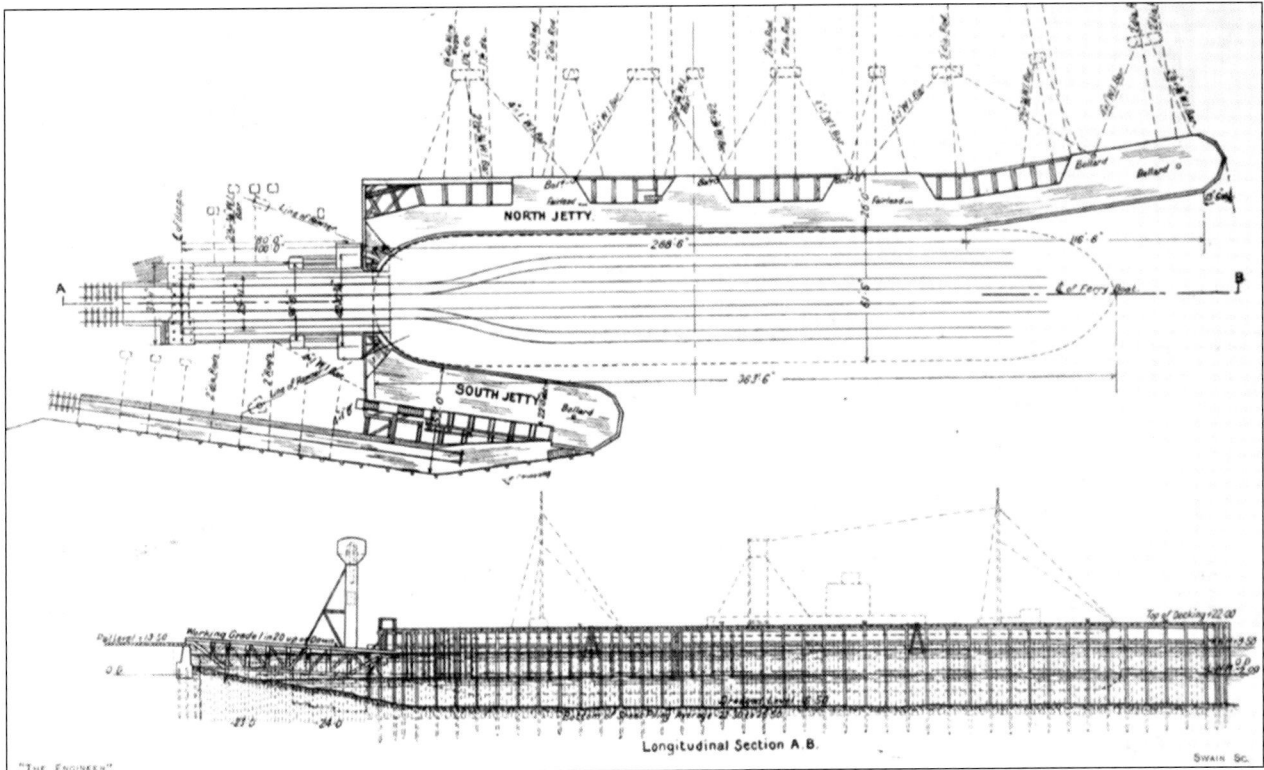

Plan of the ferry berth at Richborough. *(The Engineer)*

shorten the delivery time, the third ferry was ordered from the Fairfield Shipbuilding & Engineering Co. in Govan, near Glasgow.

The three ships, named *T.F.1, T.F.2* and *T.F.3*, were identical. A large open train deck with four lines of track, loading over the stern ramp. Two funnels, one either side, with the wheelhouse on a gantry. There was no accommodation for passengers and basic crew quarters were provided below the train deck, forward of the engine room. The ships' boilers were oil-fired in order to reduce the time needed for bunkering.

Length overall	363.5 feet	(110.8m)
Breadth extreme	61 feet	(18.6m)
Depth	17.25 feet	(5.3m)
Draught loaded		
(fwd/aft)	9/10 feet	(2.74/3.05m)
Gross tonnage	2,672	
Deadweight	1,250 tons	

Two sets of triple expansion steam engines driving two screws, service speed 12 knots.
1080 feet of track on deck, (329m) with capacity for 54 x 20' wagons.

Two ports were selected on the English side of the Channel. Richborough was an obvious choice as it was already under the control of the Inland Waterways & Docks Branch of the Royal Engineers and had extensive railway sidings. Several sites around the Solent were

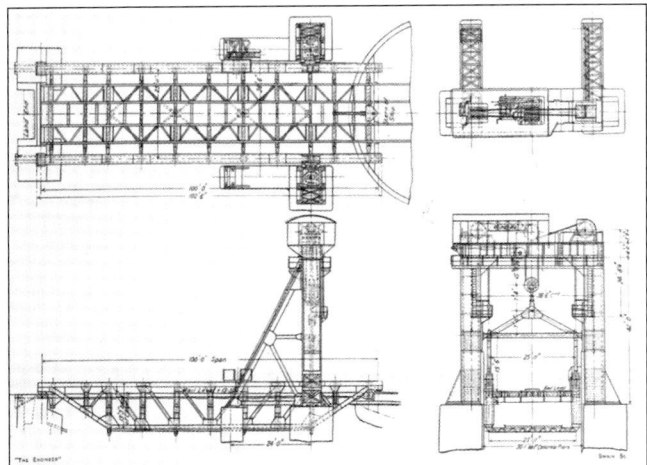

The heavy-duty gantry and linkspan bridge erected at the five Channel ports by the Royal Engineers. *(The Engineer)*

examined for the second port and Southampton was finally chosen. The selected site was immediately west of the Royal Pier as it was clear of the main shipping channel and required little dredging. A masonry pier was built for a new branch line to the dock and linkspan connecting to the London & South Western Railway at Southampton West station. A large area of the foreshore was reclaimed to provide a marshalling yard with space for 500 wagons.

On the French side, Dunkerque was chosen as the preferred port. Although it was 54 miles from Richborough, it could be entered at all states of the tide

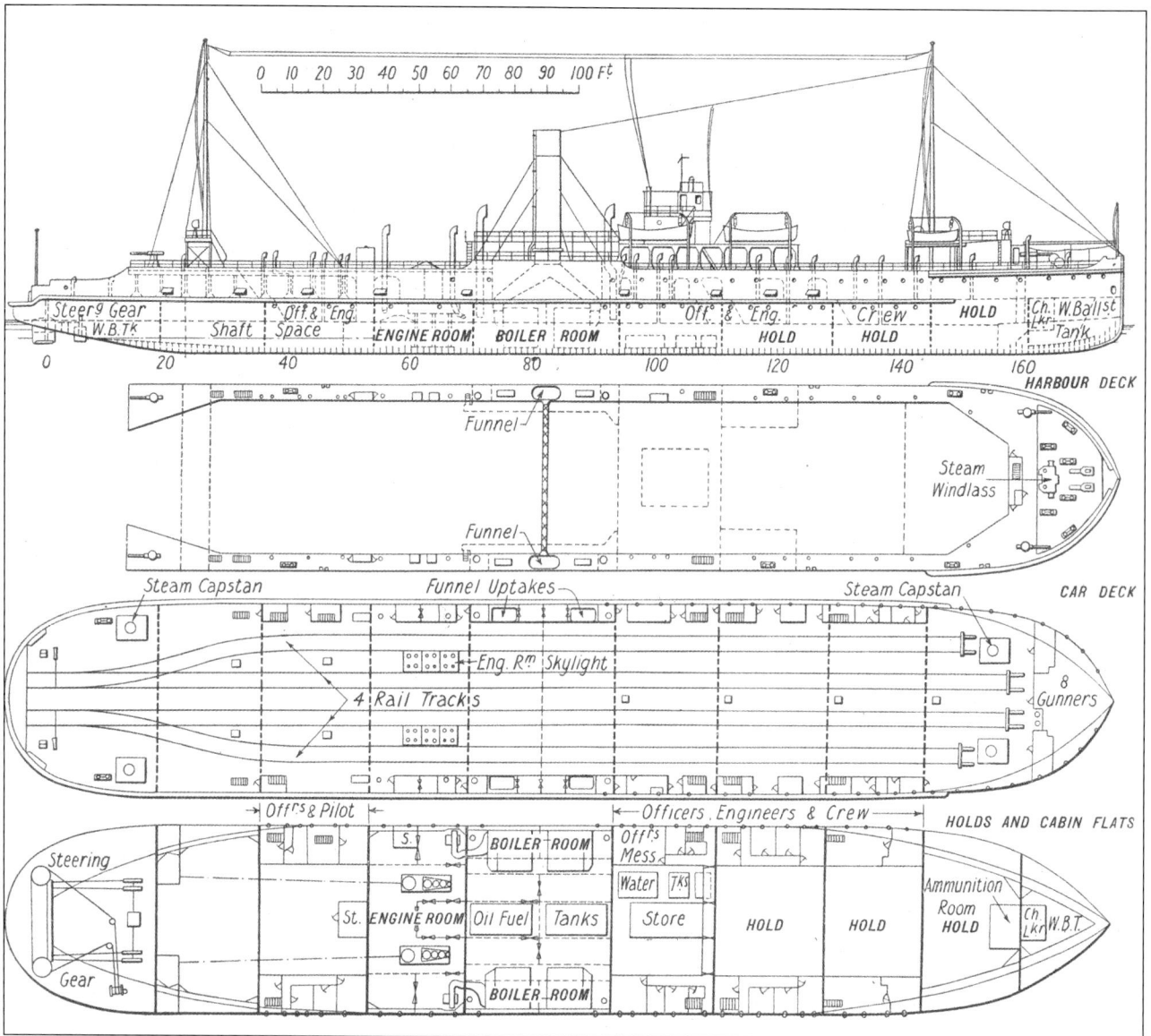

Elevation and plans of **T.F.1-3**. The train deck was enclosed in the original design, but they were built with an open deck to save material. (*Shipping Wonders of the World*)

and had space to build the necessary railway sidings. The risk was that Dunkerque was less than 20 miles from the front line and thus vulnerable to shelling. Calais was only 35 miles from Richborough but could only be accessed two hours either side of high tide and the port area was already congested with other traffic. Further west, the Royal Engineers looked at Cherbourg, Le Havre and Dieppe. Dieppe was chosen as the harbour was relatively less congested and it had the best railway connections. The terminal was located in the Arrière Port which was accessible for five or six hours around high tide. At other times the ferry had to wait in the outer port, but later dredging allowed the ferry to remain at the dock at any state of the tide. The distance from Southampton to Dieppe was 103 miles.

The ferry dock and transfer arrangements were designed by Armstrong Whitworth & Co. and were virtually identical at the five ports. The dock was formed by timber faced jetties, shaped as a semi-circle around the ship's stern. Trains were transferred over a hinged linkspan bridge suspended at the ship-end from a large steel gantry. The bridge had two lines of track and was built for a load of 2 tons per linear foot, sufficient for 30-ton wagons on both tracks or to transfer a locomotive or 12" artillery gun. The bridge was suspended on steel wire ropes over pulleys to counterweights in the gantry legs. It was raised or lowered, through a system of sheaves and pulleys, by an electrical winch, located in a machinery-house on the top of the gantry. The bridges were designed for a maximum gradient of ±5% over the tidal range, thus the length of the bridges varied between the ports: 80 feet (24m) at Dunkerque, 100 feet (30m) at Richborough and Calais and 120 feet (37m) at Southampton and Dieppe.

The bridge structure was designed to be flexible, allowing a twist of ±5° to allow for changes in the ship's heel during unloading. To connect the bridge to the ship, a slotted hole in a casting at the end of the bridge girders landed on a 7" diameter vertical steel locating pin on the stern of the ship. This allowed the bridge flaps to align the tracks on the bridge with those on the ship's deck. It also prevented the ship detaching from the bridge if its moorings failed. The gantry hoist was adjusted to ensure that the bridge put a load of around 10 tons on the ship's stern, to avoid any vertical movement in the connection.

The train ferries were completed in November 1917 and the service from Southampton to Dieppe started in December with *T.F.2*. The service from Richborough with *T.F.1* and *T.F.3* started in February 1918, although the linkspans were not fully operational until March. Even with that limitation, the ferries shipped 150 locomotives, 6,208 new war department wagons, 328 brake vans and four 14" rail-mounted guns in their first month.

From Birkenhead to the Channel, via Quebec

An additional ferry, the *Leonard*, soon renamed *T.F.4* was brought into service in the autumn of 1918. She had been built in 1914 by Cammell Laird in Birkenhead for the National Transcontinental Railway Co. of Canada. Its overall dimensions were similar to the other ferries, but there the similarity ended. The *Leonard* had a unique appearance with a huge steel gantry running the full length of the ship. The wheelhouse was perched on top of the forward end of the gantry and four tall thin funnels were arranged, two either side. She had been designed to carry passenger carriages and freight cars across the St. Lawrence river between Quebec and Levis, a distance of around 2½ miles, and her hull was strengthened for ice. As the docks on either side were at a fixed elevation, the ship compensated for variations in the river level by raising and lowering the entire train deck. This deck had three lines of track and sat within the gantry structure. It was raised and lowered by worm gears driven by a dedicated engine. This was described in 'Marine Engineering of Canada' in May 1914:

The engine is of the four cylinder high pressure type of massive design, driving through double helical spur wheels, a second motion shaft running athwart ship. At each end of this shaft, mitre wheels are arranged for driving the fore and aft line shafting arranged on both port and starboard sides of the vessel. At equal distances along the shafting, worm and wheel gearing is fitted for turning the lifting screws; the latter being driven through a loose forged steel sleeve and sliding key arrangement, fitted into the boss of the wheel. Heavy gunmetal nuts into which the screws work are fitted into the structure of the train deck, the load coming upon the screws being taken up by

The completed gantry and linkspan at Richborough in 1918. *(The Engineer)*

T.F.2 at the ferry dock in Dieppe's Arrière Port, this was well protected but not accessible at all states of tide. *(Photoship)*

special ball bearings supported by the upper structure of the vessel.

It must have been quite a task keeping the mechanism clean, greased and working smoothly. When the National Transcontinental Railway completed their Quebec Bridge in December 1917, the *Leonard* became redundant. She was bought by the British Government and renamed *T.F.4*. The three tracks on the elevating deck did not fit the existing docking arrangements, so *T.F.4* was used for a new service between Southampton and Cherbourg. She did not need linkspans and loaded directly from a new berth next to the Southampton jetty.

There was normally one round trip per day from Richborough and every second day from Southampton. The train ferries were frequently attacked by enemy aircraft while in Dunkerque and Calais and were fitted with four 12-pounder guns for protection. Eventually they stopped using Dunkerque due to constant enemy bombing.

The ferries were manned by 9 officers and 37

A train ferry returning to Richborough with an ambulance train. The decks were timbered between the rails, so that vehicles could also carried. *(National Railway Museum)*

seamen, including the gun crews, most were merchant seaman who had enlisted to the Inland Waterways & Docks Section of the Royal Engineers. A few crew members were retired Royal Navy personnel or were trained directly by the Royal Engineers. However, all the crew adopted army ranks and wore khaki uniforms.

The wagons for the train ferry were prepared on designated sidings, each with capacity for around 30 wagons, allowing the wagons to be moved quickly. The average time taken to unload and load a ferry at the terminal was 21 minutes. Once onboard, each wagon was secured by four chain slings, connecting each corner to a ring bolt on the deck. The wagons were then jacked-up at each corner, taking sufficient load off the suspension springs to avoid any movement at sea. This operation took a squad of 50 men around half an hour to complete and was often carried-out while the ferry manoeuvred out of the dock, with the men being put ashore by tug.

By the end of 1918, the ferries had transported 7,142 rail wagons with 261,000 tons of freight, plus 164 locomotives and other rolling stock for the military railways in France. They also transported 734 tanks and large numbers motor lorries and other vehicles. Just as importantly, the ferries carried ambulance trains back from France, providing the most comfortable route home for injured men.

Train ferry with dazzle painting to reduce the risk of U-boat attack in the Channel. *(Author's collection)*

After the armistice

After hostilities ended, the ferries operated largely without incident. On 1st February 1919, the American transport ship *USS Narragansett* went aground in a snowstorm, near Bembridge on the Isle of Wight. She was returning from Le Havre to Southampton with 2,500 troops onboard. *T.F.2* was among the vessels mobilised to help and managed to get alongside in very bad weather, rescuing the majority of the men onboard.

Army control of the ferry service ended on the 1st March 1919. The Southampton operation was shut down and the Richborough port and ferries were transferred to civilian control, managed by the South-Eastern & Chatham Railway Company. The ships and their crews became part of the merchant service. However, the work to demobilise the army and return personnel and equipment from France lasted well into the following year. In response to a question in Parliament in

After her return from Quebec, the *T.F.4* was used between Southampton and Cherbourg, where her elevating deck could transfer rail wagons to the dockside without a linkspan. *(Railway Wonders of the World)*

The *Leonard*, later *T.F.4,* on builder's trials from Cammell Laird in Birkenhead in 1914. *(The Engineer)*

December 1919, Sir Winston Churchill stated that 11,667 railway wagons had been returned to Britain since the Armistice with a further 22,900 wagons still to be shipped back from France. At that time around 600 wagons were being returned each week.

The *T.F.4* was sold to the Anglo-Saxon Petroleum Company, part of Shell Tankers, and had a remarkable transformation into an oil tanker. Renamed *Limax* she operated for a further decade until scrapped in Osaka in

Underneath the Train Ferry – Sketch by war artist Muirhead Bone of *T.F.3* under construction at Fairfields in Govan on the Clyde. *(Scottish Maritime Museum)*

1931.

The service from Richborough to Calais with *T.F.1, T.F.2* and *T.F.3* carried on through 1920, though after that it is unclear how regular the sailings were. The railways endeavoured to start new services. On the 11th October 1921, *T.F.2* carried temperature-controlled wagons bringing 300 tons of fresh fruit from Avignon in the South of France to London's Covent Garden fruit market. However, building a fleet of special wagons required significant investment which was not forthcoming.

Through 1922 the ferries appear largely to have been laid-up, either in Richborough or at Immingham on the Humber estuary. There were a few ad-hoc charters, transporting newly-built coaches from Immingham to Calais and moving vehicles across the Irish Sea. However, keeping Richborough operational required frequent dredging and the company which owned the port went into receivership in August. After this it was seldom used.

A plan for the Irish Sea

The success of the Channel ferries led to various schemes to re-use them after the war, one was the Irish Packing Company. This was set up in 1919 with a plan to build meat-packing plants in Dublin and Waterford and export Irish meat to Britain in chilled or refrigerated rail wagons. One of the strange quirks of railway history is that while British standard-gauge is used throughout Europe, North America and China, trains in Ireland run on a 5' 3" gauge. It has never been practical to transfer rail wagons between Britain and Ireland. Presumably, the Irish Packing Company's plan included building standard gauge lines from their plants to Dublin and Waterford harbours.

The company was reported to have started negotiations with the War Department to buy the three ferries and raised capital to build port facilities. The

Dublin Port & Harbour Board had identified a site for a ferry terminal at the Alexandra Basin and a corresponding terminal was planned for Fleetwood in agreement with the Lancashire & Yorkshire Railway Company. A second route was planned from Waterford, on the south-east corner of Ireland, with a service to South Wales and Southampton. The plan was not carried through, possibly the uncertainty of the ongoing struggle for Irish Independence may have made it hard to attract investment.

Ironically, *T.F.2* was chartered by the British Army in March 1922 to ship their motor vehicles from Cork and Dublin back to Liverpool, following the establishment of the Irish Free State.

Great Eastern Train Ferries

Great Eastern Train Ferries Ltd.	**1924–1932**
London & North Eastern Railway	**1932–1939**
Harwich – Zeebrugge	1924–1939
Harwich – Calais	1931–1936

The ferries did not have too long to wait. The Great Eastern Railway had failed to establish a freight line to the Continent in 1922. However, the following year an arrangement was made with the Belgian Government that led to two companies being established. Great Eastern Train Ferries Ltd. would own and operate the ferries and La Société Belgo-Anglaise des Ferry Boats S.A., a subsidiary of the Belgian state railway, would provide the rolling stock much of which had been bought from the British Army.

Great Eastern Train Ferries purchased the three ships and the linkspans at Richborough and Southampton from the British Government. The ferries, *T.F.1, T.F.2* and *T.F.3,* were renamed *Train Ferry No.1, No.2* and *No.3*. The linkspan and gantry at Southampton were dismantled and shipped by barge to Harwich, where a

A colourised picture of Prince George, in his borrowed uniform coat, inaugurating the Harwich ferry service in April 1924.

One of the train ferries at Zeebrugge, flying the Great Eastern Train Ferries' house flag. The ships never carried passengers, so the coaches may be new rolling stock being exported. (Author's collection)

new port area with sidings was built between Harwich Town station and Trinity Pier. The linkspan weighed around 250 tons, the gantry and counterweights around 130 tons, and they were secured on to two barges strapped together. Just six miles from Harwich, part of the load broke loose in heavy weather and the barges sank in shallow water. The linkspan was salvaged, but the gantry and barges were eventually blown-up to

One of the Great Eastern train ferries arriving at Harwich in 1920s. (Author's collection)

remove them as a hazard to shipping. A replacement gantry was built using many parts from the redundant gantry at Richborough. The gantry and linkspan from Dunkerque were erected at Zeebrugge. This linkspan was much shorter, because at Zeebrugge, as at Dunkerque, the dock was entered through a sea-lock which protected it from the tidal range.

On the 24th April 1924 the train ferry service was inaugurated and despite being a humble goods ferry service it was seen as an important event. Prince George arrived at Harwich by special train to be met by an honour guard of Boy Scouts and Girl Guides and the local Silver Band. The ferry terminal was dressed in what was described as 'a liberal display of bunting'. There was a bit of a hiatus when it was realised that the Prince, or at least his valet, had forgotten to bring the coat of his naval uniform. The band played through their repertoire while there was a mad dash to borrow a uniform coat from a local naval base. After an hour, a breathless young officer arrived with a replacement. There were suitable speeches from the LNER Directors and the Belgian Ambassador, followed by a tour around Train Ferry No.2. The party then boarded the paddle steamer Norfolk and headed for a good lunch at the Felix Hotel. The following day there was a similar ceremony at Zeebrugge with Prince Léopold and the Belgian Minister of Railways in attendance.

Cover of a sales booklet issued by the Great Eastern Train Ferry Co., in the 1920s. Illustration by the well-known marine artist, Frank Mason, (1875-1965). *(Author's collection)*

Belgian poster for 'les Ferry-Boats' guided by Mercury the god of commerce.*(Author's collection)*

One of the train ferries at sea. Note the 'crow's nest' on the forward mast, probably used to spot mines during wartime crossings. *(Author's collection)*

Unloading at Harwich in the inter-war years. *(Author's collection)*

Train Ferry No.3 started the following day and *Train Ferry No.1* arrived in July. Initially, there was one sailing a day in each direction, six days a week, with the third ferry moored at Harwich as reserve. Over the winter of 1924-25, the ferries were converted from oil-firing to coal. This seems unusual, but the company reported that the conversion reduced each ferry's fuel bill from £32,000 to £18,000 per annum. The ferries carried 4,539 wagons in their first year, rising to 19,670 wagons with 158,000 tons of cargo in 1927. The service attracted high-value, fragile and perishable goods as it avoided transhipment and the risk of damage or theft. Exports from the UK were large items of machinery and also vehicles, which could use the wooden decking between the rails. Around 80% of the cargo was from the Continent to the UK, much of it time-dependent goods, such as fruit and vegetables. By 1935, the Italian Railways had a fleet of 600 ventilated vans and 700 refrigerated wagons taking fruit directly from Sicily to London in 5-6 days, including their two ferry crossings. There were also more exotic cargoes, such as 1500 geese from Poland to a farm in Norfolk and special wagons taking four elephants to a circus in Slough.

In the recession of the late 1920s, the ferries struggled to break even and a new service providing three sailings a week between Harwich and Calais was started in November 1931 in an attempt to increase traffic. Despite this, Great Eastern Train Ferries Ltd. went into liquidation the following year and the operation was taken over directly by LNER. The service to Calais stopped in October 1936, when Southern Railways started their service from Dover, but in September 1939 all sailings came to an end with the outbreak of the Second World War.

Between the wars

Southern Railway and ALA
Dover – Dunkerque   1936-1939

Britain's railways were amalgamated into four large companies in 1923, the LNER, LMS, Southern and Great Western Railways. The Southern Railway had always resisted ferry schemes and supported plans for a Channel Tunnel, which were revived during the 1920s. The proposal finally came before Parliament in 1930 and though the vote was close, as before the opponents of the tunnel won the day, by 179 to 172 votes, based on concerns over the project cost and the military risk.

In 1927, the LMS and the French shipping company S.A. de Gérance et d'Aremement, (SAGA), created a joint venture, the Angleterre-Lorraine-Alsace Société Anonyme de Navigation, (ALA). This operated a passenger ferry service from Tilbury, east of London, to Dunkerque using four steamers transferred from LMS Irish Sea services. With the failure of the Channel Tunnel project, they announced their intention of starting a train ferry service between the two ports.

With no tunnel and the prospect of their rivals dominating the channel ferry trade, the Southern Railway and their French partners C.F. du Nord developed their own plan for a train ferry service. The Southern Railway bought the LMS holding in ALA in 1932 and moved their Dunkerque service from Tilbury to Folkestone. While the LNER and LMS had been focused purely on goods traffic, the Southern Railway also saw the opportunity to provide through passenger services from London to Paris. The Flèche d'Or, or Golden Arrow, service had started in 1926 providing a 1st class pullman service between London and Paris. While passengers still had to change from train to ship at Dover, and the reverse at Calais, they could check-in their baggage at Victoria Station and collect it at the Gare du Nord. Train ferries would allow a nightly sleeper service and carry goods wagons during the day. Initially, the plan was to run the ferries between Dover and Boulogne, but the French terminal was moved to Dunkerque, where the harbour was protected from the tide by locks and thus wagons could be loaded over a relatively simple

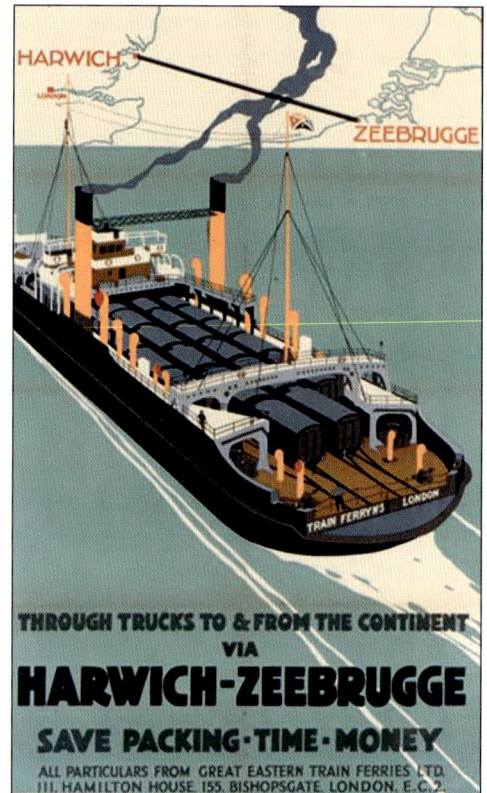

Great Eastern Train Ferry Co. poster showing *Train Ferry No.3*. (Author's collection)

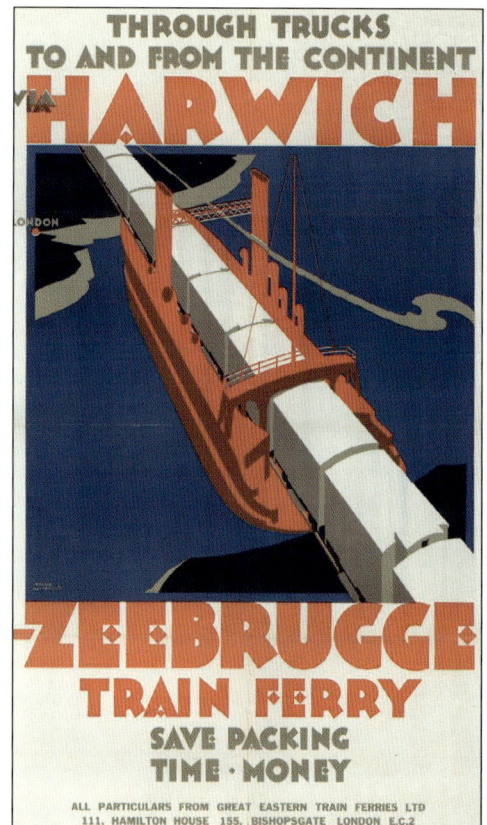

Great Eastern Train Ferry Co. poster by Frank Newbould (Author's collection)

4. Mai 1919.

27e Numéro spécial : 2 fr.

LA
SCIENCE
ET LA VIE

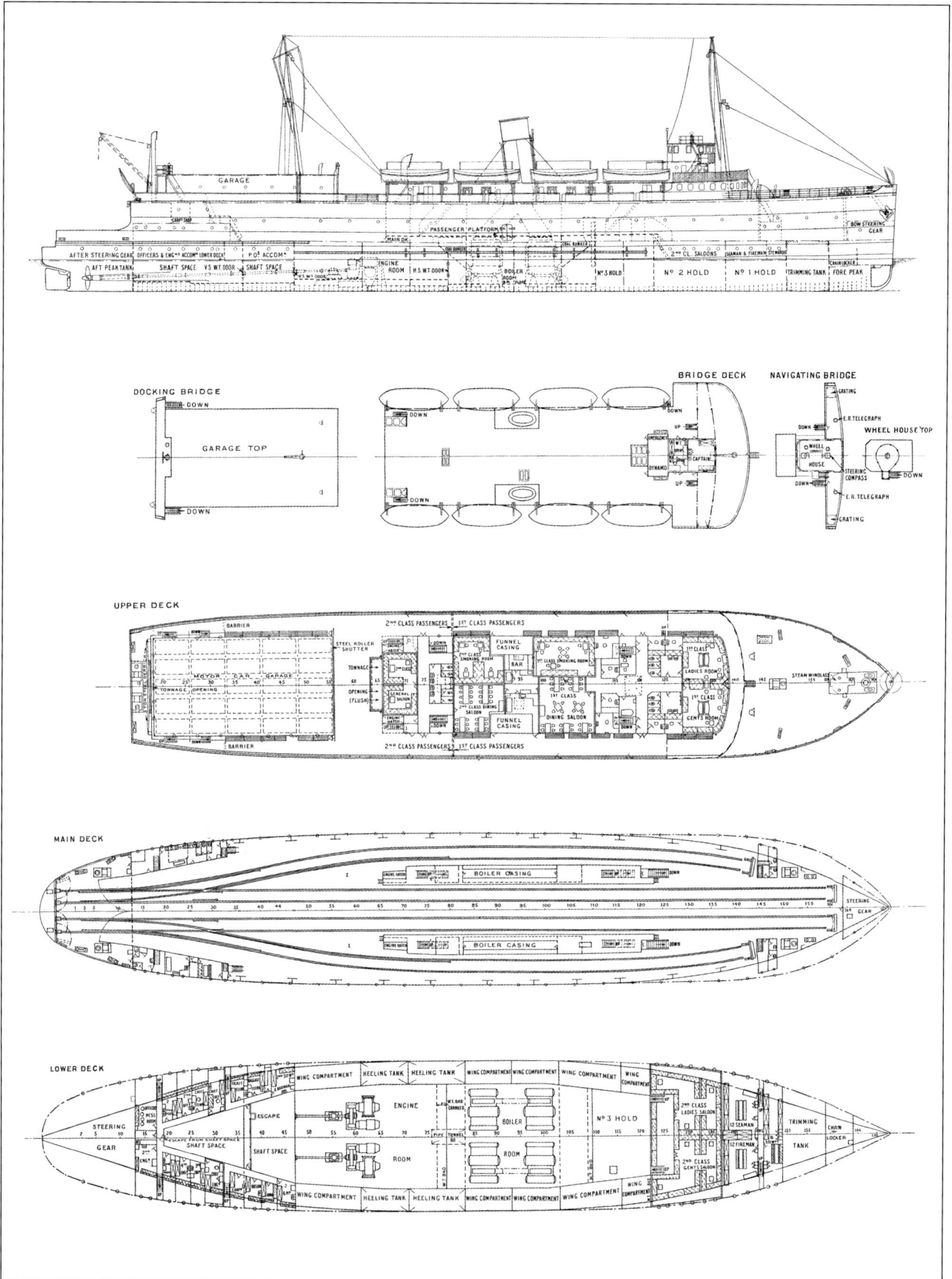

Elevation and plans of the three cross-Channel train ferries delivered by Swan Hunter & Wigham Richardson of Newcastle to the Southern Railway in 1934. *(Institution of Naval Architects)*

SECTION THROUGH BOILER-ROOM LOOKING FORWARD.

LONGITUDINAL SECTION THROUGH BOILER AND MECHANICAL STOKER.

The three Southern Railway ferries were the last large ferries in Europe built with steam propulsion. The section shows the coal-fired boilers which supplied steam turbines. *(Institution of Naval Architects)*

linkspan. Dover did not have this advantage and there was not the space to build a long sloping linkspan to cope with the 7m tidal range. The previous Dover ferry scheme in 1905 had proposed a large hydraulic elevating platform that would move the train to the elevation of the ferry. However, this was a complicated mechanism and there was also the problem that Dover harbour was vulnerable to rough seas in certain weather directions.

The train ferry dock

The chosen design was to build an enclosed dock. The ferry could enter at any state of tide and once the dock gate was closed, the water was pumped in or out to bring the ferry to the level of the short linkspan. The dock was a 141m long and 24.5m wide, which gave a gap of around 3m either side of the ferry and a metre of water below the keel at low tide. Each of the three pumps could move over 200m3/min so that at an extreme low tide it would take 30 minutes to lift the ferry 5.6 metres to the linkspan elevation. Construction started in 1933 and the plan was to sheet pile the dock sides, fit a temporary caisson over the dock end, then pump it dry to dig out the chalk floor and pour the concrete sides and base. The first part of the construction went to plan, the sheet piling and caisson were in place, but it proved impossible to pump the dock dry. Once the water level inside the dock was below the level in the surrounding harbour, the pressure forced water through fissures in the chalk floor. Solutions such as spreading clay on the surrounding seabed to block

Testing of the new Dover train ferry dock in September 1936, with coal wagons being loaded on to the *Hampton Ferry*. The new passenger terminal is still under construction at the left of the picture. *(Illustrated London News)*

fissures were tried, but to no avail. The more they pumped, the faster the water came in. The only way to continue was to work underwater. A dredger was floated into the dock to excavate the chalk floor, though it was designed for mud rather than hard chalk and made slow progress. Eventually the 1.5m thick concrete base was poured underwater, controlled by divers. The dock gate was sunk into place, it was hinged at the base and flooded to lie flat on the harbour bottom to allow the ferry to enter or leave the dock. Next to the dock, there was a Customs and Booking Hall, a Pump House and a ramp for cars to access the ferries' upper garage

77

Aerial view of the *Hampton Ferry* in the Dover train ferry dock, with export cars parked on the quayside awaiting loading. The dock was 141m long and 24.5m wide, which gave around 3m clearance either side of the ferry. *(FotoFlite)*

Wagons-Lits sleeping cars secured on the train deck. The four corners of each car have been jacked-up to prevent movement on the springs and the cars secured by chains to pad-eyes on the deck. The white frame between the tracks on the left is a gulley drain to catch waste from the sleeping cars wash-rooms. *(Author's collection)*

1930s poster for the 'Night Ferry' sleeper cars between London and Paris.

Sheperton Ferry leaving Dover's Eastern Dock. *(FotoFlite)*

deck. The dock project inevitably took longer than originally planned and it was summer 1936 before the dock was ready for use.

The three ferries were built by Swan Hunter & Wigham Richardson in Newcastle. The *Twickenham Ferry* and *Hampton Ferry* were delivered in 1934 and the *Shepperton Ferry* early the following year. However, they were initially laid-up at Southampton for over a year awaiting completion of the Dover dock. To reflect the Anglo-French ownership of the service, the *Twickenham Ferry* was changed to the French flag in September 1936. The three sisters were similar in size to the old Harwich ferries, the main difference was that the train deck was largely enclosed to support an upper deck of passenger accommodation. They were designed to carry twelve sleeping cars or 40 goods wagons and loaded over the stern to four tracks on the main deck. There were narrow platforms which allowed passengers to leave the sleeping cars and go up to the public rooms on the upper decks. The ferries could carry up to 500 passengers and had an upper deck garage for 25 cars, the first drive-on, drive-off service across the Channel. At a time when ferries in most other parts of Europe were diesel, they were powered by two sets of Parsons high- and low-pressure steam turbines, geared to twin screws. The boilers were coal-fired with automatic stokers as local coal was much cheaper than oil. The bunkers were filled by running the coal wagons on to the deck and dropping coal directly to the bunkers below.

The 'Night Ferry'

The *Hampton Ferry* made the first crossing from the Dover train ferry dock on the 3rd October 1936 and ten days later the first 'Night Ferry' sleeper train ran from Paris to London with twelve blue and gold sleeper cars provided by the Compagnie Internationale des Wagons-Lits, (CIWL). From the 15th October, the service operated in both directions every night. Trains left Victoria Station at 10pm each evening, arriving at the Gare du Nord before 9am the following morning. Each car had its own conductor who would supply drinks and refreshments at the touch of a bell and breakfast could be taken in a dining car. A 1st class single ticket on the 'Night Ferry' cost £4 19s 6d and very quickly became the fashionable way to cross the Channel. Between October 1936 and the following August, 33,000 sleeping car passengers were carried plus 30,000 seat passengers.

With the new train ferries in service, LNER stopped their service from Harwich to Calais. However, the new service had less than three years to become established. The last sleeper trains left on the 3rd September 1939, the day Britain and France declared war on Germany following the invasion of Poland.

The Second World War

The train ferries were all soon engaged in the war. *Train Ferry No.1, No.2* and *No.3* had wooden decking fitted between their rail tracks to transport vehicles to France for the British Expeditionary Force, (BEF). The two British flag channel ferries, *Hampton Ferry* and *Shepperton Ferry*, were almost immediately requisitioned by the Admiralty as minelayers, renamed *HMS Hampton* and *HMS Shepperton*, under Naval command. In 1940 they were returned to the merchant service and used to supply the BEF in France until the evacuation from Dunkerque in the first week of June.

The following week, the British Army's 51st Highland Division were pushed westwards along the French coast and encircled at Saint-Valery-en-Caux, near Dieppe. The three Harwich train ferries were ordered to assist with their evacuation but due to the weather and the speed of the German advance this never happened. *Train Ferry No.2* was held up by bunkering delays and arrived on the 13th June, having missed the signals to return to England and unaware that the Germans had taken the town. She was hit by artillery shells from the shore. Damaged and on fire, the crew tried to beach her, but she sank with the loss of 14 of her 34 crew.

The French-flag *Twickenham Ferry* escaped to England and was almost immediately sent to Brest on the French Atlantic coast, where she evacuated soldiers of the French Foreign Legion under fire. At the same time, *Shepperton Ferry, Train Ferry No.1* and *No.3* were in action evacuating civilians from the Channel Islands. On their return to the UK in September 1941, *Train Ferry No.1* and *No.3* were taken over by the Royal Navy and renamed *HMS Iris* and *HMS Daffodil*. The following year the two ships were converted to landing craft carriers, with a rail system fitted to the train deck which could launch up to fourteen landing craft over a stern chute. The two ships were also reconverted to oil-firing and their two funnels replaced by a single central funnel. In 1942, *HMS Iris* was renamed *HMS Princess Iris* and the two ships spent most of their time ferrying landing craft around the Channel ports.

The **Hampton Ferry** carried locomotives and rolling stock to France in 1944-45. The huge gantry crane on the stern was built by Cowans, Sheldon & Co. in Carlisle and could lift an 84-ton locomotive onto the quayside. *(Roy Thornton)*

The three Dover sisterships were transferred to the Ministry of War Transport in 1940 and spend the next four years ferrying road vehicles between Stranraer and Larne, supplying the military in Northern Ireland and bringing Irish farm produce to Britain.

D-Day and the French railways

In 1944, preparations started for the invasion of France. Early in the planning, the Allies agreed on the importance of getting the French Railways operational soon after the invasion to supply their armies as they advanced across France. Their assumption was that most French locomotives and rolling stock would be destroyed by the retreating Germans, so a large amount of railway equipment would need to be shipped from England as soon as the Channel ports were secure. In preparation for D-Day, the *Hampton, Shepperton* and *Twickenham* were converted back to train ferries and a huge gantry weighing 258 tons was fitted to their sterns, designed for landing 84-ton locomotives at harbours without a linkspan.

The first port to be captured by the allies was Cherbourg on the 26th June 1944, three weeks after D-Day. The docks had been destroyed by the retreating Germans and blocked by sunken ships, but within a few days a quayside was cleared, and *Twickenham Ferry* was the first ferry to enter the port, carrying four locomotives and a hospital train. Within a week, 48 diesel and steam locomotives and 184 wagons were delivered to get the French railways restarted. On her third trip, she landed a full ambulance train of fourteen coaches and four wagons.

The two remaining Harwich ferries, *HMS Princess Iris*

and *HMS Daffodil*, were converted back to train ferries in September 1944 and fitted with a stern gantry and ramp for handling locomotives and rolling stock. On her way back to Southampton, *HMS Daffodil* struck a mine after leaving Dieppe on the evening of the 17th March 1945 and sank the following morning with the loss of 33 lives.

US Navy LSTs

The US military first landed rolling stock in Cherbourg late in July 1944, using cranes and a lightering barge, but in the preparations for D-Day they had also converted a few LSTs (Landing Ship Tank) to carry rail wagons across the Channel. The LSTs were jokingly referred to by their crews as Large Slow Targets. They had three rail tracks welded to their deck and a switching rail at the bow. With limited space in Cherbourg harbour, the US Army laid tracks to the shore at Terre-Plein des Mielles, a flat open area to the north-east of the docks. There the LSTs were beached

Top left: Unloading a rail wagon from the *Twickenham Ferry* on to the quayside at Cherbourg on the 28th July 1944. *(Photos Normandie)*

Middle left: Unloading a British Army box car from the *Twickenham Ferry* on to the quayside at Cherbourg on the 28th July 1944. The censor has scribbled over the naval ships in the background. *(Photos Normandie)*

Left: Unloading a US Army Transportation Corps shunter from the *Twickenham Ferry* on to the quayside at Cherbourg on the 28th July 1944. As it weighs less than 40 tons it can be lifted on a single block. *(Photos Normandie)*

Above: The landing craft carrier HMS *Princess Iris*, formerly *Train Ferry No.1*, carrying out trials to launch landing craft over her stern chute in the Firth of Clyde. *(Imperial War Museum)*

and wagons were unloaded across a temporary bridge that sat in the shallow water and was manually connected to the bow of the LST by a squad of around thirty men. The first trials were carried-out by *LST 21* on the 31st July 1944 and the US Corps of Engineers soon had four ferry bridges in operation. There are pictures of *LST 7, LST 21, LST 392* and *LST 393* discharging wagons, though it is likely that others were also used.

The train ferries and LSTs took around 2,000 locomotives and thousands of pieces of rolling stock to France in the year following D-Day. These were also routed through Calais after it was liberated in October. One of the LSTs used on the service, LST 393, has survived and is preserved as a museum ship in Muskegon on Lake Michigan.

Top left: The HMS *Daffodil*, formerly *Train Ferry No.3*, unloading a locomotive in Dieppe, using the long ramp supported by the aft gantries. She struck a mine on her way back to Southampton on the 17th March 1945 and sank with the loss of 33 lives.

Top right: The HMS *Princess Iris*, formerly *Train Ferry No.1*, was modified in 1944 to carry rolling stock to France. The gantry structures at the stern supported a long ramp for landing locomotives and rail wagons on the quayside. *(Photos Normandie)*

Above: The US Army first landed rolling stock at Cherbourg on the 26th July 1944, these were craned off the USS *Lakehurst* to a lightering barge and towed into the port. *(Photos Normandie)*

Left middle: The US Army built tracks to the water's edge at Terre-Plein des Mielles to land rolling stock from LSTs. The town of Cherbourg in the background. *(Photos Normandie)*

Left: Unloading US Army wagons from *LST 21* at Terre-Plein des Mielles, near Cherbourg on the 31st July 1944. *(Photos Normandie)*

British Rail from Harwich

London & North Eastern Railway	**1946-1947**
British Railways/ Sealink UK Ltd.	**1948-1982**
Harwich – Zeebrugge	1946-1987
Harwich – Dunkerque	1967-1982

Of the three pre-war ferries, only *HMS Princess Iris*, the former *Train Ferry No.1*, survived the war. The LNER bought her back from the Admiralty and had her refitted on the Clyde, arriving back in Harwich in July 1946 renamed *Essex Ferry*. The service to Zeebrugge was restarted, though with only one ship, there were only three return sailings per week.

A new ship had been ordered at the end of the war and the *Suffolk Ferry* was delivered in 1947 from John Brown & Co. in Clydebank. She was the first motor ferry on cross-Channel service, powered by two Sulzer diesels with a service speed of 14 knots. She was also longer than the previous ships, able to carry 35 wagons on four tracks. Like the Southern Railway sisters, her train deck was largely enclosed, though open at the stern, and she had accommodation for 12 passengers. Her main problem on delivery was poor manoeuvrability, having twin screws but inexplicably only one central rudder. She was returned to Clydebank and had twin rudders fitted at the shipyard's expense. With the *Suffolk Ferry*, LNER was able to restart a daily service to Zeebrugge,

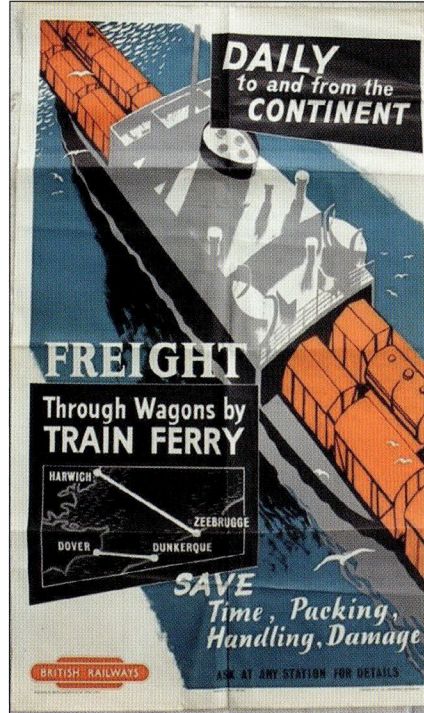

British Railways' poster from 1959 for the Harwich to Zeebrugge and Dover to Dunkerque train ferries.

An aerial view of the *Suffolk Ferry* at the Harwich train ferry berth in 1952. The linkspan was originally used in Southampton during the First World War. The pier next to the train ferry berth is used by Trinity House. *(Historic England)*

The train deck of the **Essex Ferry**, built by John Brown & Co. in Clydebank in 1957. The rails are set into the deck plating to allow road vehicles to be carried. *(Ferry Publications Library)*

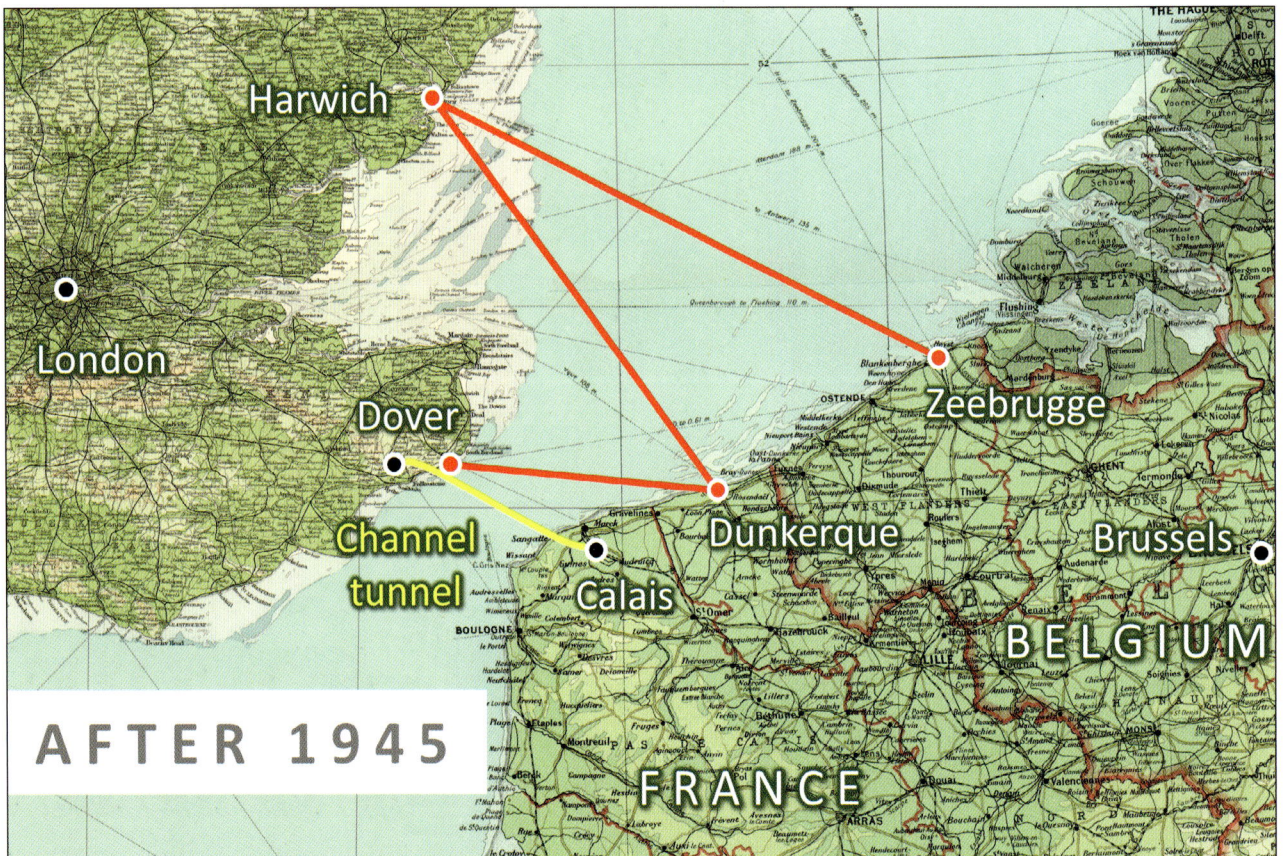

Harwich

London

Dover

Channel tunnel

Calais

Zeebrugge

Dunkerque

Brussels

BELGIUM

FRANCE

AFTER 1945

Harwich – Zeebrugge ferries

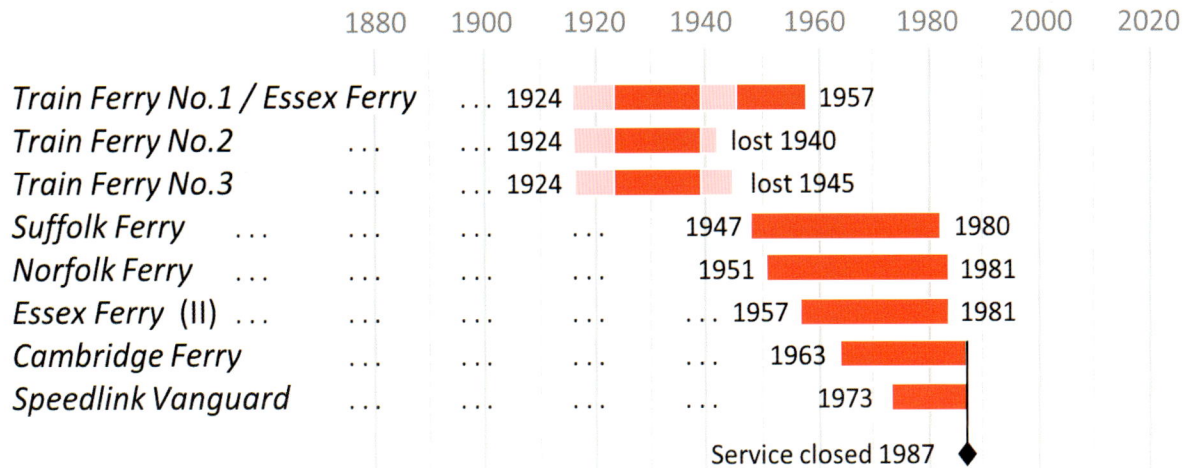

	1880	1900	1920	1940	1960	1980	2000	2020
Train Ferry No.1 / Essex Ferry	...	1924			1957			
Train Ferry No.2	...	... 1924		lost 1940				
Train Ferry No.3	...	... 1924		lost 1945				
Suffolk Ferry ...	...	...	...	1947		1980		
Norfolk Ferry ...	...	...	...	1951		1981		
Essex Ferry (II) ...	...	...	...	... 1957		1981		
Cambridge Ferry ...	...	...	...	1963				
Speedlink Vanguard ...	...	...	...	1973				

Service closed 1987 ◆

The *Cambridge Ferry* was the last of the traditional Harwich train ferries, delivered in 1963 with British Rail's black hull and buff funnel. She was built by Hawthorn Leslie and was the first post-war ferry to be built on the Tyne. *(Max Wilkinson)*

however she was their last ship as a few months after her delivery, the old railway companies were amalgamated into British Railways. A second ship, the *Norfolk Ferry*, was delivered by John Brown & Co. in 1951. She was a close sistership of the *Suffolk Ferry*, although two metres shorter. More interestingly as a sign of times, her hull plating was welded, though the welded shell plates were still riveted to the frames.

Europe's railways recovered through the 1950s and old routes, such as the ventilated fruit vans from Italy, were revived. Soon there was too much traffic for a single daily sailing, but the 2½ to 3 hours required to go in and out through the Visart locks at Zeebrugge made it impossible for the ferries to complete a daily round trip. A new terminal was built in Zeebrugge's outer harbour in 1953 with a 49m linkspan to cope with the tidal range. Avoiding the locks allowed the ferries to make two sailings per day. The old *Essex Ferry* was kept as reserve though she was too slow to deputise for the newer ships and was replaced in 1957 by a third diesel ferry. The *Essex Ferry* (II) was delivered by John Brown & Co. in 1957, as a sistership to the *Norfolk Ferry*. One innovation on the *Essex Ferry* (II), was a series of gantry cranes that allow railway containers to be handled on the train deck. With the new ferry in place, the old *Essex Ferry*, ex- *Train Ferry No.1.*, ex- *T.F.1*, was scrapped after forty years' service.

A fourth ship, the *Cambridge Ferry*, was built by Hawthorn Leslie Ltd. on the Tyne in 1963. In dimensions and layout, she was very similar to her older sisters, but she was a much more modern ship. She had a raked funnel, similar to other BR ships of the time, and was unusual in having both masts forward of the funnel. She

The Brush type 2 diesel locomotive 31 225 unloading wagons from the *Cambridge Ferry* at Harwich. *(Mickoo737)*

The **Norfolk Ferry** was the second post-war ferry from John Brown & Co. in Clydebank in 1951. Seen here after 1966 with her hull painted British Rail blue and a red funnel with the familiar double arrows. *(FotoFlite)*

The **Cambridge Ferry** looking a bit unkempt. Her upper deck was extended aft in 1977 to carry an additional 25 trade cars. *(FotoFlite)*

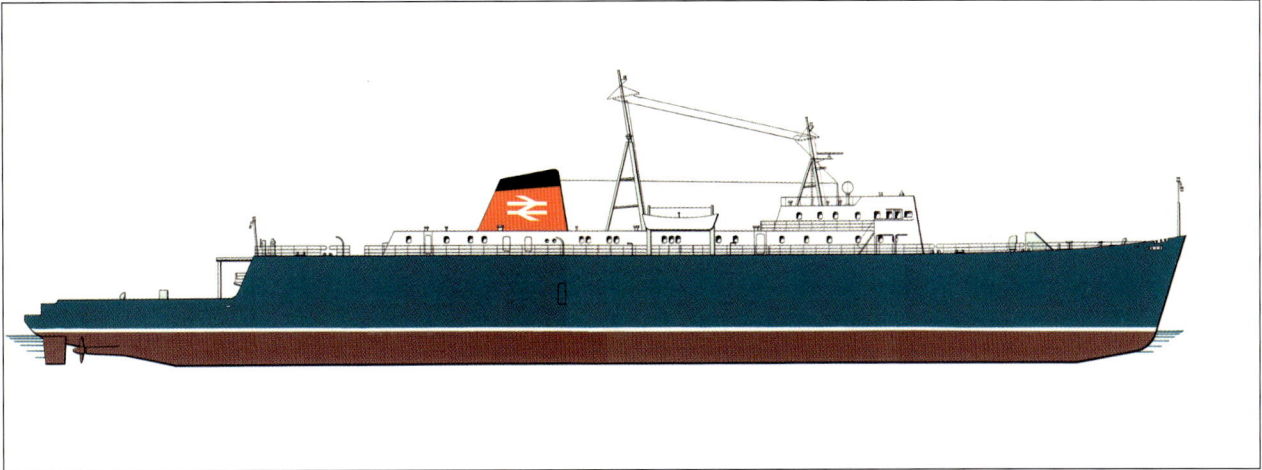

A page from British Rail's Corporate Identity Manual issued in 1966. This defined the corporate style for trains, signage, uniforms etc., as well as the paint scheme for the ferry fleet. The larger passenger ferries also had 'Sealink' painted on their sides. *(Author's collection)*

had two Mirrlees 4-stroke diesels and was the first British railway ferry to have controllable pitch propellers and bridge control. She was also fitted with flume stabilising tanks, though it was reported that these were not always correctly adjusted to her loading condition so she had a strange roll motion. Like her sisters, she had accommodation for twelve passengers though the polished wood panelling of the older ships was replaced by 1960s blue-grey Formica. The four tracks were recessed into the train deck to allow trucks or trailers to be carried. She also had a gantry crane system for handling railway containers, though this was removed after a few years as it did not have the headroom to handle the taller ISO standard containers which were becoming more common. Her arrival allowed up to three sailings a day when traffic required.

In 1966 the four ships were repainted in British Rail's new colours. The black hulls and buff funnels were replaced with BR's new blue hull and red funnel with the double-arrow logo. The following year the *Essex Ferry* and *Norfolk Ferry* were modified so that they could dock at the Dunkerque linkspan. Their stern shape was narrowed and a second locating pin was added and they started 2-3 sailings per week from Harwich to Dunkerque. During the 1970s the ferries carried a wide variety of privately-owned specialised wagons, such as gas tanks and bulk hopper wagons. In 1971, the ferries carried 36,387 wagons to Zeebrugge, 8,873 to Dunkerque and over 26,000 export cars. As the export car trade became more important, the upper deck of the *Cambridge Ferry* was extended aft to carry an additional 25 cars in 1977.

Sealink and *Speedlink Vanguard*

In 1979, British Rail's shipping services were separated into a subsidiary company, Sealink UK Ltd., which brought the loss-making train ferry service into focus. A plan was developed to replace the four small

The *Speedlink Vanguard* was chartered from Stena AB and converted to a train ferry in 1981. She carried rail wagons on both the main and upper decks, following new ferry designs introduced to the Baltic and Black Sea in the 1970s. *(Tony Garner)*

The *Speedlink Vanguard* unloading at Zeebrugge in 1983, in the last few years of the Harwich service. *(Michael Neidig)*

Unloading tank wagons at Harwich in the 1970s. The older ferries were laid-up in 1981. *(Ferry Publications Library)*

The Harwich train ferry berth on a grey morning in 2014. It was listed by Historic England as a Grade II Listed Building after the ferry service closed in 1987 and remains intact if slightly dilapidated. *(John Cooper)*

ageing ferries with two large new ships, each carrying 104 wagons and able to make three crossings per day. Wagons would be loaded on two decks, with new terminals built at both Harwich and Zeebrugge. The total cost of the project was estimated at £40 million. As a first step, Sealink chartered the ro-ro ship *Stena Shipper*, which had been built by A. Vuyk & Zonen at Capelle a/d Ijssel in the Netherlands in 1973. She was renamed *Speedlink Vanguard* and converted to a train ferry at Smith's Dock in Middlesbrough in 1981. Four tracks were fitted on both her main and upper decks and the trailer lift modified to move two rail wagons at the time between the decks. The wagons were loaded using small rubber-tyred 'Trackmobile' shunters. She was also fitted with large sponsons to improve her stability. Although she was not much larger than the older ferries, around 20m longer than the *Cambridge Ferry*, her two decks could carry over 50 wagons, compared to around 30 on the older ships. Incidentally her sistership *Stena Seatrader* had a similar conversion to a train ferry, as the *Stena Scanrail*, a few years later.

The old *Suffolk Ferry* was sold for scrap in 1980, and with the arrival of the *Speedlink Vanguard*, the *Norfolk Ferry* and *Essex Ferry* (II) were laid-up in reserve the following year. Any plans for investment in new ferries was shelved when the Government announced their

intention to privatise Sealink. The British and French Governments also set-up a group to re-examine options for a Channel Tunnel. From 1982, *Speedlink Vanguard* operated a single return trip per day, with the *Cambridge Ferry* kept in reserve.

Shortly afterwards, there was a serious accident when the *Speedlink Vanguard* was approaching Harwich on the night of the 19th December 1982, the Townsend Thoresen ferry, *European Gateway*, was outward bound from Felixstowe. The two ships should have passed in the channel, but for some reason, the *European Gateway*, failed to make a turn at a bend in the channel and ran across the *Speedlink Vanguard's* bow. The *Vanguard* ran straight into her starboard side, penetrating her vehicle deck and the generator room below. As the *Gateway* flooded, she quickly began to heel, reaching an angle of 40° within three minutes. At that point, her bilge keel rested on the seabed and she took a further 10-20 minutes to roll over onto her side. The *Gateway's* port side remained above water and most of the 70 passengers and crew managed to scramble to safety, though six lives were lost. The inquiry put most of the blame on the *European Gateway* for watchkeeping errors and running with her engine-room watertight doors open, though this was not unusual in the ferry industry. The *Speedlink Vanguard* had only superficial damage to the bow and was back in service within ten days.

The *Cambridge Ferry* came back into service in 1983, operating three or four days a week to deal with a backlog of wagons. Despite record levels of rail traffic, over half a million tons in 1985, the railways were looking to 'rationalise' the ferry services. This included concentrating train ferry services on a single route, which inevitably favoured the shorter crossing from Dover. British Rail's ferry services had been privatised as Sealink in July 1984 and operated on contract to British Rail. In September 1986, British Rail announced that their contract with Sealink for the Harwich to Zeebrugge service would finish at the end of January 1987.

The *Cambridge Ferry* was transferred to other Sealink services, carrying trucks in the Irish Sea until 1992 when she was sold to the Mediterranean and finally scrapped in 2003. The *Speedlink Vanguard* returned to Stena and was used as a ro-ro ferry on various routes, including the English Channel, before being scrapped in 2013. The train ferry berth remains at Harwich and is designated as a 'Listed Building' by English Heritage.

The Channel post-war

Southern Railway /British Rail / Sealink / ALA

	1947-1984
Sealink British Ferries	1984-1988
SNCF / SNAT	1951-1995
Dover – Dunkerque	1947-1995

The *Twickenham Ferry, Hampton Ferry* and *Shepperton Ferry* all returned to Dover at the end of the war. The train ferry dock at Dover had also survived undamaged, as had the linkspan in Dunkerque. It was reported that Hitler had ordered these to be protected in 1940, so that they could used for the invasion of Britain, and as the order was never rescinded, they had never been attacked. Initially the ferries were used to transport military supplies for the British Army in Germany. The *Shepperton Ferry* was the first to return to civilian service in February 1946, with her stern gantry removed and her boilers converted to oil-firing. The Southern Railway and its French partner Sociètè Nationale de Chemins de Fer Français, (SNCF), which had been formed in 1938, reinstated the London to Paris 'Night Ferry' sleeper service in December 1947. The *Twickenham Ferry* and *Hampton Ferry* returned the following year.

The *Twickenham Ferry* returned to her pre-war owners, ALA, and the French flag. With the two British ferries, SNCF were keen to provide their own ship for

The *Shepperton Ferry* with red funnels and British Rail's 'double-arrow' logo introduced in the mid-1960s. Together with her pre-war sisters, she was the backbone of the Channel train ferry service for more than thirty years. *(John Pegden)*

The *Twickenham Ferry* followed the mid-60s change to red funnels but kept her French identity with the ALA logo. *(John Pegden)*

the service and ordered the *Saint-Germain* from Helsingør Skibsværft in Denmark, a company with long experience of building train ferries. She was delivered in 1951 and in dimensions and layout, she was very similar

A classic cut-away drawing of the *Saint-Germain* by the marine artist Laurence Dunn, published in the 'Eagle' magazine in November 1951. *(Author's collection)*

to the pre-war ferries. However, she was a much better-looking ship, with a raked bow, rounded bridge front and single central funnel, which avoided the solid upright look of the earlier ships. Her main deck had four tracks with narrow platforms that allowed passengers to leave the carriages to use the 1st class lounge and dining saloon on the promenade deck. There was also a 3rd class lounge for foot passengers on the boat deck, and like the pre-war ships, a garage for 25 cars which were loaded directly on to the promenade deck. The main difference was that she was powered by two B&W diesels. She was not the first, as the post-war Harwich ferries were also motor ships, but British Railways continued to build steam ships until the 1960s.

Saint-Germain's first few years were not without incident, in December 1951 she collided with the Prince of Wales pier while running astern into Dover on a dark foggy morning. The damage to the stern prevented the sleeper cars from being unloaded and the passengers had to transfer to another train to finish their journey to London. In 1953 she damaged her superstructure, including two lifeboats in a collision in Dunkerque harbour. *Saint-Germain's* accommodation was changed to single class in 1956 and the following year an extra sleeping car was added to the 'Night Ferry' which ran to Brussels.

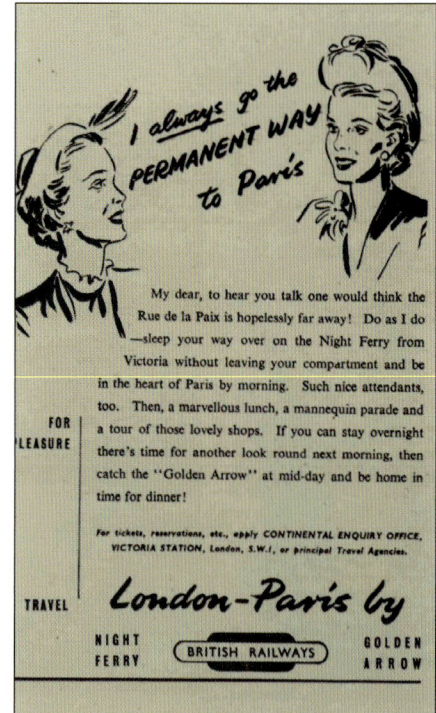

I always go the PERMANENT WAY to Paris

My dear, to hear you talk one would think the Rue de la Paix is hopelessly far away! Do as I do —sleep your way over on the Night Ferry from Victoria without leaving your compartment and be in the heart of Paris by morning. Such nice attendants, too. Then, a marvellous lunch, a mannequin parade and a tour of those lovely shops. If you can stay overnight there's time for another look round next morning, then catch the "Golden Arrow" at mid-day and be home in time for dinner!

For tickets, reservations, etc., apply CONTINENTAL ENQUIRY OFFICE, VICTORIA STATION, London, S.W.I, or principal Travel Agencies.

FOR PLEASURE

TRAVEL

London-Paris by

NIGHT FERRY

BRITISH RAILWAYS

GOLDEN ARROW

A British Railways' advert from 1949, encouraging London ladies to use the 'Night Ferry' sleeper service for shopping trips to Paris.

The *Saint-Germain* followed the blue hull and red funnel trend, with SNCF in white letters. Her passenger accommodation was expanded by a new 150-seat lounge fitted above the garage in 1976. *(FotoFlite)*

The **Saint-Germain** at the new Dunkerque West port which opened in 1976. This avoided the locks into the old harbour and reduced the crossing time by more than an hour. *(Miles Cowsill)*

The *Vortigern, Saint Eloi and Anderida*

British Rail first developed designs for replacement train ferries in 1958, as the pre-war ships were all more than 20 years old, but the history of the Channel train ferries has always been haunted by the tunnel and the spectre returned in the 1960s. The decision to build new ships was postponed as discussions on building a rail tunnel were revived. The British and French Governments agreed to build a Channel Tunnel in 1964. However, it was obvious that the project would take more than a decade to complete and it was agreed that the old train ferries needed to be replaced in the meantime. After many false starts a new multi-purpose ferry was ordered from Swan Hunter's yard at Wallsend on the Tyne and the *Vortigern* was delivered in 1969. In style, her overall appearance was similar other British Rail ferries of the time, with open boat decks and a large central funnel topped by a vertical fin. Her design had to meet many demands. She could operate as a train ferry between Dover and Dunkerque, loading through a folding stern door to four rail tracks on the main deck and with cars loaded over a side ramp to the upper garage deck. She could also operate as a drive-through vehicle ferry on the short crossings from Dover to Boulogne and Calais, carrying cars, trucks and up to 1,400 passengers. In car ferry mode, the forward rail buffers moved clear so that both bow and stern doors could be used by the 250 cars on the main deck and on movable mezzanine decks. While the access equipment provided by Cargospeed in Greenock was a success, British Rail's naval architect Tony Rogan described the layout of the passenger accommodation as a disaster, due to meddling by senior management, and it was subject to a series of later modifications. Late in the design, the naval architects realised that each of the Wagon-Lits sleeper carriages had an anthracite stove to provide heating and hot water. Burning coal in an enclosed train deck took some negotiation with the Dept. of Transport but was resolved by fitting additional deluge nozzles, so that the fire-water system provided a 'curtain' of water around the carriages.

In 1969, British Rail's shipping services were centralised as a separate division and the following year adopted 'Sealink' as their corporate brand. Over the next few years, the brand was adopted by their French, Dutch and Belgian partners and painted on the sides of the ferries.

The success of the *Vortigern* led to two near sisters being ordered by ALA and SNCF. The second ferry designed by British Rail was the *Saint Eloi*, for their French subsidiary, ALA. In size and layout she was very similar to *Vortigern*, though she had an additional deck of accommodation forward and a large funnel which incorporated the aft mast. As ALA were not involved in the car ferry routes, she was a pure train ferry. There were no mezzanine car decks or bow door, though she was designed to allow these to be fitted later when she moved to other services after the Channel Tunnel was built. She was ordered from Cantieri Navali di Pietra Ligure in the north-west of Italy for delivery in 1972. However, these were difficult times and the shipyard went bankrupt during construction. After many delays, the yard received state subsidies to complete the contract and the *Saint Eloi* was eventually delivered in 1975.

With the arrival of the *Vortigern*, the old pre-war ferries were retired. The *Hampton Ferry* was sold in 1969 and scrapped a few years later. The *Shepperton Ferry* was withdrawn in 1972 and scrapped in Spain. The delays with the *Saint Eloi* led British Rail to look for a stopgap replacement for the train ferry service. They turned to Stena AB in Sweden, (a company that would

figure large in Sealink's future), who were building two of their *Stena Carrier* ro-ro ships, at Trosvik Verksted in Brevik, Norway. Stena had converted the first of these ships to a train ferry and chartered her to the East German railways, Deutsche Reichsbahn, as the *Stubbenkamer*. The second ferry was also converted to a train ferry prior to delivery and chartered to British Railways as the *Anderida*. She was a typical ro-ro ferry in appearance, with a forward bridge and two funnels aft, and designed to carry goods wagons and trucks, with accommodation for 12 drivers. She arrived in Dover in the summer of 1972 and stayed on the Dunkerque service until 1976 when she was moved to carry trucks and trailers on the Irish Sea.

The *Chartres*

The last of the three passenger train ferries was ordered by SNCF from Dubigeon-Normandie in Nantes, although the *Chartres* was delivered in 1974 ahead of

Top: The *Chartres* was a half-sister to *Vortigern*, delivered in 1974 by Dubigeon-Normandie in Nantes. She was always easily recognised by her large distinctive funnel. *(FotoFlite)*

Above: The *Transcontainer I*, seen here on passage from Dunkerque. She was a ro-ro and container ship operated by SNCF and later she was converted to carry rail wagons in 1974 but was only occasionally used in rail service..*(FotoFlite)*

Left: The ro-ro ship *Anderida* was chartered from Stena in 1972 and converted to carry rail wagons as a stop-gap until the *Saint Eloi* was completed. *(David Ingham)*

The multi-purpose ferry *Vortigern*, delivered in 1969, was the first new train ferry for a generation. She was designed to operate both as a Dover to Dunkerque train ferry and as a short-crossing car and passenger ferry between Dover, Calais and Boulogne. (*FotoFlite*)

Saint Eloi. Like the *Vortigern*, the *Chartres* was a multi-purpose ferry designed to spend the winter carrying rail traffic between Dover and Dunkerque and the summer as a car ferry between Calais, Dover and Folkestone. She had accommodation for 1,400 passengers on three decks with the aft saloon on the upper deck used as a bar and discotheque in the summer and converted to a garage for cars loaded over the side ramp on the winter train ferry service. Her superstructure was crowned by a very large red funnel with a distinctive shape, described in the press at the time as the 'back-to-front funnel'. Her access equipment was again built by Cargospeed and included a unique 3-position stern door. This sloped forward when closed and hinged open at the top when loading trains. It could also be lowered to hinge at the bottom and serve as a car ferry ramp.

Chartres' other innovation was the Navyflux Y-thruster, developed by Alsthom. The bow thruster fitted to most ferries is in a tunnel running port and starboard through the hull. These are very effective when the ship is stationary, but the transverse thrust drops away very quickly once the ship starts moving as the water flows over the face of the thruster tunnel. Conversely, a bow rudder is effective when the ship is running astern but is of limited use at low speed. The *Vortigern* had both a bow rudder and a tunnel thruster. The idea of the Y-thruster was that it would be effective over a range of speed and perform the function of both bow rudder and thruster. The inlet was on the forefoot, facing forward, and the water was directed either to port or starboard using hydraulic flaps at the outlet ports on either side. When the ship was at sea, the flaps closed flush over the outlet ports, reducing the drag on the hull. While it seems a good idea, the Y-thruster did not catch on. Whether it was the complexity of the hydraulic flaps, or simply the cost, traditional tunnel thrusters remain the norm on modern ferries.

In 1974, SNCF converted their ro-ro container ship, *Transcontainer I*, to carry rail wagons. She spent most of her time carrying containers and trailers from Dunkerque to Harwich and Felixstowe, but the rail tracks allowed her to act as a reserve ship for the Dunkerque to Dover service. She was sold to Greece in 1986 and operated in the Red Sea for a while before being scrapped in 2000.

The *Twickenham Ferry's* boilers were no longer serviceable and with the *Chartres* now in service, the last of the old pre-war ferries was retired in 1974 and scrapped in Spain. Construction work had also started on the Channel Tunnel. However, with uncertainty about the project costs at a time when Britain was experiencing severe inflation, the Labour Government cancelled the project less than a year later. With no immediate prospect of a tunnel, the train ferry service

ALA's *Saint Eloi* was delivered in 1975, three years late after her Italian builders went into liquidation. Seen here outbound from Dover passing RMT's *Prins Philippe*. *(FotoFlite)*

was updated in July 1976 when the Dunkerque terminal moved to the new Loon-Plage Port in Dunkerque West. The new terminal had an 83m long linkspan to cope with the 7.5m tidal range in the port. Dunkerque West shortened the crossing distance by around 12km, but more importantly avoided the delay of passing through the Watier Lock in and out of Dunkerque's Eastern Docks. The crossing time was reduced by more than an hour so that each ferry could complete three round trips per day rather than the previous two.

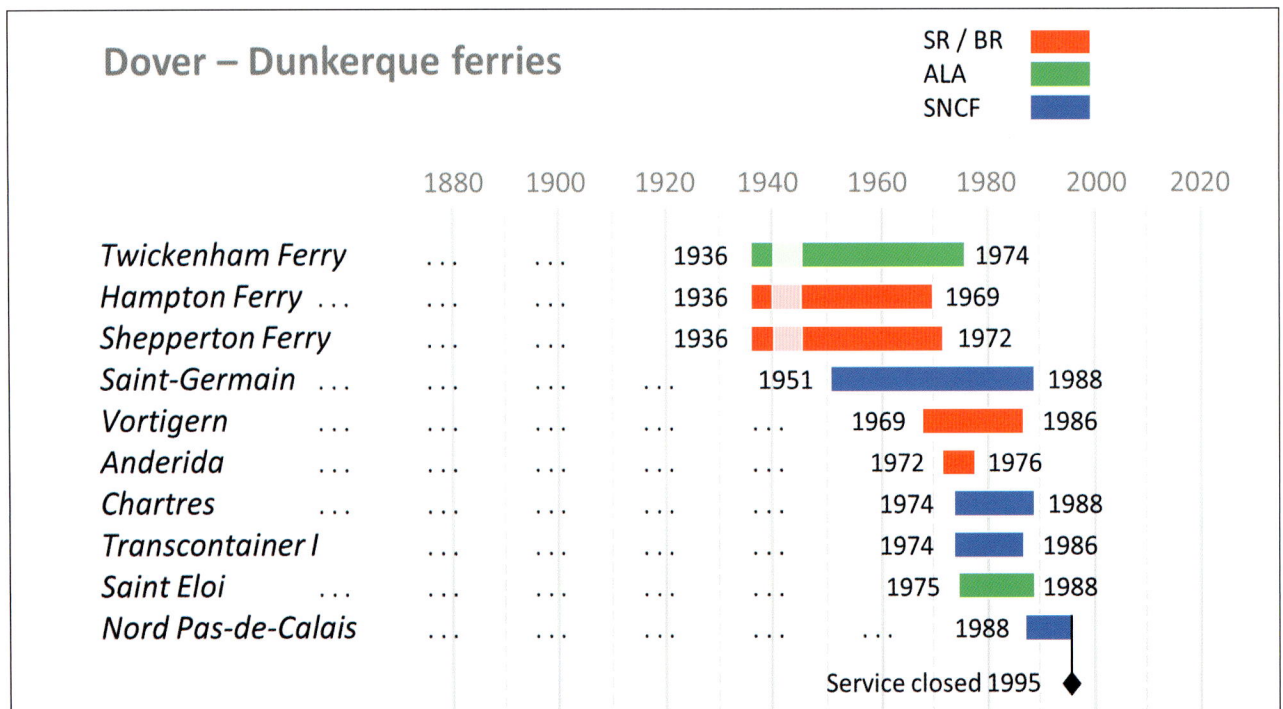

Dover – Dunkerque ferries

SR / BR
ALA
SNCF

	1880	1900	1920	1940	1960	1980	2000	2020
Twickenham Ferry	...	...	1936			1974		
Hampton Ferry	...	...	1936		1969			
Shepperton Ferry	...	...	1936			1972		
Saint-Germain	...	...	...	1951		1988		
Vortigern	...	...	...	...	1969	1986		
Anderida	...	...	...	...	1972	1976		
Chartres	...	...	...	...	1974	1988		
Transcontainer I	...	...	...	...	1974	1986		
Saint Eloi	...	...	...	...	1975	1988		
Nord Pas-de-Calais	...	...	...	...	...	1988		

Service closed 1995

The end of the 'Night Ferry'

The reduction in crossing time was a bonus to business passengers on the 'Night Ferry' train, who now arrived at 07.45, rather than the traditional 09.00. However, it was probably too late to make much difference. A typical 'Night Ferry' train of the time left London Victoria with 14 coaches and vans. The four coaches with 'seated' passengers and two restaurant / buffet cars stopped at Dover. Five CIWL sleeper cars, four for Paris and one for Brussels, a luggage van and two mail vans crossed on the ferry. Each sleeper car had nine compartments and, depending on the mix of single and double occupancy, between 12 and 15 passengers. Thus, the whole system of trains and ferries carried at best 60-70 sleeper passengers per night and often only around half that number.

CIWL's 15-year contract to operate the sleeper trains expired in 1976. British Rail and SNCF had no doubt hoped that it would have been replaced by the tunnel. In an effort to reduce costs, they decided to operate the service in-house. From 1977, SNCF bought or leased the sleeping cars, some being the originals from 1936, and BR provided the attendants. However, neither company believed the service could be profitable and from 1977, BR trimmed costs by removing the dining car which allowed passengers to have breakfast between Dover and London. SNCF did the same the following year and previous plans to upgrade the sleeping cars were shelved. British Rail's Chairman announced the end of

The *Saint Eloi* was a half-sister to the *Vortigern* and *Chartres* but was designed purely for the Dover - Dunkerque train ferry service. She did not have a bow door or portable decks for car ferry service. *(Author's collection)*

the sleeper service in 1980, claiming an annual deficit of £120,000. There was little fanfare when the last trains arrived at Victoria and the Gare du Nord on the morning of the 1st November.

All change in the 1980s

The closure of the 'Night Ferry' was just the beginning of a decade of change. Britain's new Conservative government, led by Margaret Thatcher,

The *Saint-Germain* was retired in 1988 after 37 years on the Dover to Dunkerque crossing. She was scrapped soon after. *(FotoFlite)*

The *Nord Pas-de-Calais* came into service with SNCF in 1988. Freed from the limitations of the Dover train ferry dock, she was much larger than the previous ships. *(Miles Cowsill)*

came to power in 1979 with an agenda to end public subsidies and privatise most state-owned industries. A few months earlier, British Rail had hived off their ferry business as a separate company, Sealink UK Ltd. Within a couple of years, plans for a Channel Tunnel were revived by the British and French Governments, though this time funded by private capital. The scheme for two rail tunnels, with a smaller central service tunnel, was finally approved in 1987.

In 1984, Sealink which included the *Vortigern* and *Saint Eloi* was sold to Sea Containers Inc. and renamed Sealink British Ferries. By this time, the multi-purpose ferries *Vortigern* and *Chartres* were only occasionally used as train ferries, spending more of their time on car ferry routes. The *Chartres* operated between Newhaven and Dieppe from 1982, with brief spells back as a train ferry between Dover and Dunkerque in 1986 and 1988. After this, she served on various routes until sold to Greece in 1993 and to the Persian Gulf in 2016. *Vortigern* served on a variety of Channel routes after 1986, with brief trips to the Irish Sea, until she was sold to Greece in 1988. She continued there until scrapped in 2005.

British Rail and SNCF reviewed their options for the train ferry service in the mid-1980s. The tunnel was still not approved and would take at least a decade to complete. SNCF's old *Saint-Germain* was near the end of her life as was the Dover train ferry dock. New larger ships would be more economic to operate but would

The *Nord Pas-de-Calais* was too large for Dover's old train ferry dock and a new linkspan for the train ferry service was built at the Admiralty Pier. *(Author's collection)*

need a new terminal at Dover and changes at Dunkerque. As British Rail no longer controlled the ships, they needed to offer a long-term charter to induce Sealink British Ferries to build new ships, but with the spectre of the tunnel it was difficult to forecast long-term demand. Sea Containers' naval architects prepared a design for a large new freight ferry, which would load at two levels, with rail wagons on the main deck and trucks and trailers above. They also investigated the cheaper option of lengthening the *Saint Eloi* and fitting

The **Nord Pas-de-Calai**s shipped the last rail wagons to Dunkerque in December 1995. The service was not viable after the Channel Tunnel opened the previous year. *(Miles Cowsill)*

large sponsors to let her carry trucks on the upper deck. However, British Rail and Sea Containers could not reach a commercial agreement and negotiations stopped. The agreed solution was for SNCF to build and operate a large new freight ferry and for British Rail to construct a new terminal at Dover. BR's Harwich to Zeebrugge service would also be closed to concentrate all rail traffic on the new service. From 1985, the *Saint Eloi* and *Saint-Germain* stopped carrying passengers between Dover and Dunkerque.

SNCF's new ferry was ordered from Chantiers du Nord et de la Méditerranée, (Normed) in Dunkerque. The last and largest train ferry built for the Channel and also Normed's last ship as the yard was run down for closure. The *Nord Pas-de-Calais* was a delivered in December 1987. Freed from the restrictions of the Dover train ferry dock, she was 160m long with a breadth of 23m, allowing six rail tracks on her main deck, and an open upper deck for trucks and trailers. Her gross tonnage of 13,727 was more than four times that of the old *Saint-Germain*. The *Nord Pas-de-Calais* was designed to replace not only the *Saint-Germain* and *Saint Eloi*, but also the *Cambridge Ferry* and *Speedlink Vanguard* at Harwich. As well as her size, she had a service speed of 22 knots to provide four round trips per day.

New double-deck linkspans were built at Dunkerque and at Dover's Admiralty Pier. The service was scheduled to start in January 1988, but a severe storm

in the previous October had delayed work at Dover and it was May before the terminal opened. With the *Nord Pas-de-Calais* in service, the *Saint Eloi* and the old *Saint-Germain* were retired and Dover's train ferry dock was closed. After 37 years on the route, the last of the classic ferries, the *Saint-Germain*, left Dunkerque two months later on her way to India for scrapping. The *Saint Eloi* served as a car ferry on other Channel routes and the Isle of Man and was sold to Italy in 1998. She was still operating at the *Azores Express* in 2020.

A problem with the new ferry berth led to the old train ferry dock being brought back into service for a few weeks in October 1988, with the *Chartres* and *Cambridge Ferry* pressed into service. After that, the new train ferry service operated successfully for six years, carrying over a million tons of freight per year. Ownership of the *Nord Pas-de-Calais* was transferred from SNCF to the holding company Société Nouvelle d'Armement Transmanche (SNAT) in 1989. The end came in June 1994 when the Channel Tunnel was opened for freight traffic. The *Nord Pas-de-Calais* continued for a few months, carrying mostly dangerous goods wagons that were not allowed through the tunnel, but there was not enough traffic to sustain the service. The final trip from Dunkerque to Dover on the 22nd December 1995 closed the train ferry service. The *Nord Pas-de-Calais* continued on the Channel as a truck and trailer ferry until leaving for the Mediterranean in 2016.

FOUR

Denmark

Train ferries have been more important to Denmark than to any other country. This is simply the result of geography. The largest part of the country is the Jylland peninsula in the west, which separates the North Sea from the Baltic. The capital and largest city of København is on the eastern island of Sjælland. Between Jylland and Sjælland lies the island of Fyn. Travel across Demark has always been broken by the two sea crossings. The western crossing, between Jylland and Fyn is known as the Lillebælt, (or little belt). The longer eastern crossing between Fyn and Sjælland is the Storebælt, (or great belt). Providing an unbroken transport link across the Belts, and to a lesser extent from Sjaelland to the southern island of Falster, is essential to the country's economy and identity.

Between 1872 and 1997, when the Storebælt bridge was completed, train ferries were operated on ten routes within Denmark, five by Det Danske Statsbaner, (Danish State Railways), and five by small private operators. Of these routes, the Storebælt is the most famous and probably the most iconic train ferry service in the world, both in terms of capacity and frequency. At its peak, twelve large train ferries plus several car ferries worked the crossing night and day. As with other train ferry crossings, most of the ships on the Storebælt spent their whole working lives on the route.

However, Det Danske Statsbaner is unique in having applied a standard dock and loading bridge design to all the smaller ferry ports, giving the flexibility to move ships between their four domestic routes and also the international crossing between Helsingør and Helsingborg. One big advantage enjoyed by all ferries in the Baltic is a very low tidal range. While ports in the English Channel had to allow for a tidal range of 5.8m, in the southern Baltic, the equivalent range is only around 0.14m. This allowed the ports to have short simple loading bridges. The ferries on the short routes were standardised, based on the design of the first ferry, *Lillebælt*. They were double ended with a single track on the centreline and an overall breadth of around 13.5m.

There were of course also international ferries from Denmark to Norway, Sweden and Germany and these are the subject of later chapters.

The beginnings

The railway revolution that occurred in Britain during the 1830s and 40s quickly spread across Northern Europe. In Denmark, the Sjællandske Jerbane-Selskab, (Sjælland Railway Company) was formed in 1844 and opened its first line from København, 31km west to the town of Roskilde in 1847. By 1856, the line had been extended westward across Sjælland to the port of Korsør on the Storebælt. It didn't take long for a member of the Danish Parliament, Col. A.F. Tscherning, to propose that a railway tunnel be built under the Storebælt to extend the railway westwards.

In parallel to the railways on Sjælland, a separate company had been set up to build railways on Jylland, Det danske Jerbane-Driftsselskab (The Danish Railway Operating Co.). This was essentially a British company, run by the railway entrepreneur Sir Morton Peto in partnership with his brother- in- law Edward Betts and the civil engineer Thomas Brassey. They had previously built a railway across the Duchy of Schleswig in 1854 connecting Tönning on the North Sea coast to Flensburg on the Baltic. In 1862 they opened the first railway in Jylland, between the towns of Aarhus and Randers.

The Danish Ministry of Interior, who were responsible for transport, decided to commission a report on the options for connecting the nation's railways. This report was compiled by a young army officer, Ingeniørkaptajn Niels Holst, and was published in December 1862 with a clear conclusion:

To achieve cheap and regular carriage of persons and goods on the railways, the Great and Little Belts are major and minor obstacles. Individuals and animals could easily be transferred to ordinary steamers without added expense, but freight on the other hand cannot. The transhipment of goods from railway wagons to steamships and vice versa will lead to considerable time losses and additional expense. The goods are also vulnerable to damage. It can therefore be considered that the Railway will not be able to operate major freight trains unless action is taken to avoid the transhipment of the Goods. Taking such measures will thus become an important task, in particular because it can be assumed that the larger freight traffic will lead to increased passenger traffic over the Railway. Neither the Great nor the Little Belt are suitable for the Construction of Bridges or similar means

capable of carrying Railways. The simplest and cheapest means of avoiding transhipment of goods during its transport over the belts is undoubtedly the design of steam vessels that they could load rail cars. We could not be in doubt that it is, after all, feasible to build steamers which are able to safely transfer loaded railway wagons across the Great and Little Belts. This will overcome the leading obstacles to the development of a more healthy traffic on the Danish railways.

The report proposed the construction of three steam ferries. A small ferry for the Lillebælt plus two larger ferries, one to operate on the Storebælt and one in reserve. There was also a lengthy report from kaptajnløjtnant P. Schønheyder who had visited Scotland to examine the operation of the ferries on the Firths of Forth and Tay.

Despite the clear conclusion, implementing it was more complex. The railways were operated by different private companies and ferries were opposed by the existing shipowners. Before anything could be resolved, Denmark was plunged into a war in 1864. The Duchies of Schleswig and Holstein were at the time part of Denmark. While the people in Schleswig were a mix of Danes and Germans, Holstein was almost completely German. These differences came to a head with disagreement on who should succeed to the Danish throne. The German population of the Duchies rebelled and, supported by the Prussian and Austrian armies, defeated the Danish army in a series of battles. This forced the Danish Government to accept a peace ceding Schleswig and Holstein to Germany.

The war was a national and economic disaster for

Denmark, which lost nearly 40% of its territory. However, in its aftermath there was a renewed determination to develop industry and agriculture. Essential to that was effective transport.

The lillebælt

De jysk-fyenske Jernbaner	**1872-1885**
Det danske Statsbaner	**1885-1935**
Fredericia – Strib	1872-1935

In September 1865, 'Queen Louise's Railway' was opened on the island of Fyn, connecting Middlefart to Nyborg. This was the missing link, allowing passengers to travel from west to east by train, though still having to disembark and board ferries across the Belts.

The Government reached an agreement with Det danske Jerbane-Driftsselskab, which operated the railways in both Jylland and Fyn, to provide a steam ferry across the Lillebælt, between Fredericia and Strib,

Driftsselskab. This was completed on the 1st September 1867 and the railway was renamed De jysk-fyenske Jernbaner, (The Jutland & Funen Railway).

With both the Jylland and Fyn railways in Government ownership, this should have simplified progress with the ferry, but it was not until 1870 that a revised Bill was put before Parliament to provide a steam ferry across the Lillebælt and a ferry terminal at Nyborg on the west side of the Storebælt. Despite seven years having past since the original report, there was still opposition to a Lillebælt train ferry, mostly on the grounds of cost. The Bill was eventually passed in April 1870 and 300,000 rigsdaler approved for the project.

The Lillebælt

The contract to build the Lillebælt ferry was placed in Britain, with J. Wigham Richardson & Co., Low Walker in Newcastle, who had built the ferry *Ruhr* for the German railways in 1865. 'The Engineer' reported:

Niels Holst, (1828-1889), wrote the pamphlet proposing steam train ferries on the Belts in 1862, when he was a junior army officer. He later became the first Director-General of Det Danske Statsbaner in 1885. *(Det Kgl. Bibliotek)*

Sir Morton Peto, (1809-1889), was the British railway entrepreneur who built the Jylland railway. His insolvency in 1866 led to the railways being taken over by the Danish state. *(Suffolk Archives)*

a distance of around 2.5km. A Bill was laid before parliament requiring the railway company to put a ferry in place by the 1st July 1867.

The plan then received an unexpected setback. The London bank of Overend Gurney & Co. collapsed in 1866 with debts of over £11 million, more than £1 billion in today's money. Sir Morton Peto, the Danish railway's major shareholder became insolvent. The crash revealed he had been financing his interest in the London Chatham & Dover Railway, through unsecured bank loans for which he became personally liable. This was on the edge of legality and although Peto escaped prosecution, his reputation never recovered. In Denmark, the main concern was that Peto's interest in the Danish railways might be sold to Prussian interests. To avoid this, the Danish Parliament agreed that the State should take over the assets of Det danske Jerbane-

The ferry was to be constructed as to cross the Little Belt in all weathers and at all seasons of the year. Usually the surface of the water is very calm, but occasionally in north-easterly storms there is a heavy sea running, and generally in winter time there is not only the naturally formed ice to contend with, but the drifting blocks from the north.

The current varies from one to five knots per hour, and the variations in the level of the water amount to 9 ft. Further, it was stipulated that the steamer was to be capable of taking on board 100 first and second-class passengers, 300 third-class passengers, and at the same time six of the largest trucks possessed by the railway administration, all fully loaded. The connecting bridges were also to be capable of supporting the heaviest locomotive

Lillebælt ferries

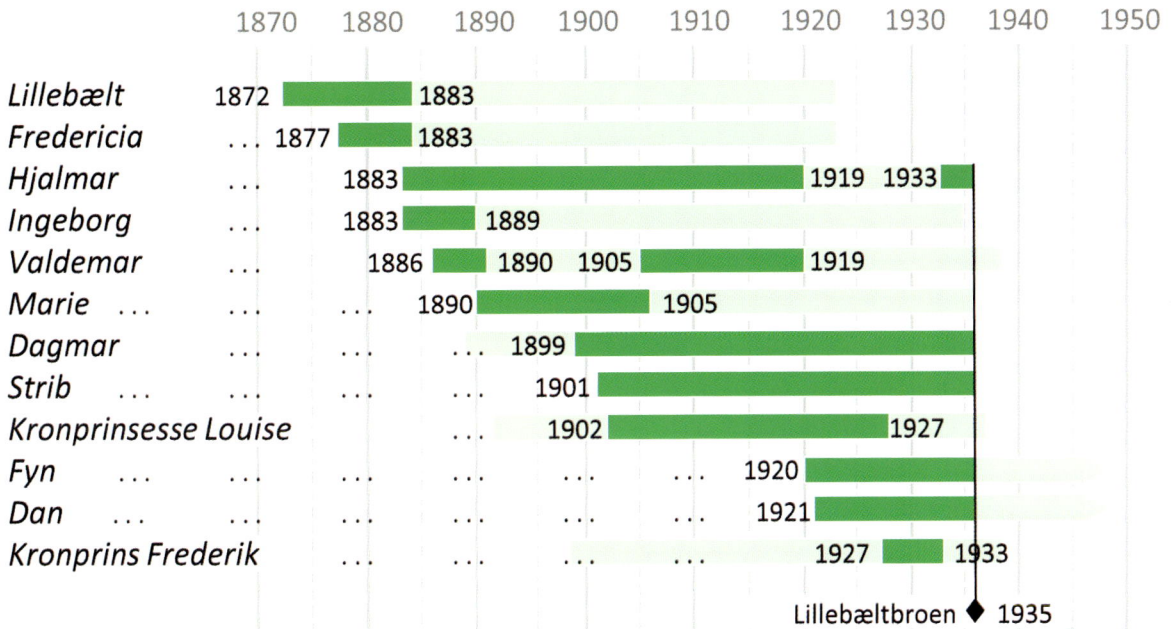

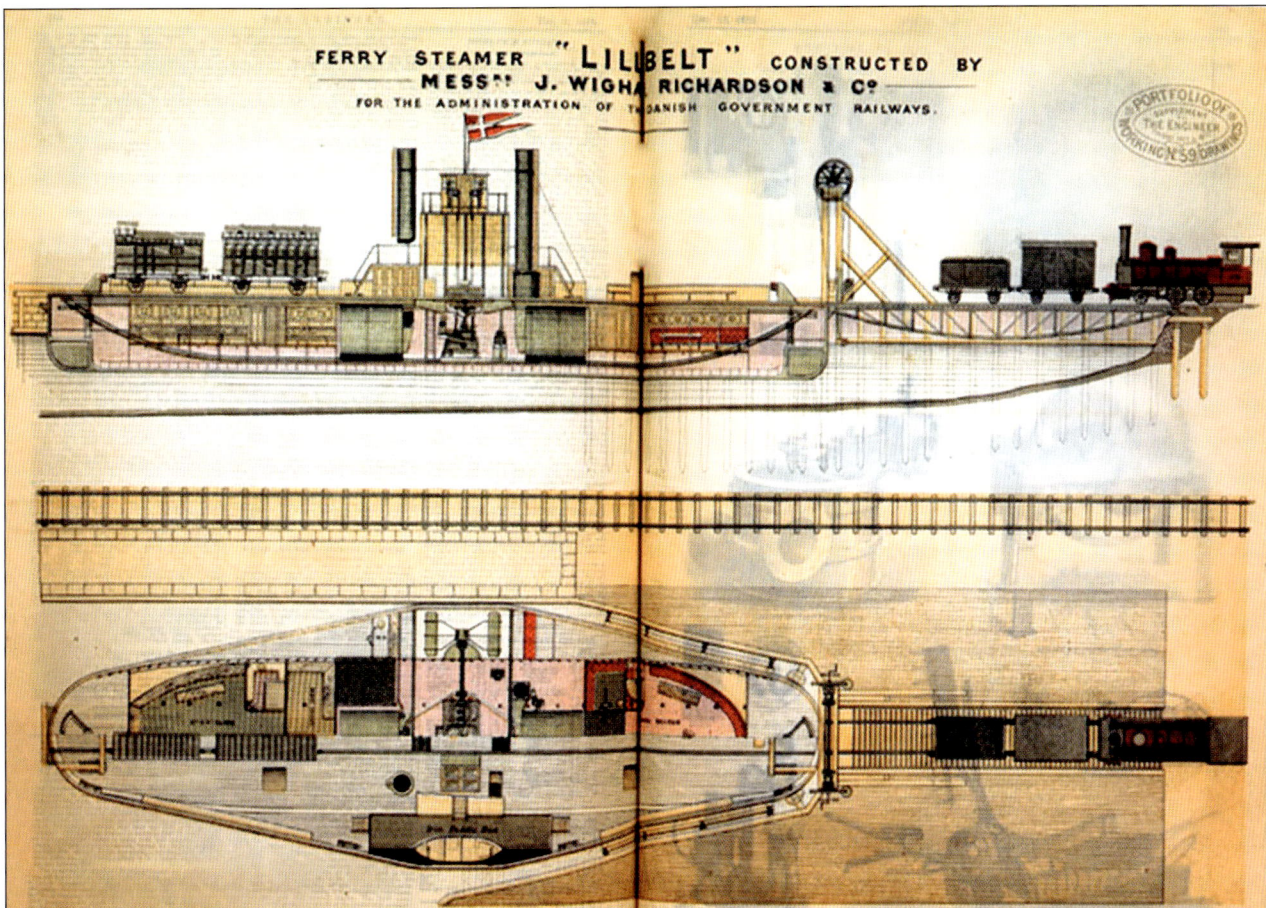

	1870	1880	1890	1900	1910	1920	1930	1940	1950
Lillebælt	1872	1883							
Fredericia	... 1877	1883							
Hjalmar	...	1883			1919	1933			
Ingeborg	...	1883	1889						
Valdemar	...	1886	1890 1905			1919			
Marie ...	...	...	1890	1905					
Dagmar	...	...	... 1899						
Strib ...	...	...	...	1901					
Kronprinsesse Louise		...	1902			1927			
Fyn ...	...	...	...	...	...	1920			
Dan ...	...	...	...	...	...	1921			
Kronprins Frederik		...	...	...		1927	1933		

Lillebæltbroen ◆ 1935

Elevation and plan of the first Danish train ferry, the *Lillebelt*, (later spelt Lillebælt), built by J. Wigham Richardson & Co., Newcastle. *(The Engineer)*

The *Lillebælt* loading wagons at Fredericia. The linkspan was built in Newcastle and delivered with the ferry. *(Museet for søfarts)*

The *Lillebælt*, with the *Hjalmar* or *Ingeborg* in the background, showing the red and white stripes of the Danish flag on their funnels. *(Museet for søfarts)*

engine and tender.

The steamer is 140 ft. long, 26 ft. beam, and draws 7 ft. of water when loaded, and the scantlings of the hull are enormously strong, far above what is required for the first classification in the register books of Lloyd's and Veritas, which classifications were both required. The engines are of the oscillating kind, of 120 horsepower collectively, *with two multi-tube boilers fitted with brass tubes. The paddle-wheels are of the radial type. The floats being of wood, with an iron plate on each side riveted through.*

The small double-ended ferry was 42.8m long with a breadth of 7.9m, 13.6m across the paddle-boxes. Similar in size and arrangement to the *Robert Napier* and *Carrier* built for the Tay crossing twenty years earlier. Originally named *Lillebelt*, the spelling was later changed to *Lillebælt*, the ferry had two tall slender funnels, located either side obliquely, forward and aft of the bridge. Unlike the Scottish ferries, *Lillebælt* had only a single rail track on deck and could carry only 5 or 6 goods wagons. There were also two passenger saloons below deck, one for 1st and 2nd class passengers, the other for 3rd class. The boilers and engines were built by Thompson & Boyd of Newcastle and gave the *Lillebælt* a speed of 8 knots.

She was meant to be delivered by September 1871, but strikes at the shipyard delayed completion, so that it was January 1872 before she set off on the delivery voyage across the North Sea. To save coal, the ferry was fitted with temporary masts and sails. However, the weather was so bad that they could not be used. *Lillebælt* arrived in Fredericia at the end of January. The transfer bridges had also been built in Newcastle and were transported on deck. These were assembled at Strib and Fredericia and regular crossings started on the 19th March 1872.

Each trip only took around 15 minutes, so many crossings could be made each day. The number of goods wagons transported rose quickly over the first few months; 136 in March, 661 in April, 1,069 in May and 1,081 in June. The following year, traffic had doubled. Having only one ferry was a problem when it had to be withdrawn for maintenance or drydocking. A second-hand passenger steamer was bought in order to maintain passenger traffic when the *Lillebælt* was

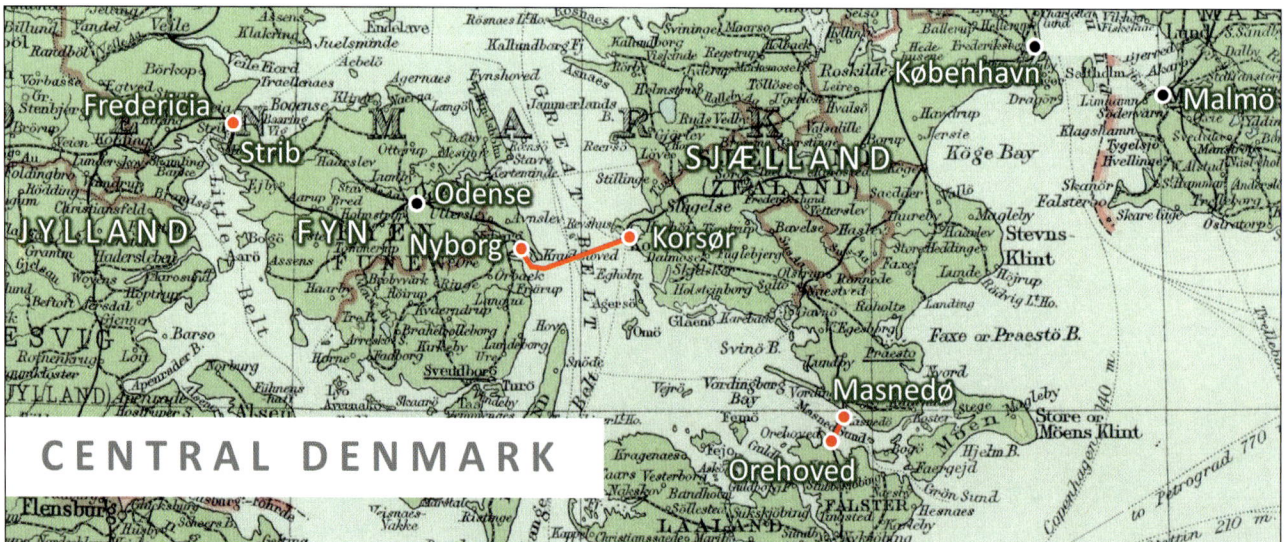

CENTRAL DENMARK

An early postcard of Fredericia harbour, showing the two loading bridges still surrounded by trees. *(Museet for søfarts)*

The *Fredericia* was the second ferry for the Lillebælt crossing, built by Schichau in Elbing, Prussia. *(Museet for søfarts)*

The *Ingeborg*, also built by Schichau in Elbing, was the last small ferry built outside Denmark. *(Museet for søfarts)*

The *Hjalmar* was the third Lillebælt ferry, built in 1883 by Schichau in Elbing, Prussia. *(Museet for søfarts)*

unavailable, but it took until 1876 before Parliament approved the funds for a second ferry.

The order was placed with Ferdinand Schichau & Co., in Elbing, East Prussia (now Elblag in Poland) and the *Fredericia* was delivered in 1877. She was virtually a copy of the *Lillebælt*, one minor change was that she had 16 blades on each paddle wheel, compared with ten on *Lillebælt*.

The two ferries operated successfully for the next five years, traffic growing every year, until it was decided that two new ferries should be built. De jysk-fyenske Jernbaner returned to Schichau & Co., in Elbing and the ferries *Hjalmar* and *Ingeborg* were delivered in July 1883. They were slightly larger than the older ferries, 51.5m long, compared to 42.8m, and could carry up to

Strib harbour in 1918, with DSB's winged wheel and crown on top of the loading bridge gantries. *(Museet for søfarts)*

700 passengers. This required four lifeboats rather than the previous two. Their appearance differed from the older boats as their two funnels were arranged either side by side, rather than obliquely.

Once the *Hjalmar* and *Ingeborg* were settled on the Lillebælt crossing, the *Lillebælt* and *Fredericia* could be used to open up new routes. *Lillebælt* was initially transferred to north Jylland to open the Oddesund crossing. Then six months later, she moved south again to start the Storstrømsund crossing, between Sjælland and Falster, and *Fredericia* took her place at Oddesund.

Hjalmar and *Ingeborg* operated the Lillebælt crossing reliably through most of the year. The one problem was that in winter their paddle wheels could become congested with ice and the ferry service would be suspended to avoid damage. The solution to this was to build an ice-breaking ferry capable of year-round operation. This was ordered from Burmeister & Wain in København and delivered, as *Valdemar* in 1886. She was slightly smaller than the other ferries, closer in size to *Lillebælt*, but more powerful and propelled by twin screws at the stern. The engines developed 575 hp, as opposed to 400 hp of the previous ships and the bow was shaped for breaking sheet ice. She could carry 500 passengers. Apart from having no paddles, *Valdemar* was similar in appearance to *Hjalmar* and *Ingeborg*. The deck was extended outboard of the hull amidships,

The **Valdemar** doing what she was designed for, breaking a channel through the ice for the paddle ferries. *(Museet for søfarts)*

similar to paddle boxes, to have the same overall breadth as the paddle ferries in order to fit the dock.

The screw propulsion was a slight disadvantage for a ferry as *Valdemar* had to turn, rather than operate double-ended, which added a few minutes to each crossing. However, she was very effective as an icebreaker. When the ice was particularly thick, the crew developed the practice of securing a coal-filled wagon at the stern. This trimmed the boat and improved propeller immersion. Once the bow was pushed hard into the ice, the crew rolled the wagon forward, which brought the bow crashing down and broke the ice.

Ingeborg moved on to the Oddesund crossing in

Top: The **Valdemar** in drydock early in her 73-year career as an icebreaker. *(Museet for søfarts)*

Above: The **Marie** moored at Fredericia in 1898, with the loading bridges in the background. *(Museet for søfarts)*

Top right: The **Marie** was the second icebreaking ferry, also built by Burmeister & Wain. *(Museet for søfarts)*

Middle right: The **Strib** was built in 1901 and spent her whole career on the Lillebælt crossing. The picture shows her after she was lengthened in 1904. *(Museet for søfarts)*

Bottom right: The **Dan** followed her sister **Fyn** as large new ferries built for the Lillebælt crossing in 1921. *(Museet for søfarts)*

1889, after six years. *Hjalmar* stayed on the Lillebælt crossing for 36 years through to 1919.

Valdemar was a success and led to a second identical ferry being ordered from Burmeister & Wain. This was the *Marie*, delivered in April 1890. *Marie* replaced *Valdemar* as the Lillebælt icebreaker and *Valdemar* moved to Oddesund, joining *Fredericia* and *Ingeborg*.

Hjalmar and *Marie* carried on but as traffic grew, additional capacity was needed. The *Dagmar*, which had served on the Storstrømmen since 1889, was transferred to the Lillebælt in 1899 and a new ferry, the *Strib*, was delivered in 1901. *Strib* was very similar to *Hjalmar*, a double-ended paddle steamer with a single rail track and with two funnels in the centre, either side

Fredericia on the 15th May 1935, the last day of the Lillebælt ferry before the bridge opened. The *Strib* on the left and *Kronprinsesse Louise* on the right. *(Museet for søfarts)*

Otto Busse, (1822-1883), was Chief Engineer of Det sjællandske Statsbaner and designer of the first Storebælt ferries. His son on the right (also Otto) later became the Technical Director of DSB. *(Det Kgl. Bibliotek)*

of the bridge. She was built by Helsingør Shipyard to carry 6 goods wagons and was licensed for 850 passengers. *Strib* was 51m long and was the last small ferry to be built for DSB with paddle wheels. She then spent her whole working life, the next 34 years, crossing the Lillebælt. In 1902, *Strib* was joined by the *Kronprinsesse Louise*, which was transferred from Helsingør and stayed for 25 years.

The two ferries on the Storstrømmen crossing, *Alexandra* and *Thyra*, were successfully lengthened in 1903. This gave DSB the confidence to do the same to the three main Lillebælt ferries, *Dagmar*, *Strib* and *Kronprinsesse Louise*, even though *Strib* was only three years old. During 1904, each ferry was lengthened in turn by adding a 12m section at A/S Københavns Flydedok.

From then through to 1919, the Lillebælt service stayed fairly constant with five ferries: *Hjalmar*, *Dagmar, Strib* and *Kronprinsesse Louise*. The *Valdemar* returned in 1905, swapping with *Marie*, which was rebuilt and moved to Storstrømmen.

The last two ferries built for the Lillebælt were ordered in 1916. Given the wartime pressure on the commercial shipyards, they were built by the Orlogsværftet, (Naval Dockyard) in København. Construction was delayed due to shortages of materials and the ferries, *Fyn* and *Dan*, were not delivered until

August 1921. Their design was traditional, 69m long with capacity for 8 goods wagons. Steam propulsion, with two side-by-side funnels. The main difference from the previous ferries was that they had screw propellers, rather than paddles.

Fyn and *Dan* allowed two old Lillebælt ferries to move on. *Hjalmar* transferred to Sallingsund and as the new ferries had no paddles to be damaged in ice the old icebreaker *Valdemar* moved to Oddesund. The five ferries: *Fyn, Dan, Dagmar, Strib* and *Kronprinsesse Louise* operated through the 1920s. The only change was that the *Kronprinsesse Louise* returned to Helsingør in 1927 and was replaced by the *Kronprins Frederik*.

However, plans were being put in place to replace the ferries with a bridge across the Lillebælt. Construction started on a combined road and rail bridge in 1929 and the 1,178m long Lillebæltsbroen opened in May 1935. While the bridge was under construction, the old *Hjalmar* returned to the Lillebælt in 1933, replacing the *Kronprins Frederik*. When the bridge opened, the *Hjalmar, Strib* and *Dagmar* were sold for scrapping, after 52, 34 and 46 years' service respectively. *Fyn* and *Dan* moved on, with long careers ahead of them at Helsingør.

The storebælt

Det sjællandske Statsbaner	**1883-1885**
Det danske Statsbaner	**1885-1996**
Scandlines Danmark A/S	**1997**
Korsør – Nyborg	**1883-1997**

It had taken ten years to get a ferry in operation across the Lillebælt. Flushed with its success, the

A postcard showing the Lillebælt ferry terminal and station at Fredericia in 1907. *(Museet for søfarts)*

Storebælt ferries

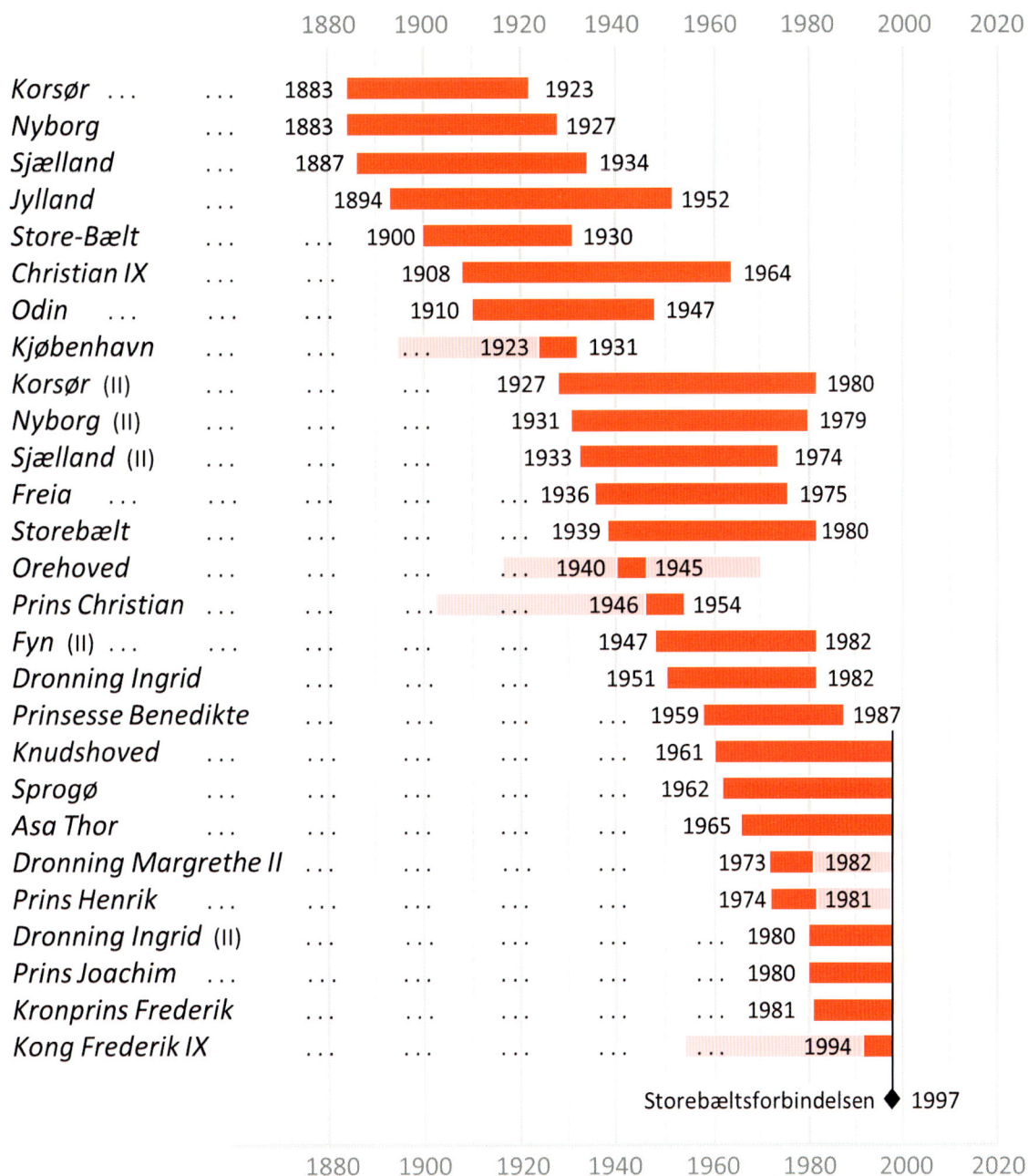

	1880	1900	1920	1940	1960	1980	2000	2020
Korsør	1883	▬▬▬	1923					
Nyborg ...	1883	▬▬▬▬	1927					
Sjælland ...	1887	▬▬▬▬▬	1934					
Jylland ...	1894	▬▬▬▬▬▬	1952					
Store-Bælt	1900	▬▬▬	1930					
Christian IX	1908	▬▬▬▬▬▬▬	1964					
Odin	1910	▬▬▬▬	1947					
Kjøbenhavn	1923	▬	1931					
Korsør (II)	1927	▬▬▬▬▬	1980					
Nyborg (II)	1931	▬▬▬▬▬	1979					
Sjælland (II) ...	1933	▬▬▬▬	1974					
Freia	1936	▬▬▬▬	1975					
Storebælt	1939	▬▬▬▬▬	1980					
Orehoved	1940	▬	1945					
Prins Christian	1946	▬	1954					
Fyn (II)	1947	▬▬▬▬	1982					
Dronning Ingrid ...	1951	▬▬▬▬	1982					
Prinsesse Benedikte ...	1959	▬▬▬▬	1987					
Knudshoved ...	1961	▬▬▬▬						
Sprogø ...	1962	▬▬▬▬						
Asa Thor ...	1965	▬▬▬						
Dronning Margrethe II ...	1973	▬	1982					
Prins Henrik ...	1974	▬	1981					
Dronning Ingrid (II) ...	1980							
Prins Joachim ...	1980							
Kronprins Frederik ...	1981							
Kong Frederik IX ...	1994							

Storebæltsforbindelsen ◆ 1997

Ministry of the Interior set up a Commission in 1872 to make proposals for a train ferry across the Storebælt. This was a much longer crossing, around 26km, and also more exposed to the weather. As Directors of the railway companies on either side of the Belt, Niels Holst, of De jysk-fyenske Jernbaner, and Viggo Rothe, of the Sjællandske Jerbane-Selskab, were key member of the Commission.

The Commission took two years to report. As with most train ferries, they identified the main commercial benefit was in moving goods wagons, including livestock and mail, without having to trans-ship cargo. The benefits to passengers were less as they could more easily transfer to passenger steamers. To build new ferries that could carry all passengers and goods would require very large vessels. However, as the railway companies ran mixed trains, with both passengers and freight, a purely freight service would not meet the demand. The Commission made three main recommendations:

The *Korsør* was built in 1883 by Kockums in Malmö as the first train ferry on the Storebælt. *(Museet for søfarts)*

An early engraving of the deck on *Korsør* showing wagons being manoeuvred by hand. *(Museet for søfarts)*

1.   That a steam ferry service should be established between Korsør and Nyborg and that two large train ferries should be procured.

2   That in addition to the port facilities at Korsør and Nyborg, secondary harbours should be built at Halsskov and Knudshoved, which would be less affected by ice in winter.

3   That three new passenger steamers should also

be acquired to operate alongside the train ferries.

The whole plan would cost around 3 million rigsdaler, ten times the budget of the Lillebælt ferry. A Bill to finance the project was presented to the Danish Parliament in 1875, but there was no enthusiasm for the committing this scale of funds. Very little happened for a few years until the Danish Government took over the private Sjællandske Jerbane-Selskab in 1880. With the state now owning the railways on both sides of the Storebælt, many of the discussions on how the project should be financed disappeared. The Bill for the ferries and ports was resubmitted to Parliament in December 1880 and finally approved in April 1881.

The 17.7m legacy of Otto Buse

Otto Busse, the Chief Engineer of the newly named Det sjællandske Statsbaner (Sjælland State Railways) was given the job of developing the specification for the new ferries. They were much larger than those built for the Lillebælt, 77m long, with two tracks on deck providing capacity for 16 goods wagons. They would also carry 900 passengers, with suitable saloons for first, second and third class passengers. The crossing time should not be more than one hour and a quarter.

The terminals at Korsør and Nyborg were designed to work efficiently with the ferries. The ferry's bow entered a tapered set of wooden piers which centred the ship to

Færgehavnene, Korsør.

the loading bridge. The centreline of the loading bridge was 8.85m out from the face of the quay, based on the ferries having an overall breadth of 17.7m. This dimension dictated the ferries' design for nearly 100 years. It was only in 1980 that DSB modified the dock to allow broader ferries. The loading bridge was supported on wire ropes from a lattice gantry structure embellished on top with DSB's winged wheel and crown. The two tracks were gauntleted to restrict the width of the bridge but avoid any need for switching.

The contract for the two ferries was placed with Kockums Mekaniska Verkstads in Malmö with the shipyard responsible for the detailed design. Busse had proposed that the paddle wheels should be able to be operated independently to improve manoeuvrability but this was lost in the final design.

The two ferries were delivered in November 1883, named *Korsør* and *Nyborg*. They were impressive ships. Double-ended, with the bridge in the centre and two funnels, forward and aft of the bridge. The wheelhouse had a distinctive pagoda roof, with a gold crown on the top. There were three lifeboats each side and a gross tonnage of 945. Two 2-cylinder steam engines, developing 1,200 hp, drove 6m diameter paddle wheels. This gave a service speed of 13 knots and a crossing time of around one hour and eight minutes. Below the train deck were passenger saloons, a ladies' room, dining room and galley.

The ferries were double ended, similar to the small ferries previously built for the Lillebælt, and loaded over the bow at one port and stern at the other. However, the paddles were curved and thus worked more efficiently in one direction. As the crossing took more than an hour, the extra speed from going in the efficient direction was worth the time lost to turn the ferry and always make the crossing with the same end as the bow.

The service was a great success and transported 4,689 wagons in the first year of operation and over 10,000 in the second year. In 1885, the two state owned railway companies were merged to form a single national railway, Det danske Statsbaner (DSB), with Niels Holst as the Director-General. One of his early decisions was to order a third ferry for the Storebælt in February 1886. The contract was placed with Burmeister & Wain

Top: The *Nyborg* was the second Storebælt ferry built in 1883 by Kockums in Malmö. *(Author's collection)*

Left: A postcard of Korsør harbour around 1907 showing the ferry berth and gantry, with *Nyborg* on the left. *(Museet for søfarts)*

Middle left: The paddle ferries always struggled in the ice and the *Jylland* was built in 1894 as an icebreaking ferry for the Storebælt. *(Museet for søfarts)*

Bottom left: As traffic increased between Kørsor and Nyborg, the *Store-Bælt* was added in 1900. *(Museet for søfarts)*

The **Store-Bælt** and the **Sjælland** in Korsør harbour in the first years of the 20th century. *(Museet for søfarts)*

The **Christian IX**, built in 1908 was radical change from the older ferries. The enclosed superstructure, upper passenger decks and forward bridge followed the design of the Prins Christian of 1903. *(Museet for søfarts)*

in København and the *Sjælland* was delivered in August 1887, virtually a replica of two earlier ferries. Over the next century DSB would build a further twenty train ferries in Denmark specifically for the Storebælt service.

As had been learned at the Lillebælt, ice and paddle wheels don't mix well, so the next ship built for the Storebælt was an icebreaker ferry. The *Jylland* was delivered by Burmeister & Wain in 1894, she was shorter than the three existing ferries and could carry 10-11 goods wagons on two tracks. She had a distinctive look with only one tall central funnel and of course screw propellers, rather than paddle wheels. The *Jylland* served in the DSB fleet for 58 years, renamed *Fenris* in 1933,

she was only sold for scrap in 1952.

Traffic continued to increase and a fourth paddle ferry, the *Store-Bælt*, was built by Burmeister & Wain in 1900. She was similar in design to *Sjælland*, though slightly longer, 85m as opposed to 76m. The four paddle ferries and the *Jylland* operated together for the next eight years before further capacity was needed.

During the first decade of the 20th century DSB had a major programme of lengthening many of its existing ferries. This mostly affected the smaller ferries, but in 1909 it was decided to lengthen the *Sjælland*, from 76 to 89m, by installing two 6m sections one forward and one aft of the machinery space. Inevitably the ship was slower than before, but it also gained a reputation for being very difficult to manoeuvre and was referred to as the 'storebælts skræk', (storebælt fright).

The design of the next two ships was a big step forward. *Christian IX* and *Odin* were delivered in 1908 and 1910 respectively, again products of Burmeister & Wain in København. Paddles had gone, they had screw propellers and an extended superstructure, so that the bridge was forward of the two funnels. Their design also abandoned the concept of being double ended, although they could load and unload at both ends, they had a defined bow and stern and a single navigating bridge forward and smaller docking bridge aft. *Christian IX* and *Odin* were also larger, 89m long, 17.7m breadth with gross tonnage of 1,503. Their two steam engines developed 2,260 hp and gave a service speed of 15 knots. In practice it was found easier to manoeuvre the ferries into the dock bow first, so after a few years they

STORABELT FERRY.

TRAFFIC DEVELOPMENT FROM 1883 TO 1903.

YEAR.

1883   1888   1893   1898   1903

700,000 Pas.
350,000,000 Kg.

600,000 Pas.
300,000,000 Kg.

500,000 Pas.
250,000,000 Kg.

400,000 Pas.
200,000,000 Kg.

300,000 Pas.
150,000,000 Kg.

200,000 Pas.
100,000,000 Kg.

100,000 Pas.
50,000,000 Kg.

- - - - - = *Passengers.*

———— = *Goods.*

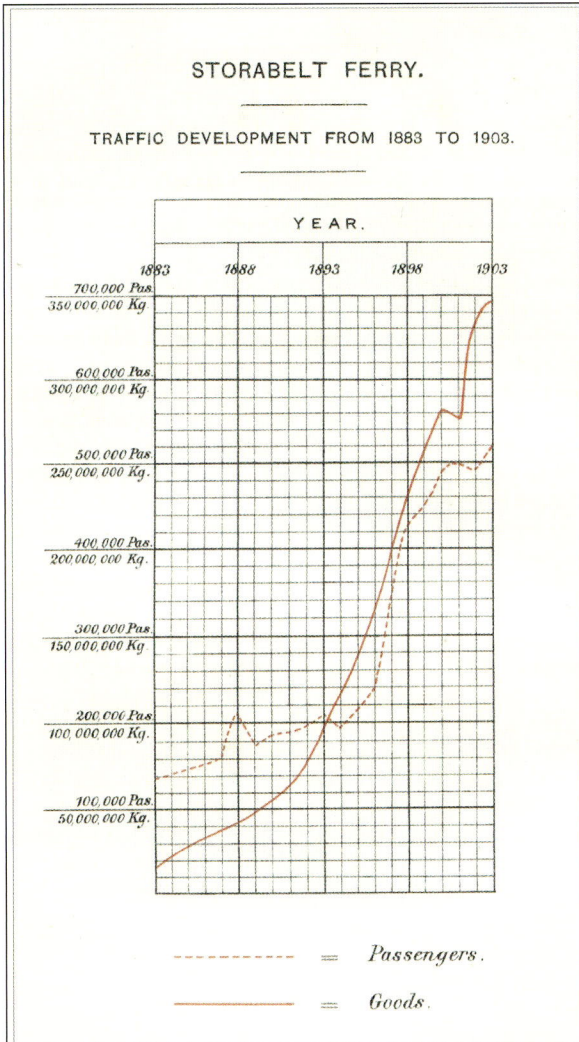

were only loaded and unloaded over the bow. In 1926, *Christian IX* and *Odin* were modified so that the tracks on their decks ran parallel to the stern, which added around 14m track capacity.

The Storebælt service had reached a plateau and continued in a largely steady state from 1910 through to the mid-1920s, with its mix of seven paddle and screw ferries: *Korsør, Nyborg, Jylland, Sjælland, Store-Bælt, Christian IX* and *Odin*. The *Kjøbenhavn* was retired from the Malmö route in 1923 and moved to the Storebælt until she was scrapped in 1931. The two old paddle ferries, *Korsør* and *Nyborg* were retired and scrapped in 1923 and 1927.

The first diesel ferries

The *Korsør* and *Nyborg* were replaced by two new ferries, reusing their names. The *Korsør* (II) was delivered by Helsingør Skibsværft A/S in 1927. She was larger than the previous ferries, both longer at 96.8m, but also with three lines of tracks on deck, giving capacity for 30 goods wagons as well as 1,500 passengers. The biggest change was in the machinery, with two Burmeister & Wain diesel engines rather than steam. *Korsør* (II) was DSB's first diesel ferry and took advantage of Burmeister & Wain's experience as pioneers of motor ships, since building the cargo ship *Selandia* in 1912. After *Korsør* (II), all Danish ferries were diesel powered.

With *Korsør's* three lines of track, the loading bridges at Korsør and Nyborg were modified to have three, rather than two gauntleted tracks. This led to the connections at the bow and stern of the older ferries being modified so that their two tracks aligned with the

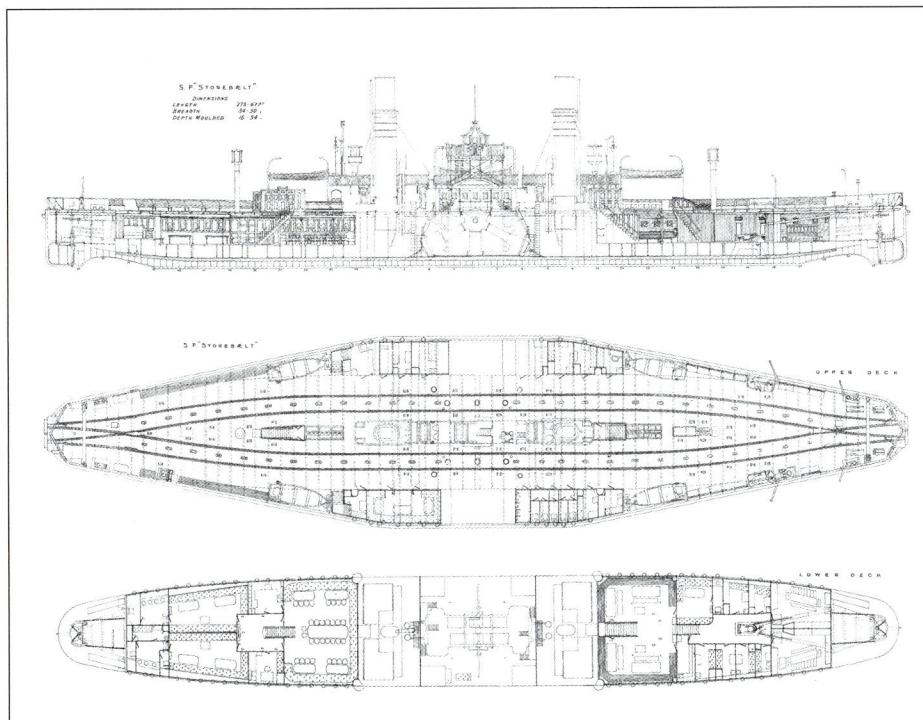

Top left: Graph showing the increase of passenger and goods traffic on the Storebælt from 1883 to 1903. *(The Channel Ferry)*

Left: Plans of the main and lower decks of the **Store-Bælt**, showing the two tracks gauntleted at bow and stern. The difference in breadth between the two decks shows the width of the paddle sponsons. *(Institution of Eng. & Shipbuilders in Scotland)*

The **Christian IX** was rebuilt after the war and was the last steam ferry on the Storebælt when retired in 1964. *(Museet for søfarts)*

The **Christian IX** hit a mine on the 20th April 1940 and sank on the Nygrund near Korsør. She was raised and returned to service the following year. *(Museet for søfarts)*

The **Korsør** entered service in 1927 and was the first large ferry in Europe to be diesel powered. *(Museet for søfarts)*

outside tracks on the loading bridges. *Korsør* was soon followed by two very similar ferries, *Nyborg* (II) in 1931 and *Sjælland* (II) in 1933, both from Helsingør Skibsværft. They were similar to *Korsør*, but 6m longer at 102.8m and could carry an extra wagon on each track, 33 in total. The old *Sjælland* was sold for scrapping 1933.

By the end of the 1920s, there was a growing number of private motor cars crossing the Storebælt. The old train ferries were not very suitable as the rail tracks limited the number of cars that could be carried on deck. The railways may also have resisted the competition. This frustration led to members of the Forenede Danske Motorejere, (Federation of Danish Motorists) deciding to build and operate a dedicated car

ferry. They formed a company, Motorjernes Færgefart A/S, (The Motor Owners Ferry Company) and ordered a diesel car ferry from Aalborg Værft. DSB woke up to the need to address this market and as a stopgap converted the old *Store-Bælt* to a car ferry in 1930. They also agreed to take over the new car ferry and build dedicated car ferry terminals at Korsør and Nyborg. The *Heimdal* was delivered in 1930, with capacity for 55 cars and 600 passengers. A second car ferry, *Freia*, was ordered from Helsingør Skibsværft and delivered in 1936 to run alongside the *Heimdal*. The old *Store-Bælt* was finally laid-up and scrapped 1938. Unlike *Heimdal* which was purely a car ferry, *Freia* was designed to fit into the DSB train ferry docks and had a single line of rail track laid on the car deck. This allowed her to carry a three-

The **Nyborg** manoeuvring in ice, she was delivered in 1931 as a sistership to **Korsør**. (Museet for søfarts)

carriage 'Lyntog' express train as back-up to the main train ferries.

DSB had one last ferry delivered before the war. A new *Storebælt* was delivered by Helsingør Skibsværft in 1939. Although her size and capacity were similar to the previous diesel ferries, she had a new modern look. The superstructure was more enclosed and instead of twin funnels side by side, the *Storebælt* had two large funnels, one in front of the other, in the style of a 1930s ocean liner.

The Second World War

When the German army invaded Denmark in April 1940, DSB had a fleet of eight ferries on the Storebælt, the six main train ferries: *Christian IX, Odin, Korsør, Nyborg, Sjælland* and *Storebælt*, plus the *Freia* and the old icebreaker *Jylland*, which had been renamed *Fenris* in 1933. While the seven ferries on the route in 1920 had a combined capacity of 928 track metres (116 x 8m goods wagons), the capacity of the eight ferries on the Storebælt in 1940 was 1,464 track metres, (180 wagons).

The occupation was not without incident. *Christian IX* hit a mine while crossing the Storebælt on the 20th April 1940. The crew managed to ground her on the Nygrund sandbank where she sank in around 8m of water. She was raised and towed to Nakskov for temporary repair, then taken round to København to be fully repaired, returning to service in June 1941.

The ferry *Orehoved* was moved from the Storstrømmen to make the night mail crossings. This was a dangerous duty as it wasn't possible to keep a lookout for mines in the dark. As *Orehoved* plodded across the Storebælt at 10.5 knots, she was jokingly nicknamed the 'Nacht Jäger', (Night Hunter), after the Luftwaffe's Ju88 fast fighter.

On the 3rd November 1943 the *Sjælland* was sabotaged by German collaborators, two bombs with time-delay fuses exploded during a crossing to Korsør. The ferry managed to reach port safely, but three people were killed and the superstructure was badly damaged by fire. She was out of service until after the war.

Christian IX, Orehoved and Freia were all seized by the German Navy in October 1944 and used as naval auxiliaries in Norway. Fortunately, they were all liberated intact in 1945, though *Christian IX* was badly damaged, and returned to Denmark for refurbishment. *Storebælt* could have suffered the same fate but she was hi-jacked by Danish resistance fighters in November 1944, on a voyage from Korsør round to København for docking. To avoid her being taken by the German Navy, they diverted *Storebælt* into the neutral Swedish port of Hälsingborg where she remained until the end of the war.

Denmark was liberated in May 1945 and the *Storebælt* returned from Sweden. Almost immediately DSB placed a contract to build a sistership. *Fyn* was delivered by Burmeister & Wain in København in April 1947. In the meantime, the fire damaged *Sjælland* had been rebuilt from the hull up at Nakskov Skibsværft. The old side by side funnels had gone and her new superstructure resembled the *Storebælt* when she was redelivered in October 1945. The last of the two-funnel 'Storebælt style' ferries was the *Dronning Ingrid*, delivered by Helsingør Skibsværft in 1951. The old *Odin* was scrapped in 1947 and the icebreaker *Fenris* was laid-up after the 1947-48 winter season, leaving the refurbished *Christian IX* as the last steam ferry on the Storebælt.

The number of cars being carried across the

A postcard of the **Storebælt** from 1940, showing her 'ocean-liner' style with wide funnels and rounded superstructure.

The **Sjælland** (II), built in 1933, being broken out of the ice by the Government icebreaker Storebjørn in 1942. *(Museet for søfarts)*

Storebælt continued to increase through the 1950s. To reduce congestion at the old railway ports, DSB opened new ferry terminals at Knudshoved and Halsskov in 1957 so that the car ferries could run in parallel with the old rail crossing between Korsør and Nyborg. A large car ferry, the *Halsskov* was delivered for this route in 1956.

The next train ferry built for the Korsør – Nyborg service had a distinctive 'fifties' look, similar to many passenger and car ferries built around Scandinavia.

Prinsesse Benedikte was delivered by Helsingør Skibsværft in 1959. She had a single rounded funnel, raked masts and a streamlined shape to the forward superstructure and wheelhouse. The dimensions and capacity were very similar to the earlier ships, though her two B&W 750-VF-90 diesels developed 8,700 hp, and a service speed of 18 knots, compared with the 5,450 hp and 16 knots of the older 'Storebælt style' ships.

The 1960's started with eight train ferries on the Storebælt. The old steam *Christian IX*, the *Korsør*, and *Nyborg* from the 1920s, the four ocean liner styled ferries; *Storebælt, Sjælland, Fyn* and *Dronning Ingrid* and the new *Prinsesse Benedikte*. The *Freia* was still around, though used only as a car ferry. The combined capacity was 1,927 track metres (234 goods wagons), up from 1,464m in 1940 and double what was available in the 1920s. DSB's timetable in summer 1961 showed 12 return sailings daily between Korsør and Nyborg and 18 between Halsskov and Knudshoved, with extra sailings at weekends.

The old *Christian IX* was sold in 1964 after 56 years' service. She spent a year sailing between the Swedish mainland and Öland, renamed *Borgholm*, before being scrapped in 1965. Four large new ferries were built based on the *Halsskov* design. The *Arveprins Knud* was a

DE DANSKE STATSBANER
TOGFORBINDELSER
til og fra UDLANDET.

The **Storebælt** was delivered in 1939, just before the outbreak of the Second World War. *(Author)*

pure car ferry. *Knudshoved* and *Sprogø* were combined train and car ferries. The fourth ship, the *Asa Thor* was designed purely to carry goods wagons with no facilities for cars or passengers. All the ferries had a similar look. The same single rounded funnel as the *Prinsesse Benedikte*, but without her elegant look. They were designed to dock at the two-level linkspans at Halsskov and Knudshoved. The result was square bow doors, which opened sideways, rather than a traditional ship-shaped bow with a lifting visor. The superstructures still had rounded corners but had a much more vertical and industrial appearance than the *Prinsesse Benedikte*. *Knudshoved* and *Sprogø* were sisterships from Helsingør Skibsværft, delivered in 1961 and 1962. Similar in dimensions and rail capacity to the earlier train ferries but with an additional car deck above the main rail deck. This allowed them to be used on the Halsskov – Knudshoved service during the day, carrying trucks on the main deck and around 200 cars on the upper car deck. At night they could carry 30 rail wagons between Korsør and Nyborg.

The *Asa Thor* was much more distinctive. Long and low, with very little superstructure, it was the first DSB ferry built at the Nakskov Skibsværft. Without the need to access passenger coaches, she had four tracks on the main deck, compared with three on the other ships. This gave it capacity for up to 50 rail wagons. The stern was

The superstructure of the **Sjælland** burned-out after bombs exploded on the 3rd November 1943. *(Museet for søfarts)*

open and with no passengers she was able to transport dangerous goods.

The 1970s saw two new ferries on the Storebælt. The *Dronning Margrethe II* and *Prins Henrik* were delivered by Nakskov Skibsværft in 1973 and 74. They maintained the standard dimensions of the previous ferries with three rail tracks on the main deck, but with a ship-shaped bow and lifting visor, had a more traditional look. The funnel was squared off and the superstructure had more glass than the 1960s ships. With the new ships in operation the old pre-war *Sjælland* was taken out of

The *Sjælland* (II) reversing into the dock at Korsør sometime in the 1950s. The three gauntleted tracks can be clearly seen. *(Museet for søfarts)*

service in 1974. More remarkably, the old *Korsør* and *Nyborg* were still working. *Nyborg* was reclassified as a goods ferry in 1975 and finally withdrawn and sold for scrap in 1979. *Korsør* had been re-engined in 1967 and was only withdrawn from service in 1980, after 53 years' service. There was an attempt to preserve her as a museum ship, but this fell through and the following year she was towed to Spain for scrapping.

The 'Inter-City' ferries

The last three ships for the Storebælt were ordered in 1978. DSB were operating hourly inter-city trains and as train lengths grew the existing ferries were barely coping. Danish shipyards were also struggling to survive the downturn in the shipbuilding industry, so there was political backing for placing new orders. The first two 'inter-city' ferries, *Dronning Ingrid* (II) from Helsingør Skibsværft and *Prins Joachim* from Nakskov Skibsværft

The growth of the Storebælt ferries

	Year built	Gross tonnage	Length (m)	Breadth (m)	No. of tracks	Track length
Korsør	1883	945	77.4	17.7	2	123
Christian IX	1908	1,510	88.9	17.7	2	157
Korsør (II)	1927	2,398	96.8	17.7	3	242
Fyn	1947	2,941	107.8	17.7	3	260
Dronning Margrethe II	1973	5,623	132.7	17.7	3	309
Dronning Ingrid (II)	1980	10,607	152.0	23.1	4	494

The **Dronning Ingrid**, delivered in 1951, was the last two-funnel ferry following the' 'Storebælt-style'. *(Author)*

The **Dronning Ingrid**, was retired in 1982, but was renamed **Sjælland** (III) for her last few years, as her name was re-used by a new ferry. *(Author)*

Aerial view of Nyborg port, with either the **Korsør** or **Nyborg** docked. *(Museet for søfarts)*

The **Asa Thor**, delivered in 1965, was unique amongst the Storebælt ferries in carrying only freight wagons. Without the need to provide space for passengers, she had four tracks on deck compared with three on the other ferries. *(Paul Haywood)*

were delivered in 1980. Their general appearance was similar to the *Dronning Margrethe II* and *Prins Henrik*, delivered seven years earlier, though they were more box-shaped and squat. The square corners at the forward end of the superstructure extended out beyond the hull. More significantly, the new ferries were much larger, the size of the Storebælt ferries had grown steadily over a century, but these last three ships provided a step change in capacity.

The increased breadth was particularly important. Every Storebælt ferry since the first *Korsør* in 1883 had followed Otto Busse's standard overall breadth of 17.7m in order to fit the train docks. New docks were required to accommodate the ferries' breadth. The new loading bridges were also much wider with two parallel tracks allowing two trains to load simultaneously compared with the old bridges with three gauntleted tracks.

The Storebælt train ferry fleet peaked in 1980 with twelve ferries on the crossing, as well as several car ferries. The old *Korsør* was in her last year. The pre-war

Top left: The ***Dronning Ingrid*** discharging at Korsør.. *(Museet for søfarts)*

Middle left: An aerial view of Korsør port, with ***Korsør*** and ***Nyborg*** docked and ***Freia*** reversing out. *(Museet for søfarts)*

Bottom left: The train deck on ***Prinsesse Benedikte,*** showing the three gauntleted tracks. *(Museet for søfarts)*

Above: The ***Prinsesse Benedikte*** was delivered by Helsingør Skibsværft in 1959. She brought a new look with a single rounded funnel and raked masts. *(Author's collection)*

Storebælt and her later sisters *Fyn* and *Dronning Ingrid* (now renamed *Sjælland*) were still operating, together with the *Prinsesse Benedikte, Knudshoved, Sprogø, Asa Thor, Dronning Margrethe II, Prins Henrik* and the brand new *Dronning Ingrid* and *Prins Joachim*. A combined capacity of 3,787 track metres (464 goods wagons), nearly twice the capacity in 1960.

The third and last 'inter-city' ferry, the *Kronprins Frederik*, was delivered from Nakskov Skibsværft in

1981. The pre-war *Storebælt* had been laid-up in 1980 and was sold the following year to be used as a barge. *Fyn* was laid-up in 1981. She made a few temporary trips between København and Malmö the following year and was sold in 1985. The *Sjælland* (ex *Dronning Ingrid*) was laid-up in 1982. Like *Fyn* she made a few temporary trips between København and Malmö and was then laid up in København and used as a music venue, restaurant and museum between 1984 and 2002. Sold on as a restaurant and disco ship, she was berthed in Tilbury and later Barrow in Furness before finally being scrapped in 2015.

It had taken the Danish Government ten years to decide on the Storebælt ferry in the 1860s. The discussion on replacing it with a fixed link, either tunnel, bridge or both, had continued for over fifty years before a final decision was made in 1986. The Storebæltsforbindelsen (Storebælt Fixed Link) provides a combination of tunnel and bridge to link road and rail across 18km of sea. Construction started in 1988 and

Top: The **Knudshoved** was built by Helsingør Skibsværft in 1961. She was a combined car and train ferry and followed the design of the earlier car ferry Halsskov. *(Author's collection)*

Middle left: The **Prins Henrik** followed the **Dronning Margrethe II** from the Nakskov Skibsværft in 1974. These two new ships allowed the last pre-war ferries to be retired. *(Tony Garner)*

Left: The Inter-City train to København, IC 932, arriving at Nyborg with the **Dronning Ingrid** waiting to load in 1994. *(Lolke Bijlsma)*

Above: The **Sprogø** followed her sistership **Knudshoved** from Helsingør Skibsværft in 1962. They were designed to sail on either of the Storebælt routes, between Korsør and Nyborg as train ferries or on the parallel car ferry service between Halsskov and Knudshoved. *(Author's collection)*

The *Dronning Ingrid* was delivered in 1980, the first of three 'Inter-City' (IC) ferries which were the last and largest built for the Storebælt. *(Bruce Peter)*

The old **Kong Frederik IX** spent her last few years as relief ship on the Storebælt. The towers of the Storebælt Bridge rising behind her. *(Bruce Peter)*

The second IC ferry, the *Prins Joachim* was delivered by Nakskov Skibsværft. The ferries had a breadth of 23.7m, the first to break Otto Busse's standard of 17.7m from 1883. *(Bruce Peter)*

The last of the IC ferries, the *Kronprins Frederik* arriving at Korsør during her last season on the Great Belt. *(Miles Cowsill)*

Above: Unloading one of the new IC3 diesel inter-city trains from the *Kronprins Frederik* in the early 1990s. *(Miles Cowsill)*

Left: The new wider linkspans for the *Dronning Ingrid* and the other IC ferries had two parallel tracks. This speeded-up loading compared to the old gauntleted tracks. *(Andreas Keller)*

The *Kong Frederik IX* was laid-up along with the other Storebaelt ferries after the bridge opened in 1997. There were plans to preserve her as a museum ship, but these fell through and she was scrapped in 2005. *(Bruce Peter)*

The Storebaelt Bridge under constuction in the mid-1990s with DSB's car ferry **Arveprins Knud** in the foreground, crossing between Halsskov and Knudshoved. *(Bruce Peter)*

the railway link opened on the 1st June 1997, the road link a year later.

With the fixed link on its way, ownership of DSB's ferry operations was transferred to a holding company, DSB Rederi A/S in 1995, with Ministry of Transport as the sole shareholder. This was renamed Scandlines Danmark A/S and took control of DSB's remaining ferries on the 1st January 1997.

The opening of the fixed link was the end of an era and the seven train ferries on the crossing were laid-up. The *Knudshoved* and the *Asa-Thor* were sold for scrapping in 1997. The *Sprogø* was sold to Saudi Arabia and operated in the Red Sea until scrapped in 2004. The old *Kong Frederik IX* was sold for conversion to a

museum ship. Several groups tried and failed to raise the necessary funding and she was eventually sold for scrapping in 2005.

The three large 'inter-city' ferries have survived. *Dronning Ingrid* was sold to a charity and converted to a hospital ship in Newcastle. She started her new life as the *Africa Mercy* in 2007 providing surgery and medical care in West Africa. *Prins Joachim* and *Kronprins Frederik* remained with Scandlines and operated as vehicle ferries between Gedser and Rostock until 2016. The *Prins Joachim* was then sold to Greek owners and the *Kronprins Frederik* remained as Scandlines reserve ferry between Rødbyhavn and Puttgarden.

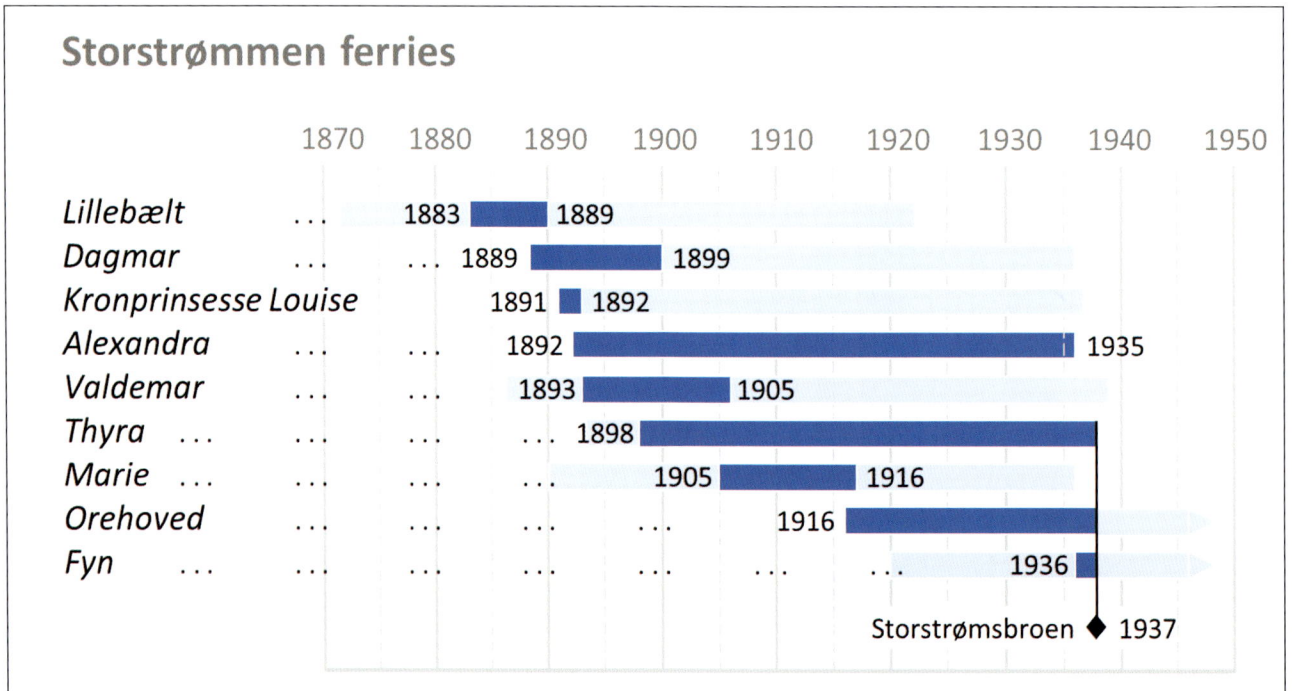

Storstrømmen ferries

	1870	1880	1890	1900	1910	1920	1930	1940	1950
Lillebælt		1883 — 1889							
Dagmar		1889 — 1899							
Kronprinsesse Louise		1891 — 1892							
Alexandra		1892 —————————————— 1935							
Valdemar		1893 — 1905							
Thyra		1898 —————————————————							
Marie		1905 — 1916							
Orehoved		1916 ———————————							
Fyn		1936 ▸							
					Storstrømsbroen ◆ 1937				

Storstrømmen

Det sjællandske Statsbaner	**1884-1885**
Det danske Statsbaner	**1885-1937**
Masnedø – Orehoved	**1884-1937**

The railway from København, west to Roskilde, then south to Vordingborg was completed by the Sjællandske Jerbane-Selskab, (Sjælland Railway Company) in 1870. The company also had the concession to continue the railway on the prosperous island of Falster, from the port of Orehoved to the main town of Nykøbing-Falster. Due to delays, this part of the railway was taken over by the Lolland-Falsterske Jerbane-Selskab and opened in 1872.

Initially the connection between the two railways was made by passenger steamer from Vordingborg to Orehoved, a crossing of around 7 km, but as always this involved trans-shipping goods and mail between the train and the steamer. In 1880, the Sjælland railway came under Government control and the proposal to introduce a train ferry was approved by Parliament in 1881. The plan was to reduce the crossing distance to around 3.7 km by extending the railway from Vordingborg to the little offshore island of Masnedø, directly opposite Orehoved. The railway and the bridge to Masnedø, plus the ferry ports on either side were completed by 1883.

After being released from the Lillebælt crossing, the *Lillebælt* was initially transferred to north Jylland to open the Oddesund crossing. After only six months she was replaced and moved south again, arriving at Masnedø in December 1883, ready to start the new Storstrømmen service at the beginning of 1884. The *Lillebælt* operated the crossing for its first five years. In 1889, she moved to Sallingsund and was replaced by a larger ferry, the *Dagmar*, newly built by Burmeister & Wain in København and a single-track paddle steamer very similar to *Ingeborg*.

In 1891, *Dagmar* was briefly joined by the brand new *Kronprinsesse Louise*. She was built for the new Helsingør crossing and only stayed a few months, leaving in March 1892, when the *Alexandra* arrived. *Alexandra* was newly built by Burmeister & Wain in Københaven, a single-track paddle steamer, 54m in length, with a single-2-cylinder steam engine of 440 hp. As always, paddle steamers had trouble with ice in the winter, so the icebreaking ferry *Valdemar* arrived from Oddesund to join the *Dagmar* and *Alexandra* in 1893.

Alexandra's sister ship the *Thyra* had been built in 1893 but was sent to the Helsingør service until replaced by the *Kronprins Frederik*. In 1898, *Thyra* came to the Storstrømmen replacing the *Dagmar*, which went to the Lillebælt.

From 1898, the two sisterships *Alexandra* and *Thyra* settled down to be the backbone of the service for the next forty years, with an icebreaking ferry in reserve. However, there was a major increase in traffic in 1903

The *Dagmar* was the first new ferry on the Storstrømmen crossing in 1889, having been operated since 1884 by the Lillebælt. *(Museet for søfarts)*

The *Alexandra* was built for the service in 1892. Like all paddlers, she and *Dagmar* had trouble in the ice and were soon joined by the *Valdemar*. *(Museet for søfarts)*

with the opening of the Warnemünde to Gedser ferry service. As well as the local traffic from Falster, the ferries had to cope with the through trains and sleeper service between Berlin and København. Rather than build new ferries, DSB decided to lengthen *Alexandra* and *Thyra* by around 11m, increasing their capacity by nearly 20%. The ferries went to Københavns Flydedok where they were cut immediately forward of the engine room and a new section installed. The infill section also included a new third-class saloon below the deck.

The lengthening was a success, particularly as the slight reduction in speed was not of great importance on a short crossing. As a result, the Lillebælt ferries and the icebreaking ferry *Marie* were also lengthened at Københavns Flydedok. *Marie* was also fitted with three new engines with an output of 800 hp and arrived at Storstrømmen in 1905 and replaced the *Valdemar*, which returned to the Lillebælt.

A third ferry, the *Orehoved* was built for the crossing

Orehoved. Dam

the closure of the Lillebælt crossing. *Fyn* moved to the Storstrømmen and the *Alexandra* was sold for scrapping in 1935. By this time, the Storstrøm bridge was under construction and the ferry service was in its last years. The bridge opened in September 1937 and the ferries were redundant. The old *Thyra* was scrapped after 44 years' service. *Fyn* went to the Helsingør crossing and *Orehoved* was laid-up and later moved to the Storebælt.

North Jylland

De jysk-fyenske Jernbaner	**1883-1885**
Det danske Statsbaner	**1885-1938**
Oddesund Syd – Nord	**1883-1938**

The north western part of Jylland is not normally considered an island, however from Thyboron in the west across to Aalborg on the east coast, this part of

Top left: Passengers disembarking from the **Alexandra** at Orehoved ferry station on the island of Falster. *(Author's collection)*

Middle left: The **Thyra** was built in 1903 as a sistership to Alexandra, seen here drydocked in København, around 1922. *(Museet for søfarts)*

Bottom left: A postcard showing the **Orehoved** at her namesake port. She was built in 1916 and the first screw ferry on the crossing. *(Author's collection)*

Above: The **Fyn** was moved to Storstrømmen when the Lillebælt bridge opened in 1935 but only two years later, the ferries were replaced by the Storstrømmen bridge in 1937. *(Author's collection)*

Jylland is completely separated by water. In the latter part of the 19th century, the only link was a pontoon bridge at Aalborg. To provide a connection in the west, the Thybanen railway between Struer and Thisted was inaugurated in April 1882. However, the line was split in the middle by the ferry crossing at Oddesund. At its narrowest point, the crossing over the Oddesund is only about 400m and originally the railway had intended to build a bridge. However, this was soon dropped due to the cost.

The existing ferries were small open boats and with strong tidal currents and exposure to the North Sea winds, the crossing was often unpleasant and

in 1916 by Helsingør Skibsværft. She was a larger ship, 68.7m long, but still the same breadth, a single rail track and powered by two 2-cylinder steam engines. Most importantly, she was a screw ferry and able to operate as an icebreaker in winter, which allowed the *Marie* to move to Sallingsund.

The three ferries worked together for 19 years, until the *Fyn*, a close sister to *Orehoved*, became free after occasionally dangerous. The railway proposed to provide a steam ferry, but this soon ran into local opposition. Like many ferry crossings, the Oddesund ferries were operated under a Royal Concession which had been in place for many generations. The owner of the Concession, Dorothea Krizsau, challenged the railway company's proposals and took her case all the way to the Supreme Court, where she won. A settlement must have been negotiated as the railway company's plan went ahead and by June 1883 the ferry ports were completed.

The Oddesund crossing started using the *Lillebælt*, which had been released from the Lillebælt crossing. The main export from north Jylland was peat, and by the time *Lillebælt* arrived around 200 wagon loads were waiting to be transported. However, *Lillebælt* was just a stopgap and after only six months she was transferred south to the Storstrømmen. She was replaced by the *Fredericia* which operated alone for six years until joined by the *Ingeborg*. Together these two ferries would operate the Oddesund crossing for nearly 40 years.

The icebreaker *Valdemar* joined them in 1890 for three years, but it was soon sent to the more important crossing at Storstrømmen. When she was replaced there in 1919, *Valdemar* returned to Oddesund and remained there until 1938.

The 45-year-old *Fredericia* was sold for scrapping in 1922, but she was rescued by A/S Mommark Færge and served as their reserve ferry until finally scrapped in 1926. The old *Kronprins Frederik* arrived at Oddesund in 1933 and allowed the *Ingeborg* to be sold for scrapping. By this time the plan for an Oddesund bridge had been approved, though it was six years before it opened in May 1938.

Once the bridge opened, the old *Kronprins Frederik*

was sold for scrapping. The *Valdemar* was even older and as all the smaller DSB ferry routes had screw ships, an icebreaker was no longer required. She was transferred to the Statens Istjenste (State Ice Service) and served as an icebreaker in the Limfjorden until 1959, when she finally retired after 73 years' service.

Det danske Statsbaner
Sallingsund : Glyngøre – Nykøbing Mors. 1889-1977

De jysk-fyenske Jernbaner completed its line from Skive north to Glyngøre in 1884. At a dinner in Nykøbing Mors to celebrate the new railway its Director, Niels Holst, declared his intention to establish a railway ferry across the Sallingsund to bring railway wagons from Glyngøre directly to Nykøbing and the island of Mors. However, despite the good intentions, Nykøbing was a small town and the focus on developing new ferries continued elsewhere. It was five years later, when Niels Holst was in his new job as Director-General of the DSB that the ferry came into being.

The *Lillebælt* had been sailing on the Storstrømmen since 1884 and was replaced by the new larger ferry *Dagmar* in 1889. This let the little *Lillebælt* come north and open its fourth service, where she would stay for 33 years until the end of her career. As always, paddle ferries struggled in the ice so when the *Marie* became redundant at Storstrømmen in 1916, she was transferred to the Sallingsund.

The *Hjalmar* arrived in 1919 and after a few years in reserve, the old *Lillebælt* was scrapped in 1922. The end of Denmark's first train ferry and after 50 years' service, the only one that was never fitted with electric lighting.

After more than 40 years of second-hand ferries, the

Dampfærgen Nyköbing—Mors

Top left: The *Lillebælt* at Nykøbing Mors, she worked the crossing for 33 years. *(Museet for søfarts)*

Top right: After retiring as a train ferry, the *Hvalpsund* continued as a car ferry until 1980. *(Author)*

Middle right: The *Morsø* was built in 1933. *(Museet for søfarts)*

Middle left: The *Sønderjylland* operated between Aarøsund and Assen. *(Author's collection)*

Above left: The *Glyngøre*, formerly the *Helsingborg*, was used as the reserve ferry on the Sallingsund crossing from 1946. *(Museet for søfarts)*

Above right: The *Mommark* was the world's first diesel powered train ferry in 1922 . *(Author's collection)*

Right:The *Langeland* was built in 1926 to connect the Langelandsbanen to Fyn. *(Schovfinn)*

Sallingsund ferries

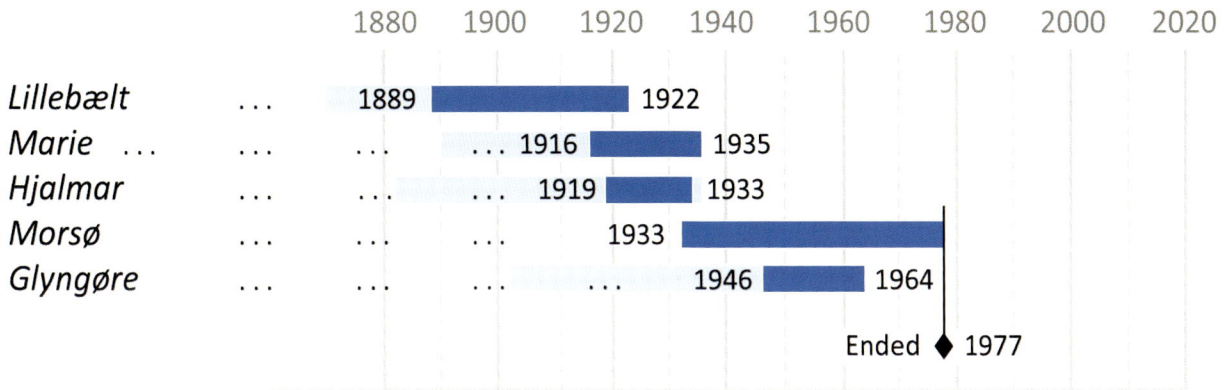

	1880	1900	1920	1940	1960	1980	2000	2020
Lillebælt	... 1889 ━━━━ 1922							
Marie ...	... ... 1916 ━━ 1935							
Hjalmar	... ... 1919 ━ 1933							
Morsø	... ... 1933 ━━━━━━							
Glyngøre	... ... 1946 ━━ 1964							

Ended ◆ 1977

Morsø was specially built for the Sallingsund crossing in 1933. She was delivered by the Nakskov Skibsværft, only 40m long and with capacity for three goods wagons, she was DSB's first small ferry to be diesel powered. With the new ferry in place, the old *Hjalmar* was returned to the Lillebælt as a reserve boat. As *Morsø* was a screw ferry, an icebreaker was no longer required, and the old *Marie* was retired and scrapped.

Morsø operated alone for more than ten years until at the end of the war the *Helsingborg* became redundant. She was renamed *Glyngøre* and came to the Sallingsund in 1946 as reserve ferry, occasionally standing in at Helsingør and other routes. She remained until 1964 when the need for major boiler repairs led to her scrapping and the *Morsø* carried on alone. Passenger services on the Skive to Glyngøre railway stopped in 1971, but she continued with goods traffic until the service was finally closed in 1977. The new Sallingsund road bridge opened in 1978.

Morsø was bought by the community, with plans to preserve her as a museum. However, this did not materialise. A final plan to sell her to America fell through in 1982 and she was sold for scrapping the following year.

A/S Aalborg-Hvalpsund Jernbaneselskab

Hvalpsund – Sundsøre   **1927-1969**

The Aalborg – Hvalpsund Jernbaneselskab was a private railway built across north Jylland. The line from Svenstrup to Aars was opened in 1899 and extended through to Hvalpsund in 1910. In 1925 the railway obtained a concession to operate a ferry between Hvalpsund and Sundsøre. Originally there was a plan to

Oddesund ferries

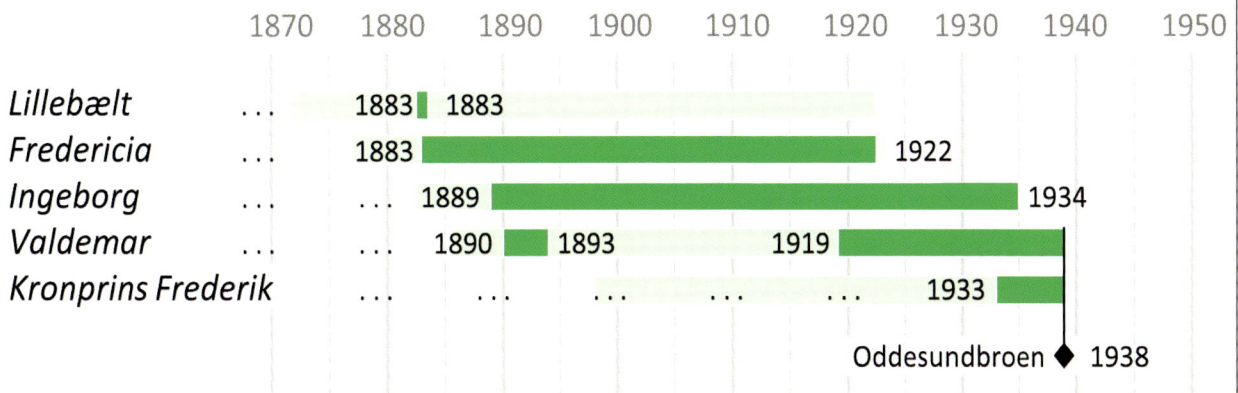

	1870	1880	1890	1900	1910	1920	1930	1940	1950
Lillebælt	... 1883 ▌ 1883								
Fredericia	... 1883 ━━━━━━ 1922								
Ingeborg	... ... 1889 ━━━━━━━ 1934								
Valdemar	... ... 1890 ━ 1893 ━━━ 1919 ━━								
Kronprins Frederik	... ... 1933 ━								

Oddesundbroen ◆ 1938

The *Lolland* was principally a car ferry but carried railway wagons from Langeland to Fyn for a short time until replaced by a bridge in 1962. *(Author's collection)*

The *Ærøskøbing* was old fashioned when she was built in 1955 and only lasted four years before being sold. *(Author's collection)*

extend the railway north from Sundsøre to connect with DSB's Sallingbanen, but this never happened.

The Danish Government approved a grant to establish the ferry in 1925. The railway company ordered a small diesel ferry from Aalborg Skibsværft and the *Hvalpsund* was delivered in May 1927. She was powered by a single Holeby diesel engine and could carry 4 wagons or up to 22 cars. At Sundsøre the railway had a goods siding and a warehouse, where wagons could be loaded and unloaded. There was never much traffic on the railway and the number of wagons declined after the Second World War. The railway eventually went into liquidation and traffic stopped in 1968. The *Hvalpsund* was used as car ferry by the local authorities until 1980, when she was replaced by a more modern ferry.

Southern islands

A/S Lillebæltsoverfarten
Assens – Aarøsund   1923-1950

Denmark got bigger in 1920. The Duchy of Schleswig had been lost to Germany in the 1864 war and a feeling of injustice remained as many people in northern Schleswig spoke and considered themselves Danish. Thus, although Denmark has been neutral during the

First World War, they took their case to the Versailles Peace Conference in 1919, where Europe's boundaries were being redrawn. The result was the Schleswig Plebiscite in 1920, a referendum to determine whether the people of Schleswig wished to be Danish or German. The result was to divide the territory. The southern part remained German, the northern area of Sønderjylland returned to become part of Denmark.

A/S Lillebæltsoverfarten was formed in 1920 to provide a ferry from Assens in the south-west of Fyn to the newly Danish town of Aarøsund in Sønderjylland. The little ferry *Sønderjylland* was built in 1921 by Schmidt-Tüchsen & Hegge, in Laboe, North Germany. She was 27.3m long and 100 gross tons and initially was purely a car and passenger ferry. She was delivered with two 2-cylinder hot-bulb oil engines, which were popular in Scandinavia at the beginning of the 20th century. However, they were not very fuel efficient and were replaced with diesel engines in 1924.

The farming area of Haderslev, inland from Aarøsund, was connected by a rural narrow-gauge railway. A group of farmers proposed extending this railway to connect with the ferry so that wagons of sugar beet could be shipped across to the sugar-factory in Assens. In 1923 the ferry was modified by Aalborg Værft and fitted with a single line of 1000mm narrow-gauge track. The first trip with three wagons of sugar beet took place in October.

This seasonal trade continued uneventfully until the war. The ferry was damaged when it struck a mine on the 22nd October 1942 but was repaired and returned to service the following year. The Haderslev County Railway was largely closed down during the 1930s, but the ferry continued to carry railway wagons until 1950. After this, she continued in service as a car ferry until she was sold to D/S Ærø in 1963 and withdrawn from service.

A/S Mommark Færge   1922-1945
Det danske Statsbaner   1946-1962
Faaborg – Mommark   1922-1962

As with the ferry between Assens and Aarøsund, the reunification of Sønderjylland created a demand to link the island Als to the Danish railway network at Faaborg on the island of Fyn. In 1920 the A/S Mommark Færge was founded as a joint venture between A/S Det sydfyenske Jerbaneselskab, (The South Fyn Railway Co.) and the shipowner Det østasiatisk Kompagni, (The Danish East Asiatic Company). They ordered the ferry *Mommark* from Nakskov Skipsværft, which was delivered in 1922. *Mommark* had two Holeby diesel engines, developing 380 hp, and the first motor train ferry in the world. This was not surprising as the East Asiatic Company had been pioneers of diesel propulsion operating the world's first large diesel ship, the *Selandia*, in 1912. Like the *Selandia*, *Mommark* did not have a

SOUTHERN ISLANDS

funnel, the diesel exhausts were two thin pipes supported by the aft mast. It took another five years before DSB followed with their first diesel ferry, the *Korsør* in 1927.

Mommark loaded over the bow and was unusual in that she had a combination track, capable of taking both standard gauge and narrow-gauge wagons. Transferring wagons from the narrow-gauge lines on Als to the standard gauge on Fyn was difficult, but a system was developed where standard gauge wagons could be pulled up onto a narrow-gauge undercarriage at Mommark, to continue their journey on Als. In 1922, A/S Mommark Færge rescued the old Lillebælt ferry *Fredericia*, built in 1877, from the scrapyard. She was renamed *Fåborg* and kept as reserve ferry until sold for scrapping in 1926.

After around ten years, the narrow-gauge railway on Als began to lose money and most of the network closed down in the early 1930s. However, the direct line from Mommark to the county town of Sønderborg was retained and upgraded to standard gauge in 1933. Apart from times during the war when the ferry was stopped by fuel shortages, the service continued until the end of 1945, when A/S Mommark Færge got into financial difficulties. The ferry and the port facilities were sold to DSB for 1 kr. in March 1946 and DSB continued transporting rail wagons until the Mommark branch line was closed in May 1962. After this, *Mommark* continued as a car ferry until she was sold for scrapping in 1964 and replaced by DSB's new car ferry *Fynshav*. With no need for a railway connection, DSB moved the service to the shorter crossing between Bøden and Fynshav in 1967.

Sydfyenske D/S
Svendborg – Rudkøbing   **1926-1962**

The Danish Government introduced a Railways Act in 1908, under which the state provided grants to develop rural railways. One of these schemes was the Langelandsbanen, which built 33km of line on the island Langeland, connecting the port towns of Rudkøbing, Spodsbjerg and Bagenkop and opening in October 1911.

As with other rural lines, transporting sugar beet was a major source of income and farmers were keen to reduce the cost of sending their crop to the sugar factory at Odense on Fyn. The obvious answer was to provide a train ferry between Langeland and Fyn, but as the Langelandsbanen was a private railway line, DSB had no interest in providing a ferry. In 1925, an agreement was reached between the railway and the Sydfyenske D/S, (South Fyn Steamship Co.) which operated a number of ferries between the southern islands. The Langelandsbanen would build the ferry port and Sydfyenske D/S would provide a ferry.

The ferry *Langeland* was built by Helsingør Skibsværft and delivered in 1926. She was 46.7m long with a single track able to carry four or five wagons and powered by two 2-cylinder steam engines. The ferry had two funnels, port and starboard. These were black and painted with red-white-red bands. At first glance, these looked like the DSB funnels, but were subtly different. On DSB ships the red-white-red bands are the same width. On Sydfyenske D/S ships, the white band is wider than the red bands above and below. Passenger saloons and a dining room were provided under the deck.

The *Langeland* carried a mix of cars, passengers and

131

The *Ærøsund* was built in 1960 and typical of Knud E Hansen ferry designs of the time, with a large dummy funnel and twin exhausts aft. *(Author's collection)*

The *Ærøsund* was the last train ferry to the Southern Islands, the rail service closed in 1995 and she was eventually sunk in 2014 to form a reef for scuba divers. *(Author)*

rail wagons throughout the year, but during the sugar beet season each autumn, up to 1,800 wagons of beet were shipped over to Fyn. The ferry's boilers were converted from coal to oil fuel in 1947 and it continued in service until March 1961, when it was sold for service as the car ferry *Citta di Ischia* in Italy.

Sydfyenske D/S had built the diesel ferry *Lolland* in 1955 for their Nakskov to Spodsbjerg car ferry service. She was similar in size to *Langeland* and had been fitted with a rail line so that it could stand-in on the Svendborg to Rudkøbing crossing. After *Langeland* was sold, *Lolland* continued the service for 18 months until the final crossing on 29th September 1962. The following day the Langelandsbroen was opened, connecting the islands by road bridge, and the Langelandsbanen railway was closed.

Dampskibsselskabet Æro
Svendborg – Ærøskøbing   1931-1995

The farmers on the island of Ærø had seen the benefits enjoyed by their counterparts on Als and Langeland from being able to ship sugar beet directly to the factory by rail. They developed a plan to build 30km of railway on the island and persuaded the shipping company, Dampskibsselskabet Ærø A/S, (Ærø Steamship Co.), to build a train ferry for their Svendborg to Ærøskøbing service. The railway was never built, only a goods yard near Ærøskøbing harbour where wagons brought over on the ferry could be loaded and unloaded.

Ærø was delivered by the Svendborg Skipsværft in 1931. It was a small ferry, 47m long, with two Holeby diesel engines. As with the other ferries to the southern islands, she mostly carried cars and passengers but had a single rail track, with capacity for four or five wagons. In 1951 she was lengthened by 10m. In 1967 she was sold to Yugoslavia and renamed *Ero*, where she served for a further 40 years as a car ferry in the Adriatic, only laid-up in 2007 and scrapped in 2011.

A second ferry *Ærøskøbing* was built by H.C. Christensens Staalskibsværft in Marstal and delivered in 1955. She was 35.2m long, shorter than *Ærø*, and rather old fashioned in design, still having a 'ladies' saloon'. The second ferry had been bought to satisfy the postal contract, but D/S Ærø quickly realised that it was not economic to run two ships in the winter. After only four years' service, *Ærøskøbing* was sold in 1959 for further service in Italy.

D/S Ærø then ordered a much larger and more modern ferry designed by the well-known naval architects Knud E. Hansen. This was the *Ærøsund*, built by Husumer Schiffswerft in Germany and delivered in 1960. She was 57.8m long and primarily a car and passenger ferry, but with a single rail track capable of transporting 5 or 6 wagons. The accommodation was very different from her predecessor, the ladies' saloon had gone, replaced by a TV lounge and a bar inside the dummy funnel.

The goods yard at Ærøskøbing was modernised in 1975, though the rail traffic continued to decline. As there were no locomotives on Ærø, wagons were loaded on and off the ferry by tractor. Most wagons were simply used to move oil, animal feed and similar products between the two ports without connecting to the rail network. The last rail wagon was shipped in 1995, but the ferry continued with cars and passengers until 1999. *Ærøsund* was then laid-up for many years while various plans for her future use came and went. She was eventually sunk off Svendborg in 2014 to form an artificial reef for recreational divers.

Kattegat & Skagerrak

Helsingør to Helsingborg

Det danske Statsbaner	**1892-1991**
Scandlines	**1991-2000**
Helsingør – Helsingborg	**1892-2000**

With the success of the Lillebælt and Storebælt train ferries, the Danish and Swedish Governments set up a committee in 1884 to look at introducing similar ferries on the Øresund, where the crossing between Helsingør and Helsingborg is only around two nautical miles. While both sides could see the benefits, the railways on the west coast of Sweden were owned by five private companies, so Det danske Statsbaner, (DSB), had no clear partner to work with. Eventually DSB took the initiative and introduced a passenger steamer in 1888.

It took some time to get approval for a ferry port in Helsingborg, but it was finally agreed that DSB would introduce a train ferry service. The ferry port at Helsingør was completed in autumn 1891 and a new ferry, the *Kronprinsesse Louise*, was built by Helsingør Skibsværft. She was similar to the *Dagmar* built two years before by Burmeister & Wain and followed DSB's small ferry standard: 54m long, 13.4m across the paddle boxes, double ended with a single track on the centreline. She had the usual passenger accommodation below the train deck: a dining room for 1st and 2nd class passengers, a ladies' saloon and a saloon for 3rd class passengers.

Kronprinsesse Louise was the first of many ships built by the Helsingør Skibsværft for DSB and was diplomatically named for the Swedish princess married to the Danish Kronprins Frederik to emphasise the links between the two countries. She was delivered in 1891, but bureaucratic delays in Sweden meant she spent her first few months on the Storstrømmen crossing.

A Danish station in Sweden

The service was officially started on the 10th March 1882 when DSB's senior officials, together with mail and luggage wagons, crossed from Helsingør to be met by a curious throng in Helsingborg. The wagons were exchanged and the *Kronprinsesse Louise* returned to Helsingør. The service was always run by DSB and in fact

Helsingborg F was a Danish station with a few DSB officials to manage the ferry traffic and ensure goods were properly dispatched to the connecting Swedish railways.

In 1893, *Kronprinsesse Louise* was joined by a near sister ship the *Thyra* built by Burmeister & Wain in København. She remained on the service for five years until the third similar ferry the *Kronprins Frederik* was delivered by the Helsingør Skibsværft in 1898. This allowed the *Thyra* to move to the Storstrømmen crossing, where she remained for the rest of her career.

In 1902 the *Helsingborg* was built by Helsingør Skibsværft. She was the first DSB ferry to have a screw propeller at each end and thus able to sail equally well in both directions. (DSB had previously built the screw ferries *Valdemar* and *Marie* as icebreakers with a propeller at the stern only) As a screw ferry, the *Helsingborg* was also a capable icebreaker in Helsingør and Helsingborg harbours. Though she was found to consume more coal than the paddle ferries. With *Helsingborg's* arrival, the *Kronprinsesse Louise*

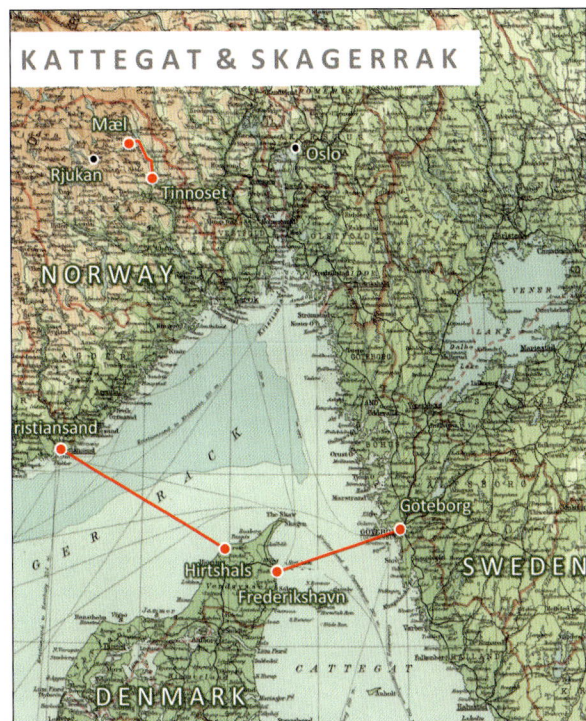

KATTEGAT & SKAGERRAK

Kronprinsesse Louise which had been lengthened by 12m to 64m in 1905 to take the carriages of the Berlin sleeper on the Storstrømmen crossing. This extra length allowed her to transfer the 3rd class passenger carriages on the through trains from København to Göteborg and Kristiania (Oslo). Although she led a largely uneventful life, *Kronprinsesse Louise* was in collision with a British cargo ship the *Chevychase* in 1934, though neither ship was badly damaged.

Dan and *Svea*

With bridges built at the Lillebælt and Storstrømmen in 1935 and 1937, a number of ferries came free. The *Dan* was moved to Helsingør in 1936, allowing the old *Kronprinsesse Louise* to be laid-up, and *Dan's* sistership the *Fyn* arrived in 1937 and was renamed *Svea*. *Dan* and *Svea* were steam screw ferries built in 1921 and 69m

Top: The ***Kronprinsesse Louise*** in Helsingborg harbour. She started the first train ferry service between Denmark and Sweden in 1892. *(Museet for søfarts)*

Above left: ***Kronprinsesse Louise*** leaving Helsingør with the imposing railway station building behind her. *(Museet for søfarts)*

Above: The ***Thyra*** at the Helsingør quay with Kronborg castle in the background. *(Museet for søfarts)*

Left: The ***Kronprins Frederik*** entering Helsingborg harbour, she operated on the Øresund crossing for nearly 30 years. *(Museet for søfarts)*

transferred to the Lillebælt. For the next twenty-five years, the *Helsingborg* and *Kronprins Frederik* maintained the service together. In these days before regular air travel, the international express and sleeper trains were the main connection between European cities. A sleeper train from Berlin arrived each morning in København and connected with the express to Göteborg which travelled via Helsingør and Helsingborg. In 1927 the *Kronprins Frederik* was swapped for the

long, which allowed them to transport three passenger carriages. Together with *Helsingborg,* they maintained the service through the German occupation, though with civilian traffic stopped, this was at a low level. *Dan* struck a mine in 1942 but was repaired and back in service the following year.

The post-war years brought a reconnection of the Danish and Swedish economies and a boom in tourist travel. The first change was to bring the *Orehoved* to

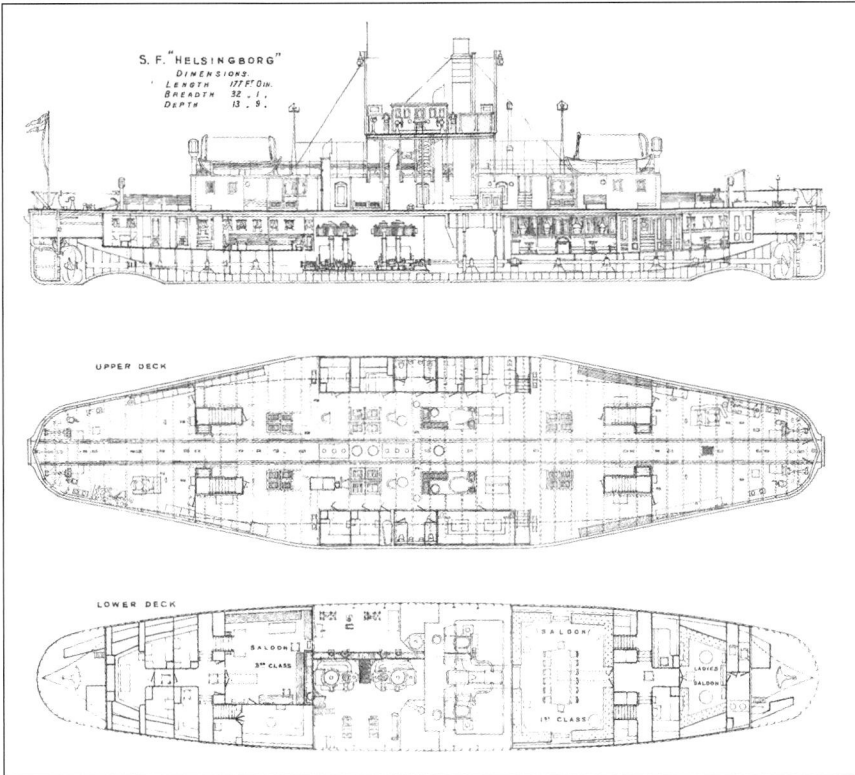

*The **Helsingborg**, built in 1902, was DSB's first double-ended screw ferry. (Museet for søfarts)*

Helsingør from her war service on the Storebælt. She was a close sister of *Dan* and *Svea* and replaced the old *Helsingborg*. After 44 years on the Øresund, *Helsingborg* was renamed *Glyngøre* and moved to Sallingsund, though she did return to Helsingør to fill-in as reserve ferry on a number of occasions.

These three ships, *Dan, Svea* and *Orehoved* were the backbone of the service until the 1970s, though all were changed radically over the years.

Svea was the first ferry to be rebuilt after the war. Over the 1948-49 winter her superstructure was extended to create long thin lounges either side of the train deck with built-in stairways to the passenger spaces below. This also created more space for carrying cars.

In 1950 the *Orehoved* had a more significant rebuild. Her superstructure was extended and the tall twin funnels replaced by a single large central funnel. Her steam boilers were converted from coal to oil firing and with her new look, she was renamed the *Kärnan* for the Øresund crossing.

Over the 1951-52 winter *Dan* had an even larger rebuild at Nakskov Skibsværft. She emerged looking similar to *Kärnan* with an extended superstructure and large central funnel, though she also had her old triple-expansion steam engines replaced by two B&W diesels developing 1400 bhp.

An early postcard of **Helsingborg** entering Helsingør harbour, with Kronborg Castle in the background. *(Author's collection)*

A century of Helsingør to Helsingborg ferries

	Year built	Gross tonnage	Length (m)	Breadth (m)	Pass. capacity	Track length
Kronprinsesse Louise	1891	414	54.9	13.4	650	52.3
Helsingborg	1902	530	54.9	13.1	870	52.0
Dan	1921	777	68.7	13.4	950	65.5
Helsingør	1955	1,123	80.0	13.4	800	76.0
Najaden	1967	1,553	87.9	13.4	800	80.4
Tycho Brahe	1991	11,148	111.2	28.2	1250	259.9

The **Dan** with her Danish 'neutral' flags painted on the hull, negotiating the ice at Helsingør during the Second World War. (Museet for søfarts)

Steam to diesel

A new ferry, the *Helsingør* was built by Helsingør Skibsværft for the crossing in 1955, the first since they had built the *Helsingborg*, more than 50 years earlier. In appearance *Helsingør* did not differ significantly from the previous ships, though the large central oval funnel was now slightly tapered and rounded at the top. The main innovation in the superstructure was a cross-corridor on the bridge deck that allowed passengers to access the kiosks and lounges on both sides of the ship. The more radical change was diesel-electric propulsion controlled from the bridge. Six B&W diesel generators were installed which fed electric motors on the forward and aft propeller shafts. *Helsingør* was 80m long, compared to around 68m for the previous ferries. This was dictated by the continual growth of sleeping cars. The pre-war Swedish cars were 21m long, but the length of the post-war German sleeping cars had grown to 26.4m

In 1958 *Svea* got her second rebuild, this time the steam compound engines were replaced by diesels. The superstructure was also updated, the twin funnels were

Commuters on the **Dan** in the 1930s. (Museet for søfarts)

replaced by a single central oval funnel and a bridge level cross-corridor was fitted, similar to *Helsingør*.

The 1960s and 70s

A fifth ferry, the *Hälsingborg* was added in 1960 and built by Svendborg Skibsværft. She was virtually identical to *Helsingør* and had diesel-electric machinery,

though in her case powered by nine Frichs diesel generators.

In the 1930s with two ferries on the service, each completed between 6 and 8 return trips per day, the crossing normally taking 20 to 25 minutes. In the 1960s, with five ferries on the route there were around 70 return trips per day, with departures every 15 minutes at peak times. In parallel with DSB's train ferries, the Swedish Linjebuss International A/B, normally called LB, started operating small car and passenger ferries on the route from 1955. The first being the *Betula*, which had previously operated as a train ferry to Öland and was originally the Mersey ferry *Perch Rock*. They were popular with commuters, partly as they were never delayed waiting for a train, but also as their ships had a bright passenger lounge above the car deck. The DSB ferries were nicknamed 'the U-boats' as their passenger lounge and cafeteria were in windowless spaces below the train deck.

By the late 1960s the three pre-war DSB ferries were showing their age, despite their upgrades. A new generation of ferries was planned, the first being the *Najaden* delivered by the Aarhus Flydedok in 1967. She was 89m long, though still maintained the standard DSB breadth of 13.4m for single-track ferries applied for

nearly a century. *Najaden* had twin tapered funnels and for the first time, a passenger saloon and cafeteria above the train deck, windows at last. She had a similar diesel-electric propulsion to earlier ships with five B&W diesel generators. *Najaden* was also fitted with a lifting visor at the bow and stern which gave the car deck more protection from water and spray in bad weather. The previous ferries had only a simple gate at either end.

For the first time, foot passengers could board the *Najaden* through a covered walkway to the upper passenger deck, rather than having to walk through the rain across the linkspan. However, the new access towers at the ports with stairs, escalators and enclosed gangways were considered by many to be an eyesore alongside the historic railway buildings.

Najaden was joined by the *Kärnan* in 1970, built by the Helsingør Skibsværft. Her arrangement was similar to her predecessor, though distinctive by having larger funnels. The main difference was that the diesel-electric propulsion used on the last three ferries was replaced by direct drive diesel engines geared to shafts with variable-pitch propellers. The old *Kärnan* was renamed *Senior* for her last few months, to free the name for her successor, and retired in September 1970 as DSB's last steamship.

Helsingør to Helsingborg ferries

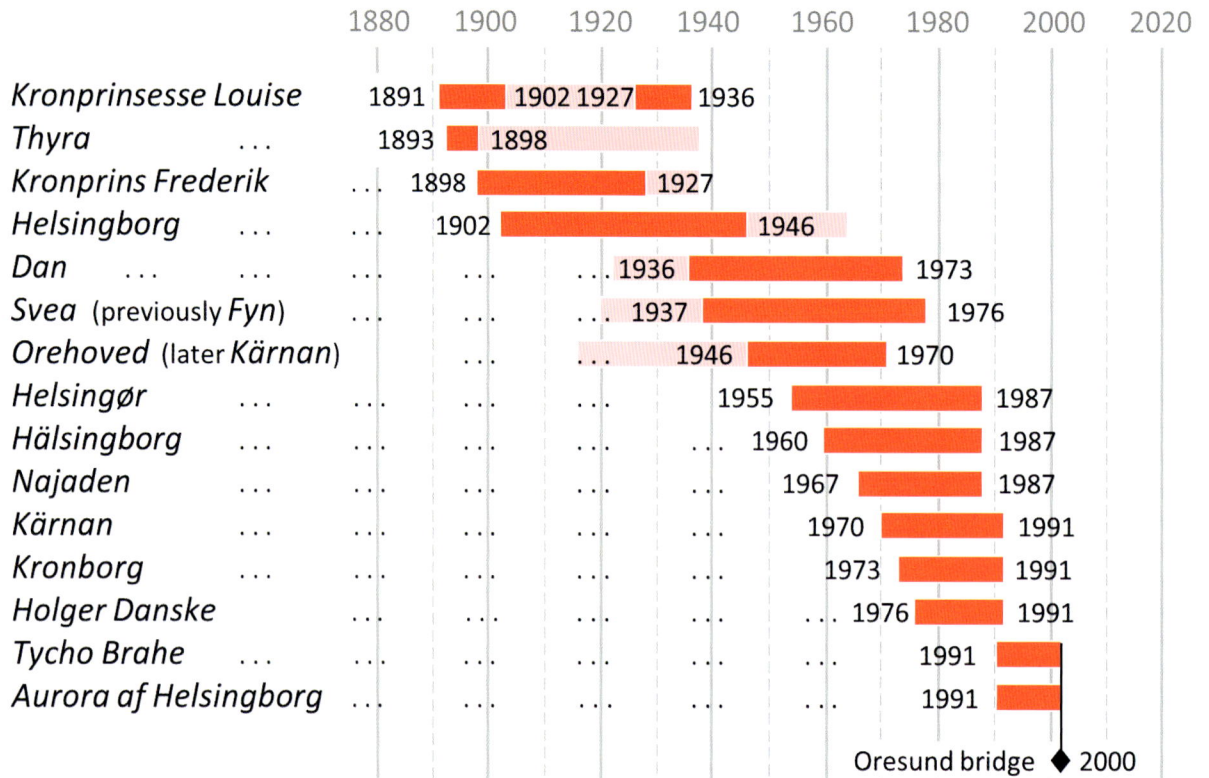

	1880	1900	1920	1940	1960	1980	2000	2020
Kronprinsesse Louise	1891	1902 1927	1936					
Thyra	1893 1898							
Kronprins Frederik	1898	1927						
Helsingborg	1902		1946					
Dan			1936	1973				
Svea (previously *Fyn*)			1937	1976				
Orehoved (later *Kärnan*)			1946	1970				
Helsingør				1955	1987			
Hälsingborg				1960	1987			
Najaden				1967	1987			
Kärnan				1970	1991			
Kronborg				1973	1991			
Holger Danske				1976	1991			
Tycho Brahe					1991			
Aurora af Helsingborg					1991			

Oresund bridge ◆ 2000

The *Helsingør* was DSB's first ferry built with diesel-electric propulsion in 1955. *(Museet for søfarts)*

The *Helsingør* on the right and the old *Helsingborg* on the left, after she had been renamed *Glyngøre*, standing in as reserve ferry at Helsingør in the late 1950s. *(Museet for søfarts)*

The last two ferries, the *Kronborg* from Aarhus Flydedok in 1973 and *Holger Danske* from Aalborg Værft in 1976 were repeats of the *Kärnan*. With their arrival, the last two pre-war ferries were retired. *Dan* was sold in 1973 and had a short further life as a barge for a Swedish contractor working on the Mukran ferry terminal in Germany. *Svea* was sold and scrapped in 1976.

With the old ships gone, DSB's fleet of six Øresund ferries remained unchanged for the next decade; *Helsingør*, *Hälsingborg*, *Najaden*, *Kärnan*, *Kronborg* and *Holger Danske*. They maintained a tight schedule transporting around 7.5 million passengers, 480,000 cars, 90,000 trucks, 136,000 goods wagons and 27,000 passenger coaches each year.

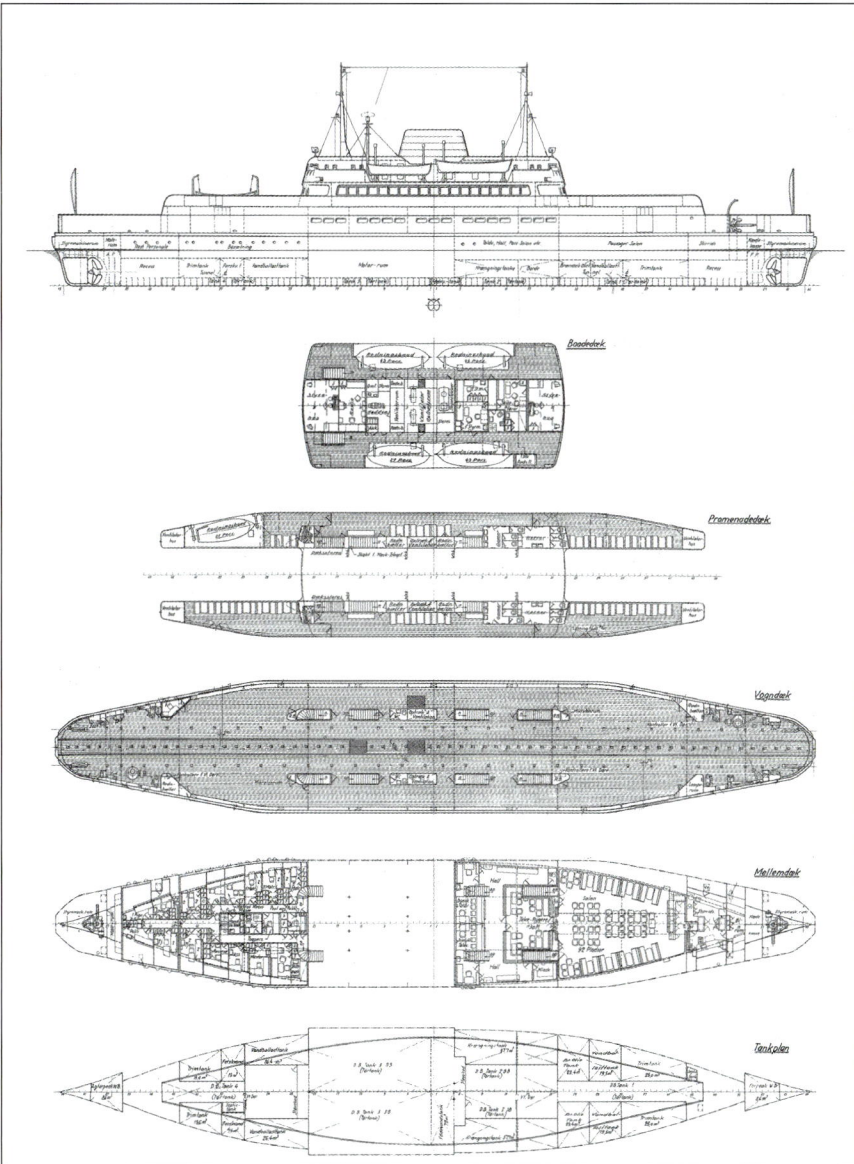

Like all the Øresund ferries, the *Helsingør* had a single rail track on the centreline and all the passenger spaces were below the train deck. *(Museet for søfarts)*

Knutpunkten

In 1984 Helsingborg City Council began a major redevelopment which moved DSB's ferry terminal and combined the city's two railway stations into a single traffic hub, known as the Knutpunkten, (the Junction). Two years later, DSB and SJ decided to close the København to Malmö service and consolidate goods traffic across the Øresund on a route between København and the new terminal at Helsingborg. The new service operated as DanLink and used two large new ferries which no longer had to meet DSB's historic dock dimensions

DanLink took the goods wagons out of the congested passenger ferry terminals. It also allowed the three older ferries, *Helsingør*, *Hälsingborg* and *Najaden* to be retired in 1987. The older two were sold to the Mediterranean and operated as car ferries for a further 12 years, *Helsingør* in Malta and *Hälsingborg* in Italy. *Najaden* was transferred to DSB's Bøjden to Fynshav car ferry service. She was sold to Germany in 1998 and then to Turkey in 2004 where she operated until sold for scrapping in 2011.

The *Kärnan* was similar to *Najaden*, but her appearance was improved by larger funnels. *(Author)*

The *Kronborg* leaving Helsingør with passenger coaches on deck. *(Author)*

The *Hälsingborg* arriving in her namesake port with a cargo of trucks. The car ferry *Regula* in the background. *(Author)*

The *Kronborg*, with the single track on the centreline framed by the linkspan hoists. *(Museet for søfarts)*

DSB, SweFerry and Scandlines

In the background to the ferry service changes, railway companies all over Europe were experiencing political change as their services were commercialised and privatised during the 1980s. In Sweden the Statens Järnvägar consolidated their ferry operations under a subsidiary company called SweFerry. DSB and SweFerry then agreed to combine the operation of their fleets under the Scandlines brand. Traffic between Helsingør to Helsingborg also continued to increase; 14.3 million passengers, 1.6 million cars, 240,000 trucks, 45,000 buses and 25,000 railway coaches crossed in 1989.

DSB and SweFerry ordered two large ferries from Langsten Slip & Båtbyggeri in Tomrefjord, Norway. The first of these, the *Tycho Brahe* was delivered to DSB in 1991. The increase in length and breadth allowed three lines of track on deck, compared with the single track on all previous ferries, so that nine railway carriages could be carried. She also had increased space for cars and two passenger decks above the train deck accommodating 1,250 passengers. The table on page 136 gives a comparison with the previous ferries.

Tycho Brahe was fitted with four azimuth thrusters (two forward, two aft) supplied by a diesel-electric power plant. She was also fitted with a sophisticated engine control system with a high level of automation. This had a number of teething problems over the first few months of service when the ferry suffered loss of power. The most dramatic incident was on the 6th November when the system stuck in 'drive' as the ship entered Helsingør harbour. The ferry collided with the dock at about 8 knots. Many of the passengers who were preparing to disembark were knocked to the deck, dishes and glass were thrown about and 55 people were taken to hospital. Fortunately, no-one was seriously injured. After this the local media referred to her as the 'Psycho Brahe' due to her unpredictable behaviour.

The *Holger Danske* was the last of the traditional DSB ferries built for the Øresund crossing in 1976. *(Museet for søfarts)*

The *Tycho Brahe* was delivered in 1991, the first of two large ferries, though her advanced engine control system suffered from teething problems. *(Museet for søfarts)*

The *Aurora af Helsingborg* leaving Helsingør in the last few years of the train ferry service. *(Arkiv Frihavnen)*

The second ferry, the *Aurora af Helsingborg* was delivered to SweFerry in March 1992. The first Swedish train ferry after 100 years of Danish operation. By this time, the gremlins in *Tycho Brahe's* automation system

had been largely resolved and the two ships settled down as the backbone of the service. A third sistership, the *Hamlet*, was delivered in 1997 though she did not carry rail traffic.

The three older ships were laid-up in 1991. *Kärnan* was sold to Malta and later to Turkey before she was scrapped in 2012. *Kronborg* was converted to an exhibition ship for København's year as European City of Culture in 1996, then sold to Italy to operate alongside *Hälsingborg* until scrapped in 2005. *Holger Danske* remained with Scandlines initially as a car ferry on the Kolby Kås route and later carrying hazardous goods vehicles between Rødby and Puttgarden.

Scandlines maintained a monopoly on the Helsingør to Helsingborg crossing until a legal challenge in 1996 required them to allow HH Ferries to use their terminals. HH Ferries introduced two of the Sunderland-built 'Superflex' car and passenger ferries. The Scandlines duo of *Tycho Brahe* and *Aurora af Helsingborg* continued to carry rail traffic until the end of June 2000. From the 1st July, all rail traffic was routed through the new Øresund bridge and tunnel.

Despite the fixed link, the Helsingør to Helsingborg ferry crossing remains busy. The *Tycho Brahe, Aurora af Helsingborg* and *Hamlet* are still in service but only carrying passengers, cars and trucks.

DSB locomotive 1438 unloading passenger coaches from the ***Tycho Brahe*** at Helsingør in 1997. *(Peter Velthoens)*

København to Malmö

Det danske Statsbaner	**1895-1986**
Statens Järnvägar	**1900-1986**
Köbenhavn – Malmö	1895-1986

A number of steam passenger ships operating between København and Malmö were brought together in the 1860s to provide a regular service by Det Forenede Dampskibsselskab, (better known as DFDS). In 1881, the company had proposed introducing a train ferry, though this hadn't been met with any enthusiasm in Sweden. However, once the Helsingør to Helsingborg service got started in 1892, there was concern in Malmö that they would be by-passed by the new service. An agreement for a ferry was negotiated between DSB and the Statens Järnvägar, (Swedish State Railways), and a ferry port was included in the plans for København's new Frihavnen which was under construction at the time. The terminal consisted of two ferry docks, a railway station, siding and a locomotive turntable. In Malmö the terminal was simpler with only one ferry dock, though a second dock was added in 1903.

The *Kjøbenhavn*

DSB ordered their first ferry for the crossing, the

An early postcard of the *Malmö*, built by Kockums Verksted in 1900. *(Author's collection)*

Kjøbenhavn, from Burmeister & Wain. She was a double-ended paddle steamer with two tracks on deck, a central wheelhouse and two tall funnels, forward and aft on the centreline. At the time, she was DSB's largest ferry, similar in design to the *Sjælland* which B&W had built for the Storebælt crossing eight years before, but 8m longer. *Kjøbenhavn* was 84.7m long with a hull breadth of 10.4m, and the standard 17.7m across the paddle

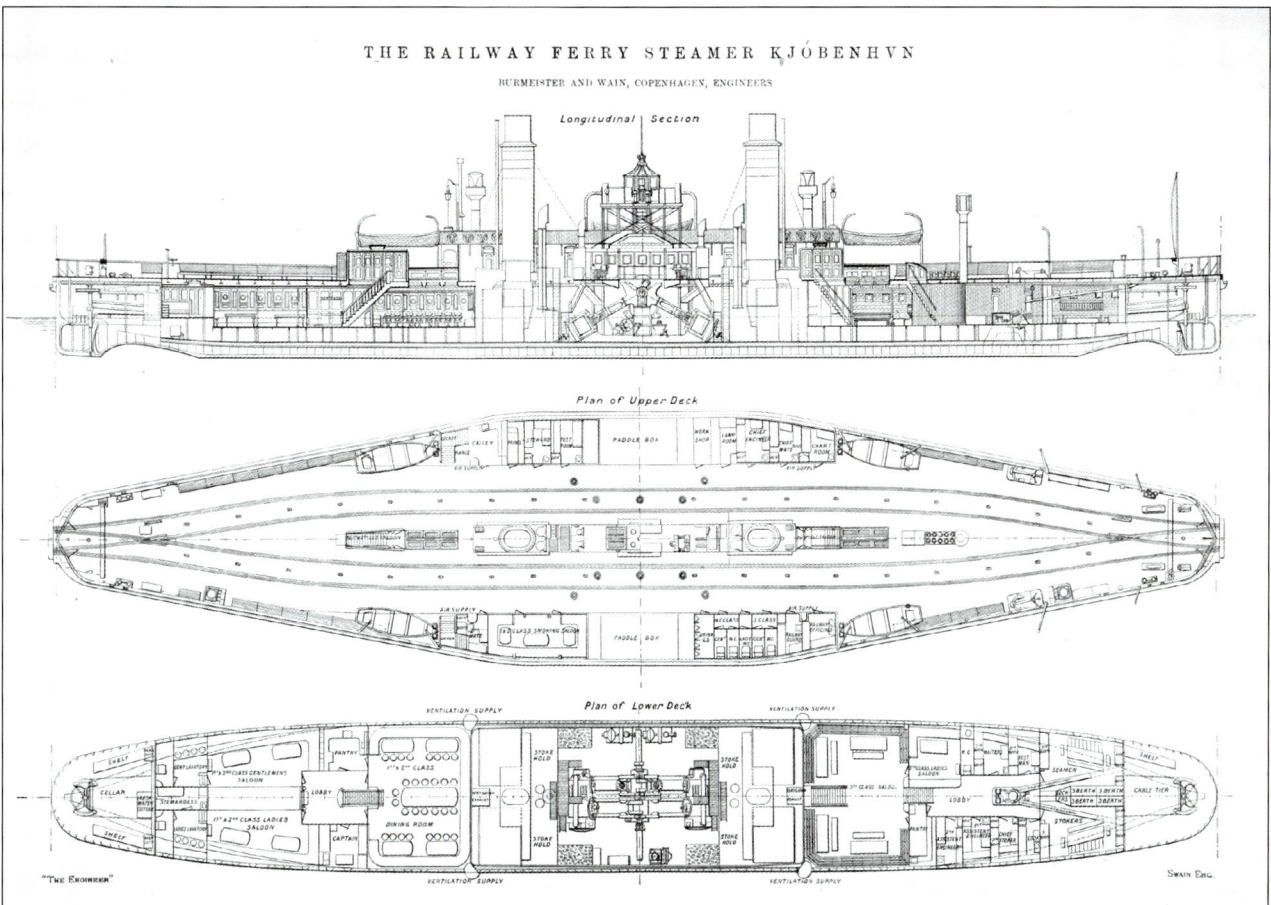

Elevation and plans of the *Kjøbenhavn* built in 1895. It shows how narrow the hull was below the paddle boxes. *(The Engineer)*

Kjøbenhavn to Malmö / Helsingborg ferries

Danske Statsbaner ▮
Statens Järnvägar ▮

	1880	1900	1920	1940	1960	1980	2000	2020
Kjøbenhavn		1895 ▬▬ 1923						
Malmö		1900 ▬▬▬ 1945						
Nyborg		1915 ▮ 1916						
Prins Christian		1923 ▬▬ 1943						
Malmöhus				1945 ▬▬▬▬				

Moved from Malmö to Helsingborg ◆ 1986

Öresund							1986 ▬	
Trekroner							1986 ▬	

Oresund bridge ◆ 2000

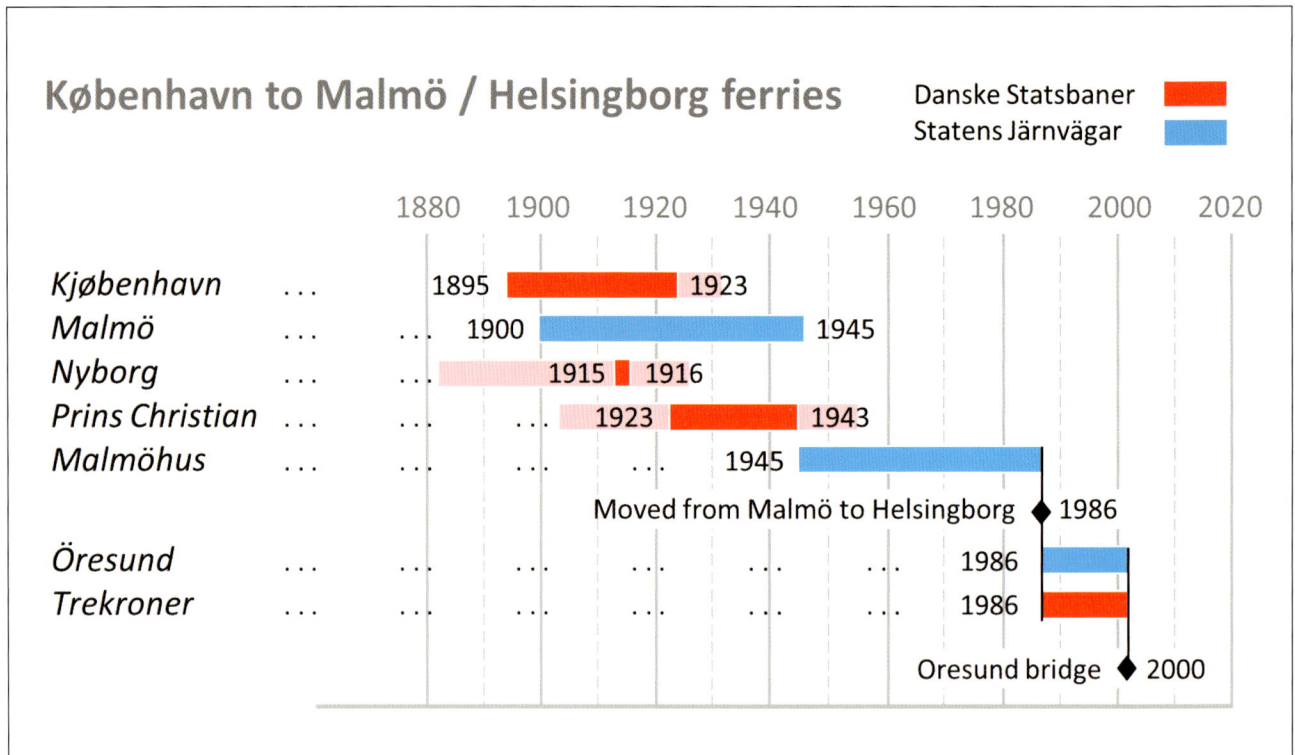

The **Prins Christian** was moved to København from the Gedser crossing in 1923. *(Museet for søfarts)*

A postcard of København's Frihavnen ferry station, around 1930, with **Malmö** on the left and **Prins Christian** in the centre. *(Jernbanen.dk)*

boxes. The 139m of track could carry 18 two-axle goods wagons.

Everything went well on trials and the service to Malmö was inaugurated on the 5th October 1895. *Kjøbenhavn* left Frihavnen at 09.30 in the morning adorned with flags and complete with railway executives, government ministers and an orchestra. On arrival in Malmö, the Swedish dignitaries came on board and the ferry returned to København for an afternoon banquet. After that the party sailed back to Malmö, the sea air having whetted their appetites sufficiently to enjoy a celebratory supper.

Once in service *Kjøbenhavn* completed two return trips each day. Like her near sisterships on the Storebælt, she had no ballast tanks to control heel, so the wagons had to be loaded carefully on her two tracks to ensure the load was balanced port and starboard. Traffic on the route quickly built up, from 12,486 wagons in 1897 to 18,771 the following year.

The *Malmö*

Under the agreement between DSB and SJ, a second ferry would be provided by the Swedish railways and the *Malmö* was delivered by Kockums Verksted in her namesake city in August 1900. She was quite different from the *Kjøbenhavn* and in many ways a more modern design. At 81.7m by 16.0m, she was slightly shorter but much broader. She was not designed to be double ended, which had limited benefit on a longer crossing, and loaded over the bow. This allowed her two tracks to run in parallel to the stern giving her 141m of track, compared with *Kjøbenhavn's* 139m. She had twin screws

The *Malmö* struck a mine in April 1943, but her crew managed to beach her so that she was salvaged and repaired. *(Author's collection)*

aft and her bow was cut-away to help with icebreaking. Though with a single rudder, she was not very manoeuvrable. Her superstructure was distinctive in that she had her wheelhouse forward with an extended deck behind, giving the passengers an open promenade deck for the first time, without being in amongst the wagons. As with all ferries of the time, the passenger saloons were below the train deck. When first built, the *Malmö* had a black hull and buff superstructure and funnel, she was repainted white in the 1930s.

Although the traffic continued to increase, from 28,552 wagons in 1901 to 36,129 in 1905, generally one ferry could cope by making four return trips per day. Thus, the two ferries took it in turn, *Kjøbenhavn* sailed for two weeks, then was laid-up while the *Malmö* sailed the next fortnight. As with all paddle steamers *Kjøbenhavn* sailed more efficiently in one direction due to the curve of the paddle blades. Thus, like the Storebælt ferries, she normally sailed with the same end as the bow. This was acknowledged in 1908 when she was fitted with new bridge in front of the forward funnel.

Direct sleeper trains were introduced between København and Stockholm in 1911, though this was short-lived as it was withdrawn in 1914 with the outbreak of war. The war also led to the suspension of the ferry between Trelleborg and Sassnitz which diverted much of the freight from Sweden to Germany through Malmö. To cope with the increased traffic, 12 to 14 return trips were made each day and *Nyborg* was temporarily transferred from the Storebælt to assist the two regular ferries. Mines were laid in the Øresund, which required the ferries to take a longer route, so that

the crossing time increased from the normal 90 minutes to nearer 2½ hours. While the peak traffic on the route was 125,835 wagons in 1915, this reduced towards the end of the war due to coal shortages. Once the Trelleborg route was re-established, it declined further to 43,654 wagons in 1922.

The sleeper trains from København to Stockholm were reinstated in 1921 and in 1923 a major improvement took place when DSB transferred the *Prins Christian* from the Gedser to Warnemünde route. Although only eight years younger than the *Kjøbenhavn*, the *Prins*, as she was known, was a much more modern ship. She was a screw steamer, much broader and more powerful than her predecessor and with a promenade deck and passenger saloons above the train deck. The loading dock at Gedser was a different shape from the Storebælt standard used at København, so the *Prins'* stern had to be modified and extended by around four metres. Her extra power and screw propulsion also made her an excellent icebreaker. The old *Kjøbenhavn* was moved to the Storebælt until she was sold for scrapping in 1931.

In 1923 through trains from Stockholm to Hamburg and Berlin were introduced and the service continued with *Prins Christian* and *Malmö* through the 1920s. As the *Prins'* bow still fitted the Gedser dock, she was periodically used as stand-in on the Gedser route and was then replaced at København with the *Odin*. Although the crossings were generally without incident, *Malmö* went aground in fog in April 1937. She ran into the breakwater on the Middelgrundsfortet, a small island fortress just outside København harbour, and stuck fast for several hours. The passengers managed to scramble

145

The *Malmöhus*, built in 1945 was an old-fashioned design, but she had an almost yacht-like appearance with a white hull and upper deckhouses painted to look like varnished teak. *Auithor's collection)*

The *Öresund* was delivered in 1986 for the København to Helsingborg route. Her bulk and flat-fronted square superstructure was similar to the Baltic super-ferries. *(Museet for søfarts)*

ashore with the help of the Danish marines from the fort. Eventually the ferry *Konung Gustav V* arrived from Trelleborg and managed to pull the *Malmö* free without serious damage. Statens Järnvägar later delivered several cases of beer to the fort to reward the marines for their assistance.

At the start of the Second World War very little changed. Large national flags were painted on the sides of the ferries to indicate they belonged to neutral countries. The 1939-40 winter was very cold and the *Prins* was regularly needed as an icebreaker. With the German occupation in April 1940, all passenger traffic stopped but the ferries remained busy with goods wagons until *Malmö* struck a mine in April 1943. Fortunately, her crew managed to beach her on the Swedish coast north of Malmö and she was salvaged and repaired. After this the service stopped completely.

The elegant *Malmöhus*

With the service suspended, the Statens Järnvägar

decided it was time to replace the 40-year-old *Malmö*. In 1944, they ordered a new diesel ferry from Kockums Verksted and the *Malmöhus* was delivered in October 1945, a few months after the service had restarted. With her fine bow, white hull and yellow funnel, the *Malmöhus* had an elegant yacht-like appearance. The upper deckhouses were even painted brown to look like varnished teak. She had a full deck of passenger saloons above the train deck, but even when new, she was old-fashioned. Her deck layout, which loaded over the stern to two tracks, was the same as the SJ's Trelleborg ferries built 40 years earlier and her rail capacity was essentially the same as her predecessor. When first delivered she suffered from serious engine vibration, but this improved after modifications by the shipyard. With the *Malmöhus* in service, the old *Malmö* was laid-up and sold for scrapping in 1947.

At the end of the war the international sleeper car services were restarted, the 'Nordekspres' between Stockholm and Paris in 1946 and a new sleeper car between Stockholm and Basel in 1947. There was also more goods traffic through Denmark to Sweden as the pre-war ferry ports of Warnemünde and Sassnitz were now in the Russian Sector which became East Germany. After 1945 the *Malmöhus* largely operated the service alone, though assisted for short periods by DSB ferries from the Storebælt, including, *Odin, Christian IX* and *Kørsor*. The old *Prins Christian* was shared as reserve ferry between København and the Storebælt until she was sold for scrapping in 1955 after 52 years' service. The Swedish ferries from Trelleborg, *Drottning Victoria* and *Konung Gustav V*, were also used occasionally. As they did not fit the main linkspans at København and Malmö, the reserve docks were modified to fit them.

While the train ferry service continued between København and Malmö, new car and passenger ferries were introduced during the 1960s on the shorter crossing between Dragør and Limhamn which took much of the passenger traffic. DSB's *Storebælt* worked in partnership with the *Malmöhus* until the through passenger trains were routed via Helsingør in 1973. With few local passengers, the passenger service was stopped in 1975. After this *Malmöhus* continued as a freight ferry and her hull was painted black.

As part of a wider review of the Øresund crossings, the Danish and Swedish State Railways decided to close the København to Malmö service in 1986 and replace it with a new route between København and Helsingborg. This would also take the goods traffic from the Helsingør to Helsingborg crossing and reduce the congestion in these ports.

Malmöhus made her last crossing on the 1st October 1986. There were plans to convert her to a floating restaurant and theatre, but these did not materialise and she was scrapped in 1988. The service continued for a further few weeks using DSB's *Prinsesse Benedikte*. The last crossing was on the 3rd Nov 1986.

Top: Loading the *Öresund* in København with DSB locomotive MZ 1458. *(Morten Jensen)*

Middle left: The *Trekroner* was converted from a ro-ro trailer ship and entered service for DSB in 1986..*(Kenn Ellersen)*

Below: The *Trekroner* loading at København's Frihavnen terminal in 1987. The original 1895 ferry dock and station building are still intact on the left. *(Arkiv Frihavnen)*

Bottom left: The *Trekroner* from the stern showing the visor and docking bridge. *(Morten Jensen)*

DSB & Statens Järnvägar (DanLink)	**1986-1991**
Scandlines	**1991-2000**
Köbenhavn – Helsingborg	1986-2000

The new Øresund service between København and Helsingborg opened with the closure of the Malmö crossing. As with the previous service, it was operated as a partnership between the Danish and Swedish railways, each of which provided a large new ferry. The two ships were operated together and marketed as the DanLink service.

The *Öresund* and *Trekroner*

The *Öresund* was first and delivered to Statens Järnvägar's subsidiary SweFerry by the Norwegian yard of Moss Rosenberg Verft A/S in October 1986. She was much larger than any previous ferries, 186m long, with a gross tonnage of 16,925 and with five rail tracks on her deck with a total track length of 817m.

DSB's ferry *Trekroner* was of similar size and converted from a seven-year-old ro-ro trailer ferry. She had been built as *Milora* at Ankerløkken Verft A/S in Florø, Norway in 1979 for trade between Northern

Europe and Africa. She was bought by DSB and converted for train ferry service at the Nakskov Skipsværft in 1986. Her hull was lengthened by 36m and fitted with sponsons. The stern door was removed and replaced with a hinged visor and the deck fitted with five rail tracks with a total length of 815m. A small docking bridge was also built at the stern.

The 800m of rail track on each of the two new ships was a step change in capacity compared to the existing fleet. The total track length on the six DSB ferries at Helsingør plus the *Malmöhus* was 625m, though of course they had shorter crossings and could make more trips per day. Apart from a minor accident in 1995, when the *Öresund* collided with the breakwater when leaving København, the two ships had uneventful lives. The ownership of *Trekroner* transferred from DSB to Scandlines Danmark A/S in January 1997. The service closed on the 30th June 2000 and the following day the railway traffic was routed over the new Öresund bridge and tunnel between København and Malmö.

The two ships were laid-up. *Öresund* was sold the following year to a subsidiary of Sea Containers Ltd. Renamed *Sky Wind* she continued as a train ferry between Sweden and Finland and later as a vehicle ferry, the *Wolin* between Poland and Sweden. *Trekroner* remained laid-up Nakskov until 2004 when she was sold to Turkish owners and renamed *Erdeniz* for further service on the Bosporus.

Frederikshavn to Göteborg

Stena A/B

Frederikshavn – Göteborg	1987-2015

The mid 1980s saw changes in the train ferry routes from Sweden to Denmark and Germany. The long-established København to Malmö service closed and the Helsingør to Helsingborg crossing stopped handling freight. The Danlink service between København and Helsinborg was started in 1986 and the following year Nordö-Link started a rail service from Malmö to Travemünde. Stena A/B had a well-established passenger and vehicle service between Göteborg and Frederikshavn and saw an opportunity to add a rail ferry to this route in competition to Danlink. The route to Frederikshavn provided a direct connection from Sweden to Jylland, creating a direct rail route to Hamburg and Rotterdam that avoided the busy Storebælt crossing. A dedicated rail ferry, not carrying passengers, was also able to transport rail wagons and trucks with hazardous cargoes.

To establish the train ferry SEK 80 million was invested in the terminals, including a 2km branch line from Frederikshavn station to the ferry terminal at Isværkshavnen. Stena also spent SEK 13 million on renovating and converting their 14-year old ro-ro *Stena Searider* to carry rail traffic.

Originally named *Stena Seatrader*, she was built as a train ferry by A. Vuyk & Zonen, Capelle aan den Ijssel in the Netherlands in 1973. She was immediately chartered to Canadian National Railways and operated as *Seatrader* on their service to Newfoundland in Canada. At the beginning of 1976, she was returned to Stena and lengthened by 27m. She spent the next few years on charter as a ro-ro ferry between Italy and the Red Sea, including a trip to Texas. Renamed *Stena Searider*, she completed several short charters around Northern Europe in the mid-1980s before Stena decided to bring her into their scheduled services. She spent four months in Cityvarvet in Göteborg being reconverted to a train ferry. Her stern was rebuilt with a full-width guillotine door, the main deck was strengthened, the tracks on the main and upper decks were reinstated and the lift

The **Stena Scanrail** in Frederikshavn in 2011, showing the large sponsons on her sides. The service closed in 2015 when the Stena Scanrail was 42 years old. *(Matthias Schalk)*

Kristiansand to Hirtshals ferries

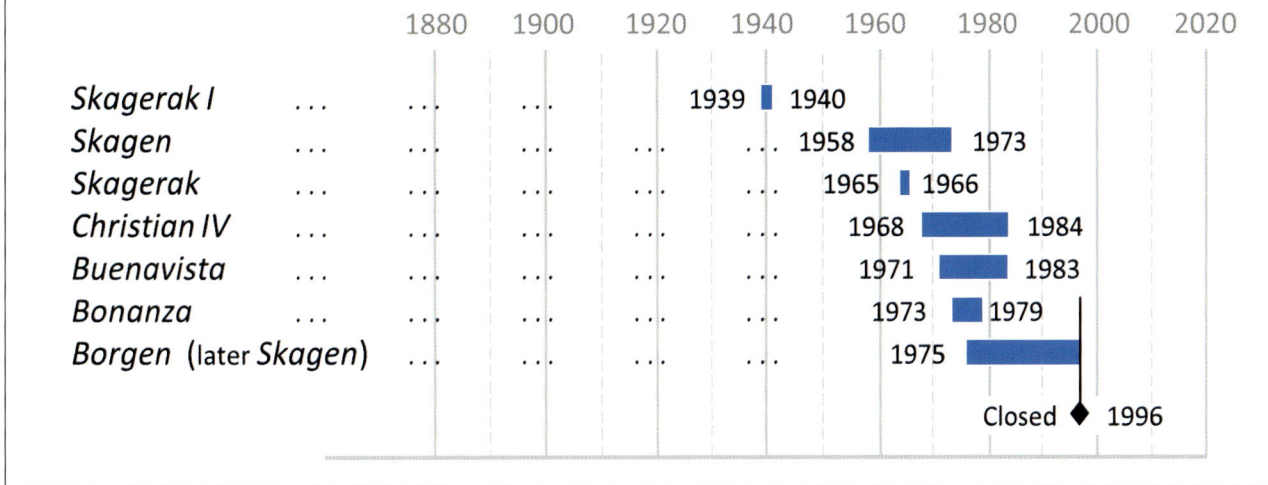

	1880	1900	1920	1940	1960	1980	2000	2020
Skagerak I ...	...	...	...	1939 ■ 1940				
Skagen ...	...	...	...	...	1958 ▬▬ 1973			
Skagerak ...	...	...	...	...	1965 ■ 1966			
Christian IV ...	...	...	...	1968 ▬▬	1984			
Buenavista ...	...	...	...	1971 ▬▬ 1983				
Bonanza ...	...	...	...	1973 ▬ 1979				
Borgen (later *Skagen*) ...	...	...	...	1975 ▬▬▬				
						Closed ◆ 1996		

refurbished. 1.4m wide sponsons were also fitted to her sides to improve stability.

The newly renamed *Stena Scanrail* started the Göteborg to Frederikshavn rail service in December 1987. Initially there was a single return trip each day, leaving Göteborg at 10.30 and Frederikshavn at 18.00. The crossing took four hours, with two hours for loading and unloading. The service quickly attracted Swedish rail traffic and hazardous goods, though Danish Railways resisted the loss of revenue to their Storebælt and Danlink crossings. Soon *Stena Scanrail* was providing two return trips daily.

Over the next three decades several passenger-car ferries came and went on Stena's Göteborg to Frederikshavn service, including a high-speed catamaran, but the *Scanrail* carried-on with no other vessel able to carry her combination of rail wagons and hazardous goods. Eventually it was decided to close the train ferry service in 2015. *Stena Scanrail* was 42 years old, a remarkable career for a ro-ro ferry and the traffic did not justify building a replacement. Her last trip was on the 25th August. After a short lay-up she was sold to Turkish owners and renamed *Birdeniz*, leaving Göteborg for the last time in October 2015.

Skagerrak

A/S Kristiansands Dampskipsselskap	**1939-1940**
	1958-1968
Fred. Olsen & Co.	**1968-1990**
Color Line A/S	**1990-1996**
Kristiansand – Hirtshals	1939-1940
	1958-1996

A/S Kristiansands Dampskipsselskap, (Kristiansand Steamship Co.), started a passenger and cargo service between Kristiansand and Frederikshavn in 1899 and

The *Skagerak I* was Kristiansands D/S' first car and rail ferry. The guillotine stern door was lifted by a counterweight over the pulleys on the top of the stern frame. Sadly, she only had one season as a ferry before being lost in the Second World War. *(Museet for søfarts)*

The service restarted in 1958 with the *Skagen*, showing the Mosvold family's Olympic rings on her funnel. *(Author's collection)*

over the years they operated several steamships on the route. In 1937 they moved their Danish port from Frederikshavn to a new harbour at Hirtshals, which reduced the crossing distance from 118 to 77 nautical miles. The route provided a shortcut for holiday traffic from Denmark and Germany to Western Norway, though in the 1930s tourist's cars were still being loaded by crane. A rival crossing was started in 1937 with the new car ferry *Peter Wessel* providing a drive on / drive off service between Larvik and Frederikshavn.

Kristiansands D/S needed to respond and ordered their first drive-on ferry, the *Skagerak I* which was delivered by Aalborg Værft in May 1939. She was a solid-looking 1930s motorship, though by modern standards quite small for such an exposed crossing, 68m long and 1281 gross tons, powered by two B&W diesel engines. *Skagerak I* was designed for passengers and cars during the summer season but had a single track fitted to the car deck for rail wagons to provide freight revenue during the winter season. Both cars and wagons were loaded through the stern. The stern door was of a novel guillotine design, secured at the sides, the door moved up and down in a frame with counterweights and pulleys. Linkspans with electric hoists were installed at both ports. The *Skagerak I* had the funnel markings of the Mosvold family who owned Kristiansands D/S as well as a fleet of deep-sea ships, a yellow funnel with the Olympic rings in white on a wide red band.

Sadly, the *Skagerak I* lasted only a single season as a ferry. When the Germans invaded Norway in April 1940, she was requisitioned by the German Navy. With her car deck and stern door she was quickly converted for use as a minelayer and renamed *Skagerrak*. In January 1944, she sailed from the Baltic coast to Bergen with mines, then to Trondheim with ammunition, before heading back south. On the 20th January her convoy was attacked by a Coastal Command squadron of the New Zealand Air Force and she was sunk by a torpedo west of Trondheim.

The Kristiansands D/S got back into business after the war by converting a Royal Navy patrol vessel, the *HMS Kilbride*, into a car and passenger ferry. She was renamed the *Jylland* and restarted the Kristiansand to Hirtshals service in 1948. *Jylland* did not carry any rail wagons and was always just a stopgap. In the mid-1950s they commissioned Knut E Hansen & Co. in København to design a new purpose-built car passenger and train ferry. Finance was tight and it was two years before they could place the order for their new ferry the *Skagen*. Her hull was built by Pusnæs mekaniske Verksted in Arendal and she was fitted out by Kristiansands Verksted and delivered in 1958. She was larger than the *Skagerak I*, but by later standards still a small ship, 1,870 gross tons and 80.8m long. She was designed principally as a car and passenger ferry with capacity for 505 passengers and 75 cars loaded through a stern door. She also had a single railway track set into

the car deck allowing her to carry 6 goods wagons. Two Nordberg 6-cylinder diesels gave her a maximum speed of 18 knots.

As the shortest route between Norway and Denmark the Kristiansand – Hirtshals crossing took 4½ hours and was marketed as the 'Skagerak-Expressen'. In winter the *Skagen* sailed a single return trip from Kristiansand each day. In summer the *Skagen* added a second trip to Arendal, sailing from Kristiansand to Hirtshals early in the morning, returning to Arendal in the afternoon, then back to Hirtshals for a late evening sailing which arrived back in Kristiansand in the early hours of the morning. The service was successful, in 1960 *Skagen* completed 375 return trips, carrying 96,000 passengers, 15,000 cars, 190 buses, 213 trucks and 2,200 freight cars with 10,500 tons of cargo. As a result, Kristiansands D/S decided to order a second, larger ship.

The *Skagerak* was delivered by Aalborg Værft in Denmark in July 1965. She was also designed by Knut E. Hansen and followed their typical Scandinavian ferry design of the 1960s. Her engine exhausts were led up the sides to two raked funnels, allowing a clear car deck, and a dummy funnel connected to the forward mast was located immediately behind the bridge. Like *Skagen* she had a pale yellow hull and white superstructure, but instead of the Mosvold Olympic rings, *Skagerak* had the Kristiansands D/S houseflag, a red swallowtail pennant with a white saltire cross, fitted to either side of the dummy funnel. The passenger areas were light and modern with terraced open decks at the stern. She was slightly larger than *Skagen*, 87m long with a gross tonnage of 2,703 and licenced for 845 passengers with space on the car deck for 140 cars. *Skagerak* had a much greater rail capacity with three tracks set into the deck able to carry 17 wagons.

One aspect of Kristiansands D/S service stood out from other Scandinavian ferry operators; no alcohol was allowed onboard. At a time when many Scandinavian ferry companies relied on duty-free sales for much of their income, particularly in the quieter winter season, this was a major lost opportunity. However, the Mosvold family were prominent members of Norway's Misjonsforbund, (Mission Covenant Church), and strongly disapproved of alcohol.

The loss of the *Skagerak*

Sadly, like her namesake, the *Skagerak* had only a single season on the Hirtshals crossing. In the latter part of August 1966, Hurricane Faith tracked westwards from Cape Verde to the Caribbean and then north and east in a huge arc across the North Atlantic. It was unusual in tracking very far north, and though no longer a hurricane when it passed the Faroe Islands into the North Sea, it brought heavy seas and winds gusting to 100km/h. In the early hours of Wednesday 7th September, *Skagerak* was in Kristiansand harbour preparing for her overnight sailing which departed at

The *Skagerak* listing to starboard after passengers and crew had been recovered from the life-rafts by Danish rescue helicopters. *(Royal Danish Air Force)*

The *Skagerak*, when newly delivered in 1965, was a typical Scandinavian ferry of the time. *(Museet for søfarts)*

01.30. The departure was delayed due to the strong winds and Captain Anstein Dvergsnes spoke to the *Skagen* which was in Hirtshals also waiting for better weather before sailing.

At 05.30, the Captain was told that the *Skagen* has sailed and so *Skagerak* made her last preparations and sailed at 06.00. There were 144 people on board, 47 crew and 97 passengers including 28 children on a school trip, and on the car deck 15 cars, two caravans and seven rail wagons. It was a rough crossing and most of the passengers stayed in their cabins. In normal circumstances *Skagerak* would have reached Hirtshals around 10.30, but progress was slow. Having headed into the seas for much of the crossing, *Skagerak* had to turn eastwards to head towards Hirtshals. The waves

were reported as between seven and ten metres in height and as she ran ahead of the sea, they were slamming on to the stern doors. At around 11.00, an off-duty member of the crew came up to the bridge, reporting that water was leaking down into the cabins below the car deck. Checking the car deck, it was found to be awash with seawater with more entering through the stern doors. It was already too deep for the crew to reach the doors and the caravans were floating. More seriously, the water was also leaking down into the engine room and soon the main engines stopped. The emergency generator then failed to start. Everything was quiet except the noise of the wind and *Skagerak* was at the mercy of the elements.

With water sloshing on the car deck, *Skagerak* soon heeled over and settled with a starboard list. A distress signal was sent at 11.21 and the radio operator was soon in contact with the Danish Coastguard at Skagen who initiated a rescue operation. Ships in the area were notified and some fishing boats which had been sheltering in Hirtshals put to sea to provide assistance. The Royal Danish Air Force also scrambled their new S-61A air-sea rescue helicopters, which had come into service only the year before. Onboard, the crew started to evacuate the passengers and managed to launch three lifeboats before they had to give up due to the increasing angle of heel. After that, they continued launching life-rafts, though some of these turned over in the waves, spilling people into the water. Berit Rostoft, at the time a 24-year old Assistant Purser, recalled climbing down the side of the ship on a rope ladder. She

The *Christian IV* continued on the Skagerak crossing with Fred Olsen until 1984. *(Author's collection)*

A summer's day at Hirtshals in the early 1970s, with the *Buenavista* waiting to load. The Hirtshalsbanen railcar connected to DSB's main line at Hjørring. *(Robert von Hirschhorn)*

could only go so far and could hear people in the life-rafts below shouting to her to jump. After a pause, she did and plunged into the cold water. She vividly remembered the time it took to surface, coughing seawater and being dragged into a life-raft already filled with around 20 people.

Five Danish helicopters arrived on the scene at 12.15, by which time the *Skagerak* was listing around 30°, and started picking up individual survivors from the water. The weather conditions were still very bad and at times the helicopters would drop below the wave crests to reach survivors. They managed to rescue and return 69 people to shore. Soon after, the Russian trawler *Joseph Greifenberger* was the first ship to arrive and started recovering survivors from the lifeboats and rafts. She was soon joined by Danish and Norwegian ships.

The Captain, ten crew and an Afghan hound remained onboard, hoping that it would be possible to get a towline onboard and salvage the ship as the

weather began to ease. They remained onboard for several hours, as the list increased to around 45°. By early evening, it was clear that no salvage was possible and the remaining crew were evacuated by helicopter before it got dark. As night fell, 39 people including 16 children were still missing. Only when the *Joseph Greifenberger* docked in Frederikshavn around 01.30 in the morning was it clear that all the missing people were safely onboard. The rescue was complete and all 144 people, plus the dog, had been recovered safely. Sadly, one elderly man later died of a heart attack.

Skagerak capsized and sank at 20.15 around 5 nautical miles off the Danish coast. The wreck lay in around 20m of water and was examined by divers a few days later to assess it for salvage. However, the ship had rolled on the seabed and the superstructure was found to be badly damaged. It was decided that salvage was not practical, but the divers did recover a valuable oil painting which had been in the passenger saloon.

There were several outcomes of the tragedy. Berit Rostoft remembers being grateful that the *Skagerak* was an alcohol-free ship, as it helped maintain discipline during the evacuation. The Marine Accident Inquiry identified that a major cause of the sinking was that the stern doors were not properly secured. Rather than a hinged ramp, *Skagerak* had two stern doors which opened by sliding sideways on rollers. When closed, the doors were secured by 28 locking pins, each of which had to be put in place and secured by the crew. This was time-consuming and the crew had become used to not fitting all the pins. On the final voyage, three pins on either side were not in place. The Inquiry fined Captain Dvergsnes for sailing under adverse conditions and the Chief Officer for not confirming that the stern doors were adequately secured. The Inquiry also criticised the ferry's design as it failed to ensure a watertight boundary between the train deck and the machinery space below, which had led to the loss of power.

One positive outcome was the success of the Royal Danish Air Force's S-61A helicopters. This was the first time that helicopters had carried-out a major rescue at sea. At the time, Norway did not have air-sea rescue helicopters and the Norwegian Government very quickly followed the Danish lead and established rescue helicopters along their coast.

To recover their business, Kristiansands D/S quickly ordered a replacement ferry from Aalborg Værft, the *Christian IV* was delivered in February 1968. She was essentially a replica of *Skagerak*, but with a more robust stern door. Car ferries normally have a stern ramp hinged at the base with locking pins on either side at the top. This provides a strong door but is not suitable for a train ferry as the rails on the deck need to align precisely with the rails on the linkspan. On *Christian IV* the reinforced stern door returned to a guillotine design, an updated version of that fitted to the *Skagerak I* before the war.

Like previous Kristiansands D/S ships, *Christian IV* had a yellow hull and red swallowtail pennants on either side of the dummy funnel. She also had 'SKAGERAK EXPRESSEN' painted on the hull. However, the livery did not last for long. In September 1968, the Mosvolds sold Kristiansands D/S to another well-known Norwegian shipowning family, Fred. Olsen & Co. Like Kristiansands D/S, Fred. Olsen had been operating passenger steamers since the turn of the century, principally from Norway to the UK and Belgium. They had dipped their toe into the booming Scandinavian ferry market by taking a share in the Jahre Line car ferries introduced between Oslo and Kiel in 1961. Buying Kristiansands D/S gave them an established service and two ships, the 10-year old *Skagen* and the brand-new *Christian IV*. The ships were soon painted in Fred. Olsen colours, grey hulls, white superstructures and the wheelhouse and dummy funnel painted buff. Fred Olsen's white and blue swallowtail pennant replaced the red Kristiansands' flag on the dummy funnel. The only remnant of the old colours was the red Kristiansands D/S shield with its white saltire which remained on the bow. Inside, the main changes were a new bar and a duty-free shop.

Fred. Olsen's new ships

In 1971 Fred. Olsen introduced the first of two new vessels on the route. The *Buenavista* looked quite different from the previous ships, more like a ro-ro trailer carrier with a forward bridge and twin funnels aft, though with a deck of passenger accommodation. The bow-fronted wheelhouse was a signature of Fred. Olsen ships of the time. She was built by Ulstein Mek. Verksted in Norway and could carry 750 passengers and 200 cars. She also had two lines of rail track to carry 12 rail wagons, though this reduced the car capacity. She was designed to carry cars and passengers between Kristiansand and Hirtshals through the summer and operate as a ro-ro freight ferry through the winter carrying tomatoes and vegetables from the Canary Islands to the Netherlands and UK. The Canaries trade was a long-established Fred. Olsen business and they developed a successful formula with the *Black Watch* and *Black Prince* built in 1966. These two ships operated in the North Sea as passenger and car ferries in summer and with cruise passengers to the Canaries, returning with tomatoes in the winter.

Her sistership *Bonanza* was delivered from Ulstein in May 1972, although Fred. Olsen chartered her to Silja Line for their summer route from Norrtälje in Sweden to the Åland islands. It was summer 1973 before she arrived at Kristiansand.

With the arrival of *Bonanza*, the old *Skagen* was chartered to Stena Line for the summer and then laid-up in September 1973 for sale. She was resold to a different part of the Fred Olsen empire which operated subsea remotely operated vehicles (ROVs) to support offshore oil and gas developments. Renamed *Borgholm*, she

The *Borgen* was Fred Olsen's last train ferry, built in 1975 by Aalborg Værft in Denmark. *(Ken Lubi)*

Fred. Olsen's ferry fleet was sold to Color Line A/S in 1990 and the *Borgen* was renamed *Skagen*. The rail freight service came to an end in 1996 and she was retired in 2004. *(Author's collection)*

operated as an ROV mothership until 1982. She then went through a number of owners and lay-ups and was finally scrapped in 2019.

Buenavista was lengthened from 95m to 106m in 1974, increasing her gross tonnage from 2,719 to 5,213. This also increased her capacity to 900 passengers, 240 cars and 15 rail wagons.

The *Borgen*

The following year Fred. Olsen took delivery of their last train ferry for the Skagerak crossing. The *Borgen* was delivered by Aalborg Værft in 1975. She was not a good-looking ship, square and boxy with upright funnels and the superstructure overhanging the ship-sides near the stern. She had the standard Fred Olsen bow-fronted wheelhouse and, as a nod to the past, her bow still carried the red Kristiansands D/S shield. She had a much-increased passenger capacity of 1,600, together with space for 270 cars and 18 rail wagons on three tracks. Unlike the previous two ships, *Borgen* did not have the benefit of winters in the sun and remained on the Skagerak crossing all year. During her first winter she also spent some time on the North Sea crossing from Kristiansand and Stavanger to Newcastle, but this was not a success as she was an uncomfortable ship in bad weather.

Bonanza continued to spend her summers on the Kristiansand to Hirtshals crossing until 1979. She operated on other routes in 1980 and was then sold to Lineas Fred. Olsen S.A. She was renamed *Benchijigua* and operated in the Canary Islands until 1999. Sold to Indonesia she was sunk in a collision in the Sunda Strait in 2012.

In 1969, 5,924 rail wagons and 3,349 trucks were carried between Kristiansand and Hirtshals. By 1980 the number of rail wagons had increased to 8,000, but the number of trucks had more than quadrupled to 14,000. Inevitably the importance of rail freight declined as more traffic moved to trucks.

Borgen returned to Aalborg Værft over the 1981-82 winter for a major conversion where she was expanded in all directions. A new 22m section increased her length from 108 to 130m. Her superstructure was jacked up to fit an additional car deck, increasing her capacity from 270 to 410 cars. Sponsons were fitted to either side of the hull to improve stability which increased her breadth by 2.3m. Square and boxy to start with, none of these modifications improved her appearance.

Buenavista continued to spend her summers on the Kristiansand to Hirtshals route until 1983. She was then sold to another Fred. Olsen associate company, COMARIT in Morocco and renamed *Bismillah*. Sold on to Mexico in 2006 she was wrecked in 2007 and scrapped the following year.

The *Christian IV* was laid-up after the 1984 season and sold to Malaysia. She has gone through many hands since then. Her superstructure was cut down to increase her freight capacity, but she was still operating in the Mediterranean in 2020.

In 1984, 2,881 freight wagons were carried, only 36% of the traffic in 1980. After this, *Borgen* was the only rail ferry on the route. The *Christian IV* was replaced by the car ferry *Bolette*, bought second hand from the Sally line, but with no rail capacity. This was also true of the *Bolero* and later the *Bayard* which served on the Skagerak crossing amongst other routes in the 1980s.

In 1990, Fred Olsen decided to withdraw from the Scandinavian ferry business, selling their fleet to the newly formed Color Line A/S which amalgamated the ferry interests of the Norway Line, Jahre Line and Fred Olsen. The *Borgen, Bolero* and *Bayard* were transferred to the new company. As a nod to the past, *Borgen* was renamed *Skagen* (II). She continued to transport small numbers of rail wagons between Kristiansand and Hirtshals until 31st May 1996, when the rail freight

service came to an end. She continued for Color Line on various routes, though demoted to a freight ferry in 2001. *Skagen* was laid-up in 2004 and sold the following year for service in the Red Sea, being finally scrapped in 2011.

Tinnsjø

Norsk Transport AS
Tinnoset – Mæl   1909-1991

Although not a seagoing service, this is probably a good place to include the only inland train ferry service in Norway on Tinnsjø, (Lake Tinn).

At the beginning of the 20th century, a young engineer, Sam Eyde, saw an opportunity to use Norway's

Sam Eyde (1866-1940) the founder of Norsk Hydro and developer of the Rjukan project. *(Norsk Hydro)*

vast untapped potential for hydroelectricity. He formed a partnership with another Norwegian, the physicist Kristian Birkeland, who had developed a process for making artificial fertiliser by capturing nitrogen from the air using an electrical arc furnace. They built a trial plant at Notodden in southern Norway in 1904 using power generated from the neighbouring Tinnfossen waterfall. The trials were successful and in 1905 Eyde formed the Norsk Hydro company, with capital from Swedish and French investors, to build a much larger plant. This was to be sited at Rjukan and draw power from the 300m drop in the Måna river at the Rjukanfossen waterfall. As this was deep in the mountainous Telemark region of southern Norway, there were major challenges to building the plant and exporting its products.

The Notodden plant was linked to the coast by canal and later by railway. In 1907 Eyde established Norsk Transport AS to build and operate a 78km rail link from Notodden to Rjukan. Rjukan is set in the bottom of a long steep-sided valley which opens to the Tinnsjø at its

The railway construction took 18 months. In spring 1908 a steam icebreaking tug *Skarfos* was put in service on the lake together with a wooden ferry barge, the *Tinnsjø*. The barge was built by Norsk Hydro in Tinn Austbygd at the north end of the lake. She was 42m long, 11m wide and had two tracks on deck carrying 8 wagons. The hull was sheathed with iron plates to prevent ice damage in winter. The ferry docks at Tinnoset and Mæl were completed in January 1909 and the first railway wagons were transported on Tinnsjø in February. The tug and barge worked together until 1929 mostly carrying stone and other construction materials until *Tinnsjø* was condemned in 1938, (its remains are under the boat marina at Mæl). The *Skarfos* was in service until 1983 and is still in use at Skien.

Top: The first wooden ferry, the *Tinnsjø* at the quay at Mæl in 1908. *(Norsk Hydro)*

Middle left: The first steam ferry, the *Rjukanfos*, was built in 1909 and could carry nine wagons. The passenger saloon was below the train deck. *(Author's collection)*

Above: The *Hydro* and *Ammonia* at Mæl the northern port on Tinnsjø..*(Author's collection)*

Left: The *Hydro* on the slipway at Tinnoset. *(Øystein O. Jonsjord)*

The steam ferry

The Rjukan railway line was opened in August 1909 and in the autumn the steam powered ferry *Rjukanfos* was put in service. She was built by Fevig Jernskibsbyggeri and assembled on the Tinnoset slipway, by Akers Mek. Verksted. 43m long with a breadth of 10m, she had two tracks on deck able to carry 9 wagons. There was a passenger saloon below the main deck for up to 120 passengers. *Rjukanfos* was loaded and unloaded over the bow using two gauntleted tracks on the loading bridges. Her first years were spent transporting construction materials and workers for the Rjukan site until the factory started production in 1911.

eastern end. Tinnsjø is one of the deepest lakes in Europe, only around 1km wide, it runs north-south for around 35km with the mountains dropping steeply to the water on both sides. At the southern end of the lake, the river Tinnåa runs south to Notodden then out to the coast. Building a railway line along the steep sides of the lake would take many years, so the chosen solution was to build two railway lines joined by a ferry. The 31km Tinnoset Line from Notodden to Tinnoset at the southern end of Tinnsjø, a 31km ferry service from Tinnoset up the lake to Mæl, then the 16km Rjukan Line from Mæl to the new industrial town at Rjukan.

It manufactured calcium nitrate, known as 'Norwegian saltpetre' which it exported in 100kg barrels. The Vermork hydroelectric station which powered the arc furnaces was the largest hydroelectric plant in the world. The Rjukan plant soon produced other chemicals such as ammonium nitrate which was exported to Notodden in railway tankers. The railway lines were electrified in 1911 with AEG equipment using 10kV (16.66 Hz). The problem of being a pioneer was that an international agreement was made the following year to standardise railway traction on 15kV, so that the electrical equipment had later to be converted.

A larger ferry was soon needed and the *Hydro* was ordered from Akers Mek. Verksted, prefabricated in their yard in Kristiania (now Oslo), and assembled on the slipway at Tinnoset. The *Hydro* was delivered in 1914 and her arrangement was similar to *Rjukanfos*, bow loading with two tracks on deck, though slightly larger, 52.6m long and able to carry 12 wagons. As with *Rjukanfos*, she had two steam engines and a service speed of 8 knots.

The two ferries were kept busy as the population of Rjukan reached 12,000 in 1920. By 1924 they had transported over 10 million barrels containing 2.8 million tonnes of calcium nitrate from the plant. A new process was introduced in 1929, producing ammonia by combining hydrogen and nitrogen. The hydrogen was recovered from water by electrolysis, using direct current. To minimise transmission losses the new hydrogen plants were built close to the power stations. The Vermork Hydrogen Plant around 5km west of Rjukan was the largest water electrolysis plant in the world with hydrogen and oxygen transported by pipeline to the Rjukan plant. A by-product of the electrolysis was the production of heavy water, initially only a few kilogrammes each month.

With the extra work in Rjukan a third steam ferry was built to run alongside *Hydro* and allow *Rjukanfos* to be kept in reserve. This was the *Ammonia*, built in 1929 by Moss Verft & Dokk on the Tinnoset slip. She was quite a bit longer than *Hydro*, 70.3m and able to carry 17 wagons on two tracks as well as 250 passengers. She was also faster, with two triple expansion steam engines she could achieve 12 knots, reducing the crossing time from a little over two hours to around an hour and a half. The superstructure had also been enlarged, providing a first-class lounge and a Directors' Lounge and dining room for senior Norsk Hydro staff on the top deck behind the bridge. Below decks there were first- and second-class lounges as well as separate ladies' lounges for each class. In her later life, these spaces were put together.

Throughout the 1930s the ferries prospered with *Ammonia* and *Hydro* in regular service and *Rjukanfos* in reserve. When Norway was invaded by the German army in 1940, the Rjukan works and in particular the Vermork Hydrogen Plant became important for reasons no-one could have imagined.

Sinking the *Hydro*

In 1939, Albert Einstein wrote a letter to the US President Franklin Roosevelt warning that he thought it possible to create a nuclear chain reaction using uranium that would result in an extremely powerful bomb. The Allies took this warning seriously, and over the next few years brought together a group of scientists to investigate whether a nuclear chain reaction was possible. This culminated in Enrico Fermi's 'atomic

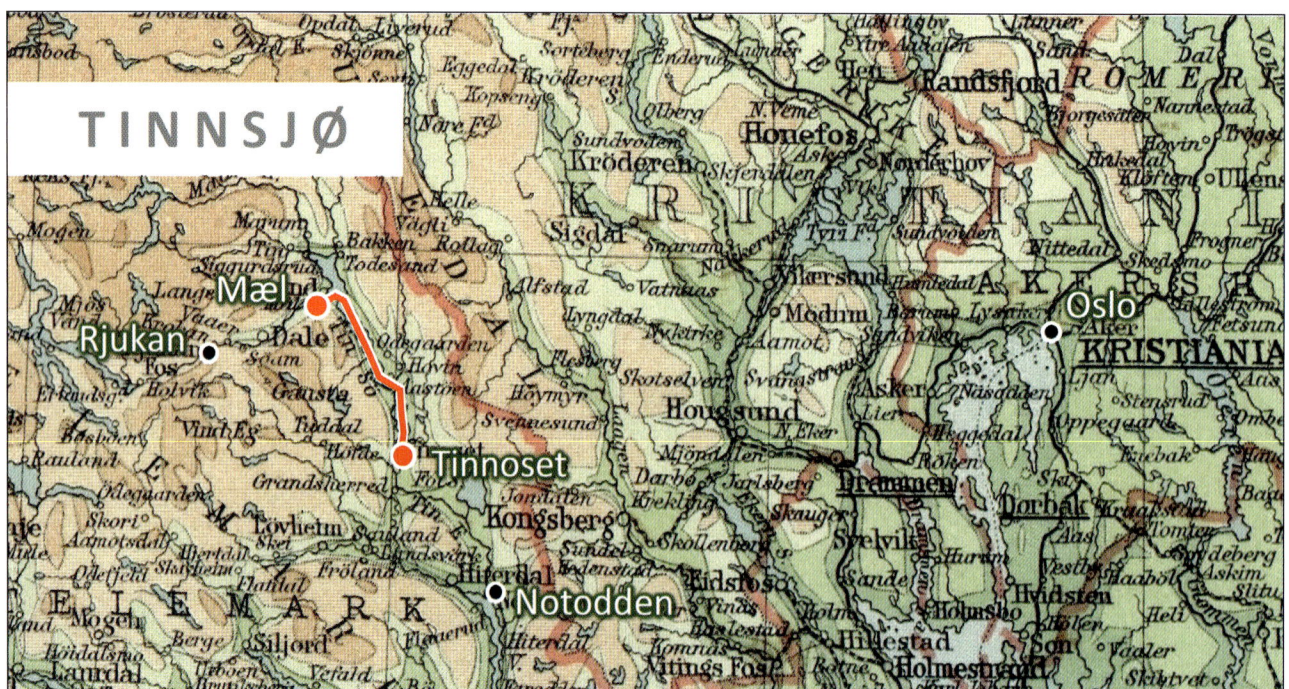

pile' achieving the first nuclear chain reaction in Chicago in December 1942. At this point, the scientists' best estimate was that it would take at least two years to develop a workable bomb.

This was worrying news, as information had come out of Norway that the Germans had increased the heavy water production at the Vermork Hydrogen Plant to 110kg per month in 1940 and to 380kg per month in 1942. Heavy water was a key material for controlling the rate of nuclear fission. There was no other purpose that could make it so important to the German military, so it had to be assumed that German nuclear research was months, maybe even years ahead of the Allies.

The Allies soon made plans to sabotage the Vermork plant. The story later told by the film 'Heroes of Telemark', which despite its Hollywood glitz, stayed very close to the true events. The first raid was planned by British Combined Operations. A small group of Norwegian commandos were flown from Scotland and parachuted into the wild mountains of the Telemark plateau, north of Rjukan. They were to prepare for a raiding party of British special forces to arrive by glider and guide them to Vermork. The gliders set off on the 19th November 1942, but in bad weather both gliders crashed on the west coast of Norway. Many of the British troops were killed and those that survived were captured and executed by the Germans. The second plan was to use a much smaller force of Norwegian commandos, trained in explosives, who would be dropped by parachute. It took several months to prepare for this operation, which meant that the first group had to spend a hard winter on the Telemark plateau, living rough with no supplies and surviving on moss and reindeer meat. The second group parachuted into Telemark in February 1943 and together they prepared for their daring raid on Vermork. On the night of the 27th February, the nine saboteurs climbed down sheer cliffs to cross the Rjukan gorge in snow and

The *Hydro* unloading wagons at Mæl in 1925. *(Author's collection)*

darkness then followed the railway track to reach the Hydrogen Plant unnoticed. They evaded the guards and climbed through a cable duct to enter the plant, carefully laying their explosives around the heavy water concentration cells. The detonation destroyed the equipment and the stocks of heavy water. Amazing as this was, the greater achievement was that they then escaped, without a shot being fired, and made their way over 200 miles cross-country to the safety of neutral Sweden.

A small group led by Knut Haukelid stayed in Norway, keeping in contact with the local Norwegian resistance and collecting information from the workers in the plant. By August 1943, the Germans had rebuilt much of the heavy water plant and were producing over 100kg per month. When this information was passed back to Britain the Allies decided the best course of action was a bombing raid though the location of the plant at the base of a deep valley made this a difficult operation. On the 16th and 18th November, the US Air Force VIII

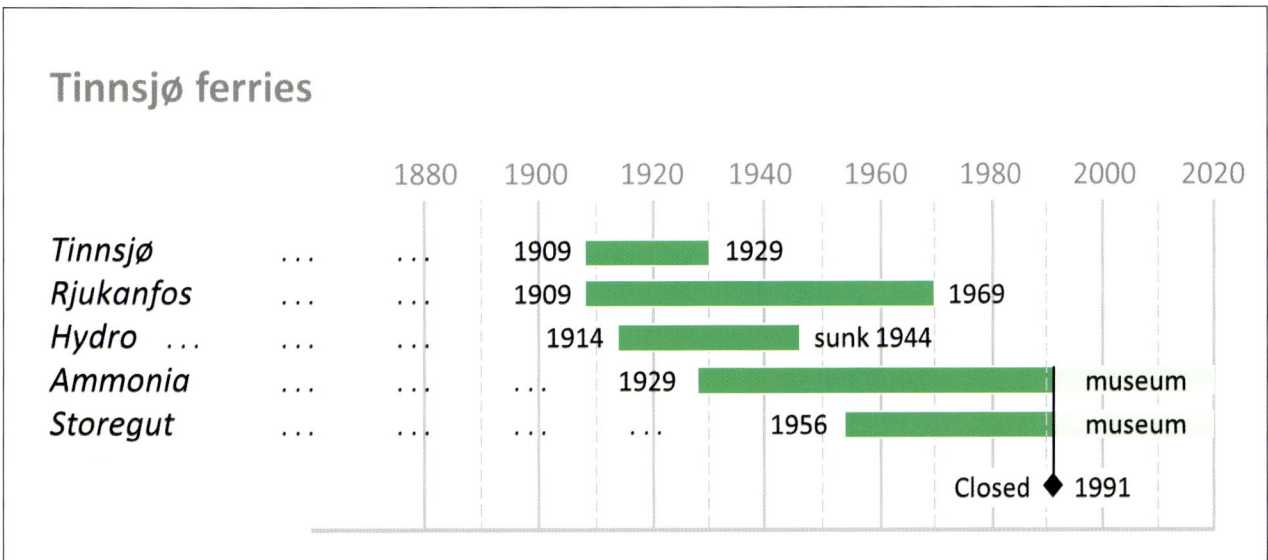

Tinnsjø ferries

			1880	1900	1920	1940	1960	1980	2000	2020
Tinnsjø	...	...		1909 ▬▬▬▬ 1929						
Rjukanfos	...	...		1909 ▬▬▬▬▬▬▬▬▬ 1969						
Hydro ...	...	...		1914 ▬▬▬▬▬ sunk 1944						
Ammonia	...	...	...	1929 ▬▬▬▬▬▬▬▬▬▬▬ museum						
Storegut	...	...	...	...	1956 ▬▬▬▬▬▬▬ museum					

Closed ◆ 1991

The *Ammonia* approaching Tinnoset with a tank wagon. *(Olle Sundström)*

Bomber Command sent around 200 aircraft on daylight raids to Rjukan. Hundreds of bombs were dropped and much of the plant was damaged, part of the railway was destroyed. Inevitably some bombs fell on residential parts of the town and twenty-two civilians were killed. The worst was that the hydrogen plant remained undamaged. The Norwegian Government in exile were not told of the raid and protested strongly at the loss of civilian lives. They proposed that any future sabotage should be left to their forces on the ground. By this time, the Germans realised that continuing heavy water production in Norway was impractical and decided to move all their stocks to Germany. The Norwegians in the plant passed on intelligence of the plan. The drums would be loaded on rail wagons, taken to Mæl, then down the lake on the ferry to Tinnoset and by train to the port of Herøya for shipping to Germany. The Allied Command in Britain made clear how important it was to prevent the heavy water leaving Norway. Haukelid and his team's first thought was to blow up the train, but getting close to the heavily guarded railway would be difficult and ensuring that all the heavy water was destroyed would be virtually impossible. The surest plan was to sink the ferry.

Word came that the train would be transported on the *Hydro* on the morning of Sunday 20th February 1944. Haukelid and two colleagues made explosive charges and got a local man to build timing devices from alarm clock parts. Their plan was to plant explosive in the bottom of the ferry close to the bow and timed to explode around half an hour into the voyage. The charge would blow a hole around 1.2m diameter sinking the ferry bow first in around 430m of water in the deepest part of the lake. If the propeller and rudder came out of the water, the Captain would not be able to turn the

The *Rjukanfoss*, with an extra 's', after being lengthened and re-engined in 1945-6. She was scrapped in 1969. *(Røkke, Arne Dag)*

ferry and try to ground her on the shore. The hope was that the ferry would say on an even keel and take a few minutes to sink, giving passengers time to escape.

On the Saturday evening the train was loaded at Vermork and ready to leave, surrounded by German soldiers, including guards on board each wagon. Haukelid and his men drove the 16km to the ferry terminal at Mael. It was quiet and the few German soldiers were playing cards in the guardhouse. The three men boarded the ferry as casually as possible and went down to the passenger saloon. They were soon discovered by one of the crew but assured him that they were simply trying to hide some contraband, in case their homes were searched by the Germans. He understood and opened the hatch leading from the passenger saloon down into the double-bottom. There they crawled forward to lay their 8 kg sausage of plastic explosive and set the timers. Their original plan was to place the charge on the bottom plates, but there was so much water in the bilges they had to fit the charge on the side shell to keep the timers dry. As soon as everything was set, the three men made their escape. Haukelid travelled cross-country overnight to take an early morning train to Oslo. Those living locally in Rjukan returned home to continue their lives as if nothing had happened, unlike the film, none of the saboteurs travelled on the ferry.

The following morning the drums of heavy water arrived at Mæl with the train under close guard. The wagons were loaded onboard *Hydro* without incident. At around 10am she set-off down the lake to Tinnoset on a clear cold morning. There were 47 people on board, 39 Norwegian passengers and crew and eight German soldiers guarding the railway wagons. Everything went to plan, at exactly 10.30 the bomb went off, blowing a hole through the plating on the port side. Very quickly the ferry started heeling over and sinking by the bow. Passengers above deck jumped into the icy water, but many down in the passenger saloon could not get out. Some wagons rolled off the deck. A few of the heavy water drums were only half full and floated free with other debris. Captain Sorensen remembered that within a few minutes he could stand on the side of the ship and in less than five minutes *Hydro* had sunk. 29 people had jumped into the water, 25 Norwegians and four German soldiers, and managed to keep afloat some using the floating drums. Farmers who lived along the lakeside had witnessed the sinking and rowed out in small boats to rescue the survivors from the cold water. 18 people drowned, four soldiers and 14 passengers and crew.

That evening Haukelid bought a newspaper in Oslo and found a small story confirming the plan had been successful. He crossed the border to Sweden and after a few weeks returned to his army unit in Britain.

The *Hydro* sank in the deepest part of the lake in 430m of water and is still there. After the war two of the drums were salvaged and were confirmed to contain heavy water. Only in 1945 when the US dropped its atomic bombs in Japan, did those involved in the sabotage begin to understand the importance of their operations. Haukelid remained in the Norwegian army and retired as a General in 1974.

With the loss of the *Hydro*, the service on the Tinnsjø relied on the *Ammonia*. With no prospect of an early replacement, the old *Rjukanfos* was lengthened and re-engined in 1945-46. Her length was increased from 43 to 69m. When she returned, her name had been changed to *Rjukanfoss*, the extra 's' being the only case of a name being lengthened as well as the ship.

A new diesel ferry was ordered from Glommens Mek. Versted in Fredrikstad and assembled on the slipway at Tinnoset. The *Storegut* was delivered in 1956. She was larger than the previous ships, 82m long and with capacity for 19 rail wagons and 400 passengers. Her design was innovative in that much the superstructure was made of aluminium, she was also the first Norwegian ferry fitted with a bow thruster.

The linkspan at Tinnoset show the overhead power cables and two gauntleted tracks. *(OleK)*

The ferry service stopped in 1991, when a road was completed along the lakeside. However the **Storegut** and the **Ammonia** have been preserved. *(Alexander Ytteborg)*

Once *Storegut* was in service, *Rjukanfoss* was kept as reserve and was scrapped in 1969. The *Storegut* and *Ammonia* maintained the service for nearly thirty years, although latterly *Ammonia* was largely kept in reserve. In 1985 a bus service replaced the passenger trains and after this *Storegut* and *Ammonia* carried only freight. The railway lines finally closed and the ferry service stopped in July 1991 when a road was completed along the western side of the lake. Between 1909 and 1991 the railway line and ferries had transported 30 million tonnes of freight, with a peak of 722,000 tons in 1962.

The ferries were laid up and ownership was transferred to Stiftelsen Rjukanbanen (the Rjukan Line Foundation) in 1997 which preserved them as museum ships in Mæl. In 2012, the *Storegut* and *Ammonia* were taken over as part of the Norwegian Industrial Workers Museum in Vermork, which maintains much of Rjukan plant as an industrial heritage site. The industrial buildings, railway and ferries were recognised by UNESCO in 2015 as a World Heritage Site.

SIX

Across the Baltic

There is no doubt that the Baltic is where the train ferry came of age in the last decades of the 19th century between the Danish islands and on the short crossings to Sweden. The next stage was for the Danish, German and Swedish railways to develop longer Baltic crossings at the beginning of the 20th century. These changed after the Second World War when Europe's new borders left many of the Baltic ferry ports behind the 'iron curtain'. This led to new routes and changed fortunes for many of the old ferry routes that survived.

The Baltic was also the location for next great innovation in train ferry design, with the introduction of multi-deck ferries on long-distance routes. This was pioneered in 1975 by the Railship ferries which ran over 1,000km from West Germany to Finland. It also led to the huge state-funded project for a ferry service between the East German port of Sassnitz and Klaipeda in the Soviet Union. The fleet of five huge ships built in the late 1980s were the world's largest train ferries.

The 1990s privatisation

Throughout the 20th century, nearly all the train ferries around Europe were operated by state-owned railway companies. This was also true in the Baltic, where the main operators were Danske Statsbaner (DSB) in Denmark, Statens Järnvägar (SJ) in Sweden and Deutsche Reichsbahn (DR) and Deutsche Bundesbahn (DB) in East and West Germany, respectively.

In 1991 this began to change, largely driven by an EEC Directive requiring countries to separate the operation of their railways from the ownership of the infrastructure. In parallel with this, there was increasing political pressure to avoid what was often seen as unfair competition between state-owned railway ferries and independent car ferry operators.

The first change followed German unification, when DB and DR merged their ferry fleets in April 1993 to form the Deutsche Fährgesellschaft Ostsee, (DFO), which became a subsidiary of the new Deutsche Bahn AG the following year. DFO inherited a fleet of seven ferries, the *Theodor Heuss, Deutschland* and *Karl Carstens* from DB. The *Warnemünde, Sassnitz, Rostock* and *Rügen* from DR.

In 1995, DSB separated its shipping division as a limited company, DSB Rederi A/S, owned by the Danish

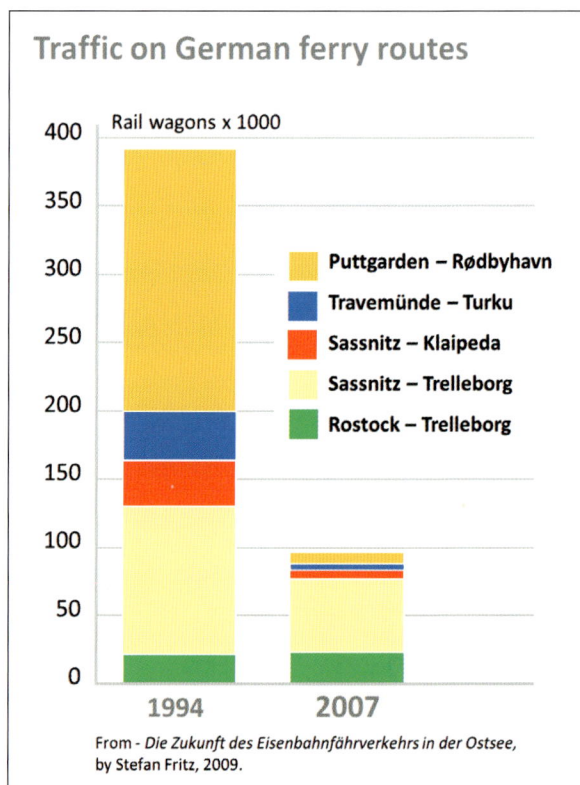

Traffic on German ferry routes

Rail wagons x 1000

Legend:
- Puttgarden – Rødbyhavn
- Travemünde – Turku
- Sassnitz – Klaipeda
- Sassnitz – Trelleborg
- Rostock – Trelleborg

From - *Die Zukunft des Eisenbahnfährverkehrs in der Ostsee*, by Stefan Fritz, 2009.

Ministry of Transport and in 1997 this was renamed Scandlines Danmark A/S.

In 1998, DFO and Scandlines Danmark A/S merged to form Scandlines AG. The new company's ultimate owners were initially the German and Danish Governments, however in 2007 they decided to sell Scandlines AG to private investors. It was initially bought by a consortium of three investors, but in 2013 the London based 3i Group bought out its partners to become the sole owners.

In Sweden, SJ was the first national railway to separate its ferry business into a limited company, SweFerry AB in 1991. In 1996 it combined its operations with DSB Rederi A/S under the Scandlines brand and later transferred ownership of its fleet to a Swedish company, Scandlines AB. In 1999, the Swedish Government decided to sell their shareholding in Scandlines AB and after negotiations with Scandlines AG and Stena AB, decided to sell to Stena for SEK 560m. Scandlines took this decision to court, as when the

Privatisation in the 1990s

WEST GERMANY
Puttgarden - Rødbyhavn

Deutsche Bundesbahn (DB)

EAST GERMANY
Warnemünde – Gedser
Sassnitz - Trelleborg

Deutsche Reichsbahn (DR)

DFO

Deutsche Fährgesellschaft Ostsee (DFO)

Scandlines AG
(no train ferry services)

DENMARK
Gedser - Warnemünde
Rødbyhavn - Puttgarden

Det danske Statsbaner (DSB)
DSB Rederi A/S

Scandlines Danmark A/S

SWEDEN
Trelleborg - Sassnitz

Statens Järnvägar (SJ)
SweFerry AB

Scandlines AB

Stena AB
Trelleborg - Rostock

GERMANY to DENMARK

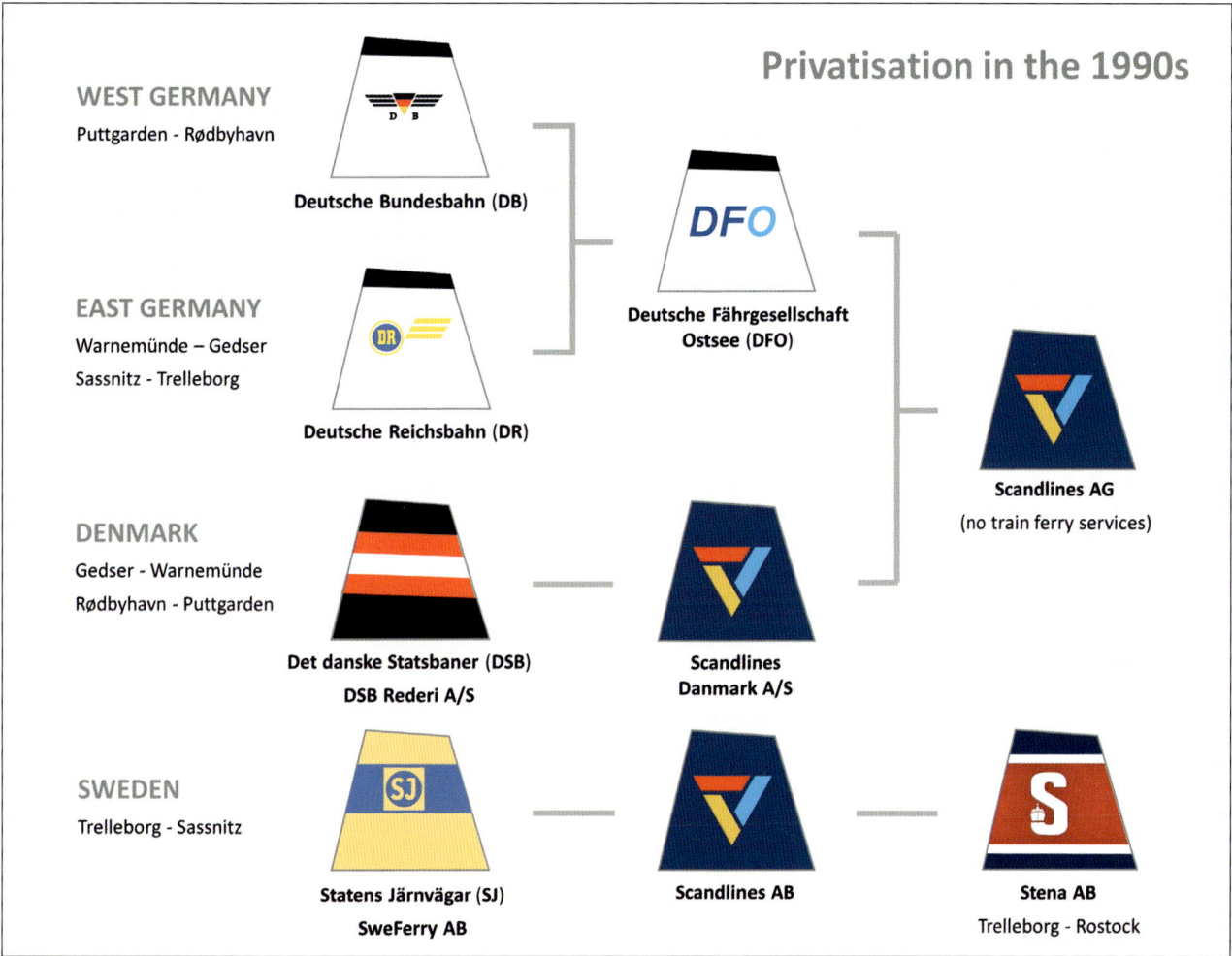

Scandlines brand had been established, DSB Rederi A/S had an agreement with the Swedish Government to have first refusal if Scandlines AB was sold. However, when DSB Rederi A/S had been merged into Scandlines AG, this agreement had not been rolled over to the new company. Stena won the court case and the four Swedish Scandlines ferries, *Götaland, Trelleborg, Skåne* and *Aurora af Helsingborg* joined the Stena fleet in July 2000.

In parallel with the consolidation of the ferry operators there was a large reduction in traffic, partly due to the fixed links across the Storebælt and Øresund, which allowed cars and trucks to be driven through Germany, Denmark and Sweden, without crossing a ferry. The loss of duty-free sales and the rise of cheap flights also reduced the number of passengers. The graph shows the huge reduction in rail traffic on routes from Germany, from around 390,000 rail wagons in 1994 to less than 100,000 by 2007. By 2020, the only train ferry service still in operation was between Rostock and Trelleborg.

Germany to Denmark

Det danske Statsbaner
G.h. Mecklenburgische Friedrich-Franz-Eisenbahn
	1903-1920
Deutsche Reichsbahn/DFO	**1920-1995**
Warnemünde – Gedser	**1903-1995**

The crossing between Warnemünde and Gedser is not the shortest between Germany and Denmark, but the ports are on a direct line between Berlin and København. The railway reached the towns in 1886 and a mail steamer service was started allowing passengers to travel between the two capital cities in 12 hours. While this was a great improvement for passengers, mail and freight still needed to be transhipped at the ports. The success of the Storebælt train ferries raised the possibility of using similar ships on this longer crossing. This needed agreement between both governments and the Germans were initially cautious as they had no previous experience of sea-going ferries. However, the principle was agreed by a state treaty in September 1897 and final parliamentary approvals were given in 1900. The impressively named Großherzoglich Mecklenburgische Friedrich-Franz-Eisenbahn, (Grand Duchy of Mecklenburg Friedrich Franz Railway), or MFFE, was to build a new station and ferry port at Warnemünde, including a large breakwater. The Danske Statsbaner (DSB) had recently bought the railway line to Gedser from a private operator and agreed to build a new ferry harbour. Four ferries were to be built for the service, two with screw propulsion and two with paddles, one of each type by both the MFFE and DSB.

The logic of building both paddle and screw propelled ferries, was essentially conservatism. Paddle ferries had been used successfully on the Storebælt and were felt to

The *Friedrich Franz IV* had a single track for carrying passenger coaches. She was the first ferry to be fitted with a hinged bow visor to cope with open-sea conditions on the Baltic. *(Wikicommons)*

be more stable than screw steamers. Thus, the two paddle steamers were designed primarily for passenger service and had a single track so that five coaches could be loaded and unloaded with minimum delay. The two screw steamers would principally be used for freight and were fitted with two tracks which could carry 16 wagons. However, all four ferries had similar passenger accommodation as the screw ferries would be used to stand-in on the passenger service, particularly when winter ice made it difficult to operate the paddle steamers.

The two paddle steamers were built by Ferdinand Schichau in Elbing, the *Friedrich Franz IV* for the MFFE and the *Prinsesse Alexandrine* for DSB. Both were 85m long and distinctive for their four funnels, two either side. The two screw steamers were the MFFE's *Mecklenburg* built by Schichau in Danzig, and the *Prins Christian* built by the Helsingør shipyard for DSB. The two screw ferries had a more enclosed superstructure and much more modern appearance than the paddle steamers. They were nearly sisterships, though the *Mecklenburg* had a single central funnel, while the *Prins Christian* had two funnels on the centreline, though her profile would have been more elegant if the funnels had been slightly further apart. All four ferries loaded over both bow and stern, but always sailed in the same

Top: The four-funnelled **Friedrich Franz IV** was the first of two paddle steamers built by Ferdinand Schichau in Elbing for the Warnemünde to Gedser crossing in 1903. *(Author's collection)*

Middle: The **Prinsesse Alexandrine** for Det Danske Statsbaner was the second paddle ferry delivered by Schichau in Elbing in 1903. She was the last paddle ferry built for DSB. *(Ferry Publications Library)*

Bottom: After only two years' service, the **Prinsesse Alexandrine** was lengthened in Helsingør and two tracks fitted to replace the single track on deck. Her four funnels were removed and replaced by two new funnels on the centreline, which greatly improved her appearance. *(Museet for søfarts)*

direction with a lifting visor fitted to the bow to give better weather protection on the more exposed route. While the *Prinsesse Alexandrine* was DSB's last paddle train ferry, the *Prins Christian* became the model for DSB's next generation of Storebælt ferries, the *Christian*

IX and the *Odin*, built five years later.

Unlike the more utilitarian ferries on domestic routes, the ships were an expression of national pride and their passenger accommodation was built to ocean liner standards. They had electric lighting throughout and the 1st and 2nd class public rooms had polished wood panelling and leather armchairs. The Ladies' Lounge had delicate white-lacquered furniture with a gold inlay.

The service started in September 1903 with the *Prins Christian* and the German ferries. The *Prinsesse Alexandrine* followed two months later. For the first time, direct express trains could run between Berlin and København. A day service left each city in the morning and a Wagons-Lits sleeper service each evening taking just under ten hours. With a service speed of 14 knots, the ferry crossing took around two hours.

The ferries made eight to ten round trips per day and in their first year carried 80,000 passengers and 18,000 goods wagons with over 80,000 tons of freight. Within a few years, more capacity was needed and it was decided to rebuild the two single-track paddle ferries. The *Prinsesse Alexandrine* was rebuilt at the Helsingør shipyard over the 1904-05 winter. She was lengthened by 15m to 102m and the deck reconfigured to have two tracks. To create more space on deck, the four funnels were removed and replaced by two new funnels on the centreline. The lengthening also increased the size of the 3rd class saloons below the main deck. The following year, the *Friedrich Franz IV* had the same treatment at the Neptun-Werft in Rostock. The rebuilding increased the ferries' track length from 79.5m to 152m, allowing them to carry a seven-carriage train, plus luggage and mail vans. Although the conversion improved their appearance, the downside was a loss of speed and manoeuvrability, which resulted in a number of minor collisions in their later careers.

The passenger service stopped at the outbreak of the First World War and the German ferries were used for military transport between various ports. The Danish ships were initially laid-up in København, but a limited freight service was soon restarted with their neutrality signposted by 'DANMARK' and Danish flags painted on their sides. The German ferries were taken over by Deutsche Reichsbahn in 1920, when the railways were nationalised, and it was only in 1922 that the passenger train service restarted.

DSB ordered a new ferry in 1919, though with the material shortages after the war, it was the end of 1922 before the *Danmark* was delivered by the Helsingør shipyard. She was quite similar in appearance to the *Prins Christian*, with a large enclosed superstructure extending the full width of the ship. As befitted the flagship of a national railway she was outfitted to much higher standard than domestic ferries. She was larger, 102m long and with 157m of track compared to her predecessor's 129m. This allowed her to carry seven passenger coaches or up to 20 goods wagons as well as

Ostseebad Warnemünde
Mittelmole und Fährschiff Friedrich

Ostseebad Warnemünde. Fährschiff S

Top: The *Friedrich Franz IV* followed her sistership and was lengthened over the 1905-06 winter. *(Author's collection)*

Above: The screw ferry *Mecklenburg* on the Warnemünde to Gedser crossing after the Friedrich-Franz Eisenbahn had been amalgamated into Deutsche Reichsbahn in 1920. *(Carl Bellingrodt)*

Top right: The *Danmark* was delivered by Helsingør Skibsværft in 1922 as DSB's flagship. She replaced the *Prins Christian* and was the last steam ferry built for DSB. *((Ferry Publications Library))*

Middle right: The *Schwerin* was built for DR in 1926 replacing the old paddle steamer *Friedrich Franz IV*. She was used by the military during the Second World War, including a brief spell as a minelayer in the English Channel, before being destroyed by Allied bombing in 1944. *(Author's collection)*

Bottom right: Deutsche Reichsbahn's *Mecklenburg* was rebuilt in 1924 replacing her single funnel. In April 1940 she started the invasion of Denmark by landing the first German soldiers on Danish soil. *(Museet for søfarts)*

1,100 passengers. She was fitted with two triple-expansion steam engines, though she was the last steam ferry built for DSB. The following year the old *Prins Christian* was moved to the København to Malmö service.

The *Mecklenburg* was rebuilt in 1924 and her large single funnel was replaced by two funnels, so that in profile she looked very like the *Prins Christian*. This upgrade was purely a stopgap and in 1926, DR introduced a new ferry, the *Schwerin*. Like the previous German ferries, she was built by Schichau in Elbing and was a close sister to the *Danmark*. The main difference was that she was powered by steam turbines, rather than reciprocating engines as fitted to the *Danmark*.

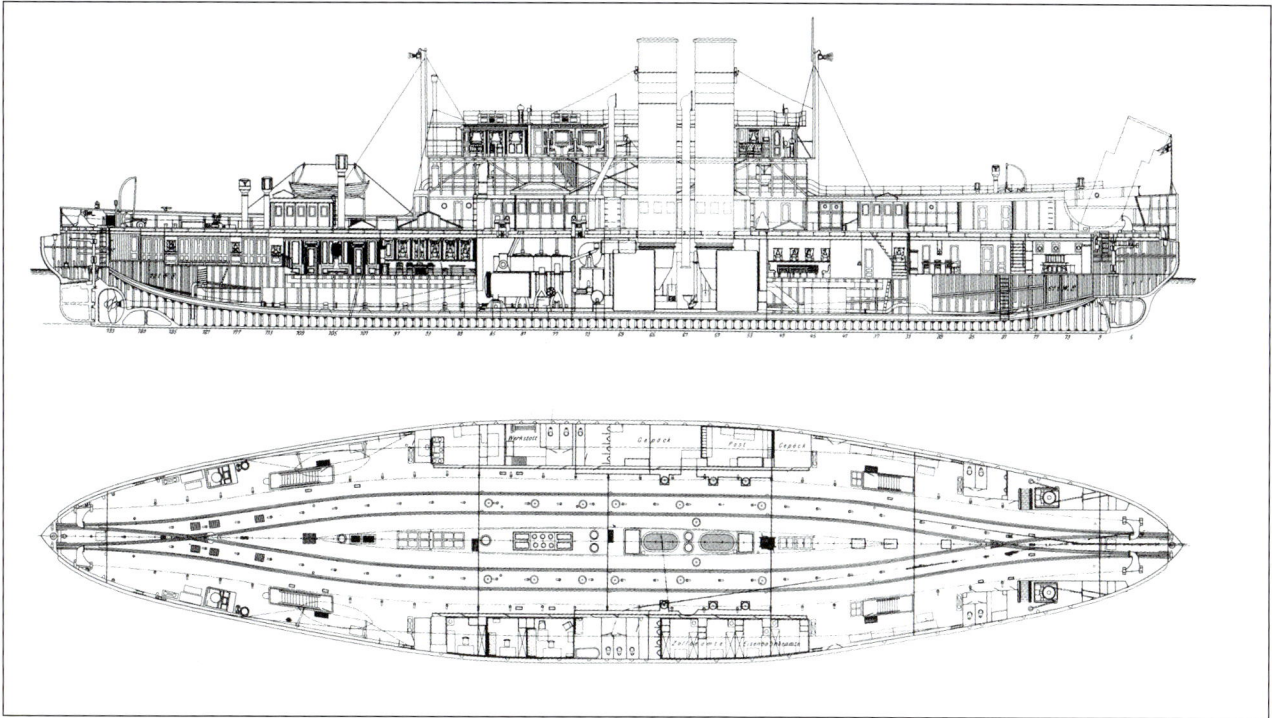

Section and Deck Plan of the **Prins Christian**. She became the model for DSB's later Storebælt ferries and served in their fleet for 52 years. *(Museet for søfarts)*

Another sign of the times was that *Schwerin* was designed to allow motor cars to be driven directly on to the train deck. On the older ferries, cars could only be carried as freight in rail wagons. When she came into service, the *Friedrich Franz IV* was retired and scrapped. The last paddle steamer, *Prinsesse Alexandrine* was laid-up in 1933 and scrapped two years later.

The winter of 1928-29 was very severe and both *Mecklenburg* and *Schwerin* were trapped in the ice off the German coast for over a week. Food supplies were dropped by aircraft and the ships were eventually freed by Russian icebreakers chartered by the German Ministry of Transport. This was also a time of economic difficulty and it was only in the 1930s that traffic began to recover. The opening of the Storstrøm Bridge in Denmark in 1937 reduced the time from Berlin to København by an hour to nine hours. On the eve of the Second World War, the three ferries, *Mecklenburg,*

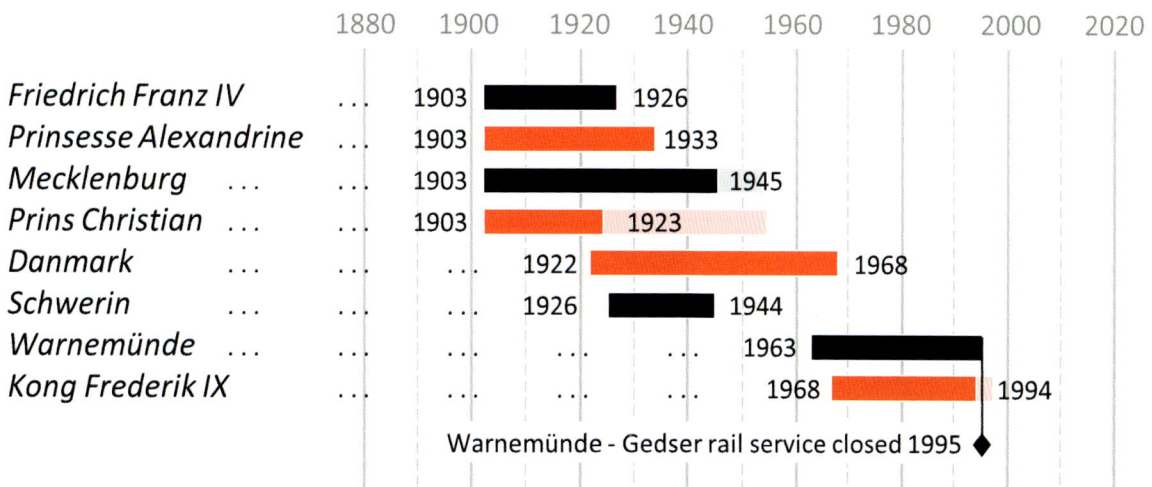

Warnemünde to Gedser ferries

Deutsche Reichsbahn
Danske Statsbaner

	1880	1900	1920	1940	1960	1980	2000	2020
Friedrich Franz IV		1903 — 1926						
Prinsesse Alexandrine		1903 — 1933						
Mecklenburg		1903 — 1945						
Prins Christian		1903 — 1923						
Danmark			1922 — 1968					
Schwerin			1926 — 1944					
Warnemünde				1963 —				
Kong Frederik IX				1968 — 1994				

Warnemünde - Gedser rail service closed 1995 ◆

It was 1963 before Deutsche Reichsbahn built a ferry for the service Denmark. The *Warnemünde* had a distinctive profile with her two squat funnels. *(Bernd Bauer)*

The 1954 built *Kong Frederik IX* took over the Gedser to Warnemünde route when the old Danmark was retired in 1968. *(Bernt Skjøtt)*

Schwerin and *Danmark* carried over 200,000 passengers and 167,000 tons of freight and 7,500 private cars in 1938.

The invasion of Denmark

The railway ferries played an important part in the German invasion of Denmark on the 9th April 1940. Soldiers were transported from Warnemünde on the *Mecklenburg*, hidden under tarpaulins on deck, and the first German boots on Danish soil arrived at Gedser at 03.55 in the morning. In the twilight of a summer morning, the town was quickly taken and the *Schwerin* arrived shortly later with more troops and vehicles, for the German army's advance north towards København. A few months later, the *Schwerin* made a voyage to the English Channel as an auxiliary minelayer, to support preparations for the invasion of England. After a few weeks, the operation was cancelled and she retuned to her ferry service in the Baltic. Although the passenger trains were stopped, the ferry service continued during

The *Warnemünde* unloads a diesel railcar at her namesake port in the 1980s. Although she seldom carried many passengers, she had a crew of 140. *(Author's collection)*

the war under military control. However, the *Schwerin* was bombed and burned out in 1944, while at the Neptun Werft in Rostock for boiler repairs, and scrapped after the war. In March 1945, the *Danmark* was sunk in Gedser harbour by the Danish resistance to prevent the German military using the port. Only the old *Mecklenburg* escaped unscathed and was captured by the Soviet Army at the end of the war and later transferred to Poland.

In post-war Germany, the port of Warnemünde was

in the Soviet Zone, which later became the German Democratic Republic, the DDR. The *Danmark* was refurbished at Burmeister & Wain in København and restarted the service in the summer of 1947, though there was limited traffic and frequent bureaucratic interruptions. A through train from København to Prague was started in 1948 but discontinued after a few years. In 1956, the Baltic ice was so severe that the ferry service stopped for six weeks.

The state railways in East Germany retained the name Deutsche Reichsbahn and in 1963 they took delivery of the *Warnemünde* from Neptun Werft in Rostock. She had a very distinctive appearance, long and low with two squat white funnels, one behind the other. She was powered by supercharged diesels connected to twin screws with variable pitch propellers, (a lesson learned from DR's first ferry *Sassnitz* which had fixed propellers). Her train deck had 317m of track able to carry 11 passenger coaches or 31 wagons, loaded through bow and stern doors. The accommodation was designed for 800 passengers, with a dining room, cafeteria, smokers lounge and wine bar. These were served by 140 crew, who for most of the year must have outnumbered the passengers. New linkspans were also built to align with her three gauntleted tracks. Her delivery allowed the reintroduction of a through train from Berlin to København, the 'Neptun', which used a diesel railcar and reduced the journey time to 7 hours, 44 minutes.

The *Danmark's* last trip was in April 1968 after which she was sold for scrapping. She was replaced on the route by the *Kong Frederik IX*, which had herself been replaced on the Rødbyhavn to Puttgarden route by the *Danmark* (II). The traffic on the route never justified two full-time ferries and after 1977, the *Kong Frederik IX* split her time between the Warnemünde and Puttgarden services.

For her first ten years, the *Warnemünde* operated to Gedser through the summer and between Sassnitz and Trelleborg in the winter. After 1973, she ran full-time between Warnemünde and Gedser and from 1984 maintained the summer service on her own with two round trips per day. The *Kong Frederik IX* operated a replacement service in winter. In 1985 the service carried 300,000 passengers, 10,000 goods wagons and 38,000 vehicles. This compared with more than 6 million passengers between Puttgarden and Rødbyhavn.

The *Warnemünde* collided with the pier at Warnemünde in 1992, due to a problem with the propeller variable pitch controls, though there was no serious damage. The following year, the operation was taken over by Deutsche Fährgesellschaft Ostsee, (DFO), which amalgamated the Deutsche Reichsbahn and Deutsche Bundesbahn ferry services, and the old *Kong Frederik IX* moved to spend her final years on the Storebælt after 25 years. DFO did not see a long-term business in the train ferry service and the *Warnemünde*

The *Danmark* loading at Gedser in the 1950s with the *Deutschland* on the right preparing to sail to Grossenbrode. *(Author's collection)*

Deutsche Bundesbahn's *Deutschland* was delivered in 1953 and allowed passenger trains between Denmark and West Germany to cross from Gedser to Grossenbrode. *(Author's collection)*

was laid-up after her last trip in September 1995 and the old ferry station at Warnemünde was closed. She was sold to an Italian ferry company and operated as a car ferry from Sardinia until scrapped in 2003.

DFO moved their operations to a new ferry terminal around 4 km south of Warnemünde in the Port of Rostock. Now part of Scandlines AG, they continue to operate a passenger and car ferry service to Gedser.

Det danske Statsbaner	**1951-1998**
Deutsche Bundesbahn / DFO	**1953-1998**
Scandlines	**1998-2019**
Großenbrode – Gedser	**1951-1963**
Puttgarden – Rødbyhavn	**1963-2019**

The shortest ferry crossing from Germany to eastern Denmark is only around 19km between the islands of Fehmarn and Lolland. The idea of developing this route, known as the Vogelfluglinie, (or Fugleflugtslinien in Danish), as it followed the bird migration route, was first raised in the 1930s. The plan was revived after the

The *Deutschland* loading DB diesel railcars at Grossenbrode. *(Author's collection)*

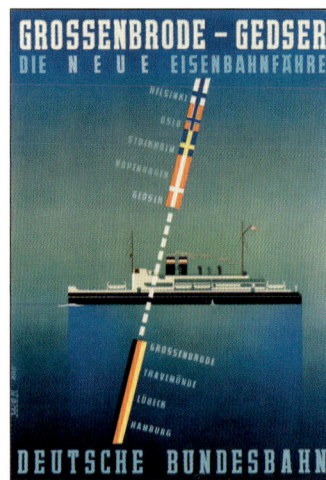

German Occupation of Denmark in 1940 with a new ferry port proposed at Rødby on the Danish island of Lolland. On the German side, a new port would be built at Puttgarden on the island of Fehmarn and a bridge linking to the mainland. The Danish firm of naval architects, Knud Hansen A/S, were approached to develop designs for large diesel train ferries. In September 1941, the Danish Transport Minister, Gunnar Larsen, was invited to ceremoniously turn the first sod for the new ferry port at Rødbyhavn. Symbolically, the spade broke, and as the war progressed and German resources were diverted to other priorities, the project came to halt.

After the Second World War most of the German Baltic coast, including Warnemünde, became part of East Germany and a new crossing was needed for a rail link from København to what had become West Germany. The short crossing was not viable until a bridge to Fehmarn and new ferry ports could be built, so in July 1951 a service was started between Grossenbrode and Gedser. The crossing was 69 km and took around 2½ hours. This was initially served by the *Danmark* which was under-utilised on the service to Warnemünde and alternated with crossings to Grossenbrode. A connecting railcar ran from Hamburg to Grossenbrode, but there was no through train, only goods wagons, vehicles and passengers crossed on the ferry.

Through trains were revived with the delivery of Deutsche Bundesbahn's new ferry the *Deutschland* in 1953. Regular direct trains were started from København to Hamburg and the 'Skandinavien-Italien-Express' from København to Roma. The *Deutschland* was a solid looking motor ferry built by Howaldtswerke

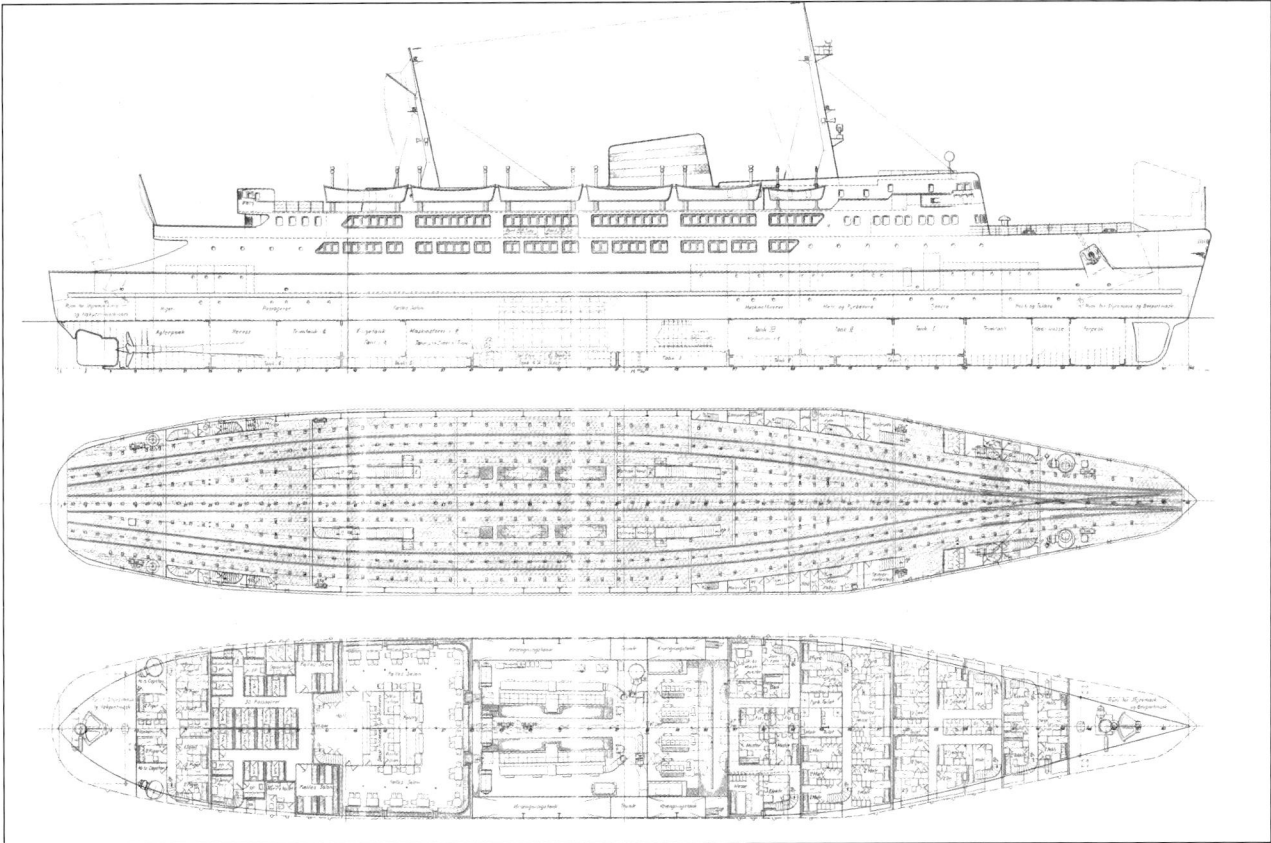

The elegant profile of the *Kong Frederik IX*, built by Helsingør Skibsværft in 1954. Her rounded funnel and bridge top and sweeping aft bulkheads were typical of Scandinavian ferries of the 1950s. *(Museet for søfarts)*

The train deck of DSB's *Kong Frederik IX* when delivered in 1954. The rails and tie-down points are set flush with the timber deck to allow cars to be carried. *(Museet for søfarts)*

The train deck of DSB's *Kong Frederik IX* when delivered in 1954. The rails and tie-down points are set flush with the timber deck to allow cars to be carried. *(Museet for søfarts)*

Deutsche Werft in Kiel. She could carry 1,200 passengers and was powered by two MAN diesels. The train deck had space for ten carriages or 24 wagons carried on three tracks that were gauntleted over the stern ramp. DSB had built the dock at Rødbyhavn to their 'Storebælt standard', so that ferries could be transferred between routes, and they insisted that the DB ferries conformed to the same hull shape and breadth. Thus, the *Deutschland* had a breadth of 17.7m with the forward part of the hull tapered to fit the piling of DSB's ferry dock.

Traffic on the crossing increased quickly and DSB modified the Storebælt ferry *Dronning Ingrid* for stern loading in 1953 to allow her to run alongside the *Deutschland*. For much of her career she time-shared between this crossing and the Storebælt. DSB's new flagship, the *Kong Frederik IX* was delivered in 1954 by the Helsingør Skibsværft and was a close sister to *Deutschland* in terms of dimensions and capacity, but with her black hull and round funnel top she had a more elegant profile.

DB's second ferry, the *Theodor Heuss* was delivered

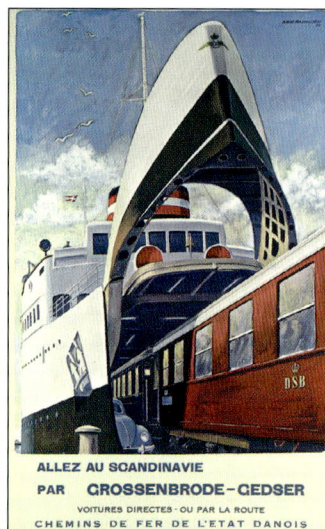

Top left: Deutsche Bundesbahn's second ferry, the *Theodor Heuss*, unloading at Grossenbrode Kai in the early 1960s. *(Author's collection)*

Left: A Deutsche Bundesbahn VT 12 railcar rolling off the *Theodor Heuss* at Grossenbrode on a snowy day in 1959. *(Flodur 44)*

Above: DSB's new flagship, the *Danmark* (II) took over from the *Kong Frederik IX* between Rødbyhavn and Puttgarden in 1968. *(Mariolu04)*

Left: The *Theodor Heuss* in 1981 with DB's later livery of a blue hull and grey stripe on the superstructure. The large ugly ventilation shafts were also retrofitted aft of the funnel. *(Mariolu04)*

in 1957, named after the Federal President. Like her predecessor, she was built by Howaldtswerke Deutsche Werft in Kiel, though she was 20m longer than the *Deutschland* and *Kong Frederik IX*, which gave her 318m of track, compared to the older ferries' 256m. Her main innovation was diesel-electric propulsion, with nine Maybach diesel engines driving generators which fed four DC electric motors geared to the propeller shafts. Compared to the other ferries on the route, she had an ungainly appearance which was made worse when two huge ventilators were later fitted aft of the funnel.

In November 1957, the *Deutschland* ran aground near the entrance to Grossenbrode harbour in bad weather. Efforts by the Fehmarnsund ferry, the *Schleswig-Holstein*, to tow her free failed when she ended on the beach herself. The *Deutschland* was refloated and towed free after 42 hours, fortunately without significant damage. She had a more serious incident in 1969 when she hit the Puttgarden Ostmole in dense fog. Several passengers were thrown off their feet by the impact and some needed hospital treatment.

The Vogelfluglinie revived

It was not until 1958 that the Danish and West German Governments agreed to revive the Vogelfluglinie project for a short crossing between Puttgarden and Rødbyhavn. The new ports were built and the Fehmarnsund bridge opened in April 1963 allowing the *Deutschland, Theodor Heuss* and *Kong Frederik IX* to move to the new route the following month. The crossing time was reduced to an hour and the port at Grossenbrode was closed.

Increased traffic meant that they were soon joined by the Storebælt ferry *Knudshoved* which had her stern doors widened in 1963 to fit the Rødbyhavn linkspans and, just as importantly, the rear saloon was enlarged to incorporate a duty-free shop. She went to Rødbyhavn the following year and in the summer of 1965 the four ships operated 28 sailings per day in each direction.

Larger ships were needed and DSB built a new flagship, the *Danmark* (II), which joined the route in 1968 allowing the *Kong Frederik IX* to move to Gedser. The *Danmark* (II) was built by Helsingør Skibsværft and was 30m longer than her predecessor with space for 1,500 passengers. The three tracks on her main deck could carry 12 coaches or 30 wagons and there was a separate car deck above. Despite the height of the superstructure and the bow door, *Danmark* (II) was one of the most elegant train ferries ever built. She had a fine bow and a central rounded funnel. The sweeping line separating the black hull from the white superstructure created the illusion of gentle curves that the slab-sided hull did not have in reality.

In 1972 DB build their new flagship, the *Deutschland* (II), which replaced her older namesake. She was built by Nobiskrug Werft in Rendsburg and essentially a sistership of *Danmark* (II), in terms of dimensions and

DB's new flagship, the *Deutschland* (II), was delivered by Nobiskrug Werft in Rendsburg in 1972 and took over from her older namesake. *(mariolu04)*

After German unification, the Deutsche Bundesbahn and Deutsche Reichsbahn ferry fleets were merged under the Deutsche Fährgesellschaft Ostsee, *(Pieter Inpyn)*

capacity. However, she had quite a different look, with a more angular superstructure and a sharp-edged funnel with a skip. The hull was painted blue and the height of the superstructure was broken by a horizontal grey stripe through the saloon windows.

The old *Deutschland* was laid-up and there were negotiations to sell her to either DSB or Polish Railways, however in the end she went to Greece as a car ferry. As the *Nisos Rodos*, she suffered a major fire in 1978 and was scrapped the following year.

The *Theodor Heuss, Danmark* (II) and *Deutschland* (II) continued through the 1970s with part-time assistance from the *Knudshoved* and *Kong Frederik IX*. In the summer of 1977, there were five ships on the route providing 33 sailings in each direction. When DSB's large new 'Inter-City' ferries arrived at the Storebælt in 1980, the older *Prins Henrik* and *Dronning Margrethe II* were moved to Rødbyhavn. The six-year-old *Prins Henrik* went to Nakskov for conversion first, where she was lengthened by 12m and her superstructure jacked-up to create a new car deck, to match the facilities on *Danmark* (II). She arrived at Rødbyhavn in 1981 and the following winter her sistership *Dronning Margrethe II* had the same treatment. With these two large ferries on the route, the *Knudshoved* and *Kong Frederik IX* returned to the Storebælt.

DB's last and largest ferry was the *Karl Carstens*,

Top left: An aerial view of Rødbyhavn in the 1980s with DSB's three ferries. The **Prins Henrik** on the left is loading cars to the upper deck. **Danmark** (II) in the middle is unloading both cars and passenger coaches, while D*ronning Margrethe II* is at the reserve berth on the right. *(Bruce Peter collection)*

Top right: DSB's **Prins Henrik** was transferred to Rødbyhavn in 1981 when the new large 'Inter-City' ferries were introduced to the Storebælt service. *(Bruce Peter collection)*

Middle right: The **Dronning Margrethe II** was lengthened and had her superstructure raised to include a car deck, before joining her Storebælt sistership **Prins Henrik** in 1982. *(Miles Cowsill)*

Right: The last ferry built for Deutsche Bundesbahn was the **Karl Carstens**, delivered in 1986. *(Author's collection)*

Bottom Right: The **Prins Richard** was delivered to Scandlines A/S in 1997. The Danish and German ferries have differently shaped superstructures and wheelhouses. *(Sebastian Ziehl)*

Above: The German flag ferry, **Schleswig-Holstein**, was delivered in 1997. Like her sisterships she has only a single rail track for a six-coach train. *(Jan Huismann)*

Großenbrode to Gedser and Puttgarden to Rødbyhavn ferries

Deutsche Bundesbahn ▬
Danske Statsbaner ▬

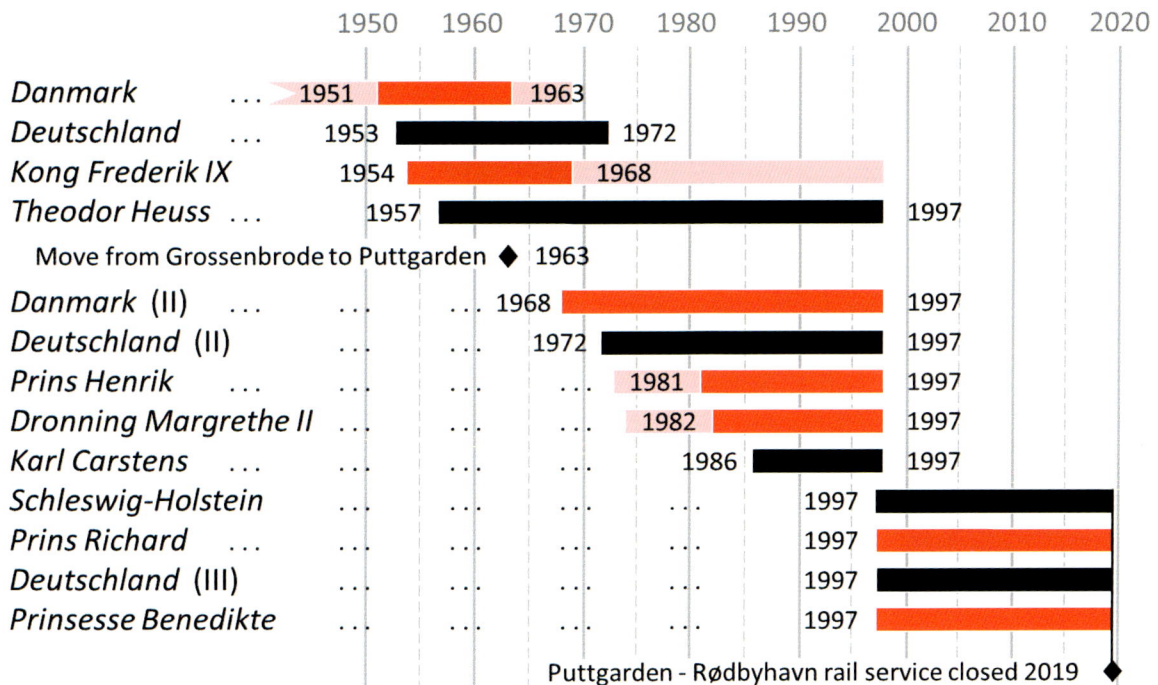

	1950	1960	1970	1980	1990	2000	2010	2020
Danmark ...	1951 ▬▬▬ 1963							
Deutschland ...	1953 ▬▬▬▬▬ 1972							
Kong Frederik IX	1954 ▬▬▬▬ 1968 ▬▬▬▬							
Theodor Heuss ...	1957 ▬▬▬▬▬▬▬▬▬▬ 1997							
Move from Grossenbrode to Puttgarden ◆ 1963								
Danmark (II) ...			1968 ▬▬▬▬▬▬ 1997					
Deutschland (II) ...			1972 ▬▬▬▬ 1997					
Prins Henrik ...			1981 ▬▬▬ 1997					
Dronning Margrethe II			1982 ▬▬ 1997					
Karl Carstens ...			1986 ▬▬ 1997					
Schleswig-Holstein				1997 ▬▬▬▬				
Prins Richard ...				1997 ▬▬▬▬				
Deutschland (III)				1997 ▬▬▬▬				
Prinsesse Benedikte				1997 ▬▬▬▬				
Puttgarden - Rødbyhavn rail service closed 2019 ◆								

delivered in 1986 by Howaldtswerke Deutsche Werft in Kiel. In appearance she was a stretched version of *Deutschland* (II), the main difference was that the aft mast was no longer attached to the funnel. Like her predecessors, she had diesel electric propulsion, with six Krupp MaK diesel generators driving two DC motors. Ironically, she was the last ship built to DSB's 'Storebælt standard' introduced more than a century before in 1883. This restricted her breadth to 17.7m so that to increase capacity the *Karl Cartstens* could only be made longer. The restricted breadth also limited stability and prevented an upper vehicle deck that could take heavy trucks. The new ferry had a length of 164m, which gave her an L/B ratio of 9.3, and this long thin shape must have made her difficult to manoeuvre. By comparison, DSB's 'Inter-City' ferries built a few years earlier had an L/B ratio of 6.4.

The *Danmark* (II) spent 29 years reliably sailing on the same crossing. The only recorded incident was in 1995, when she suffered an engine breakdown in bad weather. With reduced power, it was too dangerous to enter the narrow channel to Rødbyhavn, so she made a nine-hour diversion to Nyborg, where the cars on the upper deck had to be landed with a mobile crane. This was one occasion when the multiple diesel-generator sets on the DB ferries would likely have been more reliable than *Danmark's* two direct drive diesels.

The Scandlines quartet

DFO and Scandlines A/S reviewed the future of the Vogelfluglinie in the mid-1990s. Their older ships were expensive to operate and needed replacement while much of their rail freight traffic was likely to disappear when the Storebælt fixed link opened. They decided to retire their six old ships and replace them with four new double-ended ferries. The challenge was for the new ships to maintain the existing timetable, with a sailing every half-hour at peak times. With six ships, each crossing took an hour with a 30-minute turnround in port. To maintain the timetable with four ships, the crossing time had to be reduced to 45 minutes with a 15-minute turnround. Two pairs of almost identical ships were built. The *Schleswig-Holstein* and the *Deutschland* (III) were built for DFO by Van der Giessen de Noord BV in Krimpen a/d Ijsel in the Netherlands. The *Prins Richard* and the *Prinsesse Benedikte* were built in Denmark for Scandlines A/S by Ørskov Stålskibsværft in Frederikshavn.

The German ferries were delivered in the DFO livery, but all four ships were soon painted in Scandlines colours with dark blue funnels carrying Scandlines' triangular logo. The four ships had identical hulls and propulsion, though with minor differences in the accommodation layout. The ends of the superstructure are semi-circular on the two German ferries, while on

Deutsche Bundesbahn's ICE train rolling on to the *Prinsesse Benedikte* at Puttgarden in 2013. *(Hans & Jeanny de Rond)*

the Danish ferries, they are sloped with an overhanging bridge. To reduce the crossing time, the ships maintain a service speed of 16-18 knots and are fully double ended, so that they do not turn. The docks have been rebuilt for their 25.4m breadth with an automatic locking system to minimise connection time. The hull design is unique with a semi-detached bulbous bow and two azimuth thrusters at each end. All four thrusters are used together, with 40% of the power distributed through the forward thrusters and 60% through the aft. With no requirement to carry goods wagons, they have a single 118m rail track on one side of the deck to carry two DSB IC3 three-car trains, each 58.8m long.

When the four new ships entered service in 1997, the six old ferries were retired. The old *Theodor Heuss* was scrapped, having spent 40 years on the crossing. The *Deutschland* (II) was sold to the Red Sea as a car ferry but was scrapped in 1999. The *Karl Carstens* had the most remarkable second career as she was converted to an oil production vessel. Renamed the *Helix Producer 1*, she is still in service in the Gulf of Mexico. The *Danmark*, *Prins Henrik* and *Dronning Margrethe II* were laid-up in 1997, joining the other seven old DSB train ferries made redundant by the Storebælt fixed link. The *Danmark* was scrapped in 1999 and in the same year, the *Prins Henrik* was sold to Italy where she ran as a car ferry until scrapped in 2007. Only the *Dronning Margrethe II* survived in the Baltic for a few years, running as a goods vehicle ferry alongside the *Prins Richard* and *Prins*

Enthusiasts witness the last Hamburg to København train crossing between Puttgarden and Rødbyhavn on the 14th December 2019. The end of 147 years of Danish train ferries. *(Author's collection)*

Benedikte until 2001. After this she ran between Rostock and Gedser until sold for scrapping in 2005.

The four new ferries lives have not been uneventful, no doubt partly due to their tight timetable. The *Schleswig-Holstein* collided with the breakwater entering Puttgarden in 1997, the *Prinsesse Benedikte* did the same in 1999 as did *Prins Richard* in 2001. *Prinsesse Benedikte* was also damaged in 2015 while being drydocked in Gdansk. The floating dock she was in heeled over and she fell off the blocks.

Scandlines have been leaders in applying 'green' technology to their fleet and the ferries were converted to hybrid power in 2013-14. One of their five diesel generators was replaced by a 50-ton battery bank that could store 1.9MWh. The thrusters are driven from the battery bank which is charged by the remaining diesel generators. This allows the generators to be run at their optimum fuel efficiency all the time, with the battery bank taking account of variable loads. A programme started in 2019 to replace the ferries' four azimuth thrusters with a more fuel-efficient and quieter design.

The last through train from Hamburg to København across the ferry was on the 14th December 2019. After this, the train was routed over the Storebælt link which allowed longer trains. The last passenger train in Northern Europe to cross on a ferry was unloaded at Rødbyhavn at 20.02, bringing Denmark's 147 years of train ferry operation to an end. Since then, the four ships continue as passenger and vehicle ferries. The plan to replace them with a tunnel between Rødbyhavn and Puttgarden has been discussed for several decades and preparatory work is underway. It would be brave to state when the tunnel will be completed, as most of these large projects have several false starts and delays, as did the Vogelfluglinie itself.

Germany to Sweden

Statens Järnvägar / SweFerry	
Königlich Preußische Staatseisenbahnen	1909-1920
Deutsche Reichsbahn/DFO	1920-2000
Stena AB	2000-current
Sassnitz – Trelleborg	1909-2020
Rostock – Trelleborg	1993- current

Mail steamers had operated from the Swedish port of Ystad, and later from Malmö, to Stralsund on the German coast since the 1860s. In 1897, the route was shortened when a train ferry was put in place from Stralsund to the island of Rügen and the railway extended north to the little fishing port of Sassnitz. The opening of the train ferry between Gedser and Warnemünde in 1903 saw much of the traffic from Sweden to Germany routed through Denmark and started discussion between the Swedish and German Governments about introducing a similar ferry.

Agreement was reached in 1906 and after competition with the port of Ystad, Trelleborg was chosen to be the Swedish terminal. A huge amount of civil works was needed to build the harbours and ferry ports at both Trelleborg and Sassnitz, including dredging, breakwaters and lighthouses. In Sassnitz, the railway had to be extended from the existing town

station down a steep gradient to the new port. The Swedish railways also built forty-five new passenger coaches, including sleeping cars, baggage and mail vans specifically for the service. They were built to the German rail standard which was 200mm narrower than the coaches normally used in Sweden.

The two railway companies, Königlich Preußische Staatseisenbahnen, (Prussian State Railways) and the Swedish Statens Järnvägar each ordered two ferries in 1908. The *Deutschland* and the *Preussen* were built by AG Vulcan in Stettin. The first Swedish ferry, the *Drottning Victoria*, was built by Swan, Hunter & Wigham Richardson in Newcastle and her sistership, the *Konung Gustav V*, by Lindholmens Verkstad in Göteborg. The four ships were nominally identical, 113m long with accommodation for 975 passengers and two tracks on main deck able to carry eight coaches or 16-18 wagons loaded over the stern. They were all painted white and their fine hulls and high bow gave an almost yacht-like appearance, topped off with two tall yellow funnels. The accommodation on the *Drottning Victoria* was described in 'The Engineer' magazine of June 1909:

The smoke-room is in fumed oak, Old English in

175

The **Deutschland** leaving the narrow mouth of Trelleborg harbour. The Kungsleden, (Royal Route) between Sassnitz and Trelleborg started in 1909. *(Järnvägsmuseet)*

style, and in colour harmonises with the covering of the furniture, which is in blue antique morocco leather; a touch of colour is given by the inlaid metal marqueterie in the pilasters and by three beaten copper panels at the fore and aft ends of the room. . . .

The lounge is treated as a drawing room, and the woodwork is of grey sycamore, finished with a high polish in a free treatment of German Renaissance. The furniture is inlaid mahogany Sheraton, covered with fine French repp in two shades of rose pink, and the curtains are silk tapestry of a similar delicate shade. The carpet is Axminster and harmonises in colour with the rest of the furniture. Leading forward from the grand entrance, which is Grecian in style, is the Regal room. This compartment, set aside for the exclusive use of Royalty, is carried out in the Adams style. The wood is sycamore with grey silk panels. The fireplace is richly carved, and the white tiles behind the radiator are decorated with purple Adams ornament.

To be fair, 3rd class was a bit plainer, but still featured *'pine panels finished in white enamel and green repp sofa seats'*. There was also accommodation for six Customs Officers, ten Post Office sorters and eight railway officials. On the train deck, the coaches were held down by turnbuckles and then screw jacks were placed under the cars to relive the springs. Given the severity of winter weather in the open Baltic, there was an additional screw attachment which connected the roofs of the coaches to the deck girder above the train deck.

Deutsche Reichsbahn's second ferry, the **Preussen** in Trelleborg harbour. *(Author's collection)*

The service was inaugurated in July 1909, by Kaiser Wilhelm II and King Gustav V, and was marketed as the Kungsleden, (the Royal Route). The sea crossing of 105km took around four hours. Initially served by the *Deutschland, Preussen* and *Drottning Victoria*, the *Konung Gustav V* was delivered in 1910. There were direct trains from Stockholm to Hamburg and Berlin, the journey to Berlin took just less than 24 hours and with faster locomotives on both sides was reduced to 21½ hours by 1914.

When the First World war broke out in July 1914, the ferry service was stopped. The *Deutschland* was requisitioned by the military as a minelayer. However, after a few months the other three ships were back in service. In fact, the war proved less of an interruption than the harsh winters of the 1920s. In the winter of 1924 both the *Deutschland* and the *Konung Gustav V* were stuck in metre-thick ice off the German coast for

Sassnitz & Rostock to Trelleborg ferries

Deutsche Reichsbahn ▬

Statens Järnvägar ▬

	1880	1900	1920	1940	1960	1980	2000	2020
Deutschland		1909		1944				
Preussen		1909		1944				
Drottning Victoria		1909			1967			
Konung Gustav V		1910			1967			
Starke			1931		1971			
Trelleborg					1958 1977			
Sassnitz					1959 1986			
Skåne					1966 1989			
Drottningen					1968 1976			
Stubbenkamer					1971 1977			
Rügen					1972	2004		
Götaland					1973 1994			
Svealand					1973 1982			
Rostock					1977 1993			
Trelleborg (II)					1981		2014	
Sassnitz (II)					1989			

Sassnitz service closed 2020 ◆

Rostock service opened 1993

	1880	1900	1920	1940	1960	1980	2000	2020
Rostock						1993 1998		
Götaland						1994 1998		
Mecklenburg-Vorpommern						1996		
Skåne (II)						1998		

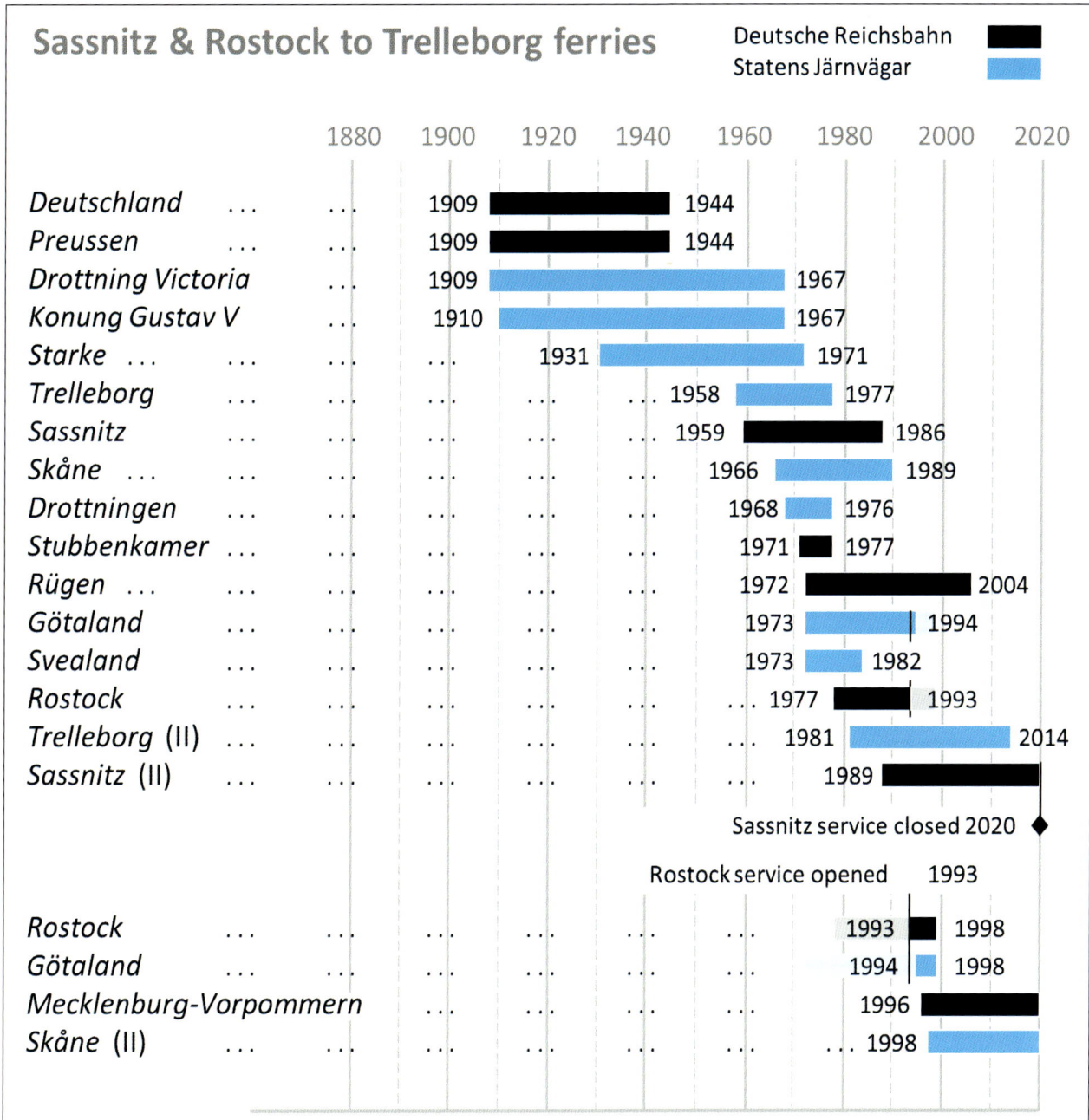

several days and supplies were carried across the ice to the trapped passengers and crew. In 1929, conditions were even worse and the service was interrupted for several weeks, with the ferries trapped in their harbours by ice. The *Drottning Victoria* had a close escape in January 1929. A large amount of frozen spray had built-up on the superstructure and in severe weather she rolled heavily, breaking the chains securing several goods wagons. The wagons rolled back and forward on the train deck several times, causing more damage as they went. Only at the last moment did some of the crew manage to clamp the brake shoes and stop the wagons breaking through the stern gate. Within a few days, the *Deutschland* was holed when she struck a rock while entering Trelleborg harbour in a snowstorm and had to be towed to Kiel for drydock repairs.

As a result of these problems, Swedish railways decided to build an icebreaking freight ferry to maintain the winter service and assist the regular ferries if they got trapped in ice. The design was prepared by AB Lindholmen and the *Starke* was built by Deutsche Werke in Kiel and delivered in 1931. She was shorter than the older ferries, but with three tracks on deck she could carry 22 goods wagons. She was also painted white, but with a single funnel. More importantly, she was reinforced for icebreaking with 20-25mm thick plate around the waterline and double bottoms separated into seven watertight compartments. She also had large forward and aft trimming tanks to help with icebreaking, connected by an 800t/h pump.

The *Konung Gustav V* loading the Stockholm – Berlin Express at Trelleborg, with the *Drottning Victoria* on the right. *(Järnvägsmuseet)*

The *Preussen* suffered an accident in 1926, when drydocked at AG Vulcan in Stettin. She fell off the blocks when the floating drydock partially flooded and developed a list. *(Author's collection)*

The first Swedish ferry, the *Drottning Victoria* shows off her yacht-like lines with her white hull and buff funnels. *(Museet for søfarts)*

Despite the *Starke*, the ice remained a problem. In the winter of 1937, the *Konung Gustav V* took 25 hours for one crossing and the *Drottning Victoria* had to go to assist the *Preussen* which had been trapped in the ice for a week and run out of coal. The *Victoria* managed to manoeuvre within 50m of the trapped ship and the crew carried 40 tons of coal across the ice in sacks. That was not the end of the *Preussen's* problems as in December 1937 she ran aground near Sassnitz in a blizzard and was stranded for 20 days before she was refloated.

With the outbreak of the Second World War, the ferry service was only briefly suspended and the *Deutschland* was once again requisitioned to act as a mine layer, this time in the English Channel. After the invasion of Norway in 1940, German troops were allowed to transit through neutral Sweden and there was a daily military train from Trelleborg to the Norwegian border. In February 1942, the *Starke* came to the assistance of the *Koning Gustav V* which was trapped in the ice near the German coast. The *Starke* struck a mine, a fire spread through her accommodation and she started flooding. The crew pushed six wagons overboard in an attempt to keep her afloat, but after several hours she sank in shallow water. Fortunately, the crew escaped to the *Gustav* without any casualties. In October of the same year, the *Deutschland* was not so lucky. She was torpedoed by a Russian submarine and the aft end of the train deck was curled upwards to the height of the bridge. The *Deutschland* managed to reach Trelleborg harbour, but around 30 passengers and crew were killed.

More than a hundred years later, the 1909 linkspans are still in use at Trelleborg, with the winged wheel, crown and supporting dolphins at the top of the gantry. *(Rick Skateboard)*

After the ferries had been trapped by ice a number of times, the Swedish Railways built the *Starke* as an icebreaker and goods wagon ferry in 1932. She struck a mine and sank in 1942 while trying the break the *Konung Gustav V* out of the ice. *(Järnvägsmuseet)*

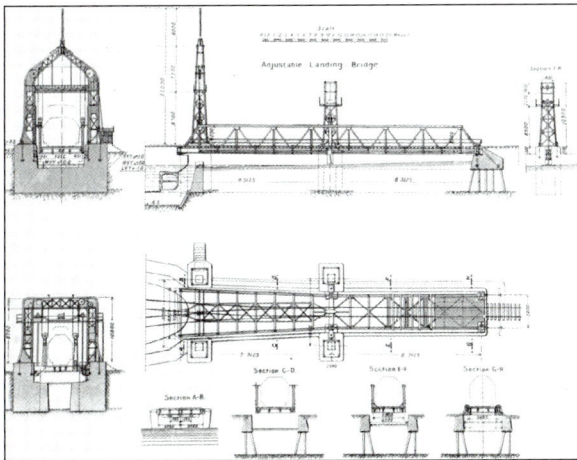

Although there is little tide in the Baltic, the ferry ports had substantial linkspans, with two gauntleted tracks. *(The Engineer)*

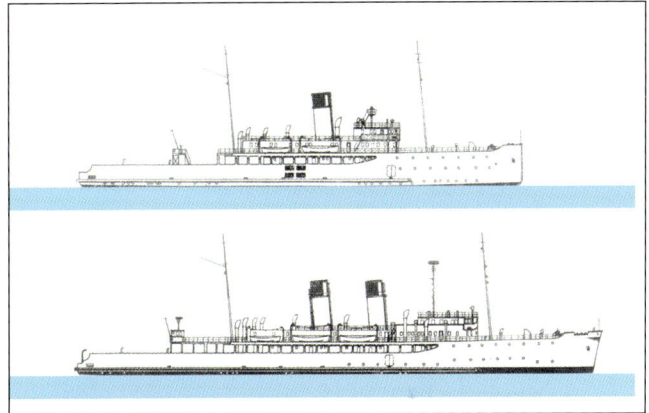

The *Starke* was salvaged in 1943 and completely rebuilt at Kockums in Malmö. She was lengthened by 18.7m and emerged in 1946 with passenger accommodation and a second funnel. *(Kramer, Kramer & Foerster)*

The *Starke* was raised the following year and towed to Malmö for rebuilding, but the Swedish Government stopped the ferry service in September 1944. The *Deutschland* and *Preussen* were used to evacuate German civilians as the Soviet Army advanced along the Baltic coast. At the end of the war, they were used by the Allies for a few months and in 1946 handed over to the Soviet Union, who renamed them Анива, *(Aniva),* and Крильон, *(Krillon)*. The two ships were sailed to Vladivostok and used as passenger ships on Russia's Pacific Coast. The *Aniva* (ex- *Deutschland*) sank in 1960 and the *Krillon* (ex- *Preussen*) was in service until 1975 and after this used as a floating hostel.

After the war

The *Starke* was completely rebuilt at Kockums, lengthened by 18.7m, re-engined and emerged in 1946 fitted with a second funnel. The port of Sassnitz and the bridge to the island of Rügen had been badly damaged during the war and SJ initially restarted the ferry service with a longer crossing to

The *Konung Gustav V* going astern into Trelleborg in the 1950s. She had been updated to oil-firing and the boat and promenade decks enclosed, though she kept her slender funnels. *(Museet for søfarts)*

Warnemünde in June 1947. The ships returned to Sassnitz in March of the following year. Sassnitz, like Warnemünde, was in East Germany and initially there was limited traffic. Statens Järnvägar used the ferries on other routes, from Trelleborg to Travemünde in West Germany and to Swinoujscie in Poland. Following a grounding in 1952, the *Drottning Victoria* was modernised, her boilers were converted from coal to oil-firing and new wider funnels were fitted, which did not improve her appearance. Internally, new furniture replaced some of the worn-out Edwardian splendour. The *Konung Gustav V* had the same modifications soon after but managed to retain her slender funnels.

Only in the 1950s did freight traffic increase and the Swedish and East German railways build new ships. SJ's *Trelleborg* was delivered by Helsingør Skibsværft in 1958. She was the first motor ship on the route, powered by two B&W diesels. She was also the first to have four rail tracks, giving space for around 36 goods wagons, and a separate mezzanine car deck and, like her predecessors, she loaded over the stern. The *Trelleborg* was as elegant as the older ferries, with a white hull and rounded yellow funnel, carrying the SJ crest. Diners in the restaurant were served by stewards in crisp white jackets and her accommodation was finished like an ocean liner. The public rooms were panelled with Bangkok teak and decorated with glass and ceramics by well-known artists. Her accommodation was a tour of the world's forests with Swiss cherrywood panels in the dining room, polished rosewood furniture in the

The *Drottning Victoria* was rebuilt in 1952. She was converted from coal to oil-firing, the promenade deck was enclosed and she was fitted with new wider funnels which spoilt her appearance. *(Sjöhistoriska Museet)*

cafeteria, bulkheads clad in Oregon pine and furniture from Guadelopé mahogany.

Deutsche Reichsbahn took delivery of the *Sassnitz* the following year, built by VEB Schiffswerft Neptun in Rostock. Her dimensions and capacity were similar to the *Trelleborg*, but with her two funnels, she had quite a different appearance. She was the first ferry built in East Germany after the war and some of her equipment was fairly basic. In particular, her fixed-pitch propellers made her difficult to manoeuvre at low speed. After a few near-misses, she was refitted with variable-pitch propellers in 1962. Like many ships, she could break ice

The *Trelleborg* running builders' trials in 1958. She was built by Helsingør Skibsværft and was one of the best-looking train ferries ever built. *(Museet for søfarts)*

Deutsche Reichbahn's first post-war ferry, the *Sassnitz* on trials in the Baltic in 1959. *(Gena Anfimov)*

The *Sassnitz* arriving at Sassnitz harbour in 1962, the ferries had to turn at sea and run astern into the small harbour. *(Deutsche Fotothek)*

better when going astern, and it is reported that in the severe winter of 1963, on one trip she reversed all the way across from Sassnitz to Trelleborg. The ferry berths were also rebuilt and expanded to accommodate the *Sassnitz* and *Trelleborg*, with high-level ramps to align with their upper car decks.

A second Swedish ferry, the *Skåne*, was delivered in 1966 by Uddevallavarvet AB. She was 148m long with four tracks on deck. At the time, she was the largest train ferry in Europe, with capacity for 40 wagons. She could also carry trucks as well cars on her mezzanine deck and had capacity for 1780 passengers. Her accommodation reflected the age, more Swedish pine and colourful fabrics than polished teak, and like many of the Baltic ferries built in the mid-60s she had a large dummy funnel containing a 'sky bar' lounge with panoramic windows. The twin diesel uptakes were integrated with the aft mast. With her delivery, the two old steam ferries, *Drottning Victoria* and *Konung Gustav V*, were finally retired after 58 and 57 years' service respectively and the *Starke* moved to Stockholm to start a new service to Finland.

SJ's next ferry the *Drottningen* was delivered in 1968, also from Uddevallavarvet AB. She was primarily designed to operate as a car ferry between Trelleborg and Travemünde and act as reserve on the Kungsleden. She was much smaller than the *Skåne*, 116m long and with three tracks, and could carry only 23 wagons. The *Drottningen's* career started badly when she collided with an East German Torpedo Boat which sank with

The *Skåne* in Trelleborg showing the large 'Sky Lounge' in the dummy funnel. The vertical extensions to the engine exhausts had been retrofitted to reduce fumes on deck. *(Pieter Inpijn)*

The coaches of the 'Sassnitz Express' on its way from München to Malmö being unloaded from the *Skåne* at Trelleborg in 1982. The funnel of the new *Trelleborg* (II) is just visible above the loco cab on the right. *(Author's collection)*

The *Drottningen* was delivered in 1968 and designed to open a new route from Trelleborg to Travemünde. Although a smart-looking ship, she was never a success and was laid-up in 1976 after only eight years service. *(Author's collection)*

seven casualties and the following year she was moved to Stockholm for the service to Finland. This did not work out and though she spent some time on the Travemünde route, she was chartered-out for several years and finally laid-up in 1976. She was sold to the Mediterranean the following year and operated as a car ferry until 1993. After this, she was based in Hong Kong as a casino ship until scrapped in 2004. The *Trelleborg* had largely been a reserve ship since the arrival of the *Skåne* and she was transferred to Stockholm to replace the *Drottningen* in 1972.

Over the next two years four new ships joined the Kungsleden, the first two provided by Deutsche Reichsbahn. The *Stubbenkamer* was built for Stena AB in 1971 by the Norwegian yard of Trosvik Verksted in Brevik. She was one of Stena's successful series of *Stena Carrier* ro-ro ships, built by various Norwegian yards. This also included the *Anderida* used by Sealink on the English Channel. The *Stubbenkamer* was lengthened after launching and completed as a train ferry for charter to Deutsche Reichbahn. She was purely a freight carrier, with four tracks able to carry 40 wagons. One problem was that she did not have an aft bridge, so she had to turn inside Sassnitz and Trelleborg harbours, rather than turn outside the breakwaters and run astern like the passenger ferries. She must also have had stability issues as flume tanks were fitted after a few months service to reduce her roll. DR's second ship was the *Rügen*, a more traditional passenger, vehicle and train ferry delivered in 1972 by VEB Schiffswerft Neptun in Rostock. She was similar in dimensions to the *Skåne*, with capacity for 850 passengers and four tracks on the train deck with capacity for around 40 wagons. She looked more modern than the previous DR ferries, with twin side-by-side funnels, though a bit ungainly in appearance. With the *Rügen's* arrival, DR's *Warnemünde*, no longer had to stand-in on the Sassnitz service in the winter.

Götaland and Svealand

The Swedish railways had two new freight ferries built by Nakskov Skibsværft in Denmark in 1973. The *Götaland* and the *Svealand*. The *Götaland* was owned by Statens Järnvägar, the *Svealand* was owned by Lion Ferry AB and on a long-term charter to SJ, presumably to circumvent the capital financing bureaucracy common to the public sector. The breadth of the previous ferries had been limited to 18.8m to fit the docks in Sassnitz and Trelleborg. The two railways agreed to modify the docks to increase the breadth to 22.6m to allow the *Götaland* and *Svealand* to have five tracks on deck, giving space for 45 wagons plus trucks on the upper deck.

DR took delivery of a new freight ferry, the *Rostock*, in 1977. She was largely a replica of the *Götaland* and *Svealand* built in Norway by Bergens Mekaniske Verksted A/S. She was 10m longer than her half-sisters and the first to have more than 600m of track with space for 49 wagons. With the *Rostock* on the route, the *Stubbenkammer* was laid-up after only six years' service. DR had bought her from Stena shortly after delivery and she was initially used as a deep-sea ro-ro by another East German operator. She was sold to Norway in 1983 and went through several hands before being scrapped in 2007.

The old *Sassnitz* was largely used as reserve ship after 1977, spending her summers on a car ferry service from Sassnitz to Rønne on the Danish island of Bornholm. In 1986, she was sold to Greek owners and served in the Mediterranean until she was scrapped in 2000.

By the end of the 1970s the passenger service was largely maintained by the *Skåne* and the *Rügen*, with the *Götaland*, *Svealand* and *Rostock* carrying freight and the old *Sassnitz* in reserve. It was a time when shipyards all over Europe were struggling to survive and Sweden was no exception. As a public enterprise, SJ were supported to order a large new ferry from Öresundvarvet in Landskrona. The *Trelleborg* (II) was delivered in October 1981 and billed as the largest train ferry in the world. However, she was found to have insufficient stability margin to meet two-compartment damaged conditions. This was fixed over winter at the Cityvarvet in Göteborg and she finally entered service in May 1982 fitted with sponsons which increased her breadth by 1.3m. She was much larger than any previous ferry, 170m long with a gross tonnage of 10,882 and capacity for 800 passengers and 55 wagons. Her sharp square-edged superstructure and large boxy funnel was also very different from earlier ferries, though followed the style of similar large Baltic ferries of the time. Internally, the passenger spaces were light and colourful with no sign of the polished hardwoods of her namesake 23 years earlier. The central feature was the 'Avenue' on the boat deck which linked the lounges, bars, restaurants, shops and conference rooms. This was also a time when the duty-free shop was an important feature and source of revenue for Baltic ferries. Each of the four engines was also located in its own watertight and acoustically insulated compartment to allow a single engine to be withdrawn for servicing, while the other three were operating. She also had two bow thrusters, as well as bow and stern rudders to help manoeuvring in the confined harbours.

With the delivery of the *Trelleborg* (II), the *Skåne* became reserve ferry. The *Svealand's* charter had also expired in 1981 and she was sold the following year to Rederi AB Nordö. With two passenger and two freight ships on the route, *Trelleborg*, *Rügen*, *Rostock* and *Götaland*, 321,400 passengers and 20,785 rail wagons were shipped in 1985, together with 41,043 trucks and coaches and 38,403 cars.

The *Sassnitz* (II) was delivered to Deutsche Reichsbahn in 1989 as their running mate for the

The **Drottningen**'s open train deck with three tracks and movable mezzanine car decks which allowed a flexible mix of cars, trucks and wagons. *(Järnvägsmuseet)*

The **Rügen** in Trelleborg. She was delivered to Deutsche Reichsbahn in 1972 by the Neptun Shipyard in Rostock and was the largest train ferry in Europe at the time. *(Pieter Inpijn)*

Trelleborg (II). She was built in Denmark by Danyard A/S in their Aalborg and Frederikshavn yards and was similar in size and capacity to her running mate, with space for 900 passengers and five tracks on deck for 56 wagons. Her profile was similar to the *Trelleborg* (II), but her superstructure and large funnel were more rounded in appearance. After the *Sassnitz* (II) was delivered, the *Rügen* replaced the *Skåne*, as reserve ferry. The *Skåne* was sold to Italy and used as a car ferry until scrapped in 2002. The *Rügen* was used as a car ferry from Sassnitz to Rønne and other routes. She returned briefly to the Sassnitz to Trelleborg route in 2001 after the *Sassnitz* (II) suffered fire damage. *Rügen* was laid-up in 2004 and scrapped in 2005.

The *Sassnitz* (II) had a near miss in November 1995 when a number of freight wagons overturned in heavy weather. Their cargo of steel rolls broke loose and the ship arrived in Trelleborg with a heavy list. She was the last ship built for Deutsche Reichsbahn and after German reunification, the *Sassnitz* (II), *Rügen* and *Rostock* were transferred to the new holding company DFO in the early 90s, together with the former Deutsche

SJ's two new freight ferries *Svealand* and *Götaland* in Trelleborg harbour in the 1970s. The new ferry berth in the foreground with the old 1909 ferry station behind. *(Järnvägsmuseet)*

Bundesbahn ferries. The *Rostock* and *Götaland* were transferred to the new Rostock service in 1993 and in January 1998 the *Sassnitz* (II) and *Trelleborg* (II) moved from the old rail terminal in Sassnitz harbour to the new port at Mukran, a few kilometres south. Mukran was renamed Sassnitz Ferry Port. While this improved access for both rail freight and trucks, it did not bring Sassnitz any closer to the autobahn and traffic to Trelleborg began to move over to the new route from Rostock.

Through passenger trains from Sweden to Germany disappeared after the privatisation of the railways. However, in 2012 a private rail company, Snälltåget, restarted an overnight sleeper service between Malmö and Berlin, which ran at weekends and holidays during the summer.

The *Trelleborg* (II) transferred to Stena AB in 2000 after they bought Scandlines AB from the Swedish Government, however both *Trelleborg* and *Sassnitz* continued to operate in Scandlines livery. Only after Stena bought the *Sassnitz* in 2012, were the two ships repainted in Stena colours. The *Trelleborg* had only a couple of years with her red Stena funnel before she was laid-up in 2014 and sold to the Middle East. The *Sassnitz* (II) carried on alone until 2020, when Stena announced the suspension of the service due to reduced traffic during the Covid-19 pandemic. A few weeks later, they announced that the service would not reopen. Some of *Sassnitz's* 126 crew members who lost their jobs had served onboard since she was delivered 31 years previously. The *Sassnitz* (II) made the last crossing from Trelleborg on the 16th March and left Sassnitz Ferry Port for lay-up on the 28th April. The Kungsleden

The second Swedish freight ferry, the *Svealand*, was built for Lion Ferry AB in 1973 and put on long-term charter to Statens Järnvägar. *(Museet for søfarts)*

was closed after 111 years.

The new service from Rostock

The disappearance of the border between West and East Germany was an opportunity to develop new ferry routes between Germany and Sweden. While Sassnitz offered the shortest crossing, its location on the island of Rügen was a long drive from the autobahn network. DFO saw the opportunity to provide a vehicle and rail ferry service from Warnemünde to Trelleborg. However, the old ferry station at Warnemünde was too small for their large modern ferries and did not have the space for marshalling ro-ro traffic.

In 1993, DFO's freight ferry *Rostock* was converted at the Schiffswerft Neptun, adding a new car deck and accommodation for 400 passengers and in June opened

The *Götaland* near the end of her career as reserve ship at Trelleborg in 2008. *(Svenja Welge)*

Deutsche Reichsbahn's freight ferry *Rostock* loading at Trelleborg in the early 90s with the short-lived 'TS Line' logo on her hull. *(Pieter Inpijn)*

a ferry service to Trelleborg from a new ferry terminal in the Port of Rostock. The new terminal was around 3 km south of the old Warnemünde ferry station, on the east side of the river directly opposite the Neptun shipyard. The crossing took around six hours, compared to four for the Sassnitz crossing.

The *Götaland* had been similarly converted at Öresundsvarvet in Landskrona the previous year. Her superstructure was raised by 2.7m to provide a new deck with space for 35 cars and increase her passenger accommodation from 36 to 400. She returned to the same yard in the winter of 1993-94 and was lengthened by 33.6m to 183m. After this, she joined the *Rostock* on the service to Trelleborg.

The Rostock route proved very successful and DFO and SweFerry decided to build the two last and largest

railway-owned train ferries. In December 1996, DFO took delivery of the *Mecklenburg-Vorpommern* from Schichau Seebeckwerft AG, in Bremerhaven. In gross tonnage she was 80% larger than the *Sassnitz* (II) with space for 890 passengers, 440 cars and around 75 rail wagons on six tracks. Despite her size, she recovered a little of the elegance of the older ferries, with the front of her superstructure raked and with rounded corners. She was first delivered with DFO markings on her funnels and the word 'HANSA' in large blue letters on her sides. Following DFO's merger with Scandlines, she was repainted with the words 'Scandlines HANSA' on her sides and dark blue funnels with Scandlines' triangular logo. In 1998 Scandlines AG sold her to an investment company, chartering her back on a long-term lease.

Skåne

The second ferry was the *Skåne* (II), built for SweFerry by Astilleros Espanoles, in Puerto Real near Cadiz and delivered in 1998. She was slightly larger than the *Mecklenburg-Vorpommern* and is the largest passenger train ferry ever built, with a gross tonnage of over 42,000 and 1,110m of rail track. Designed by the Danish naval architects Knud E Hansen, the raked superstructure front and funnels give her a purposeful appearance from a distance. Close-up, the angular bulges for the vehicle deck side doors and the gantry crane on the top deck give her a more industrial look. Like the *Mecklenburg-Vorpommern*, she has six tracks on the rail deck but, uniquely for a passenger ferry, there is also a lift that takes wagons down to a lower deck. The lift is a rectangular frame, 102m long and 7.2m wide, which contains two tracks that can carry 16

185

The growth of the Kungsleden ferries

	Year built	Gross tonnage	Length (m)	Breadth (m)	No. of tracks	Track length
Dronning Victoria	1909	3,302	112.3	15.3	2	165
Trelleborg	1958	6,164	137.7	18.8	4	403
Skåne	1966	6,534	147.7	18.8	4	465
Trelleborg (II)	1981	20,028	170.2	23.8	5	755
Sassnitz (II)	1989	21,154	171.5	24.1	5	711
Mecklenburg-Vorpommern	1996	37,987	200.0	28.2	6	945
Skåne (II)	1998	42,705	200.2	29.6	6+2	1,110

The **Trelleborg** in 2009 after Scandlines AB had been bought by Stena, though still operating in Scandlines colours. *(Jens Taxwedel)*

The **Sassnitz** (II) was delivered in 1989, built in Denmark, she was the last ferry built for Deutsche Reichsbahn before German reunification. *(Fuerbi1)*

The *Sassnitz* (II) in Stena colours with coaches of the RST 302 Berlin to Malmö express being unloaded at Trelleborg in 2015. (*Steffen Haase*)

The *Sassnitz* (II) at Trelleborg in 2019, in what turned out to be the last year of the Kungsleden service. She was laid-up in April 2020. (*Markus Klausnitzer*)

wagons weighing up to 816 tons. In concept, the lift is similar to those fitted on the *Railship* vessels, however their lifts are 20-30m long carrying only a few wagons at a time. On the *Skåne*, the lift is more than half the ship's length and the wagons stay in the lift frame during the voyage. Loading and unloading requires only a single lift operation which allows all the shunting to be done at train deck level. The efficiency of this lift is hugely important to achieving the design turnround of 75 minutes. Both *Skåne* and *Mecklenburg-Vorpommern* make three crossings a day, two 6-hour daytime crossings and a 7¼-hour night sailing. Including three 75-minute turnrounds, this schedule accounts for 23 hours per day, leaving very little margin for delays.

The *Mecklenburg-Vorpommern* was delivered to DFO in 1996, the first ship built for the Rostock – Trelleborg service. As she was much broader than the previous ferries, the stern door is offset to starboard to align with the linkspan. *(Pieter Inpijn)*

The growth in size of the Kungsleden ferries over the century is shown in the table on page 186. The two ferries remaining on the Rostock to Trelleborg route being by far the largest.

With the *Skåne* in service, the *Rostock* and *Götaland* were retired. The *Rostock* was laid-up in 1998 and sold to Seawind Line of Stockholm the following year who renamed her *Star Wind*. The *Götaland* operated as a freight ferry between Travemünde and Trelleborg until 1998. In 2010, she was sold to VG Transport Terminal Company in Moscow and renamed *Apollonia*. She was used irregularly between Sassnitz and Baltijsk for two years, then sold to the Mediterranean and scrapped in 2013.

Although the *Skåne* was bought from the Swedish Government by Stena in 1999, both the *Skåne* and *Mecklenburg-Vorpommern* operated in Scandlines colours until 2012. Stena then took over the lease of the *Mecklenburg-Vorpommern* and the following year the two ferries were rebranded in Stena colours.

AB Nordö-Link/Finnlines
Travemünde – Malmö 1982-2007

In the post-war years, both Sassnitz and Warnemünde were in East Germany. Shipping goods by rail from West Germany to Sweden required either the delays and paperwork of crossing the border to the east, or the longer journey through Denmark with two ferry crossings. To provide a direct link, the Swedish company Rederi AB Nordö bought the *Svealand* from Lion Ferry AB, which had finished her charter to Statens Järnvägar. She had a major conversion at Howaldtswerke in

Like her running-mate, the *Mecklenburg-Vorpommern*, the Skåne's stern door is offset to starboard to align with the linkspans at Rostock and Trelleborg. *(Author)*

A drawing showing the *Skåne*'s wagon lift built by the Finnish cargo handling specialist MacGregor-Navire. The wagons stay on the two tracks inside the 102m long lift frame during the voyage. *(MacGregor-Navire)*

Repainted in Stena's colours in 2013, the **Skåne** was designed for functionality rather than elegance, with a square extension for the car deck door and a gantry crane on the top deck. *(Frank Lose)*

Rederi AB Nordö introduced the old SJ ferry **Svealand** on the Malmö to Travemünde route as the Svealand av Malmö in 1982. She was further modified and renamed **Svea Link** in 1987. *(Tony Garner)*

Hamburg, lengthening the hull by 35m and fitting new machinery before starting a new service from Travemünde to Malmö in 1982, renamed *Svealand av Malmö*.

In 1984 Nordö bought the ro-ro ferry *Polaris*, which had been built by Wärtsilä, Helsinki, as the *Finncarrier* in 1969. She was renamed *Scandinavia* and operated as a vehicle ferry for a few years. In 1986 the ownership of the company changed and it was renamed Rederi AB Nordö-Link. The new owners decided to convert the *Scandinavia* to a train ferry. Rails were fitted to the main deck and she was lengthened by 41m by Wärtsilä, Turku, and returned to service in April 1987 renamed *Scandinavia Link*. She was followed into the yard by the *Svealand av Malmö* whose superstructure was jacked-up to create an upper vehicle deck and returned to service the following month renamed *Svea Link*.

In 1989, Nordö-Link bought two Finnish ro-ro ships, the *Finnrose* and *Finnhawk*, which had been built in

The ***Scandinavia Link***, built as ***Finncarrier***, was lengthened and converted to a train ferry for Nordö-Link's service in 1987. *(Pieter Inpijn)*

Sweden in 1980. They were converted into bow-loading train ferries and passenger accommodation was added at Gdynia. Renamed *Lübeck Link* and *Malmö Link* they came into service in the summer of 1990, replacing the *Svea Link* and *Scandinavia Link*, which were sold to Stena.

The company also bought an old Canadian train ferry, which had been built as the *Frederick Carter* in 1967, and renamed her *Hansa Link*. She spent most of her time chartered-out as a ro-ro ferry and was sold in 1991. Nordö-Link was bought by Finnlines in 2002 and though the ships were later repainted in Finnlines colours, they retained the Nordö-Link brand on the superstructure. With the opening of the fixed links across the Storebælt and Öresund in 2000, the benefit of the direct ferry reduced. The *Lübeck Link* and *Malmö Link* were sold in 2007 and the rail service came to an end.

T-T Line GmbH
Travemünde – Trelleborg   planned

The Swedish railways, Statens Järnvägar, had experimented with a train ferry service between Travemünde and Trelleborg in the early 1970s, using the *Drottningen*, though this had not been successful. In the mid-80s, a plan to revive the service was developed with T-T Line, which had operated car and passenger ferries on the route since 1962. Two ferries were ordered from Schichau Seebeckswerft in Bremerhaven, the *Robin Hood* by T-T Line GmbH and the *Nils Dacke* by Swecarrier Rederi AB. The sisterships were delivered in 1988, designed to carry 36 wagons on six tracks on their main deck, and road trailers on their upper deck.

In the event, the companies had picked the wrong time to start a rail ferry service. The reunification' of Germany in 1990, allowed rail freight to use the shorter ferry routes from Sassnitz and later Warnemünde. The

The ***Malmö Link***, formerly the ro-ro ship ***Finnhawk***, was introduced to Nordö-Link's service in 1990 after conversion to a train ferry in Poland. *(Mathias Lu)*

ferries carried trucks for a few years and in 1993 were converted into passenger and vehicle ferries. The rails tracks were removed, a bow door fitted, and the superstructure extended to provide accommodation for 1,044 passengers.

Poland to Sweden

Statens Järnvägar	1945-1950
Polskie Koleje Państwowe	1950-1953
Gdańsk / Gdynia – Trelleborg	1945-1948
Swinoujscie – Trelleborg	1948-1953

At the end of the Second World War, the railways of Germany and Poland had been destroyed. The port of Sassnitz was not operational and the Swedish ferries *Drottning Victoria* and *Kong Gustav V* first restarted a ferry service from Trelleborg to Gdańsk in November 1945. Over the winter this was used to transport more than a thousand goods wagons from Sweden to help get the Polish railways restarted and in particular to start

The *Lübeck Link* arriving in Travemünde. Like her sister she entered service as a train ferry in 1990. Her livery was changed after Finnlines bought Nordö-Link in 2002. *(Eero Isotalo)*

The *Nils Dacke* and her sistership *Robin Hood* were built to operate as train ferries between Travemünde and Trelleborg. The service did not materialise and they were converted to passenger/car ferries in 1993. *(Pieter Inpijn)*

the movement of coal. The following spring a more regular service, with two return trips each week, began between Trelleborg and Gdynia and in the summer of 1947, a sleeping car service was started from Stockholm to Warsaw. When the *Drottning Victoria* and *Kong Gustav V* were moved to start a service to Warnemünde in 1947, the rebuilt *Starke* continued the sailings from Trelleborg to Gdynia. In 1948 the Polish terminal was moved westwards to Odra Port, formerly Ostswine, across the river from Swinoujscie. This reduced the crossing distance from Trelleborg to 178 km, compared with 407 km to Gdynia.

The old German ferry *Mecklenburg*, which had been built for the Warnemünde to Gedser crossing in 1903, had survived the war and was taken over by the Soviet authorities in 1946 and renamed *Turgenev*. The

The Polish railways *Kopernik* in 1950, with the winged wheel crest of PKP on her funnel. She was formerly the German *Mecklenburg*, built in 1903, and transferred to Poland as reparations after the Second World War. *(Author's collection)*

The *Mikolaj Kopernik* later in her career with the sponsons added in 2001 and the Unity Line funnel. *(Author's collection)*

following year she was transferred to Poland, who suffered from indecision in renaming her, first the *Waza*, then *Kruszewski* and then *Kopernik*. As *Kopernik*, the Polskie Koleje Państwowe, Polish State Railways, (PKP) put her in service between Odra Port and Trelleborg in 1950, mostly carrying coal north to Sweden. The old ferry's two funnels were linked together and fitted with a red PKP shield. In 1950, there were 650 sailings on the route transporting 11,350 wagons. However, traffic declined once the much shorter Sassnitz route was restarted. In 1953 there were only 245 trips carrying 3,100 wagons and at the end of the year, the service was stopped and the old *Kopernik* was laid-up. After a few years as an accommodation ship and workshop in Gdańsk, she was scrapped under her sixth and final name, the *Kolejarz*, in 1958.

Polskie Linie Oceaniczne	1974-1995
Unity Line	1995-2019
Swinoujscie – Ystad	1974-2019

Through the 1960s, rail traffic from Poland to Sweden was routed through East Germany and the crossing from Sassnitz to Trelleborg, though a car ferry service was started between Swinoujscie and Ystad. In 1972, Statens Järnvägar and PKP signed an agreement to start a train ferry service between the two ports.

The PKP did not have marine experience, so a combined rail and freight ferry was ordered by Polskie Linie Oceaniczne, Polish Ocean Lines, (POL) from Trosvik Verksted in Brevik. The *Mikolaj Kopernik* was delivered in 1974. She was not a large ship, 126m long and designed to carry 36 wagons on three tracks on her main deck and 16 trucks on the upper deck. She had twin funnels

Swinoujscie to Ystad & Trelleborg ferries

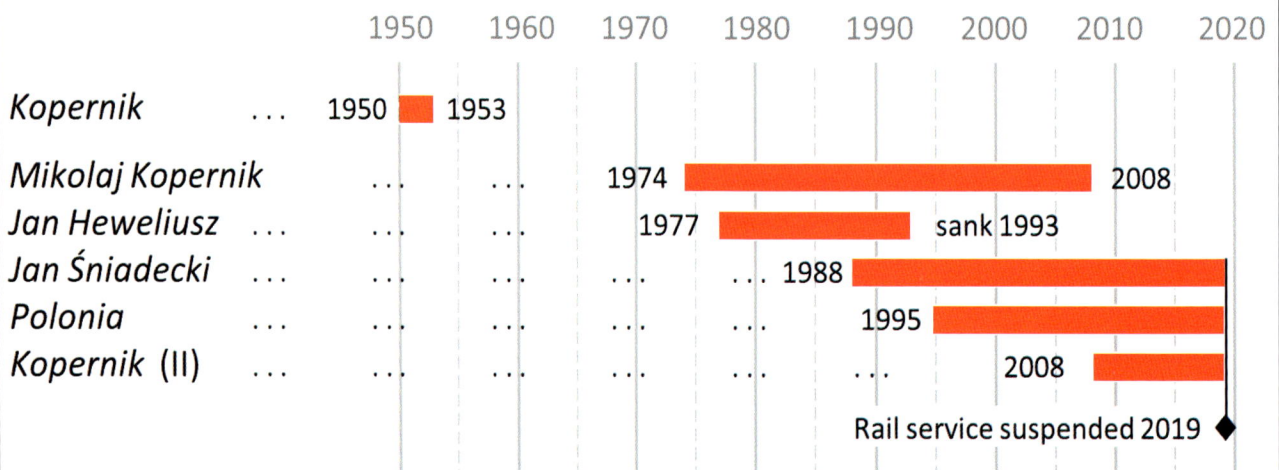

	1950	1960	1970	1980	1990	2000	2010	2020
Kopernik ...	1950 ▬ 1953							
Mikolaj Kopernik ...	...	...	1974 ▬▬▬▬▬▬▬▬▬▬▬▬▬ 2008					
Jan Heweliusz ...	...	...	1977 ▬▬▬▬ sank 1993					
Jan Śniadecki ...	...	...	...	... 1988 ▬▬▬▬▬▬▬▬▬▬▬▬▬▬▬				
Polonia ...	...	...	...	...	1995 ▬▬▬▬▬▬▬▬▬▬▬			
Kopernik (II) ...	...	...	...	...	...	2008 ▬▬▬▬▬		

Rail service suspended 2019 ◆

POLAND to SWEDEN

aft and a square dummy funnel, painted yellow with the POL crest on a red stripe.

The service was a success and 15,300 wagons were shipped in 1976, which prompted an order for a second ship. The *Jan Heweliusz* was delivered to POL by Trosvik in 1977, essentially a replica of the previous ferry. The ownership of the *Mikolaj Kopernik* was transferred to another state-owned company, Polskie Zeluga Baltycka at the same time. With two ships on the 6½ hour crossing, POL scheduled two return trips per day and quickly attracted through-traffic from Sweden to Hungary and the Balkans. In 1979, 35,000 wagons were shipped on the route with 550,000 tons of cargo.

Right from the start, the *Jan Heweliusz* was accident prone. On her first trip she suffered an engine failure and a few weeks later she collided with the harbour wall in Ystad. In August 1982, she had a major accident when she lost stability and capsized while unloading cement wagons at Ystad. She would have capsized completely if the harbour had been deeper, but came to rest at an angle of around 45°, leaning on the dock wall with her bilge keel stuck in the mud. The trucks on the upper deck all slid to the port side and the train deck and machinery spaces were flooded. Fortunately, there were no casualties, but it took a month before she could be righted using two large floating cranes and towed to Göteborg for repair. Initially, the accident was blamed

on a failure of the trimming pumps, but a later report suggested that the root cause was unloading the heavy cement wagons before discharging the trucks from the upper deck, together with slack fuel and ballast tanks. Three months later, the *Mikolaj Kopernik* was out of action for two weeks following a cable fire and SJ's *Skåne* was briefly chartered to maintain the service .

The *Jan Heweliusz* continued to have a series of minor collisions, but her next major accident was in 1986 when a refrigerated trailer on the upper deck caught fire. The fire spread to five other vehicles and did considerable damage to the superstructure before the crew brought it under control. She was repaired quickly in Hamburg and returned to service a few weeks later. The fire had buckled much of the steelwork around the upper deck, but rather than replace the steel, the owners opted for a quicker repair, using concrete to fair the surface and reinforce the damaged structure.

POL added a third ship in 1988, the *Jan Śniadecki* was built by Falkenbergs Varv. AB in Sweden. She was also principally a freight ferry, with accommodation for 57 drivers, and was both longer and wider than the previous ships. She was 155m long with five tracks on the main deck able to carry more than 60 wagons plus trucks and trailers on an upper deck. The service continued with the three ships until 1993.

193

The *Mikolaj Kopernik* in 2006, showing the large sponsons fitted five years earlier to improve her stability. The sloping rails are under the rescue boat so that it can be launched without snagging on the sponson. *(Author's collection)*

The accident-prone *Jan Heweliusz* in 1986, before her superstructure was damaged by fire. *(Author's collection)*

The *Jan Heweliusz* lost stability while unloading heavy wagons in August 1982 and capsized against the harbour wall in Ystad. *(Author's collection)*

The loss of the *Jan Heweliusz*

The sinking of the *Jan Heweliusz* in the early morning of the 14th January 1993 is without doubt the greatest tragedy involving a train ferry in Northern Europe. It began four days earlier when her stern door was damaged while docking at Ystad. The damage was not reported to the authorities and the owners told the crew to carry-out repairs as time permitted. Her departure from Swinoujscie on the night of the 13th had been delayed by two hours as the crew tried to repair the door. When she finally departed at 23.25, the door was still not watertight. There were 64 people on board, 29 crew and 35 passengers, mostly truck drivers. A severe storm was forecast, but as she left port the weather was not remarkable. As she was behind schedule, Captain Ułasiewicz set a direct course to Ystad, rather than sail west to take shelter from the German coast. The wind grew stronger as she sailed north and as she heeled over under the force of the wind, the crew decided to use the heeling tanks to keep her upright. This was the first indication that something was wrong. The tanks should have only been used when handling cargo in port, so their use at sea suggests that the wind force had caused a serious list.

For the first half of the voyage, the *Jan Heweliusz* was in the lee of the island of Rügen and the sea conditions were not extreme. Once north of Rügen, at around 03.30, she was exposed to the full force of a Baltic storm. The weather was much worse than forecast with the wind gusting to over 100 knots. She altered course to the west keeping her head to sea, but the heeling tank system had failed, so that she now had a permanent list. The captain altered course towards Rügen, seeking some protection from the storm and the first distress call was issued indicating they had a problem. An hour later at 04.35, a second distress call was broadcast saying that some of the trucks on the upper deck had broken loose and the list had increased to 30°. Two minutes later, the first emergency signal was broadcast seeking immediate assistance. At 04.45, a 'mayday' signal stated that the list was now approaching 70°. The last signal from the *Jan Heweliusz* was at 05.27 and at 05.50 she turned over, floating bottom up.

In the dark of a winter morning, most of those onboard had managed to escape to liferafts, but many died of hypothermia before they could be rescued. The water temperature was around 2°C and only the crew had survival suits, many of the passengers were in pyjamas. A rescue helicopter snagged a line on a liferaft, tipping it over and drowning several of the occupants. Of the 64 people onboard, only nine survived. The *Jan Heweliusz* finally sank around 11.00 near the coast of Rügen, where she lies in around 30m of water.

The sinking was investigated by three inquiries which rumbled on for six years. Their final conclusion in 1999 was that the vessel was not seaworthy, the stern door was not watertight and that the repairs after the fire

The *Jan Heweliusz* in Ystad harbour after being righted. She was towed to Göteborg for repair. *(Wolfgang Fricke)*

had added 60 tons of concrete to the superstructure which seriously compromised her stability. Her capsize in Ystad harbour eleven years earlier had indicated that there was little margin of stability even before the repairs. However, little blame was attributed to the owners for these defects. Most of the responsibility was put on Captain Ułasiewicz, who had not survived. The court criticised him for failing to adequately secure the cargo, for taking an inappropriate route and for not providing accurate positions in the emergency signals. The families of the casualties challenged the findings and eventually took their case to the European Court of Human Rights, which ruled that the Polish inquiries had been defective, but apart from a small amount of compensation to the bereaved families, no further action was taken.

Rebranding as Unity Line

Partly as a result of the accident, but also the reorganisation of Polish shipping after the end of communism, the consortium of owners rebranded the ferry service as Unity Line in 1995. The ownership of the *Mikolaj Kopernik* and the *Jan Śniadecki* was transferred to offshore holding companies. A large new ferry was ordered, this time with accommodation for 920 passengers, 204 cabins and the usual restaurants, shopping arcade, nightclub and other facilities common for large Baltic ferries of the time. The *Polonia* was delivered in 1995 by Langsten Slip & Båtbyggeri A/S, Tomrefjorden in Norway. She had five tracks on the train deck with a truck deck above. As she was much broader than the previous ferries, the rail tracks at the stern door are offset from the centreline to align with the existing ramps. With a large single funnel positioned well aft, she is the best-proportioned of the three large multi-purpose train ferries built in the mid-90s, *Polonia, Skåne* and *Mecklenburg-Vorpommern*.

The old *Mikolaj Kopernik* was upgraded in 2001 and fitted with large sponsons to improve her stability,

POL's freight ferry *Jan Śniadecki* at Ystad shortly after her delivery in 1988. She has the yellow funnel with red stripe and crest of the Polskie Linie Oceaniczne and the PKP logo at the aft end of the superstructure. *(Pieter Inpijn)*

though in her later years she was used mostly for trucks rather than rail wagons. Unity Line's next move was to expand their capacity with two old train ferries. The opportunity to buy second-hand ships was always restricted due to the need for ice-strengthening. In 2007, they bought the *Sky Wind* (ex- *Öresund*), and renamed her *Wolin*. She was used between Swinoujscie and Trelleborg but only carrying road vehicles. The following year they bought her old running-mate the *Vironia* (ex- *Star Wind*, ex- *Rostock*) from Estonia for the Ystad service and renamed her *Kopernik* (II). She replaced the old *Mikolaj Kopernik*, which was sold to Turkey after 34 years' service between Swinoujscie and Ystad. After a few years in the Mediterranean, she was scrapped in 2014.

The regular train ferry service between Swinoujscie and Ystad stopped at the end of 2018, when the Swedish rail operator Green Cargo AB withdrew. A few rail cargoes were carried in 2019, but since then the service has been closed. After spending eleven years with Unity Line, the *Kopernik* (II) was sold in 2019. Despite 42 years as a Baltic train ferry, she was

The *Jan Śniadecki* at Swinoujscie in 2010 in the Unity Line's blue and yellow colours. The PKP logo still at the aft end of the superstructure. *(Poul Erik Olsen)*

Unity Line's large passenger vehicle and train ferry *Polonia*, built in Norway in 1995. *(Mirek Kubicek)*

The *Wolin* leaving Swinoujscie for Trelleborg in 2013. She was previously the *Sky Wind* and originally built as the *Öresund* in 1986. *(Pieter Inpijn)*

converted for further service as a vehicle ferry in Greece. Unity Line still operate the *Polonia, Jan Śniadecki* and *Wolin*, together with four other ferries, carrying vehicles and passengers from Swinoujscie to Ystad and Trelleborg.

Sweden to Finland

Statens Järnvägar
Stockholm – Naantali   **1967-1975**

Given the huge ferry traffic between Sweden and Finland, it would be expected that train ferries were well established between the two countries. However, the traffic has always been limited by the change of gauge. Swedish railways are standard gauge, but as Finland was part of the Russian empire when the railways were built in the 19th century, they adopted a 1,534mm gauge.

Statens Järnvägar started a freight service from Stockholm to the small town of Naantali, just west of Turku, in March 1967 using the *Starke*. Initially there were three return trips each week, which was increased

to five the following year. From 1969 the service was shared between the *Starke* and the *Drottningen* until the *Starke* was retired and scrapped in 1971. The *Trelleborg* replaced the *Drottningen* in 1972, though it could hardly have been economic to operate such a large passenger ferry to carry a few goods wagons. The service was stopped at the end of 1975, partly due to the sudden increase in the oil price, but also because the opening of the Railship service took away through-traffic from Germany.

FinnLink OY
Hargshamn – Uusikaupunki   **1989-1996**

In 1989, Finnlines began operating a train ferry service between Hargshamn in Sweden and Uusikaupunki in Finland on behalf of the FinnLink consortium. This was owned by a group of industrial companies, including the steelmaker Rautaruukki, who exported much of their product through Sweden. FinnLink chartered two ro-ro ferries, the *Finnmaid* and

SWEDEN to FINLAND

The *Starke* running astern into the terminal at Värtan on the east of Stockholm. *(Järnvägsmuseet)*

The **Drottning Victoria** loading at the Värtan terminal. *(Järnvägsmuseet)*

the *Finnfellow*. The *Finnmaid* was kept as a vehicle ferry, while the *Finnfellow* was converted to a train ferry at HDW in Kiel. This included cutting the hull horizontally along its full length and jacking-up the superstructure to increase headroom on the train deck. The fleet of rail wagons were designed to allow the bogies to be changed from Finnish to Swedish gauge before being loaded at Uusikaupunki.

After a few years, the service struggled to maintain sufficient traffic, partly because of the extended rail journey north to Hargshamn compared with the rival SeaWind Line service. The *Finnfellow* suffered grounding damage on the Finnish coast in 1996 and though she was repaired, the service was closed.

SeaWind Line/Tallink
Stockholm – Turku   1989-2011

Silja Line has long been the main ferry operator between Sweden and Finland and they did not want Finnlines competing on these routes. As a response to the FinnLink service, Silja Line's parent company created a subsidiary, SeaWind Line, to provide a rival train ferry service between Stockholm and Turku. Silja Line were ultimately successful and the FinnLink service closed. However, it was also a time when Silja Line's ferries were increasingly becoming like luxury cruise liners and the

The **Drottningen** loading at the Värtan terminal in the Stockholm winter. *(Järnvägsmuseet)*

SeaWind Line provided an alternative 'cheap and cheerful' brand for car and passenger traffic.

SeaWind chartered the Swedish ro-ro ferry *Saga Wind*, built at Helsingør in 1972, and had her converted to a four-track rail ferry by Blohm & Voss in Hamburg and renamed *Sea Wind*. She started on the Stockholm to Turku route in 1989 and apart from a grounding incident in 1997 continued on the service for over

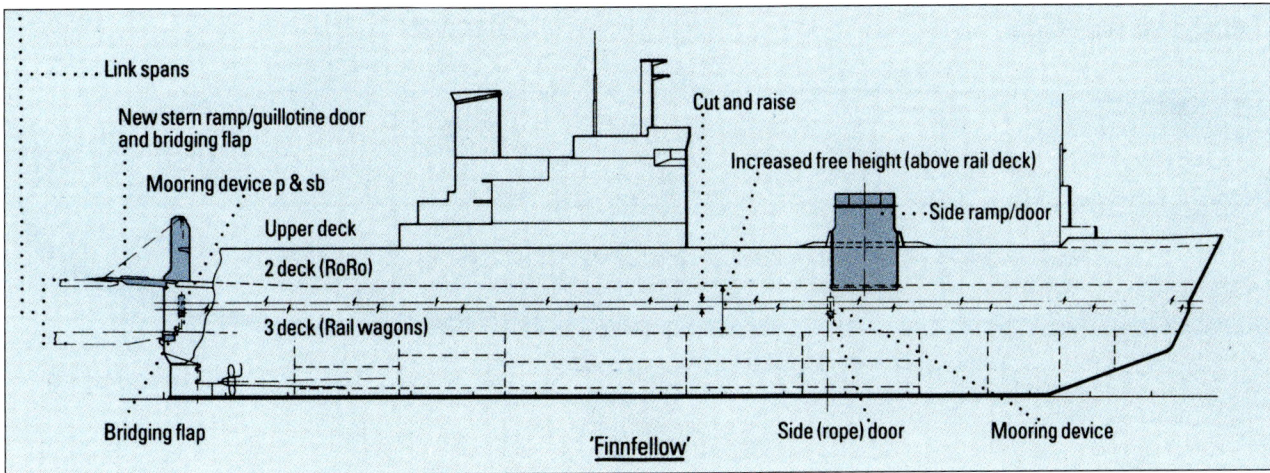

The 1973 built *Finnfellow* was converted to a train ferry in 1989. New doors and ramps were fitted and the hull was split along its length and jacked-up to increase headroom on the train deck. *(MacGregor-Navire News)*

twenty years. The *Sea Wind* was bought by SeaWind Line AB in 1993. Historically, the ferries between Sweden and Finland have relied on duty-free sales for much of their revenue, particularly during the winter months. This was planned to end in 1999 when duty-free sales ended on trips between EU ports, however a special tax status was negotiated for the Åland Islands which allows ships to continue duty-free sales by calling in at the port of Långnäs on their way between Stockholm and Turku.

Second-hand ice-strengthened train ferries are a bit of a niche market, so SeaWind was quick to buy Scandlines' *Rostock* in 1999 after she was replaced by the *Skåne* on the Rostock to Trelleborg route. She was renamed *Star Wind,* her rear ramp was rebuilt and she joined *Sea Wind* between Stockholm and Turku.

In 1999, the London-based Sea Containers Ltd. had bought Silja Line and the following year a second opportunity came when Dan-Link's freight ferry *Öresund* was laid-up with the opening of the Øresund Bridge. She was nine years younger than the *Star Wind*, with 30% more cargo capacity. The *Öresund* was bought by Sea Containers and rebuilt at the Remontowa Yard in Gdańsk. They added 1,300 tons of lightship weight, extending the superstructure to provide cabin accommodation for 364 passengers, fitting a new stern door and internal ramps and SOLAS upgrades required for a passenger ship. She was delivered to SeaWind Line in 2002 renamed *Sky Wind.*

With *Sky Wind's* arrival, the *Star Wind* was refurbished and used as a passenger and vehicle ferry between Helsinki and Tallinn. Like many Baltic ferry services, the revenue relied on duty-free sales which disappeared when Estonia joined the EU in 2004. The following year the *Star Wind* was sold to the Saaremaa Shipping Company in Estonia and renamed *Vironia*, for a short-lived ro-ro service between Sillamäe in Estonia and Kotka in eastern Finland.

The Estonian ferry company Tallink bought Silja Line

The *Finnfellow*, in later service as *Fellow*, navigating through the ice. The horizontal chine in the hull, where it was jacked-up during conversion, can be clearly seen. *(Jukka Koskimies)*

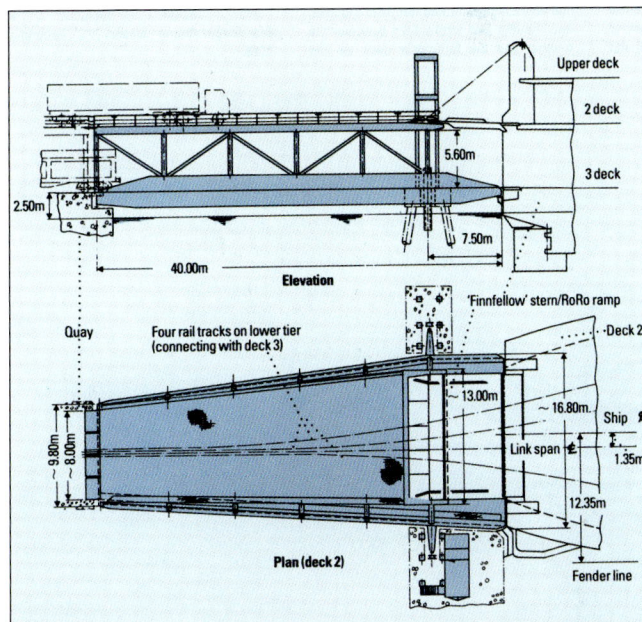

The heavy-duty two-level linkspan installed at Uusikaupunki for the FinnLink service to Hargshamn. *(MacGregor-Navire News)*

Top: The *Sea Wind* in 1996 in her original livery, showing the heavy guillotine stern door and the additional car space at boat deck level. *(A. Spörri)*

Above: The *Sky Wind*, previously the *Öresund*, on her way through the Stockholm archipelago in winter. *(Author's collection)*

from Sea Containers in 2006. Right from the start, they made clear that the train ferry business was not part of their long-term strategy. The *Sky Wind* was sold the following year to Unity Line in Poland and renamed *Wolin*. From 2008, the *Sea Wind* no longer carried passengers and the following year the SeaWind brand was ended and she was repainted in Tallink colours. After a change of policy by Finnish railways, the transport of rail wagons ended in 2011. The 48-year-old *Sea Wind* still operates as part of the Tallink fleet, carrying freight vehicles between Finland and Estonia.

Germany to Finland

Railship AG

Travemünde – Hanko	1975-1998
Travemünde – Turku	1998-2002

The economics of a direct ferry service between West Germany's Baltic coast and Finland is far from obvious, the sea distance is over 1,000 km. However, in the 1970s, the route was the centre of two of the most

innovative ferry projects in the world. Finnlines introduced the first high-speed cruise-ferry, the *Finnjet*. She was over 200m long, and able to carry over 1800 passengers at 30 knots, powered by two Pratt & Whitney gas-turbines, developing 75,000 shp. She was a hugely impressive ship, but for all the attention she rightly received, she was a one-off and ultimately the victim of high fuel costs and cheap air travel. The second project built the *Railship I*, far less glamourous than the *Finnjet*, but the biggest step change in train ferry design since the *Leviathan* 125 years earlier.

Since the days of the *Leviathan*, most train ferries have been operated by railway companies. They saw the ferry as part of the rail network, able to transport individual trains as part of the timetable. It is fair to say that no railway actually wants to have a ferry, they are expensive to build and operate, but the alternative of a bridge or tunnel is often not practical. The biggest problem in making a train ferry economic is that no matter how many wagons can be squeezed on to the rail deck, the ship's entire cargo is carried in a 2.5m high

GERMANY to FINLAND

and Uniwaggon AG from Switzerland and Finska Ångfartygs AB, The Finland Steamship Co. The *Railship I* was built by Rickmers Werft at Bremerhaven with H.M. Gehrckens acting as the managing owners. Apart from the rail handling system, she was a conventional ro-ro ship of the time, 150m long, with forward accommodation and medium-speed diesel engines below the main deck. Given the Baltic weather, the train decks were fully enclosed and the hull was ice-strengthened.

The wagon handling system was provided by the Finnish company, MacGregor-Navire. The heart of the system was the hydraulic lift. It was a framed box which could carry wagons on two-levels, when the top was flush with the upper deck the bottom would be flush with the main deck, when the bottom level was flush with the lower deck, the top was flush with the main deck. The benefit of this was that the lift could serve three decks, while only having to move the height between two decks, which limited the stroke of the hydraulic rams to around 5.5m. Each movement of the lift took 90 seconds and it could carry an 84-ton wagon on each level. Once a wagon had been moved to the upper or lower deck it was shunted forward on the centre rail to the switching track, fitted in the bow. This was pivoted at its forward end and could switch the wagon to the other tracks. The wagons were shunted using six small diesel-powered Unilok shunters built by Hugo Aeckerle in Hamburg. In addition to the driving wheels on the rails, the shunters had rubber tyres and could jack themselves off the rails and move independently. Managing heel and, to a lesser extent trim, is important on all train ferries but particularly when loading or unloading heavy freight wagons. *Railship I* had a cargo loading control room, located next to the stern door, where ballasting could be adjusted during the loading operation. The console also provided audible alarms if trim or heel limits were approached.

slice of wagons, the rest of the ship earns nothing unless it can be filled with trucks or passengers. As the ferry becomes larger the cargo in the rail wagons becomes an ever-smaller proportion of the displacement.

The answer to carrying more cargo is simple in principle, to carry wagons on several decks. On a ro-ro ferry this can be achieved by ramps, but rail wagons can only manage slight gradients. The first ship fitted with an elevator to carry wagons on a second deck was the *City of New Orleans*, built in 1959 for the route between Florida and Cuba. Less than two years later, this service was stopped by the Cuban revolution. The idea was not developed until the *Railship I* was built in 1975. She was loaded over a conventional linkspan at the stern, but carried wagons on three train decks, each with five tracks. This required two main innovations: a lift to transfer wagons up or down from the main deck to the upper and lower decks and on these decks a pivoting track to switch wagons between the five tracks. These allowed the ship to carry sixty 20m wagons on 1,307m of track. The downside of the arrangement was that it took some time to load and unload the ship, but on a long crossing this was less important.

A second complication with the project was that Finland used the Russian rail gauge. Thus, as well as the ferry, the transport system had to build a fleet of 500 special rail wagons with replaceable bogies and a facility for changing bogies at the port. To manage both these aspects of the project, Railship's partners were a consortium of shipowners and freight forwarders. H.M. Gehrckens and Schenker from Germay, Kühne & Nagel

With its distinctive blue hull and orange funnel, *Railship I* started operation between Travemünde and Hanko in Finland in February 1975. Hanko was chosen as its location at the south-west corner of Finland makes it relatively ice-free. The 1,000 km crossing took around 30 hours with a turnround of six hours at each port, so *Railship I* managed two round trips per week. The tracks

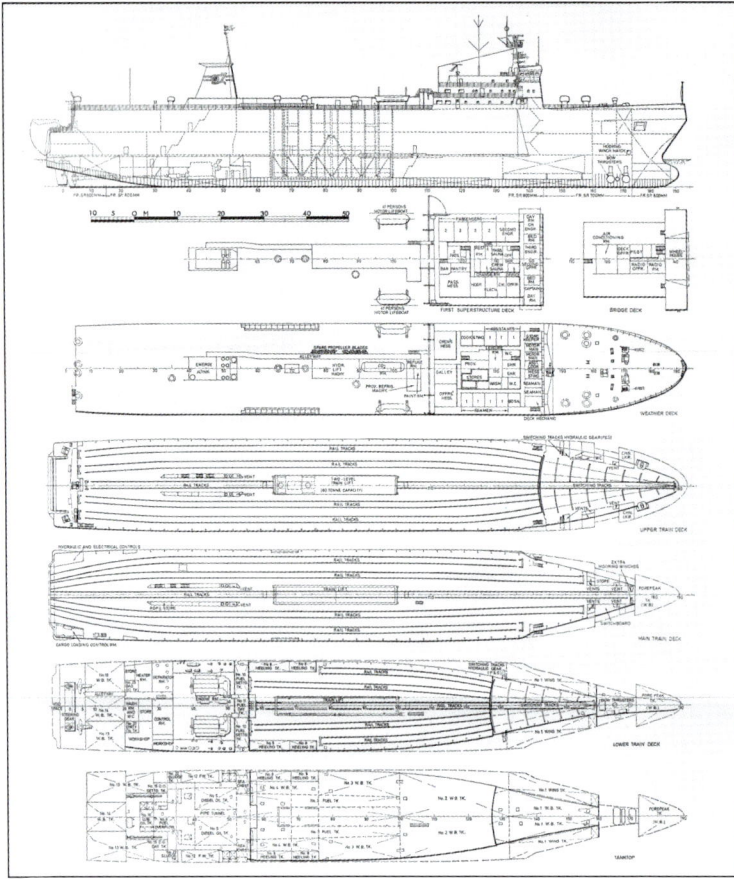

Top: The *Railship I* carried wagons on three decks with a central lift and forward switching rails. She had many imitators over the following decade. *(The Motor Ship)*

Above: The *Railship I* was built in 1975 as the first multi-deck rail ferry. She was used on a 1000 km route from Travemünde in West Germany to Hanko in Finland. *(Jukka Huotari)*

Top right: *Railship II* joined her earlier sister in 1984. She was 10m longer and with a much wider funnel and protected bridge wings. *(Jukka Huotari)*

Middle right: Close-up of the forward switching rail fitted on *Railship III*'s upper and lower decks. *(MacGregor-Navire News)*

Right: Each Railship had six Unilok diesel shunters, (similar to the picture) which moved wagons between the decks. The shunter could move off the rails on rubber tyres. *(Unilok)*

Bottom right: Some of Railship's fleet of 'Habis' closed wagons being discharged from *Railship III* at Hanko in 1991. *(Richard Latten)*

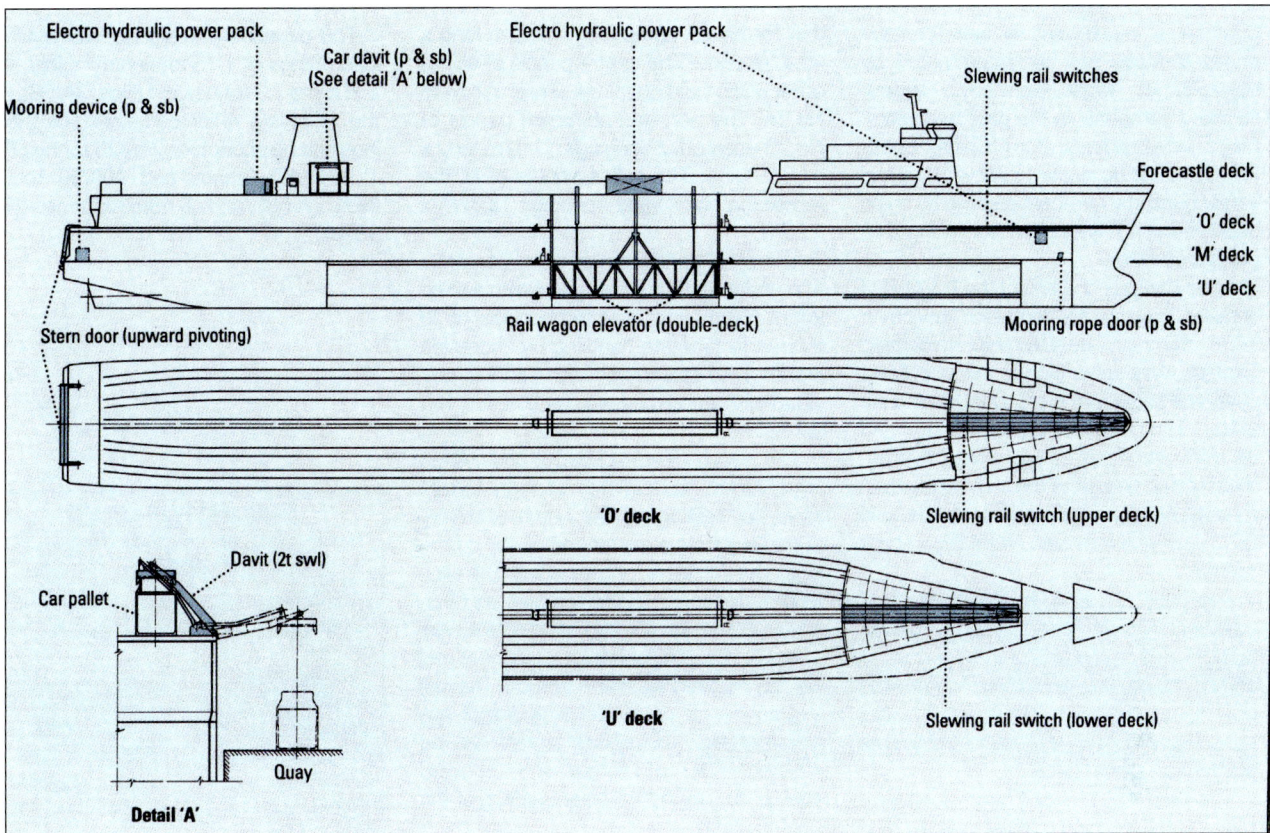

The heart of the wagon handling system on *Railship III* is the two-level lift on the centre track, which moves wagons to upper and lower decks, where they are moved between tracks by the forward switching rails. *(MacGregor-Navire News)*

on the ship were standard gauge and there was a large shed at Hanko, where the bogies were exchanged to the Finnish gauge. The service was successful, with 76,000 tons transported in the first year, rising to 206,000 tons in 1976 and 276,000 tons 1978. Much of the traffic was relatively high-volume timber and paper products from Finland south, which always exceeded the volume of northbound cargoes. The *Railship I* was lengthened by 27m in 1979, increasing her track length by 30% to over 1,700m. In 1982 the *Railship I* suffered an engine room fire and was out of service for six weeks, which highlighted the vulnerability of operating with a single ship.

A second ship, *Railship II* was delivered by Schichau Seebeckwerft in Bremerhaven in 1984. It was an endorsement of the success of *Railship I*'s design that she was essentially identical to her older sister, though 10m longer at 187m and able to carry 85 wagons. Visually her funnel was much wider, but the only significant change was that she had two Krupp-MaK diesels rather the four smaller diesels fitted to *Railship I*. The two ships provided four return trips per week and the wagon fleet was increased to 886 wagons, which carried 509,000 tons in 1985.

The third and last ship, the *Railship III*, was delivered in 1990. Again, virtually a replica of *Railship II* and built by Schichau in Bremerhaven. Visually the main change

was the bow-fronted section in the middle of the wheelhouse, similar to Fred. Olsen ships of the time. The three ships provided six roundtrips per week across the Baltic. Rail transport experienced many changes through the 1990s. The old national railway companies were privatised in most of Europe and the reunification of Germany brought competition from shorter routes across the Baltic. Traffic peaked in the late 1990s with around 600,000 tons of cargo.

Finnlines takeover

In 1997, Finnlines became the majority shareholder in Railship AG and moved the Finnish terminal from Hanko to its base in Turku to save costs the following year. *Railship I* was sold for scrapping in 2001. At the end of 2002, Railship AG was liquidated. The fleet of railway wagons was sold off to other operators and the *Railship II* and *Railship III* were amalgamated into the Finnlines fleet, renamed *Finnrider* and *Finnrunner*. They continued under Finnlines management as ro-ro ships on the Travemünde to Turku service with their names shortened to *Rider* and *Runner* in 2004. The *Rider* was sold to Russian owners in 2006. The *Runner* was laid-up in 2009 and sold to Russia the following year.

The Railship ferry design spawned several imitations which resulted in twelve of the largest train ferries ever built. The *Geroite na Odessa, Geroite na Sevastopol,*

Finnlines moved the route's Finnish terminal to Turku in 1998 and amalgamated *Railship III* into their fleet in 2002, renamed *Finnrunner* and later *Runner*. *(Author's collection)*

Geroi Shipki and *Geroi Plevny* were built in 1978 for service between Bulgaria and Ukraine, followed by the *Garibaldi* for Italian Railways in 1982. The five huge Baltic ferries delivered between 1986 and 1989 are discussed in the following section and two Romanian ships, *Mangalia* and *Eforie*, were completed in 1988 and 1991. The last and largest version of the MacGregor-Navire train lift was supplied to the *Skåne* in 1998.

Germany to the USSR

VEB Deutfracht Seereederei Rostock
Lithuanian State Shipping Co/DFDS Seaways
Mukran – Klaipeda   1986-2013

The *Rider*, previously *Finnrider* and originally *Railship II* was sold to Russian owners in 2006. *(Folke Österman)*

The success of the Railship project, and the Black Sea ferries which followed it, spawned the largest ever train ferry project. A multi-national plan to build two huge ports and a fleet of six of the world's largest train ferries. The roots of the project were political as much as commercial. In the early 1980s, the bulk of East Germany's trade was with the Soviet Union. The Soviet Union also maintained a large army in East Germany, in total around half a million people when families and civilian workers were included, plus thousands of tanks, military vehicles and aircraft. Supplying this army from Russia, and reinforcing it should there ever be a conflict, required military trains to transit through Poland. The Polish railways were never very efficient and it was not unusual for wagons to take four days to travel the 700km across the country. Poland was also becoming less politically reliable. There had been a series of strikes and protests during the 1970s and in 1980, the

Solidarność trade union was founded to directly confront the communist government. For the East Germans and Russians, by-passing Poland with a direct ferry connection across the Baltic looked attractive, it would be quicker and safe from political interference. The final issue was cost, trade between the Comecon countries of Eastern Europe used 'transferable rubles', a standard measure by which goods and services were exchanged under a barter arrangement. Poland used this system to receive transit fees for wagons using their railways until 1981. The Polish government then demanded that the fees should be paid in hard currency, such as US dollars. This was the final straw and provided an economic as well as a political justification for the ferry project. The plan was approved by the Soviet and East German Governments in 1982.

The new port at Mukran

Ferry ports were planned at Mukran, near Sassnitz on the island of Rügen, and at Klaipeda in Soviet Lithuania. A fleet of six large ferries would be built, each able to carry over a hundred rail wagons on two decks. This would avoid any payments to Poland and reduce the transit time between East Germany and the Soviet Union from four days to 18-20 hours. With a turnround of between four and six hours, the six ships would provide a sailing from each port every eight hours. Construction of the Mukran ferry port started in 1982 and was planned on a large scale. A new breakwater extended along the coast for around a kilometre, protecting a 200m-long finger pier with a linkspan on either side. The terminal extended inland for around 5 km, with 120km of track in the marshalling yards and a large shed for changing the wagon bogies between standard-gauge and Russian-gauge. The tracks on the ferries were Russian gauge, so the transfer shed was referred to as the western terminal of the Trans-Siberian Railway. The whole area was fenced-in and monitored by the DDR's State Security as a closed military site. A new town was built nearby, providing apartments for many of the 2,000 people who worked on the site.

The Project's engineers had visited the ferries and terminals in Ukraine, where similar large ferries had been built a few years earlier to run between Iliychevsk and Varna in Bulgaria. Coincidently, these ferries had a similar purpose, as they provided a route from the Soviet Union to Bulgaria that by-passed Romania where the Ceaușescu regime was increasingly distrusted by the Kremlin. The Ukrainian ferries followed the Railship model, with wagons loaded through the stern to the main deck and then transferred by lift to the upper or lower decks. The East German engineers disliked the reliance on the lift, which was a complicated piece of foreign-made equipment and slowed down the turnround. With a fleet of six ferries, that had to unload and load 200 wagons in four hours, it was more efficient to keep the ships as simple as possible and invest in double-deck linkspans that gave direct access to both the main and upper decks. The existing Sassnitz ferry terminal had a similar arrangement for loading cars to the upper deck, though obviously cars could deal with a steeper ramp than trains. The distance between the ships' main and upper decks was 6.2m. They designed a ramp with a gradient of around 1:100 to the upper linkspan. It was made up of a 550m-long earthworks ramp followed by a 90m concrete bridge that allowed the upper and lower tracks to converge on the 60m linkspans. The linkspans fanned-out to a breadth of around 25m connecting to the five tracks on both the main and upper train decks. Although simple in concept, the double-deck linkspans created a problem. A ferry will always heel a few degrees either way as heavy wagons are loaded or unloaded from the outboard tracks. This can be partially compensated by heeling tanks, but there is always a certain amount of twist which is accommodated by the linkspan. However, with two linkspans at different elevations, a small amount of heel creates a horizontal misalignment as well as twist. A few centimetres of misalignment do not matter on a ro-ro ramp but are a big problem with rails. The East German engineers solved this by developing a patented system of fenders which locked against both sides of the ship, at main and upper deck levels, to counteract the heel and keep the tracks at both levels horizontally aligned with the linkspans. It obviously

The *Mukran* arriving at Klaipeda on her inaugural voyage in October 1986. She was fitted with transverse thrusters forward and aft, which perhaps were not working as she is being assisted by two tugs. *(Gena Anfimov)*

worked and identical facilities were built at the other end of the route at Klaipeda in Soviet Lithuania. The ferries did not load both decks simultaneously, as there was insufficient headroom between the linkspans. Wagons on the upper deck were unloaded first, then the upper linkspan was raised to unload the main deck. Once the main deck was reloaded. The upper linkspan was reconnected to load the upper deck.

The world's largest train ferries

Six ships were ordered from VEB Mathias-Thesen Werft (MTW) in Wismar, called Type EGF-321. Three ships to be operated by the East German VEB Deutfracht Seereederei and three by the Soviet Lithuanian State Shipping Co. The lead ship, the *Mukran* was delivered in October 1986. She was 191m long with a gross tonnage of 21,890, with two train decks, each with five broad-gauge tracks. There was space for 103 wagons, 49 on the main deck and 54 on the upper deck. Above the cargo decks, there were three decks of accommodation with single cabins for the 42 crew and six double cabins for passengers. The crews worked two-week shifts and were reported by the magazine 'Seewirtschaft' to have 'an indoor swimming pool with sauna, sports room, hobby room and photo laboratory to provide opportunities for relaxation and recreation.' Given the strategic importance of this national project, the crew members were largely selected on the basis of party membership and security clearance. Unlike the comparative luxury of the crew accommodation, a space was provided below the main deck for transporting troops. This troop space was reached by a

Klaypeda in her original Soviet colours, showing the structure supporting the aft guillotine door and the 'Christmas tree' mast between the funnels. *(Author's collection)*

companionway ladder from the main deck and apart from a row of toilets and washbasins, it was a bare compartment with painted steel bulkheads and electric strip lights. Theoretically up to 300 soldiers could be carried, crammed together on camp beds, though normally only smaller numbers were transported. Their officers used the passenger cabins upstairs. One disturbing aspect of the troop-carrying role was that the ships were fitted with two 54-man lifeboats and three 20-man life rafts, sufficient for those above decks, but there was no life-saving provision for the soldiers below.

The ships were designed purely to carry rail traffic with the tracks set on top of the decks. Early in the construction phase, the Soviet military asked if the rails could be set into the decks to allow wheeled vehicles to

The *Petersburg*, ex- *Mukran* in 1998 with her superstructure extended to provide passenger accommodation. She was operated between Travemünde and St. Petersburg by Euroseabridge. *(Gena Anfimov)*

The *Greifswald* was also converted to carry passengers and operated on various routes around the Baltic for Euroseabridge before going to the Black Sea in 2003. *(Ulf Kornfeld)*

be carried. However, this this was refused on the grounds of cost and all vehicles had to be carried on flat rail wagons.

Mukran's trials were not uneventful and one of her four main engines was destroyed when the overspeed protection failed. Once in service with Deutfracht Seereederei, she was followed by two ships for the Soviets, the *Klaypeda* and *Vilnyus* in 1987, then the East German *Greifswald* in 1988 and the Soviet *Kaunas* in 1989. By the end of the 1980s, the East German economy was in serious trouble and the sixth ship, to have been called *Wismar*, was cancelled. The five ships did achieve their purpose. The planned capacity of the service was 5.3 million tons per year. In 1980, 8.5 million tons of goods had been shipped between East Germany and the Soviet Union by Polish railways. By

1988, this had reduced to 4.6 million tons and the difference of around 4 million tons was being shipped by ferry, not much short of the original plan. Only around a quarter of the Russian wagons had their bogies changed on arrival at Mukran and continued their journey on German railways. The rest had their loads transferred to German wagons in the huge sidings, work that employed hundreds of men. Around 30% of the ferries' capacity was reserved for the Soviet military.

The end of the USSR and the new Europe

The ferries only operated as originally planned for a few years before the world changed around them. The DDR disappeared with German reunification in 1990 and at the same time Lithuania declared its independence from the Soviet Union. The ownership of the three Soviet ships transferred to the Lithuanian Shipping Co. (LISCO) and the German ships to Deutsche Seereederei GmbH. For the first few years of the 1990s, the ships were busy shipping the Soviet army and its equipment back home, but it was clear that there would not be sufficient rail traffic in the future. One by one, the ships were converted to carry trucks, cars and passengers as well as rail wagons.

Mukran was sold in 1994 to Euroseabridge (Reederei F. Laeisz) and the following year converted to carry trucks and 140 passengers at Remontowa in Gdansk. She was renamed *Petersburg* and started a new service carrying trucks and rail wagons between Travemünde and St. Petersburg. Apart from charters in 1996 and 1999 to carry NATO military equipment to the Balkans, she remained in the Baltic, chartered to Scandlines on

The *Klaipeda* was not converted for passengers and remained on the Mukran to Klaipeda train ferry service for nearly twenty years, longer than any of her sisterships, before being sold in 2006. *(Jirka)*

various routes from 2003 to 2009 and was sold to the Russian operator Black Sea Ferry & Investments (BFI) in September 2010. Like her sister, the *Greifswald* was sold to Euroseabridge and converted to carry passengers and ro-ro traffic in 1994. She operated between Mukran and Klaipeda until 1997 and later between Travemünde and Klaipeda. From 1999 until 2002 she was on various short-term charters around the Baltic and in 2003 she was the first of the sisters to head south to the Black Sea, chartered to the Ukrainian operator UkrFerry.

LISCO continued the Mukran to Klaipeda service through the 1990s with the *Klaypeda*, renamed with the Lithuanian spelling *Klaipéda*. Her two sisters, *Vilynus*, (renamed *Vilnius*), and *Kaunas* were converted to carry ro-ro traffic and passengers. *Vilnius* was converted at Cammell Laird's yard at Birkenhead in 1993. The rail tracks were kept on the main deck but the upper deck was converted for ro-ro trailers, accessed by an internal ramp. The accommodation was also extended for 112 passengers together with fire protection and stability improvements needed to meet SOLAS passenger ship rules. *Kaunas* had essentially the same conversion at Blohm & Voss in Hamburg the following year, though she had accommodation for 210 passengers, including a casino and duty-free shop. LISCO put the two ships on new services mostly carrying trucks and ro-ro trailers between Klapeida and Kiel and later Mukran to Baltijsk and Riga to Travemünde. LISCO was bought by the Danish ferry operator DFDS in 2001.

The *Klaipéda* remained on the Mukran to Klaipeda route as a train ferry for nearly twenty years but was

Kaunas with her new DFDS funnel arriving at Klaipeda on an icy morning in January 2009. *(Gena Anfimov)*

The *Vilnius Seaways*, ex-*Vilnius*, after the LISCO name was dropped and the ferries were rebranded by DFDS Seaways in 2010. *(Folke Österman)*

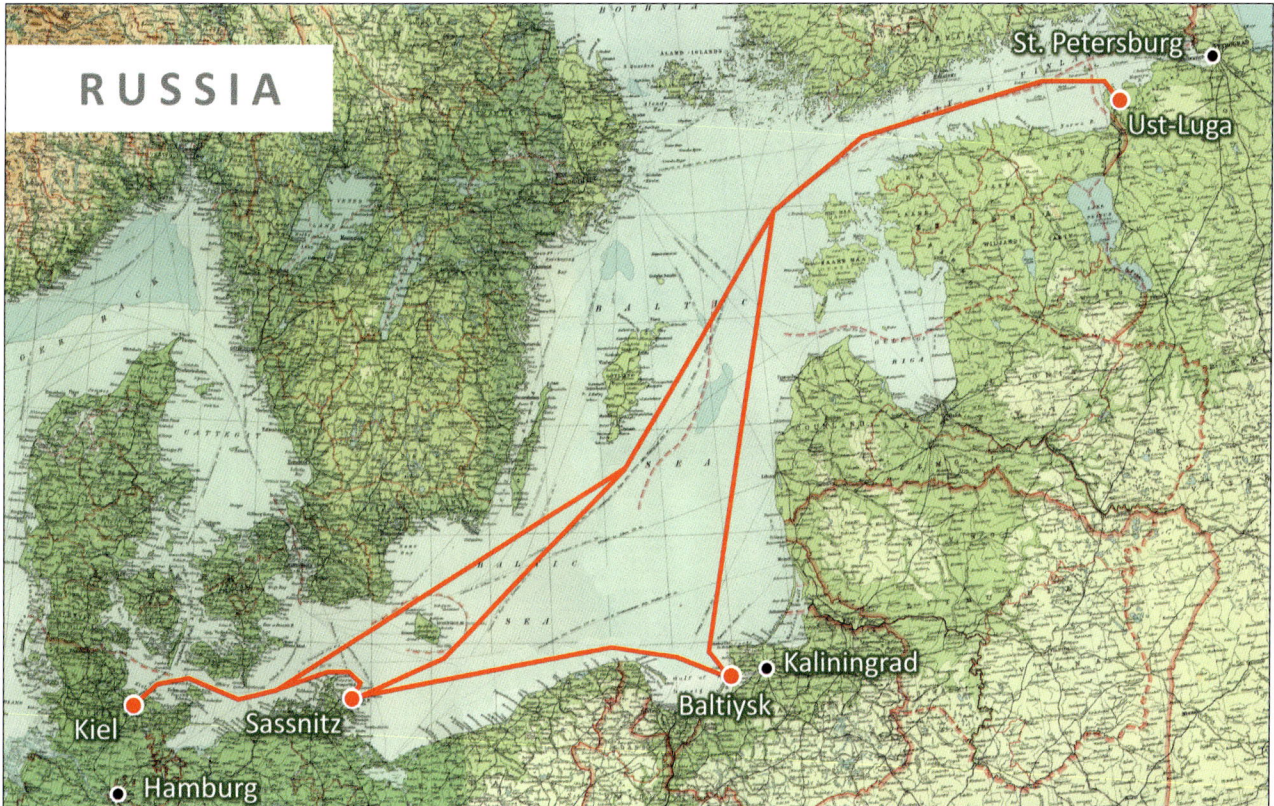

RUSSIA

St. Petersburg

Ust-Luga

Kaliningrad

Baltiysk

Kiel

Sassnitz

Hamburg

eventually retired in June 2006. By 2005, only around 7,000 wagons were being shipped on the route compared to over 100,000 at its peak. The steep decline followed Poland, Latvia, Lithuania and Estonia joining the EU in 2004. As their land borders opened it became much simpler to ship goods overland by truck or rail. The *Klaipéda* was sold and used briefly between Portsmouth and Cherbourg in 2007, renamed *Celtic Mist*. Since then she has operated as a ro-ro ferry on various routes around the Mediterranean and since 2019 in the Red Sea.

After the *Klaipéda*'s departure, the *Vilnius* included occasional sailings between Mukran and Klaipeda with her other routes. LISCO was rebranded as DFDS Seaways in 2010 and provided three sailing a week using the ferries then renamed *Vilnius Seaways* and *Kaunas Seaways* between Kiel, Mukran and and Ust-Luga. DFDS Seaways ended the regular service between Mukran and Klaipeda in September 2013. The *Vilnius Seaways* was chartered to UkrFerry for service in the Black Sea. The *Kaunas Seaways* was briefly chartered to BFI for services around the Baltic before joining her sisters in the Black Sea in 2015, chartered to UkrFerry. The two ships were sold in 2018 and went back to their old names.

Russia

The break-up of the Soviet Union opened the borders between Poland and the Baltic States but simultaneously created barriers to overland transport between Russia and

The *Kaunas Seaways* in 2015, her last year in the Baltic before being transferred to the Black Sea. (*Gena Anfimov*)

The *Baltiysk*, originally *Railship II*, was operated by Trans-Exim between Baltiysk in Kaliningrad and Ust-Luga near St. Petersburg from 2006. (*Author collection*)

Anship operated the **Apollonia**, formerly the Swedish ferry **Götaland**, on a service to Baltiysk for a short time in 2011-12. *(Gena Anfimov)*

its neighbours. This created an island of Russian territory around the city of Kaliningrad, surrounded by Poland and Lithuania. While train ferry services from Germany to Lithuania were replaced by overland transport, new ferry services connected Russia to the Kaliningrad enclave and Germany.

DFDS Seaways
Ust-Luga – Kiel – Mukran (Sassnitz)   2011-2012

DFDS Seaways started a triangular service between Ust-Luga, 150 km west of St. Petersburg, and the German ports of Kiel and Sassnitz in May 2011. The *Kaunas* made a single round-trip between the three ports each week carrying passengers, trucks and railway wagons. The service continued for a little over a year before the *Kaunas*, by then renamed *Kaunas Seaways*, was transferred to other Baltic routes.

Anship
Baltiysk – Mukran (Sassnitz)   2011-2012

The Swedish train ferry *Götaland* was sold to VG Transport Terminal Company of Moscow in 2010 and renamed *Apollonia*. The following summer she was put in service between Baltiysk in Kaliningrad and Sassnitz (Mukran) operated by Anship, part of AnRussTrans. However, the service lasted less than a year before she was laid-up and then sold in 2012 for service in Mediterranean and scrapped the following year.

The **Ambal**, originally **Railship III**, shortly after she was bought by Anship for the Ust-Luga to Baltiysk service in 2011. *(Muhsen Hussein)*

Trans-Exim/Anship/Oboronlogistika LLC
Ust-Luga – Baltiysk   2006- current
Ust-Luga – Sassnitz   2010-2016

The *Rider* (ex- *Finnrider*, ex- *Railship II*) was bought by Rosmorport in 2006, part of the Russian Ministry of Transport. She was renamed Балтийск, *(Baltiysk)*, and put into service between Ust-Luga and Baltiysk, nominally operated by Trans-Exim, though they describe themselves as 'agents' for the ferry line. Apart for a short break at the start of 2007 for repair after an engine room fire, she has been on this service ever since.

As the *Baltiysk* only carried freight, the *Petersburg*, (ex-*Mukran*) was bought by Black Sea Ferry & Investments (BFI) in 2010 to provide a passenger service again operated by Trans-Exim. From 2012, she also ran between Ust-Luga and the Sassnitz Ferry Port at Mukran. After

The *Petersburg*, ex- *Mukran*, was bought by BFI in 2010 to provide a passenger service from Ust-Luga to Baltiysk and Sassnitz. *(Gena Anfimov)*

The *Petersburg,* ex- *Mukran*, with the blue hull on one of her last visits to the Mukran terminal in 2015. The old rail tracks look overgrown and there is a new wind turbine assembly quay is on the left. *(Author's collection)*

Two new ferries are under construction, designed by the Odessa Marine Engineering Bureau, they can carry 80 wagons on six tracks on the main deck. *(Author's collection)*

Russia's annexation of Crimea in 2014, she was temporarily used in the Black Sea and replaced in the Baltic by her sistership *Kaunas Seaways*, chartered from DFDS Seaways. *Petersburg* returned to Baltic service and made her last trip to Sassnitz in 2016. After a shipyard visit to Tallinn in 2018, the *Petersburg* was detained due to non-payment of bills. The *Baltiysk* was also detained around the same time for arrears in crew wages, though whether the problems lay with Trans-Exim or the owners is opaque. The *Baltiysk* returned to service but the *Petersburg* was laid-up and sold to OFW Ships the following year. Renamed *Odeep One*, she was converted in Gdansk for a new career as a floating water extraction plant in the Mediterranean.

In 2011 the *Baltiysk* was joined by her near sister the *Runner* (ex- *Finnrunner*, ex- *Railship III*), renamed *Амбал*, (*Ambal*). She was initially owned by Rosmorport and operated by Anship, but later transferred to Oboronlogistika LLC, a civilian arm of the Russian Ministry of Defence. The two ships provide seven round trips per month between Ust-Luga and Baltiysk carrying 1.5 million tons of freight per year.

The *Baltiysk* and *Ambal* are both over thirty years old and in 2018 the Russian Government announced an order with the Nevsky Shipyard near St. Petersburg to build two large replacement ferries. These have been designed by the Odessa Marine Engineering Bureau with space for 80 wagons on six tracks on the main deck and trucks and trailers on an upper deck. The main innovation will be dual-fuel engines which will normally run on LNG.

SEVEN

The Baltic Coast

The previous chapter dealt with the larger train ferries on international routes across the Baltic, but there have also been many smaller ferries around the Baltic coast. Some linking offshore islands, others on river estuaries and harbours. This chapter takes an anti-clockwise trip around the Baltic, from Germany through Poland and Russia to Sweden.

Kiel Canal

Nord-Ostsee Kanal

Rader Insel fähre	1914-1937

The most westerly ferry on Germany's Baltic coast, was not actually on the Baltic, but on the Nord-Ostsee Kanal, (more often called the Kiel Canal in English). The canal links the Baltic to the North Sea, from Holtenau, near Kiel, 98 km to Brunsbüttel on the Elbe estuary. Originally built in 1895, it was widened and straightened between 1912 and 1914 and a new straight section of canal was dug near the village of Borgstedt, cutting off a bend in the old canal. This created an island, the Rader Insel, between the old and new lines of the canal.

Although a small island, it contained a coke plant and brickworks, which had lost their connection to the railway east of the canal. The canal resolved this by providing a small train ferry. They bought the *Weichselmünde* in 1914 from the Westpreußische Kleinbahnen, (West Prussian Light Railway) and renamed her the *Rade*. She was nearly new, having been delivered

The ferry *Rade* was used to the link the Rader Insel to the east bank of the Nord-Ostsee Kanal, (generally called the Kiel Canal in English) from 1914 until 1937. *(Author's collection)*

by J.W. Klawitter in Danzig the previous year. The *Rade* was a double-ended single-track ferry, 36m long and able to carry four wagons.

The service across the canal continued for over twenty years, though some of the factories on the island closed during the depression of the 1920s. In 1937, a road bridge was opened from the west of the island to Borgstedt and the ferry service closed. The fate of the *Rade* is not clear, but she may have been converted to a vehicle ferry and used at the naval air base at Pillau-Neutief, (now Baltiysk) near Königsberg.

Fehmarnsund

Kreis Oldenburger Eisenbahn AG	1903-1941
Deutsche Reichsbahn	1941-1949
Deutsche Bundesbahn	1949-1963
Großenbroder fähre – Fehmarnsund	**1903-1963**

Fehmarn is the furthest west of Germany's Baltic islands and best known for the ferry port of Puttgarden and the Vogelfluglinie ferry to Denmark. This ferry relies on the road and rail bridge to the mainland, but before this was built, Fehmarn was connected by train ferry. The Kreis Oldenburger Eisenbahn (KOE) built a line to Großenbroder fähre in 1900 and started the train ferry service to Fehmarnsund in October 1903. In its first two years, many of the wagons carried construction materials to extend the railway across the island. Fehmarn is an agricultural island and much of the traffic was farm produce, sometimes shipping cattle on the train deck rather than wagons.

The *Fehmarnsund* was built by J.W. Klawitter in Danzig, a small double-ended screw ferry, only 23m long and able to carry two wagons. Like most steam ferries of the day, she had a central wheelhouse on a gantry with a funnel either side. The service was not always reliable and the small ferry struggled to cope with ice in the winter. In 1921, she broke loose from her moorings in a storm and ran aground at high tide. It was several months before she could be refloated and returned to service.

A new larger ferry, the *Fehmarn* was built in 1927 by Werft Nobiskrug in Rendsburg. She was 38m long, able to carry four wagons or two passenger coaches, and had small passenger saloons on either side of main deck giving passengers some protection from the weather. She was still steam powered, at a time when diesels were becoming popular, with a single screw at either end and two tall central funnels. The terminals were also modernised with new electrically powered linkspans replacing the old hand winches. The *Fehmarnsund* was kept in reserve.

The idea of the Vogelfluglinie from Puttgarden to Denmark was first developed in the 1930s and in preparation, Deutsche Reichsbahn took control of the Fehmarn railway in 1941. However, no progress was made during the Second World War and in the

KIEL & FEHMARN

The *Fehmarnsund* broke her moorings in a storm in 1921 and ended up beached at high tide. It took several months and a lot of digging to get her refloated and back in service. *(Author's collection)*

A larger ferry, the *Fehmarn* was built in 1927 able to carry four wagons or two passenger coaches. A new electrically powered linkspan was also installed. *(Author's collection)*

The *Fehmarn* was rebuilt in 1951, lengthened by 15m and with her steam engines replaced by diesels. *(Author's collection)*

The military ferry *Frauke* was rebuilt as a train ferry after the war and joined the *Fehmarn* crossing as the *Schleswig-Holstein* in 1947. *(Author's collection)*

post-war world, the railway became part of Deutsche Bundesbahn in 1949. They introduced a new ferry, the *Frauke*, which had been built by Otto Kuczewski in Königsberg for the Kreigsmarine in 1940. She had operated between Pillau and the naval air base at Neutief during the war and escaped westward with German refugees as the Soviet Army approached in 1945. She was rebuilt as a train ferry by Werft Nobiskrug in Rendsburg in 1947, lengthened by 5m to

43.5m, and renamed the *Schleswig-Holstein*. With the arrival of the new ferry, the old *Fehmarnsund* was sold, but had a long further life as a workboat.

In 1951 the *Fehmarn* was rebuilt. She was lengthened by 15m, her steam engines were replaced by two MaK diesels and the two tall funnels replaced by a short funnel. However, the increased capacity was soon overwhelmed by the number of cars using the ferries. This increased rapidly through the 1950s, from 46,000

213

The *Schleswig-Holstein* went to assist the grounded ferry *Deutschland* in November 1957 and ended up on the beach herself. Her newly refurbished engine-room was flooded, but otherwise there was no serious damage. *(Author's collection)*

The *Schleswig-Holstein* was lengthened in 1957 and a new passenger saloon fitted on one side of the car deck. *(Author's collection)*

in 1953 to 87,000 in 1957, and there were often long queues at summer weekends.

In 1957, the *Schleswig-Holstein* was refurbished. She was lengthened by 4.6m and her two Deutz diesels were replaced by a single MWM engine. One of her funnels was removed and a new cafeteria was fitted above the train deck. In November of the same year, the ferry *Deutschland* ran aground at Großenbrode and the *Schleswig-Holstein* went to help tow her off. In the high winds, the *Schleswig-Holstein* herself ended up on the beach and her newly refurbished machinery space was flooded. Fortunately, there was no serious damage and

she was refloated a week later and towed to Nobiskrug for repair.

By the end of the 1950s, plans were revived to build a bridge to Fehmarn providing a route to a new ferry terminal at Puttgarden. The Fehmarnsund bridge was finally opened in April 1963 and the ferry service came to an end. Both *Fehmarn* and *Schleswig-Holstein* were sold to Italian owners and had long careers as car ferries. The *Ferry Capri*, (ex-*Schleswig-Holstein*) was scrapped in 2008 and the *Peloritano* (ex-*Fehmarn*) was only scrapped in 2010 after 73 years' service.

Rügen

Königlich Preußische Staatseisenbahnen	1883-1920
Deutsche Reichsbahn	**1920-1936**
Stralsund – Altefähr	1883-1936

Rügen is Germany's largest island and the long sandy beaches of its east coast first became popular with tourists in the latter half of the 19th century when Sassnitz and later Binz were developed as seaside resorts. The railway reached Stralsund, on the mainland opposite Rügen, in 1863 but it was twenty years before a railway was built on the island. The main line from Altefähr to Bergen was opened by the Königlich Preußische Staatseisenbahnen (Royal Prussian State Railways) in 1883 and was extended to Sassnitz in 1891.

The railway's first train ferry the *Prinz Heinrich* was delivered in 1882 and used to transport equipment to the island before starting the ferry service between Stalsund and Altefähr the following year, when she was joined by a sistership the *Rügen*. Both steam ferries were built by F. Schichau Werft in Elbing, who had recently built ferries for the Danish railways. They were 36m long with a single track for three wagons and a central bridge on a gantry between two tall funnels. The ferries had a closed stern with a single screw propeller and loaded over the bow. The forward part of the hull had a spoon-shape, strengthened for navigating in ice. It is interesting that the Prussian railway built screw steamers from the start. The early Danish ferries all had paddles, which were often damaged in ice, and only built their first screw ferry for icebreaking, the *Valdemar*, in

The Fehmarnsund bridge was opened in 1963, replacing the ferries and providing a direct route to Puttgarden and the ferry to Denmark. *(Gerhard Hohm)*

1886. The crossing between Stralsund and Altefähr was only around 2.5 km and the downside of screw propulsion was that the ferries needed to turn, which added a few minutes to the 15 minute crossing. The ferry docks were similar to those built in Denmark, with timber piling leading to a linkspan suspended from an iron gantry. The railway had expected around 30-40,000 passengers per year but in the first year they carried 90,000. A third similar ferry, the *Stralsund,* was ordered from Schichau in Elbing and delivered in 1890.

A regular mail steamer service from Sassnitz to Trelleborg in Sweden was started in 1897 and with it a direct express train

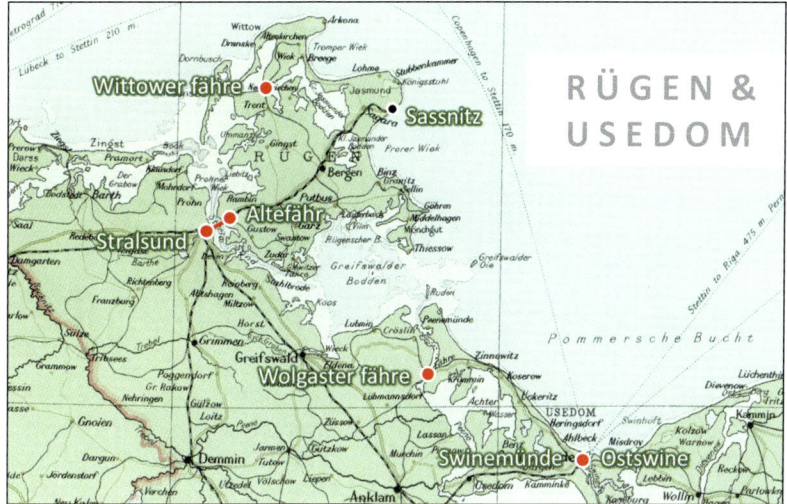

The ferry *Stralsund* was built in 1890. She was soon replaced by larger ferries, but had a long career on other routes. *(Author's collection)*

Passengers leave the Berlin express to take the air while crossing on the *Putbus*. *(Author's collection)*

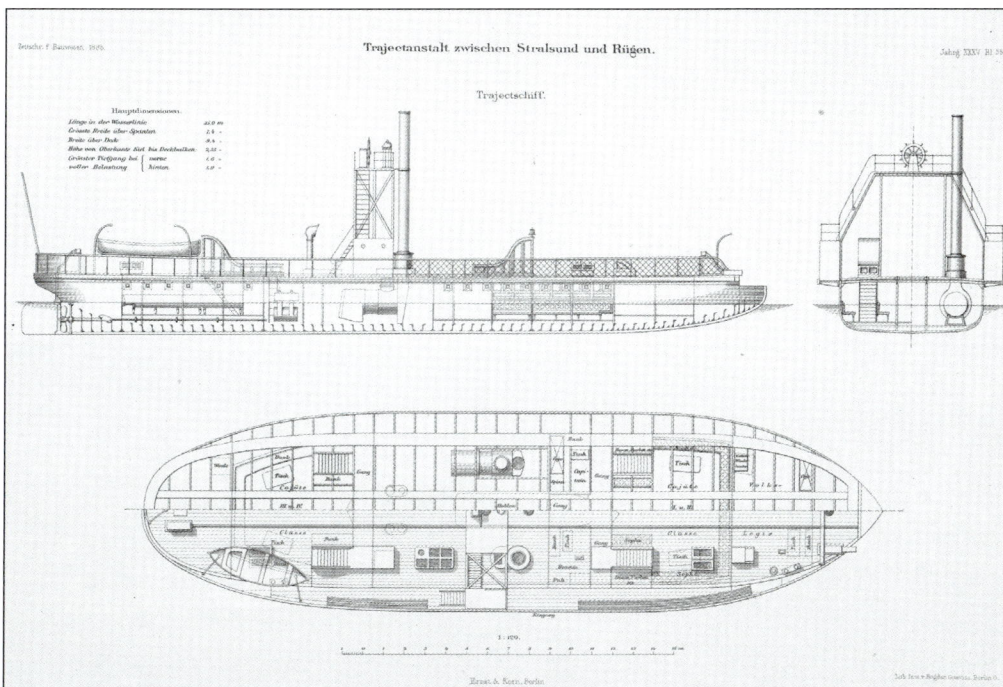

The ferry service from Stralsund to Altefähr on Rügen started in 1883 with two ferries, the *Prinz Heinrich* and the *Rügen*, built by F. Schichau in Elbing. The spoon-shaped bow and propellers were designed for icebreaking and was later copied by Danish ferries. *(Berlin Architekturmuseum)*

service was started from Berlin to Sassnitz. The existing ferries were too short for the passenger coaches and longer ferries were needed. The 65m long *Saßnitz* was delivered by Schichau in Elbing in 1897 which could carry three coaches, followed by the 81m long *Putbus* in 1899. As well as being longer, the new ferries were double-ended with twin screws and a rudder at both ends. A second ferry dock was built on each side of the crossing, so that the express train could be split and loaded on to two ferries simultaneously. With the two new ferries in service, the original three ferries, *Prinz Heinrich*, *Rügen* and *Stralsund* were moved to Swinemünde (now Swinoujscie in Poland) in 1901. Two further 81m ferries, were delivered, the *Rügen* in 1902 and the *Bergen* in 1906. The four ships operated more than forty crossing every day and carried 85,000 wagons and coaches in 1907. One unique thing about the Stralsund ferries was that the bands on their funnels were painted different colours, so that the ferries could be distinguished from a distance. The rail ferry service from Sassnitz to Trelleborg started in 1909 and prompted proposals to build a bridge to replace the ferries. Like all such discussions, it carried on for several years. The plan for the bridge was finally approved in 1914, but was overtaken by the First World War.

After the war, a fifth ferry was built, the *Altefähr* was delivered by Schichau in Elbing in 1920. She was similar to the previous ferries, 83m long with space for eight wagons on a single track. In 1927, the *Bergen* was lengthened to 88m and the old *Saßnitz* was lengthened to 83m the following year. While the five ships could manage the railway traffic, they struggled to manage the increasing number of private cars during the 1920s. At peak holiday times there were up to 90 return trips each day and long queues of cars built up on each side of the crossing. In 1931, Deutsche Reichsbahn began the project to build the Rügendamm road-rail bridge. The railway crossing opened in October 1936 and the road

Top: The *Putbus* was built in 1899 to join the *Sassnitz* on the Stralsund crossing, each taking half of the express train. *(Author's collection)*

Middle right: The *Wittow* was built in 1896 to carry narrow-gauge wagons on a short crossing to the Wittow peninsula on Rügen. The picture was taken in the 1920s after she had been converted from steam to motor. *(Author's collection)*

Right. The last ferry built for the Stralsund crossing was the *Altefaehr* in 1920. The number of cars increased through the 1920s and the ferries were replaced by the Rügendamm road-rail bridge in 1936. *(Author's collection)*

Bottim right: The Wittow railway closed in 1968, but the *Wittow* continued as a car ferry until 1994. After this she was laid-up in Barth as attempts were made to preserve her as a museum ship. *(Author's collection)*

crossing in the following May. The *Saßnitz, Rügen, Bergen* and *Altefähr* were transferred to Swinemünde. The *Putbus* was initially put up for sale but later joined her sisterships at Swinemünde.

Rügensche Kleinbahn	1896-1949
Deutsche Reichsbahn	1949-1968
Wittower Fähre – Fährhof	1896-1968

In addition to the main line train to the ferry port at Sassnitz, there were also narrow-gauge railways linking small towns on the island of Rügen. While the island's east coast was popular with tourists, the Rügensche Kleinbahn's line to the north-west was financed by local farmers in order to export milk and other produce. The line ran 38km from Bergen to Wittower Fähre where a train ferry crossed the Breetzer Bodden to Fährhof on the Wittow peninsula.

Two steam ferries were built in 1896, the *Wittow* and the *Jasmund*. They were small double ended ferries built by AG Vulcan in Stettin with a propeller and rudder at each end. Their single track could carry three wagons, though often the locomotive would cross with two wagons. The ferry docks had a linkspan and a simple gantry. The 350m crossing took less than ten minutes, including loading and unloading. In 1911, a third ferry was built by AG Vulcan the *Jasper von Moltzahn*. She was externally similar to the other ferries but fitted with a 45 hp petrol engine. Thus despite her humble appearance she was the first motor train ferry in the world. The new motor ferry proved very economic as there were normally only two or three trains in each direction and keeping a steam ferry's boiler hot all day for only a few short crossings burned a lot of coal. With the *Jasper von Moltzahn* in service the *Jasmund* was scrapped in 1912.

The two ferries continued on the same crossing for more than fifty years, largely unaffected by two World Wars. The *Wittow* had her steam engine replaced by a petrol engine in 1922, which was in turn replaced by a diesel in 1937. After the war, the area became part of the DDR and the ferries were taken over by Deutsche Reichsbahn in 1949. The only change being that the *Jasper von Moltzahn* was renamed the *Bergen*. The rail ferry service ended in 1968 when the line on the Wittow peninsula was closed and the rest of the narrow-gauge railway closed two years later. The *Wittow* and *Bergen* were taken over by the Weiße Flotte and continued to carry passengers and cars until they were replaced by a new car ferry in 1994. The *Bergen* was scrapped in 1997. The *Wittow* was laid-up and a first attempt to preserve her as museum was made in 2005. After many delays she was finally taken over by the Association for the Conservation of Rügenschen Kleinbahnen and is now preserved as a museum ship. The old linkspans are also still in place.

Built in 1890, the **Stralsund** worked on several routes and survived war service at Peenemünde to operate the Wolgaster crossing from 1946 to 1990. *(Author's collection)*

Unloading tank wagons from the **Stralsund** at Wolgast in 1986. It was never a busy route. *(Jörg Meyer)*

Usedom

Deutsche Reichsbahn
Wolgaster fähre   1946-1990

Situated around 30km east of Rügen, the island of Usedom stretches along the Baltic coast for around 60km. Famous for its beaches, it is the seaside resort closest to Berlin and has been popular since the mid-19th century. At its northern tip, the village of Peenemünde is remembered as the site of the research station where the V-2 rocket was developed during the Second World War. The railway first reached the island in 1876 when the Berlin-Stettiner Eisenbahn Gesellschaft (Berlin-Stettin Railway Co.) built a line to Swinemünde which crossed to the island by a swing-bridge at Karnin. Over the following few years, the line was extended along the full length of the northern coast and direct trains ran from Berlin during the summer months bringing holidaymakers to the Baltic beach resorts. The old swing-bridge was replaced by a double-track lift-bridge in 1933.

After working for a hundred years, the *Stralsund* retired in 1990 and has since been preserved as a museum ship in Wolgast. *(Pieter Inpijn)*

The holiday traffic came to an end with the Second World War and in April 1945, as the Soviet Army advanced along the coast, the retreating German Army blew-up the Karnin lift-bridge, (though its giant rusting gantry still remains). After the war, the eastern tip of the island was ceded to Poland and the town of Swinemünde was renamed Swinoujscie. This left the Isedom with no access from the east and the road and railway bridges destroyed. Fortunately, during the retreat of the German

Army, the old train ferry *Stralsund* had managed to survive. Built in 1890, she had been used on the Swinemünde crossing until 1936 and then used for carrying equipment to the Peenemünde military base, narrowly escaping damage when the base was bombed in August 1943. As the Soviet Army approached, she was sailed to Rügen to avoid being caught in the conflict. The crossing from Wolgast Hafen on the mainland and Wolgast Fähre on Isedom is only around 400m. To reconnect the island's railways, the Soviet Military Administration built ferry terminals on either side and in 1946 the *Stralsund* resumed her career as a train ferry. The operation was handed over to Deutsche Reichsbahn in 1949. A new road bridge was built in 1950, but the rail service continued to rely on the ferry and what was meant as a temporary stopgap continued for nearly forty years. In 1986, her steam engines were removed for repair and she continued the ferry service taken back and forward by a tug. The old engines were declared to be past repair and she continued with the tug for another four years, celebrating her centenary of service in October 1990, before making her last trip two months later.

The *Stralsund* was bought by the Wolgast Town Council for preservation as a museum ship and taken over by a Preservation Society in 2014. Like many such projects, she has been slowly restored over several years and remains as a museum ship in Wolgast Hafen. A new rail bridge to Usedom was finally opened in 2000.

Königlich Preußische	
Staatseisenbahnen	1901-1920
Deutsche Reichsbahn	1920-1945
Swinemünde – Ostswine	**1901-1945**

The port of Swinemünde, at the eastern tip of Usedom, was separated from Ostswine on the mainland to the east by the river Swine which allows the river Oder to flow out to the Baltic. The channel is only 200m wide, but a bridge has never been practical as it is the access to the port city of Stettin, (now Szczecin) 60km to the south.

The railway reached Swinemünde in 1876 and Ostswine in 1900. This prompted the Prussian State Railway to start a train ferry service the following year transferring goods wagons between the two lines which would otherwise need to have been routed south through Stettin. The redundant ferries from the Stralsund crossing, the *Prinz Heinrich, Rügen* (renamed *Swinemünde*) and *Stralsund* were moved to Swinemünde in 1901. The *Prinz Heinrich* was moved to

THE *RÜGEN's* INLAND VOYAGE

Danzig in 1905, but the other two ferries continued on the service until 1936.

With the completion of the Rügendamm in 1936, the five larger Stralsund ferries became redundant. Four were transferred to Swinemünde, the *Saßnitz*, *Rügen*, *Bergen* and *Altefähr*. This allowed the *Stralsund* to be transferred to Peenemünde, later Wolgaster Fähre and become the great survivor. The *Saßnitz* was broken up in 1938. The fifth Stralsund ferry, the *Putbus* was converted into a car ferry and arrived in Swinemünde in 1938, renamed *Pommern*. The last of the old ferries, the *Swinemünde* (ex *Rügen*) was transferred to Stettin in 1939 and sank the following year.

The *Bergen*, *Rügen* and *Altefähr* continued the ferry service during the war and were joined in 1943 by the small ferry *Tyras* transferred from Stettin and renamed *Swinemünde 2*. The area was taken over by the Soviet army in 1945 and after the war, the border between Germany and Poland was moved west. Swinemünde became Polish territory, renamed Swinoujscie, and was separated from the German railway system. The train ferry service was not restarted. The *Swinemünde 2* moved back to Stettin, now the Polish city of Szczecin. The *Bergen* and *Altefähr* were sent to the Soviet Union in 1946 as reparations. The *Rügen* had left Swinemünde in 1944 in more unusual circumstances.

The *Rügen*'s inland voyage

In the late summer of 1944, the Allied Armies were advancing eastward through France and Belgium towards the German border. Allied bombing had destroyed many of the railway bridges over the river Rhein to interrupt supply lines to the German Army in the west. To keep supplies moving, it was important for Deutsche Reichsbahn to maintain its rail links across the river and as a contingency, they decided to transfer a train ferry to the Rhein. In September 1944, the Reichsbahn office in Stettin received an order from Berlin to transfer the *Rügen* from Swinemünde to Bingen on the Rhein. The order was approved at the highest level and whatever difficulties had to be overcome.

In normal times, the voyage would have taken around a week. The *Rügen* would have sailed through the Kiel Canal to the Elbe, down the North Sea coast to Rotterdam and up the Rhein to Bingen. However, by September 1944, the Allies were already in southern Holland and any German ship sailing down the Dutch Coast would be attacked. The only alternative was to make an inland voyage using rivers and canals. The job was given to Johannes Nagel, First Officer on the train ferry *Deutschland*. He planned a route from Stettin through the Kiel Canal, then turning left, to Hamburg and up the river Elbe to Magdeburg. From there westward via the Mittellandkanal for 300km to Ibbenbüren to join the Dortmund-Ems Kanal. This led south and in turn connected to the Rhein-Herne-Kanal which joined the Rhein at Duisburg.

The *Rügen* was taken to Stettin to prepare for the voyage. The funnels and superstructure were dismantled and secured flat on the deck. Hatches and openings were secured for the sea voyage. On the 19th September, she was towed out into the Baltic and west, past her original ferry route at Stralsund, to Holtenau at the north end of the Kiel Canal. From there, through the canal to reach Hamburg the following day.

One of the biggest problems with the route was the depth of water in the river Elbe, in several places as little as 1.2m, while the *Rügen*'s draught was 1.95m. The solution was ingenious, to lift the *Rügen* using two river barges. She was taken to the Wilhelm Bauer Shipyard at Reihersteig in the Hamburg docks where two barges had been requisitioned, each around 60m long. They were ballasted down and lashed either side of the *Rügen*'s hull. It took around 400 tons of upward force to reduce the *Rügen*'s draught, so a series of heavy girders were laid across the decks of the barges and ferry and attached by chains and turnbuckles. The fifteen girders were 80cm deep and 21m long, around 80 tons of steel in total. Once the ballast was pumped out of the barges, the *Rügen* was lifted by around 67cm, reducing the draught to 1.19m forward and 1.43m aft. Fortunately, the river level was rising so the decision was made to proceed upriver. The *Rügen* with barges alongside set off up the Elbe on the 8th October, towed by the tug *Odin*. It took around three days to reach Magdeburg as the tug could only make around 3 km/h against the river current.

Once at Magdeburg, the barges were disconnected and the temporary girders removed. The *Rügen* was manoeuvred into the boat lift at Rothensee on the 19th October, where she was lifted 16m to start her voyage on the Mittellandkanal. The voyage down through the three canals was not without incident. There were frequent air raids when the crew would tie-up and seek shelter ashore. Power cuts would cause delays at locks and sluices. It took four weeks for the *Rügen* to emerge from the canal system at Duisburg, arriving at the Rheinwerft shipyard at Walsum on the 16th November. Safely on the Rhein, the shipyard started rebuilding the ferry. Funnels and superstructures were reassembled and the ship was trimmed to refit the propellers which had been removed to prevent grounding damage. The shipyard had very few workers and the ferry crew had to help with the rebuilding, but after a few weeks the *Rügen* left the shipyard under her own power and proceeded upriver to Bingen. The whole voyage had taken nearly three months.

After the adventure of the voyage, the arrival was an anti-climax. Despite Johannes Nagel's achievement, the *Rügen* was never used on the Rhein and during the confusion at the end of the war was sunk at Assmannshausen, a few kilometres downstream from Bingen. The wreck was raised after the war and presumably scrapped.

Stettin (Szczecin)

Stettin was one of Prussia's great port cities on the south coast of the Baltic and in the 19th century developed a large shipbuilding industry. At the end of the Second World War, most of Germany's Baltic coast came under Soviet control. Poland's border moved west to the Oder river and Stettin became the Polish city of Szczecin.

Stettiner Maschinenbau AG Vulcan
Stettin Hafen   **1858-1930s**

The Stettin shipyard that became AG Vulcan was founded in 1851 in Grabow, around 3 km north of the old city centre. Without a railway connection, material had to be transhipped from the railway sidings in the city. In 1858, the shipyard decided to build themselves a ferry to transport wagons from the city centre downriver to the shipyard. She was named the *Pikas*, and was 27m long, able to carry two or three wagons. Details are scarce, but what was most unusual for the time was that she had a screw propeller powered by a 60 hp steam engine supplied by a vertical boiler sitting on the deck. Most ferries at the time had paddles, though screw propellers were probably chosen as they worked much better in ice. The *Pikas* served the shipyard until the 1930s, though her exact fate is unclear.

Hans Knust Eisenbahn-Trajektschiffart und Wasserbauamt GmbH
Stettin Hafen   **1882-1945**

Hans Knust was a ship's captain in Stettin who saw the opportunity to deliver goods wagons by ferry around the shallow channels of Stettin harbour. He founded his company in 1882 and built a series of small steam ferries designed to carry three or four wagons. The wagons were loaded at the railway yards on the east side of the river and delivered to the docks and shipyards where they were unloaded. Return cargoes or empty wagons were loaded in the docks and returned by ferry to the railway. Capt. Knust operated a fleet of bow-loading ferries in the late 19th century, including the alphabet sisters, *Anton, Bertha, Caesar* and *Dora*. The company operated successfully until the Second World War, when the dock area and shipyards were heavily bombed and in 1945 most of the pre-war German population moved westward.

Two of Knust's ferries survived the war, the *Sultan*, built in 1884, remained in Stettin. The *Tyras*, built in 1887, had been transferred to the Swinemünde ferry service in 1943 and renamed *Swinemünde 2*.

Polskie Koleje Państwowe
Szczecińska Stocznia Remontowa Gryfia SA
Port Szczecin   **1946-1983**

The two surviving ferries, *Sultan* and *Swinemünde 2* were taken over by the Polish Authorities after the war and renamed the *Prom Kolejowy 1* and *Prom Kolejowy 2*, which translates as 'Railway Ferry 1 and 2'. The *Prom Kolejowy 1* (ex-*Sultan*) was used in Szczecin harbour, then laid-up in 1952. She was refurbished by the Polskie Koleje Państwowe, (Polish State Railways) in 1961, who replaced her steam engine with a diesel and brought her back into service around the harbour. However, she only worked for a few years and was reportedly scrapped around 1966.

The *Prom Kolejowy 2* (ex-*Swinemünde 2*) had been sunk at the end of the war and though she had been raised, she remained laid-up in poor condition. In 1952, the Stocznia Remontowa 'Gryfia', (Gryfia Ship Repair Yard) was founded on Gryfia island, opposite the old AG Vulcan shipyard. They took over the *Prom Kolejowy 2* and refurbished her, putting her back into service in 1955 renamed the *Gryfia*. She continued taking wagons with materials across the river to the shipyard until 1983, when the rail connection ended and she was replaced by a vehicle ferry. The *Gryfia*, ex-*Prom Kolejowy 2*, ex-*Swinemünde 2*, ex-*Tyras*, had worked in and around Szczecin for 96 years. Since ending her work, she has been preserved by the shipyard and remains moored in Szczecin harbour. In 1990, her steam engine was removed and put in a museum, as it was no longer safe to operate. However, she was fitted with a diesel engine and *Gryfia* still makes occasional trips around the harbour as Poland's oldest operating vessel.

Danzig and the Vistula

Danzig lies around 350km east of Stettin and was Prussia's other great port city. After the First World War, much of Prussia became the newly independent Polish Republic, with the Vistula as Poland's eastern

STETTIN (SZCZECIN)

border. As the main port for both the German and Polish hinterlands, Danzig became a 'Free City', not officially part of either country until annexed by the Germans in 1939. At the end of the Second World War, this area became part of Poland and Danzig became the Polish city of Gdańsk.

Königlich Preußische Staatseisenbahnen
Stocznia Gdańska
Kaiserhafen (Polnocny) – Holm (Ostrów)   1905-current

The old city of Danzig lies on a branch of the river Vistula a few kilometres inland from the Baltic coast. Over many centuries its docks and shipyards developed along both sides of the river. However, like many old ports, the river was increasingly too shallow for the larger ocean-going ships that were around at the end of the 19th century. The solution was to build a new harbour with a deep-water channel east of the river. The Kaiserhafen opened in 1904 and created an island which separated the docks on the eastern side of the river from the railway. The island does not appear to have a name and was referred to as Holm in German, and later Ostrów in Polish, which just means small island in both languages.

The Königlich Preußische Staatseisenbahnen (Royal Prussian State Railways) restored the rail connection to the docks using a train ferry across the Kaiserhafen channel to the new island. In 1905, they bought the train ferry *Prinz Heinrich*, which had been built in 1882 for Stralsund and had been working in Swinemünde since 1901. The *Prinz Heinrich* could only carry three wagons and was a stopgap until a new steam ferry, the *Danzig,* was delivered in 1907 by the local shipyard of Asmus W. Johannsen & Co. She was larger than her predecessor, 52m long and able to carry four or five wagons.

With the creation of the Danzig Free City in 1920, the Danziger Werft took over the ferry. The shipyard occupied much of the northern part of Holm and was the main user of the ferry. In 1926 the shipyard built a second ferry, the *Gedania*. She was similar to her older sister and followed the standard pattern for a small double-ended ferry, with a screw at either end and a central wheelhouse with a tall funnel either side. The two ferries operated through the Second World War, though by 1945 the *Danzig* was badly damaged and the *Gedania* was sunk in the harbour.

After the war, Danzig became the Polish city of Gdańsk and the ruined shipyards were rebuilt to become the Stocznia Gdańska. The *Gedania* was salvaged and repaired and put back in service in 1949, renamed *Gedanja*. The ferry port at Kaiserhafen was renamed Polnocny and Holm became Ostrów. The *Danzig,* now fifty years old, was rebuilt and returned to service in 1957 as the *Gdańsk*. The *Gdańsk* was retired in 1966

An early postcard showing a ferry passing AG Vulcan's shipyard in Stettin, perhaps one of those operated by Hans Knust. *(Author's collection)*

The *Gryfia* is preserved and makes occasional trips around Szczecin harbour after more than 130 years, though her steam engine was removed in 1990 and replaced by a diesel. *(Roman Huzar)*

and the *Gedanja* carried on into the 1970s, though by then she was also needing replaced.

The shipyard designed two new ferries which were built by Stocznia Rzeczna in Płock. The *Ostrów-1* was delivered in 1977. She is 57m long and built to carry four heavy wagons each with 100t of shipbuilding steel. She was joined by a sistership, the *Stogi-2*, in 1979. Shortly after this, the shipyard became famous for the Solidarność movement and the strikes which led to the downfall of Poland's Communist Government. The shipyard has declined from its heyday, when it employed over 20,000 people, now there only around 2,000 workers in the yard, but the ferries are still operational.

Westpreußische Kleinbahnen	1905-1920
Danzig Free City / Deutsche Reichsbahn	1920-1945
Polskie Koleje Państwowe	1948-1956
Schiewenhorst – Nickelswade	**1905-1956**

The main branch of the Vistula river flows into the Baltic around 15 km east of Danzig. The mouth of the river is surrounded by a flat delta area of farms and

DANZIG & VISTULA

DANZIG (GDANSK)

The **Ostrów-1** was built in 1977 to serve the Stocznia Gdańska (Gdansk Shipyard) carrying heavy wagons with steel and machinery. (Author's collection)

small villages and in 1899 the Westpreußische Kleinbahnen, (West Prussian Light Railway) was formed to link this area to the city of Danzig. A line was built east from Danzig along the coast to the small town of Stutthof and a ferry was put in place where is crossed the river between Schiewenhorst and Nickelswade.

The ferry *Schiewenhorst II* was built in 1903 by Leopold Zobel in Bromberg, (now Bydgoszcz). She was a standard small double-ended steam ferry, 29m long, with a single track able to carry three wagons. She had propellers forward and aft, each driven by a 120 hp compound engine. Leopold Zobel's main business was boiler-making and he only tried shipbuilding for a few years, launching tugs and barges into the Brahe river. It was not a success as the river level was frequently so low that ships were left on the building berth for several months before they could be launched. The ferry *Schiewenhorst II* started on the crossing between Schiewenhorst and Nickelswade in 1905 and continued there for over fifty years, despite several changes of name and nationality. The area was German West Prussia until 1920, the Free City of Danzig until 1939, Germany again until 1945 and, after the Soviet occupation, finally Poland.

The Westpreußische Kleinbahnen built a second ferry, the *Weichselmünde*, which was delivered from J.W. Klawitter & Co. in Danzig. She was similar to the *Schiewenhorst II*, though slightly larger, and started service in November 1913. For some reason, she was only there for four months before she was sold to the Nord-Ostsee Kanal and renamed *Rade*, (see the beginning of this chapter).

The *Schiewenhorst II* carried on alone through the border changes of 1920. When the area came under German control in 1939, the railway system was taken over by Deutsche Reichsbahn and she was renamed the *Aegir*. The ferry continued until 1945, when she was sunk during the fighting at the end of the war. The *Aegir* was raised and repaired in 1946 and handed over to the Polskie Koleje Państwowe, (PKP), the Polish State Railways. The PKP changed her name to the *Swibno* and returned her to her old service in 1948 with the towns' names changed from German to Polish, Schiewenhorst became Swibno and Nickelswade became Mikoszewo.

The ferry service was stopped in 1956 and the *Swibno*, ex-*Aegir*, ex-*Schiewenhorst II*, was most probably scrapped in 1961.

The steam ferry *Parom-Ledokol No.1*, (*Ferry-Icebreaker No.1*) was built by the Baltic Shipyard in 1948 to connect the yard to the docks on the south side of the River Neva. (*Author's collection*)

Kleinbahn Marienwerder
Mewe – Johannisdorf   **1900-1920**

There was a second small ferry across the Vistula around 60km upstream from Schiewenhorst. The Kleinbahn Marienwerder, (Marienwerder Light Railway) started a train ferry across the river between Mewe and Johannisdorf, (now the Polish towns of Gniew and Janowo).

The ferry *Landrat Brückner*, was built by AG Vulcan in Stettin in 1900. She was a small double-ended steam ferry, 27m long, with the standard central wheelhouse on a gantry and two tall funnels. She operated until 1920, when the change of borders after the First World War, made the Vistula the boundary between Germany and Poland. With the crossing now an international border, the ferry service was stopped and it is not clear what happened to the *Landrat Brückner*.

St. Petersburg
Baltiysky Zavod (Baltic Shipyard)
New Port – Vasilyevsky Island 1913-current

Looking out from the St. Petersburg's Winter Palace, the grand buildings across the River Neva are on the eastern end of Vasilyevsky Island. West of the old city, much of the southern part of the island is taken by the Baltiysky Zavod, (Baltic Shipyard). Today the shipyard builds most of Russia's icebreakers, but like many Baltic shipyards it had British origins, founded in 1856 under the name of Carr & MacPherson.

At the southern tip of Vasilyevsky Island, the shipyard operates a small train ferry across the Neva, shipping heavy equipment by rail from the sidings on the south side of the river. The first ferry and the linkspans were put in place in 1913. Unfortunately, there are no details of this ferry as much of the shipyard, and probably the ferry, was destroyed during the Second World War. After the war, the shipyard built themselves a new ferry named the *Паром-Ледокол №1*, (*Parom-Ledokol No.1*), which simply translates as 'Ferry-Icebreaker No.1', which started service in 1948. She was a double-ended steam ferry, around 50m long, and able to carry four

The diesel electric ferry *Parom-Ledokol No.2* was built in 1967 and continues to service the Baltic Shipyard as one of the last small ferries in Europe. (*Baltiysky Zavod*)

A winter view from the bridge of the *Parom-Ledokol No.2* while unloading wagons at the Baltic Shipyard. *(Oleg Kuleshov)*

The *Lidingöfärjan 1* carried an electric tram to the island of Lidingö in the eastern suburbs of Stockholm between 1909 and 1914. *(Spårvägsmuseet)*

wagons on a single track. The shipyard used her to develop their welding procedures and the ferry was the first to have a fully welded hull. The hull was ice-strengthened to operate all year, though in one very severe winter it was reported that she took 15 hours, to make the 500m crossing. Her steam engine was replaced with a diesel in the 1950s.

The *Parom-Ledokol No.1* was replaced by a new diesel-electric ferry in 1967, unsurprisingly named the *Паром-Ледокол №2*, (*Parom-Ledokol No.2*). Like her predecessor, she was built in the shipyard and designed to carry four wagons on a single track. She is still in service today, though her name was shortened to *ПЛ-2* (*PL-2*) in 2002. As Europe's oldest working ferry, it is appropriate that she can boast the oldest working ferryman. Nikolay Spiridonov joined the crew in the early 1960s and nearly sixty years later, still works on the ferry at the age of 93.

Stockholm

Lidingö Trafik AB
Ropsten – Lidingö   1909-1914

A little ferry that only operated for a few years carried trams to the Swedish island of Lidingö. The island lies to the east of Stockholm and at the beginning of the 20th century was developed for suburban housing. To allow its new residents to commute into the city centre, Lidingö Trafik AB built an electric tramway on the island connected by a ferry to Ropsten on the mainland.

The ferry *Lidingöfärjan 1* was built by the electrical company Allmänna Svenska Elektriska AB, (ASEA), and delivered in 1907. She was a small double-ended steam ferry, 36m long and able to carry two tram cars. It took some time to complete the tracks and ferry docks and the service did not start until the summer of 1909. The novel feature was that the electric trams could drive directly on and off the ferry using an overhead electric cable extended over the dock. The tram rails at either end of the ferry's deck sat on a hinged ramp which was raised once the ferry was docked to bring the tram's trolley pole in contact with the overhead wire.

The service was suspended in August 1914, due to a coal shortage caused by the First World War, and the ferry was laid-up. The service did not restart after the war and was replaced by a bridge in 1925. The *Lidingöfärjan 1* was sold for use as a car ferry across Göteborg harbour on Sweden's west coast. She was renamed *Färjan 2* and operated until 1966.

Öland

Statens Järnvägar
Kalmar – Färjestaden   1947-1961

Öland is the long thin island that sits off Sweden's east coast. A narrow-gauge railway was built on the island at the beginning of the 20th century and the Ölands Järnväg's main business was moving timber in

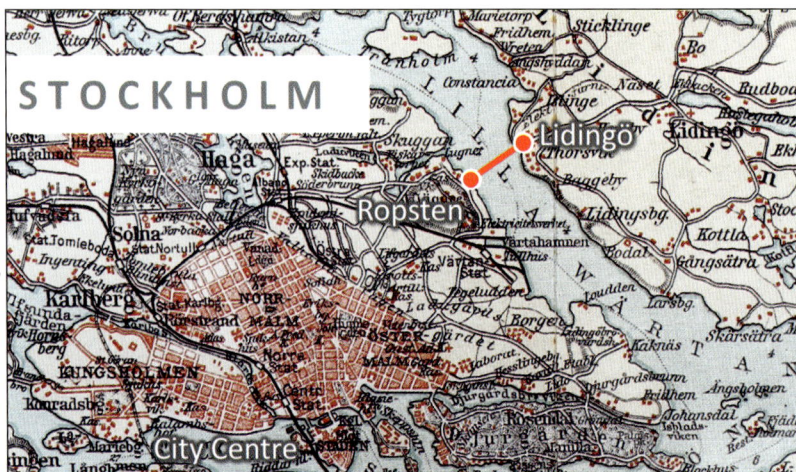

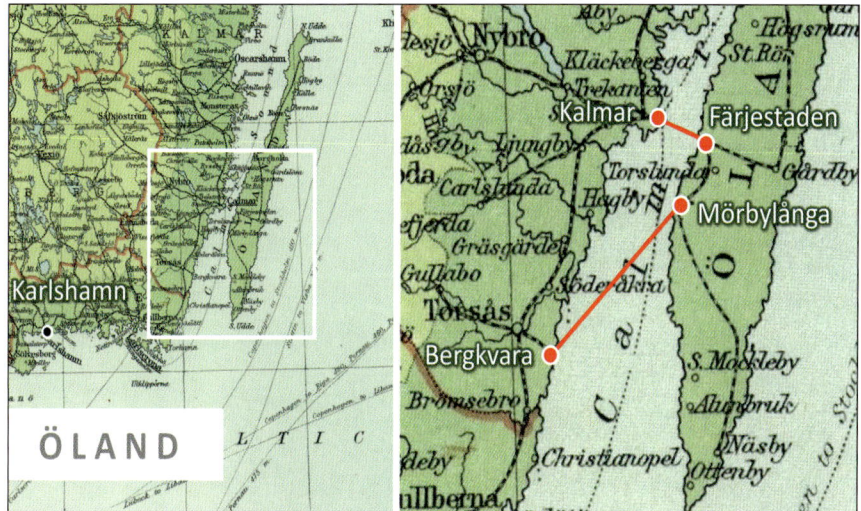

the north of the island and shipping sugar beet to the mill at Mörbylånga in the south-west. During the Second World War, there was a shortage of narrow-gauge wagons on the mainland. As Ölands Järnväg's sugar beet wagons sat idle for much of the year, they were shipped to the mainland and returned to Öland for the sugar beet season. Initially, the wagons were shipped on barges, though this was time consuming.

In 1947, the Ölands Järnväg was nationalised and amalgamated into the Statens Järnvägar (SJ), who decided to ship the wagons by ferry. They chartered a small diesel ferry belonging to the Swedish Navy's Coastal Artillery, named *J321 Balder*, and fitted temporary rails to the deck. The ferry was 28m long and could carry three wagons, the rails were adjustable so that she could carry either narrow or standard-gauge wagons. The service between Kalmar and Färjestaden started in September 1947 and the following year 14 standard-gauge and 177 narrow-gauge wagons were shipped.

SJ chartered a second similar ferry, the *Ane,* from the Swedish Navy in 1950 and the following year there were 911 return crossings, carrying 550 standard-gauge and 1,950 narrow-gauge wagons. The *Ane* had suffered engine problems from the beginning of the charter, and in 1954 SJ replaced her engines with two Scania Vabis D814 diesels. SJ's plan was to recoup the cost of the engines from the charter rate, however the following year the Navy terminated the charter. The *Balder* was temporarily brought back into service and SJ considered buying the *Ærøskøbing* from D/S Æro in Denmark, but decided she was too large. Their solution was to order a new ferry from AB Bröderna Larsson, in Kristinehamn to a standard design developed by the Swedish Roads Administration. The *Bure* was delivered in October 1957, a smart little double-ended diesel ferry that could carry four wagons on either narrow or standard-gauge track. SJ also fitted new hydraulically powered linkspans at Kalmar and Färjestaden.

By the time that the *Bure* was delivered, the rail traffic had begun to decline and the sugar mill were also running their own seasonal ferry. The old narrow-gauge lines on Öland were in poor repair and after a few years, SJ decided to close the narrow-gauge railway. The Öland railway stopped operating in October 1961 and the *Bure* was used to ship the last of the rolling stock off the island. Her last trip as a train ferry was in May 1962. After a period of lay-up, she was sold to the Roads Administration where she operated as the car ferry *Färja 61/264* until 1985.

With no linkspan, the arrangements for getting wagons on and off the **Balder** were fairly primitive. (*Järnvägsmuseet*)

A second ferry, the **Ane**, was chartered from the Navy's Coastal Artillery in 1950. Statens Järnvägar had to replace her engines. (*Author's collection*)

The Öland railway closed in 1961. The **Bure** removed rolling stock from the island until the following year, then served as a car ferry on other routes until 1985. *(Järnvägsmuseet)*

Svenska Sockerfabriks AB
Bergkvara – Mörbylånga   1953-1957

Svenska Sockerfabriks AB operated a number of sugar mills around Sweden including the factory at Mörbylånga on Öland. In 1953, they closed their sugar mill at Karlshamn on the mainland and decided to ship the sugar beet across to their Mörbylånga mill for processing. Rather than rely on the SJ ferry at Kalmar, and the problems of adjusting wagons from mainland standard-gauge to Öland narrow-gauge, they decided to operate their own ferry.

They found a ferry in an unlikely location. The *Perch Rock* had been built by Caledon Shipbuilding & Engineering in Dundee for the Borough of Wallasey in 1929. She was described as a 'luggage boat' carrying goods and vehicles across the Mersey from the Wirral to Liverpool. She was very broad, 44m long and 15m wide, with side ramps for loading to the Mersey landing stages. There was no passenger accommodation, only a small wheelhouse on a bridge in front of the large central funnel. Svenska Sockerfabriks bought the *Perch Rock* in 1953 and renamed her *Betula*. They fitted standard-gauge rails set into the deck, allowing her to load sugar beet wagons over the stern. The ferry ran between Bergkvara on the mainland and Mörbylånga, where a length of standard-gauge track was laid from the harbour to the sugar mill. This allowed the mill to receive standard-gauge wagons directly from the mainland as well as narrow-gauge wagons from local farmers on the Öland railway.

The sugar beet trade was limited to the autumn and Svenska Sockerfabriks chartered her out as a passenger

After her few years on the Öland crossing, the **Betula** was sold to Linjebuss International and completely rebuilt as their first car ferry operating between Helsingør and Helsingborg. *(Author's collection)*

and car ferry during the summer months. For this work, the *Betula* was fitted with a large superstructure aft of the funnel with a passenger deck and saloon. She spent the summer of 1954 chartered to Skandinavisk Linietrafik between Korsör and Nyborg and the following three summers chartered to Linjebuss International AB between Helsingør and Helsingborg.

The sugar beet ferry service ran for five years until 1957. After this the *Betula* was sold to Linjebuss International and continued as a full-time car and passenger ferry between Helsingør and Helsingborg. In her later years, she was completely rebuilt and became unrecognisable from the original *Perch Rock*. She was eventually retired and cut down for use as a barge in 1972. Her old wheelhouse lives on as the clubhouse for the Råå boat club, just south of Helsingborg.

EIGHT

The Rivers

The Netherlands

Hollandsche Ijzeren Spoorweg Maat.
Enkhuizen – Stavoren   1900-1936

Although this chapter is about train ferries on rivers, the first is an exception as it crossed the Zuiderzee which at the time was a large bay separating the Dutch provinces of Noord-Holland and Friesland and open to the North Sea. From 1886, passenger steamers had connected the railway at Enkhuizen around 50 km north-east of Amsterdam with the port of Stavoren. This linked the railways on either side of the Zuiderzee and provided a shortcut between the cities of western Holland and the agricultural province of Friesland.

The steamers were initially owned by a local operator but were taken over by the Hollandsche Ijzeren Spoorweg-Maatschappij, (Hollands Iron Railway Company) in 1896. As in other places with railway-owned steamers, the railway's directors soon decided to ship loaded wagons by ferry to reduce the cost of transhipping freight. Their first train ferry, the *Stavoren*, was delivered by the Rotterdam shipyard of Rijkee & Co. in 1899. She was a simple barge-shaped vessel, designed for goods wagons, 66.6m long, 12m wide with two lines of track on deck. Ten 15-ton wagons were loaded over the bow on gauntleted lines. The wheelhouse was supported on a spidery iron gantry located forward of the two funnels on the centreline. Below the deck there were two 2-cylinder compound steam engines.

Although the *Stavoren* was delivered in September 1899, problems with the foundations for the linkspans delayed the opening of the service until January 1900. The 20km crossing took around an hour and forty minutes. Traffic increased quickly and a second ferry, the *Enkhuizen* was delivered by the same shipyard in 1901. She was virtually identical to the *Stavoren*, the only visual differences were that the wheelhouse gantry was a bit more substantial and the funnels were around two metres taller. The third and last ferry, the *Leeuwarden* was delivered in 1909 and was a sistership of *Enkhuizen*. The three ships provided five round trips a day.

The project to build the 32km long Afsluitdijk and seal off the Zuiderzee from the North Sea was approved by the Dutch Parliament in 1918 but work only began in

The last of the three ferries, the *Leeuwarden*, joined her sisters in 1909, the three ships provided five round trips per day. *(Author's collection)*

1927. The dyke was completed in 1932, forming the Ijsselmeer and allowing the reclamation of the polders. Even before the dyke was completed rail traffic had begun to decline and the *Stavoren* was sold in 1927. When the highway across the Afsluitdijk was opened in

The *Spoorpont* at the simple terminal at Distelweg in 1915. This served the developing industrial areas on the north side of Amsterdam harbour. *(Author's collection)*

The Hollandsche Ijzeren Spoorweg started a ferry service across Amsterdam harbour in 1914. The *Spoorpont* was the second motor ferry to be built in Europe, powered by a Kromhout hot-bulb engine. *(Author's collection)*

The diesel ferry *Spoorpont II* entered service in 1957, serving both Distelweg and the new terminal at Ketjen. *(Author's collection)*

1933, the ferries had to compete directly with road transport and rail traffic quickly disappeared. The last ferry ran in April 1936.

None of the three ships were used as train ferries again. The *Enkhuizen* was used a barge, the *Leeuwarden* ended up in Venezuela and the old *Stavoren* was moored on the River Zaan and used as a Chinese restaurant until the 1980s. Though the rails have gone, the old linkspan at Stavoren is still in place.

Hollandsche Ijzeren Spoorweg Maat.	**1914-1938**
Nederlandse Spoorwegen	**1938-1983**
Rietlanden – Distelweg	1914-1983
Rietlanden – Ketjen	1955-1983

The Hollandsche Ijzeren Spoorweg-Maat. (HSM) also ferried rail wagons across Amsterdam harbour. The service ran from the Rietlanden station, in the docklands east of the city centre, to the industrial area of Distelweg on the north side of the harbour. The ferry *Spoorpont* was built in 1914. She was a basic double-ended ferry, 36m long with a single track for three wagons and a simple wheelhouse on an elevated frame on one side of the deck. What singled her out was that she was powered by a 130 hp hot-bulb oil engine built by the local firm of Kromhout Motoren Fabriek. This made her the second motor train ferry in Europe, following the German ferry *Jasper von Moltzahn* which had been fitted with a much smaller petrol engine three years earlier. The hot-bulb engine was an early form of the diesel engine that used an external vapouriser or 'hot-bulb' to ignite the fuel-air mixture. The engines operated at much lower pressure than the later diesel engines, which made them large and heavy for the power developed, though this was not a disadvantage on a ship. They were also not too fussy about fuel quality, while the fuel injector nozzles on a diesel engine were easily clogged. Diesel engines were inevitably more efficient and once they became more reliable in the 1930s, the hot-bulb engines largely disappeared.

The ferry dock was built at Rietlanden around 3km east of Amsterdam's Centraal Station. Prior to the Second World War, the wagons were loaded by a steam shunting locomotive and unloaded one-by-one at Distelweg using a winch and a horse. The HSM was amalgamated into the state-owned Nederlandse Spoorwegen in 1938 and afterwards the ferry took a diesel shunter across to Distelweg on the first trip each morning. This unloaded and shunted the wagons during the day and returned to Rietlanden on the last crossing each evening. Throughout this period, the Koppe company managed the ferry's day-to-day operation.

In 1955, a new service was started from Rietlanden directly across the harbour to Ketjen. This was just over 1 km, compared to the longer 5 km trip to Distelweg. With more traffic a new ferry, the *Spoorpont II*, was delivered in 1957 by the Scheepwerf Vooruit in Zaandam. She was 48m long with a single track that could carry five wagons. The wheelhouse was fitted centrally on a gantry over the train deck. With the new ferry in service, the old *Spoorpont* was retired, though remained in general use around the harbour for the next decade.

A third ferry, the *Spoorpont III* was delivered in 1962 from the same shipyard and was essentially identical to her predecessor. However, the two ferries did not operate together for very long. During the 1960s several of the older industrial plants began to close and the *Spoorpont II* was laid-up in 1970. By then only a few wagons were being shipped to Distelweg and the remaining traffic was concentrated on the shorter crossing to Ketjen. This also declined until the service was no longer viable and the last crossing was in April 1983.

Haarlem Alkmaar Tramweg
Velsen Zuid – Velsen Noord   1906-1924

The port of Amsterdam is linked to the North Sea by the Nordzeekanaal, (North Sea Canal) which runs west from the city to Ijmuiden on the coast. In 1897, a steam tram service was opened from Haarlem running north to Alkmaar and crossing the canal by a swing bridge at Velsen. In 1900 a plan was developed to widen and deepen the canal. The new width of around 200m was too long for a swing bridge and two ferries were ordered to make the crossing between Velsen Zuid and Velsen Noord.

The first ferry, the *Kennemerland I* was delivered by the De Maas Shipyard in Rotterdam at the end of 1900 and her sistership, the *Velsen* at the beginning of the following year. They were 37m long and 15m wide

powered by two compound steam engines and paddles. A rail track was fitted on the centreline to carry the Haarlem to Alkmaar tram, normally a small steam locomotive with two passenger cars and a freight wagon. There was also space on one side of the track for road vehicles, mostly horses and carts, and the other side was shared by foot passengers and the two funnels. The ferries were much admired, their passenger saloon had central heating and electric lighting and the main deck was covered by a glass roof to keep the trams and foot passengers dry.

The *Velsen* started her first test runs in early 1901 and things quickly went wrong. Although she had sailed from the builders successfully, she proved completely unsteerable at slow speeds. Docking the ferries proved

The *Spoorpont III* leaving Distelweg for Rietlanden with a locomotor and two wagons. She was built in 1962 by Scheepwerf Vooruit in Zaandam. *(J.C. de Jongh)*

The *Rotterdamse Tramweg* operated steamers and light railways connecting the islands of Goeree-Overflakkee and Schouwen-Duiveland to the mainland. Rail wagons were taken over on barges. *(Jan Voerman / NVBS-Railverzamelingen)*

Empty wagons being unloaded from the Rotterdamse Tramweg barge. Wagons loaded with sugar beet for transport to the mainland are lined-up on the shore. *(Author's collection)*

next to impossible if there was any wind, not a rare occurrence in western Holland. The glass was removed from the roof to reduce windage, though it made little difference and by this time, questions were being asked in Parliament. In May 1902 one of the ferries got stuck in the neighbouring footbridge early in the morning and passengers were trapped onboard until she could be pulled free by a passenger steamer in the late afternoon. The *Kennemerland I* got stuck a few months later blocking all shipping traffic in the canal. Manoeuvrability was not the only problem. In August 1902, the hinged flaps that connected the *Kennemerland I* to the linkspan got stuck, trapping the tram onboard the ferry for two hours. The whole saga became an increasing embarrassment to the Tramway and Canal Authorities. The Amicitia Theatre Society in Velsen even set the ferries' problems to music as a comic opera.

Throughout this saga, people were still able to cross the canal on a temporary footbridge and connect with the tram on either side. The Canal Authority were keen to demolish the bridge but needed to demonstrate that

the ferry was a reliable alternative. The next plan was to convert the ferries to run on a guide chain. A heavy iron chain was fixed on one side of the Canal and tensioned by a steam winch on the other bank which could lower the chain to the canal bed to allow shipping to pass. The first tests were carried out with the *Kennemerland I* in November 1902, though they revealed a new problem. The winter had come early and the ferry simply pushed the floating ice ahead of her into the dock, preventing the bow from connecting to the linkspan. Further trials were postponed until the spring while various other changes were made. It was August 1903 before the ferry returned from docking in Amsterdam. Her paddles had been removed and replaced by screw propellers, the roof over the deck was completely gone and the wheelhouse and gantry were replaced by small cabins fitted at either end of the main deck. Test runs continued through the winter and became more reliable, though the *Kennemerland I* still struggled to cope with ice. It was March 1904 before test runs with the tram began. These were only partly successful as it took around five minutes to load the tram for a crossing that only took seven minutes. However, with practice and small modifications this improved and by the end of 1905 the ferry was sufficiently reliable to allow the footbridge to be demolished. The *Velsen* was then converted to run alongside her sistership and by July 1906 the two ferries were running together and a tram journey became a reliable routine.

Apart from recriminations on the delay and huge cost of the project, the ferries continued uneventfully from then until 1924 when the tram service was stopped. After this, *Kennemerland I* and *Velsen* continued transporting passengers and vehicles until 1940, when they were replaced by new larger ferries.

N.V. Rotterdamse Tramweg Maatschappij

Zijpe – Anna Jacobapolder	**1900-1953**
Zijpe – Numansdorp	**1900-1953**

The last of the Dutch ferries was run by the Rotterdamse Tramweg Maatschappij, (Rotterdam Tramway Co.) which operated light trains and ferries south-west of Rotterdam and connected to the islands of Goeree-Overflakkee and Schouwen-Duiveland. The RTM opened a steam tram line on Schouwen-Duiveland in 1900 and goods wagons were transferred to the mainland on barges secured alongside a tug. The three barges *Sleepschip 1, 2* and *3* were towed between loading ramps at Zijpe on Schouwen-Duiveland and the mainland docks at Anna Jacobapolder and Numansdorp. The traffic varied throughout the year and was particularly busy for a few weeks each autumn when the sugar beet harvest was sent to the mainland. RTM also connected the islands by car ferry and particularly after the Second World War most freight came by road.

The rail service ended when the islands of South

Holland and Zeeland were inundated by the disastrous flood of February 1953 which killed several hundred people. Many buildings and roads on the islands were destroyed and large sections of the Schouwen-Duiveland railway were washed away. The track was never reinstated and the dykes built by the Delta Project to prevent future floods provided new road links between the islands and mainland.

The first Rhein ferry

From the 1850s through to 1900 there were ten train ferries at different points on the Rhein. One of the reasons for this was political rather than technical. Like other parts of Europe, railway construction boomed in the German states from 1850 through to 1880. In Germany, this coincided with a period of political upheaval. The North German Confederation was created in 1866 as an amalgamation of twenty-two small German states, dominated by Prussia. Inevitably, France saw this as a threat to the balance of power. Fearing a French invasion, the Prussian military refused to permit new bridges to be built across the Rhein in case they were used by an invading army. The few that were built, such as at Köln and Koblenz, were heavily defended. In the event, when the Franco-Prussian war did break out in 1870, the Germans turned it into a military victory and annexed the French regions of Alsace and Lorraine. After the war, there were no new ferries over the Rhein and those already in operation were gradually replaced by bridges as they then helped the Prussian military to defend their expanded territory.

Ruhrort-Crefeld-Kries Gladbach E.G.	**1852-1866**
Bergisch-Märkische Eisenbahn Gesellschaft	
	1866-1885
2 Homberg – Ruhrort	1852-1885

The first train ferry service in Germany started in November 1852, less than three years after the first ferry on the Firth of Forth. However, the two projects were largely planned in parallel. The Ruhrort-Crefeld-Kries Gladbach Eisenbahngesellschaft, (RCG) operated on the western side of the Rhein. They wanted to deliver coal from the Ruhr coalfields to the cities on the eastern side of the river and also transport freight to and from the Belgian ports. A second railway company, the Cöln-Mindener Eisenbahn Gesellschaft, (CME) ran from Köln to Duisburg and eastwards through the coalfields to Minden. As in Britain at the same time, the railways were private companies and in competition which each other. However, in this case both sides were set to benefit and in March 1847 the two companies reached an agreement. The CME would build a branch line to Ruhrort on the east side of the river, just north of Duisburg. The RCG would build a line to Homberg on the western bank and ferry wagons across the river.

The loading arrangements had to cope with steep

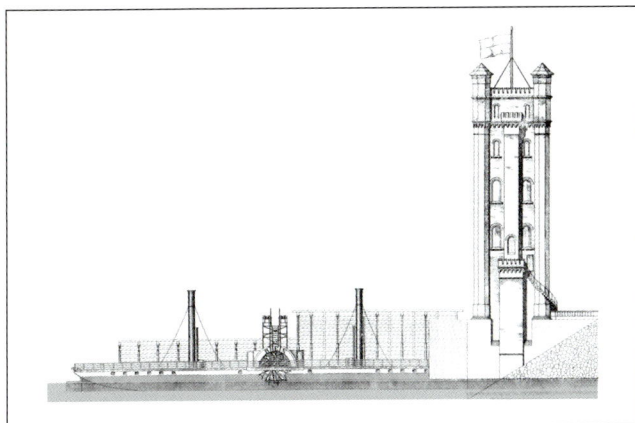

The tugs, barges and winches were too slow. In 1856 a new system was started with a large steam ferry and hydraulic lifts to raise wagons from the ferry's deck to the riverbank. *(Z.f. Bauwesen, 1857)*

riverbanks and changes in the river-level during the year. The railway companies chose a cheap and simple system, using barges each able to carry three wagons. A basin was built on either side of the river, to protect the barges from the current, with rails set on a ramp sloping down into the water with a 1:12 gradient. A string of three wagons was attached to a locomotive by a long chain and run down the slope and over a moveable loading bridge on to the barge. The locomotive remaining on the horizontal track at the top of the riverbank. The loaded barge was then taken across the river by steamer and the wagons were pulled up the ramp on the other side in the same way, using a chain attached to a locomotive at the top of the slope. The RCG built six barges and three steamers, named *Delphin*, *Adler* and *Emscher*. The barges were attached either side of the steamer and taken across the river two at a time, which took around 15 minutes. Initially, the pulling chains often broke causing the heavy coal wagons to career down the slope and over the barge into the water. The chains were then replaced by wire ropes which proved more reliable. The service was also interrupted by floods and ice for a few weeks each year. Initially around 700 wagons were transported each month, rising to over 2,600 in 1855. However, this was pretty much the limit of the system and a re-think was required if more wagons were to be shipped.

Armstrong's hydraulic lift

Having proved the demand for a ferry, the RCG decided to increase capacity by building a new system, using a steam ferry and hydraulic lifts on each bank to raise and lower the wagons. The steam ferry *Rhein* was built by a local shipyard, Jacobi, Haniel & Huyssen in Sterkrade and delivered in 1856. She was a double-ended paddle steamer, 52m long with three tracks on deck set close together, so that she could carry six wagons or four passenger coaches on the centre track or twelve wagons on the two outside tracks. The open

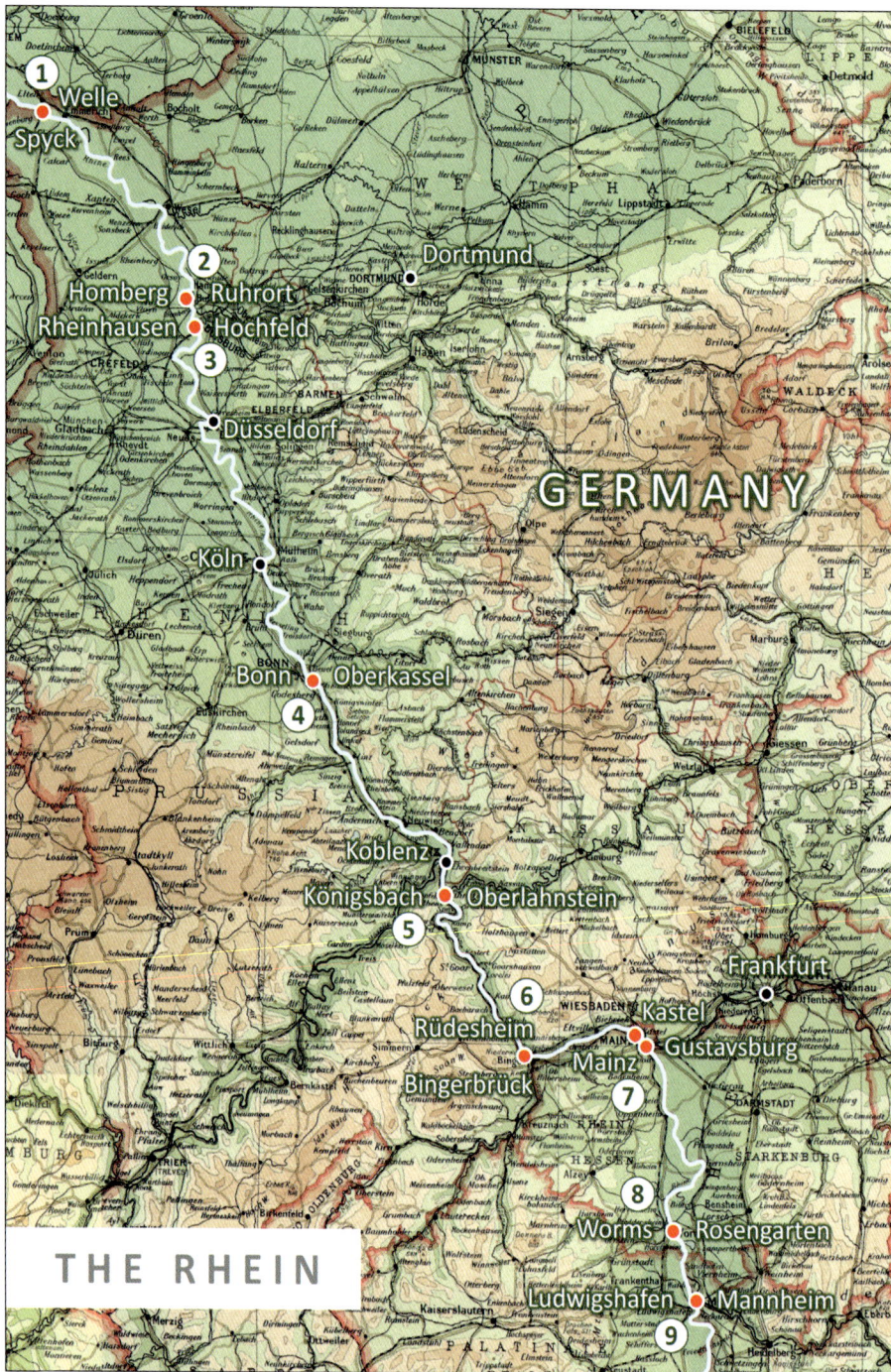

THE RHEIN

in stone with arched windows, turrets and a flagpole on top, like medieval castles.

The new system went into operation in May 1856 and soon transported 4,000 wagons a month. Wagons were still ferried on the old steamers and barges when traffic demanded, though the *Adler* and *Emscher* were mostly used as passenger ferries. In the event, passenger coaches were seldom shipped across the river, as they reduced the number of more-profitable goods wagons that could be carried. A second ferry, the *Ruhr*, was ordered from J. Wigham Richardson & Co. in Newcastle and delivered in 1865. She was similar to the *Rhein*, 51m long with three close-set tracks on deck which matched the rails in the lift, and able to carry 12 wagons. With the two ferries running, RCG was able to transport more than 8,000 wagons a month.

In 1866 the RCG was taken over by the Bergisch-Märkische Eisenbahn Gesellschaft, (BME), and the competing Rheinsche Eisenbahn Gesellschaft, (REG) opened their own ferry service between Rheinhausen and Hochfeld around 6km to the south. In the short-term, there was enough traffic to keep both ferry routes busy and the ferry continued even after the Rheinhausen ferry was replaced by a bridge in 1874. The Ruhrort tower was repaired after a fire in 1876 and nearly 7000 wagons a month were still crossing between Ruhrort and Homberg in 1881.

The various railways companies were nationalised between 1880 and 1882 and absorbed into the Preußische Staatseisenbahnen (Prussian State Railways). With the end of competition between the railway companies, the costly ferry operation could no longer be justified and all rail traffic was routed over the Rheinhausen bridge. The ferry stopped in 1885. The ferry basins still remain and though the lift-tower in Ruhrort was demolished in 1971, the Homberg tower is still in place and now part of the Ruhr Industrial Heritage Trail.

bridge was on a gantry between the paddle boxes surrounded by four tall funnels. The *Rhein* was the first train ferry designed to carry passenger coaches and had a passenger saloon below the train deck. For the hydraulic lifts, RCG turned to William Armstrong & Co. in Newcastle. The lifts on either side of the river were set in a 35m tower and each could carry two wagons side-by-side or a single passenger coach over a height of 8.5m. The hydraulic system was driven by a 30 hp steam engine in a neighbouring engine house. Like the best of Victorian engineering, the lift towers were not left as simple industrial structures. Their iron frames were clad

Hartwich's cable ferries

Rheinische Eisenbahn Gesellschaft

Of the ten ferry crossings on the Rhein, four were operated by the Rheinische Eisenbahn Gesellschaft, (REG). They were the work of the civil engineer Emil Hartwich. He was born in 1801 and when he qualified started work for the Prussian Civil Service. He stayed there for most of his career, gaining a reputation for bridges and canal works. In 1856, he left the civil service and took the position of Chief Engineer with the REG. He introduced many changes, but the problem of river ferries focused his attention. Hartwich could see that neither of the solutions at the Homberg – Ruhrort ferry were ideal. The simple ramps and barges were relatively cheap but slow and unreliable. The steam ferry and hydraulic lifts were complicated and expensive, both to build and operate. In the first few years of his new position, he visited Britain to see the rail ferries on the Firths of Forth and Tay, though their operating conditions were very different from a river crossing. What impressed him more were the steam-powered chain ferries crossing the tidal estuaries of England's south coast at Plymouth, Portsmouth and Southampton. The crossing between Plymouth and Devonport was around 700m and the slipways on either side were joined by a heavy chain tensioned by counterweights. The ferry carried passengers and wheeled carts and was powered by a small 30 hp engine driving two chain wheels. It took around seven minutes to cross the estuary in a virtually straight line despite the fast-flowing currents.

5 Königsbach – Oberlahnstein   1862-1864

The REG's first ferry was designed purely as a temporary measure. They needed to transport iron ore from the Lahn valley to the steelworks on the western side of the Rhein. After negotiation between Prussia and the Duchy of Naussau, an agreement was made in 1857 to extend the Nassauische Staatsbahn, (Nassau State Railway) from Limberg to Oberlahnstein on the east bank of the river and to connect this to the REG lines with a bridge, defended by the fortress at Koblenz. Inevitably, the bridge would take some time to complete and the REG were concerned that their competitor the Cöln-Mindener Eisenbahn Gesellschaft, (CME) would get in first and ship the ore via their bridge at Köln. To secure the trade, the REG and the Nassau State Railway agreed in March 1862 to establish a temporary wagon ferry between Königsbach and Oberlahnstein until the bridge was completed.

Emil Hartwich proposed developing a chain ferry, though the design would need some time. His proposal was rejected by REG's directors as they were not prepared to wait. They approved a simpler scheme using

In the event, four ferry slips were built at Rheinhausen and Hochfeld. They had a 1:48 gradient which allowed wagons to be loaded and unloaded by locomotive. *(Berlin Architekturmuseum)*

The first three ferries, the *Ruhr*, *Lahn* and *Mosel* were 47m long. They could carry five passenger coaches or eight coal wagons. *(Berlin Architekturmuseum)*

barges that would be taken across the river by steamer, similar to the first ferries at Ruhrort. Each of the companies were responsible for building the ferry slipway on their side of the river and the REG took responsibility for building and operating the ferries. Five flat barges were built with a single track able to carry three wagons and small paddle steamship, which also carried passengers. The system was in operation in less than a year and continued through until June 1864 when the Pfaffendorfer Bridge was opened.

Hartwich took advantage of the bridge works to carry out some experiments for his chain-ferry scheme. He set up a ¾" chain across the river at Koblenz and fitting a chain-wheel on the side of a 30m barge, driven by an 8 hp engine, it successfully crossed the river in around seven minutes. Using it to tow a second barge, it crossed in around twelve minutes. This convinced Hartwich that a chain ferry could operate with a fraction of the power needed for a paddle or screw steamer. It could also stop at any time without the need for anchors or mooring lines.

Once the coaches were onboard, the buffers were locked in place, though it is not clear how the coaches were secured. *(Berlin Architekturmuseum)*

The locomotive stayed on the slipway when unloading the *Sieg* and reversed the spacer wagons over the bridging ramp to pull the coaches off the ferry. *(Author's collection)*

1 Spyck – Welle   1865-1912

The next railway ferry continued the competition between the REG and the Cöln-Mindener Eisenbahn Gesellschaft, (CME). The Dutch Nederlandsche Rijnspoorweg operated a line on the north side of the Rhein from Amsterdam and Rotterdam eastwards through Arnhem to Elten on the German side of the border where it connected with the CME. However, the Dutch railway were keen to get a connection to southern Germany through the REG's line at Kleve. As always, a bridge over the Rhein would have been the best solution, but this was opposed by the Prussian military and the Dutch government did not want a bridge on their side of the border financed by a German railway. The solution agreed in 1862 was for the REG to build a line north from Kleve to Griethausen and from there via the bridge over the old river course to Spyck on the southern bank of the Rhein. From Spyck a ferry would cross to Welle on the northern side of the river and a branch line would connect to the Nederlandsche Rijnspoorweg at Elten.

This was Emil Hartwich's opportunity to develop his chain ferry. His design was to have a steam ferry with a chain wheel on either side running on two chains, a bit like a paddle steamer. Wagons would be carried on two barges which would be pulled across the river, one attached to either side of the ferry. The steam ferry and barges were built by Jacobi, Haniel & Huyssen and delivered in October 1863. The ferry was 28m long with a central funnel and passenger saloons below deck. The barges were 45m long, with iron hulls and wooden decks able to carry six goods wagons or five passenger coaches on a single track. On the riverbanks, two rails were set 11m apart to align with the rails on the barges.

The previous ferries further upriver had to cope with steep riverbanks, but near the Dutch border the land was flat and low, though the river level could still vary by around 10m. This allowed long loading ramps with a gentle gradient of 1:48, so that the wagons could be loaded and unloaded using a locomotive with spacer wagons rather than by ropes or chains. The bridge that allowed the wagons to run up from the ramp to the ferry was positioned using a small winch.

The first trials in January 1864 were a failure when the barges grounded on the riverbed in front of the ramps. After further dredging, the Government Railway Inspectors were invited to the next trial trip in March. However, this time the current pushed the ferry downstream and it stuck on the riverbank trying to approach the ramps. The Government Inspectors had to be taken off by rowing boat, with red faces all round. Several further trials followed with various adjustments to the chain tension. However, the problem remained that increasing the chain tension sufficiently to guide the ferry on to the ramp caused the chain to jump off the drive sprockets.

Hartwich was forced to rethink. After what must have been a difficult meeting with the REG Directors, the new steam ferry was scrapped. The two barges were converted into independent ferries, each with a locomotive engine and two driving wheels on the side. The chain was also abandoned and replaced by two wire ropes, each 1,280m long: a strong 45mm diameter guiding rope, which was anchored at several points to the seabed and ran over rollers on the side of the barge, and a lighter 30mm driving rope which passed through the driving wheels.

The railway line and approach bridges had been completed by April 1864, but with the redesign of the ferry system, it took a full year until April 1865 before trials were complete and the first wagons were shipped across the river. The first passenger coaches were transported the following month, though with no facilities on the barges, passengers had to stay in their coaches during the crossing. The schedule allowed 20 minutes for the crossing, but in general it took only around four minutes at either side for loading and unloading and eight minutes for the crossing. Over the first few months, several modifications were made to the wire guides and rollers to minimise wear on the rope, but the system was at last working reliably. REG's Directors had to report to shareholders that as well as being a year late, the final cost of the project was 1,215,000 thalers, 60% more than the original budget of 750,000.

An average of around 2,000 wagons were shipped each month and daily express trains were run from Köln to Zevenaar over the ferries. A third ferry was built as a reserve in 1868 and the three ferries were named the *Yssel, Waal* and *Maas*. However, the flat land by the river was vulnerable to flooding and most years the crossing was closed for two or three weeks due to flooding or ice.

When the REG's Rheinhausen to Hochfeld ferry was replaced by a bridge in 1874, its five ferries became redundant. Three of these, the *Lahn, Ruhr* and *Mosel* were transferred to the Spyck – Welle crossing in 1877 and the old *Yssel, Waal* and *Maas* were retired. After the German railways were nationalised in 1880, the express trains were rerouted over the old CME line north of the river and goods declined. The Dutch railway company, Maat. tot Exploitatie van Staatsspoorwegen took over the operation of the ferry in 1890 and continued until it was finally closed in 1912. A small passenger ferry continued the crossing until the 1920s when the train services were finally closed.

3 Rheinhausen – Hochfeld   1866-1874

REG's next project was at Duisburg where they wanted a share of the lucrative coal trade which had been the monopolised by the Ruhort-Crefeld-Kries Gladbach Eisenbahngesellschaft, (RCG) ferry between Ruhrort and Homberg. Ideally, they would have built a bridge, but as this was not approved by the military, the next best thing was their own ferry. Approval for a ferry between Rheinhausen and Hochfeld, around 6km upstream of RCG's Homberg – Ruhrort crossing, was received in July 1863.

Construction of the railway lines began almost immediately, but the ferry contract was wisely delayed until the Spyck-Welle ferry was completed and its lessons could be incorporated in the design. It was the end of 1864 before their rebuilt barges and wire ropes were working effectively. The plan for the Rheinhausen to Hochfeld crossing was to repeat the Spyck-Welle design, with cable ferries running on guiding and driving cables, but with five ferries running in parallel, rather than the two at Spyck-Welle.

To avoid some of the previous problems with silting, ferry basins were dug to bring the ferry ramps out of the river current and the incline of the ramps was kept at 1:48 to allow wagons to be loaded and unloaded by locomotive. The tracks at Spyck-Welle were 11 metres apart, to suit the original design. Experience suggested this was too close together so the Rheinhausen tracks were initially set with a 22m spacing, though this was

later reduced to 18m. The wire ropes were heavier, 65mm for the guide ropes and 33mm for the driving ropes.

Five ferries were ordered from Kölner Maschinenanstalt in Bayenthal. They were more substantial than the previous ferries, with an iron sheathed deck. They were also longer, the first three the *Ruhr, Lahn* and *Mosel* were 47m long and could carry eight coal wagons or five passenger coaches. The fourth ferry, the *Rhein* was 63m long and could carry ten wagons or seven coaches. The fifth ferry, the *Eisponte* was only 32m long and built as an icebreaker, though was later lengthened to 63m, similar to the *Rhein*, and renamed *Emscher*. All the ferries had a steam engine offset to one side which drove 2.5m diameter rope wheels fitted on the side. There was also a guide shoe and roller arrangement for the guide rope.

The first three ferries were delivered early in 1866 and after trials, the service started shipping goods wagons with two ferries in August. The first passenger coaches were carried the following month. The third and fourth ferries were put in place in 1867 and the decision was taken not to install the fifth route.

The main problem for the ferries was wear on the wire ropes. The rope strands were made of wrought iron and were much more vulnerable to damage than the later steel wires. To protect the guide wires, soft metal bearings, cast from lead, antimony and tin, were fitted to the guide tubes on the ferries. These had to be replaced every three weeks and were made in a foundry at the railway workshops. The contact surfaces on the driving rope sheaves were made from oak.

The ferries were kept working hard. They transported 400,000 tons of coal in 1867, rising to 1.4 million tons in 1873. Like the previous ferries at Spyck-Welle, the crossing was closed for a few weeks each year due to ice and flooding. When capacity was limited, the passenger trains were stopped to ensure as much coal as possible was transported. In the longer term, the only way for REG to ensure that coal deliveries were not interrupted was to build a bridge. After the Franco-Prussian War of 1870, official attitudes changed and permission was given to build a bridge at Rheinhausen in 1872. However, the approval still demanded that the railway provide gunboats to defend it.

The Rheinhausen bridge was completed early in 1874 and the ferries were laid-up. The three 47m ferries, the *Lahn, Ruhr* and *Mosel* were transferred to replace the older boats on the Spyck – Welle crossing. The 63m ferries, the *Rhein* and *Emscher*, were sold in 1877 to the Alföld – Fiumaner Railway and transferred for further use on the Danube.

4 Bonn – Oberkassel   1870-1914

After the REG had opened the Pfaffendorfer Bridge near Koblenz in 1864, the Prussian Government encouraged them to extend their line on the east bank of the Rhein north from Niederlahnstein to Oberkassel and connect by ferry to Bonn. Approval was given in 1866, though there were a number of delays in securing the land to build the railway. After the success of the Rheinhausen ferries, the REG was confident they had a standard design that could be copied for the new service.

Work to build the ferry ramps on the riverbanks started in 1869. Three ferry ramps were built, similar to those at Rheinhausen, though the gradient was slightly increased to 1:38. The wire rope cables were laid between Oberkassel on the eastern side and Spannhäusern on the southern outskirts of Bonn. Unlike the previous ferries which crossed the river at a right angle, the ferry crossing was between 520m and 560m long and set at 45° to the river flow. Three ferries were ordered, the *Agger, Sieg* and *Wupper*. They were 70m long and 9.5m wide, able to carry ten goods wagons or seven passenger coaches.

While most of the traffic was goods wagons, REG also ran six daily passenger trains from Niederlahnstein to Bonn. As with the other ferries, the crossing time was scheduled to take 20 minutes including loading and unloading. It was a slick operation, with a team of shunters and switchers in the sidings, who broke each train for loading on the ferry and connected it on the other side. Each ferry was operated with a crew of five, the helmsman, two sailors, the engineman and a stoker. In its first full year, the service carried nearly 4,000 wagons a month, rising to 8,000 in 1873. After this the traffic declined, first as other railways were built and then when the Bonn road bridge was opened in 1898. The service continued until it was suspended at the beginning of the First World War in 1914. The ferries were laid-up, but the service never restarted after the war and was officially closed in 1919.

The Oberrhein

On the upper part of the Rhein, there were five more ferry crossings. These were simpler than the cable ferries operated downstream and used steamers and barges rather than self-propelled ferries. In Mainz and Mannheim, these only operated for a few years before being replaced by bridges.

Rhein-Nahe Eisenbahn Gesellschaft
6 Bingerbrück – Rüdesheim   1862-1900

As with many of the river train ferries, the Bingerbrück to Rüdesheim crossing was primarily to move coal. The Rhein-Nahe Eisenbahn's line from Bingerbrück on the west side of the river south-west to Neunkirchen was opened in 1860 connecting with the coalfields and ironworks of Saarland. This started a discussion with the railways on the east side of the river to provide a ferry that would allow the high-quality

Saarland coal to be shipped onwards to the cities of Weisbaden and Frankfurt.

In 1861, the Rhein-Nahe Eisenbahn and Nassauische Bahn agreed to build two paddle steamers and three wooden barges, known as 'schaldes', for the crossing. On the Bingerbrück side, the loading ramp was built on a bend of the river sheltered by the charmingly named Mäuseturminsel, (Mouse Tower Island). The wagons were winched up and down the ramp on to the barges, initially using chains and later by wire ropes. At Rüdesheim on the eastern bank, there was a much longer ramp, around 130m, where the gentler gradient allowed wagons to be loaded using a locomotive with spacer cars.

The passenger service started using a chartered steamer in November 1861 and the wagon service started the following June using the steamers, *Bingerbrück* and *Rüdesheim*, together with the three barges. The barges were built at Mainz and could carry three wagons on a single track. In 1864, two larger barges were added, 31m long and able to carry four or five wagons. The barges had fixed buffers at the bow and loaded wagons over the stern. This meant that the paddle steamers had to turn as they approached the offloading ramp and run astern to land the barge on the ramp, which must have been a difficult manoeuvre when there was a strong river current. The two steamers completed around 15 return trips each day and carried around 2,500 wagons per month in 1890. Though as with other Rhein ferries, the crossing was often stopped for around four weeks a year due to flooding or ice.

Few passengers used the ferry as the Bingerbrück terminal is around 2.5 km from Bingen town station and there was a more direct passenger steamer between Bingen and Rüdesheim. The wagon ferry stopped in 1900, though passenger steamers continued between Bingen and Rüdesheim and there is still a car ferry operating between the two towns.

Hessische Ludwigs Eisenbahn Gesellschaft
7 Mainz – Mainz-Gustavsburg   1858-1862
Mainz – Mainz-Kastel   1861-1863

The city of Mainz on the west bank of the Rhein had two train ferries for a short time. This is because the river Main joins the Rhein opposite the city and so the ferries ran to Gustavsburg, south of the Main and to Kastel further north. The Hessische Ludwigs Eisenbahn Gesellschaft, (The Hessian Ludwig Railway Co.) was authorised to build a railway from Darmstadt to Mainz in 1856. The line was opened in 1858 from Darmstadt through to Mainz-Gustavsburg on the east side of the Rhein, though the completion of a bridge to the centre of Mainz was delayed, mostly due to finance. To provide a temporary ferry, HLEG bought two old river steamers which could ferry passengers across the river and two barges which could be lashed alongside to transport wagons. The detail of the loading arrangements is not clear, but the wagons were probably pulled up and down a ramp using a chain attached to a shunting engine. The passenger ferry started in August 1858 and wagons started being transported in November.

To relieve the traffic on the Gustavsburg ferry, HLEG decided to start a second service in 1861, transporting wagons from Mainz to Kastel on the east bank north of the Main. This connected with the Taunusbahn which ran north to Weisbaden and Frankfurt. Three paddle steamers and barges were bought, named *Taunus-Eisenbahn Nr. 1, 2 & 3*. In Kastel, a steep ramp was built on the riverbank and the wagons loaded on to the barges over a movable 'transfer car'. This was probably a loading ramp that bridged between the tracks on the barge and the tracks on the ramp, allowing the wagons to be pulled up the slope either using a winch or a shunting engine on the riverbank. In Mainz, there was a high bank around the city and no space to build a ramp, so the wagons were lifted on and off the barges using a 30 ton steam crane and a lifting cradle. The 6m cradle was landed on the barge deck and the wagons pushed on to it and secured. The cradle was then lifted by the crane, rotated through 90° and landed in a pit that aligned the rails with the tracks on the quayside. The wagon was then pulled out of the cradle by a shunting engine. This obviously took some time, so only a limited number of wagons could be shipped.

The trains to Darmstadt were routed over the Mainz Südbrücke when it opened in December 1862 and the Gustavsburg ferry service was stopped. In January 1863, a new line to Frankfurt was opened connecting over the Südbrücke and the Kastel ferry stopped transporting rail wagons, though it continued as a passenger service until replaced by a road bridge in 1885.

Hessische Ludwigs Eisenbahn Gesellschaft
8 Worms – Rosengarten   1870-1901

By the late 1860s, there were railway bridges across the Rhein at Mainz and 67 km further south at Mannheim. However, the distance between these bridges meant that many journeys need a substantial detour. The HLEG got approval in 1868 to build a line westward from Darmstadt to Rosengarten on the east bank of the Rhein and construct a bridge across to Worms. The lines were completed in 1870 but as there no finance for the bridge, a ferry was put in its place.

Three paddle steamers were built in Rurhort, named *Ludwigsbahn 1, 2 & 3*. There were also three barges, each able to carry three wagons on a single track. These had a pointed bow and loaded over the stern. The riverbanks were low and flat, so the wagons were loaded without any complicated system. A long ramp with a gentle gradient was built parallel to the riverbank on either side and the wagons shunted directly on and off the barge using a locomotive and spacer wagons. The

problem with this simple arrangement was the sharp change in gradient between the tracks on the barge and the tracks on the ramp. Only short wheelbase wagons could be shipped and if their buffers interlocked as they came off the barge, the forward wheels of the following wagon could lift off the track and derail.

The ferry was busy, handling roughly a train every hour, and as with the Bingerbrück ferry, the steamer had to turn in the river and run astern to land the barge stern-first on to the ramp. The crews presumably put up with the difficulties of the system on the understanding that it was only temporary. However, the project to replace the ferry with a bridge dragged on for many years. The bridge project was approved in 1890, the construction contract was placed in 1896 but the nationalisation of the railways delaying the start of building work until 1898. The bridge finally opened in November 1900 and after thirty years, the 'temporary' ferry service stopped early the following year.

Pfälzische Ludwigsbahn Gesellschaft
9 Ludwigshafen – Mannheim   1863-1867

The Pfälzische Ludwigsbahn Gesellschaft, (Palatine

The ferry between Worms and Rosengarten started in 1870. Wagons were shipped across on a barge attached to a paddle steamer. *(Stadarchiv Worms)*

At Worms and Rosengarten the wagons were unloaded on to a long ramp on the riverbank. The sharp change in gradient as the wagons came off the barge could easily derail the locomotive. Getting it back on the tracks involved a lot of muscle and wet feet. *(Stadarchiv Worms)*

Ludwig Railway Co.) operated a line from the Saarland coalfield eastward to the Rhein at Ludwigshafen. Providing a bridge to Mannheim on the eastern bank gave a connection to the Großherzoglich Badische Staatseisenbahnen, (Grand Duchy of Baden State Railways) to ship coal to Karlsruhe and other cities of Southern Germany and Switzerland. A state treaty was signed between Bavaria and Baden in 1862 approving the construction of a bridge and as a temporary measure, a ferry was put in place starting early in 1863. Each of the railway companies provided a paddle steamer and a barge with a track for four or five wagons. The ferries operated between ramps on either side of the river, though exactly how the wagons were loaded and unloaded is not clear.

In their first year of operation, the ferries transported around 3,500 wagons a month. This continued for four years while the bridge construction progressed. The Rhein bridge between Ludwigshafen and Mannheim opened in August 1867 and the ferry service stopped.

The Elbe and Havel

Königlich Hannöversche Staatseisenbahnen & Lübeck-Büchener Eisenbahngesellschaft
Lauenburg – Hohnstorf   1864-1878

The first ferry over the Elbe was between Hohnstorf and Lauenburg and was arguably the world's first international train ferry. Hohnstorf on the south side of the river was in the German Kingdom of Hanover. Lauenburg on the north side was in the Duchy of Lauenburg and ruled by King Christian IX of Denmark. However, things changed quickly and within a year Lauenburg had been annexed by Germany as a result of the Schleswig war between Denmark and Prussia.

The railway line from Lauenburg north to the Baltic port of Lübeck dated back to 1851 when the Berlin to Hamburg Railway, which ran along the north bank of the Elbe, built a branch line from Büchen to Lauenburg. This connected with the Lübeck-Büchener Eisenbahngesellschaft railway which ran north from Büchen to Lübeck. The Königlich Hannöversche Staatseisenbahnen, (Royal Hanoverian State Railways) operated south of the Elbe and wanted to build a line north from Lüneberg to Hohnstorf with a bridge across the river giving them a direct route to Lübeck. However, partly through lack of finance and the usual resistance from the Prussian military, the bridge was not approved. It was not until 1862, that the three railway companies jointly agreed to provide a ferry. This was to be owned 50% by the Hannoverian Railway, 37.5% by the Lübeck-Büchener Railway and 12.5% by the Berlin – Hamburg Railway.

As the riverbanks were relatively steep, it would have been expensive to build long ferry ramps with a gentle gradient as had been used on the lower Rhein. The solution was to copy the ferry ramps used by the Forth and Tay ferries in Scotland. A steep ramp was built down the riverbank, with a gradient of 1:9, and the wagons were raised and lowered on a 'flying bridge' which was winched up and down the ramp by a stationary steam engine. A steam paddle ferry, the *Lauenburg*, was built by Maschinenfabrik Buckau in Magdeburg and delivered in 1863. She looked very similar to the *Leviathan*, built fourteen years earlier, with tall thin funnels and a bridge on a gantry structure between the paddle boxes. She was 44.7m long with a single track on deck that could carry five wagons. There were also saloons for 1st & 2nd and 3rd class passengers below the train deck. The main difference from her predecessor was that she had a single 150 hp steam engine. This meant that the paddles could not be used independently for steering and despite having rudders forward and aft, she proved difficult to manoeuvre in the river currents. The service started in March 1864 and the river crossing took around ten minutes, but with the time to load and unload on either bank, it took the *Lauenburg* around an hour for a return trip.

The railways also built a passenger steamer, the *Hohnstorf*, and a barge that could carry three wagons. When the *Lauenburg* was unavailable for any reason, wagons were shipped across the river on the barge attached to the side of the *Hohnstorf*. The service was soon working to capacity, though there were frequent interruptions in the winter due to ice. The political situation changed in 1876 when the Duchy of Lauenburg was incorporated into Schleswig-Holstein. There was no longer any military opposition to building a bridge and an iron railway bridge was completed in November 1878 which brought the ferry service to an end.

Hamburg, Dep. fur Strom und Hafenbau
Waltershof – Neuhof   1912-1972

While the old city of Hamburg sits on the north bank of the Elbe, many of the shipyards and industrial areas lie on an island between the north and south branches of the river. When the dock area expanded to the west in the early 20th century, a train ferry service was started across the Köhlbrand linking the Steinwerder docks to the Waltershof area on the mainland south of the river. The ferry was built by the Port Authority and operated by the Hamburger Hafenbahn (Hamburg Harbour Railway). In theory, the ferry was a temporary measure and the Port Authority was to replace it by a tunnel within 24 years, though in the event it operated for sixty years.

Two ferries were built at A.G. Vulcan in Stettin in 1912 named rather unimaginatively the *Fährschiff I* and *Fährschiff II*, but were popularly known as the Mississippi-Dampfer, (Mississippi Steamers). They were short and wide, 36.6m long with a breadth of 15.5m, but quite different from other ferries in that the whole deck was supported by a gantry. This allowed the deck to move up and down to align with the quayside over the harbour's

The *Lauenburg* had a single steam engine, so the paddles could not be used independently to manoeuvre in the river currents. The ferry was replaced by a bridge in 1878. (*Author's collection*)

The vehicle ferry *Finnieston* was built in 1890 and crossed the Clyde in Glasgow. Her elevating deck was the model for the *Fahrschiff I & II*. (*Author's collection*)

The *Fährschiff I & II* crossed the Köhlbrand between areas of the Hamburg docks on the south side of the Elbe. (*Author's collection*)

tidal range of around 4.5m. The deck had two tracks, with space for six wagons, and a small passenger shelter. While this was largely a new design for a train ferry, it owed its parentage to a river ferry in Glasgow. The *Finnieston*, built for the Clyde Navigation Trust in 1890 carried passengers and road vehicles across the river on a similar elevating deck. While this was a complicated ship, with steam powered screws to raise and lower the deck, its benefit was that it needed only a small linkspan which took up very little space on the quayside.

The crossing between Neuhof and Waltershof was only around 400m and the ferries provided up to fifty trips per day in each direction. In 1938, they carried 91,000 wagons and a third ferry was ordered from A.G. Vulcan in Stettin. However, this was delayed by the Second World War and the new ferry was damaged when the shipyard was bombed and never completed. At much the same time, the *Fährschiff I* was sunk by Allied bombing of Hamburg's docks in the summer of 1943. She was raised the following year and refurbished at the end of the war.

After 1945, harbour rail traffic never recovered to pre-war levels but the number of cars and trucks continued to increase. The *Fährschiff I* and *Fährschiff II* were supplemented by car ferries in 1956 and 1960 and after this were mostly in reserve, used only occasionally when required for rail traffic. They were finally retired in 1972 and rail traffic was rerouted over the Kattwykbrücke lift-bridge the following year. The promised tunnel between Neuhof and Waltershof never materialised, but the car ferries were replaced by a high-level road bridge in 1974.

Faserstoff GmbH
Fürstenberg / Havel   1934-1993

The last and smallest German river ferry crossed the Havel river around one kilometre east of the town of Fürstenburg/Havel. The factory of Faserstoff GmbH was set-up in 1911 to make mantles for gas and kerosene lamps. The business failed in the 1920s and the factory

was taken over by the Government to manufacture shell casings for the military. The name of Faserstoff GmbH was retained to disguise the production of munitions that were not allowed under the Versailles Treaty. The shell casings were shipped by rail to an air base at Strelitz and a rail ferry was built to connect across the river. The ferry was a simple rectangular barge, 34.2m long and 5.2m wide, with a single track on deck and powered by a single diesel engine. It was not named when delivered by the Schichau yard in Elbing in 1934. The crossing was only around 150m and simple linkspans were built on either side of the river. The ferry was used regularly during the Second World War as the munitions factory expanded using forced labour from the nearby Ravensbrück concentration camp.

In 1945, the area came under Russian control. Some of the old facility continued to be used as a repair workshop for the Soviet Army's tanks and vehicles and a nearby sawmill used the ferry to transport wagons of sawn timber. In 1957, the ferry's ownership was transferred to VEB Holzindustrie and she was given an official

The ferry across the Danube from Gombos to Erdöd was in the Austro-Hungarian empire when it started in 1872. Gombos is now in Serbia and Erdöd is Erdut in Croatia. *(Author's collection)*

The *Duna* and *Drava* operated on the Danube for more than thirty years, eventually being replaced by a bridge in 1910. *(Author's collection)*

registration number, *15 B 22-19*. A new 34 hp engine was fitted in 1960 and the ferry continued in service until after German reunification. With the withdrawal of the Soviet Army, the plant was closed in 1993 and the ferry and linkspans were abandoned. In 2007, students at the local school in Fürstenburg/Havel decided to rescue the ferry from the undergrowth as a history project. They cleared the area around the track and terminals and raised money from the community to have the old ferry lifted out of the water and repainted. It remains on display and has now been officially listed as an Industrial Heritage Site.

The Danube

Alföld – Fiumaner Railway
Gombos – Erdöd   1872-1910

The Alföld is the great plain of eastern Hungary which stretches south into Serbia. In the 1860s, the Alföld – Fiumaner Railway was developed to link this agricultural area to the port of Fiume on the Adriatic coast, (now Rijeka in Croatia). The railway crossed the Danube between the towns of Gombos, (now in Serbia) and Erdöd, (now Erdut in Croatia), though at the time all this area was part of the Austro-Hungarian Empire.

The train ferry across the river was reported to have

started in 1872, though it is not clear what ferries were used for the first few years. However, when the Rheinhausen bridge opened in 1874, the Rheinische Eisenbahn's five cable ferries became redundant. The three smaller ferries were transferred to the Spyck-Welle crossing and the two 63m ferries, *Rhein* and *Emscher*, were sold to the Alföld – Fiumaner Railway in 1877. They were dismantled into pieces that could be transported by rail and reassembled on the Danube, renamed *Duna* and *Drava*. The flat floodplains either side of the river suited Emil Hartwich's design. Long ramps with a gentle gradient were built on either side of the river connected by guiding and driving ropes as they had been at Rheinhausen. The ferries operated successfully for over thirty years until they were replaced by a bridge in 1910.

Bulgarian State Railways
Giurgiu – Ruse   1940-1954

When the first Orient Express train left Paris with great fanfare in October 1883, only the small print on the ticket would have revealed its final destination as the small town of Giurgiu in Romania. Once there, passengers had to leave the train and cross the Danube by passenger ferry to Ruse in Bulgaria. From there, they took a local train to the port of Varna and a steamer to İstanbul. The Orient Express later changed to a more southerly route direct to İstanbul, but the Danube remained a barrier to railway traffic between Romania and Bulgaria.

During the Second World War, both Romania and Bulgaria were initially neutral, however both relied on Germany for much of their trade and their railways were an important route for transporting Black Sea oil to Germany. In 1939, the three countries agreed to establish a train ferry between Giurgiu and Ruse. Two ferries were ordered from German shipyards, one for the Romanian Railways and one for the Bulgarians. The Romanian ferry, the *Bucharest*, was destroyed by Allied bombing in Hamburg and never delivered. The Bulgarian ferry, the *София*, (*Sofia*), was built by Rheinwerft AG at Walsum, near Duisburg. She was 65m long with three tracks for 15 wagons on deck and a central wheelhouse on a gantry. The most important innovation was that she was powered by two MAN diesels driving Voith-Schneider propellers, forward and aft. Voith-Schneider propellers were developed in Germany during the 1920s and 30s and allowed thrust to be applied in any direction, making them ideal for manoeuvring a ferry. The river level on the Danube can vary by up to 7.5m and two huge linkspans were constructed, 200m long and supported on six piers, which limited the gradient to around 1:30.

The ferry service started in May 1940 and the *Sofia* was kept busy throughout the war, particularly as the German army moved east into Russia. The *Sofia* was slightly damaged by Allied bombing in the summer of 1944 as the German army retreated and the service was stopped for around ten days. The Soviet army took over

THE DANUBE

The *Sofia* linked the main line from Romania to Bulgaria, crossing from Giurgiu to Ruse, until replaced by the 'Friendship Bridge' in 1954. *(Author's collection)*

the area in 1944 and continued to operate the ferry. After the war, the Bulgarian State Railways continued to operate the service, which remained busy in the post-war Soviet zone of eastern Europe. The ferry finally stopped in June 1954 when the 'Friendship Bridge' was completed providing a road and rail link across the Danube. The huge linkspan structure in Giurgiu remained abandoned for over fifty years and has only recently been dismantled.

Bulgarian River Shipping Co.
Vidin – Calafat **1952-2013**

A second railway ferry was operated across the Danube between Vidin in the north-west of Bulgaria and Calafat in Romania. The Bulgarian River Shipping Co.

operated a number of ferries, mostly carrying road vehicles, but the *Бонония, (Bononia)*, also carried rail wagons. Details of the ship are a bit vague, but it was unusual in that rail wagons were loaded port to starboard across the deck, rather than bow to stern. The ferry had twelve short strips of track across the deck and was able to carry around 30 wagons in total. Similar ferries used for trucks were catamarans, formed by fitting a large flat deck across two river barges connected side by side. The ferry operated from 1952 until 2013, though latterly mostly carried trucks rather than rail wagons. The ferry service came to an end with the opening of the 'New Europe Bridge' in June 2013. Although the new bridge has a rail line, it appears that it carries hardly any rail traffic.

NINE

Alpine lakes

The Bodensee

The Bodensee, also called Lake Constance, is one of Europe's largest lakes and famous for its beautiful scenery. It is around 70km west to east and 14km north-south at its widest point. In the days before German unification, the lake shores were shared by five different states. The German states of Baden, Württemberg and Bayern along the northern shore, Austria at the eastern end and Switzerland along the southern side of the lake. Long before the railways, the towns around the lake were linked by passenger steamers.

The first railway to arrive at the northern side of the lake was the Königlich Württembergische Staats-Eisenbahnen, (Royal Württemberg State-Railways) which built a line from Ulm south to Friedrichshafen in 1847. A port station was built in 1850 to connect with the lake steamers. This was followed by the Königliche Bayerische Staats-Eisenbahnen, (Royal Bavarian State-Railways) line from Augsburg to Lindau in 1854. On the southern shore, the Schweizerische Nordostbahn, (Swiss

The *Trajekteschiff I* was the first international train ferry, operating between Germany and Switzerland from 1869. Her huge coal consumption made her very expensive to operate and she was laid-up in 1883. *(Stadtarchiv Friedrichshafen)*

North-eastern Railway) line arrived at Romanshorn in 1855 and the harbour was soon extended to include warehousing and a shipyard. These lines provided a direct route from German cities south to Switzerland and onwards to Italy, but they were only connected by steamer across the lake. Initially, the steamers carried mostly passengers, but from 1856 to 1868 the goods traffic crossing the lake rose from 15,000 to 124,000 tons annually. Handling this freight between train and

steamer on both sides of the lake became a major expense for the railway companies and moving the loaded wagons by ferry was the obvious solution. Rail wagons were ferried across the lake from 1869 to 1976 with breaks only during the wars. While most of the ferry services described in this book are simply from A to B, the Bodensee is more complex. At different times, five ferries and thirteen barges have connected six ports. They were initially owned by five different railway companies which over the years have been amalgamated and renamed.

Before the First World War

Königlich Württembergische Staats-Eisenbahnen
	1869-1917
Friedrichshafen – Romanshorn	**1869-1917**

In 1867 the Württemberg Railway and the Nordostbahn decided to build a steam ferry to carry wagons between Friedrichshafen and Romanshorn. The ship was to be operated by the Württemberg Railway,

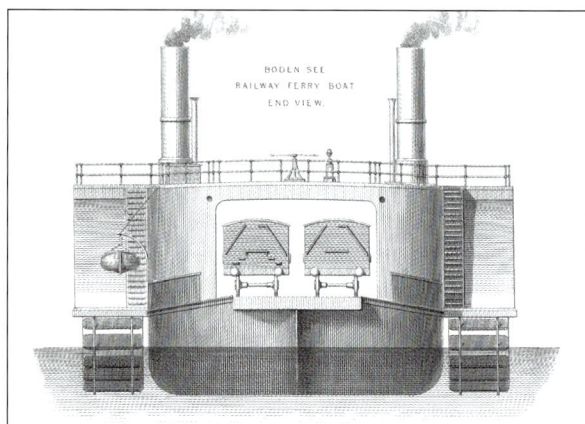

End view of the *Trajectschiff I*, showing her huge, 8m diameter, paddle wheels. *(Royal Institution of Naval Architects)*

with the Nordostbahn meeting half the costs. The British naval architect John Scott Russell was appointed to prepare the design. He was one the leading naval architects of his generation who developed several hydrodynamic theories, though is probably best remembered for his ill-fated partnership with Isambard Kingdom Brunel to build the world's largest ship, the *Great Eastern*. Born in Glasgow, Russell was an outstanding student of mathematics and physics and

Bodensee ferries

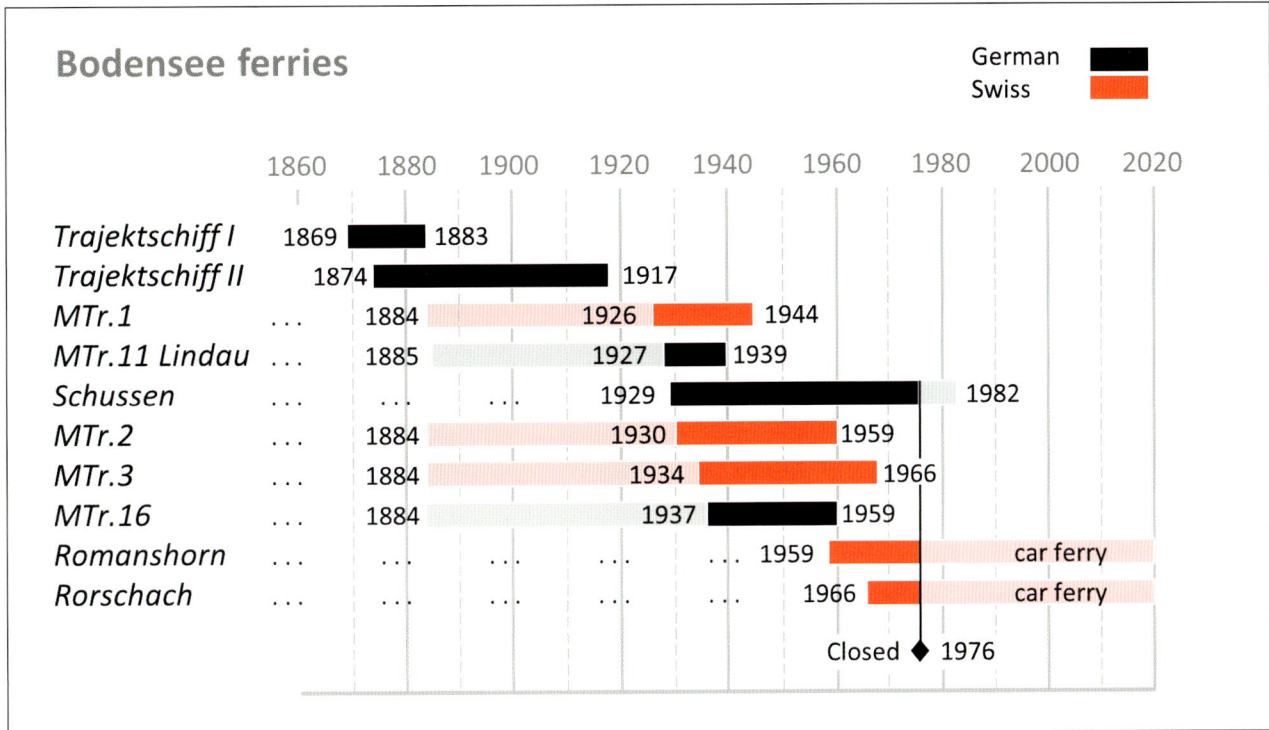

	1860	1880	1900	1920	1940	1960	1980	2000	2020

German ■ (black)
Swiss ■ (orange)

Trajektschiff I — 1869 – 1883
Trajektschiff II — 1874 – 1917
MTr.1 — … 1884 – 1926 – 1944
MTr.11 Lindau — … 1885 – 1927 – 1939
Schussen — … … … 1929 – 1982
MTr.2 — … 1884 – 1930 – 1959
MTr.3 — … 1884 – 1934 – 1966
MTr.16 — … 1884 – 1937 – 1959
Romanshorn — … … … … … 1959 – car ferry
Rorschach — … … … … … 1966 – car ferry

Closed ◆ 1976

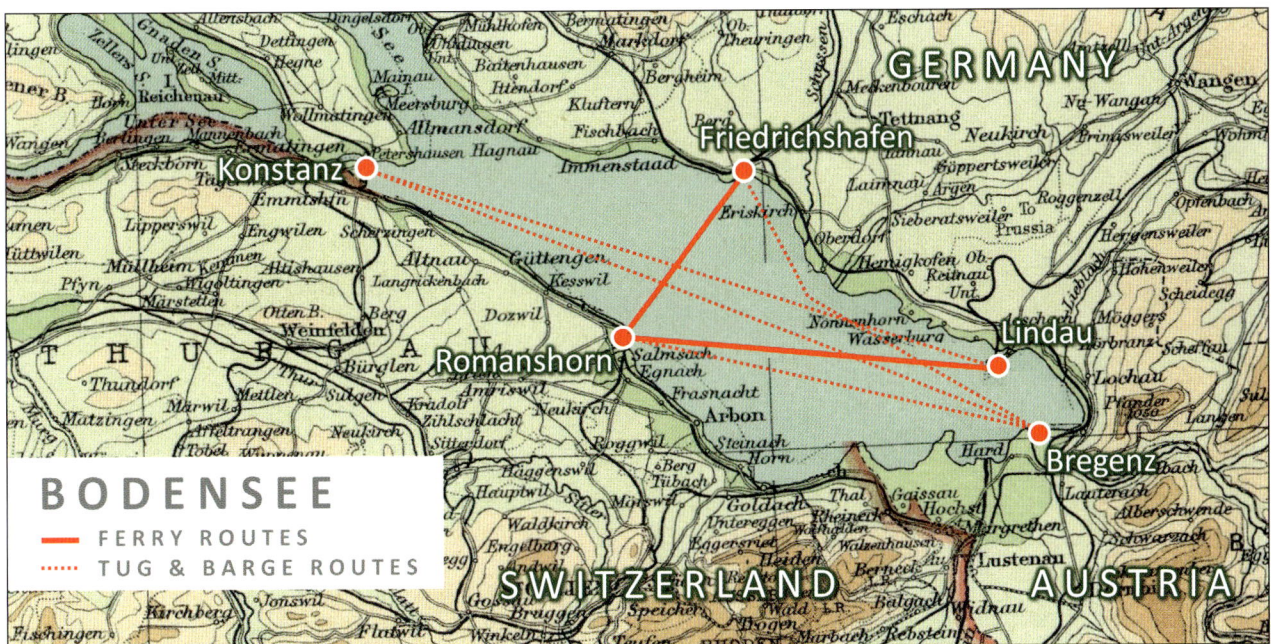

BODENSEE
▬ FERRY ROUTES
⋯ TUG & BARGE ROUTES

briefly lectured at Edinburgh University before leaving academia to learn practical shipbuilding on the Clyde. He moved to London in 1848 and took over the Millwall shipyard. Russell was known to the Nordostbahn directors as he had built the first Swiss steamship, the *Stadt Schauffhausen*, which was prefabricated in Millwall and reassembled on the upper Rhine in 1851. However, since then he had been bankrupted by his involvement in Brunel's *Great Eastern* project and by the 1860s, Russell spent his time on academic work and consulting.

The design he prepared for the Bodensee lent heavily on the success of the *Leviathan* on the Firth of Forth. A double-ended ferry, 70m long, with two tracks on deck able to carry 18 wagons. The paddle wheels were very large, 8m in diameter, and each was driven by two 50 hp steam engines. An engine arrangement that was essentially a small-scale version of the *Great Eastern*. The paddle wheels were not connected so that they could be operated separately to steer and turn the ship. One novel feature was an engine speed indicator. This showed the Captain on the bridge the revolutions of each paddle wheel and was also repeated in the port and starboard engine rooms, so that when the ferry was crossing the lake the engineers on either side of the ship

Loading a barge at Romanshorn in the early 20th century. The cast iron columns and counterweights were designed by John Scott Russell for the *Trajekteschiff I* in 1869. *(Stadtarchiv Friedrichshafen)*

The *Trajektschiff II* leaving her home port of Lindau. She operated until the First World War and was scrapped in the 1920s. *(Stadtarchiv Lindau)*

could match the speed of their engines without needing input from the bridge.

Rather than a simple gantry for the wheelhouse, the superstructure was a solid iron box, with the bridge and a promenade deck on the top. The reason for this was that Friedrichshafen harbour was very shallow and the ferry's draught was restricted to 1.3m. The ship's longitudinal strength was limited by the depth of the hull between the train deck and the keel. As Russell could not increase the depth of the hull, his solution was to use a load-bearing superstructure to reinforce the central part of the ship, probably the first time this had been done.

Although there is no tide on the Bodensee, the water level can vary by around 2m at different times of year, so that linkspans were needed at the two harbours. These were around 16m long with the free end supported by chains and counterweights that allowed the level to be adjusted by a hand winch. The linkspans

were built to carry the weight of a standard locomotive, though the wagons were normally unloaded using flat 'spacer cars' so that the locomotive stayed on the quayside. The cast iron columns supporting the Romanshorn linkspan are still in place, after 150 years.

The ferry was built by the Swiss engineering company Escher Wyss & Co. and launched in Romanshorn in January 1869. She was not formally named, though was officially listed as *Trajektschiff I*, (Ferry-ship 1). However, she was more often referred to as 'der Kohlenfresser', (the coal-eater) as her four engines swallowed more than 600kg of coal every 12km crossing.

The service started on the 22nd February 1869 and the *Trajektschiff I* carried 2,100 wagons in her first year and 7,845 in the second. To provide additional capacity, the Württemberg Railway had a barge built by Escher Wyss in 1877 which could be towed behind a passenger steamer. This was 44m long and could carry eight or ten wagons on two tracks.

The *Trajektschiff I* remained an expensive ship to operate and by 1883 her boilers needed to be replaced. Rather than spend more money on the ship, she was laid-up. A second barge was built in 1885 and the ferry was scrapped after only 16 years' service. The service continued with the two barges and in 1891 a dedicated tug, the *Buchhorn*, was built to allow the goods wagons to be ferried independently of the passenger steamers. The service with the tug and two barges continued through to the First World War, when it was suspended in 1917.

Königliche Bayerische Staats-Eisenbahnen 1869-1917
Lindau – Romanshorn   1869-1917

The Bavarian State Railway's line reached the Bodensee at Lindau, a tiny medieval town built on an island in the lake and connected to the shore by bridge. The town was soon transformed as the railway built a harbour and a causeway to the mainland. Not wanting to lose out to the Württemberg Railway, the Bavarian State Railway developed their own plan for a ferry service and also formed a 50/50 partnership with the Swiss Nordostbahn. They chose a simpler solution, loading wagons on to barges and towing them the 23km from Lindau to Romanshorn using the existing passenger steamers. Three barges were built by Escher Wyss on a temporary slipway at Lindau in 1869. They were 39.6m long with two tracks able to carry eight wagons and loaded over the stern. Each barge had a tall wheelhouse perched on the bow and when they were towed into harbour, they were released by the towing ship and had to drift on to the mooring dolphins steered by the helmsman. This must have required a lot of skill, particularly if there was any wind. Once connected to the linkspan, the wagons had to be loaded and unloaded in strict sequence as with a draught of only 0.55m the barges could easily heel over. When first built, the barges were also fitted with a mast and sail, but this was soon abandoned as impractical.

The Bavarian Railway managed to beat their rivals by starting their service at the beginning of February 1869 just a fortnight before the Württemberg Railway's *Trajektschiff I* was ready. In the years up to the First World War, the Bavarian Railway also carried much more traffic. From 1869 to 1913, an average of 35,900 wagons went through Lindau each year, while only 9,400 went through Friedrichshafen. The Austrian Vorarlberg Railway built a line around the eastern end of the lake in 1872 that connected Lindau in Bavaria, through Bregenz to St. Margarethen in Switzerland. In principle, this could have been the end of the ferry service. However transporting goods in and out of Austria involved a two-hour customs delay, plus loss of revenue to another railway company, so very little traffic was sent by this route.

In 1873 the Bavarian Railway and the Nordostbahn decided to follow the Württemberg Railway's example and build a steam ferry. She was similar to her predecessor, built by Escher-Wyss and also because she does not appear to have been formally named and was therefore referred to as *Trajektschiff II*. She was around 70m long with two tracks able to carry 16-18 wagons. The main difference was that her paddle wheels were much smaller, only 3.64m in diameter, and each was driven by a single steam engine. This reduced her coal consumption to around two-thirds that of *Trajektschiff I*. Without the draught restriction, her hull did not need reinforced and she had a simple wheelhouse on a gantry over the train deck. She also had forward and aft ballast tanks, which allowed the trim to be altered to match the linkspans. Like her predecessor, the paddle wheels operated independently to help her manoeuvre in the small harbours. Her engines developed 290 hp and she was often used to tow one or two of the old rail barges, though this could double the crossing time from one hour to two. With two round trips she could move more than a hundred wagons in a day.

An accident occurred at Lindau in 1905 when wagons on a goods train broke loose around 5 km from the harbour. The wagons ran downhill arriving in Lindau at high speed where they ran on to the linkspan and over a barge into the water. Fortunately, no-one was killed but the barge was badly damaged and the harbour closed until the wagons could be recovered. A similar accident occurred in 1908. The *Trajektschiff II* and the three barges maintained the service until the First World War when trade between Germany and neutral Switzerland declined sharply. The ferry service stopped in 1917 and the *Trajektschiff II* was laid-up in Lindau harbour. She remained there until she sank at her moorings in 1927 and was scrapped the following year. The three barges were also disposed of after the war.

The *Schussen* was rebuilt in 1954, allowing wagons to load over the bow as well as the stern. A new passenger saloon was also fitted behind the bridge, replacing the old saloon below the train deck. *(Werner Friedli)*

A barge being loaded in Lindau early in the 20th century. Wagons broke loose from a train outside Lindau in 1905 and careered down the hill, through the station and crashed over a barge into the harbour. *(Author's collection)*

Großherzoglich Badische Staatseisenbahnen

Konstanz – Lindau	1873-1899
Konstanz – Bregenz	1884-1899

The last of the German railways to reach the Bodensee was the Großherzoglich Badische Staatseisenbahnen, (Grand Duchy of Baden State Railways) which arrived in Konstanz at the western end of the lake in 1863. Unlike the other railways, they already had a line to Switzerland that ran west of the lake. With the opening of the Vorarlberg line from Lindau to Bregenz, they saw an opportunity to send freight to Austria using a ferry to Lindau. They ordered a 40m barge from Escher Wyss that could carry eight wagons on two tracks which they named the *Ludwigshafen*. This started a service between Konstanz and Lindau in 1873, towed by a passenger steamer. Drifting the barges into the dock at Konstanz was particularly difficult as they could easily be caught by the current flowing from the lake to the Rhein and carried past the harbour.

The service carried an average of 2,400 wagons per

The **MTr.3** was built as a barge in 1884 and motorised in 1934. When she retired from ferry service in 1966, her hull was 82 years old. *(Author's collection)*

Swiss Railways' **Rorschach** was built as a freight ferry in 1966, the last ferry built to carry rail wagons on the Bodensee. *(Author's collection)*

year, but it was not a commercial success. The barges could not be operated with the scheduled passenger steamers, as they stopped at several ports along the lake, and had to use a passenger steamer simply as a tug. They also had to pay the Bavarian Railway a fee for each wagon landed at Lindau and transferred to the Vorarlberg Railway.

The Austrian Railways started operating their own barges on the lake in 1884 after the opening of the Arlberg tunnel connected the Vorarlberg Railway to the rest of the network in Austria and Hungary. This increased traffic to Bregenz and the Baden State Railways built a second slightly larger barge in 1893, the *Baden*, to operate a joint service. The two barges had an accident in 1895 when they broke free from their tug in a storm and ended up beached on the Lindau causeway. Fortunately, they were recovered without much damage.

However, with the opening of the Bodenseegürtelbahn (Bodensee Belt Railway) along the north side of the lake between 1899 and 1901, most of the traffic went overland and the ferry services stopped.

K.K. Österreichische Staatsbahnen
Schweizerische Nordostbahn/Bundesbahnen

Bregenz – Friedrichshafen	1884-1913
Bregenz – Romanshorn	1884-1915
Bregenz – Konstanz	1884-1917

The Austrian Vorarlbergbahn (Vorarlberg Railway) built a line around the eastern end of the lake in 1872 that connected Lindau in Bavaria, through Bregenz to St. Margarethen in Switzerland. Though this had little effect on the existing ferries. The change came in 1884 with the opening of the Arlberg tunnel connecting the Voralberg Railway to the rest of the Austrian network. At the same time, the Voralberg Railway was absorbed into the newly established K.K. Österreichische Staatsbahnen, (Imperial Royal Austrian State Railways).

The new Austrian Railways decided to operate their own ferry service, in particular to connect to the Swiss Nordostbahn at Romanshorn. Six new 44m ferry barges were delivered in 1884, each able to carry 8-10 wagons on two tracks. Four were built for the Austrian Railways in Bregenz by the Linz Shipyard, numbered *I, II, III* and *IV*. The other two were built for the Nordostbahn by the Sulzer Bros. in Romanhorn and named '*A*' and '*B*'. The original plan was for the Swiss barges to operate between Romanshorn and Bregenz and the Austrian barges from Bregenz to Friedrichshafen and to Konstanz in partnership with the Baden State Railways. The barges were towed by passenger steamers on the shorter routes, but the Austrian Railways also built a tug to take the barges on the 45 km route to Konstanz.

In the event, there was limited traffic to Friedrichshafen. From 1884 through to 1913 an average of 14,200 wagons per year were shipped between Bregenz and Romanshorn, 13,200 between Bregenz and Konstanz and only 4,400 between Bregenz and Friedrichshafen. In 1902, the Swiss Nordostbahn was amalgamated into the new Schweizerische Bundesbahnen, (Swiss Federal Railways) who took over their part of the service.

The peak traffic was in 1911 when 85,000 wagons were transported on the three routes, but this soon declined with the coming of the First World War. As the war continued, the services were stopped one by one and the barges laid-up.

After the First World War

Deutsche Reichsbahn / Bundesbahn
Schweizerische Bundesbahnen

Friedrichshafen – Romanshorn	1920-1976
Lindau – Romanshorn	1920-1938

The German railways were nationalised after the First World War and amalgamated into the Deutsche Reichsbahn (DR) in 1920. While they inherited the Bodensee steamers and barges, very few were fit for service. They replaced the old tug *Buchhorn* (I) in 1920 with a new more powerful vessel, the *Buchhorn* (II). This worked from Friedrichshafen using the old Württemberg Railway barges and the Swiss Railways (SBB) still had their barges '*A*' and '*B*' from the Bregenz service. The Austrian Railways did not restart their services after the war and in 1925, DR took over two of their barges, *III* and *IV*. The other two were sold to a dredging contractor.

The first new investment was in 1926 when the SBB fitted two 90 hp Sulzer diesel engines to barge '*A*' and renamed her *MTr.1*. Apart from the engines, little else changed and she still had the wheelhouse perched on the bow, though now operated with a crew of four. The same improvement was made to barge '*B*' in 1930, she was given 125 hp engines and renamed *MTr.2*. A third barge, probably one of the old Austrian barges, was also motorised by SBB. She was lengthened by 7m, in order to carry 10 wagons, given two 180 hp engines and renamed *MTr.3* in 1934.

DR built the first new ferry for the lake in 1929, fifty-five years after the *Trajektschiff II*. The *Schussen* was delivered by Bodan-Werft in Kreßbronn for the Friedrichshafen to Romanshorn service. In size she was closer to the motorised barges than the old steam ferries, 54.4m long with two tracks for ten wagons and loaded over the stern. She had two diesel engines, each 240 hp, with bridge control. Unlike the previous ships, which were designed only for goods wagons, *Schussen* was also designed to take cars and had a gloomy passenger lounge below the main deck.

In parallel with the *Schussen,* DR followed the SBB's lead and fitted engines to two of the old barges for the service to Lindau. The newer of the Württemberg

Railway barges, built in 1885, was fitted with diesel engines in 1927 and renamed *MTr.11 Lindau*. The wheelhouse was also moved from the bow and raised on to a gantry amidships. The last of the old Austrian Railway barges had a similar conversion in 1937 and was renamed *MTr.16*. As the Second World War approached there were six ferries on the Bodensee crossing from Friedrichshafen and Lindau to Romanshorn, DR's *Schussen, MTr.11 Lindau* and *MTr.16* and SBB's *MTr.1, MTr.2* and *MTr.3*. However, after Germany's annexation of Austria in 1938, DR had access to Switzerland via the Austrian rail network and running the ferries became an unnecessary cost. The crossing from Lindau closed in 1938 and from Friedrichshafen in May 1939. During the war, Friedrichshafen was a strategic target for the Allies as the home of the Dornier aircraft company and the MTU diesel engine plant. The *Schussen* was fitted with anti-aircraft guns and moored off the port as an air-defence ship. In the event, the only casualty was in neutral Switzerland. The SBB ferry *MTr.1* was damaged in a collision with her sistership *MTr.2* in 1944 and scrapped the following year.

The Friedrichshafen to Romanshorn service was restarted by SBB in 1948 using the *MTr.2* and *MTr.3*. Much of the traffic was taking scrap iron from Germany to Switzerland. The DR's assets were taken over by the Deutsche Bundesbahn, (DB) in 1949 and the *Schussen* and *MTr.16* were brought back into service. The *Schussen* was modified in 1952 with a new passenger saloon aft of the bridge and her bow was rebuilt to allow her to load over both bow and stern. Her engines were also replaced later by two 500 hp MWM diesels, which more than doubled her power. After this, she operated

The *Romanshorn*, continues as a car ferry on the Bodensee, largely unchanged after sixty years service. The car ferry *Euregia* in the background. *(Schweizerische Bodensee-Schiffahrtsgesellschaft AG)*

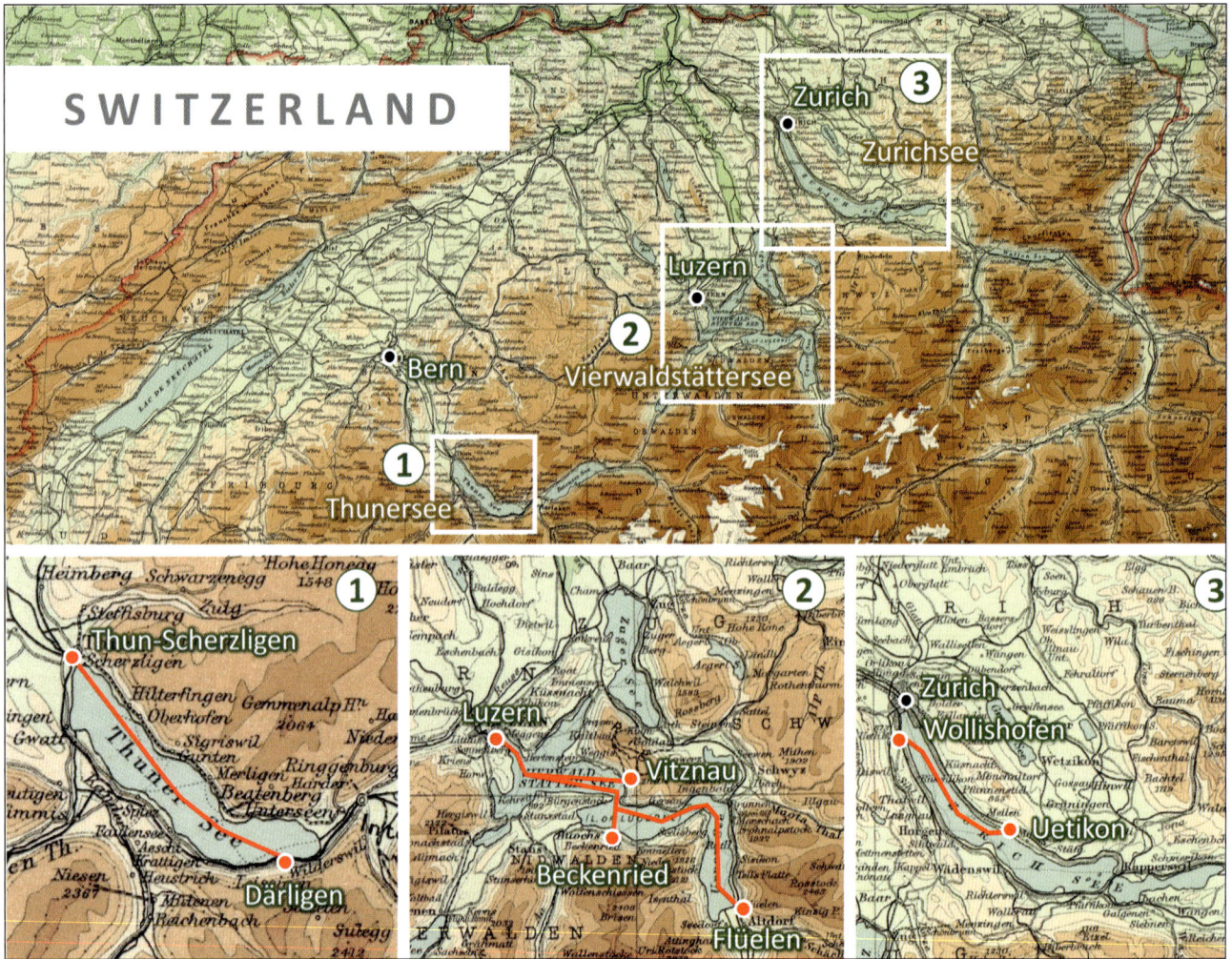

as a car ferry during the tourist season and only carried rail wagons in the winter.

The two old SBB ferries were getting towards to end of their lives, by the mid-1950s their hulls were 70 years old. SBB ordered their first new ferry from Bodan-Werft, the *Romanshorn*, which started service in 1959. She was similar in size to the *Schussen*, double ended and able to carry either 10-12 rail wagons or 35 cars on her main deck. She also had a full deck of passenger accommodation above the train deck. Her main innovation was to have a Voith-Schneider propeller forward and aft. Unlike most other rail ferries, the Swiss ferries did not have flat decks, they were built with sheer so the deck sloped upwards towards the bow and stern. This design was reportedly a safety measure to prevent a rail wagon running off the end of the ferry if it came loose. With the *Romanshorn* in service, SBB's old *MTr.2* and DB's *MTr.16* were retired in 1959.

The last rail ferry built for the Bodensee was the *Rorschach*, delivered from Bodan-Werft in 1966. She was similar in size to the *Romanshorn*, with two 600 hp MTU diesels and Voith Schneider propellers, but without the passenger deck. With her in service, the last old barge conversion, *MTr.3,* was retired in 1966, by which

time her hull was 82 years old. From 1948 to 1968, an average of 32,000 rail wagons were carried across the lake each year. However, the cost of running the ferries continued to increase and it was cheaper for rail traffic to take the slightly longer route around the lake. The *Schussen*, *Romanshorn* and *Rorschach* continued carrying rail wagons but more and more of their traffic was cars and trucks. The last rail service was in May 1976. After this, the three ferries continued as car ferries. The *Schussen* was retired in 1983 and there were plans to keep her as a museum. This did not happen, but her superstructure was preserved as a clubhouse by the Friedrichshafen Yacht Club. The *Rorschach* had a passenger deck added for use as a car ferry and was chartered to DB in 1983 and renamed the *Friedrichshafen*. The *Romanshorn* and *Friedrichshafen* are still in service as car ferries more than four decades later.

The Swiss lakes

While the ferries on the Bodensee were an integral part of the railway network, most other ferries on alpine lakes were used to connect an isolated factory or quarry to a railhead on the other side of the lake. Most had fairly short lives as they were replaced by new roads or railways.

Bödelibahn
Thunersee
Thun-Scherzligen – Därligen   1873-1893

The railway from the city of Bern to Thun was completed in 1859 and extended to Scherzligen at the north shore of the Thunersee two years later. This allowed passengers to connect with the lake steamers operated by the impressively named Vereinigte Dampfschiffahrts-Gesellschaft für den Thuner- und Brienzer-See, VDGTB, (United Steamship Co. for Lakes Thun and Brienzer) which linked the small towns along the lakeside down to Interlaken in the south-east. Even then, Interlaken was a popular tourist resort with its wealthy visitors enjoying the elegant spa and mountain scenery.

In 1872, the first section of the Bödelibahn railway was opened, running from Interlaken a few miles west along the south shore of the lake to Därligen. The new railway tried to persuade the VDGTB to introduce a rail ferry linking the Bödelibahn to the main line at Thun. The discussions failed, so the Bödelibahn decided to set up their own service. They ordered a small steam ferry, the *BB I*, which was prefabricated by Escher Wyss & Co. in Zürich and assembled on the lakeside. She was 37m long with a single track able to carry four or five wagons and a simple 60 hp steam engine able to make around 7 knots. The *BB I* was the first ferry to be powered by a propeller rather than paddles. This improved her fuel efficiency and made it easier to operate in winter ice. Paddles had an advantage when operating in shallow water, but this was not normally an issue on the lakes. She started operating between Thun-Scherzligen and Därligen in 1873, taking around an hour and forty minutes for the 18km trip. Wood products and ice from the Grindelwald glacier were transported north with food and general goods going south to Interlaken.

The service was a success and a second ferry, *BB II*, was delivered by Escher Wyss in 1886. She was larger and faster than her predecessor, with a 110 hp steam engine and space for five or six wagons. She only sailed for a few years before a new railway line was built down the west side of the lake, connecting Thun to the end of the Bödelibahn at Därligen. When this opened in 1893, the ferries were laid-up and offered for sale. The *BB I* and *BB II* were bought by the D.G. des Vierwaldstättersees in 1895.

Schweizerische Nordostbahn
Zürichsee
Wollishofen – Uetikon   1885-1894

The train ferry service that lasted the shortest time was on the Zürichsee. It was operated by the

The *Nordostbahn* operated another Escher Wyss ferry serving a chemical works on the Zürichsee from 1885. *(Author's collection)*

The *D.G.V. 1*, around 1920 with an enclosed wheelhouse towards the end of her career on the Vierwaldstättersee. *(Author's collection)*

Nordostbahn from their station at Wollishofen on the southern edge of Zürich to Uetikon on the eastern side of the lake where the Schnorf Brothers' chemical works made sulphuric acid. The ferry was built by Escher Wyss & Cie., 42m long with a single track able to carry five wagons. She had a screw propeller linked to a single steam engine and a steering bridge on a simple gantry. Though, like the previous ferries on the Bodensee, she does not appear to have had a name.

In 1894 the Rechtsufrige Zürichseebahn (Zürichsee right-bank railway) was opened along the east side of the lake. This provided a direct link from Zürich to Uetikon and the ferry became redundant. The hull was later used as a landing stage at Rapperswil.

D.G. des Vierwaldstättersees
Vierwaldstättersee
Luzern – Vitznau / Beckenried / Flüelen   1891-1920

The Vierwaldstättersee is probably better known as Lake Lucerne. It is not the largest lake in Switzerland, but it has a complex shape with over 140km of shoreline. As a result, the quickest route from Luzern to many towns and villages around the lake is by water and passenger steamers have operated on the lake since 1830. The largest fleet was, and still is, operated by the Dampfschiffahrts Gesellschaft des Vierwaldstättersees, or DGV. Their steamers carried passengers and small freight, but bulk goods such as lime or coal were transported in barges towed by the steamers. By the 1880s, the number of barges had become a problem for

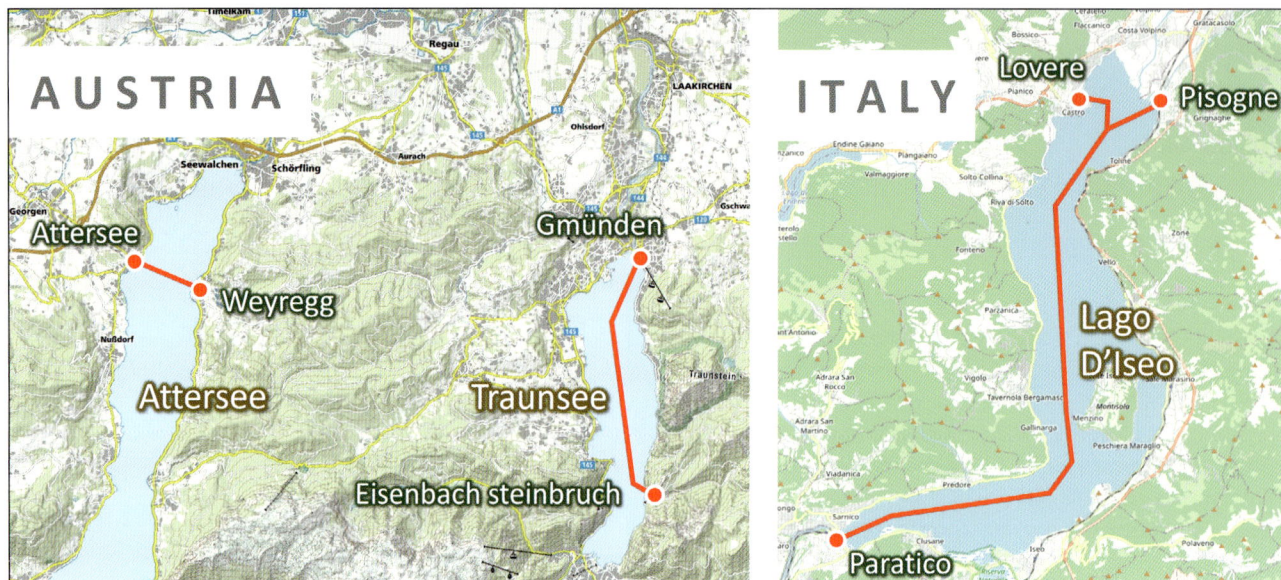

the steamers and discharging their cargoes on the quayside in the middle of Luzern was a growing inconvenience. In 1889 the company decided to build a ferry to transport bulk goods in rail wagons, having seen the success of similar operations on the Zürichsee and Thunersee.

They ordered a ferry, the *D.G.V. 1,* from Escher Wyss & Co. in Zurich, 42m long with a single track able to carry five wagons and an open navigating bridge on a truss structure amidships. The ferry largely followed what was by now the Escher Wyss standard design, though she had two engines and twin screws, compared with the previous single engined ferries. The rail track was also arranged for both narrow- and standard-gauge wagons.

D.G.V. 1 started service in February in 1891 and was principally used between Luzern and three main ports around the lake. Vitznau for coal and wood, Beckenried for lime and cement and Flüelen for cattle for the Altdorf market. The service was a success and the DGV decided in 1895 to buy the two Bödelibahn ferries, *BB I* and *BB II*, laid-up on the Thunersee. Recording that they got them on 'relatively cheap terms'. The *BB II* was dismantled and transported to Luzern where she was rebuilt and named *D.G.V. 2.*, starting service in May 1896. The *BB I* was left on the Thunersee for a few years and was eventually dismantled and brought to Luzern in 1899. The pieces were resold in 1902 and shipped to Lake Como in Italy.

The two ferries, *D.G.V. 1* and *2*, operated on the lake until 1920 with only a few incidents. In 1916, the *D.G.V. 1* collided with another ship in the dark and damaged her bow. In 1918, a wagon of lime on the *D.G.V. 2* caught fire but was extinguished without damaging the ferry. One interesting difference between the two ships, which were of similar size and speed, was that the twin-engined *D.G.V. 1* burned 15kg of coal per km, while the older single-engined *D.G.V. 2* burned only 8.8kg.

DGV stopped the service in 1920. *D.G.V. 1* was sold to Germany and was most probably scrapped within a few years. *D.G.V. 2* became the great survivor. She remained laid-up on the Vierwaldstättersee and was used occasionally for transporting cattle or heavy loads. In 1930 she was leased, and later sold, to a Luzern company Seeverlad & Kieshandels AG, (Seekag), to carry cement wagons on the lake. When this trade finished, she was laid-up until 1963 when her steam engine and rail tracks were removed and Seekag rebuilt her as a diesel-powered gravel barge, named *Luzern*. In 1970 she capsized and sank in Flüelen harbour. However, she was raised and refurbished and the *Luzern* (ex *D.G.V. 2*, ex *BB II*) is still working on the lake after more than 130 years.

Austrian and Italian lakes

Franz Häupl Sägewerk GmbH
Attersee – Weyregg   1935-1966

The Attersee is a fairly small lake in Upper Austria, around 40 km east of Salzburg. It is approximately 19 km north-south and 3 km wide. The western shore is gently sloping with farms and villages, while on the eastern side the mountains rise steeply from the lakeside, broken only by deep wooded valleys. Like the small ferries on the Swiss lakes, the ferries on the Attersee were purely for industrial purposes. Franz Häupl were a family business with a large sawmill at Weyregg on the east side of the lake and exported sawn timber by barge. In 1913, the Attergaubahn railway was built on the west side of the lake. This ran electric railcars, essentially trams, on a narrow-gauge track from the main line station at Vöcklamarkt to the lakeshore village of Attersee.

The first rail ferry across the lake was introduced in 1935. It was a small barge that could carry two wagons on a single track and powered by a diesel engine at the stern. The timber wagons were pushed on to the ferry close to the Weyregg sawmill and then towed off at Attersee by electric railcars. From there the wagons went to Vöcklamarkt where the timber was transferred to main line trains. The demand for timber increased during the war and Franz Häupl Sägewerk GmbH had a second larger barge built in Linz Shipyard in 1942. This was named *Resi*, it could carry three wagons and had a small raised wheelhouse at the stern. The *Resi* continued to ferry wagons of sawn timber until 1966 when a new road down the east side of the lake made road transport a cheaper option.

Gmünden Kalkwerke
Traunsee
Gmünden – Eisenbach steinbruch approx. 1909-1968

Around 20km east of the Attersee is the Traunsee, a similar but slightly smaller lake. The town of Gmüden lies at the north end of the lake and on its eastern shore there is a limestone quarry at Eisenbach. The Gmünden Kalkwerke operated limekilns at the quarry from 1870 making lime for cement manufacture. The lime was transported in wooden wagons running on narrow-gauge lines. These were loaded on barges taken up the lake to the railhead at Gmünden until the works closed in 1968.

Società di Navigazione del Lago d'Iseo
Lago d'Iseo
Paratico – Lovere   1907-1998
Paratico – Pisogne   1916-1994

The last of the alpine ferries lies further south on the Lago d'Iseo in Northern Italy, though like the Traunsee, it was a tug and barge operation, rather than a powered ferry. Lovere is a picturesque town which nestles under the mountains at the north-west end of the lake. Like many towns in northern Italy, it has a history of industry and metalworking. The steel plant in Lovere was founded in 1856, but in 1907 Giovanni Gregorini expanded it to become one of the largest manufacturers of train wheels and axles which it still is today. To export these to the industrial cities further south it was obvious to ship them down the lake to Paratico. From there, a branch line had been built in 1880 to connect with the main line between Bergamo and Brescia.

Gregorini built four iron barges in 1906, each of which could carry four wagons, and linkspans at the Lovere works and at Paratico. After a few years, they sold the barge operation to the Società di Navigazione del Lago d'Iseo, who then ordered four new barges made of reinforced concrete in 1909. In 1916, a new linkspan was built at Pisogne in the north-east corner of the lake, which allowed wagons to connect with the Valcominca Railway. During the 1920s and 30s, the service expanded using a mix of small wooden and iron

The ferry service on Lago d'Iseo started in 1907. This postcard showing wagons being loaded at Paratico-Sarnico at the southern end of the lake. *(Author's collection)*

The raft of barges, three either side of the now diesel-powered tug, approaching Paratico in 1986. *(Franco Faglia)*

barges which mostly carried only two wagons. Another four iron barges, carrying four wagons, and a second steam tug were ordered in 1924.

Unlike other barge operations, where one or two barges were towed behind the tug, on the Lago d'Iseo the barges were secured to either side of the tug. Often the tug had three barges on either side, carrying 24 wagons in total, and moved down the lake like a giant raft taking two and a half hours for the 25km trip. Traffic peaked in the 1930s and though it recovered after the war, it continued a slow decline thereafter. The old steam tugs were replaced by diesel towage and the Pisogne service stopped in 1994 when the linkspan needed repair. The final wagons were ferried between Paratico and Lovere in 1998, after that all freight went by road. Though the rails have gone, the linkspans in Paratico and Pisogne are still part of the waterfront and a reminder of a previous age.

TEN

Mediterranean

Sicilia

Società per le Strade Ferrate della Sicilia

	1899-1905
Ferrovie dello Stato Italiane	**1905-2000**
Rete Ferroviaria Italiana	**2000- current**
Reggio di Calabria – Messina	1899-1979
Villa San Giovanni – Messina	1905- current

Like Germany, the Italy we know today was only created in the latter half of the 19th century. The various kingdoms and Papal States came together and the northern borders with France and Austro-Hungary, were settled. As a result, it took some time for the railways to extend the length of the country. On the island of Sicily, the port town of Messina was connected to Catania and Syracuse in 1869, but it took until 1880 before the line extended westwards to the capital, Palermo. On the mainland, the line first reached Reggio di Calabria, at the toe of Italy, by a rather tortuous route down the east coast of Calabria in 1875. The line down the west coast, which gave a more direct route to Napoli and the north, did not open until 1895.

Even before these lines were completed, proposals were developed to link Sicily's railways to the mainland. Plans for a tunnel, then later a bridge across the Strait of Messina were put forward in the 1860s and 70s. However, these were soon abandoned as impractical and the naval architect Antonio Calabretta was asked to prepare a scheme for train ferries in 1881. He initially proposed two ferries, referred to as 'piro-pontone'. The first was a single-track double-ended paddle ferry, with wheelhouses and a passenger saloon above the train

deck and a hinged loading ramp at each end. He also proposed a much larger screw-driven ferry with three tracks capable of carrying 24 wagons. Despite local support, the Ministry of Public Works in Rome had no appetite to support this investment.

The Compagnie Internationale des Wagons-Lits (CIWL) introduced Pullman cars between Napoli and Palermo in 1886, though passengers had to disembark and cross between Reggio and Messina on the passenger steamer. By 1891, the two passenger steamers on the Strait were struggling to cope with the traffic and a proposal was made to tow rail wagons across on barges. This prompted Calabretta's third proposal for a steam ferry, but the plan to use barges was approved by the Ministry of Public Works, despite opposition from senior naval officers who considered it impractical due to the strong currents. Fortunately, another change of government brought a change of mind before the barge scheme was implemented. Officials from the railways and the Ministry of Public Works visited Denmark and having been impressed by the Lillebælt operation, all agreed that steam ferries were the best solution. The project was finally approved in November 1893.

The *Scilla* and *Cariddi*

The railway company, Società per le Strade Ferrate della Sicilia, turned again to Antonio Calabretta to design two ships following the Danish model, much smaller and simpler than his previous proposals. These were built by Odero de Sestri Ponente, Genova and named the *Scilla* and *Cariddi*. They were small double-ended paddle ferries, 50.2m long with a breadth of 8.2m and a single

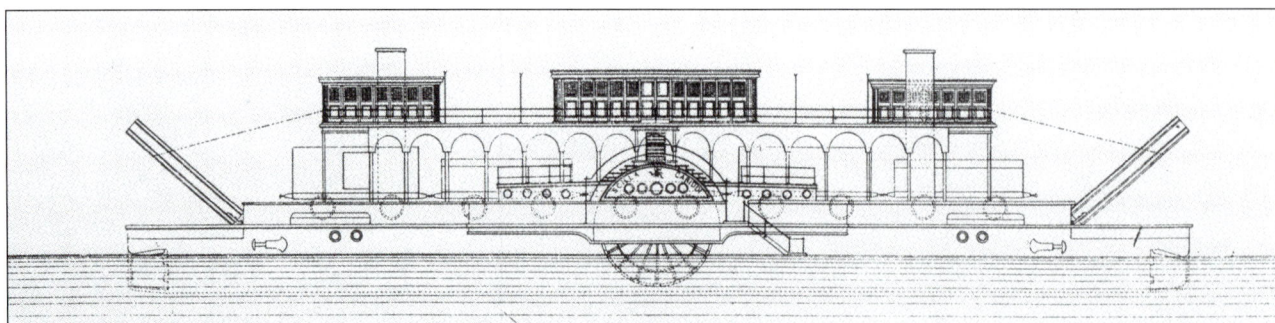

Antonio Calabretta's first design for a Messina Strait ferry in 1881. It was double-ended with hinged ramps for unloading the wagons and a passenger saloon on the upper deck. *(Author's collection)*

rail track on the centreline which could carry five railway wagons. There was a small bridge on a gantry between the paddle boxes and saloons for the different classes of passenger below the main deck. The ferries had a 2-cylinder double expansion steam engine developing 780 hp and could manage 10.5 knots. They also had electric lighting including two large arc lamps for loading at night. When they were delivered in 1896, the ferry ports Messina and Reggio di Calabria were not complete and so for the first few years they carried only passengers and mail.

After a few trial runs, the first rail wagons were carried in November 1899. There was no big ceremony to start the service, but the local people soon took the smart white-painted ferries to heart. While the ferries had been referred to as 'piro-pontoni' in official reports, the more affectionate English term 'ferribotti' was soon adopted. The first through passenger train from Roma to Syracuse started in August 1901 with two coaches crossing on the ferry. The following year, CIWL introduced their 'Napoli-Palermo Express', allowing wealthy northerners to travel to the Sicilian sun in comfort. The Sicilian Railway also started shipping fruit to the mainland in temperature-controlled box cars.

The last paddle steamers

Two additional ships were delivered in 1905, the *Sicilia* was built in Palermo and the *Calabria* in Ancona. They were essentially copies of the original two ferries and were the last paddle train ferries built for service in Europe. The railway line on the mainland was also linked to a new ferry port at Villa San Giovanni, north of Reggio, which reduced the crossing distance from around 12km to 8km. In the same year, the Società per le Strade Ferrate della Sicilia was amalgamated with Italy's other regional railways to form the nationalised Ferrovie dello Stato Italiane (FS), which took over the four ferries.

Traffic on the crossing had risen to 17,000 wagons per year, so the new state railways soon decided to order two larger ferries for the crossing. However, before these could be delivered the area was devastated by a major earthquake in December 1908. The towns of Messina and Reggio were almost completely destroyed and around 80,000 people were killed. The tsunami that followed destroyed the harbours and several kilometres of track that ran close to the coast. Fortunately, the

ferries were not badly damaged and in the days after the quake they provided accommodation for survivors from the shattered towns. The ferry service restarted a few days later, but only carrying passengers and relief supplies as it took several weeks before the terminals and track could be rebuilt.

The two new ships were delivered in 1910. The *Villa* was built by C.N. Fratelli Orlando in Livorno and the *Reggio* by Cantieri Napoletana Pattison in Napoli. They were both 77.6m long, 10.3m wide and able to carry eight wagons. More significantly, they had screw propulsion.

During the First World War the *Calabria* and *Sicilia* were requisitioned by the Admiralty and used as gunboats with a large rail-mounted gun secured to the track. The gun could not traverse, so aiming relied on steering the ship to point towards the target. Whether

Strait of Messina ferries

Ship	Start	End
Scilla	1896	sunk 1917
Cariddi	1896	1923
Sicilia	1905	1933
Calabria	1905	1927
Villa	1910	1979
Reggio	1910	1950
Scilla (II) later *Aspromonte*	1922	sunk 1942
Messina	1924	1981
Scilla (III)	1931	1974
Cariddi (II)	1931	1991
Secondo Aspromonte	1948	1990
Mongibello	1948	1994
Reggio (II)	1960	1990
San Francesco di Paola	1964	1998
Iginia	1969	2013
Sibari	1969	2008
Rosalia	1973	2010
Riace	1983	2012
Scilla (IV)	1985	
Villa (II)	1985	
Fata Morgania	1988	2012
Logudoro	2012	
Messina (II)	2013	

253

this was ever used successfully is not recorded. The other four ferries remained on the Messina Strait. The major casualty was the *Scilla*, which hit a mine laid by a German U-boat in August 1917 and sank with the loss of several lives. At the end of the war, the five remaining ferries continued the service until the second *Scilla* was delivered by Castellammare di Stabia in 1921. She was an improved version of *Reggio*, slightly longer at 82.6m, and with her arrival the old *Cariddi* was sold and scrapped in 1923.

The *Messina*

The early 1920s were a turbulent time in Italy with Mussolini's fascist government taking power. However, it was also a time of investment in national projects, which included the railways. The next ferry built was a leap forward from the existing fleet. The *Messina* was delivered in 1924 and was designed principally to carry freight wagons for the summer fruit trade. She was only

Promenaders admiring the 'ferribotti' at the Messina Stazione Marittima in the first decade of the 20th century. *(Author's collection)*

slightly larger than *Scilla* (II), but without the open space needed for passengers, she had three lines of track on deck able to carry 20 wagons. Unlike the previous ships, she was not double-ended, the three tracks ran to buffers at the stern and were switched to a single track forward to load over the bow from the existing linkspans. However, the biggest innovation was diesel propulsion. She was the first large motor ferry in Europe as only a few small Danish ferries had previously been fitted with diesel engines. Like many of the early diesel ships, she had two thin diesel exhausts rather than a conventional funnel. The row of spindly white columns along her sides that supported the superstructure soon earned her the nickname 'iaddennaro', the henhouse. The *Messina* made a huge change to the traffic across the Strait. In the peak months of the Sicily fruit harvest she could make eight round trips each day, carrying 320 wagons. To cope with this traffic, the ports were also extended, with a third berth and linkspan built in Messina to reflect the two in Villa San Giovanni and one

in Reggio. The old *Calabria* was laid-up and scrapped in 1927 and the *Scilla* (II) was renamed *Aspromonte*, in 1931.

The next two ships reused the old names, *Scilla* (III) and *Cariddi* (II). Delivered in 1932, they took the technical developments of the *Messina* to the next level. They were amongst the most advanced ships in the world at the time, with diesel electric propulsion and bridge control. Like the *Messina*, they had a closed stern with three tracks on deck converging to a single track at the bow, however the curves on the outside tracks were gentler than on the *Messina*, allowing them to load the longer passenger coaches. The deck could carry ten coaches, enough to transport a full express train. They also provided a completely new experience for passengers. Instead of the dingy saloons below deck, their large superstructure had a promenade deck with separate lounges for different classes of passenger and four restaurants. However, it is hard to see how

The four ferries in Messina harbour after the *Scilla* and *Cariddi* were joined by two further sisterships, the *Sicilia* and *Calabria* in 1905. *(Author's collection)*

passengers could relax to enjoy a meal as their speed of 15 knots reduced the crossing time to Villa San Giovanni from 35 to 25 minutes. As part of the spirit of modernisation, the ferry terminal at Messina Marittima was rebuilt in 1939 in the rationalist style. The architect Angiolo Mazzoni introduced light open spaces with sweeping curves, large windows and mosaic walls.

Although each of the new ships cost more than 20 million lire, their size made them much more economic than the old steamers. At the end of the 1930s the estimated cost of transporting a wagon across the Strait using the old *Villa* or *Reggio* was 100-110 lire, on the *Aspromonte* it was 84 lire and on the new *Scilla* (III) and *Cariddi* (II), 55 lire. However, the *Messina* was always the most efficient ship with a cost of 40 lire. The number of wagons transported had also increased from 107,000 in 1921 to 190,000 in 1937.

The Second World War

At the outbreak of the Second World War, the Strait

of Messina was declared a military zone and the six ferries were taken over as naval auxiliaries and fitted with 75mm guns. The *Aspromonte* was sunk by the Royal Navy while sailing as part of a convoy in December 1942. The ferries and ports were bombed by the Allies in the run-up to the invasion of Sicily and the *Reggio* and *Scilla* (III) were sunk in Messina harbour in May 1943. After the Allied landing in July, the remaining ferries were kept busy as German and Italian troops and vehicles moved back to the mainland. The *Villa* was scuttled by retreating German troops in Villa San Giovanni on the 16th August. On the same day, the *Cariddi* (II) had suffered an engine-room fire and was at anchor loaded with German military vehicles. To prevent her being bombed, her crew decided to scuttle her, first by opening the seacocks but as this took too long, they eventually blew holes in her hull with explosive.

Only the *Messina* escaped as she had sailed to Taranto for repairs. With no working ports and only one

Smaller and with more basic passenger accommodation, they were essentially utility versions of the pre-war *Scilla* (III) and *Cariddi* (II). The following year, the *Aspromonte* (II) was renamed *Secondo Aspromonte*. The traffic across the Strait began to recover, from a high of 248,000 wagons in 1941-42 to a low of 977 in 1943-44, it had returned to 283,000 in 1948-49, plus 12,500 cars. The old *Reggio* which had not been rebuilt after the war was scrapped in 1950.

The last of the pre-war ferries, the *Cariddi* (II) did not return to service until 1953 and was completely unrecognisable from the pre-war ship. Rebuilt at Riva Trigoso, she was lengthened by 11m, re-engined and fitted with a high forecastle and two large, rounded funnels. There were also four tracks on deck, rather than the previous three, increasing her capacity from 26 to 36 wagons. Another new feature was an upper car deck served by a separate side ramp. The people of Messina marked her return with great festivities as it

The *Sicilia* was built in 1905 to an old-fashioned design. She and her sistership *Calabria* were the last paddle train ferries built in Europe. *(Author's collection)*

The *Messina* was purely a freight ferry and could carry 20 wagons on three tracks. She loaded over the bow and the tracks ran to buffers at the stern. *(Author's collection)*

ship afloat, the Messina Strait ferries were out of action for over a year. Goods were transported on makeshift barges until the *Messina* managed to get back in service, late in 1945. The three ferries sunk in the harbours were raised first, the *Villa* in 1944 and the *Reggio* and *Scilla* (III) in Messina the following year. Salvaging the *Cariddi* (II) was a much longer operation as she had capsized and sunk in deeper water. The cargo and much of the superstructure had first to be removed by divers. They worked through from 1946 until the summer of 1949 before the hull was finally raised.

The service began to return to its pre-war condition in 1948 when the refurbished *Villa* and the *Scilla* (III), rebuilt with a new raised forecastle and bow-door, returned to service alongside *Messina*. They were also joined by two new ships, the *Mongibello* and the *Aspromonte* (II), which had been laid down during the war but with the shortage of materials took many years to complete. They were diesel ferries, capable of carrying 20 wagons or eight coaches on three tracks.

finally drew a line under the losses and privations of the war.

With *Cariddi's* return, the two oldest ferries were modernised. The last steam ferry, the *Villa* was reconstructed, lengthened by 5m, and returned 18 months later with two tracks on deck, a single funnel and new Fiat diesel engines. The *Messina* was modernised in 1956 and fitted with new Fiat diesel engines. Her superstructure was extended to provide additional passenger accommodation and the two slender diesel exhausts replaced by a large central funnel.

The six ferries maintained the service until the end of the 1950s. Rail traffic had continued to increase with 516,000 wagons carried in 1955-56, but after this it began to level off. The main change in the 1950s was the increase in tourism which led to a doubling of road vehicles, from 76,000 in 1955-56 to 148,000 by the end of the decade. In addition, more than five million passengers were carried.

The *Scilla* (III) was salvaged and returned to service in 1948 with her open bow replaced by a large forecastle and bow door. *(Author's collection)*

To complement the new ferries, the ferry terminal in Messina was rebuilt in the rationalist style in 1939. Designed by Angiolo Mazzoni, Messina Marittima features sweeping curves, marble floors and huge mosaic panels. *(Author's collection)*

The 1960s

The first new ferry of the 1960s was the *Reggio* (II) built by Cantieri del Tirreno in Genova. Slightly larger than the rebuilt *Cariddi* (II), she had four tracks on the train deck and a separate car deck above. The four tracks were switched to a single track for bow loading and for the first time a hinged bow visor was fitted. A new feature was a lifting bulwark allowing her to load over two tracks at the stern. This feature was to allow her to be used on the new service to Sardegna and was never used on the Messina Strait. She also had modern spaces for 1800 passengers and was the first ship fitted with a bow thruster. A second ferry, the *San Francesco di Paola* was delivered by the same yard in 1964. She was a close sister to *Reggio* (II) but had a cleaner more elegant profile and a few improvements such as a larger car deck and controllable pitch propellers. As with *Reggio* (II), she had a stern door for the Sardegna service.

The design progression of the Messina ferries over seventy years is remarkable. The very first *Scilla* and *Cariddi* were based on the Danish Lillebælt ships, small upright double-ended ferries with the train deck open at bow and stern. As the ferries got larger, they began to look more and more like seagoing ships. The pre-war *Scilla* (III) and *Cariddi* (II) had a closed stern and though built with an open bow, they were rebuilt after the war with an extended forecastle and bow doors. The *San Francesco di Paola* looked like a mini cruise liner, with her white hull, a fine raked bow and large rounded central funnel. An illusion helped by the Mediterranean sunshine.

The main change throughout the 1960s was the increasing number of cars and trucks on the crossing with more than half a million by the end of the decade. There was also competition for the first time as private operators started car ferry services. These were more convenient for motorists as they did not need to wait for the trains to load. To compete, FS converted the old *Villa* and *Messina* to car ferries, by removing the track from the deck and fitting a stern ramp. The longer-term solution was to order three large new ferries. The first two sisters, the *Iginia* and *Sibari* were delivered in 1969, the third the *Rosalia* in 1973. They were similar to the *San Francesco di Paola* but 12m longer and with more car carrying capacity. With a large funnel and huge forward mast, their profile was not as elegant as their predecessor and they were designed purely for the Messina crossing with no stern door. The three sisters were the backbone of the service for the next 15 years as some of the older ships were disposed of. The *Scilla* (III) was laid-up in 1974 and scrapped in 1979 and the longest survivor, the *Villa*, was scrapped in 1979 after an amazing 70 years of service. The *San Francesco di Paola* was moved to the Sardegna service between 1974 and 1982. The *Secondo Aspromonte* and *Mongibello* were modernised in 1979-80 and the old *Messina* was finally withdrawn and scrapped in 1985 after more than 60 years' service. The train ferry service to Reggio de Calabria was also stopped in 1979, after this all rail traffic crossed through Villa San Giovanni.

By the mid-80s the ferries were making around 60 crossings in each direction every day and carrying 650,000 rail wagons, 10 million passengers and 570,000 car and trucks each year. Four new ships were added to the fleet. The *Scilla* (IV) and *Villa* (II) were delivered in 1985 and were largely an update of the *Iginia* sisters delivered 15 years previously. Their profile was long and low, with a square funnel and if anything looked more balanced than their predecessors. Their dimensions and rail capacity were similar with four tracks on the main deck able to carry 43 wagons or 16 carriages and space for 150 cars on the deck above. Like the *San Francesco di Paola*, they were also fitted with a stern door that allowed them to fit the linkspans on the Sardegna route. The other two ships were completely different. The *Riace* delivered 1983 and *Fata*

Morgania in 1988 were double ended ferries around 100m long with an open deck and an upright central superstructure. They could carry 12 wagons on three tracks or a mixture of cars and trucks. They were the first Italian train ferries to have a Voith-Schneider propeller at either end. Their design was developed from the two car ferries, *Agata* and *Pace,* built in the 1970s and in profile they were much more like the first Messina Strait ferries 90 years earlier, than the more recent mini cruise liners.

At the end of the 1980s, the Messina Strait train ferry fleet had reached its peak with 12 ships in service. The four new ferries, plus the *Iginia, Sibari* and *Rosalia*, the *San Francesco di Paola*, back from Sardegna, the *Reggio* (II), the post-war sisters *Mongibello* and *Secondo Aspromente* and the last pre-war survivor, the *Cariddi* (II). FS had built its first car ferries in the 1970s and since the 1990s, the number of train ferries has slowly declined as newer ships have been designed only for cars and trucks.

The *Secondo Aspromonte* and *Reggio* (II) were withdrawn in 1990, with the *Reggio* (II) sold to be a temporary hotel ship for the Barcelona Olympics. After this she was laid-up and sank twice, first alongside her berth in Barcelona in 1992, then raised and re-sunk at L'Estartit on the Costa Brava as an artificial reef for scuba divers. The old *Cariddi* (II) after several engine failures was laid-up in 1991 then sold the following year to the Provincial Government for conversion to a museum. However, this did not progress and she remained laid-up and uncared-for in Messina harbour. After a fire in 2000, she was moved to a different berth and eventually sank at her moorings in 2005. On the 4th July 1993, the *Mongibello* collided with a cargo ship in the Messina Strait. She suffered significant damage and it was not worth repairing a 45-year-old ship. She was laid-up and scrapped in 1995. The *San Francesco di Paola* was withdrawn in 1998.

Reorganisation and RFI

As with other European railways, EU regulations required the Ferrovie dello Stato to split its activities between two separate companies in 2000. Trenitalia was created to operate the railways, while Rete Ferroviaria Italiana (RFI) owned the track, signalling and other infrastructure. As the ferry connection to Sicily was an integral part of the network, ownership was transferred to RFI who created a subsidiary called Bluvia to operate the ships. Unlike other countries, this reorganisation was only a theoretical privatisation, as both Trenitalia and RFI remain subsidiaries of the state-owned Ferrovie dello Stato.

Bluvia took over a fleet of eight train ferries on the Messina Strait and the three old *Iginia* sisters were withdrawn over the next decade. The *Sibari* was laid-up 2008 and the *Rosalia* in 2010. Although the oldest of the three, *Iginia* continued through until the ferries were

A postcard of the *Reggio* (II) at Messina in the 1960s. Cars are being loaded over the side-ramp to the upper deck, while passenger coaches load through the bow. *(Author's collection)*

The *Mongibello* had three tracks and a closed stern, loading over the bow like her sister Aspromonte and the pre-war ferries. *(Author's collection)*

reorganised again. In 2012, a further reorganisation separated the car and train ferry services. Bluvia was replaced by a new company, Bluferries, which operated the vehicle and passenger services in competition with private operators and took over the *Riace* and *Fata Morgania*. The subsidised train ferry operation remained with RFI and they became the operator of the *Iginia*, *Scilla* (IV) and *Villa* (II). The *Logudoro*, which had been laid-up in Civitavecchia following the closure of the Sardegna operation, was transferred to Messina in 2012. *Iginia* was laid-up 2013 and scrapped in 2015. With the expansion of cheap air travel, fewer passengers were using long distance trains and some of the classic sleeper trains, such as the 'Treno del Sole' from Torino and the 'Frecia della Laguna' from Venezia came to an end. In 2020 there were still at least five through trains in each direction daily, two intercity and two sleeper trains from Roma and a sleeper from Milano.

In the background, successive Italian Governments had promised to build a Messina Strait bridge, as first proposed in the 1870s. A detailed plan was made for a

Top left: The *San Francesco di Paola* was delivered in 1964 and was probably the most elegant of all the Italian ferries. She also had a larger car deck and controllable pitch propellers *(Author's collection)*

Middle left: The open deck on *Riace* has three rail tracks, though since the separation of the train and vehicle ferry operations in 2012, she has only carried road vehicles. *(Author's collection)*

Above: The *Riace*, delivered in 1983, went back to the upright double-ended design of the early ferries. *(Author's collection)*

Top right: A locomotive being pushed on to the *Scilla* (IV) in Messina to unload the coaches of the 'Peloritano' express from Roma. The naming of express trains stopped in 2009. *(Roberto Copia)*

Middle right: The *Logudoro* was built for the Sardegna service in 1989 and a close sister to *Scilla* (IV) and *Villa* (II). *(Phil English)*

Right: The Milano sleeper coaches crossing to Sicily on the *Messina* (II), the last ferry to carry passenger coaches in Europe. *(Marco Bereth)*

With the *Scilla* (IV) and *Villa* (II) in service, the older ferries *Secondo Aspromonte* and *Reggio* (II) were retired in 1990 and the even older *Cariddi* (II), the following year. *(Author's collection)*

Messina (II) has an open train deck as RFI no longer carries cars. A second similar ferry, the *Iginia (*II), is under construction to maintain train ferry service. *(Captain Peter)*

single-span suspension bridge in the 1990s that would have been the longest span in the world, 60% longer than the Akashi Bridge in Japan. The project was cancelled in 2006, then revived by Berlusconi's government in 2009. This time some of early construction work was started before the project was again suspended in 2013.

Without a commitment to a bridge, RFI decided to order a new train ferry to replace their aging fleet. The *Messina* (II) was delivered in 2013. With four tracks and capacity for 27 wagons or 15 coaches, plus 138 cars and 900 passengers, she is similar in size to her running mates, *Scilla* (IV), *Villa* (II) and *Loguoro*. However, she has a unique and stylish appearance, with a reverse rake on the bow and square funnels either side of the open

The *Fata Morgana* was operated as a car ferry by Bluferries after 2012, when the car and train ferry fleets were separated. *(Miles Cowsill)*

When the Messina Strait bridge project was again delayed, RFI ordered the *Messina* (II) which was delivered in 2013, replacing the old *Iginia*. *(Malcolm Cranfield)*

train deck. A new ferry is under construction, the *Iginia* (II), which will be similar to the *Messina*, and is due to be delivered in 2021. The railways of Sicily remain an integral part of the Italian rail network and as more than 8% of Italians live on the island, it is inevitable that a Messina Strait bridge will be built at some point in the future. With the end of passenger trains on the Baltic ferries, RFI's ships on the Strait of Messina remain as Europe's last great train ferry route.

Sardegna

Ferrovie dello Stato Italiane	1961-2000
Rete Ferroviaria Italiana	2000-2009
Civitavecchia – Golfo Aranci	**1961-2009**

The island of Sardinia was not immune from the 19th century railway boom and the Ferrovie Reale Sarde, (Royal Sardinian Railway), opened their first line in 1871. By 1883, there was more than 400km of track connecting the main town of Cagliari on the south coast to the north and east of the island. However, unlike the other regional railways, the Sardinian railway was not amalgamated into the Ferrovie dello Stato Italiane (FS) until 1920, by which time their rolling stock had become completely dilapidated.

The FS decided on a wholesale replacement of the island's rolling stock and the simplest way to transport it was to use one of their own ferries. In 1928, the *Messina* spent ten weeks shuttling back and forth between Civitavecchia and Olbia transporting 88 locomotives, 46 coaches and 1,292 wagons. The practicality of a train ferry service between the mainland and Sardegna had been demonstrated, though it took more than 30 years before it was realised.

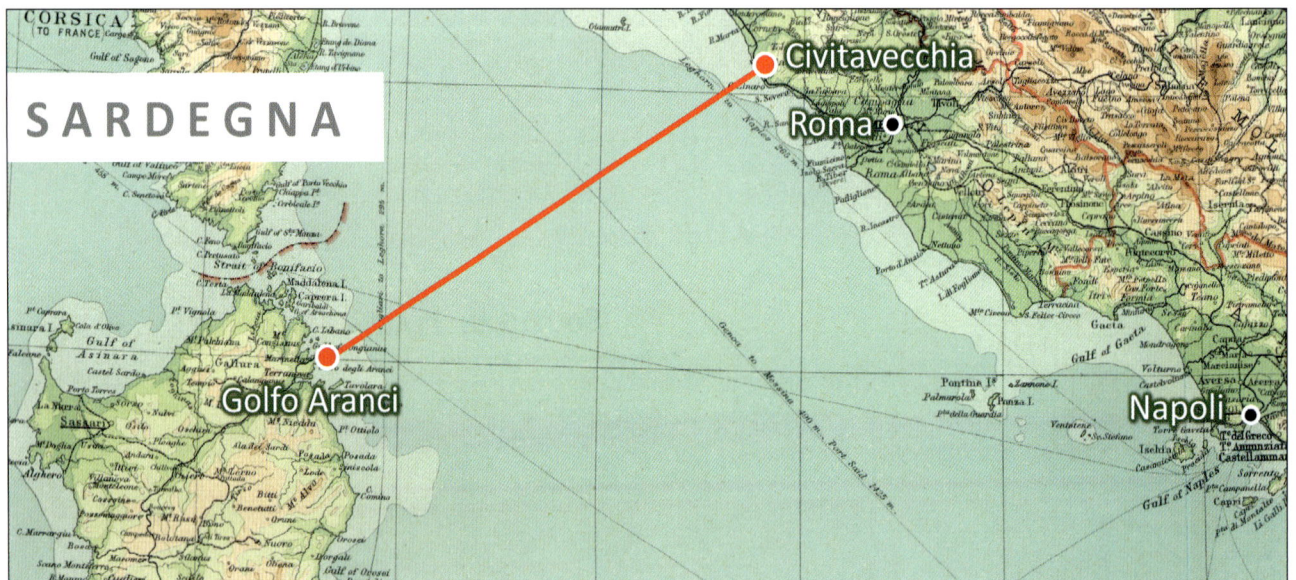

The *Gennargentu* was delivered in 1965 by Cantieri Navale del Tirreno in Ancona. *(Author's collection)*

The *Gallura* being launched at Cantieri Navale del Tirreno e Riuniti at Ancona in November 1968. *(Author's collection)*

The regular train ferry service between Civitavecchia, north of Roma, to Golfo Aranci on the north-east coast of Sardegna started in 1961. At the time, the crossing of 120 nautical miles, 222km, was the longest train ferry route in the world. The service was designed for foot passengers, vehicles and rail wagons, passenger coaches were never carried. Initially, two ships were built by Cantieri Navale Riuniti in Palermo, the *Tyrsus* delivered in 1961 and her sistership, the *Hermaea* the following year. They were similar in dimensions to the *Reggio* (II) built in 1960 for the Messina crossing, but with no bow door they had a finer hull and a more elegant appearance. With only three tracks on deck, they could carry 30 wagons plus 180 cars and 711 passengers, with berths for 194.

The service grew very quickly and by 1964 carried 33,150 rail wagons, 100,000 passengers and 44,000 cars. As a consequence, two more ships were built to allow up to four sailings a day. This time they were built by Cantieri Navale del Tirreno e Riuniti in Ancona, the *Gennargentu* was delivered in 1965 and the *Gallura* in 1969. They were similar in size and capacity to the previous ships, though their appearance was modernised by a more steeply raked bow and large forward mast. *Gallura* was distinctive with a skip on the aft of her funnel. All four ships were powered by a pair of Fiat S.G.M. 600.62 6-cylinder diesels. They were also fitted with stabilisers for the eight-hour crossing.

The *Garibaldi*

By 1969, rail traffic had increased by 50% to 46,785 wagons and passenger and car traffic had doubled to 232,000 passengers and 88,000 cars. More capacity was needed and the *San Francesco di Paola* was transferred from Messina in 1974. She stayed until 1982 when FS took delivery of their largest train ferry, the *Garibaldi*, from Cantieri Navale Riuniti in Palermo. The *Garibaldi* was completely different from all other FS ferries and designed purely to carry freight wagons and trucks on three decks. Her design was evolved from the *Railship I* which had been introduced on the Baltic in 1975 and her state-of-the-art cargo handling system was provided by the same Finnish company, MacGregor-Navire. *Garibaldi* could carry up to 80 wagons which were loaded through the stern to four tracks on the main deck. Hydraulic lifts were fitted on the two centre tracks, each able to lift two 40-ton wagons at a time. The lifts served two tracks on the open upper deck and four tracks on the lower deck. The *Railship* had a pivoting switching rail and manually driven diesel shunters on each deck, but the *Garibaldi* had a more sophisticated system. On the lower deck, wagons were moved sideways from the lifts to the outside tracks on hydraulic traverser platforms. Wagons were moved forward and aft by remotely operated shunters fitted to a rack and pinion drive on each of the ten tracks. To load and unload 80 wagons in less than five hours took careful sequencing and she was fitted with a computer system with 'pre-programmed cassettes' to operate the loading equipment, all monitored from a central control-

The *Garibaldi* was built in 1982 and could carry 80 wagons on three decks. *(Dave Wilkinson)*

The Scomenzera linkspans in the 1970s, by which time most of the traffic was on trucks rather then rail wagons. *(Author)*

After the passenger service closed in 2000, *Logudoro* continued as a freight ferry, with all but the forward lifeboat removed. She was refurbished in 2012 and transferred to Messina. *(Author's collection)*

room. *Garibaldi* was also fitted with a 25-ton crane on the port side for loading up to twenty-five 20-foot containers which were stacked on the upper deck. This was seldom used and the crane was removed after a few years' service. Despite the technology, no-one could describe the *Garibaldi* as a good-looking ship, with a high bow and square box superstructure. Her funnel was initially just a truss frame to support the exhaust stacks but was later plated-out to look more conventional. She made a daily round trip between Civitavecchia and Golfo Aranci, taking around seven hours on the crossing with five hours either end to load and unload. Her large capacity freed-up the other ships to carry passengers and road vehicles.

The last ship built for the service was the *Logudoro* in 1989. She was a close sister of the Messina twins *Scilla* (IV) and *Villa* (II), but with cabins and improved passenger spaces for the longer crossing. In addition to 689 passengers, she had four tracks on the main deck for 43 wagons, plus an upper deck for 150 cars. With *Logudoro* in service, the *Tyrsus* was withdrawn in 1991 and sold for further service as a car ferry. The remaining five ships continued through the 1990s, though the service became increasingly uneconomic as rail freight traffic began to decline and competing private operators offered cheaper fares for passengers and vehicles. Cheap flights also reduced the number of passengers. As plans were developed in the late 1990s to reorganise the Ferrovie dello Stato in line with EU regulations, a decision was taken to stop the Sardegna passenger and car ferry services. *Hermaea* was withdrawn in 1998 and *Gennargentu* in 1999 and both were sold for scrapping.

Gallura and *Logudoro* continued carrying passengers until 2000 when the service transferred to the Rete Ferroviaria Italiana (RFI). After this, *Gallura* was laid-up and sold for scrap in 2002. *Logudoro's* passenger accommodation was mothballed and she operated as a freight ferry for a few years though after 2006 she was mostly laid-up. *Garibaldi* continued RFI's rail freight service through to 2009 when government subsidies were withdrawn and the service closed. *Garibaldi* was sold for scrap in 2010, but the *Logudoro* was retained in lay-up at Civitavecchia and used for occasional rail freight, such as moving rolling stock to the mainland for maintenance. In 2012 she was refurbished and transferred to the Messina Strait, bringing the Sardegna route to a final close.

Laguna di Venezia

Società per le Strade Ferrate Meridionali	**1897–1905**
Ferrovie dello Stato Italiane	**1905–1982**
Società Veneziana di Navigazione SpA	**1982–1992**
Scomenzera – Giudecca / Murano	1897–1992
Santa Lucia – Murano	1899–1919

Soon after the Messina Strait ferries were delivered, the idea of moving rail wagons by sea was also being developed in the Laguna di Venezia. The railways had first arrived in Venezia around 1860 and the grand Santa Lucia station was built on the western edge of the old city. To the south of the station, a branch line served a large goods yard built in the Santa Croce district, bounded on its western side by the docks and industrial areas on the Canale Scomenzera. The nature of Venezia, with the main island divided by a network of canals and industrial sites on outlying islands, meant that water transport was inevitable. Initially, goods were unloaded at the sidings and transferred to small barges for distribution around the city. In 1897 the railway decided to simplify this by running the wagons directly on to barges and the first service took wagons to the southern island of Giudecca. This was arguably not a train ferry as the wagons were not unloaded from the barges at their destination. The barges were towed around the island's various shipyards and factories where goods were lifted from and to the wagons by crane. The barges were then returned to the Canale Scomenzera, where the wagons were unloaded over a small linkspan. In the first full year of operation, 3,796 wagons were carried. The success led to a second linkspan being built on the north side of

Barges **PP5** and **PP21** with a diesel tug at Scomenzera in the 1970s. The last rail wagon was transported in 1992. *(Author)*

Santa Lucia station in 1899 for barges taking wagons to the famous glassworks on the northern island of Murano.

With the amalgamation of the railways, the Ferrovie dello Stato (FS) took over the operation in 1905. It had carried 8,343 wagons in the previous year. FS inherited two steam tugs and ten barges, six wood and four iron. The vast majority of wagons were loaded at Scomenzera and in 1919 the second linkspan at Santa Lucia was closed. FS built another tug and seven iron barges, *PP 11* to *PP 17*, capable of carrying six wagons each, then added another five barges during the 1920s. They also built a second linkspan at Scomenzera.

The system was allowed to run down during the Second World War and rail traffic never really recovered. In 1947, the barges carried 2,400 wagons and 3,300 trucks. Over the next three decades most of the traffic was road vehicles as the number of rail wagons continued to decline. FS eventually sold the operation to a local company, Società Veneziana di Navigazione SpA, in 1982. By 1991, they only carried around 12 wagons a month and in 1992, the last rail wagon carried sand to the Murano glassworks. Since then, the barges have continued to carry trucks and heavy equipment around the Laguna di Venezia and are still loaded over the old linkspans in the Canale Scomenzera.

Camargue

Cie. des Salins du Midi
Salin de Giraud – Port St. Louis du Rhône   1958–2006

While the train ferries operated by SNCF on the English Channel are well known, there was another little train ferry at the opposite end of France. On the flat muddy delta at the mouth of the river Rhône, the Mediterranean sun has been used to produce sea salt for centuries. This grew from being a cottage industry when a group of salt producers amalgamated in 1868 to form

The *Esquineau* was one of two small ferries built for the Cie. des Salins du Midi in 1958 to transport salt wagons across the Rhône. *(Author's collection)*

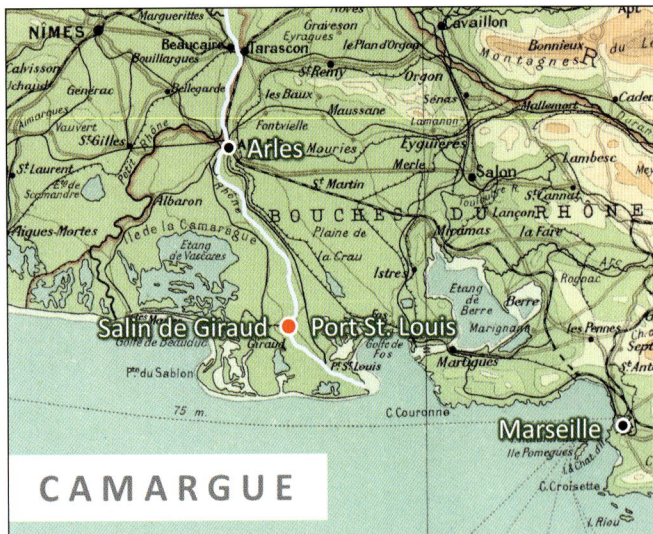

CAMARGUE

The *Victoria* at Ibiza shortly after delivery in 1953, with her black hull and Empresa Nacional Elcano funnel. *(Jordi Piera Costa)*

the Compagnie des Salins du Midi. In 1890 they produced 80,000 tonnes of salt and much of this was exported by rail using the Chemin de Fer de Camargue's metre-gauge line. This ran northwards from the saltpans at Salin de Giraud for 40km up the western side of the Rhône to Arles, where the salt was transferred to mainline trains.

By the 1950s the Camargue railway's infrastructure was crumbling and the Cie. des Salins du Midi decided to change their export route by connecting to the standard gauge line at Port St. Louis de Rhône on the eastern side of the river. This avoided the cost of upgrading the narrow-gauge line and of trans-shipping the salt at Arles. A short branch line was laid from the salt works at Salin de Giraud to the riverside and two ferries were ordered to ship the salt wagons across the river.

The *Beauduc* and the *Esquineau* were delivered in 1958 by the Chantiers Navals de Barriol in Arles. They had a simple rectangular hull, 39m long, with a central track able to carry two salt wagons. The wheelhouse

was fitted on one side and the engine exhausts on the other. The ferries had a Voith-Schneider propeller at the bow and stern each driven by a Deutz diesel. The ferry docks were located around 500m south of the existing Bac du Barcarin road ferry where the river was around 400m wide. The 50m linkspans on either side were longer than the ferries.

By 2000 the saltpans of Salin de Giraud were producing more than 300,000 tons per year. Most of this was exported on barges and coasters from the company's quayside on the Rhône, but there were also regular rail shipments that crossed the ferry on their way to a chemical plant at Château-Arnoux-Saint-Auban in Provence. When this contract ended in 2006, the ferry was discontinued after 48 years of operation. Since then the tracks, gantries and linkspans have been removed and only the concrete mooring dolphins remain on the riverbanks.

Spain

Empresa Nacional Elcano S.A.   1952-1955
Trasmediterránea S.A.   1955-1966

The last two train ferries on the Mediterranean served for more than thirty years, but never regularly carried trains. Built for Empresa Nacional Elcano, a state-owned shipping company, the *Victoria* was delivered by Union Naval de Levante S.A. in Valencia in 1952 and was joined by her sistership the *Virgen de Africa* the following year. They were the first drive-on / drive-off ferries built in Spain and from delivery were chartered to the Cia. Trasmediterránea S.A., which operated ferries from the Spanish mainland to the Canary and Balearic Islands and Spain's North African territories.

They were smart little diesel-powered ships which loading over the stern. The main deck had two rail tracks with space for either 12 rail wagons or 100 cars. The tracks were set into the deck, with cover plates to give a flat surface for cars when no wagons were being carried. The three decks above provided accommodation of 808 passengers with separate first, second- and third-class lounges.

Victoria was put in service between Algeciras and Ceuta on the North African coast. Once *Virgen de Africa* was delivered, she took over the Ceuta service and *Victoria* moved to run from Barcelona and Valencia to Palma de Mallorca. In June 1953, she carried a special cargo of electrical power equipment on three rail wagons. The ships were bought by Cia. Trasmediterránea in 1955 and repainted with white hulls and the distinctive gold coloured funnels with a red band. Apart from occasional heavy cargoes the two ships spent their lives as car and passenger ferries. The rail tracks were removed, or more probably plated over, around 1966. *Victoria* was withdrawn and scrapped in 1982 and *Virgen de Africa* a few years later in 1986.

ELEVEN

Russia, Turkey, the Black Sea and Caspian

The Volga

Ryazan-Ural Railway Co

Saratov (Uvek) – Pokrovskaya Sloboda 1896-1935

In 1839, the Russian government sent a bright young army Colonel from the Corps of Transport Engineers to the United States. He was to study their railways and recommend technology for building railways in Russia. On his return, Col. Pavel Melnikov worked as the supervising engineer on the first main railway, 650 km from St. Petersburg to Moscow. When this opened in 1851 it was the longest double-track railway in the world. By the end of the 1860s, Col. Melnikov was the Minister of Transport and presided over a great expansion of Russia's railways.

It was not surprising that the Russians decided to learn from the United States as the vast flat plains of Russia were much more like the American west than the crowded countryside of Western Europe. Just as the American railroads had to cross the Mississippi and other major rivers as they headed west, the main obstacles to the Russian railways as they headed east were a series of large rivers, the Volga running south to the Caspian, the Ob and Yenisei running north to the Arctic Ocean.

By 1871 the Ryazan-Ural Railway had reached the city of Saratov on the Volga. While this gave them access to the river traffic, their ambition was to extend the railway east of the river. To cross the Volga, a 1,700m long bridge was required with an estimated cost of 10 million rubles. This was a huge sum and remained a block to developing the railway for 20 years. In 1892 the railway started building a line from Pokrovskaya Sloboda, on the east bank of the Volga opposite Saratov, towards the city of Uralsk, (now Oral in Kazakhstan). Initially, rail wagons were taken across the river on barges, but this was slow and unreliable. As the railway line extended eastwards, the number of wagons bottle-necked at the river crossing became a problem. The estimated cost of a train ferry was around 2.5 million rubles, much cheaper than a bridge, but not without its own challenges. The river level could change by more than ten metres throughout the year, when it was low there were shallows and sandbanks, and in winter the river

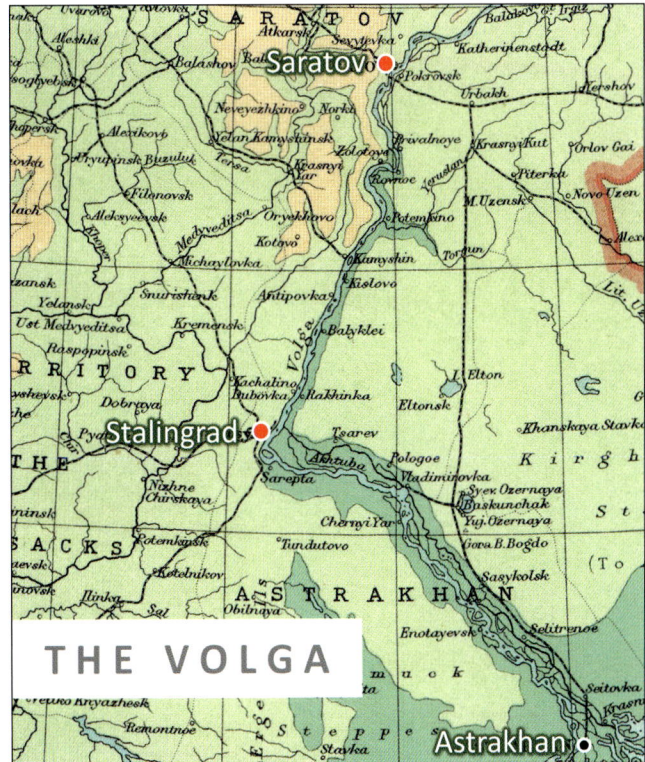

THE VOLGA

froze and could be blocked by rafts of ice.

The Tyne to the Volga

An order was placed in 1894 with Sir W.G. Armstrong, Mitchell & Co. in Newcastle to build a train ferry for goods wagons and an icebreaking passenger steamer. These were both remarkable vessels as in addition to a shallow-draft and being able to operate in ice, they had to get from Newcastle to Saratov. Once they had sailed across the North Sea and Baltic, the ships had to transit the Mariinsk Canal system to reach the Volga. This links the river Neva at St. Petersburg through rivers and canals to the city of Rybinsk on the Upper Volga, however the limiting breadth for the canal system was 8.5m. The solution was to split the ships longitudinally, bow to stern, into two separate sections which could be floated through the canals. Each section had its own engine-room, propeller and funnel.

The icebreaker *Саратовский ледокол*, (*Saratovskiy Ledokol*), the name translates simply as *Saratov*

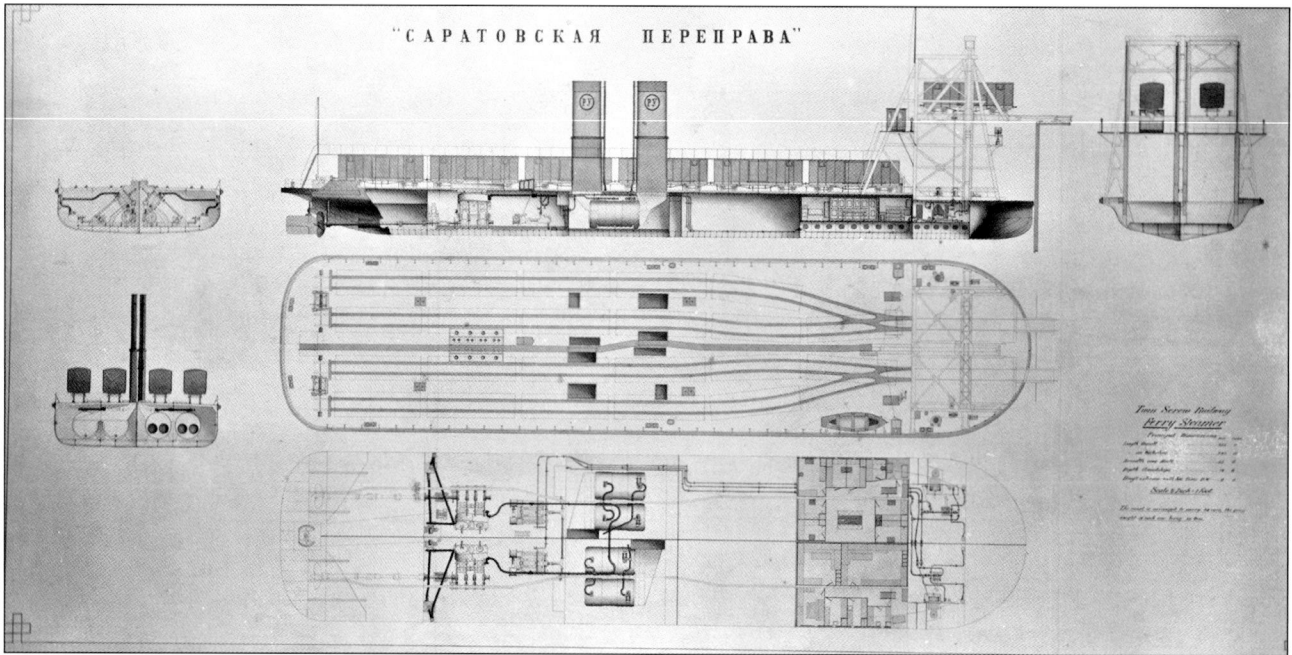

The **Saratovskaya Pereprava** was built for the Ryazan-Ural Railway Company by Armstrong Mitchell & Co. in Newcastle in 1895. *(Author's collection)*

Icebreaker, was 42.7m long with a breadth of 10.9m and capacity for 400 passengers. She had longitudinal bulkheads bow to stern and separate engine-rooms and accommodation in each side of the ship. The plating around her bow was 25mm thick and closely framed for icebreaking.

The train ferry *Саратовская переправа,* (Saratovskaya Pereprava), which translates as *Saratov Crossing*, was built to the limits of the canal system, 74.1m long, with a breadth of 17m and a loaded draft of 2.74m. She had four tracks on deck that could carry 28 wagons and two funnels offset to either side of the centreline bulkheads. The forward funnel served the starboard engine room and the aft funnel the port. There was a large gantry frame at the bow, which was split on the centreline, and supported two independent

hydraulic lifting platforms. These could raise a wagon to a height of 25 feet (7.62m) above the deck. Both ships were completed on the Tyne in 1895 and sailed to St. Petersburg, where the two sections were disconnected, then towed through the canal system to the river Volga, where they were then reassembled.

The ferry crossing started in 1896. Two landing stages with timber piers were built on each side of the river. These were at different elevations, so that the ferry could use the dock closest to the water level depending on the time of year. In summertime, it took around four hours for the *Saratovskaya Pereprava* to make a return trip including loading and unloading, though in winter this could take much longer. The *Saratovskiy Ledokol* operated independently as a tug and passenger ferry in summer, but in winter was used

The **Saratovskaya Pereprava** completing trials on the Tyne in 1895 in preparation for departure to St. Petersburg. *(Author's collection)*

On the deck of the **Saratovskaya Pereprava**, the funnels are slightly offset from the centreline as the forward funnel serves the starboard engine room and the aft funnel the port. *(Author's collection)*

to break a channel through the ice for the train ferry. In addition to the ferries, the Ryazan-Ural Railway operated a substantial fleet of barges and other vessels on the Volga. At the ferry port at Uvek, just south of Saratov city, they had a large harbour, with floating grain elevators, an oil depot and a floating drydock for maintaining their ships. As oil fuel could be shipped upriver from Baku, both the ferry and icebreaker had oil fired boilers.

The first Russian-built ferry

Traffic increased such that in 1908, the Ryazan-Ural Railway ordered a second ferry. This was essentially a replica of the *Saratovskaya Pereprava*, though fitted with its own passenger accommodation. The new ferry *Переправа вторая*, (*Pereprava Vtoraya*), or *Second Crossing*, was built at the Sormovsky Shipyard further up the Volga at Nizhny Novgorod and so did not need to be split in two for a canal transit. The most obvious change from her predecessor was a large passenger saloon on a platform at the stern. In addition, the wagon lift at the bow of the *Pereprava Vtoraya* was built for heavier loads and could be used to transport locomotives. These had previously been handled on the *Saratovskaya Pereprava* and the lift had been overloaded and damaged.

The *Saratovskaya Pereprava* had transported 44,000 wagons across the river in 1907 and with the *Pereprava Vtoraya* coming into service in 1909, this rose to over 73,000 in 1910 and 128,000 by 1915. By this time, the railway employed a total of 585 people on the Saratov ferries and marine operations. The level of traffic became an increasing problem during the winter when the ferry crossings were delayed by the need to clear ice. In 1916 the river was frozen so hard that they gave up trying to clear a channel and laid a temporary rail track across the ice. The wagons were initially pushed by hand across the river and later pulled by horses in groups of two or three. The traffic peaked in 1916, with 147,000 wagons crossing the river, including more than 5,000 on the temporary ice track.

Over the next few years Russia was plunged into Civil War. Rail traffic was greatly reduced and the *Saratovskiy Ledokol* was requisitioned by the Red Army and fitted with guns to fire on anti-Soviet uprisings in cities further upriver. A major accident occurred on Christmas Day 1918. The *Pereprava Vtoraya* made a sharp turn as she approached Uvek pier. As she heeled over, water flooded in through a number of portholes which had carelessly been left open. Within a few minutes, she had sunk at the pier and lost several wagons of grain into the river. With the pier blocked, the ferry service was stopped and a salvage operation was quickly organised. Diving in the Volga in winter could not have been much fun and it took until March before the *Pereprava Vtoraya* was raised. She was refurbished and back in service in May and the salvage team received a

The second ferry, the *Pereprava Vtoraya* was fitted with a large passenger saloon aft and was built by the Sormovsky Shipyard in Nizhny Novgorod in 1908. *(Author's collection)*

The *Pereprava Vtoraya* towards the end of her career with the aft passenger saloon removed. *(Author's collection)*

personal telegram of thanks from V.I. Lenin and the People's Commissar of Railways, L.B. Krasin.

The Russian economy recovered during the 1920s and in 1928 it was decided to replace the Saratov ferries with a railway bridge. Construction took many years and suffered a major setback in 1934 when a large section failed and fell into the river killing over 100 workers. After this the military took over construction and the bridge finally opened in April 1935. The ferries were redundant and laid-up at Uvek.

The battle for Stalingrad

Soviet Railways

Stalingrad (Latoshinka) – Shadrinsky	1941-1942
	1943-1961

The Germans invaded the Soviet Union in June 1941 and by the end of year had captured large areas of the country and paralysed the railway network. It was increasingly difficult to supply the city of Stalingrad from the west and railway connections were quickly built on the east side of the Volga to the town of Shadrinsky, slightly north the city. The laid-up ferries at Saratova were refurbished and moved down river to Stalingrad. The *Saratovskaya Pereprava* had been renamed the *Иосиф Сталин*, *(Josef Stalin)*, to celebrate the leader's 60th birthday. A ferry terminal was established on the west bank of the Volga at Latoshinka, close to the giant tractor factory a few miles north of the city centre. Through the 1941-42 winter and on into the spring, the *Pereprava Vtoraya* and *Josef Stalin* worked twenty-four hours a day taking goods wagons across to the city, despite numerous air-raids. In July the river was mined as the Germans prepared their final attack on Stalingrad and the only way in or out of the besieged city was across the river. By mid-August the Germans had broken through and hand-to-hand fighting continued at the tractor factory and railway sidings next to the ferry terminal. Throughout the fighting, the ferries continued to transport supplies and evacuate civilians and the wounded from the city.

On the night of the 24th August, the *Josef Stalin* carried-out a daring operation to recover wagons of supplies trapped in the German-occupied sidings near the Latoshinka terminal. Under a full black-out, the ferry crossed the river and docked on the west bank. The crew climbed up the embankment to the railway sidings and silently pushed the wagons by hand one by one down to the ferry. Once loaded, Captain Samoilov and his crew headed back across the river. By this time, it was close to dawn and the *Josef Stalin* was spotted by the Germans once she was out in the channel. They opened fire, but the old ferry got back to the east bank unscathed.

With the west bank ferry pier in enemy hands, the ferries could no longer transport wagons, but continued to move men and supplies across to Stalingrad each night, returning with the injured. During the day, the two ferries were camouflaged and moored in a creek a few miles north on the eastern bank. The Germans soon spotted them from the air and they were regularly shelled. To prevent their destruction, the 27th Railway Brigade were given orders to scuttle the ferries. All delicate equipment was removed and, on the 17th September, the *Pereprava Vtoraya* and *Josef Stalin* were sunk at their moorings during an artillery bombardment. Old oily ropes were hung from the ferries' gantries and set alight to create clouds of smoke so that the Germans would assume the ships had been completely destroyed.

By the end of November 1942, the Russian army had encircled the Germans and were pushing them back towards the centre of the city. The Latoshinka pier became accessible again and the order was given to raise and refurbish the ferries. For the second time, divers had to work in the *Pereprava Vtoraya* in mid-winter, and by the end of the year, both ships were refloated. It took some time to refurbish the machinery and to clear mines from the ferry channel, so it was the

24th April before the *Josef Stalin* started taking wagons across the river again. The *Pereprava Vtoraya* took longer to repair but soon both ferries were back in service.

The two ferries continued to operate across the Volga at Stalingrad after the war, though by this time they were both old and in poor condition. It is not clear how long the service continued or when the ferries were finally scrapped. However, they were gone by 1961 when the Volgograd dam was completed and provided a permanent road and rail link across the river. The *Saratovskiy Ledokol* lasted longer. She was used as a workboat during the construction of the new Saratov bridge and laid-up when this opened in 1965. There were plans to preserve her, but she sank in 1968.

The Arctic and the Kerch strait

USSR - Transpolar Main Line

Labytnangi – Salekhard	1951-1953
Yermakovo – Igarka	1951-1953

The Russian Arctic is certainly on the fringe of what can be considered as Europe. In 2018, Russia's Transport Minister and other dignitaries held a ceremony to inaugurate construction of a 2km railway bridge over the River Ob as a vital link in the new Northern Latitudinal Railway. The project revived a much darker episode from Russia's past. In the 1940s, Stalin ordered a branch line to be constructed from the Arkhangelsk railway to develop new coalfields at Vorkuta. The mine and railway were built by forced labour from Stalin's infamous Gulag camps. The next phase of the plan was to extend the railway eastwards, creating the Трансполярная магистраль, or Transpolar Main Line, linking the rail network to the port of Salekhard on the river Ob and finishing at Igarka on the river Yenisei.

Approved by the Kremlin in 1947, the planned railway was a huge project, 1,500km long and crossing five main rivers. The Nadym, Pur and Taz with bridges and the Ob and Yenisei by ferry. By any standards, the Ob and Yenisei are huge rivers, both are more than 3,000km long and flow north to the Arctic Ocean. The Yenisei discharges more water than either the Mississippi or the St. Lawrence and the Ob only slightly less.

In 1949, the General Directorate of Railway Construction Camps placed an order for four train ferries with Shipyard No. 402, later renamed the Northern Machine Building Enterprise (Sevmash) in Severodvinsk, near Arkhangelsk. The ferries were to follow the 'Project 723' design developed a few years earlier for river ferries in Eastern Siberia by Central Design Bureau No. 51. The Bureau later became the Vympel Design Bureau and has been responsible for designing many Russian ferries and icebreakers. They are based in Nizhny Novgorod, where the *Pereprava Vtoraya* had been built forty years earlier, so it was not surprising that the design owed much to the old Volga river ferries.

Like their predecessors, the Arctic ferries had four tracks on deck, two funnels on the centreline and a large gantry at the bow with lifts designed to raise 80-ton wagons around 5m. They were 90.7m long with a breadth of 18.3m and could carry 32 wagons and 130 passengers. While the arrangement was traditional, the ships were very modern, with welded hulls and diesel-electric propulsion. Their four Kharkov D-50 diesel generators developed 6,700 hp and drove twin screws. The hulls were ice-strengthened, but the ships were not designed as icebreakers. The intention was that once the rivers had frozen hard, the ferries would be laid-up and a temporary rail track laid across the ice for the winter.

The first two ships were the *Надым*, *(Nadym)* and the *Заполярный*, *(Zapolyarnyy)*. They were delivered in July 1951 in time to make their delivery voyage along the north coast of Russia before the ice closed in. The *Zapolyarnyy* went to Salekhard on the Ob and the *Nadym* had a longer voyage up the Yenisei river to Yermakova. Work had been progressing on the railway while the ferries were under construction. The line was built from both ends with large Gulag camps at Salekhard and Yermakovo and small labour camps every 10-12 km along the line as the work progressed. These were forced labour camps with prisoners sent for many years hard labour often for political offences or minor crimes. The conditions were appalling, swamps with clouds of mosquitos in summer and temperatures falling to -50°C in winter.

The second two ferries, the *Северный*, *(Severnyy)*, and the *Чулым*, *(Chulym)*, were completed in July 1952. They were almost identical to *Zapolyarnyy* and *Nadym*, the only difference being that the wagon lift platforms were slightly longer to allow them to transfer passenger coaches. However, by 1952 work was slowing down on the railway construction, and the two ferries were laid-up in the shipyard.

By the time Stalin died in March 1953, only around half the line had been completed. Within a month, the Council of Ministers in Moscow decided to stop the project, considering that it had no real economic value. Over the next few years, the system of Gulag camps was dismantled. The railway itself was mostly abandoned, only the section west of the Ob to Labytnangi remained in use. Most of the track between the Ob and Yenisei sank into the arctic mud and the wooden trestle bridges rotted away. There are widely varying estimates of the number of prisoners who worked on the line between 1947 and 1953, somewhere between 100,000 and 300,000, but no disagreement that many tens of thousands did not survive.

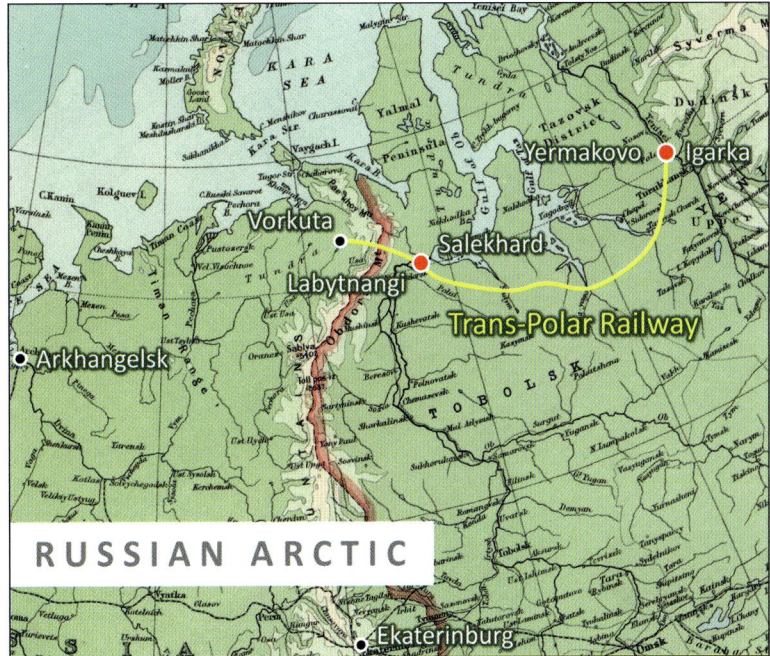

RUSSIAN ARCTIC

The ***Chulym*** on sea trials in the White Sea, 1952. The first two ferries were deployed on the Ob and Yenisei river crossings, but by the time she was delivered, the Transpolar Railway project was winding down. *(Author's collection)*

Prisoners from Stalin's Gulag camps building the Transpolar Railway from Salekhard to Igarka. Many thousands of them did not survive the harsh conditions. *(Author's collection)*

The Kerch Strait ferry service was restarted in 2004 using the **Annenkov** which had been converted from a river cargo ship. *(Alex)*

The **Annenkov** had capacity for 24 wagons on four tracks, here she is loading passenger coaches at Port Krym on the Crimean Peninsula. *(Alex)*

With the Transpolar Railway project cancelled, all four ferries were laid-up in 1953 and a decision made to transfer them to the Black Sea.

The idea of a railway between the Ob and Yenisei, this time with bridges across the great rivers, was revived in 2008. Now called the Northern Latitudinal Railway, its purpose is to allow oil, gas and nickel to be exported south. Various sections are under construction and it is due to be completed in the mid-2020s.

USSR - Azov Shipping Co.	**1954-1995**
Anship LLC	**2004-2020**
Port Krym – Kavkaz	**1954-1995**
	2004-2020

The four Arctic ferries arrived in the Black Sea in 1953, after a 5,000-mile voyage around the top of Norway, through the English Channel and Mediterranean. The main change from their arctic service was the removal of the forward gantry and wagon lift, as there is virtually no tide in the Black Sea.

The Crimean Peninsula has always been important to Russia and their Black Sea naval fleet has been based in Sevastopol for over two hundred years. At its eastern end, the peninsula is separated from the Russian mainland by the Kerch strait, around 4km wide at its narrowest point. In April 1944, the Russian army had built a temporary road and rail bridge across the strait, though this lasted less than a year as the piers were damaged by ice the following winter. The bridge was not repairable and there was no budget to build a permanent bridge, so when the four Arctic train ferries became available, they presented an opportunity to re-establish the Kerch Strait rail link at much less cost. Linkspans were built at the harbour of Port Krym in Crimea and at Port Kavkaz at the end of the long Chuska Spit, which extends out from the Russian mainland.

The ferry service started in 1954 and the following year two of the ferries were renamed. *Nadym*, became the *Восточный, (Vostochnyy)* and *Chulym* was renamed the *Южный, (Yuzhnyy)*. The names of the four ferries; *Zapolyarnyy, Severnyy, Yuzhnyy* and *Vostochnyy*, translate as *Polar, North, South* and *East*.

The four ships continued the Kerch Strait service for nearly 40 years. There were slight modifications over the years, such as extending the bridge decks aft to provide more passenger accommodation. The open space at the bow, created by the removal of the wagon lifts, also allowed them to carry a few cars as well railway coaches and wagons. As the number of cars grew, they were joined by two car and passenger ferries in the late 1980s.

Through-trains with passengers were stopped around 1987 and afterwards passengers were only carried on the car ferries. As the train ferries got older and more difficult to maintain, they were decommissioned one-by-one. *Vostochnyy* in 1987, *Yuzhnyy* in 1989 and *Zapolyarnyy* in 1991. *Severnyy* continued transporting goods wagons until 1995, when the rail service closed. She was laid-up until finally scrapped in 2002.

In 2002 there was an attempt to restart the rail ferry using the *Sakhalin-6*, which had been renamed the *Юрий Долгорукий*, *(Yuri Dolgorukiy)*. However, her draught was too deep and she could not use the existing harbours without extensive dredging, so the plan was abandoned.

The train ferry service was finally restarted in November 2004 by the Russian shipowner Anship LLC, a subsidiary of the AnRussTrans Group. They converted two cargo ships built in Ukraine in the 1980s, the *Slavutich-3* and *Slavutich-6*, into rail freight ferries and renamed them the *Анненков*, *(Annenkov)* and the *Петровск*, *(Petrovsk)*. They were long flat ships designed for river service, with a forward bridge and shallow draft, 110m by 16.4m wide. They loaded over the stern, with four lines of track on the deck able to carry 24 wagons.

The importance of the ferry crossing was suddenly changed in 2014, when Russia annexed the Crimean Peninsula and the northern border to Ukraine was closed. Overnight, all rail traffic was diverted to the Kerch Strait. In 2015, the two ships transported 77,000 wagons, many of them tank wagons with oil products. In July 2018, the *Annenkov* suffered a structural failure while unloading at Port Krym. This led to a crack in the side shell, which flooded the stern compartments. However, the damage was limited and she was soon repaired.

Prior to the political fall-out, an agreement had been signed between Russia and Ukraine in 2010 to build a road-rail bridge across the Kerch strait. This remained in the planning stages until 2014, but with the Ukrainian border closed and the Kerch ferries struggling to cope, the Russian Government accelerated the bridge project. Construction started in 2016 and the road crossing opened in 2018. The first St. Petersburg to Sevastopol passenger train crossed the bridge on the 25th December 2019, a trip scheduled to take 43 hours, 30 minutes. The regular ferry service stopped in July 2020 when freight trains started crossing the bridge, although some of the ferries may be retained for hazardous goods.

The Black Sea

USSR / Ukraine – Black Sea Shipping Co.	1978-1995
UKRferry	1995- current
Navigation Maritime Bulgare	1978- current
Varna – Iliychevsk	**1978- current**
Varna / Iliychevsk – Poti/Batumi	**1999- current**
Varna / Iliychevsk – Derince	**2001- current**

While train ferry routes have declined throughout most of Europe in the last few decades, the Black Sea has been the exception. Many new routes have opened, though the expansion has been driven as much by politics as by economics. In the decades following the Second World War, Bulgaria and Romania on the

The *Petrovsk* was a sistership of the *Annenkov* and converted from a cargo ship to a train ferry. *(Author's collection)*

western coast of the Black Sea were members of the COMECON group of countries linked economically to the Soviet Union. Rail traffic with the Soviet Union had always been hampered by different railway gauges as Bulgaria and Romania both use standard gauge. In the 1960s, the Soviets had proposed converting the north-south lines through Romania to their broader gauge, but this was understandably rejected. By the mid-70s, President Ceauşescu of Romania had a strained relationship with the Kremlin and the Bulgarian and Soviet governments agreed to establish a rail ferry service to by-pass the Romanian railways.

The success of the newly established Railship project in the Baltic provided a model solution, though the Black Sea project was on a much larger scale. Four large ships were delivered in 1978, two for Navigation Maritime Bulgare (Navibulgar), the Bulgarian state shipping company and two for the USSR's Black Sea Shipping Co. The Bulgarian ships were built by two Norwegian shipyards, the *Героите на Одеса*, *(Geroite na Odesa)* by A/S Fredriksstad M/V and the *Героите на Севастопол*, *(Geroite na Sevastopol)* by A/S Framnaes M/V in Sandefjord. The Soviet ships, the *Герои Плевни*, *(Geroi Plevny)*, and the *Герои Шипки*, *(Geroi Shipki)* were built by the Uljanik Shipyard in Pula, Yugoslavia (now Croatia).

The two pairs of ships were virtually identical and followed the Railship layout, with rail wagons carried on three decks. There were five tracks on the main deck with an elevator on the centre track taking wagons to the upper and lower decks. On these decks, a slewing rail at the forward end was pivoted at the bow to transfer wagons between the three tracks on the lower deck and five tracks on the upper deck. The ferries were designed to carry 108 wagons, 16 on the lower deck, 49 on the main deck and 43 on the open upper deck. These wagons were larger than those often used in Western Europe, 14.73m long with a weight of 70 tons. The ferries loaded through the stern, from a wide fan-

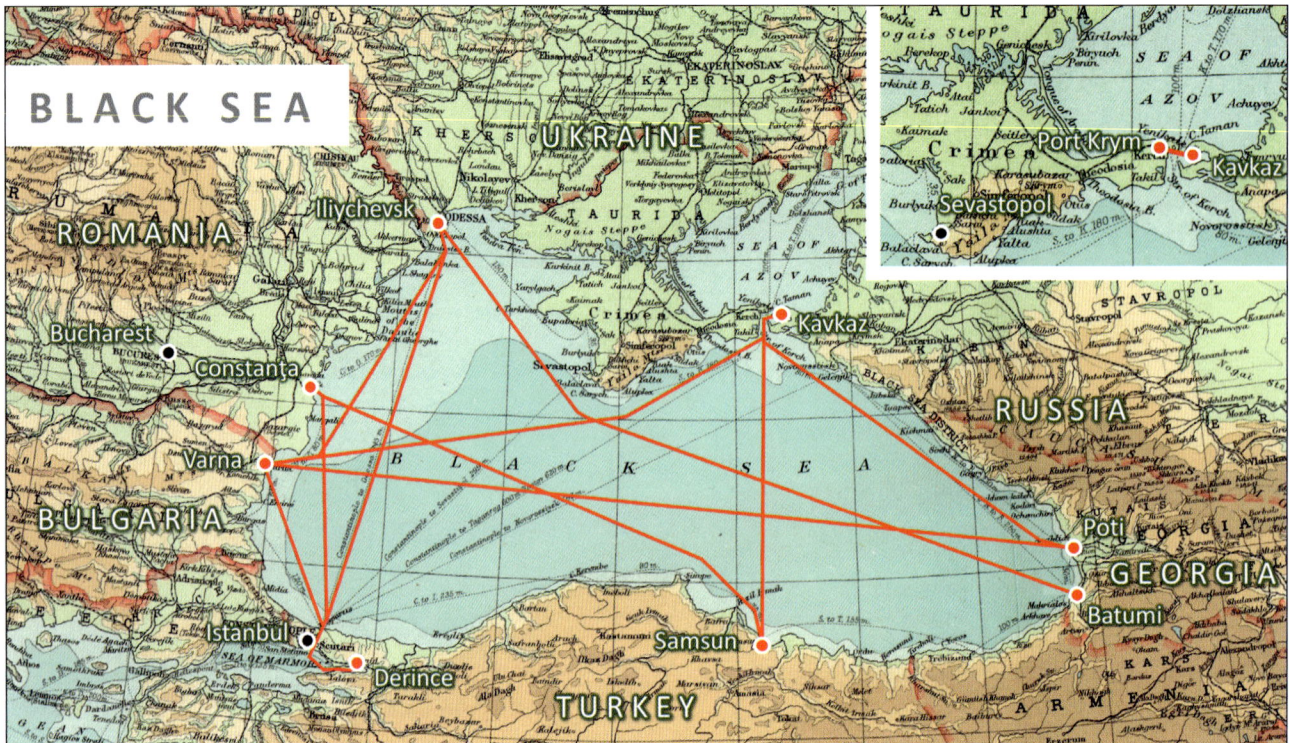

shaped linkspan connecting to all five tracks on the main deck. The stern door, elevator and slewing rail were built by the Finnish cargo equipment company MacGregor-Navire. They also built the linkspans at Beloslav, near Varna and Iliychevsk, now called Chornomorsk in Ukraine.

The track on the ferries is to the 1,524mm Russian gauge, with the wagons' gauge changed to 1,435mm at a large siding built west of the Beloslav terminal. The main goods carried from the USSR were wood, oil products, industrial equipment and chemicals and the ships returned with Bulgarian exports of fruit, vegetables, manufactured goods and food products. The round trip took around 60 hours, with the voyage between Varna and Iliichevsk taking around 19 hours and 11 hours for the turnround at each port. For wagons arriving at Beloslav, it took another four hours to change gauge before they continued their journey on Bulgarian Railways. Freight traffic increased from 2 million tons in 1979 to 3.4 million tons by 1988. A second linkspan was installed at both ports in 1982.

Ukraine became independent after the break-up of the Soviet Union in 1990 and took ownership of the Black Sea Shipping Company. The operation of the two Ukrainian ships, *Geroi Plevny* and *Geroi Shipki* was taken over by a private company, UKRferry in 1995.

With the break-up of the Soviet Union and the economic disruption that followed, freight traffic between Bulgaria and Ukraine reduced. However, these changes opened-up a new opportunity to transport freight east-west across the Black Sea to newly independent Georgia. The Georgian ports were connected by rail to the Caspian, through Azerbaijan,

and from there by ferry to Kazakhstan and Turkmenistan. The Black Sea and Caspian ferries created a rail corridor from Europe to Kazakhstan and ultimately to China that by-passed the restrictions and bureaucracy of the Russian railways. UKRferry started their freight service from Iliychesk to the Georgian ports of Poti and Batumi in 1996. This was soon extended to a triangular service including Varna and was formalised in 1999 by an agreement between the Bulgarian, Ukrainian and Georgian governments.

By 2001, traffic had nearly recovered to its previous levels, with 3.2 million tons of freight moved in 120,000 wagons. The ferries were also modified to carry around 60 passengers, mostly truck drivers, and a service was started from Ilychevsk to Derince in Turkey. The longer crossings required a fifth ship and the former East German ferry the *Griefswald* was chartered by UKRferry in 2003. She was larger than the older ships and also had accommodation for 150 passengers.

The five ships maintained the Ukraine - Bulgaria - Georgia service through until 2013 and by then the four older ferries were 35 years old. To upgrade their fleet, UKRferry chartered the *Griefswald's* sisterships from DFDS, the *Vilnius Seaways* in 2013 and the *Kaunas Seaways* in 2015. With the arrival of these two ships, the *Geroi Plevny* and *Geroi Shipki* were laid-up.

Navibulgar was privatised in 2005 and their two ferries, *Geroite na Odesa* and *Geroite na Sevastopol*, continued operating. The *Vilnius Seaways* and *Kaunas Seaways* were sold by DFDS to a holding company in 2018 but remain on charter to UKRferry operating alongside the *Griefswald* with their names shortened to *Vilnius* and *Kaunas*.

By 2020, the *Geroite na Odesa* was laid-up and *Geroite na Sevastopol* continued on a triangle service between Chornomorsk, Poti and Varna, with Batumi as an alternative Georgian port. She operated a joint schedule with the *Griefswald, Vilnius* and *Kaunas* of UKRferry, which principally ran between Chonomorsk and Batumi, taking traffic from Kazakhstan on the southern route to Europe.

CNM Romline S.A.	**1988-1998**
CFR Marfă	**1998-2009**
Constanța – Samsun/Derince	1988-2009

The Romanian Government decided to copy the success of the Soviet and Bulgarian ferries and in the mid-1980s established a train ferry service between Romania and Turkey. This was partly to provide work for their shipbuilding industry but also in the hope that they could attract through rail traffic from Turkey to Europe by-passing the congestion of the Bosporus ferries.

The ships were ordered from the Santierul Naval Yard in Constanța by the two state-owned shipping companies, NAVROM and Romline. The first ship, the *Eforie* was launched in 1987 and her sistership, the *Mangalia*, the following year. They were virtually replicas of the previous Ukrainian and Bulgarian ferries, loading through the stern to three rail decks. The main differences were that their tracks were standard gauge, as opposed to Russian gauge on the previous ships, and they had Romanian built MAN diesels, as opposed to B&W.

The delivery of *Eforie* was delayed until 1991 and the ships were initially put in service between Constanța and Samsun on the Turkish Black Sea coast, though they suffered from frequent engine problems. The level of traffic appears to have been very low, only 6,561 tons in 1995 rising to 121,662 tons in 2002. Even accepting that they were running two ships rather than four, this was less than 4% of the freight moved between Varna and Ilychevsk.

In 1998, Romanian Railways, Căile Ferate Române (CFR) was reorganised into separate divisions and the loss-making ferry business was transferred to the freight division, CFR Marfă. The Turkish port was moved from Samsun to Dernice, east of İstanbul, and a second route to Batumi in Georgia was planned, though this required a change of gauge.

When CFR was privatised in 2007, the ships were transferred to a subsidiary company, CFR Ferry-Boat S.A., to keep their losses separate from other rail freight operations. However, the ferry service soon closed. The *Mangalia* was laid-up in 2008 and the *Eforie* the following year. Their ownership was transferred to the Ministry of Transport and the ships kept as a 'Strategic Military Reserve' for a number of years while they rusted away in Agigea harbour south of Constanța.

The *Geroite na Odesa* was the first of the two large Bulgarian ferries built in 1978 for the service between Varna and Iliychevsk. *(Author's collection)*

The second Bulgarian ferry, the *Geroite na Sevastopol*, seen here with a full load of boxcars on the top deck. *(Mick Warrick)*

Black Sea Ferry & Invest (BFI)

Kavkaz – Poti	2007- current
Kavkaz – Samsun	2010- current

Black Sea Ferry & Invest was created to operate a train ferry service between Kavkaz and Poti in Georgia, which started in 2007. The service was part of an agreement between the Russian, Georgian and Armenian governments to provide a rail connection from Russia, through Georgia, to land-locked Armenia. In 2008, RZD the Russian State Railways took over the operation of the Armenian Railways and the following year bought a majority shareholding in BFI.

The port of Kavkaz was originally developed for the small ferries crossing the Kerch strait and is not deep enough for seagoing ships. As a result, shallow-draught ice-strengthened ferries were designed for BFI's service by the Odessa Marine Engineering Bureau and ordered from the Kherson Shipyard in Ukraine. The first ship, the *Smat*, was delivered in 2007, followed by a sistership the *Feruz* the following year. No-one could call them good-looking ships, flat and low with a forward superstructure

Unloading at Beloslav port near Varna, showing the five tracks on the upper rail deck and the hatch open to the elevator on the centre track. Once onshore, the wagons will be changed from Russian to European standard gauge. *(UKRferry)*

The Soviet ferry, **Geroi Plevny**, loading wagons of timber at the port of Iliychevsk, (now called Chornomorsk). *(Author's collection)*

and open aft deck. They were 150m long with a breadth of 22m and had five tracks on deck designed to carry up to fifty 88-ton tank-wagons.

The ferries made around 40 round trips a year between Kavkaz and Poti and a second route was started in 2010 between Kavkaz and Samsun in Turkey. As Turkey's railways are standard gauge, this also required a wheel change facility at Samsun port. Traffic to Turkey started slowly with 7 trips the first year and 18 in 2012, with 65,000 tons of cargo.

A third ferry was added to the fleet in 2012, the *Ulfat* had started life in 1978 as a ro-ro trailer ship, the *Norwegian Crusader*. She was converted into a train ferry in 2012 by Sefine in Altinova, Turkey. The side-shell was cut-down and sponsons added so that only her bow and the bridge-front remained recognisable from her previous life. Like the other ferries, her main deck had five lines of track though she was slightly shorter and carried 45 tank wagons.

Feruz was renamed БФИ-1, (BFI-1) in 2013 and *Smat* renamed ТФМ-1, (TFM-1) in 2014. BFI-1 was laid-up in 2017 and *Ulfat* withdrawn from service in 2018 and scrapped the following year.

Anship LLC
Varnaferry OOD
Kavkaz – Varna   2009- current

The relationship between Ukraine and Russia deteriorated following the so-called 'Orange Revolution' in 2004. This led to a desire for a direct ferry route between Bulgaria and Russia, by-passing the route from Varna to Iliychevsk in Ukraine. A new service between Varna and Kavkaz was started in 2009 by the Russian shipowner Anship LLC and later joined by the Bulgarian operator, Varnaferry OOD.

Anship provided two ships for the route, the *Славянин, (Slavyanin)*, and the *Авангард, (Avangard)*. Both were old Scandinavian ro-ro ships which were converted to train ferries at the Sevmorverf yard in Sevastopol to a design by the Odessa Marine Engineering Bureau. As with the previous Black Sea ferries designed in Odessa, they were low and flat with a single train deck

The **Geroi Shipki** and **Geroi Plevny** at the Beloslav terminal near Varna. The linkspan fans out with five tracks connecting through the 18.4m wide stern door. *(UKRferry)*

UKRferry expanded their operations across the Black Sea starting services to Turkey and Georgia. The fleet was expanded by chartering the former East German ferry **Greifswald** in 2003. *(Frank Behrends)*

The Romanian ferry **Mangalia**, seen here in the Bosporus, started sailings between Constanţa and Derince in Turkey in 1988. *(Wil Weijsters)*

The **Smat**, later renamed **TFM-1**, was delivered to Black Sea Ferry & Invest in 2007 for their service between Kavkaz in Russia and Poti in Georgia, connecting through to landlocked Armenia. *(Evgeny)*

The **Slavyanin** discharging tank wagons over the five-track linkspan at the Beloslav terminal west of Varna. The **Geroite na Sevastopol** is on the left-hand berth. *(Author's collection)*

TFM-1 was not a good-looking ship but the five tracks on the aft deck could carry up to fifty wagons. *(Evgeny)*

and the shallow draught needed for the port of Kavkaz. They were similar in size to the *Ulfat* carrying 45 wagons on five tracks. However, with a finer bow and larger funnels, they were marginally better looking than the *Smat* and *Feruz*.

They were joined in 2011 by Varnaferry's Bulgarian flag ferry, the *Varna*. She was converted from the ro-ro ferry *Sondos*, which had been built in the Okean Shipyard in Nikolayev in 1994. She is similar in size and layout to the two Russian ships, but slightly better-looking as more of her original superstructure has been retained. Each of the three ships makes a weekly round trip between Kavkaz and Varna.

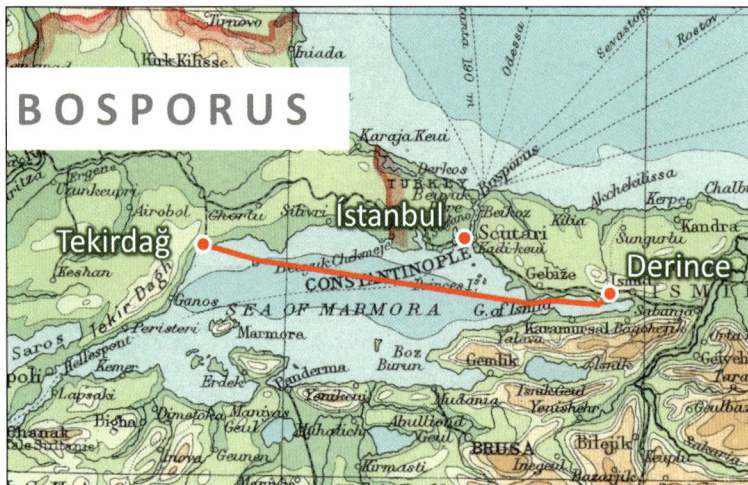

The Bosporus

Turkiye Cumauriyeti Deviet Demiyollari, (TCDD)
Sirkeci – Haydarpaşa   1959-2012

İstanbul is one of the world's great cities, with a population of 15 million, it sits astride the Bosporus strait and has always been the main crossing point on the overland route from Europe to Asia. This is reflected by the railways, the line from Europe reached Sirkeci station on the west side of İstanbul in 1872 and the Orient Express started running from there to Paris in 1889. At the same time, the Anatolian Railway was being built eastwards across the Ottoman Empire with German financial and technical assistance. Its western terminus was the magnificent Haydarpaşa railway station which dominates the waterfront on the eastern side of the Bosporus. When Kaiser Wilhelm visited Turkey in 1898, the imperial train was shipped across between the two stations by barge. At various times, it was proposed to join the two stations by a tunnel or ferry to allow international trains to run directly from Europe to the Middle East and establish through-trains from Berlin to Baghdad and from London to Cairo.

A barge was introduced in 1926, allowing locomotives and wagons to be occasionally shipped across the Bosporus. However, it took until 1958 before the Turkish State Railways (TCDD) built a train ferry to provide a regular service. The *Demiryolu*, which simply means *'Railway'*, was built by Denizcilik Bankasi's Haliç Shipyard in İstanbul. 74m long with a breadth of 15m, she was a twin-screw diesel ferry with three tracks on deck and loaded over the bow. The middle track only extended for around half the ship's length, as the aft section was filled by a central superstructure and funnel. The *Demiryolu* was built purely for goods wagons and had no passenger accommodation as she ran alongside the frequent passenger steamers on the 5km crossing. The train ferry service started in 1959 between the two stations, Sirkeci on the west and Hardarpaşa on the east. As there is no tide, the terminals did not need linkspans, the three parallel tracks simply stopped at the edge of the quay. On arriving at the terminal, *Demiryolu* trimmed the bow down by pumping water out of an aft ballast tank until the rails on the deck were level with the quayside. The bow was then locked to the quay and the aft ballast tank refilled, so that the bow exerted an upward force on the rail connection. This allowed the wagons to be offloaded without any movement between the ferry and the quayside.

A second ferry, the *Demiryolu II* was built in 1966 by the same shipyard. She had a more conventional design, with three tracks running the full length of the main deck and the superstructure above with funnels either side. Unlike her predecessor, she also had a deck of passenger accommodation below the bridge.

The *Demiryolu* was later rebuilt to look very much like the *Demiryolu II*. Her old central engine casing and funnel were removed. The central track was extended for the full length of the main deck and a new superstructure was fitted above with passenger accommodation and twin funnels. The *Demiryolu* was also renamed *Demiryolu I* in 1995.

The third and last of TCDD's ferries, the *Demiryolu III*, was built in 1982 again in the Haliç Shipyard. She was similar in size and layout to *Demiryolu II* but had a more modern square-edged appearance with two raked

The *Demiryolu* was rebuilt, with a new superstructure above the train deck and twin funnels, and later renamed *Demiryolu I*. *(Martin Penwright)*

The *Demiryolu III* was the last of TCDD's three Bosporus ferries, built in 1982 and distinctive with her square raked funnels. *(Derek Lilley)*

The *Demiryolu II* was built in 1966, seen here crossing the Bosporus with a full load of freight wagons. *(Frank Behrends)*

The *Demiryolu III* loading at the Haydarpaşa station terminal. There is no linkspan and the ferries adjust their ballast to align with the quayside. *(Kees Wielemaker)*

funnels. The ferries generally operated without incident, though *Demiryolu III* lost a goods wagon off the stern in 2004 while loading at Sirkeci. Fortunately, it was recovered from the water without any injuries or significant damage to the ship.

The long-discussed plans for a Bosporus rail tunnel finally materialised around the millennium and construction started in 2004. The Marmaray Tunnel opened in October 2013, providing a route under the Bosporus for both local and long-distance rail traffic. After this, the ferries became largely redundant and the *Demiryolu II* and *III* were laid-up at Haydarpaşa.

Alyans Chartering & Shipping Co.

Ereğli – Zonguldak	2004-2013
Tekirdağ – Derince	2013-2020

The Alyans Chartering & Shipping Co. bought the ferry *Trekroner* from Scandlines in Denmark in 2004 and renamed her *Erdeniz*. She was initially used on Turkey's Black Sea coast, carrying wagons around 45km between the Ereğli steelworks and the railhead at Zonguldak.

With the opening of the Marmaray Tunnel in 2013, İstanbul's citizens could travel by train between the two sides of the city for the first time. New suburban lines meant that the tunnel carried a huge amount of local traffic as well as long-distance trains. To reduce congestion in the tunnel, Turkish Railways, (TCDD) chartered the *Erdeniz* to start a new freight service across the Sea of Marmara, between Tekirdağ and their port at Derince, which bypassed İstanbul. The 815m of track on the *Erdeniz* gave more capacity than the three old *Demiryolu* ferries put together and also provided a route for hazardous or oversize goods that were not allowed in the tunnel.

It was announced that the service would close in 2020 as a cost-cutting measure and most freight would be routed through the tunnel. Newspaper reports suggested that the *Demiryolu II* and *III* would be refurbished and restart the service from Haydarpaşa to Sirkeci to carry hazardous and oversize cargoes.

Van Gölü

Turkiye Cumauriyeti Deviet Demiyollari, (TCDD)
Tatvan – Van   1971- current

Van Gölü, or Lake Van, is as beautiful as any Alpine Lake and lies in the mountains of eastern Turkey, 1,640m above sea level. It is over 100km across and 450m deep and remarkable in having several small rivers running in, but no outflow. The water level in the lake is maintained purely by evaporation, with the result that its clear blue water is highly alkaline and seldom freezes.

It is the rather unlikely location for a train ferry service which runs from Tatvan in the west, 96 km across to Van on the eastern shore on the railway line between Turkey and Iran. The ferry principally carries goods wagons but is also part of the Trans-Asia Express

between İstanbul and Tehran. The passenger service closed after Iran's Islamic Revolution in 1981 then reopened between Ankara and Tehran in 2001 and ran until 2015 when it was again suspended. However, it was not a through-train, the Turkish train stopped at Tatvan and after crossing on the ferry, passengers boarded an Iranian train for the onward journey from Van, only the baggage car actually crossed on the ferry. The Trans-Asia Express restarted in 2019 with one train per week on the 57-hour, 2,394km journey.

A railway line between Turkey and Iran was initially approved in 1937, but only a small part of the line was built. The project was revived in the 1960s as part of a cold-war military pact, called CENTO, between Iran, Iraq, Pakistan and Turkey and supported by the United Kingdom and the United States. CENTO was modelled on NATO and developed military cooperation between its members from 1955 until it dissolved with the Iranian Islamic Revolution in 1979. CENTO funded the completion of the railway from Turkey to Iran to create a strategic transport link between its members. The line from the west reached Tatvan at the western end of the lake in 1964. The lake remained a major obstacle as the southern shore is very mountainous and a diversion around the northern end of the lake would add significantly to the distance. The compromise was to provide a train ferry across the lake. This opened in 1971 at the same time as the eastern line from Van to the Iranian border.

Two ferries were built by Denizcilik Bankasi's Haliç Shipyard in İstanbul, then dismantled and the components transferred by rail to Tatvan where they were reassembled. The *Van* and *Tatvan* were sisterships, 82m long with a breadth of 14.5m and 1,766 gross tons.

The ferry pier at Tatvan with the **Van** on the left, one of the original ferries, and the slightly newer **Refet Ünal** loading freight wagons and **Orhan Altiman** moored on the right. (Author's collection)

The ferry **Van** was built in İstanbul and reassembled on the lakeside at Tatvan to start Turkish Railways' service on Lake Van in 1971. (Author's collection)

They looked much more like seagoing ships than the Bosporus ferries, with a high bow and a full deck of passenger accommodation below the bridge. The ferries loaded over the stern and carried 9 or 10 wagons on three parallel tracks. Like the Bosporus ferries, there was no linkspan, the rails simply stopped at the edge of the quay and the ferry adjusted ballast to align the tracks on the deck with the quay.

Two more ferries were built, the *Orhan Atliman* was completed in 1976 and the *Refet Ünal* in 1977. They were also products of the Haliç Shipyard and reassembled at Tatvan. They were nominally identical to *Van* and *Tatvan*, though with some minor changes to the superstructure. The bridge deck was extended aft to provide a promenade deck, a small docking bridge was added at the stern and the lifeboats were replaced by rafts.

Flat-pack ferries

The rail service between Turkey and Iran was interrupted from time to time by the politics of the region but by 2010 the older ships had been in service nearly 40 years. TCDD decided to build two large new ferries to replace the four old ships. The ferries were prefabricated at the Özata Shipyard in Antinova near İstanbul and, before assembly could start at Tatvan, a new construction building and drydock were built next to the Tatvan ferry pier. Construction of the first ferry, the *Sultan Alparslan*, started in 2011 and was completed 2016. She is an impressive double ended ferry, 136m long with a breadth of 24m and four tracks on deck, capable of carrying 50 goods wagons with a total weight of 4,000 tons. Powered by four diesel generators, driving steerable Schottel propellers, she has a service speed of 15 knots which reduces the crossing time from 4½ to 3¼ hours. The four-track layout, compared with three tracks on the older ferries, also required new ferry

Passengers scuttle onboard the **Refet Ünal** on a cold winter day. The passenger coaches of the train from Turkey to Iran did not cross on the ferry, so passengers had to cross on foot. Only the luggage van and goods wagons crossed by ferry. (Peter Velthoen)

The **Sultan Alparslan** at the new Tatvan pier, with its four-track linkspan and mooring dolphins. In the background, her sistership the **İdris-i Bitlisi** is under final assembly in the drydock. (Özata Shipyard)

Caspian ferries

	1950	1960	1970	1980	1990	2000	2010	2020
SOVIETSKIY AZERBAIDZHAN		1962						
SOVIETSKIY TURKMENISTAN		1963						
GAMID SULTANOV	...	1966						
SOVIETSKIY UZBEKISTAN	...	1967						
SOVIETSKIY KAZAKHSTAN...	...	1968						
SOVIETSKIY DAGESTAN ..	...	...	...	1984				
SOVIETSKIY TADZHIKSTAN	...	...	1984	sank 2002				
SOVIETSKAYA GRUZIYA ...	...	...	1985					
SOVIETSKAYA KALMKIYA...	...	...	1985					
SOVIETSKAYA ARMENIYA...	...	...	1985					
SOVIETSKIY KIRGIZIYA	...	...	1986					
SOVIETSKAYA BYELORUSSIYA	...	...	1986					
SOVIETSKIY NAKHICHEVAN	...	...	1986					
SHADAG	...	...	...	2005 / 2011				
KARABAKH	...	...	...	2005 / 2008				
AGDAM...	...	...	...	2006 / 2011				
AKADEMIK ZARIFA ALIYEVA	...	...	...	2006 / 2008				
BARDA	...	...	...	...	2012			
BALAKEN	...	...	...	...	2012			

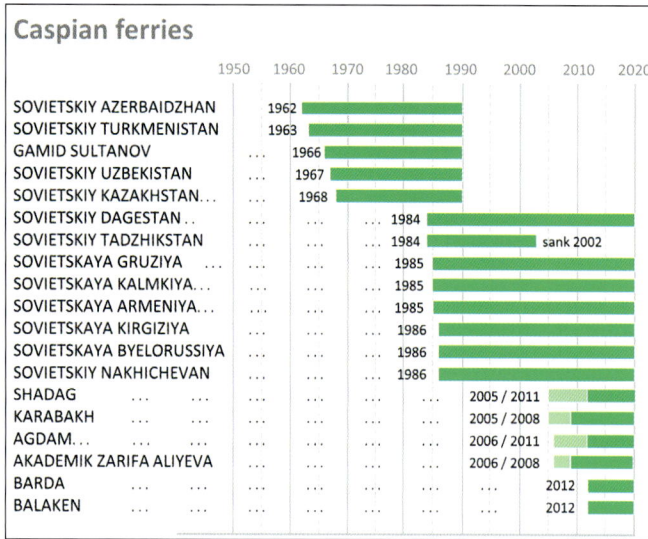

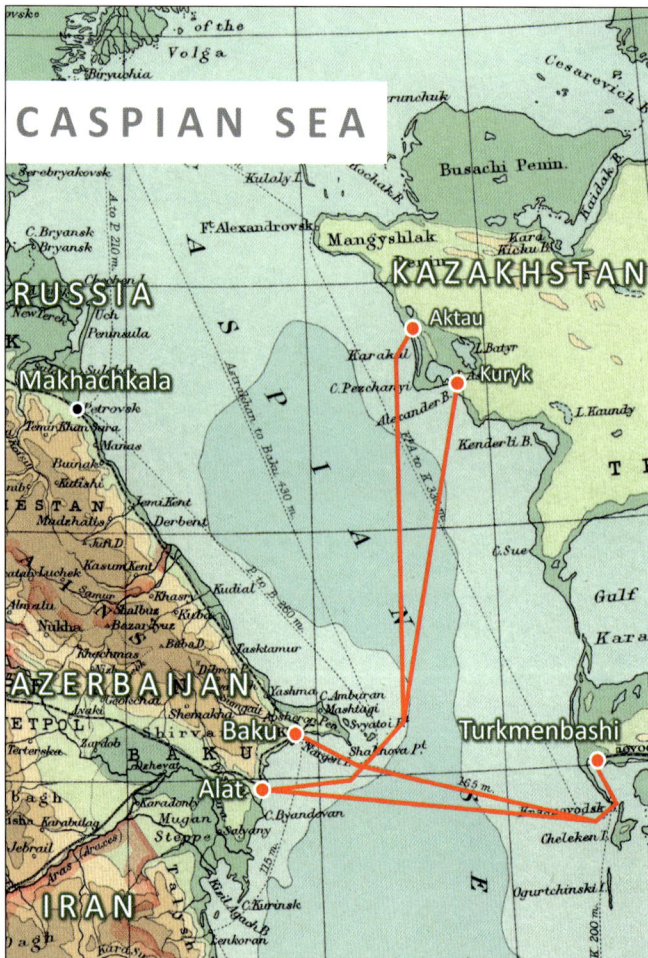

terminals which were provided with linkspans to adjust for variations in the lake's water-level. The *Sultan Alparslan* took over the service on the 15th January 2018 and was joined by her sistership, the *İdris-i Bitlisi* in July, when the four old ferries were retired. The *Van, Tatvan, Orhan Atliman*, and *Refet Ünal* remain laid-up in Tatvan.

The Caspian

USSR - Caspian Shipping Co.	1962-1991
Azerbaijan State Caspian Shipping	1991- current
Baku/Alat – Krasnovodsk (Türkmenbasy)	
	1962- current
Baku/Alat – Aktau/Kuryk	c.1992- current

It is probably difficult to achieve a consensus on the eastern boundary of Europe using geographic or cultural criteria, but the Ural River has long been considered the boundary between European and Asian Russia. The river flows into the Caspian Sea and if for no other reason than Azerbaijan has won the Eurovision Song Contest, it is worth including the Caspian ferries as the last section of this book.

The Caspian is rightly called a sea, rather than a lake. It is more than 1000 km north to south and in area is bigger than all the North American Great Lakes put together, plus Lake Victoria. As a result, it can experience weather as severe as any ocean. The main city on the Caspian is Baku, capital of Azerbaijan and one of the first cities to make its fortune from oil. The first oil well was drilled in 1846 and by the 1870s the oil industry had attracted a large and wealthy expat community from all over Europe, including the Nobel family. To support this development, the first railway linking Baku westwards to the Black Sea coast opened in 1883 and by 1900 a second rail line connected northwards to the rest of the Russian Empire.

Since the middle of the 19th century Russia had also been extending its empire east of the Caspian through what is now Kazakhstan, Uzbekistan and Turkmenistan to the boundaries of China and British India. To consolidate their control over this huge area, they started building the Trans-Caspian Railway in 1879. By the end of the century, this connected the old Silk Road cities, such as Ashkabad, Samarkand and Tashkent back to the port of Krasnovodsk on the east side of the Caspian. The main export trade was cotton sent west to Russia, with kerosene, wood and manufactured goods travelling east. As early as 1905, there are references to a 'train ferry' across the Caspian between Baku and Krasnovodsk, though this may have simply been a passenger steamer that connected with the trains or a barge for transferring rolling stock. After the Russian Revolution, the whole area became part of the Soviet Union and the first plan to start a train ferry across the Caspian was announced in the Moscow paper 'Вечерняя Москва' in 1929. Nothing came of this at the time, but a train ferry was established sometime in the 1950s. Details are scarce and the only clue is a picture of a ship in Baku harbour with goods wagons on four lines of track.

A major project was approved in the late 1950s to build five large passenger train ferries for service between Baku and Krasnovodsk. These ships were

A postcard from the 1970s showing the two berths at the ferry pier in Baku. *(Author's collection)*

The *Sovietskiy Uzbekistan* leaving Baku in 1983. *(Author's collection)*

designed by Central Design Bureau No. 51 as 'Project 721' and built by the Krasnoye Sormovo Shipyard No. 112 in Gorky, (the name of Nizhny Novgorod from 1932 to 1990). The lead ship was the *Советский Азербайджан, (Sovietskiy Azerbaidzhan)*, delivered to the Caspian Shipping Co. in 1962.

The *Sovietskiy Azerbaidzhan* was a large modern ship, 134m long with a breadth 18.3m and a gross tonnage of 8,840, the largest train ferry in the world at the time. She had an enclosed train deck with four tracks capable of carrying 30 goods wagons loaded through a stern door. Unusually for the time, she had an aluminium superstructure which contained saloons and cabins for 290 passengers. The ship had four Kharkov diesel-electric generators geared to three propellers which were controlled from the bridge. There was also a bow thruster. Like other Soviet merchant ships of the time, she had a grey hull and a white funnel with a narrow red band on which was the hammer and sickle in gold.

The Baku to Krasnovodsk service started in November 1962 and immediately made a huge difference to life in both cities. The overnight crossing took 12 hours and for people in the small town of Krasnovodsk in Turkmenistan, it opened their eyes to an exciting new world. An overnight trip on the ferry, a whole day in Baku's markets or window-shopping, then back home on the following night's ferry. The market traders from Baku took their wares in the other direction. The cheapest ticket was only three rubles and for two rubles more you could get a berth in a cabin.

The weather in the Caspian can be quite severe. Sometimes ferry sailings were cancelled and occasionally the ships could be stuck at sea for a day or two before being able to enter the harbours. Railway wagons were sea-fastened using chains and turnbuckles then jacked-up at the corners to take their weight off the suspension. In the early days there were very few trucks and cars. All vehicles were checked to ensure they were not dripping any oil or coolant. Car drivers were required to switch their engine off, then on again to prove they had a working battery.

The voyages were not always uneventful, on one occasion the *Sovietskiy Azerbaidzhan* misjudged her position when approaching Baku and grounded at speed on the Shakhova sand spit. Fortunately, there were no injuries or significant damage.

The second ferry, the *Советский Туркменистан, (Sovietskiy Turkmenistan)*, was delivered in 1963. Like her earlier sistership, the delivery voyage was a long tow from the shipyard around 1,500km down the Volga river to the Caspian. She had to pass under several bridges and so left the shipyard without her funnel, masts, radar etc. These were all fitted in Baku by a team from the shipyard.

The ferry service was a great success and in their first year the two ferries carried more than 1.8 million tons of freight. The third ferry, the *Гамид Султанов, (Gamid Sultanov)*, arrived in 1966. Right from the start, she was unlucky. On her first voyage on the 23rd November 1966 she collided with a tanker on her way out of Baku and was badly damaged. She was out of service for repair for more than a year.

The *Советский Узбекистан, (Sovietskiy Uzbekistan)*, was the fourth sistership, delivered in 1967, and the last ship, the *Советский Казахстан, (Sovietskiy*

The ill-fated *Merkuri-2*, formerly the *Sovietskiy Tadzhikistan*, during her charter on the Baltic in the late 1990s. *(Capt. Jan Melchers)*

The *Akademik Topçubaşov*, formerly the *Sovietskaya Kalmkiya*, departing from Aktau in Kazakhstan on an icy morning. *(Asker)*

Kazakhstan) was delivered the following year.

The fleet then operated without serious incident until the mid-1970s, when *Gamid Sultanov* suffered a major fire while under repair in June 1976. The aft section of the superstructure was completely burned out and the aluminium decks destroyed. As it was impossible to obtain aluminium to make proper repairs, the internal decks were replaced in steel, riveted to the surviving aluminium bulkheads. The passenger saloons were rebuilt, but the cabins were not reinstated. After this she was used as a freight ferry and seldom took passengers. Her hull was repainted black.

In April 1977, the *Sovietskiy Kazakhstan* had a collision in fog while leaving Baku harbour. She hit a small cargo ship, though fortunately it was a glancing blow without serious damage. The *Sovietskiy Uzbekistan* had a more serious collision in the following July. She entered the long narrow channel that that leads to Krasnovodsk just after midnight. An hour later she received a message from Port Control that the cargo ship *Zangelan* had left the port and that they would pass in the channel. It was a foggy night and as visibility deteriorated the *Sovietskiy Uzbekistan* slowed to a crawl, however the *Zangelan* continued at speed and the two ships collided in the channel with significant damage, though fortunately no casualties.

In 1984, 4.3 million passengers and 825,000 of rail freight were transported across the Caspian. The five ships were getting older and it was decided to replace them with a class of eight new train ferries. These were designated as Project 0379 and ordered from the Uljanik Shipyard in Pula, Yugoslavia (now Croatia) by Sudoimport on behalf of the Caspian Shipping Co.

The long way round

The lead ship was the *Советский Дагестан, (Sovietskiy Dagestan)*. Her appearance was very different from the older ferries and much less elegant. Long and low with a forward bridge, twin funnels aft and a square stern, her dimensions had to fit the existing terminals at Baku and Krasnovodsk and also the delivery route from the shipyard on the Adriatic to the Caspian Sea. The shortest route was via the Black Sea, River Don and the Volga-Don canal, however the limiting dimensions of the canal locks were a length of 140.2m and breadth of 16.5m. The existing ferries had a breadth of 18.3m, so ideally the new vessels should be the same, both to fit the linkspans but also for stability.

The alternative delivery route that was chosen was via the North Sea, Baltic and the Volga-Baltic Canal to the Volga. This was the route taken by the *Saratovskaya Pereprava* nearly ninety years earlier, through the Mariinsk Canal, which had since been enlarged and renamed. The limiting dimensions to fit the canal locks were a length of 210m and breadth of 17.6m. The *Sovietskiy Dagestan* was built to fit the locks, she was 154.5m long and although her final breadth was 18.3m, it could be reduced to 17.6m by removing the protective belting on the side shell. The low bridge and funnels allowed her to transit under the Volga bridges with only the masts and radar removed. These were refitted when she reached Baku after a delivery voyage of more than 10,000km.

The train deck on the *Sovietskiy Dagestan* had two tracks at the stern, opening out to four tracks, forward of the engine room casings. As with the older ferries, wagons were loaded through the stern. She was 21m longer, giving a track length of 414m with space for 28 wagons, compared to 360m previously. A ramp on the train deck went down to a car deck below, with space for 70-80 cars. This was always a frustration to motorists, as cars could only be disembarked once all the rail wagons had been unloaded. She had twin screws, a bow thruster and like the older ferries, the superstructure was made of aluminium to improve stability. There was accommodation for 200 passengers, with a mixture of aircraft-type seats and two or four berth cabins. Another innovation was an automatic heel adjustment system. In the older ferries the crew had to ensure the weight of rail wagons was equalised between the two sides of the ship. *Sovietskiy Dagestan* had an automatic system, which detected the ship's heel and pumped ballast port or starboard to compensate.

Sovietskiy Dagestan started service between Baku and Krasnovodsk late in 1984 and was soon followed by seven sisterships:-

Советский Таджикистан, (Sovietskiy Tadzhikistan) at the end of the same year. *Советская Грузия, (Sovietskaya Gruziya)* in 1985, *Советская Калмыкия, (Sovietskaya Kalmkiya)* in 1985, *Советская Армения, (Sovietskaya Armeniya)* in 1985, *Советская Киргизия, (Sovietskaya Kirgiziya)* in 1986, *Советская Белоруссия, (Sovietskaya Byelorussiya)* in 1986 and *Советская Нахичевань, (Sovietskiy Nakhichevan)* in 1986.

With Russia's economic difficulties a few years later, the *Sovietskiy Dagestan* was laid-up in Baku over winter in 1989 due to a lack of spare parts.

With the new ships in service the old 'Project 721' ferries were redundant. In most places, the old ships would have been sold on, either for further service or scrapping. In the Caspian Sea, there was no way to move them to different routes or a market for scrap. The *Gamid Sultanov* was taken out of service in the late 1980s and was used for a while as a hotel and restaurant before being scrapped. The *Sovietskiy Turkmenistan* remained in service longer than her sisterships and was laid-up in Baku in the late 1990s. There were various plans to re-use her as a bar and hotel, but after a few years of deterioration, she was scrapped in 2009. The *Sovietskiy Uzbekistan* was laid-up in the late 1980s. Her aluminium superstructure was removed and scrapped but her hull was abandoned was still rusting on the beach in 2014.

After the Soviet Union

With the break-up of the Soviet Union in 1991, the Soviet republics around the Caspian became independent countries, Azerbaijan, Turkmenistan and Kazakhstan. Dagestan remained part of Russia. The Caspian Shipping Company was taken over by the government of the newly independent Republic of Azerbaijan.

The *Sovietskaya Kalmkiya* suffered a terrorist attack during the conflict between Azerbaijan and neighbouring Armenia. A bomb exploded just as the ferry arrived in Baku from Krasnovodsk on the 8th January 1992 and the passengers were waiting to disembark. The explosion was followed by a fire which quickly spread through the accommodation, leaving 25 people dead and 88 injured. The ferry was repaired, though the burnt-out accommodation was not replaced and since then she has only been used for freight.

The Azerbaijan Caspian Shipping Co. renamed the

The *Professor Gül*, formerly the *Sovietskaya Byelorussiya*, in 2014, blowing out a lot of black smoke from her elderly Uljanik-B&W diesels. *(Asker)*

The *Qarabağ*, formerly the *Makhachkala-2*, was built in 2005 and bought by the Azerbaijan Caspian Shipping in 2008. *(Asker)*

ferries during the 1990s and repainted their hulls blue: *Sovietskiy Dagestan* was renamed the *Dağistan*, *Sovietskiy Tadzhikistan* was renamed the *Mercuri-2*, *Sovietskaya Gruziya* was renamed the *Mercuri-1* in 1992, *Sovietskaya Kalmkiya* was renamed the *Kalmkiya* in 1993, then the *Mercuri-3* in 1994 and finally the *Akademik Topçubaşov* in 1995. *Sovietskaya Armeniya* was renamed the *Azerbaijan* in 1994 and then the *Şəki, (Sheki)* in 2019 to release the name for the new ferry building in Baku Shipyard, *Sovietskaya Kirgiziya* was renamed the *Kirgizstan* in 1992, then the *Akademik Həsən Əliyev, (Akademik Hasan Aliyev)* in 1995, *Sovietskaya Byelorussiya* was renamed the *Belorus* in 1994, then the *Professor Gül*, a month later. *Sovietskiy Nakhichevan* was renamed the *Naxçivan, (Nakhchivan)*.

With the changed politics of the area, the port of Krasnovodsk in Turkmenistan lost its Russian name and was renamed Türkmanbaşy. The Azerbaijan Caspian Shipping Co. also started a new service from Baku to

The *Akademik Zarifa Aliyeva*, formerly the *Makhachkala-4*, loading at the new port of Kuryk in Kazakhstan. *(Author's collection)*

The *Barda* and one of the 'Dagestan' ferries at the Alat ferry terminal, 80 km south of Baku. It opened in 2014 to replace the old ferry pier in the city centre. *(Author's collection)*

Aktau in Kazakhstan. This created a route for rail and road freight from Kazakhstan through Azerbaijan and Georgia to the Black Sea ports without going through Russia.

In 1995, the *Mercuri-1* and *Mercuri-2* were chartered to operate as ro-ro ferries in the Baltic and made the long journey up the Volga and through the canals to St. Petersburg, returning in 2000. Unfortunately for the *Mercuri-2*, her return to the Caspian did not last for long.

The loss of the *Mercuri-2*

One of the saddest events in the history of train ferries was the loss of the *Mercuri-2*, formerly the *Sovietskiy Tadzhikistan*, on the 22nd October 2002. She had left the port of Aktau the previous day at around 14.30 hrs, heading south-west towards Baku. There were officially 51 people on board, 43 crew and 8 passengers. On the train deck were 16 tank wagons, each containing around 60 tons of crude oil.

In good weather, the voyage took around 30 hours but when she left Aktau the weather was poor by any standards, with a forecast of storm force winds and high seas. However, the *Mercuri-2* was a large seaworthy vessel and the weather was not thought to be a risk to her safety. The voyage continued overnight but on the Tuesday morning the weather was worse than forecast. The wind was gusting at over 100km/h and the ship was rolling violently in 6m waves. Sometime after 08.00 in the morning, the chains and turnbuckles securing one of the tank wagons broke. The loose wagon then crashed into its neighbours and very soon all the wagons were loose and piled up on one side of the train deck, releasing crude oil and causing the ship to list. A distress signal was sent at 09.00 and a rescue operation was initiated.

At 10.43 hrs, the *Mercuri-2* capsized and sank around 130 km east of Baku. When helicopters reached the scene, they managed to recover thirteen people from the water, though sadly five of them did not survive. There were no reports of lifeboats or life rafts having been launched. Efforts to recover bodies from the sea over the next few days were hampered by the large oil slick from the released cargo.

In the aftermath of the sinking, there were criticisms of the rescue operation as several hours had passed from the initial distress signal before the helicopters reached the scene. There were also questions on how many people had actually been onboard. One man came forward to state that he had put his wife and 6-year-old daughter on the ferry. The ticket office had been closed, so he had paid a crew member to get them onboard. The shipping company later admitted that there were probably eight unregistered passengers onboard and at least 51 people had died in the accident.

The post-Soviet ferries

In 2005, the first of four rail freight ferries was delivered to the Russian company Marin Investment & Development by the Uljanik Shipyard in Pula, Croatia. These were designed to operate a new service between the Russian port of Makhachkala in Dagestan and Aktau in Kazakhstan. The Махачкала-1, (*Makhachkala-1*) was, like the Project 0379 ferries, designed for the long trip from Croatia to the Caspian via the Volga-Baltic Canal. She was 155m long and 17.8m wide. Like the previous ships she was long and low, with a forward bridge and twin funnels aft. The main difference was that there was no passenger accommodation and wagons could be carried on two decks. The main train deck was open and had four tracks with capacity for 36 wagons. At the forward end, there was a lift on the two centre tracks, taking wagons down to a lower train deck. This had two tracks able to carry a further 16 wagons. The total capacity of 52 wagons was nearly twice the 28 carried on the older *Dağistan* class ferries. The *Makhachkala-1* was followed by the *Makhachkala-2* later in 2005 and the *Makhachkala-3* and *Makhachkala-4* in 2006.

The service to Makhachkala was not successful and the Russian owners sold the ferries to the Azerbaijan Caspian Shipping Co. *Makhachkala-2* and *Makhachkala-4* were sold in 2008 and renamed *Qarabağ* and *Akademik Zərifə Əliyeva, (Akademik Zarifa Aliyeva)*. *Makhachkala-1* and *Makhachkala-3* changed hands in 2011 and were renamed *Şahdağ* and *Ağdam*.

The Azerbaijan Caspian Shipping Co. ordered two more double-deck train ferries from Uljanik following the *Makhachkala* design. These were the *Bərdə, (Barda)* and the *Balakən, (Balaken)* which were delivered in 2012.

Since 2012 the Azerbaijan Caspian Shipping Co. has been operating thirteen train ferries across the Caspian. The seven surviving *Dağistan-class* ferries carrying 28 wagons and 290 passengers:

Dağistan,	*Mercuri-1,*
Akademik Hasan Aliyev,	*Sheki,*
Professor Gül,	*Nakhchivan,*
Akademik Topçubaşov, (freight only).	

The six Makhachkala-class ferries carrying 12 passengers and 52 wagons:

Qarabağ,	*Şahdağ,*
Akademik Zarifa Aliyeva,	*Ağdam,*
Barda,	*Balaken.*

Much of the traffic across the Caspian is tank wagons with oil products hence the number of freight-only ships which are required for carrying hazardous goods. However, the ferry to Kazakhstan also provides a through rail route from China allowing goods to reach Turkey and the Black Sea ports without going through Russia. While traffic from China is currently modest, it is seen as an opportunity for future growth. The rail links, marshalling yards and terminals have been expanded and rebuilt to provide more capacity. In October 2014, the old ferry pier in Baku city was closed and the operation moved to a new terminal at Alat, 80km south of the city. In 2017, the Kazakhstan terminal was moved from Aktau 70 km south to a new port at Kuryk to reduce the crossing distance. At Türkmanbaşy a new ferry terminal was opened in 2018 on the eastern edge of the city for both rail and road traffic. All these terminals have two train ferry docks with linkspans. Although there is no tide in the Caspian, linkspans are needed to adjust for changes in the water level. This has varied by around 2.5m over the past two decades due to changes in rainfall and evaporation.

With cheaper air travel and new ports moved away from city centres, the demand from passengers has declined. The ferries have also suffered a lot of criticism from western travellers over the years for the lack of timetables, the difficulty in getting tickets, dirty and dilapidated accommodation and poor food. However,

The new ferry terminal at Türkmanbaşy, opened in 2018. The passenger and ro-ro terminal is on the left and the train ferry berths on the right. *(Author's collection)*

The new ***Azerbaijan***, under construction at Baku Shipyard, interestingly the cargo is assumed to be tank wagons rather than general freight. *(Odessa Marine Engineering Bureau)*

there are signs of improvement. The shipping company now has a timetable on their website and tickets can be bought online. Some of the older ships have also been refurbished. The *Mercuri-1* was upgraded in 2017 and the *Dağistan* was given a major refurbishment in 2018, including replacing the old Uljanik-B&W engines with new Wartsila diesels and up-to-date control systems.

Two new passenger-train ferries were ordered in 2016 from the Baku Shipyard, to a design developed by the Odessa Marine Engineering Bureau. These two vessels will be similar in size and layout to the Makhachkala-class ferries and have space for 56 tank wagons on two decks. Without the need to pass under the Volga bridges, the forward superstructure is higher with accommodation for 100 passengers on two decks and a helicopter landing pad. The new ships are reported to be named the *Azerbaijan* and the *Akademik Zarifa Aliyeva* and were due for delivery in 2020-21 but their completion has been delayed.

Sources - General

Ransome-Wallis, Patrick, Train Ferries of Western Europe. Ian Allan, 1968.
Hader, Arnulf & Günther Meir, Eisenbahnfähren der Welt. Koehlers Verlag GmbH, 1986.
Asklander, Micke, Faktaomfartyg.se website.
Lloyd's Register of Ships
Grace's Guide to British Industrial History
The Times Survey Atlas of the World, J.G. Bartholomew, 1922.
Engineering
The Engineer
The Illustrated London News
The Motor Ship
The Naval Architect

Chapters 1 to 3 - Early ferries and the UK

Abell, Sir Westcott, Channel Train Ferry Steamers for the Southern Railway. Paper to the Institution of Naval Architects, April 1935.
Alexander, W., Letter to the Edinburgh Evening News, October 1936.
Behrend, George, & Gary Buchanan, Night Ferry. Jersey Artistes, 1985.
Belcher, Vice-Admiral Sir Edward, The Channel Passage, Vessels and Piers. Paper to the Institution of Naval Architects, 6th April, 1870.
Brodie, Ian, Steamers of the Forth. David & Charles, 1976.
Brodie, Ian, Steamers of the Tay. Stenlake Publishing, 2003.
Dupuy de Lôme, Henri, Calais a Douvres sur des Navires Porte-Train. Société de Géographie, Paris, March 1874.
Egerton, Hugh Aldersey, Improvements in the Construction of Ships, Ferry Boats and other Vessels. Patent No. 3936, 1st December 1873.
Egerton, Hugh Aldersey, On Double and Triple Cylindrical Vessels. Paper to the Institution of Naval Architects, 6th April, 1876.
Ellson, George, Dover Train Ferry Dock. Paper to the Institution of Civil Engineers, Nov. 1937.
Grace's Guide to British Industrial History. (gracesguide.co.uk)
Grahame, Thomas, Letter to M. Huerne de Pommeuse, Paris, March 1835. Mitchell Library, Glasgow.
Hall, William, On the Floating Railways across the Forth and Tay, Ferries in connection with the Edinburgh, Perth & Dundee Railway. Paper to the Institution of Civil Engineers, April 1861.
Henderson, Roy, Crossing the Channel. Silver Link Publishing, 1997.
Hendy, John, Saint-Germain, Vintage Train Ferry. Ferry Publications, 1990.
Hoggett, Kevin, Rails across the Sea. Mainline & Maritime, 2020.
Leigh, Evan, On a Plan for Conveying Railway Trains across the Straits of Dover. Paper to the Institution of Naval Architects, 30th March 1871.
Leigh, Evan, Improvements in the Construction and Propelling of Ships for Railway Ferries and other Purposes. Patent No. 205, 23rd January 1872.
Mackay, Thomas, The Life of Sir John Fowler, Engineer. John Murray, 1900.
McKean, Charles, Battle for the North. Granta Books, 2006.
Marshall, Peter, Burntisland - Fife's Railway Port. Oakwood, 2001.
Martin, Don, The Monkland & Kirkintilloch Railway. Strathkelvin District Libraries & Museums, 1976.
Martin, Don, The Forth & Clyde Canal - A Kirkintilloch View. Strathkelvin District Libraries & Museums, 1985.
Mitchell, Vic and Keith Smith, Branch Line to Hayling. Middleton Press, 1984.
Rapley, John, Thomas Bouch - The Builder of the Tay Bridge. Tempus Publishing, 2007.
Renau, Jean-Pierre, Louis Joseph Aimé Thomé de Gamond, (1807-1876). L'Harmattan, Paris, 2001.
Ripley, Don & Tony Rogan, Designing Ships for Sealink. Ferry Publications, 1995.
de Rodakowski, Ernest, The Channel Ferry. Harrison & Sons, 1905.
Thomas, John, revised by J.S. Paterson, A Regional History of the Railways of Great Britain: Volume VI, Scotland, the Lowlands and Borders. 1984.
Arbroath Guide
The Dover Express and East Kent News
Dundee, Perth and Cupar Advertiser
Dundee Courier
Glasgow Herald
The Graphic
Hansard
Leicester Daily Post
Marine Engineering of Canada
North British Mail
Paisley Advertiser
Practical Mechanic's Journal
The Scotsman

Chapters 4 to 7 - Denmark and the Baltic

Brogren, Klas, Anders Bergenek & Rickard Sahlsten, Stena Line - the story of a ferry company. Stena Line / ShipPax Information, 2012.
Cooke, Anthony, The Fred. Olsen Line and its Passenger Ships. Carmania Press, 2007.
Dahlberg, Rasmus, Danske Katastrofer. Gyldenhal, 2017.
Danish State Railways, Ferry Services Timetable, May–September 1961.
Foerster, Horst-Dieter and Karl Heinz Lossow, Die Älteste Eisenbahnverbindung Über Die Ostsee - Warnemünde-Gedser. Hinstorff Verlag Rostock.
Fritz, Stefan, Die Zukunft des Eisenbahnfährverkehrs in der Ostsee. Technische Universität Berlin, 2009.
Id, Kalle, Silja Line, from De Saseglande to Tallink. Ferry Publications, 2013.
Jansson, Christer, Tågfärjor till och från Sverige. Trafik-Nostalgiska Förlaget, 2016.
Jensen, Niels, Danske jernbanefærger. Clausen bøger, 1978.
Klietz, Wolgang, Ostseefähren im Kalten Krieg. Ch. Links Verlag, Berlin, 2012.
Kramer, Kramer and Foerster, Die Schiffe der Königslinie. Verlag Delius, Klasing & Co., 1981.
Krause, Lohar, and colleagues. DD247800A3 : Method and Arrangement for loading and unloading railway freight ferries. DDR Patentschrift, 1987.
Nellemann, Torben, Jernbanefærger på Øresund og Strelasund. Dansk Jernbane Klub, 1983.
Olsen, Harold, Danish State Railway Ferries. Paper to the Institution of Engineers & Shipbuilders in Scotland, 23rd March 1909.
Olesen, Mogens Nørgaard, Danske Jernbane-Dampfærger. Lamberths Forlag I/S, 1987.
Peter, Bruce, DSB Ferries. Ferry Publications, 2013.
Peter, Bruce, Knud E. Hansen - 75 years of Ship Design. Ferry Publications, 2012.
Rjukan-Notodden Industrial Heritage Site - Nomination for UNESCO World Heritage List. Riksantikvaren, Oslo, 2015.
Schwartzkopf, Karl-Aage, 50 år till sjöss. SJ Reklamavdelning, Stockholm, 1959.
Svarer, Capt. Jørgen, A/S Dampskibsselskabet Ærø, 1874-1974.
Tuxen, Capt. I.C., Danish Steam Railway Ferries and Icebreaking Steamers. Paper to the International Congress of Naval Architects and Marine Engineers, London, July 1897.

Chapters 8 & 9 - Rivers and Lakes

Both, J.C. De Rotterdamsche Tramweg Maatschappij op Goeree-Overflakkee.
Fritz, Karl F., Vom Raddampfer zur Weißen Flotte: Geschichte de Bodenseeschifffahrt. Sutton Verlag, 2013.
Hartwich, Emile, On Railway Ferries. The Engineer, August 7, 1868.
Liechti, E., Meister, J., Gwerder, J. & Jeanmarie, C. Schiffahrt auf dem Vierwaldstättersee. Verlag Eisenbahn, 1974.
Van der Linden, Jan, Hoe ver is de overkant. HGMK Ledenbulletin 29, 2006.
Schlieper, Hans, Eisenbahntrajekte über Rhein und Bodensee. Alba Publikation GmbH, Düsseldorf, 2009.
Scott Russell, John, On Railway Communication Across the Sea. Paper to the Institution of Naval Architects, 18th March, 1869.
Szymanski, Hans, Die Dampfschiffahrt in Niedersachsen und in den angrenzenden Gebieten von 1817 bis 1867. Europäischer Hochschulverlag GmbH, Bremen, 2011.
Weis, Helmut, Die Unternehmung, Stern & Hafferl I. Verlag Pospischil, Wien, 1980.

Chapters 10 & 11 - The Mediterranean & Eastern Europe

Annuario, Vincenzo, & Antonio D'Angelo, Sette Anni in Fondo al Mare. Associazione Ferrovie Siciliane, 2006.
Carboncini, Adriano Betti, Ferry-Boats un Secolo. Calosci Cortona, 1997.
Kalla-Bishop, Peter M., Railway Histories of the World : Italian Railways. David & Charles, 1971.
Migliau, Dott. Ing. Elia, L'Apparato Motore Diesel-Elettrico della Nave Traghetto 'Scilla'. Ercole Marelli & C.S.A, 1933.
Opalev, Maxim Nikolaevich, Construction and Operation of Railway Bridges and Crossings on the Lower Volga. Volgograd State Technical University, 2014.
Robert, Gianni, Treni e Navi. Quaderni delle Ferrovie dello Stato, 1955.
Zarzana, Antonio, Traghettamento dei Treni in Italia e Studio di Fattibilita' e Progettazione di un Deviatoio Triplo di Bordo. Politechnico Milano, 2012

SHIP INDEX